ORGANIZATIONAL SHOCK

W. CLAY HAMNER
Duke University

ORGANIZATIONAL SHOCK

John Wiley and Sons
New York   Chichester   Brisbane   Toronto

To three people I love:
Ellen, Tony and Julia

Library of Congress Cataloging in Publication Data:

Hamner, W Clay.
    Organizational shock.

    (St. Clair series in management and organizational
behavior)
    Includes index.
    1. Organizational behavior. 2. Psychology,
Industrial. I. Title. II. Series.
HD58.7.H347   658.3   80-11910
ISBN 0-471-06251-0

Printed in the United States of America

10 9 8 7 6 5 4 3 2 1

PREFACE

This is a nontraditional book in organizational behavior and psychology. Its purpose is to show that many of the theories taught in organizational behavior and organizational psychology courses often must be modified in applying them to the world of work. I have pointed out many of the organizational behavior shocks that students often experience when they enter the world of work for the first time. I have emphasized the politics of the work place and the reality of the organizational setting.

This book is unique for several reasons. First, the readings do not come from traditional academic journals. Instead, they were selected from various sources including fiction, poetry, and the popular press. They are not superficial readings; indeed, they show a great deal of insight into work. Second, I have selected topics that are controversial in traditionally taught organizational behavior courses. In an educational environment it is important to discuss the controversies as well as the consistencies in our organizational behavior theories. Third, the format of the book is intended to deal with the entire work life of an employee in the organization. I begin the book by discussing "getting people in the door"; that is, what attracts people to work. I then discuss how people are socialized to accept the corporate way of thinking, how long-term commitments are made, how people are motivated, how the treatment of the rank-and-file employee is distinguished from that of the upward mobile elite, and how people are encouraged to leave. In addition, I discuss the social ethics of organizational behavior and the changing world of work we shall face in the next 20 years.

This book is intended to be used as a companion to a narrative text. As a complementary volume it has the flexibility to suit either undergraduate or graduate, introductory or intermediate level courses. The material was selected not only to be readable and enjoyable but also relevant.

I thank the authors and publishers who have generously allowed me to include their publications in this book. Although I have edited some of the articles for inclusion in this volume, I have been careful to maintain their

v

integrity. I find their insight into the world of work without the benefit of theory very disconcerting because it threatens the underpinnings of my education. However, I feel an obligation to reveal their insight. They have discovered through life experiences what we are attempting to teach students who are taking this course.

W. Clay Hamner
Duke University
February, 1980

CONTENTS

1 GETTING PEOPLE IN THE DOOR   **1**

**RECRUITMENT, TRAINING, AND PERFORMANCE: THE
CASE OF BALLET**   **3**
RONALD C. FEDERICO

WE MUST CULTIVATE OUR GARDENS   **11**
VOLTAIRE

2 INDOCTRINATING THEM TO YOUR WAY
OF THINKING   **15**

HOW THEY BEND MINDS   **17**
NEWSWEEK

**FLATTERY WILL GET YOU SOMEWHERE: STYLES AND
USES OF INGRATIATION**   **22**
EDWARD E. JONES

ORIENTATIONS IN THE PROCESS OF SOCIALIZATION   **28**
ERICH FROMM

**PEOPLE PROCESSING: STRATEGIES OF ORGANIZATIONAL
SOCIALIZATION**   **33**
JOHN VAN MAANEN

BIG MAGIC: THREE SPECIFIC TABOOS   **49**
FRITZ STEELE

3 ENCOURAGING THEM TO STAY: GAINING
LONG-TERM COMMITMENT   **60**

RELIGION AND THE CORPORATION   **62**
ANTONY JAY

THE COMPANY MAN   **67**
MICHAEL MACCOBY

THE GREAT MALE COP-OUT FROM THE WORK ETHIC   **75**
BUSINESS WEEK

SEDUCTION AND COMMITMENT IN THE ORGANIZATION   **80**
ROY J. LEWICKI

4 MOTIVATING THEM TO WORK **95**

DEPARTMENTAL 98
ROBERT FROST

PATH BETWEEN THE SEAS 99
DAVID MCCULLOUGH

CREATING A NEW WORLD OF WORK 107
IRVING BLUESTONE

STONEWALLING PLANT DEMOCRACY 115
BUSINESS WEEK

**THE "JACKASS EFFECT" IN MANAGEMENT
COMPENSATION** 119
DALE P. MCCONKEY

5 THE UPWARD MOBILE ELITE **131**

CAREER DEVELOPMENT AND PLANNING 133
DOUGLAS T. HALL AND MARILYN A. MORGAN

SPOT THE WINNER 151
ANTONY JAY

THE GAMESMAN 155
MICHAEL MACCOBY

MAJOR MAJOR MAJOR MAJOR 168
JOSEPH HELLER

6 THE NONUPWARD MOBILE: ARE THEY
SECOND CLASS CITIZENS? **177**

RITES OF PASSAGE 179
JOANNE GREENBERG

WORK—IT WILL MAKE YOU UGLY 185
DAVID JENKINS

IN THE SANDING BOOTH AT FORD 201
RICK KING

7 INDIVIDUAL AND GROUP DIFFERENCES IN
THE ORGANIZATION **210**

**HOMOGENIZING THE AMERICAN WOMAN: THE POWER OF
UNCONSCIOUS IDEOLOGY** 212
SANDRA L. BEM AND DARYL J. BEM

WORKAHOLICS: THIS LAND OF OURS HAS TO HAVE THEM 227
WAYNE OATES

**BANANA TIME—JOB SATISFACTION AND INFORMAL
INTERACTION** 231
DONALD F. ROY

DEVELOPMENTAL SEQUENCES IN SMALL GROUPS 249
BRUCE W. TUCKMAN

8 CULTURAL DIFFERENCES
IN ORGANIZATIONS **256**

EUROPEAN EXECUTIVES: "UNION NOW" 258
JEAN ROSS-SKINNER

MANAGEMENT CAN LEARN FROM JAPAN 264
JOHN DIEBOLD

9 DESIGNING A STYLE OF LEADERSHIP FOR
TODAY'S ORGANIZATION **269**

REBIRTH OF THE LEADER 271
EUGENE E. JENNINGS

DON QUIXOTE'S ADVICE TO SANCHO PANZA 280
CERVANTES

TOM SAWYER, MASTER WHITE-WASHER 284
MARK TWAIN

BOSS: RICHARD J. DALEY OF CHICAGO 288
MIKE ROYKO

COACH: A SEASON WITH LOMBARDI 292
TOM DOWLING

MILES' SIX OTHER MAXIMS OF MANAGEMENT 299
RUFUS E. MILES, JR.

10 ENCOURAGING THEM TO LEAVE:
THE REAL SHOCK **311**

BICYCLES FOR AFGHANISTAN 313
KURT VONNEGUT

DEATH OF A SALESMAN 314
ARTHUR MILLER

NOW THE REVOLT OF THE OLD 321
TIME

HOW BUREAUCRATS DEAL WITH DISSIDENTS 328
DAVID EWING

11 THE ETHICS OF ORGANIZATIONAL BEHAVIOR **333**

**ESCALATION OF THE VIETNAM WAR: HOW COULD IT
HAPPEN?** 335
IRVING L. JANIS

WATERGATE AS A CASE STUDY IN MANAGEMENT 352
MAX WAYS

AIR FORCE A-7D BRAKE SCANDAL 362
CONGRESSIONAL RECORD

**CATCH 20.5: CORPORATE MORALITY AS AN
ORGANIZATIONAL PHENOMENON** 372
JAMES A. WATERS

12 REDESIGNING THE ORGANIZATION TO
REDUCE THE SHOCK **388**

THE COMING DEATH OF BUREAUCRACY 390
WARREN G. BENNIS

LINE AND STAFF AT ITT 398
THOMAS S. BURNS

POWER FAILURES IN MANAGEMENT CIRCLES 404
ROSABETH MOSS KANTER

IS BUSINESS REALLY CHANGING? 418
CHARLES PERROW

CHAPTER I
GETTING PEOPLE IN THE DOOR

ORGANIZATIONAL SHOCKS

- Society does not prepare us very well for deciding what will be an appropriate career.
- The greater the number of skills needed in a particular career, the younger one must be when making a career choice.
- Once people enter the world of work, they feel trapped.
- Our self-image is determined by our new job, not our past relationships or accomplishments.

There are four major "shocks" that people tend to experience as they leave school and enter the world of work. The *first* shock is that society does not prepare us very well for deciding what would be the appropriate career for us.

The *second* shock is that the greater the number of skills the person will need in a particular career, the younger he or she must be when deciding which career to choose. For example, if you want to be a physician it is imperative that you know this by the time you enter college. Even though more and more people are changing careers during their lifetime, certain jobs will still require expertise that is developed at a relatively young age (professional athlete, for example).

The *third* shock is that very often once people enter the world of work they feel trapped. Most relationships before this time have been temporary. Even our families have been temporary to the extent that we are prepared to graduate from one family and enter into another. This is not true with work. Work is one of the longest commitments a person will make in life. A person is expected to work from the time he is between the ages of 18 to 22 until he is at least 65. Whereas it is possible to change jobs, it is almost impossible under our economic system to do without a job for long periods of time. This is in contrast to other areas of our life where we have more freedom of choice; for example, to be married, to have children, to attend or not attend church.

A *fourth* major shock we face when entering the world of work is that who we are (our self-identity) is determined to a great extent by the occupation we pursue. Prior to entering the world of work our self-image was partially determined by the employment of our parents (were they professional?, blue-collar?, etc.) Now our own self-identity will be tied to our own jobs and no longer to that of our parents. For many of us it will mean a decrease in our self-image and for others of us it might mean an increase in our self-image. Nevertheless the reality is that we are now on our own, and who we are is determined by our own contribution to society and to our jobs. We are no longer able to hide behind others or temporary environments such as college.

The two readings in Chapter 1 will be relevant to discussion of these realities. The article by Federico on the recruitment and training of professional ballet dancers shows the ways in which professional dancers are socialized at a very young age through informal recruitment and training procedures. It shows also that many dancers succeed because of their political nature rather than their dancing abilities. People prepare for this occupation at a relatively young age and end their career usually by the age of 30. Of course, this presents a unique problem because while training for this occupation, ballet dancing, one must also think about what to do upon leaving it.

In the second selection by Voltaire, Candide is being trapped into marriage. By various means, he was able to escape this entrapment, and marry his rich mistress. He now felt that life would be without responsibility. Having no responsibility, however, led Candide to examine the question of whether the drudgery of work or the boredom of doing nothing was the greater burden to suffer. He learns the secret of work from a Turk; that is, work keeps at bay the three great evils: boredom, vice, and need. Thus he discovers that people are not born for idleness but that instead they must cultivate whatever garden that life brings their way.

RECRUITMENT, TRAINING, AND PERFORMANCE: THE CASE OF BALLET

RONALD C. FEDERICO

Any occupation must work within limits set by its recruitment and training systems. These provide the human resources vital to occupational stability and growth, and affect resource utilization, worker productivity, and worker satisfaction. These systems are themselves affected by societal values and institutional structures which may complement or conflict with the values and organization of the occupation. This [article] will look at the recruitment and training systems in the occupation of professional ballet dancing. It will relate these systems to major societal values and two occupational products, choreography and performance.

RECRUITMENT AND PERFORMANCE

Recruitment procedures are those techniques an occupation uses to involve a potential member in the training system. Such procedures may be formal or informal, depending on the degree to which there is a structured mechanism to acquaint potential professionals with the occupation. In ballet most recruitment is informal as there are few structured mechanisms for bringing potential professionals into the training system. A few formal procedures exist, most of them being in formal public educational organizations where ballet instruction is part of the curriculum, or in which lecture-demonstrations are provided. Schools exist at the grade school, high school, and university levels; examples include the High School of Performing Arts in New York City, the University of Utah's professional dance program in Salt Lake City, and the public grade schools and high schools incorporating dance in their curricula. Such programs are formal structures to train professional dancers or expose general students to dance as an art and a potential occupation. These programs also maximize exposure and recruitment utility by being part of the institutionalized public educational system.

However, most recruitment programs exist in the private, profit-oriented educational and per-

Source: From *Varieties of Work Experience* by Stewart and Cantor. Copyright © 1979. Reprinted by permission of Phyllis Stewart.

formance spheres, and do not provide systematic, institutionalized exposure. The majority of such private educational programs seem to be quite selective in their recruitment since they depend on parents, peer influence, or referral through such unlikely channels as doctors who prescribe ballet lessons to help correct a variety of physical problems. Table 1 compares the formal and informal recruitment networks by describing the reason the dancers studied began ballet lessons. Table 2 shows the age at which lessons were initiated, and it suggests that the informal recruitment network tends to operate considerably earlier than the formal one, especially for women.

There are major differences in recruitment patterns for men and women in ballet resulting from the differential use of formal and informal recruitment structures. Whereas almost the same percentage of men as women were influenced in starting to dance by the peer group, only eleven percent of the men were influenced by the family compared with fifty-four percent of the women, while forty-four percent of the men were influenced through non-family institutions compared to slightly over ten percent of the women. The effects of these differences can be seen in Table 2, which shows that eighty-five percent of the girls have begun lessons by age eleven, compared to only twenty-two percent of the boys. Given the family's early, total, and long-term socialization potential through the association of social values with physical needs, it becomes a powerful informal recruitment mechanism which reflects the societal belief that ballet is an activity appropriate primarily for females. Occupational choice is obviously affected since it depends on exposure, but professional comptence is also affected. With ballet requiring strength and flexibility in the joints and feet, training begun at a young age is likely to produce a professional with greater technical competence than one who begins his training later. The body is more flexible at the younger age and there is more time to develop the necessary strength and stamina. Greater competence increases the probability of occupational success, an important reward for members of the occupation.

Early entry into the training system also enables a pre-professional to enter the profession soon enough and for a long enough period to

Table 1

Reason for Beginning Ballet Lessons by Sex[a]

	Parental Influence		Peer Influence		Own Desire		After Seeing Dance		Other Institutional Exposure[b]	
	N	%	N	%	N	%	N	%	N	%
Males (N = 54)	6	(11.1)	8	(14.8)	8	(14.8)	8	(14.8)	24	(44.4)
Females (N = 92)	50	(54.4)	13	(14.1)	13	(14.1)	6	(6.5)	10	(10.9)
Total (N = 146)	56	(39.0)	21	(14.4)	21	(14.4)	14	(9.6)	34	(22.6)

[a] Shown is the respondent's first mentioned reason for beginning ballet lessons.
[b] The major components of this category are as follows:
  For girls: at a doctor's suggestion to help solve a medical problem, e.g., underweight.
  For boys: motivation by a school teacher or athletic coach in the course of a school extracurricular activity.

Table 2

Entry into the Field: Age Respondents Began Ballet Lessons by Sex[a]

	Under 6		6 through 10		11 through 16		17 through 20		21 and over	
	N	%	N	%	N	%	N	%	N	%
Males (N = 54)	0	(0)	12	(22.2)	17	(31.5)	22	(40.7)	3	(5.6)
Females (N = 92)	26	(28.3)	55	(59.8)	10	(10.9)	1	(1.1)	0	(0)
Total (N = 146)	26	(17.8)	67	(45.9)	27	(18.5)	23	(15.7)	3	(2.1)

[a] Lessons in other dance forms or participation in athletic activities may have begun earlier.

experience strong professional socialization. Ballet has many rigorous requirements, such as exhausting physical work, long and erratic work hours, isolation from non-dancers, and low pay. These occupational characteristics are defined as acceptable by professional norms. The occupational socialization process supports such norms, and also helps to counteract negative societal evaluation of them. Yet even with strong socialization, Table 3 indicates that ballet dancers leave the profession early. It shows that only nineteen respondents were thirty years or over, suggesting that the occupation loses most of its members before they attain occupational maturity.

The inverse relationships between socialization and occupational longevity are shown in Table 3. Women tend to enter the occupation younger than men, thereby receiving stronger occupational socialization and more extensive technical training. Yet is is the men who are more heavily represented in the upper age groups in this sample. Explanations for these data are tentative, but several can be suggested. One is that the societal definitions of the woman's role places female dancers in

Table 3

Age Distribution by Sex

	Less than 19		19 through 22		23 through 29		30 and over	
	N	%	N	%	N	%	N	%
Male (N = 54)	0	(0)	18	(33.3)	24	(44.4)	12	(22.2)
Female (N = 92)	16	(17.4)	43	(46.7)	26	(28.3)	7	(7.6)
Total (N = 146)	16	(11.0)	61	(41.8)	50	(34.2)	19	(13.0)

increasing role conflict. The major commitment required by ballet's rigorous use of a trained body makes it an occupation that is practically impossible to pursue on a part-time basis. Therefore, it is work that is most feasible before the woman marries. After marriage the demands of married life intrude on career aspirations. By then the female dancer has been in the ballet world for many years, has experienced the frustrations of a demanding and competitive profession, and has felt a diminution in societal approval when her participation in ballet moves from avocation to career. All of these factors generate discrepancies with values learned in previous socialization, and apparently the occupational structure cannot offer adequate rewards.

Men face societal norms which tend to denigrate the male role in artistic and female dominated occupations. However, men typically do not experience the conflict between family and work that women do, so the transition from dance as an avocation to a vocation is more socially acceptable. The fact that men enter the occupational system later than women may also minimize the early development of boredom and frustration. It seems that the major pressures against professional male ballet dancers exist in the informal recruitment system, where men are systematically neglected, and where ballet is not presented as a viable occupational alternative. If a man does enter the occupational system, weak socialization and difficulty in attaining technical competence create additional barriers to professional commitment. Once the commitment is made, however, it receives some societal support as a meaningful work commitment. This helps a male dancer to cope with the other problems of such an occupation (low pay, erratic hours, hard physical work, the homosexual stigma, etc.). An interesting pattern seems to emerge. Women are readily recruited in an informal recruitment system, but then experience role conflict when approaching occupational maturity.

The recruitment of men is weak, but those who are recruited can move into a career orientation more easily than women. More women than men are recruited overall, but the sex imbalance is related to age.

There are several effects of the sex imbalance that tend to result from the informal recruitment system. This sex imbalance affects: (1) types of roles which can be performed; (2) choreographic styles and artistic performing opportunities; (3) the public image of the occupation; (4) the self-image of the members of the occupation; and (5) interaction patterns between occupation members. With female dominance in ballet, the socialization structure tends to focus on behavior appropriate to women. Men are a minority group, so their occupational and personal needs are not often given special consideration. The resulting homogeneity can be functional to the extent that it encourages men and women to interact easily as equals. This is helped by the occupational minimization of sexual attractiveness inherent in an activity where bodies are in close contact according to set, objective rules. However, the women also seem to minimize the appropriateness of ballet men as sex partners because of this occupational distance and personal proximity. They also seem to adopt the societal image of male ballet dancers as potential homosexuals. One dancer summarized the problem the female dancer faces in considering stigmatized male dancers as appropriate sex partners by saying, "I could never be sure."

As noted when discussing Table 3, an occupation with only thirteen percent of its members over age thirty clearly loses the majority of its members in their most mature period. This places the burden of principal and solo roles on the young: Table 4 indicates that fourteen of the principals and fifty-two of the soloists were under thirty. This use of the young in major occupational positions directly influences (1) types of ballets performed, and (2) the quality of performance. In dance, youth has the great ad-

Table 4
Age and Company Position

	Principal		Soloist		Corps		Total	
	N	%	N	%	N	%	N	%
Less than 19	0	(0.0)	5	(31.3)	11	(68.8)	16	(11.0)
19 through 22	5	(8.2)	22	(36.1)	34	(55.7)	61	(41.8)
23 through 29	9	(18.0)	25	(50.0)	16	(32.0)	50	(34.2)
30 and over	11	(57.9)	5	(26.3)	3	(15.8)	19	(13.0)
Total	25	(17.1)	57	(39.0)	64	(43.8)	146	(100.0)

vantage of strength and suppleness but the disadvantage of artistic immaturity. In addition it affects performances indirectly through the loss of experienced artists who can coach younger dancers, influence management planning and provide mature talents to be used by a choreographer.

Given the physical and socialization benefits of early occupational entry, we have seen that the recruitment of women is likely to be more successful. However, although data are lacking, the late occupational recruitment of the men may have latent advantages for them. Any occupational socialization establishes certain value and behavior patterns, implying a certain narrowing of horizons. Art occupations value creativity. Perhaps the breadth of male experiences before occupational socialization results in greater creativity. Most major choreographers are men, while women tend to be performers and to a lesser extent teachers and administrators. Choreography involves the creation of dances, while performing is the somewhat less creative task of interpreting choreography. Teaching and administration require even less creative skills. On the other hand, choreography does not require great facility in performing. Therefore, it seems that choreography provides an outlet for the late-entering

male's somewhat lower physical facility and more diversified life experiences (i.e., weaker occupational socialization). Performing, teaching, and administration are more direct results of the female dancer's earlier occupational entry and stronger socialization. It is interesting to compare ballet with modern dance. In the latter, both male and female dancers seem to enter the art relatively late in their lives, and there is much more major choreography done by women than is the case in ballet. Although clearly speculative at this point, it does seem that the nature of occupational socialization, its duration, and its place in the growth cycle of the individual are important in the development of a professional ballet dancer.

TRAINING AND PERFORMANCE

The occupational training system is comprised of formal and informal occupational structures which socialize recruits into the professional subculture. When there are cohesive, clearly defined means to train recruits in such a way that they can meet professional certification standards, formal entry into the profession is facilitated. There are several problems in the training system in ballet which create an informal structure very loosely connected to actual professional entry and participation.

Certification procedures do not exist. This makes it difficult for training structures to develop pre-professional curricula. Consequently, a highly competitive, informal career entry system is created that is based on random opportunity. Without certification procedures, the schools training dancers offer quite divergent training which potential dancers find difficult to evaluate. This requires a commitment on the part of the recruit to a given training ideology in order to assure oneself that one's training pattern is logical. However, there is no concrete evidence to show that one training system is better than the others. The recruit is therefore exposed to a training system offering him: (1) little systematized instruction, (2) little personal protection in assuring him competent training, and (3) little security in knowing that his training will ultimately lead him into a professional position. This is the case even in schools directly associated with companies, perhaps the most formal of the training systems. Problems are even greater in the other schools. The development of university level training may help this situation to the extent that such graduates are certified for teaching positions in public schools or universities, but it does not help those hoping for performing careers.

The training problem is further accentuated by severe competition resulting from an oversupply of recruits. The lack of a formal recruitment system allows anyone to enter the training network. At the other end, societal demand severely restricts resources for professional dance performances. This greatly limits the number of companies and dancers able to be supported in the profession. The oversupply for scarce positions combines with the ambiguity created by the lack of professional certification to result in severe competition in the field. This competition results in two practices affecting the occupational products of performing and choreography: politics, and a belief in the importance of "being in the right place at the right time."

Politics refer to a wide variety of informal interpersonal bargains between aspiring pre-professionals and teachers or directors in the aspirants' attempts to obtain a professional position. The recruit has little security in his training. He has to commit himself to a particular style with no assurance it will facilitate his success. His training does not lead to formal certification, and he is faced with many competitors in substantially the same position. Under such circumstances, any "break" or advantage is to be sought, and politics is one way to obtain such an advantage. Such politicking runs the gamut from dispensing sexual favors to being willing to do extra work or even returning part of one's pay check. "Being in the right place at the right time" highlights the capricious nature of such an informal system. Another way to obtain an advantage is to be willing and able to do a needed task on very short notice. This can occur when a dancer becomes ill, when dancer-director conflicts develop, or because of carefully calculated plans to discredit another dancer for one's own potential benefit. Both politics and "being in the right place at the right time" well illustrate the opportunities for random factors to operate in an informal occupational structure.

Ballet's informal training system has several weaknesses in addition to those already mentioned. It utilizes scarce resources poorly to the extent that: (1) teachers must try to teach whomever enrolls, (2) talented students unknowingly enroll in incompetent schools, and (3) potential talent is overlooked by teachers caught up with having to teach too many students. Competent dancers may be ignored because of their unwillingness to bargain, while directors can obtain excessive personal and artistic power. The training diversity may create chaos rather than achieving artistic diversity.

The result is a system which encourages personal frustration by emphasizing chance factors, and which jeopardizes its own resource base.

The flow of professionals through the informal recruitment and training structures existing in ballet has the result of placing a great deal of responsibility on the individual. From early in the recruitment and training processes, the dancer must make decisions about his technical training, his artistic development, and his career strategy. This allows the individual dancer substantial autonomy in planning his career pattern, and permits him to try to become the type of artist which he respects. On the other hand, such autonomy lacks security. The individual has few assurances that his decisions will make him a marketable product or a competent performer. Given that artistic creativity is not easily codified, such lack of security is probably inherent in most artistic occupations. However, the structure of ballet as an occupation tends to accentuate the dancer's insecurity.

The common reliance on luck or intrigue as a means of professional advancement is one response to the insecurity generated. Such a pattern relinquishes the dancer's personal autonomy in favor of blind luck or manipulation of or by others. The group nature of ballet requires that the dancer subjugate himself to the needs of the total production, itself a restraint on personal and artistic autonomy. However, when insecurity encourages a dance student or a dance professional to blindly put his faith in a teacher, coach, or director, he has further relinquished autonomy. It is somewhat ironic that the professional structure encourages autonomy from the earliest recruitment experiences, since the loose professional structure and overcrowded conditions encourage the voluntary relinquishing of potential autonomy for some measure of occupational security. Between the demands of working cooperatively in a group, and finding a career in a very uncertain professional structure, the average ballet dancer is a performing artist with little professional autonomy.

CONCLUSION

Since choreography and performances are important parts of the occupational product in ballet, these should be closely related to major structural features of the occupation. Two major structural parts of any occupation are the recruitment and training systems, which bring potential members into the occupation and provide the necessary socialization. Such systems will vary in the complexity and formality of their structure, and the degree to which they are tied to other parts of the occupational structure. This paper has suggested that ballet as an occupation has informal recruitment and training procedures which are poorly integrated with performing needs. These structural characteristics create competition resulting from uncontrolled entry into the training system and ambiguous criteria for professional certification. Competition and ambiguous criteria encourage politics, whereby dancers are rewarded for non-dance related abilities. The informal recruitment system recruits differentially between the sexes, and is dysfunctional in that much of the occupational socialization which occurs never results in occupational productivity.

The flexibility that leads to relatively poor occupational resource utilization can also have functional consequences. Compared with the typical state-supported rigidly structured European ballet system, the American structure permits a wider recruitment effort, varied teaching philosophies, and greater opportunities for dancers with unusual physical and/or emotional characteristics. This is reflected in a distinctive body of choreography, and a more or less distinctive American type of dancer. On the other hand, the problems such a system creates for the occupation's survival in a competitive artistic and non-artistic environment, and for the individual's gratification within the occupational system, may ultimately outweigh the advantages of the system. With government support of the arts increasingly suggested as necessary, the choice of the more preferable occupational structure will soon have to be made.

WE MUST CULTIVATE OUR GARDENS

VOLTAIRE

At the bottom of his heart Candide had not the least wish to marry Cunegonde. But the Baron's extreme impertinence determined him to complete the marriage, and Cunegonde urged it so warmly that he could not retract. He consulted Pangloss, Martin and the faithful Cacambo. Pangloss wrote an excellent memorandum by which he proved that the Baron had no rights over his sister and that by all the laws of the empire she could make a left-handed marriage with Candide. Martin advised that the Baron should be thrown into the sea; Cacambo decided that he should be returned to the Levantine captain and sent back to the galleys, after which he would be returned by the first ship to the Vicar-General at Rome. This was thought to be very good advice; the old woman approved it; they said nothing to the sister; the plan was carried out with the aid of a little money and they had the pleasure of duping a Jesuit and punishing the pride of a German Baron.

It would be natural to suppose that when, after so many disasters, Candide was married to his mistress, and living with the philosopher Pangloss, the philosopher Martin, the prudent Cacambo and the old woman, having brought back so many diamonds from the country of the ancient Incas, would lead the most pleasant life imaginable. But he was so cheated by the Jews that he had nothing left but his little farm; his wife, growing uglier every day, became shrewish and unendurable; the old woman was ailing and even more bad-tempered than Cunegonde. Cacambo, who worked in the garden and then went to Constantinople to sell vegetables, was overworked and cursed his fate. Pangloss was in despair because he did not shine in some German university.

As for Martin, he was firmly convinced that people are equally uncomfortable everywhere; he accepted things patiently. Candide, Martin and Pangloss sometimes argued about metaphysics and morals. From the windows of the farm they often watched the ships going by,

Source: Voltaire, *Candide,* William, Belasco & Meyers, 1930.

filled with effendis, pashas and cadis, who were being exiled to Lemnos, to Mitylene and Erzerum. They saw other cadis, other pashas and other effendis coming back to take the place of the exiles and to be exiled in their turn. They saw the neatly impaled heads which were taken to the Sublime Porte. These sights redoubled their discussions; and when they were not arguing, the boredom was so excessive that one day the old woman dared to say to them:

"I should like to know which is worse, to be raped a hundred times by negro pirates, to have a buttock cut off, to run the gauntlet among the Bulgarians, to be whipped and flogged in an *auto-da-fé,* to be dissected, to row in a galley, in short, to endure all the miseries through which we have passed, or to remain here doing nothing?"

" 'Tis a great question," said Candide.

These remarks led to new reflections, and Martin especially concluded that man was born to live in the convulsions of distress or in the lethargy of boredom. Candide did not agree, but he asserted nothing. Pangloss confessed that he had always suffered horribly; but, having once maintained that everything was for the best, he had continued to maintain it without believing it.

One thing confirmed Martin in his detestable principles, made Candide hesitate more than ever, and embarrassed Pangloss. And it was this. One day there came to their farm Paquette and Friar Giroflée, who were in the most extreme misery; they had soon wasted their three thousand piastres, had left each other, made it up, quarrelled again, been put in prison, escaped, and finally Friar Giroflée had turned Turk. Paquette continued her occupation everywhere and now earned nothing by it.

"I foresaw," said Martin to Candide, "that your gifts would soon be wasted and would only make them the more miserable. You and Cacambo were once bloated with millions of piastres and you are no happier than Friar Giroflée and Paquette."

"Ah! ha!" said Pangloss to Paquette, "so Heaven brings you back to us, my dear child? Do you know that you cost me the end of my nose, an eye and an ear! What a plight you are in! Ah! What a world this is!"

This new occurrence caused them to philosophise more than ever.

In the neighbourhood there lived a very famous Dervish, who was supposed to be the best philosopher in Turkey; they went to consult him; Pangloss was the spokesman and said:

"Master, we have come to beg you to tell us why so strange an animal as man was ever created."

"What has it to do with you?" said the Dervish. "Is it your business?"

"But, reverend father," said Candide, "there is a horrible amount of evil in the world."

"What does it matter," said the Dervish, "whether there is evil or good? When his highness sends a ship to Egypt, does he worry about the comfort or discomfort of the rats in the ship?"

"Then what should we do?" said Pangloss.

"Hold your tongue," said the Dervish.

"I flattered myself," said Pangloss, "that I should discuss with you effects and causes, this best of all possible worlds, the origin of evil, the nature of the soul and pre-established harmony."

At these words the Dervish slammed the door in their faces.

During this conversaion the news went round that at Constantinople two viziers and the mufti had been strangled and several of their friends impaled. This catastrophe made a prodigious noise everywhere for several hours. As Pangloss, Candide and Martin were returning to their little farm, they came upon an old man who was taking the air under a bower of orange trees at his door. Pangloss, who was as curious as he was argumentative, asked him what was the name of the mufti who had just been strangled.

"I do not know," replied the old man. "I have never known the name of any mufti or of any vizier. I am entirely ignorant of the occurrence you mention; I presume that in general those who meddle with public affairs sometimes perish miserably and that they deserve it; but I never inquire what is going on in Constantinople; I content myself with sending there for sale the produce of the garden I cultivate."

Having spoken thus, he took the strangers into his house. His two daughters and his two sons presented them with several kinds of sherbet which they made themselves, caymac flavoured with candied citron peel, oranges, lemons, limes, pine-apples, dates, pistachios and Mocha coffee which had not been mixed with the bad coffee of Batavia and the Isles. After which this good Mussulman's two daughters perfumed the beards of Candide, Pangloss and Martin.

"You must have a vast and magnificent estate?" said Candide to the Turk.

"I have only twenty acres," replied the Turk. "I cultivate them with my children; and work keeps at bay three great evils: boredom, vice and need."

As Candide returned to his farm he reflected deeply on the Turk's remarks. He said to Pangloss and Martin:

"That good old man seems to me to have chosen an existence preferable by far to that of the six kings with whom we had the honour to sup."

"Exalted rank," said Pangloss, "is very dangerous, according to their testimony of all philosophers; for Eglon, King of the Moabites, was murdered by Ehud; Absalom was hanged by the hair and pierced by three darts; King Nadab, son of Jeroboam, was killed by Baasha; King Elah by Zimri; Ahaziah by Jehu; Athaliah by Jehoiada; the Kings of Jehoiakim, Jeconiah and Zedekiah were made slaves. You know in what manner died Croesus, Astyages, Darius, Denys of Syracuse, Pyrrhus, Perseus, Hannibal, Jugurtha, Ariovistus, Caesar, Pompey, Nero, Otho, Vitellius, Domitian, Richard II of England, Edward II, Henvy VI, Richard III, Mary Stuart, Charles I, the three Henrys of France, the Emperor Henry IV. You know . . ."

"I also know," said Candide, "that we should cultivate our gardens."

"You are right," said Pangloss, "for, when man was placed in the Garden of Eden, he was placed there *ut operaretur eum,* to dress it and to keep it; which proves that man was not born for idleness."

"Let us work without arguing," said Martin; " 'tis the only way to make life endurable."

The whole small fraternity entered into this praiseworthy plan, and each started to make use of his talents. The little farm yielded well. Cunegonde was indeed very ugly, but she became an excellent pastry-cook; Paquette embroidered; the old woman took care of the linen. Even Friar Giroflée performed some service; he was a very good carpenter and even became a man of honour; and Pangloss sometimes said to Candide:

"All events are linked up in this best of all possible worlds; for, if you had not been expelled from the noble castle by hard kicks in your backside for love of Miss Cunegonde, if you had not been clapped into the Inquisition, if you had not wandered about America on foot, if you had not stuck your sword in the Baron, if you had not lost all your sheep from the land of Eldorado, you would not be eating candied citrons and pistachios here."

" 'Tis well said," replied Candide, "but we must cultivate our gardens."

QUESTIONS FOR DISCUSSION

1. Examine the recruitment practices of various recruiters and their companies who are interviewing at your school. How realistic is the information they give you in describing the negative as well as the positive aspects of the jobs you are being offered?

2. Discuss among your friends or in your study group how each of you chose the college and the college courses you have taken. Are these courses preparing you for a job that you truly desire?

3. In the introduction to this chapter we discussed four major shocks that many people experience as they enter the world of work. How many of these have you experienced and how have you managed to deal with them?

4. Knowing what you know now, what career development advice will you give your children as they grow up?

5. What other realities or organizational shocks have you experienced as they relate to entering the world of work?

CHAPTER II
INDOCTRINATING THEM TO YOUR WAY OF THINKING

ORGANIZATIONAL SHOCKS

- Organizations attempt to socialize employees to accept the organizational "mind-set."
- Often the socialization process produces unhealthy results both for the organizations and the individual.
- The socialization process in organizations restricts our freedom to discuss certain topics.

When you enter an organization one of the first things it attempts to do, either consciously or unconsciously, is to break down the old norms and values that you carry with you and to replace them with new norms. For many people this socialization process is an organizational shock.

One of the purposes of this process is to develop a team player. Too much emphasis on being a team player however, may lead to conformity, which will not help the organization. Many examples in history have shown the unhealthy side of socialization and conformity in organizations, as noted in the article from *Newsweek*. For example, the followers of Reverend Jim Jones, Adolf Hitler, Charles Manson and the Kamikaze pilots in World War II were socialized to truly believe what they were doing was right. It is, therefore, reasonable to expect from organizations a great ethical responsibility to be sure that the socialization process enhances productivity on the job and is not detrimental to the individual or society. A second organizational shock occurs when employees find that the socialization process often produces unhealthy results for the employees and the organization.

The article by E.E. Jones talks about how to ingratiate others in such a way that they find you more pleasant. According to Jones, the message is clear; success in one's chosen line of work is dramatically furthered by practicing the art of ingratiation.

In the next article by Fromm, we learn that there are three orientations to socialization. The first is based on a *symbiotic relationship,* where a person tries to lose his independence and identity by becoming part of another person, either by being swallowed by that person or by swallowing him. Often this is viewed as a necessary consequence of sacrificial duty or love, but as Fromm notes, it rarely is. As we saw in the *Newsweek* article on cult followings, socialization often takes this unhealthy form. The second orientation of the socialization process is *withdrawal* and *destructiveness.* When a person is socialized to belong, join, or relate to others, he may react in such a way that he withdraws or else becomes destructive to the group and its processes. Third, to Fromm, is *love;* here the socialization process takes the productive form of relatedness to others and to oneself. In this article he describes how we can turn unproductive socialization processes into productive ones. He gives us great insight into the *underpinnings* of the socialization process and how we can differentiate healthy from unhealthy ones.

In the last two readings we find examples of strategies of organizational socialization. According to John Van Maanen, organizations attempt to socialize in order to change the behaviors and attitudes of people. Although each organization may use different methods, the purpose is often very similar.

In the last article Steele discusses the three specific taboos the socialization process teaches should not be discussed among employees. The restriction of this freedom of speech often is a shock to new employees. These taboos include discussions about salaries, career decisions, and personal feelings. In the readings in following chapters, however, we shall learn that the discussion of these three topics is imperative for effective organizational behavior.

HOW THEY BEND MINDS

NEWSWEEK

How could more than 900 people be twisted to the point of swallowing fatal doses of poison?

Clearly, the immolation at Jonestown wasn't entirely voluntary. But the orderly rows and heaps of dead and the linked arms of family groups were powerful testimony that Jim Jones's disciples hadn't enough will to resist his orders, backed up by a few armed guards. And perhaps the greatest horror in the scene lay in the realization that more or less ordinary people had been so indoctrinated—and in the seed of fear that nearly anybody might be manipulated the same way.

In a sense, such mind-bending is only an extreme form of familiar human experience. In military training, soldiers are taught to take appalling risks in the name of discipline and love of country; extending that process, Japan's kamikaze pilots in World War II accepted certain death. Jailers can be permitted to abuse and even torture their prisoners, and citizens easily shut their eyes. At the extreme, Adolf Hitler engineered the Holocaust that massacred 6 million Jews. Powerful personalities often gather groups of dependent admirers: the demonic charisma of Charles Manson mesmerized his ghoulish groupies to murder total strangers with sadistic pleasure. Jones was only the latest extreme in the wave of cult leaders of the past decade.

To many scholars who have studied the new American cults—and to many ex-cultists themselves—the behavior of Jones's following was shocking but not surprising. "As a Moonie, I would have done exactly what they did," maintains Erica Heftmann, 26, who left the Unification Church of self-styled Korean messiah Sun Myung Moon more than two years ago, "I was drilled and instructed to kill." Isolated from the real world and pressured by their peers, converts become wholly accepting of the leader's power—and his paranoia—and they put their welfare and their will totally in his hands. Jones's people even practiced suicide drills, in which they swallowed a drink of bitter liquid he said was poison. "I would think, before being told it wasn't poison, that soon I would be dead," recalls Wanda Johnson, 42, who spent eight years in the Peoples Temple and lost her youngest child at Jonestown. "I would think, 'It doesn't matter if I'm dead.' I felt relief."

Almost any passionate enthusiasm can generate cultic behavior if there is a charismatic figure to beguile disciples. In recent decades, cults have coalesced around crusading politicians, rock stars, visionary intellectuals and gurus of the human-potential movement.

CHARISMATIC LEADERSHIP

In religion, sociologists typically distinguish cults from mainline churches, which serve as custodians of normative values, and from sects, which partially withdraw from society in order to purify established doctrine. Cults emerge when groups wholly withdraw from prevailing religious practices and members commit themselves completely to the leadership of charismatic and highly authoritarian figures. Although today's cults vary widely in their ideologies, the most successful use much the same methods of indoctrinating converts.

Most cults know exactly which kind of recruits they are looking for. Synanon guru Charles Dederich prefers drug addicts, whom he can rehabilitate and then bind to his community for life. Jones sought out the oppressed—especially poor blacks, prostitutes and other outcasts—who would welcome his message of egalitarianism and his offer of a communal home. But religious groups such as the Moonies, the Children of God and the Hare Krishnas prefer college students of above-average intelligence and idealism who will be a credit to the cult. In her own interviews with more than 300 former cult members, University of California psychologist Margaret Singer found that no more than a third were suffering from marked psychological distress at the time of their induction.

"A SENSE OF BELONGING"

Timing is the key factor in seeking converts. Religious recruiters like to hit the college campuses at exam time, sit in libraries, waiting to make "eye contact" with students who are having difficulty deciding on a course of major study or recovering from a broken romance. In cities and resort areas, proselytizers seek out footloose backpackers who have taken time off from school to "find" themselves. "These kids are looking for a sense of significance and belonging," says UCLA law professor Richard Delgado, who has been studying cults for years. "Everybody is vulnerable. You and I could be Hare Krishnas if they approached us at the right time."

Studies indicate that the Moonies have devised the most sophisticated methods of luring converts. They call the first phase "love bombing." Once recruiters spot lonely students, they draw them into friendly conversation that typically ends with an invitation to dinner. Surrounded by smiling strangers who hold their hands and shower them with compliments, the students are then invited to a weekend retreat. "As instructors, we didn't tell them the truth," recalls Erica Heftmann. "If we had told them that we believed Moon was the Messiah or that we stayed up all night praying in the snow, they'd never join."

During the retreat, guests are subjected to an endless round of games, singing, exercise and vague religious discussions, with little time for sleep. Only the most discerning recruits realize that they are not being allowed to ask probing questions or make close friends. Yet every recruit is assigned a monitor who accompanies him everywhere, even to the bathroom. On Sunday, the potential converts are pressured to stay on for one last party. "Once they called their family or employer and told them they weren't coming in on Monday, we knew we had them for seven full days," said Heftmann. "And if they stayed seven days, they almost always became a member."

Isolation—from family, friends and all contact with the outside world—is the first step in what Los Angeles psychiatrist Frederick Hacker calls "the washing stage" of cultic mind control. Next, recruits are made to feel guilty about their past lives and recognize their need to be reborn like their all-knowing "brothers and sisters" in the new family of the cult. Several cults, such as the Children of God and Hare Krishna, even give recruits new names or devise private measurements of time to underscore the cult's new reality. But the development of a new personality is gradual. It requires various forms of sense deprivation, inculcated through loss of sleep, low-protein diets and exhausting rounds of chanting, praying and indoctrination in the thought of the new father figure.

TOOL OF SATAN

"It's all so simple," observes Tufts University psychiatrist Stanley Cath, who has studied the conversion techniques used by cults. "Converts have to believe only what they are told. They don't have to think, and this relieves tremendous tensions." Indeed, at Synanon, members tell recruits, "We will do your thinking for you," and inside Moon's camps independent thought is labeled a tool of Satan.

A critical point in the conversion process occurs when recruits are forced to make a major commitment to the cult. This may mean signing over one's property, bank account or children to the group, as in some religious cults, or even joining in drug or sex orgies, as demanded by Charles Manson in his "family." "Once you've done something that major, it's very hard to admit even to yourself that you've made a mistake, and subconsciously you will go to great lengths to rationalize what you did," explains Stanford University psychiatrist Donald T. Lunde. "It's a very tricky mental defense mechanism exploited to the hilt by the charismatic leader."

Cults may also exploit members by sending them into the streets to solicit funds or sell things like flowers, usually on behalf of pseudonymous organizations. "The leader tells you to go out and get $250," says Sherry Dietrich, 28, who joined the Children of God after a divorce in 1974. "Believe me, you beat your brains out to get that $250, and you don't come home until you get it."

In virtually all cults, sex is a central means of controlling members' lives. Some cult leaders, like Manson and Jones, use some of their followers—both male and female—for their own pleasure. But most religious cults rigidly segregate males and females and teach them that sexuality itself is evil. "Father" Moon not only arranges all marriages but also demands such powerful repression of sexual feelings that many members revert to pre-puberty innocence. "Women stop having their periods sometimes and men may find that they do not shave as often," reports ex-Moonie Christopher Edwards, 24. "People begin to look younger. I was 22 when I came out and people told me I looked 15."

OUTLET FOR AGGRESSION

To bind members tighter to the cult, its leaders create the image of an evil outgroup that is supposedly trying to destroy them. For Hitler, it was the Jews. For Manson, it was blacks. For Jones, it was the FBI, the CIA and the Ku Klux Klan. For Synanon's Dederich, it is the government and the news media. And for most of the militant religious cults, the enemy is the members' natural parents. "Cults allow people to hate without feeling guilty and provide a safe, group-sanctioned outlet for aggression against the enemy," observes psychiatrist Hacker. Cult leaders also persuade members that they will die, either at the hands of enemies or cult loyalists, if they defect. The Children of God tell defectors that either God or Satan will strike them dead, and perform exorcisms on those who persist in leaving. Ex-Scientologists recall warnings of the "2-45" solution—anyone who drops out should get two .45-caliber slugs.

BASIC NEEDS

What transforms some cult leaders from spirited humanitarians into frenzied despots? Jones, for one, began his career by providing a humane haven for society's outcasts, yet ended up crushing those in his care. In such cases, a charismatic leader, who may be slightly disturbed, discovers that he is fulfilling a basic human need for increasing numbers of people. "Pretty soon, he is believing more and more in his own power, and it grows so that he begins to be burdened by it and a little paranoid," reasons psychiatrist Ari Kiev of the Cornell University Medical College. So he develops new, more punitive measures for binding his followers to him. "And if there comes a threat, a terminal illness or exposure, the leader resents the idea of anyone surviving him," adds New York psychiatrist Herbert Hendin. "He doesn't want any part of whatever is left to survive."

Jim Jones's Peoples Temple differs from other cults because of its emphasis on suicidal imagery, says Yale psychiatrist Robert J. Lifton, a specialist on death and thought control. [This] atrocity, Lifton believes, "was a mixture of submitting to mass suicide and submitting to murder." As his own mind deteriorated into paranoia, Jones prepared his people for collective death by running them through suicide rehearsals. This enforced group commitment and the illusion that death for them would merely be a transition to an eternal community. "When Jones asked them to die for him, some may have gone willingly with him, but a large number probably just didn't know how to resist," Hendin argues. "You're dealing with a suicide, not of the mass group, but of the leader, who is taking the group with him."

Thus the tragedy at Jonestown was only superficially like past cases of mass suicide—the Jewish Zealots at Masada who killed themselves rather than be captured by the Romans, for example, or the Japanese who died on Saipan rather than surrender to the Americans in World War II. Instead of patriotism, religious faith or a cause larger than themselves, Jones's followers were ensnared by Jones himself. And like most charismatic figures, he left no one who could replace him as the personal embodiment of the cult. Although survivors in San Francisco insist that the Peoples Temple will go on, ex-members say it cannot survive without Jones.

Inevitably, the Jonestown atrocity has triggered national debate over cults and whether they can—and should—be curbed. Church scholars caution that the religions of Jesus, Muhammad and Buddha all began as cults, and civil libertarians warn that religious practices, no matter how odious, are protected by the First Amendment. The only legal way to attack them would be to prove that the psychological techniques practiced by some cults amount to coercive mind control, leaving their victims legally impaired. But the theory is tenuous. Dr. Stephen P. Hersh, assistant director of the National Institute of Mental Health, believes that the brainwashing attributed to cults is, in most cases, "high-pressure salesmanship." "Just because converts adopt beliefs that seem bizarre to their families, it does not follow that their choices are dictated by cult leaders," he says.

Historians say cults emerge whenever there is a serious break in the structure of society. The Industrial Revolution in England, the French Revolution and the westward movement in the U.S. all spawned new religious sects. Some scholars believe that the traumas of the '60s attracted young Americans to charismatic politicians and then, after the war in Vietnam, to equally charismatic religious figures. Although some experts think the current interest in cults has peaked, most insist that the better-financed groups, such as Moon's, will be around as long as the basic institutions of society—the family, schools and established churches—continue to turn out emotional orphans susceptible to a cult leader's blandishments.

A HEAVY PRICE

Even critics concede that many of today's cults work for social good and individual need by drawing recruits away from drugs and anomie into a steady life of service. But at best, the price is a heavy one in a free society: in joining a cult, the recruit surrenders a large measure of personal responsibility and potential growth in exchange for spiritual security. The mass deaths at Jonestown may yet do some good if they make searching young people think twice before seeking a family among the cultists.

—KENNETH L. WOODWARD with MARY HAGER in Washington, JANET HUCK in Los Angeles, MICHAEL REESE in San Francisco, RACHEL MARK and WILLIAM D. MARBACH in New York and bureau reports.

FLATTERY WILL GET YOU SOMEWHERE: STYLES AND USES OF INGRATIATION

EDWARD E. JONES

Dale Carnegie, author of *How to Win Friends and Influence People,* was enraged at the implication that he would advocate using compliments just to get something out of people: "Great God Almighty!!! If we are so contemptibly selfish that we can't radiate a little happiness and pass on a bit of honest appreciation without trying to screw something out of the other person in return—if our souls are no bigger than sour crab apples, we shall meet with the failure we so richly deserve." The chapter containing this observation (entitled "How to Make People Like You Instantly") is composed of anecdotes describing precisely how complimenters *do* gain advantages. The message is clearly stated in other chapters as well: success in one's chosen line of work may be dramatically furthered by practicing the arts of ingratiation along the way.

Carnegie is not the only advocate of "applied human relations" who has had trouble distinguishing between the legitimate and illegitimate in social behavior. In certain business and political circles, for example, "sincere" is used as a synonym for agreeable. Self-serving flattery is usually deplored—but when does "honest appreciation" become flattery? Everyone likes a cooperative, agreeable attitude, but where is the line between manipulative conformity and self-effacing compromise? Many see great evil in ingratiation. Milton considered it hypocrisy, which he called "the only evil that walks invisible, except to God alone." Norman Vincent Peale, on the other hand, is much more tolerant; he considers pleasantness a mark of Christian virtue, from which peace of mind and prosperity flow naturally—and rightly.

Between these two extremes we find the charmingly honest Lord Chesterfield:

> Vanity . . . is, perhaps, the most universal principle of human actions . . . if a man has a mind to be thought wiser, and a woman handsomer than they really are, their error is a comfortable one for themselves, and an innocent one with regard to other people; and I would rather make them my

Source: Published by permission of Transaction, Inc. From *Transaction,* Vol 2, No. 4. Copyright © 1965 by Transaction, Inc.

friends, by indulging them, than my enemies by endeavoring (in that to no purpose) to undeceive them.

Adlai Stevenson was also willing to counsel moderation with the remark, after being given a glowing introduction, "I have sometimes said that flattery is all right if you don't inhale."

What is custom and what is manipulation depends on time, place, the society, and often the individual. In those cultures where fulsome compliments are the norm, like the more traditional groups in Japan, anything less may be considered insulting. On the other hand, in many masculine circles in our own society praise is considered an affectation—a man who pays compliments easily will be thought untrustworthy or effeminate.

Most theories of social structure make the strong assumption that persons adjust their actions to what is generally accepted and expected. Ingratiation can be defined as impression-management which stretches or exploits these expectations or norms. Acts of ingratiation are designed to increase an individual's attractiveness beyond the value of what he really can offer to his target. Ingratiation is the illegitimate—the seamy—side of interpersonal communication.

BREAKING THE SOCIAL CONTRACT

But how do we determine when behavior is "legitimate"? Relationships and associations involve, in normal circumstances, an unstated contract between the actors. Different authorities describe this contract in different ways. Sociologist Erving Goffman, in his book *The Presentation of Self in Everyday Life,* emphasizes what he calls "ritual elements" in social interaction. Goffman believes that not only does communication take place in its usual sense but the communicators also engage in a "performance"—each transmits and receives clues about his definition of the situation, his

view of himself, and his evaluation of the other. Mutual adjustment occurs. *Perhaps most important, the actors enter into a silent compact to help each other save face.* Each becomes involved in "face-work"—give-and-take actions that smooth over potentially embarrassing threats, lend mutual support, and make for coherent and consistent performances. Each person has a "defensive orientation toward saving his own face and a protective orientation toward saving the other's face."

Within this frame of reference, the ingratiator may be seen as exploiting this contract while seeming to support it. He neither violates the control openly, nor merely fulfills it. Rather, he keeps sending out reassuring signals that he accepts the terms of the contract; but all the while he is actually working toward other goals.

To put it in slightly different terms: while relying on his target to stick to the rule that each should get out of a relationship what he brings to it, the ingratiator deliberately violates the rule himself in hopes of gaining a one-sided advantage. By definition, ingratiation occurs when a person cannot or does not want to offer as much as he hopes to get from the other, so he tries to make his "offer" appear more valuable by fancy packaging, misrepresenting how much he brings to the relationship, or advertising the effort or cost involved in his contribution. For instance, the worker may apply himself with greatest industry when he expects the supervisor to appear momentarily, he may try to convince others that his job is more difficult than it really is, or attempt to convince his boss that it requires considerable experience or specialized education.

While the dependent member of a relationship has more to gain from successful ingratiation than the more powerful member, the latter may be also quite concerned about his image. It has often been noted that men rising in organizations tend to lose the spontaneity of old relationships and certainty about the loyalty and reliability of old colleagues. In spite of their increasing power, they are dependent on subordinates for signs of their own effectiveness and—perhaps as a way of hedging their bets—they will use ingratiating tactics to increase morale and performance.

Ingratiation raises important problems in human relations and self-knowledge. Much of our understanding of the world around us, and of ourselves, comes to us indirectly through the impressions we get from others. In particular, self-evaluation is to a large extent determined by how others judge us—personal qualities like friendliness, respectability, or moral worth can only be assessed by social means or mirrored in the reactions of others. Since ingratiation subverts this response, it is a threat to normal interactions and to reliable information. Like the traditional Hollywood producer and his yes-men, the executive surrounded by ingratiators may find himself adrift in a sea of uncertainties in which the only markers are the selfish interests of his advisers.

Ingratiation takes three general tactical forms.

Other-Enhancement

The ingratiator may try to elicit favorable reactions to himself by building up his target. At the extreme this involves obvious flattery; but there are also more subtle and indirect ways. The ingratiator may, for instance, concentrate on playing up the real strong points of the target, passing over or playing down the weak ones.

The ultimate design is to convince the target that the ingratiator thinks highly of him. We tend to like those who like us. Sometimes, however, the tactics are not simple or direct. The higher the target's regard for himself, the less he needs the ingratiator's praise, and the more he accepts it as obvious and routine. Targets may prefer praise, as Lord Chesterfield puts it, "upon those points where they wish to excel, and yet are doubtful whether they do or not. . . . The late Sir Robert Walpole, who was certainly

an able man, was little open to flattery upon that head . . . but his prevailing weakness was, to be thought to have a polite and happy turn of gallantry; of which he had undoubtedly less than any man living . . . (and) those who had any penetration—applied to it with success."

Conformity

People tend to like those whose values and beliefs appear similar to their own. Again, however, the relationship is not always direct. The ingratiator must seem sincere. His agreement must seem to be arrived at independently, for no ulterior purpose. The tactical conformer might be wise to disagree on nonessentials in order to underline the "independence" and value of his agreement on essentials. Agreement may be more valued if it seems to result from a *change* in opinion, made at some psychological cost, seeming to reflect a sincere change of conviction.

Self-Presentation is the explicit description or presentation of oneself in such a way as to become attractive to the target. This includes avoiding those characteristics the target might consider unpleasant, and subtly emphasizing those he might approve. The ingratiator walks a tightrope: he must boast without seeming to, since open boasting is frowned on in our society; he must "be" those things his target considers ideal for his situation, and yet appear sincere; he must seem admirable to the target and yet not a threat. He may have to ride a paradox—to be both self-enhancing and self-deprecating at the same time. This may not be difficult for someone with strong and obvious credentials—someone widely acknowledged to be the best in his field may gain by not mentioning it, and instead acknowledging his all-too-human failings. But those with dubious credentials must be more blatant in advertising their strengths.

In sum, in each of these classes the main

problem of the ingratiator is to seem sincere and yet impressive and engaging. It is also better if his tactics and stated opinions support some pet but not universally admired or accepted ideas of the target.

Little research has been done on ingratiation. To carry the inspection of the subject beyond anecdote and intuition, we conducted a number of experiments in which college student subjects were given strong or weak incentives to make themselves attractive to a particular target. Sometimes targets knew that the ingratiators were dependent on them for benefits and therefore had selfish reasons to be attractive; sometimes they did not know. In other experiments, subjects were exposed to ingratiating overtures by others and their impressions of these others were assessed.

One experiment, designed to test ingratiation tactics in an organization hierarchy, used as subjects 79 male volunteers from the Naval ROTC unit at Duke University. Pairs of freshmen (low-status) and pairs of upper-classmen (high-status) were brought together in units of four. Each subject in the experimental condition (designed to promote ingratiation) was told that the purpose of the study was to find out if "compatible groups provide a better setting in which to test leadership potential than do incompatible groups." The experimenter's instructions continued: "For this reason I hope that you will make a special effort to gain (the other's) liking and respect, always remembering your position as commander (or subordinate)." With the remaining subjects, in the control condition, emphasis was on the importance of obtaining *valid* information: "We are not especially concerned with whether you end up liking each other or not. . . . We are interested only in how well you can do in reaching a clear impression of the other person."

Another experiment used 50 male volunteers from the introductory psychology course at the University of North Carolina in what was supposed to be a game designed to simulate a business situation. An experimental accomplice, presented as a graduate student from the School of Business Administration, was introduced as the "supervisor," conducting and scoring the games. Actually, the "business games" were used to discover and measure ingratiation tactics which might be used to gain advantage in comparable professional or business contexts.

From the results of the experiments thus far completed *there is no doubt that the average undergraduate behaves differently when he wants to be liked than when he wants only to be accurate in presenting himself socially.*

Specifically, let us break down the results in terms of the three major types of ingratiation tactics.

Self-Presentation

Generally, when instructed to try to make a good impression, our subjects played up their strong points and played down their weaknesses. (These varied according to the situation.) However, there were a few significant exceptions:

In a status hierarchy, tactics vary according to the ingratiator's position. In the ROTC experiment, the lower-classmen usually inflated only those qualities they considered unimportant. Apparently they felt that to inflate the important qualities might make them seem pushy, and perhaps even threatening. Upper-classmen became more modest about all qualities. They felt secure, and their high status was obvious because of age and rank—therefore they did not feel it necessary to assert superiority. Modesty, we infer, helped them build up the impression of friendliness toward the lower ranks, which they considered desirable.

Who and what the target is influences how the ingratiator describes himself. In the business games, those trying to impress the supervisor favorably emphasized their competence and respectability rather than their geniality.

"Attractiveness" can, therefore, be sought by emphasizing what is more desired in a given situation—perhaps efficiency, perhaps compatibility, perhaps trustworthiness or integrity. If the ingratiator knows that the target is aware of his dependence, his tactics are apt to be subtle or devious. He may very well deprecate himself in those areas he does not consider important in order to built up his credibility in areas he *does* consider important. If, however, the ingratiator believes the target is innocent enough to accept him at face value, he will be tempted to pull out all stops.

Conformity

Perhaps the clearest research finding was that to be successful, ingratiation must result in greater public agreement with the target's stated opinions. (Hamlet asked Polonius, "Do you see yonder cloud that's almost in the shape of a camel?" "By the mass, and 'tis like a camel, indeed." "Methinks it is like a weasel." "It is backed like a weasel." "Or like a whale?" "Very like a whale.")

Such conformity was true of both high-status and low-status students—with some significant differences. The low-status freshmen conformed more on relevant than irrelevant items. "Upper-classmen conformed more on the irrelevant than the relevant—presumably they were eager to appear good fellows, but not at the price of compromising any essential source of power or responsibility.

Further, as the business games showed, an ingratiator will cut the cloth of his agreement to fit the back of what is important to his target. If the target clearly values tact, cooperation, and getting along with others, the ingratiator will understand that the strategic use of agreement will probably result in personal advantage. Subjects were quick to reach this conclusion and to act on it, in contrast to their show of independence when the target appeared to be austerely concerned with the productivity of sub-ordinates rather than the congeniality of their views.

When the ingratiator happens to agree closely with the target anyway, there is some evidence that too much agreement is deliberately avoided. Actually, agreement is almost never total. In most of the experimental cases of conformity, the ingratiator's final stated views were a compromise between his original opinion and that of his target. He might be described as avoiding extreme disagreement rather than seeking close agreement; nevertheless, the evidence is clear that expressed opinions are influenced by a desire to create a good impression.

Other-Enhancement

In this tactical area the results were quite inconclusive. There was some evidence that low-status subjects, after being instructed concerning the importance of compatibility with their superiors, were more complimentary than when operating under instructions to be accurate. High-status subjects did not show this same tendency to flatter more under conditions stressing compatibility. On the other hand, they were more inclined to view the low-status complimenter as insincere in a final private judgment, when the instructions stressed compatibility. The low-status subjects showed no such suspicions of their superiors.

THE BOUNDS OF VANITY

Our experiments have answered a few questions and posed many more which may be profitably studied. Among the more important questions raised:

Given the ethical barriers to deceit and social manipulation, what *are* the modes of rationalization or self-justification in ingratiation? How does the ingratiator keep his self-respect? Though our data consistently revealed differences between experimental (compatibility) and control (accuracy) conditions, we were unable to detect any intent to win favor, or the *conscious* adoption of attraction-gaining strategies.

How are power differences affected by ingratiation tactics? Does ingratiation by the follower subvert or augment the power of the leader?

How precisely do the distortions of ingratiation affect our perceptions of ourselves and others?

What of the psychology of favor-giving as part of ingratiation? When does it help and when does it hurt the ingratiator? Is it possible that sometimes targets will like us more if we let *them* do favors for *us*? Why might this be so?

There remains the problem of defining ingratiation. Microscopic examinations of ingratiating behavior keeps revealing an evanescent "something" that in any given case can be identified under more familiar headings such as: social conformity, deference to status, establishing credibility. It is my contention, however, that the concept of ingratiation links together various kinds of communicative acts that would otherwise be separately viewed and studied. By recognizing that there is a strategic side to social interaction, we open to examination the forms in which one person presents his "face" to another, when that other occupies an important position in his scheme of things.

Perhaps by acknowledging that ingratiation is part of the human condition, we may bring its facets into the light of day. As psychologists, if not as moralists, we may, in this vein, admire Lord Chesterfield's candor:

> Vanity is, perhaps, the most universal principle of human actions. . . . If my insatiable thirst for popularity, applause, and admiration made me do some silly things on the one hand, it made me, on the other hand, do almost all the right things that I did. . . . With the men I was a Proteus, and assumed every shape to please them all; among the gay, I was the gayest; among the grave, the gravest; and I never omitted the least attention to good breeding, to the least offices of friendship, that could either please or attach them to me. . . .

ORIENTATIONS IN THE PROCESS OF SOCIALIZATION

ERICH FROMM

We can differentiate between the following kinds of interpersonal relatedness: *symbiotic relatedness, withdrawal-destructiveness, love.*

In the *symbiotic* relatedness the person is related to others but loses or never attains his independence; he avoids the danger of aloneness by becoming part of another person, either by being "swallowed" by that person or by "swallowing" him. The former is the root of what is clinically described as *masochism.* Masochism is the attempt to get rid of one's individual self, to escape from freedom, and to look for security by attaching oneself to another person. The forms which such dependency assume are manifold. It can be rationalized as sacrifice, duty, or love, especially when cultural patterns legitimatize this kind of rationalization. Sometimes masochistic strivings are blended with sexual impulses and pleasureful (the masochistic perversion); often the masochistic strivings are so much in conflict with the parts of the personality striving for independence and freedom that they are experienced as painful and tormenting.

The impulse to swallow others, the *sadistic,* active form of symbiotic relatedness, appears in all kinds of rationalizations, as love, over-protectiveness, "justified" domination, "justified" vengeance, etc.; it also appears blended with sexual impulses as sexual sadism. All forms of the sadistic drive go back to the impulse to have complete mastery over another person, to "swallow" him, and to make him a helpless object of our will. Complete domination over a powerless person is the essence of active symbiotic relatedness. The dominated person is perceived and treated as a *thing* to be used and exploited, not as a human being who is an end in himself. The more this craving is blended with destructiveness, the more cruel it is; but the benevolent domination which often masquerades as "love" is an expression of sadism too. While the benevolent sadist wants his object to be rich, powerful, successful, there is one thing he tries to prevent with all his power: that his object become free

Source: From *Man For Himself* by Erich Fromm. Copyright 1947. Reprinted by permission of Holt, Rinehart and Winston.

and independent and thus cease to be his.

Balzac in his *Lost Illusions* gives a striking example of benevolent sadism. He describes the relationship between young Lucien and the Bagno prisoner who poses as an abbè. Shortly after he makes the acquaintance of the young man who has just tried to commit suicide, the abbè says: "I have picked you up, I have given life to you, and you belong to me as the creature belongs to the creator, as—in the Orient's fairy tales—the Ifrit belongs to the spirit, as the body belongs to the soul. With powerful hands I will keep you straight on the road to power; I promise you, nevertheless, a life of pleasure, of honors, of everlasting feasts. You will never lack money, you will sparkle, you will be brilliant; whereas I, stooped down in the filth of promoting, shall secure the brilliant edifice of your success. I love power for the sake of power! I shall always enjoy *your* pleasures although I shall have to renounce them. Shortly: I shall be one and the same person with you. . . . I will love my creature, I will mold him, will shape him to my services, in order to love him as a father loves his child. I shall drive at your side in your Tilbury, my dear boy, I shall delight in your successes with women. I shall say: I am this handsome young man."

While the symbiotic relationship is one of *closeness* to and intimacy with the object, although at the expense of freedom and integrity, a second kind of relatedness is one of *distance,* of *withdrawal* and *destructiveness.* The feeling of individual powerlessness can be overcome by withdrawal from others who are experienced as threats. To a certain extent withdrawal is part of the normal rhythm in any person's relatedness to the world, a necessity for contemplation, for study, for the reworking of materials, thoughts, attitudes. In the phenomenon here described, withdrawal becomes the main form of relatedness to others, a negative relatedness, as it were. Its emotional equivalent is the feeling of indifference toward others, often accompanied by a compensatory feeling of self-inflation. Withdrawal and indifference can, but

need not, be conscious; as a matter of fact, in our culture they are mostly covered up by a superficial kind of interest and sociability.

Destructiveness is the *active* form of withdrawal; the impulse to destroy others follows from the fear of being destroyed by them. Since withdrawal and destructiveness are the passive and active forms of the same kind of relatedness, they are often blended, in varying proportions. Their difference, however, is greater than that between the active and the passive form of the symbiotic relatedness. Destructiveness results from a more intense and more complete blocking of productiveness than withdrawal. It is the perversion of the drive to live; it is the energy of *unlived life* transformed into energy for the destruction of life.

Love is the productive form of relatedness to others and to oneself. It implies responsibility, care, respect and knowledge, and the wish for the other person to grow and develop. It is the expression of intimacy between two human beings under the condition of the preservation of each other's integrity.

It follows from what has been set forth that there must be certain affinities between the various forms of orientations in the process of assimilation and socialization, respectively. The following chart gives a picture of the orientations which have been discussed and the affinities between them.

ASSIMILATION   SOCIALIZATION

I. Nonproductive orientation

(a) Receiving   Masochistic
    (Accepting)   (Loyalty)

(b) Exploiting   Sadistic
    (Taking)   (Authority)

} symbiosis

(c) Hoarding   Destructive
    (Preserving)   (Assertiveness)

(d) Marketing   Indifferent
    (Exchanging)   (Fairness)

} withdrawal

II. Productive orientation

    Working   Loving, Reasoning

Only a few words of comment seem to be needed. The receptive and exploitative attitude implies a different kind of interpersonal relationship from the hoarding one. Both the receptive and the exploitative attitudes result in a kind of intimacy and closeness to people from whom one expects to get the things needed either peacefully or aggressively. In the receptive attitude, the dominant relationship is a submissive, masochistic one: If I submit to the stronger person, he will give me all I need. The other person becomes the source of all good, and in the symbiotic relationship one receives all one needs from him. The exploitative attitude, on the other hand, implies usually a sadistic kind of relationship: If I take by force all I need from the other person, I must rule over him and make him the powerless object of my own domination.

In contrast to both these attitudes the hoarding kind of relatedness implies remoteness from other persons. It is based not on the expectation of getting things from an outside source of all good but on the expectation of having things by not consuming and by hoarding. Any intimacy with the outside world is a threat to this kind of autarchic security system. The hoarding character will tend to solve the problem of his relationship to others by attempting to withdraw or—if the outside world is felt to be too great a menace—to destroy.

The marketing orientation is also based on detachment from others, but in contrast to the hoarding orientation, the detachment has a friendly rather than a destructive connotation. The whole principle of the marketing orientation implies easy contact, superficial attachment, and detachment from others only in a deeper emotional sense.

BLENDS OF VARIOUS ORIENTATIONS

In describing the different kinds of nonproductive orientations and the productive orientation, I have dealt with these orientations as if they were separate entities, clearly differentiated from each other. For didactic purposes this kind of treatment seemed to be necessary because we have to understand the nature of each orientation before we can proceed to the understanding of their blending. Yet, in reality, we always deal with blends, for a character never represents one of the nonproductive orientations or the productive orientation exclusively.

Among the combinations of the various orientations we must differentiate between the blend of the nonproductive orientations among themselves, and that of the nonproductive with the productive orientation. Some of the former have certain affinities toward each other; for instance, the receptive blends more frequently with the exploitative than with the hoarding orientation. The receptive and exploitative orientations have in common the closeness toward the object, in contrast to the remoteness of the person from the object, in the hoarding orientation. However, even the orientations with lesser affinity are frequently blended. If one wants to characterize a person, one will usually have to do so in terms of his dominant orientation.

The blending between the nonproductive and productive orientation needs a more thorough discussion. There is no person whose orientation is entirely productive, and no one who is completely lacking in productiveness. But the respective weight of the productive and the nonproductive orientation in each person's character structure varies and determines the *quality* of the nonproductive orientations. In the foregoing description of the nonproductive orientations it was assumed that they were *dominant* in a character structure. We must now supplement the earlier description by considering the qualities of the nonproductive orientations in a character structure in which the *productive* orientation is *dominant*. Here the nonproductive orientations do not have the negative meaning they have when they are dominant but have a different and constructive quality. In fact, the nonproductive orientations as they have been described may be considered as distortions of orientations which in themselves are a normal and necessary part of living. Every human being, in order to survive, must be able to *accept* things from others, to *take* things, to *save,* and to *exchange.* He must also be able to *follow authority,* to *guide others,* to be *alone,* and to *assert* himself. Only if his way of acquiring things and relating himself to others is essentially nonproductive does the ability to accept, to take, to save, or to exchange turn into the craving to receive, to exploit, to hoard, or to market as the dominant ways of acquisition. The nonproductive forms of social relatedness in a predominantly productive person—loyalty, authority, fairness, assertiveness—turn into submission, domination, withdrawal, destructiveness in a predominantly nonproductive person. Any of the nonproductive orientations has, therefore, a positive and a negative aspect, according to the degree of productiveness in the total character structure. The following list of the positive and negative aspects of various orientations may serve as an illustration for this principle.

RECEPTIVE ORIENTATION (ACCEPTING)

Positive Aspect	*Negative Aspect*
accepting	passive, without initiative
responsive	opinionless, characterless
devoted	submissive
modest	without pride
charming	parasitical
adaptable	unprincipled
socially adjusted	servile, without self-confidence
idealistic	unrealistic
sensitive	cowardly
polite	spineless
optimistic	wishful thinking
trusting	gullible
tender	sentimental

EXPLOITATIVE ORIENTATION (TAKING)

Positive Aspect	*Negative Aspect*
active	exploitative
able to take initiative	aggressive
able to make claims	egocentric
proud	conceited
impulsive	rash
self-confident	arrogant
captivating	seducing

HOARDING ORIENTATION (PRESERVING)

Positive Aspect	*Negative Aspect*
practical	unimaginative
economical	stingy
careful	suspicious
reserved	cold
patient	lethargic
cautious	anxious
steadfast, tenacious	stubborn
imperturbable	indolent
composed under stress	inert
orderly	pedantic
methodical	obsessional
loyal	possessive

MARKETING ORIENTATION (EXCHANGING)

Positive Aspect	*Negative Aspect*
purposeful	opportunistic
able to change	inconsistent
youthful	childish
forward-looking	without a future or a past
open-minded	without principle and values
social	unable to be alone
experimenting	aimless
undogmatic	relativistic
efficient	overactive
curious	tactless
intelligent	intellectualistic
adaptable	undiscriminating
tolerant	indifferent
witty	silly
generous	wasteful

The positive and negative aspects are not two separate classes of syndromes. Each of these traits can be described as a point in a continuum which is determined by *the degree of the productive orientation which prevails;* rational systematic orderliness, for instance, may be found when productiveness is high, while, with decreasing productiveness, it degenerates more and more into irrational, pedantic compulsive "orderliness" which actually defeats its own purpose. The same holds true of the change from youthfulness to childishness, or of the change from being proud to being conceited. In considering only the basic orientations we see the staggering amount of variability in each person brought about by the fact that

1. the nonproductive orientations are blended in different ways with regard to the respective weight of each of them;
2. each changes in quality according to the amount of productiveness present;
3. the different orientations may operate in different strength in the material, emotional, or intellectual spheres of activity, respectively.

If we add to the picture of personality the different temperaments and gifts, we can easily recognize that the configuration of these basic elements makes for an endless number of variations in personality.

PEOPLE PROCESSING: STRATEGIES OF ORGANIZATIONAL SOCIALIZATION

JOHN VAN MAANEN

Socialization shapes the person—a defensible hyperbole. Organizational socialization or "people processing" refers to the manner in which the experiences of people learning the ropes of a new organizational position, status, or role are structured for them by others within the organization. In short, I will argue here that people acquire the social knowledge and skills necessary to assume a particular job in an organization differently not only because people are different, but, more critically, because the techniques or strategies of people processing differ. And, like the variations of a sculptor's mold, certain forms of organizational socialization produce remarkably differrent results.

Socialization strategies are perhaps most obvious when a person first joins an organization or when an individual is promoted or demoted. They are probably least obvious when an experienced member of the organization undergoes a simple change of assignment, shift, or job location. Nevertheless, certain people-processing devices can be shown to characterize every transition an individual makes across organizational boundaries. Moreover, management may choose such devices explicitly or consciously. For example, management might require all recruits or newcomers to a particular position to attend a training or orientation program of some kind. Or management may select people-processing devices implicitly or unconsciously. These strategies may simply represent taken-for-granted precedents established in the dim past of an organization's history. The precedent could perhaps be the proverbial trial-and-error method of socialization by which a person learns how to perform a new task on his own, without direct guidance.

Regardless of the method of choice, however, any given socialization device represents an identifiable set of events that will make certain behavioral and attitudinal consequences more likely than others. It is possible, therefore, to identify the various people-processing methods and evaluate them in terms of their social consequences.

BACKGROUND

Three primary assumptions underlie this analysis. First, and perhaps of most importance, is the notion that people in a state of transition are more or less in an anxiety-producing situation. They are motivated to reduce this anxiety by learning the functional and social requirements of their new role as quickly as possible.

Second, the learning that takes place does not occur in a social vacuum strictly on the basis of the official and available versions of the job requirements. Any person crossing organizational boundaries is looking for clues on how to proceed. Thus colleagues, superiors, subordinates, clients, and other work associates can and most often do support, guide, hinder, confuse, or push the individual who is learning a new role. Indeed, they can help him interpret (or misinterpret) the events he experiences so that he can take appropriate (or inappropriate) action in his altered situation. Ultimately, they will provide him with a sense of accomplishment and competence or failure and incompetence.

Third, the stability and productiveness of any organization depend in large measure on the way newcomers to various organizational positions come to carry out their tasks. When positions pass from generation to generation of incumbents smoothly, the continuity of the organization's mission is maintained, the predictability of the organization's performance is left intact, and, in the short run at least, the survival of the organization is assured.

A concern for the ways in which individuals adjust to novel circumstances directs attention not only to the cognitive learning that accompanies any transition but also to the manner in which the person copes emotionally with the new situation. As sociologist Erving Goffman

rightly suggests, new situations require individuals to reassess and perhaps alter both their instrumental goals (the goals they wish to achieve through their involvement in the organization) and their expressive style (the symbolic appearances they maintain before others in the organization).

In some cases, a shift into a new work situation may result in a dramatically altered organizational identity for the person. This often happens, for example, when a factory worker becomes a foreman or a staff analysis becomes a line manager. Other times, the shift may cause only minor and insignificant changes in a person's organizational identity; for instance, when an administrator is shifted to a new location or a craftsman is rotated to a new department. Yet any of these shifts is likely to result in what might be called a "reality shock" for the person being shifted. When people undergo a transition, regardless of the information they already possess about their new role, their *a priori* understandings of that role are bound to change in either a subtle or a dramatic fashion. Becoming a member of an organization will upset the everyday order of even the most well-informed newcomer. Matters concerning such aspects of life as friendships, time, purpose, demeanor, competence, and the expectations the person holds of the immediate and distant future are suddenly made problematic. The newcomer's most pressing task is to build a set of guidelines and interpretations to explain and make meaningful the myriad of activities observed as going on in the organization.

To come to know an organizational situation and act within it implies that a person has developed some beliefs, principles, and understandings, or, in shorthand notation, a *perspective* for interpreting the experiences he or she has had as a participant in a given sphere of the work world. This perspective provides the rules by which to manage the unique and recurring strains of organizational life. It provides the person with an ordered view of the organization that runs ahead and directs experience, orders and shapes personal relationships in the work setting, and provides the ground rules to manage the ordinary day-to-day affairs.

STRATEGIES OF PEOPLE PROCESSING

Certain situational variables associated with any organization transition can be made visible and shown to be tied directly to the perspective constructed by individuals in transit. The focus here is not on perspectives *per se,* however, but rather on the properties peculiar to any given people processing situation. These properties are essentially process variables akin to, but more specific than, such generic processes as education, training, apprenticeship, and indoctrination. Furthermore, these properties can be viewed as organizational strategies that distinctly pattern the learning experiences of a newcomer to a particular organizational role.

The people-processing strategies examined below are associated to some degree with all situations that involve a person moving from one organizational position to another. Although much of the evidence comes from studies concerned with the way someone first becomes a member of an organization, the techniques used to manage this passage are at least potentially available for use during any transition a person undergoes during the course of a career. Thus the term "strategy" is used to describe each examined aspect of a transition process because the degree to which a particular people-processing technique is used by an organization is not in any sense a natural condition or prerequisite for socialization. Indeed, by definition, some socialization will always take place when a person moves into and remains with a new organizational role. However, the form that it takes is a matter of organizational

choice. And, whether this choice of strategies is made by design or by accident, it is at least theoretically subject to rapid and complete change at the direction of the management.

This is an important point. It suggests that we can be far more self-conscious about employing certain people-processing techniques than we have been. In fact, a major purpose of this article is to heighten and cultivate a broader awareness of what it is we do to people under the guise of "breaking them in." Presumably, if we have a greater appreciation for the sometimes unintended consequences of a particular strategy, we can alter the strategy to benefit both the individual and the organization.

Seven dimensions on which the major strategies of people processing can be located will be discussed. Each strategy will be presented alongside its counterpart or opposing strategy. In other words, each strategy as applied can be thought of as existing somewhere between the two poles of a single dimension. Critically, across dimensions, the strategies are not mutually exclusive. In practice, they are typically combined in sundry and often inventive ways. Thus, although each tactic is discussed in relative isolation, the reader should be aware that the effects of the various socialization strategies upon individuals are cumulative—but not necessarily compatible (in terms of outcome) with one another.

I do not claim that these strategies are exhaustive or that they are presented in any order of relevance to a particular organization or occupation. These are essentially empirical questions that can only be answered by further research. I do claim and attempt to show that these strategies are recognizable, powerful, in widespread use, and of enormous consequence to the people throughout an organization. And, since organizations can accomplish little more than what the people within them accomplish, these people-processing strategies are of undeniable importance when it comes to examining such matters as organizational performance, structure, and, ultimately, survival.

Formal (Informal) Socialization Strategies

The formality of a socialization process refers to the degree to which the setting in which it takes place is segregated from the ongoing work context and to the degree to which an individual's newcomer role is emphasized and made explicit. The more formal the process, the more the recruit's role is both segregated and specified. The recruit is differentiated strictly from other organizational members. In an informal atmosphere, there is no sharp differentiation and much of the recruit's learning necessarily takes place within the social and task-related networks that surround his or her position. Thus informal socialization procedures are analytically similar to the familiar trial-and-error techniques by which one learns, it is said, through experience.

Generally, the more formal the process, the more stress there is influencing the newcomer's attitudes and values. The more concerned the organization is within the recruit's absorption of the appropriate demeanor and stance, the more the recruit is likely to begin to think and feel like a U.S. Marine, an IBM executive, or a Catholic priest. In other words, formal processes work on preparing a person to occupy a particular *status* in the organization. Informal processes, on the other hand, prepare a person to perform a specific *role* in an organization. And, in general, the more the recruit is separated from the day-to-day reality of the organization, the less he or she will be able to carry over, generalize, and apply any abilities or skills learned in one socialization setting to the new position.

From this standpoint, formal socialization processes are often only the "first round" of socialization. The informal second round occurs when the newcomer is placed in his designated organizational slot and must learn informally the actual practices in his department. Whereas the first wave stresses general skills and attitudes, the second wave emphasizes specified actions, situational applications of the rules, and the idiosyncratic nuances necessary to perform the role in the work setting. However, when the gap separating the two kinds of learning is large, disillusionment with the first wave may set in, causing the individual to disregard virtually everything he has learned in the formal round of socialization.

Even when formal socialization is deliberately set up to provide what are thought to be practical and particular skills, it may be still experienced as problematic by those who pass through the process. In effect, the choice of a formal strategy forces all newcomers to endure, absorb, and perhaps become proficient with *all* the skills and materials presented to them, since they cannot know what is or is not relevant to the job for which they are being prepared. For example, in police training academies, recruits are taught fingerprinting, ballistics, and crime-scene investigation, skills that are, at best, of peripheral interest and of no use to a street patrolman. One result is that when recruits graduate and move to the mean streets of the city, a general disenchantment with the relevance of all their training typically sets in.

Even in the prestigious professional schools of medicine and law the relevance of much training comes to be doubted by practitioners and students alike. Such disenchantment is apparently so pervasive that some observers have suggested that the formal processes that typify professional schools produce graduates who have already internalized standards for their everyday work performances that are "self-validating" and are apparently lodged well beyond the influences of others both within and outside the professional and intellectual community that surrounds the occupation.

Formal strategies appear also to produce stress for people in the form of a period of personal stigmatization. This stigmatization can be brought about by identifying garb (such as the peculiar uniform worn by polce recruits); a special and usually somewhat demeaning title (such as "rookie," "trainee," or "junior"); or an insular position (such as an assignment to a classroom instead of an office or job). A person undergoing formal socialization is likely to feel isolated, cut off, and prohibited from assuming everyday social relationships with his more experienced "betters."

Informal socialization processes, wherein a recruit must negotiate for himself within a far less structured situation, can also induce personal anxiety. Indeed, the person may have trouble discovering clues as to the exact dimensions of his or her assigned organizational role. Under most circumstances, laissez-faire socialization increases the influence of the immediate work group on the new employee. There is no guarantee, though, that the direction provided by the informal approach will push the recruit in the right direction so far as those in authority are concerned. Classical examples are the so-called goldbricking and quota-restriction tactics invented by employees in production situations to thwart managerial directives. Such practices are passed on informally but quite effectively to newcomers against the desires of management.

Left to his own devices, a recruit will select his socialization agents. The success of the socialization process is then determined largely on the basis of whatever mutual regard is developed between the agent and the newcomer, the relevant knowledge possessed by an agent, and of course, the agent's ability to transfer such knowledge. In most Ph.D. programs, for example, students must pick their own advisors from among the faculty. The advisors then act as philosophers, friends, and guides for the students. And among professors—as among organization executives—it is felt that the student who pushes the hardest by demanding more time, asking more

questions, and so forth, learns the most. Consequently, the recruit's freedom of choice in the more informal setting has a price. He or she must force others to teach him.

Individual (Collective) Socialization Strategies

The degree to which individuals are socialized singly or collectively is perhaps the most critical of the process variables. The difference is analogous to the batch versus unit modes of production. In the batch or mass production case, recruits are bunched together at the outset and processed through an identical set of experiences, with relatively similar outcomes.

When a group goes through a socialization program together, it almost always develops an "in-the-same-boat" collective consciousness. Individual changes in perspective are built on an understanding of the problems faced by all members of the group. Apparently as the group shares problems, various members experiment with possible solutions and report back. In the course of discussions that follow, the members arrive at a collective and more or less consensual definition of their situation.

At the same time, the consensual character of the solution worked out by the group allows the members to deviate more from the standards set by the agents than the individual mode of socialization does. Therefore, collective processes provide a potential base for recruit resistance. In such cases, the congruence between managerial objectives and those adopted by the group is always problematic— the recruit group is more likely than the individual to redefine or ignore agent demands.

Classic illustrations of the dilemma raised by the use of the collective strategy can be found in both educational and work environments. In educational settings, the faculty may beseech a student to study hard while the student's peers exhort him to relax and have a good time. In many work settings, supervisors attempt to ensure that each employee works up to his level of competence while the worker's peers try to impress on him that he must not do too much. To the degree that the newcomer is backed into the corner and cannot satisfy both demands at the same time, he will follow the dicta of those with whom he spends most of his time and who are most important to him.

The strength of group understandings depends, of course, on the degree to which all members actually share the same fate. In highly competitive settings, group members know that their own success is increased through the failure of others. Hence, the social support networks necessary to maintain cohesion in the group may break down. Consensual understandings will develop, but they will buttress individual modes of adjustment. Junior faculty members in publication-minded universities, for instance, follow group standards, although such standards nearly always stress individual scholarship.

Critically, collective socialization processes can also promote and intensify agent demands. Army recruits socialize each other in ways the army itself could never do; nor, for that matter, would it be allowed to do. Graduate students are often said to learn more from one another than from the faculty. And, while agents may have the power to define the nature of the collective problem, recruits often have more resources available to them to define the solution—time, experience, motivation, expertise, and patience (or the lack thereof).

Individual strategies also induce personal changes. But the views adopted by people processed individually are likely to be far less homogeneous than the views of those processed collectively. Nor are the views adopted by the isolated newcomer necessarily those that are the most beneficial to him in his transitional position, since he has access only to the perspectives of his socialization agents, and they may not fully apprehend or appreciate his immediate problems.

Certainly, the newcomer may choose not to accept the advice of his agents, although to reject it explicitly may well lose him his job. Furthermore, the rich, contextual perspectives that are available when individuals interact with their peers will not develop under individual strategies. In psychoanalysis, for example, the vocabulary of motives a recruit-patient develops to interpret his situation is quite personal and specific compared with the vocabulary that develops in group therapy. Of course, individual analyses can result in deep changes but they are lonely changes and depend solely on the mutual regard and warmth that exist between agent and recruit.

Apprenticeship modes of work socialization bear some similarity to therapist-patient relationships. If the responsibility for transforming an individual to a given status within the organization is delegated to one person, an intense, value-oriented process is likely to follow. This practice is common whenever a role incumbent is viewed by others in the organization as being the only member capable of shaping the recruit. It is quite common in upper levels of both public and private organizations. Because one organizational member has the sole responsibility, he or she often becomes a role model. The recruit emulates that person's thoughts and actions.

Succession to the chief executive officer level in many firms is marked by the extensive use of the individual socialization strategy. Outcomes in these one-on-one efforts depend on the affective relationships that may or may not develop between the apprentice and his master. In cases of high affect, the process works well and the new member internalizes the values of the particular role he is eventually to play quickly and fully. However, when there are few affective bonds, the socialization process may break down and the transition may not take place.

Overall, individual socialization is expensive in terms of both time and money. Failures are not recycled or rescued easily. Nor are individual strategies particularly suitable for the demands of large organizations, which process many people every year. Hence, with growing bureaucratic structures, the use of mass socialization techniques has increased. Indeed, collective tactics, because of their ease, efficiency, and predictability, have tended to replace the traditional socialization mode of apprenticeship.

Sequential (Nonsequential) Socialization Strategies

Sequential socialization refers to transitional processes marked by a series of discrete and identifiable stages through which an individual must pass in order to achieve a defined role and status within the organization. Many banks groom a person for a particular managerial position by first rotating him or her across the various jobs that will comprise the range of managerial responsibility. Similarly, police recruits in most departments must pass successively through such stages as academy classroom instruction, physical conditioning, firearm training, and on-the-street pupilage.

Nonsequential processes are accomplished in one transitional stage. A factory worker may become a shop supervisor without benefit of an intermediary training program. A department head in a municipal government may become a city manager without serving first as an assistant city manager. Presumably, any organizational position may be analyzed to discover whether intermediate stages of preparation may be required of people taking over that position.

When examining sequential strategies, it is crucial to note the degree to which each stage builds on the preceding stage. For example, the courses in most technical training programs are arranged in what is thought to be a progression from simple to complex material. On the other hand, some sequential processes seem to follow no internal logic. Management training is often disjointed, with the curriculum jumping from topic to topic with little or no integration across stages. In such cases, a person tends to learn the material he likes best in the sequence. If, on the other hand, the flow of topics or courses is harmonious and connected functionally in some fashion, the various minor mental alterations a person must make at each sequential stage will act cumulatively so that at the end, the person may find himself considerably different from the way he was when he started.

Relatedly, if several agents handle different portions of the socialization process, the degree to which the aims of the agents are common is very important to the eventual outcome. For example, in some officers' training schools of peacetime military organizations, the agents responsible for physical and weapons training have very different attitudes toward their jobs and toward the recruits from the agents in charge of classroom instruction. Officer trainees quickly spot such conflicts when they exist and sometimes exploit them, playing agents off against one another. Such conflicts often lead to a more relaxed atmosphere for the recruits, one in which they enjoy watching their instructors pay more attention to each other than they do to the training program. An almost identical situation can be found in many police training programs.

In the sequential arrangement, agents may not know each other, may be separated spatially, and may have thoroughly different images of their respective tasks. University-trained scientists, for example, apparently have considerable difficulty moving from an academic to an industrial setting to practice their trade. The pattern disconcerts many scientists as they discover that their scholarly training emphasized a far different set of skills and interests from those required in the corporate environment. It is often claimed that to become a "good" industrial scientist, you must learn the painful lesson that being able to sell an idea is as important as having it in the first place.

Consider, too, the range of views about a particular job an organizational newcomer may receive from the personnel department, the training division, and colleagues on the job, all of whom have a hand (and a stake) in the recruit's transition. From this standpoint, empathy must certainly be extended to the so-called juvenile delinquent who receives "guidance" from the police, probation officers, judges, social workers, psychiatrists, and correction officers. Such a sequence may actually teach a person to be whatever his immediate situation demands.

Besides the confusion that comes from the contradictory demands that are sometimes made on people, there is also likely to be misinformation passed along by each agent in a sequential process as to how simple the next stage will be. Thus, the recruit may be told that if he just buckles down and applies himself in stage A, stages B, C, D, and E will be easy. Agents usually mask, wittingly or unwittingly, the true nature of the stage to follow. Their reasoning is that if a person feels his future is bright, rewarding, and assured, he will be most cooperative at the stage he is in, not wishing to jeopardize the future he thinks awaits him.

When attempts are consistently made to make each subsequent step appear simple, the individual's best source of information on the sequential process is another person who has gone through it. If the recruit can find organizational members who have been through the process he can use them to help him obtain a more reality-oriented perspective. But some organizations go out of their way to isolate recruits from veteran members. Certain profit-making trade schools go to great lengths to be sure their paying clientele do not learn of the limited job opportunities in the "glamorous and high-paying" worlds of radio and TV broadcasting, commercial art, or heavy equipment operation. Door-to-door sales trainees are continually as-

sured that their success is guaranteed; the handy-dandy, one-of-a-kind product they are preparing to merchandise will "sell itself." When recruits are officially allowed the privilege of interacting with more experienced organizational members, those controlling the process invariably select a veteran member who will present a sanitized or laundered image of the future.

The degree to which an individual is required to keep to a schedule as he goes through the entire sequence is another important aspect of the sequential socialization strategy. A recruit may feel that he is being pressured or pushed into certain positions or stages before he is ready. This position is similar to that of the business executive who does not want a promotion but feels that if he turns it down, he will be damaging his career. A professor may feel that he cannot turn down the chairmanship of his department without rupturing the respectful relationships with his faculty members that he now enjoys.

On the other hand, if the person does not slip, falter, fail, or seriously discredit himself in any fashion, sequential socialization over his full career may provide him with what has been called a "permanent sense of the unobtained." Thus the executive who, at thirty, aims toward being the head of his department by the time he is forty, will then be attempting to make division head by fifty, and so on. The consumer sequence that stresses accumulation of material goods has much the same character as the artistic sequence that stresses the achievement of the perfect work. Sequential socialization of this sort has a rather disquieting Sisyphus-like nature as the person seeks perpetually to reach the unreachable.

Fixed (Variable) Socialization Strategies

Organizational socialization processes differ in terms of the information and certainty an individual has regarding his transition timetable.

Fixed socialization processes provide a recruit with a precise knowledge of the time it will take him to complete a given step. The time of transition is standardized. Consider the probationary systems used on most civil service jobs. The employees know in advance just how long they will be on probation. Educational systems provide another good illustration of fixed processes. Schools begin and end at the same time for all pupils. Students move through the system roughly one step at a time. Fixed processes provide rigid conceptions of "normal" progress; those who are not on schedule are considered "deviant."

Variable socialization processes do not give those being processed any advance notice of their transition timetable. What may be true for one is not true for another. The recruit has to search out clues to his future. Prisoners who serve indeterminate sentences such as the legendary and properly infamous "one to ten," must dope out timetable norms from the scarce materials available to them. Apprenticeship programs often specify only the minimum number of years a person must remain an apprentice and leave open the precise time a person can expect to be advanced to journeyman.

Since the rate of passage across any organizational boundary is a matter of concern to most participants, transition timetables may be developed on the basis of the most fragmentary and flimsiest information. Rumors and innuendos about who is going where and when characterize the variable strategy of socialization. However, if a recruit has direct access to others who are presently in or have been through a similar situation, a sort of "sentimental order" will probably emerge as to when certain passages can or should be expected to take place. And whether or not these expectations are accurate, the individual will measure his progress against them.

The vertically oriented business career is a good example of both variable socialization and the "sentimental order" that seems to characterize such processes. Take the promotional systems in most large organizations. These systems are usually designed to reward individual initiative and performance on current assignments and are therefore considered, at least by upper management, to be highly variable processes. But, for those deeply concerned with their own (and others') progress in the organization, the variable process is almost inevitably corrupted, because would-be executives push very hard to uncover the signs of a coming promotion (or demotion). These people listen closely to stories concerning the time it takes to advance in the organization, observe as closely as possible the experiences of others, and develop an age consciousness delineating the range of appropriate ages for given positions. The process is judgmental and requires a good deal of time and effort. However in some very stable organizations, such as government agencies, the expected rate of advancement can be evaluated quite precisely and correctly. Thus, the process becomes, for all practical purposes, a fixed one.

In some cases, what is designed as a fixed socialization process more closely approximates a variable process for the individual described by the cliché, "always a bridesmaid, never a bride." The transition timetable is clear enough but, for various reasons, the person cannot or does not wish to complete the journey. Colleges and universities have their "professional students" who never seem to graduate. Training programs have trainees who continually miss the boat and remain trainees indefinitely. Fixed processes differ, therefore, with regard to both the frequency and the rate of the so-called failure—the number of recruits who for one reason or another are not able to complete the process.

Some organizations even go so far as to provide a special membership category for certain types of role failures. Some police agencies, for example, give recruits unable to meet agent demands long-term assignments as city jailers or traffic controllers. Such assignments serve as a signal to the recruit and to others in the organization that the individual has left the normal career path.

To the extent that these organizational "Siberias" exist and can be identified by those in the fixed setting, chronic sidetracking from which there is rarely a return is a distinct possibility. On the other hand, sidetracking is quite subtle and problematic to the recruit operating in a variable socialization track. Many people who work in the upper and lower levels of management in large organizations are unable to judge where they are going and when they might get there because a further rise in the organization depends in part on such uncertain factors as the state of the economy and the turnover rates above them. Consequently, variable processes can create anxiety and frustration for people who are unable to construct reasonably valid timetables to judge the appropriateness of their movement or lack of movement in the organization.

It is clear that to those in authority within the organization time is an important resource that can be used to control others. Variable socialization processes give an administrator a powerful tool for influencing individual behavior. But the administration also risks creating an organizational situation marked by confusion and uncertainty among those concerned with their movement in the system. Fixed processes provide temporal reference points that allow people both to observe passages ceremonially and to hold together relationships forged during the socialization experiences. Variable processes, by contrast, tend to divide and drive apart people who might show much loyalty and cohesion if the process were fixed.

Tournament (Contest) Socialization Strategies

The practice of separating selected clusters of recruits into different socialization programs or tracks on the basis of presumed differences in ability, ambition, or background represents the essence of tournament socialization processes. Such tracking is often done at the earliest possible date in a person's organizational career. Furthermore, the shifting of people between tracks in a tournament process occurs mainly in one direction: downward. These people are then eliinated from further consideration within the track they have left. The rule for the tournament socialization strategy, according to Yale University sociologist James Rosenbaum, is simple: "When you win, you win only the right to go on to the next round; when you lose, you lose forever."

Contest socialization processes, on the other hand, avoid a sharp distinction between superiors and inferiors of the same rank. The channels of movement through the various socialization programs are kept open and depend on the observed abilities and stated interests of all. In perhaps 75 percent of American public high schools, school administrators and teachers have made student tracking decisions by the ninth grade (and even before). Thus only students on a college-bound track are allowed to take certain courses. But some schools practice a contest mode. They give their students great freedom to choose their classes and allow for considerable mobility in all directions within the system.

Although little empirical research has been done along these lines, there are strong reasons to believe that some version of the tournament process exists in virtually all large organizations. Often someone who is passed over for a management job once is forever disqualified from that position. And accounts from the women's movement strongly suggest that women in most organizations are on very different tracks from men and have been eliminated from the tournament even before they began. A similar situation can be said to exist for most minority-group members.

Even the so-called "high potential employee" has something to worry about in the tournament process. Often the training for the "high potentials" is not the same as that for the other employees. The "high potential" track will differ considerably from the track afforded the average or typical recruit. But tournament strategy dictates that even among the "high potentials" once you are dropped from the fast track you can't get back on it.

As you move through higher and higher levels in the organization, the tournament strategy becomes even more pervasive. Perhaps this is inevitable. The point here is simply that the tournament socialization process (particularly if an extreme version is used across all levels in an organization) has widespread consequences.

One consequence is that when tournament processes are used, the accomplishments of an employee are more likely to be explained by the tracking system of that organization than by the particular characteristics of the person. Thus the person who fails in organization X might well have succeeded in organization Y. Also, those who fall out of the tournament at any stage can expect only custodial socialization in the future. They are expected to behave only in ways appropriate to their plateaued position, are treated coolly, and are discouraged from making further efforts. The organization, in other words, has completed its work on them. As can be seen, tournament socialization, more than the contest mode, can shape and guide ambition in a powerful way.

Consider, too, that in tournament processes, where a single failure has permanent consequences, those passing through tend to adopt the safest strategies of passage. Low risk taking, short cycles of effort, and ever-changing spheres of interest based primarily on what those above them deem most desirable at any given time are the norm. It follows that those who remain in the tournament for any length of time are socialized to be insecure, obsequious to authority, and differentiated, both socially and psychologically, from one another. On the other hand, those who do not remain in the tournament tend to move in the other direction, becoming fatalistic, homogeneous, and, to varying degrees, alienated from the organization.

The attractiveness and prevalence of tournament socialization strategies in work organizations appear to rest on two major arguments. One is that such processes promote the most efficient allocation of resources. Organizational resources, its proponents say, should be allocated only to those most likely to profit from them. The other, closely related argument, is based primarily on the faith that an accurate and reliable judgment of an individual's potential can be made early in one's career. They believe that the principles of selection and personnel psychology (which are uncertain at best) can be used to separate the deserving from the undeserving members of the organization. Various tracks are then legitimized by testing and classifying people so that each test and the resulting classification represent another level in the tournament process. The American Telephone & Telegraph Co. is perhaps the foremost proponent and user of this socialization process. Each transition from one hierarchical level to another is accompanied by the rigorous evaluation of the ever-declining cadre still in the tournament.

Contest socialization, on the other hand, implies that preset norms for transition do not exist in any other form than that of demonstrated performance. Regardless of age, sex, race, or other background factors, each person starts out equal to all other participants. As in educational systems, this appears to be the stated policy of most American corporations. However, those who have looked closely at these organizations conclude that this Horatio Alger ideal is rarely even approximated in practice.

There is some evidence (primarily from studies conducted in public schools) that contest socialization processes, where they do exist, encourage the development of such characteristics as enterprise, perseverance, initiative, and a craftlike dedication to a job well done. We also have the occasionally impressive results of the workplace experiments that are designed to create autonomous work groups, open and competitive bidding for organizational jobs, and the phasing out of the predictive types of psychological tests used to locate people in the "proper" career track (sometimes in secrecy). Instead of tests, a few organizations have moved toward simply providing people with more reliable career information and voluntary career counseling so that people can make more knowledgeable choices about where to go in the organization.

In summary, tournament socialization seems far more likely than contest socialization to drive a wedge between the people being processed. In tournament situations, each person is out for himself and rarely will a group come together to act in unison either for or against the organization. Contest strategies, as the label implies, appear to produce a more cooperative and participative spirit among people in an organization. Perhaps because one setback does not entail a permanent loss, people can afford to help one another over various hurdles and a more fraternal atmosphere can be maintained.

Serial (Disjunctive) Socialization Strategies

The serial socialization process, whereby experienced members groom newcomers about to assume similar roles in the organization, is perhaps the best guarantee that an organization will not change over long periods of time. In the police world, the serial feature of recruit socialization is virtually a taken-for-granted device and accounts in large measure for the remarkable stability of patrolman behavior patterns from generation to generation of patrolmen. Innovation in serial modes is unlikely, but continuity and a sense of history will be maintained—even in the face of a turbulent and changing environment.

If a newcomer does not have predecessors available in whose footsteps he can follow, the socialization pattern may be labeled disjunc-

tive. Whereas the serial process risks stagnation and contamination, the disjunctive process risks complication and confusion. The recruit who is left to his own devices may rely on definitions for his task that are gleaned from inappropriate others.

But the disjunctive pattern also gives a recruit the chance to be inventive and original. Without an old guard about to hamper the development of a fresh perspective, the conformity and lockstep pressures created by the serial mode are absent. Most entrepreneurs and those people who fill newly created positions in an organization automatically fall into a disjunctive process of socialization. In both cases, few, if any, people with similar experiences are around to coach the newcomer on the basis of the lessons they have learned.

Similarly, what may be a serial process to most people may be disjunctive to others. Consider a black lawyer entering a previously all-white firm or the navy's recent attempts to train women to become jet pilots. These "deviant" newcomers do not have access to people who have shared their set of unique problems. Such situations make passage considerably more difficult, especially if the person is going it alone, as is most often the case.

Sometimes what appears to be serial is actually disjunctive. Newcomers may be prepared inadequately for spots in one department by agents from another department. This is often true when the personnel department handles all aspects of training. Only later, after the newcomers have access to others who have been through the same process, do they discover the worthlessness and banality of their training. Agent familiarity with the target position is a very crucial factor in the serial strategy.

Occasionally, what could be called "gapping" presents a serious problem in serial strategies. Gapping refers to the historical or social distance between recruit and agent. For example, a newcomer to an organization has the greatest opportunity to learn about his future from those with whom he works. But the experiences passed on to him—no doubt with the best of intentions—by those with whom he works may be quite removed from his own circumstance.

Typically, recruits in the first class will set the tone for the classes to follow. This is not to say that those following will be carbon copies, but simply that it is easier to learn from people who have been through similar experiences than it is to devise solutions from scratch. So long as there are people available in the socialization setting the recruits consider to be "like them," these people will be pressed into service as guides, passing on the consensual solutions to the typical problems faced by the newcomer. Mental patients, for example, often report that they were only able to survive and gain their release because other, more experienced, patients "set them wise" as to what the psychiatric staff deemed appropriate behavior indicating improvement.

From this perspective, serial modes of socialization provide newcomers with built-in guidelines to organize and make sense of their organizational situation. Just as children in stable societies are able to gain a sure sense of the future by seeing in their parents and grandparents an image of themselves grown older, employees in organizations can gain a sense of the future by seeing in their more experienced elders an image of themselves further along. The danger exists, of course, that the recruit won't like that image, and will leave the organization rather than face what seems to be an agonizing future. In industrial settings, where worker morale is low and turnover is high, the serial pattern of initiating newcomers into the organization maintains and perhaps amplifies an already poor situation.

The analytic distinction between serial and disjunctive socialization processes is sometimes brought into sharp focus when an organization cleans house, sweeping old members out and bringing new members to replace them. In extreme cases, an entire organization can be thrown into a disjunction mode of socialization, causing the organization to lose all resemblance to its former self. For example, in colleges with a large turnover of faculty, long-term students exert a lot of control. Organizations such as prisons and mental hospitals, where inmates stay longer than the staff, are often literally run by the inmates.

Investiture (Divestiture) Socialization Strategies

The last major strategy to be discussed concerns the degree to which a socialization process is set up either to confirm or to dismantle the incoming identity of a newcomer. Investiture processes ratify and establish the viability and usefulness of the characteristics the person already possesses. Presumably, recruits to most high-level managerial jobs are selected on the basis of what they bring to the job. The organization does not wish to change these recruits. Rather, it wants to take advantage of their abilities.

Divestiture processes, on the other hand, deny and strip away certain entering characteristics of a recruit. Many occupational and organizational communities almost require a recruit to sever old friendships, undergo extensive harassment from experienced members, and engage for long periods of time in what can only be called "dirty work" (that is, low-status, low-pay, low-skill, and low-interest tasks). During such periods, the recruit gradually acquires the formal and informal credentials of full and accepted membership.

Ordained ministers, professional athletes, master craftsmen, college professors, and career military personnel must often suffer considerable mortification and humiliation to pay the dues necessary before they are considered equal and respected participants in their particular professions. As a result, closeness develops among the people in that occupation and a distinct sense of solidarity and mutual concern can be found. Pervasive and somewhat closed social worlds are formed by such diverse groups as policemen, airline employees, railroad workers, nurses, symphony musicians, and funeral directors.

Investiture processes say to a newcomer, "We like you as you are; don't change." Entrance is made as smooth and troublefree as possible. Members of the organization go to great lengths to ensure that the recruit's needs are met. Demands on the person are balanced to avoid being unreasonable. There is almost an explicit "honeymoon" period. At times, even positions on the bottom rung of the organizational ladder are filled with a flurry of concern for employee desires. Orientation programs, career counseling, relocation assistance, even a visit to the president's office with the perfunctory handshake and good wishes, systematically suggest to newcomers that they are as valuable as they are.

Ordinarily, the degree to which a setting represents an ordeal to a recruit indicates the degree to which divestiture processes are operative. Rehabilitation institutions, such as mental hospitals and prisons, are commonly thought to be prototypical in this regard. But even in these institutions, initiation processes will have different meanings to different newcomers. Some "rehabilitation" settings, for example, offer a new inmate a readymade home away from home that more or less complements his entering self-image. Thus, for some people, becoming a member of, say, the thief subculture in a prison acts more as an investiture than a divestiture socialization process. In such cases, one's preinstitutional identity is sustained with apparent ease. Prison is simply an annoying interval in the person's otherwise orderly career. The analyst must examine socialization settings closely before assuming powerful divestiture processes to be acting homogeneously on all who enter.

Yet the fact remains that many organizations consciously promote initiation ordeals designed primarily to make the recruit whatever the organization deems appropriate. In the more extreme cases, recruits are isolated from former associates, must abstain from certain types of behavior, must publicly degrade themselves and others through various kinds of mutual criticism, and must follow a rigid set of sanctionable rules and regulations.

This process, when voluntarily undergone, serves, of course, to commit and bind people to the organization. In such cases, the sacrifice and surrender on the part of the newcomers is usually premised upon a sort of institutional awe the recruits bring with them into the organization. Such awe serves to sustain their motivation throughout the divestiture process. Within this society, there are many familiar illustrations: the Marine Corps, fraternal groups, religious cults, elite law schools, self-realization groups, drug rehabilitation programs, professional athletic teams, and so on. All these organizations require a recruit to pass through a series of robust tests in order to gain privileged access to the organization.

In general, the endurance of the divestiture process itself promotes a strong fellowship among those who have followed the same path to membership. For example, college teaching, professional crime, dentistry, and the priesthood all require a person to travel a somewhat painful and lengthy road. The trip provides the newcomer with a set of colleagues who have been down the same path and symbolizes to others on the scene that the newcomer is committed fully to the organization. For those who complete the ordeal, the gap separating recruits from members narrows appreciably while the gap separating members from nonmembers grows.

Clearly, divestiture rather than investiture strategies are more likely to produce similar results among recruits. And, it should be kept in mind, the ordeal aspects of a divestiture process represent an identity-bestowing, as well as an identity-destroying, process. Coercion is not necessarily an assault on the person. It can also be a device for stimulating personal changes that are evaluated positively by the individual. What has always been problematic with coercion is the possibility for perversion in its use.

SUMMARY AND CONCLUSIONS

I have attempted to provide a partial framework for analyzing some of the more pervasive strategies used by organizations to control and direct the behavior of their members. For instance, the tightness or looseness of day-to-day supervision could also be depicted as a socialization strategy. So, too, could the degree of demographic and attitudinal homogeneity or heterogeneity displayed by the incoming recruits, since it could affect the probability that a single perspective will come to dominate the group of newcomers. What I have tried to do here, however, is describe those processes that are most often both ignored by organizational researchers and taken for granted by organizational decision makers.

It is true that someone undergoing a transition is not *tabula rasa,* waiting patiently for the organization to do its work. Many people play very active roles in their own socialization. Each strategy discussed here contains only the possibility, and not the actuality, of effect. For example, those undergoing collective socialization may withdraw from the situation, abstaining from the group life that surrounds other recruits. Or a person may undergo a brutal divestiture process with a calculated indifference and stoic nonchalalance. A few exceptions are probably the rule in even the most tyrannical of settings.

However, the preponderance of evidence suggests that the seven strategies discussed here play a very powerful role in influencing any individual's conception of his work role. By teasing out the situational processes variables that, by and large, define an organization passage, it becomes apparent that for most people a given set of experiences in an organization will lead to fairly predictable ends.

If we are interested in strategies that promote a relatively high degree of similarity in the thoughts and actions of recruits and their agents, a combination of the formal, serial, and divestiture strategies would probably be most effective. If dissimilarity is desired, informal, disjunctive, and investiture strategies would be preferable. To produce a relatively passive group of hardworking but undifferentiated recruits, the combination of formal, collective, sequential, tournament, and divestiture strategies should be used. Other combinations could be used to manufacture other sorts of recruits with, I suspect, few exceptions.

At any rate, the single point I wish to emphasize is that much of the control over individual behavior in organizations is a direct result of the manner in which people are processed. By directing focused and detailed attention to the breakpoints or transitions in a person's work career, much can be gained in terms of understanding how organizations shape the performances and ambitions of their members. And, most critically, the strategies by which these transitions are managed are clearly subject to both empirical study and practical change.

Increased awareness and interest in the strategies of people processing may be a matter of some urgency. The trend in modern organizations is apparently to decrease control through such traditional means as direct supervision and the immediate application of rewards and punishments and increase control by such indirect means as recruitment, selection, professionalization, increased training, and career path manipulation. To these more or less remote control mechanisms, we might well add the seven strategies described in this paper.

Certain features of organizations promote behavioral styles among subordinates, peers, and superiors. Since many of the strategies for breaking in employees are taken for granted (particularly for employees beyond the raw recruit level), they are rarely discussed or considered to be matters of choice in the circles in which managerial decisions are reached. Furthermore, those strategies that are discussed are often kept as they are simply because their effects are not widely understood.

People-processing strategies are also frequently justified by the traditional illogic of "that's the way I had to do it, so that's the way my successors will have to do it." Yet, as I have attempted to show, socialization processes are not products of some fixed, evolutionary pattern. They are products of both decisions and nondecisions—and they can be changed. Unfortunately, many of the strategies discussed here seem to be institutionalized out of inertia rather than thoughtful action. This is hardly the most rational practice to be followed by managers with a professed concern for the effective utilization of resources—both material and human.

BIG MAGIC: THREE SPECIFIC TABOOS

FRITZ STEELE

There are two major control systems that limit discussion topics in organizations. One is the informal norm system, which consists mainly of taboos and various rules of the game about what to say and where. The other is the formal policy system. In the formal system, certain topics are declared to be officially out of bounds, and they therefore function as a more definite kind of taboo.

When the formal and informal taboos are combined, they provide a two-dimensional system for classifying topics, as shown in Table 1. For example, in most organizations salaries and money constitute one topic that is prohibited by both formal policy and informal group taboos (cell a). Career plans and movement of personnel to new positions are usually defined by policy to be secret, yet are open topics for informal discussion, speculation, etc. (cell b). Feelings and "personalities" are seldom defined officially as out of bounds, yet are taboo topics according to the informal rules (cell c). Various safe topics fall in the free area (cell d).

Any topic can theoretically be placed in one of the four cells, depending on how it is handled in the particular group or organization. I have found that being specific about where a topic falls in the table helps the system and allows people to have greater influence over factors related to that topic. Your strategy for change should vary, depending on the cell in which you are working, since it determines whether you

Table 1

System for Classifying Topics

	Informal Norms	
Formal policy	Taboo—not discussable	Free—open for discussion
Secret—not discussable	Salaries (a)	Career plans (b)
Free—open for discussion	Feelings, "personalities" (c)	Various nonthreatening topics (d)

are trying to loosen up the way group members treat one another, to change the formal reward system, or both.

TABOO 1: SALARIES

Freud once described two major requirements of successful psychoanalysis—the patient had to be able to talk openly about both sex and money. Today, the barrier to discussions about sex is fairly steadily being lowered, but the one relating to money is just about as high and solid as it ever was.

In work organizations, the taboo against the open discussion of salaries is probably the most consistent one that I have found. Money is discussed incessantly, but primarily as a score-keeping mechanism for the organization as a whole—costs, gross sales, profit margins, budgets for future operations, and the like. When it comes to disclosing personal salaries and other individual financial affairs, the climate of most organizations is not much different from that existing in the early 1900's. In short, discussion of salaries is to be kept secret and is also a taboo, according to formal organization policy and informal norms, respectively (cell a in Table 1).

One source of this attitude is American society as a whole; there are generally strong norms against discussing personal finances with anyone outside a very small circle of people. In many cases, the norm says that personal finances should be discussed with neither friends nor relatives, but only with an impersonal financial agent (such as a banker or an accountant), and then not with much comfort. Different generations of the same family are generally embarrassed when the subject of salaries arises, and many otherwise close friends have never disclosed to each other how much money they make, how much their houses cost, and so on. In his research on self-disclosure, Jourard found that money consistently fell near the bottom in terms of frequency of disclosure. Attitudes, work, tastes, and personality areas all rated higher in frequency, and only specifics about the body rated lower.[1]

One indicator of the strength of this norm is the fact that it is often invisible to people—they do not see it as a choice, but rather as a natural law. When I point out this pattern, people will say, "Of course that's not discussed—it just isn't done. What's the point in even bringing that up? Are you obsessed with money or something?" To me, this is a perfect indicator that I have just violated a taboo, and my action must be explained away as demonstrating overconcern about money, just plain stupidity, or perversity. Under no circumstance must the discussion continue to explore disclosure about money as an alternative, a choice to be made. I try to make the point that I am not saying that everyone has to *want* to discuss salaries all the time, but only that it would be easier to deal with certain issues if there were a choice. Nonetheless, people respond as though I had proposed that salaries be the only topic of every meeting.

In addition to informal norms against discussing salaries, organizations often have quite explicit policies which forbid employees from disclosing their salaries to one another or managers from discussing salaries with their subordinates. In several organizations for which I have been a consultant, an individual is not even allowed to know his or her own salary grade (general category), even though the specific salary is, of course, known. If organizations had an effective means for hiding from a person his or her own salary, I am sure that many of them would try it.

When the organization legislates rules to keep people from knowing what others are paid, and even the system by which they are paid, we indeed have a pure example of the unilateral relevance test, with top management making policy decisions about what people should *not* need to know in order to do their jobs. The reasoning behind this policy varies, but usually has to do with the (predicted) inability of people to cope with the sheer titillation if salaries were disclosed. Most executives appear to believe that: (1) people don't really want to know salaries and that this information is not useful or interesting to them, so why make it available; and (2) people are obsessed with curiosity about money and will make all sorts of negative comparisons if that information is available. The fact that these two views are somewhat incompatible does not keep them from being used in the same breath, as many executives have done with me.

To me, this inconsistency is simply an indicator of the strength of emotions that lie behind these policies. The tip-off of this emotionalism is the policy of making salaries secret and then justifying this policy on the grounds that the only other alternative would be to publish "all that information," which would take too much time and energy. What has been left out, of course, is the third alternative—having salary information available for those who request it. That possibility is usually disregarded because it would obviously violate the taboo, without providing the cop-out that the "energy drain" concept of full publishing does. To control-minded bosses, the policy of information-available-on-request also has the drawback of placing responsibility and choice in the hands of the persons seeking the information rather than with those doling it out.

Consequences of Salary Secrecy

One of the justifications for secrecy about pay is that disclosure would result in invidious comparisons and create a great deal of dissatisfaction in the organization. This long-standing assumption was never really tested until Edward Lawler did his research on pay systems. His findings indicate that just the opposite is true. On the average, organizations in which salary information is kept secret tend to have more employee dissatisfaction with salaries than do those in which such information is public.[2] This difference could be explained away as simply

the result of the fact that the open system has to pay more, were it not for Lawler's finding that when pay was secret, people tended to see themselves as worse off, relatively speaking than they actually were. They inflated the imagined salaries of their peers, superiors, and when they didn't know them, of their subordinates.

Lawler also found that open salary information tended to cut down the number of *rumors* about pay and that curiosity about such information tended to die out fairly quickly after a group had changed to a more open system. This is not a surprising result, since it is usually the absence of verifiable data that leads to rumors. Yet this knowledge has had little effect, and executives still make policies based on the assumption that they can reduce speculation by imposing rules of secrecy.

A graphic example of this lack of connection between data about the effects of secrecy and impact on the way we have occurred on a British television show not long ago. In the context of a discussion about the financial hardship that almost all members of a losing party (but not the prime minister) suffer when they leave office, Prime Minister Harold Wilson was questioned about the earnings he had received on his memoirs:

Dimbleby [the interviewer] went on: "But you are said to have earned something between £100,000 and £250,000 from your book. Has this been any consolation to you?"

Mr. Wilson replied: "I wouldn't believe any of the stories you read in the press about this . . . my press handling over a long period of time has been one of rumour. If they get the facts, they twisted them . . . if they didn't get the facts they invented them, so we can dismiss that right away. I got a fair, I think, compensation for what I wrote, but I wouldn't accept those views."

Dimbleby: "You couldn't set our minds at rest—the vexed question of what the *Sunday Times* did pay you for the book?"

Wilson: "No, No. I don't think it's a matter of interest to the BBC or anyone else."[3]

Since he had just been told that it *was* a matter of interest and had admitted as much with his rumor comments, Mr. Wilson obviously felt that it wasn't a matter that *he wanted* to disclose, not that it was of no interest to anyone else. Unfortunately, his choice tended to do that which he was just complaining about—foster rumors unsubstantiated by facts. In fact, he was quite angry that the question was even asked, and the whole segment was cut out of the show as a "courtesy" to him. It may have been a courtesy, but the decision-makers colluded with Wilson to continue the rumors unchecked by accurate information.

At that time, several newspapers pointed out that the issue of earnings from memoirs was *not* just a personal matter for a man whose public position gives him the opportunity to make those earnings. Money happened to be the medium, but the message was the relationship of public service to private gain. Mr. Wilson's reticence is regrettable, but from the discussion here it was quite predictable. Similarly, many American congressmen have been reluctant to fully disclose their own financial affairs. However, the political impact caused by President Nixon's long series of half-disclosures about his financial gains on his California and Florida homes has led to more moves toward financial disclosure by members of Congress and state political leaders.

A second major consequence of secrecy about salaries is the leeway it gives management to set salaries as they will, whether justified or not. If salary information is not shared, most people never see the whole pattern. Obvious discrepancies and inequities are hidden and thus keep functioning without constraint. This lack of constraint is often described positively as the manager's right to remain "flexible."

This flexibility is gained at a price, as are most benefits of low-disclosure policies. When secrecy is the rule, salary schemes are invented right and left, but none is usually much of an improvement over the previous plans, because the kind of information that would lead to real learning in this area is never shared. Questions about what high-quality contribution is in each area are left up to the executive who controls that sector and are not discussed by all those who might have a useful input. Compromises and bad decisions, which are used to take pressure off a boss who does not know how else to deal with a subordinate, can be kept secret through the taboo on salaries, which means that the boss is not confronted with the results of choices he or she has made. The following, for example, is a wonderful anecdote from the biography of Robert Benchley, which describes the managerial climate of a magazine for which Benchley worked:

One policy memorandum dated October 14, 1919, ran as follows:

POLICY MEMORANDUM
Forbidding Discussion
among Employees of
Salary Received

"It has been the policy of the organization to base salaries on the value of the service rendered. We have, therefore, a long established rule that the salary question is a confidential matter between the organization and the individual.

It is obviously important that employees live up to this rule in order to avoid invidious comparison and dissatisfaction. Recently several cases have come to the notice of management where employees have discussed the salary question among themselves.

This memorandum should serve as a warning that anyone who breaks this rule in the future will be instantly discharged."

The day that memorandum was distributed, Sherwood and Parker and Benchley went into action. The first thing they they did was to decide to answer the memorandum with one of their own, which Robert wrote and which went:

POLICY MEMORANDUM
Concerning the For-
bidding of Discus-
sion among Employees

"We emphatically resent both the policy and working of your policy memorandum of October

14. We resent being told what we may and what we may not discuss, and we protest against the spirit of petty regulation which has made possible the sending out of such an edict. . . ."

They then made signs, on which they wrote their salaries, and went through the office wearing the signs around their necks. That was the end of the no-talking-about-your-salary policy.*

In this instance, if the management had truly believed that salary was based on service rendered, there would have been no need for secrecy in the first place—unless, of course, it was to be a secret that employees were or were not in fact rendering services. Instead, management was trying to reserve an area about which they would not be constrained to base decisions on so rational a basis.

This Benchley-type response to such a policy is, in my experience, quite unusual. When I ask groups of managers whether they have ever pushed the secrecy-about-salary issue or whether they have ever *demanded* to know their own salary grade, as the natural right of an adult person in the system, they just smile knowingly at me and say, "Well, of course you don't really understand our way of doing things . . .," which means: "No, we haven't, and nobody in his right mind would risk it." Benchley, Parker, and Sherwood were most definitely in their right minds, however, and they rejected the policy because they were willing to back one another up and to violate the policy in a manner that highlighted management's highhandedness. By contrast, most employee groups do accept such policies and also make them an informal group norm.

A surprising consequence of secrecy about salary is that it can *reduce* managerial discretion rather than add to it, as is usually claimed. For all except those few executives at the top who can see the whole picture, remuneration is an area over which little control can be de-

veloped by the manager in his or her own area of responsibility. When the manager cannot foster open discussion of salaries or tell a person his or her salary grade (or find out), that manager definitely has less influence on the factors that are influencing his or her own performance.

This reduces a manager's sense of not only real responsibility for the job, but also self-worth. This is the heart of the message in the Benchley example; the trio refused to accept management's definition of them as immature, inadequate people who could not handle salary discussions without breaking down. Although they were undoubtedly called "immature" when they refused to play ball, I think they were just the opposite. I wish that more employees had the maturity to reject infantilizing policies, such as salary taboos imposed "for the good of the employees, who need our guidance." Fewer childlike rules and more real guidance in the open working-through of difficult issues would lead to both more performance and more learning from experiences.

TABOO 2: CAREER DECISIONS

A second major taboo area concerns career decisions. Unlike the topic of salaries, which is kept secret by both formal policies and informal group norms, no such agreement exists on the topic of career decisions, which falls in cell (b) of Table 1. In other words, informal norms permit open discussion of career decisions, but formal policy does not. The following is an excerpt from an interview I once held with an executive:

Interviewer: Do you ever discuss planned job changes with people to get their reactions or to give them warning?

Executive: No, we don't. We have a policy of keeping new assignments secret until they are formally announced.

Interviewer: Why do you have that policy?

*From *Robert Benchley: A Biography* by Nathaniel Benchley. Copyright 1955 by McGraw-Hill. Used with permission of McGraw-Hill Book Company.

Executive: We don't announce our preliminary considerations, because the
ones who don't get new jobs or
promoted might think that they
were being passed over.

Interviewer: Well, aren't they? In any particular instance there are some who
are moved and some who are
not. Isn't that just reality?

Executive: Well, uh, not really. You see,
there could be a lot of reasons,
and it might just create confusion, or false expectations, to talk
beforehand about what *might* be
done.

We might add what the executive did not say in
that particular interview: "Our people are not
mature enough to understand possibilities, and
therefore we must protect them in advance from
disappointments."

In the area of planning for job assignments
and management changes (the careers of
members of the organization), there is a strong
tendency in the United States, as a policy of top
management, for most information to be kept
secret. On the other hand, there is less of a
tendency for the informal norms of groups
within the organization to forbid discussion of
this area; hence, its placement in cell (b) of the
table—informally free but formally secret.

Another informant called this pattern the
"management change mystique." In his organization, executives took great pleasure from
their roles as manipulators of the careers (and
fates) of large numbers of employees. They saw
themselves as the people with the "big picture,"
the ones who knew what was best, both for the
company's manpower plans and for the lower-
level managers whose careers were being affected. As they talked about the importance of
this mode of operating, I had the feeling that
they were describing a chess game, with themselves as the players and other employees as
the pieces on the board.

As with many aspects of disclosure, the policy of secrecy about management changes allows these executives to maintain their position
of control, but it also has certain attendant
costs. First, individual managers, who naturally
are concerned about where they are going in
the system, spend a good deal of time and
energy speculating about their future chances,
looking for cues in small interactions between
themselves and those above, and generally trying to milk the environment for whatever information it can yield about their mysterious career
pattern. They perform this search without a
great deal of help from those above. In fact, in
some cases I have found intentional hindrance
as a result of the career-secrecy policy.

One example comes from several organizations which used "promotability ratings" of one
sort or another. These ratings were made by
various superiors and were attached to each
employee's record. Yet these ratings were considered to be confidential information, *not* to be
shared with the person involved. Thus, managers at quite high levels of responsibility did not
know what their ratings were and therefore did
not know what the company's overall evaluation
of them was. They obviously did not have the
option of challenging the accuracy of their own
rating, let alone that of the system as a whole.
Without information, who was to say whether or
not the information was accurate? The cost is
one of individuals' expending energy to obtain
a sense of mastery over their own fate that organizational policy does not encourage.

A parallel example is the increasing use of
"independent credit checks" on American citizens. Financial files are being developed on individuals, with no disclosure to them of what
evidence is in the files, who is developing them,
or the sources and reliability of the "data."

A second cost is to the system itself. Executives often make management moves and
placement decisions without getting the input of
the people who are going to be moved. To the
extent that a quality job requires that a person

be interested, motivated, and accepting of the demands, that person's decision about whether she or he wants the job is extremely relevant to whether the person *should* be moved. Thus, executives often get very angry when an employee rejects a planned move, for the rejection can be seen as either employee ingratitude *or a* poorly designed decision process.

This pattern, as in many other instances of low disclosure, also makes it hard to *learn* from past experiences. If there is no open discussion of possible shifts in job assigment, it is difficult to confront issues about selection criteria and their accuracy. The top executives in the organization may be consistently mediocre in their placement decisions, yet never have to look at their basis for decisions, since the area is out of bounds for member comment.

I think that this is an inadequate stance toward organizational issues, from the standpoint of both performance and the relationship between the individual and the system. I believe that this relationship ought to be aimed at people's experiencing themselves as competent human beings whose choices can influence their fate. As Argyris has documented so well, the dominant forces in formal organizations tend to thwart this sense of competence, and secrecy about career plans is a major input to these forces.[4]

For example, consider the following statement made by an executive at a behavioral science seminar. The question was: "When do you think that it is impossible to share with a man what plans his superiors have for his future in the organization?" The executive replied:

> We had a case of this not long ago. There was a man who was very good at his specialty. We knew that there would be no need for him when our market for his products phased out, in about three years. We also felt that he was not really a good long-term bet for promotion, although he was good at what he was doing.
> Our problem was whether to tell him about his limited future or not. We decided that we couldn't,

because it would have devastated him, and because his motivation to produce would have been adversely affected. We really need his output over the next three years.

This illustrates the touchiest aspect of the career-secrecy pattern. Top management decided, through a unilateral relevance test, that this man should not be told what his superiors had in mind for him in the organization. The price of affecting his motivation was considered to be too high, as was the probable impact of disclosure on him. But even though they talked about concern for his feelings, their choice shows very little *real* concern for him. They opted to let him work himself into being obsolete, without giving him the benefit of the choice to leave, to continue to the end, or to continue and be looking for something else. In addition, since they did not disclose their long-term evaluation to him, he wasn't given the opportunity to confront them with the possibility that they might be wrong. Indeed, they opted to hold his fate solely in their hands.

I believe that this is the wrong way to handle career information, especially when a person's future has been decided. That information should be disclosed as soon as possible, so that the individual can plan and/or influence the judgments that have been made. It is true that the company in the example above might have suffered if the man had decided to leave before the three years were up, but I think this would have been preferable to maintaining an exploitative system which milks employees for their last juices before shipping them out. The image is nineteenth-century sweatshop, but the practice, as in the example above, is still current when it comes to managerial changes.

I also believe that hiding career plans from the people affected is basically unethical. Although most managers would not admit it to themselves or to others, it has a quality of out-and-out dishonesty, as in the following example from an interview:

Our company held a one-of-a-kind Friday afternoon meeting (with drinks) in October. Top management wanted to put everyone's mind at rest about layoffs. A small section of the plant had been given the axe, but they assured us that this would never happen to Research and Development.

Three weeks later there was a major layoff, with R&D hit very hard. I later learned that the firings had been planned for months. It appears that the cocktail party was designed to be the last time that group of people would be together as a working group. At that meeting, when the question of the future arose, the Head Lier said that we were approaching Fat City, and all was secure. Sure, as secure as the Titanic . . .

No doubt top management rationalized their actions as necessary for "corporate responsibility," or some other high-sounding reason, but their actions were still patently dishonest.

This same kind of bending the truth also occurs when good news is involved. The basic assumption is that the people in the organization might take information the wrong way, e.g., treating possibilities as certainties. True, possibilities can raise anxieties about uncertainty or change, but people are also capable of hearing speculations or alternatives as just that—speculations and alternatives—if information is communicated that way *and* there is a history of trustworthy communication from management. The tentativeness must be communicated in order to be received, and it must be taken at face value in order to be believed. If the top group has a past history of disclosing "possibilities" which turn out to have been decisions already made, tentative discussions will be sifted by the lower levels in order to get clues about what is really true. Under these conditions, people will indeed be unable to cope adequately with disclosure of career possibilities; but this says more about failings in the organization's climate than it does about their inherent limitations at dealing with uncertainty.

The point is that organizational leaders have a way of making career information taboo (in order to avoid having to deal with the reactions of others), then using the resultant fear and curiosity about personal futures as evidence that people are too immature to handle that kind of information. It is just as likely, however, that the problem is caused by the fact that the superiors' are engaged in a confused (and confusing) process of promotions and job changes. As long as disclosure of career decisions is taboo, that confusion will never be directly confronted and challenged.

TABOO 3: PERSONAL FEELINGS

The final taboo that will be specifically discussed here is that connected with personal feelings and emotions. This taboo is located in cell (c) of Table 1, i.e., personal feelings and emotions are a taboo according to informal group norms, but are not treated as such in the organization's formal policies. In most kinds of organizations in the United States, even in those whose mission is to process feelings, e.g., counseling centers, and in which discussion of clients' feelings is legitimate, there is a strong norm against staff members talking about their own feelings while working on a task. To tell someone else that you feel angry, happy, apprehensive, confused, etc., is supposed to bear no relation to the work at hand. To talk about feelings, therefore, is to waste people's time and to lead the task astray. There is not usually a formal policy against talking about feelings, but rather a strong informal norm within the system which is carried in from the outside culture, where it is generally bad form to talk about feelings except in a very small circle defined as the "private" world.

When feelings *are* expressed in work organizations, they tend to take the form of innuendoes or other subtle cues, such as "I suspect there's another point of view," as a substitution for "I can't stand that idea—or you!" This follows the "satellite theory" of communication, which emphasizes indirect communication. Presumably, the goal here is an intentionally ambiguous message to which a person may choose not to respond. The sender is courteous enough to communicate his or her feelings in such a way that the receiver has the option of responding or behaving as though the message had not been sent. (Of course, if the sender doesn't like the response, he or she also has the option of denying the message.) We can assume that on the whole, people do not value their own feelings highly in a work setting, nor do they expect others to respond to them.

In some organizations, talking about feelings is automatically associated with personal criticism or prying into others' affairs. It is usually dismissed with "We don't talk about personalities here!" In most cases when I have heard this closing-off phrase, it was misapplied (perhaps intentionally), since the feelings expressed were caused as much by the situation and the behavior of others as by the "personalities" (stable traits and predispositions) of the people involved. Calling feelings the "personality area" is a means of avoiding having to deal with the effects of people's behaviors on one another.

Consequences of the Feelings Taboo in Operation

What happens to group and organizational performance when a taboo against dealing with feelings is in effect? Argyris provides a very nice summary of the cycle this creates:

> Under these conditions the individual may tend to find it very difficult to develop competence in dealing with feelings and interpersonal relationships: Also, in a world where the expression of feelings is not valued, individuals may build personal and organizational defenses to help them suppress their own feelings or inhibit others in such expression. Or they may refuse to consider ideas which, if explored, could expose suppressed feelings.
> Such a defensive reaction in an organization

could eventually inhibit creativity and innovation during decision making. The participants might learn to limit themselves to those ideas and values that were not threatening. They might also decrease their openness to new ideas and values, and as the degree of openness decreased, the capacity to experiment would also decrease, and fear of taking risks would increase. This would reduce the *probability* of experimentation, thus decreasing openness to new ideas still further and constricting risk taking even more than formerly. We would thereby have a closed circuit which could become an important cause of loss of vitality in an organization.[5]

Certain topics of discussion become the approved ones, and others, particularly those dealing with emotions, become disapproved, even when those emotions are the only real facts that are known about the problem at hand.

The quote also illustrates one of the most important features of taboos—once they begin operating, they are hard to stop. They have a self-maintaining quality, since it requires the risk of violating the taboo in order to question the taboo openly to the others in your group. For instance, the taboo against expressing feelings tends to roll on, since in order to complain about it, a person must express negative-feelings, which by definition violates the taboo itself. Someone must risk looking foolish, negative, or weak in order to promote a chance for change. This is a big order for most of us.

Taboos against the open expression of feelings also have a way of leveling out our day-to-day experiences. When people are constrained to share only nonemotional aspects of their lives, they develop blank spots in their relationships, aspects of other people about which they know very little. Nor can they learn from comparing similarities and differences of reactions to the same situation, since they can't share what those reactions were. Life on the job is just less rich than it would be if people were free to disclose what they think and feel without the necessity of mentally screening out the feelings in advance. Participants in human-relations training laboratories often report that the most significant revelation to them was the meaningfulness of being able to disclose and receive disclosures about feelings, as well as the discovery that things do not fall apart when these feelings are shared. Their belief before the experience was that talking about feelings would lead to a total breakdown in rational discourse. If anything, the discourse tends to become *more* rational (or, rather, *sensible*), since it includes all aspects of life experience.

When the feelings taboo has operated in a system for a long time, it is difficult to move toward the more open disclosure pattern just described. I once told a client group that I was bothered by something that had been said, and they immediately became anxious that I was about to break down altogether. In their world, feelings are seldom expressed, and someone had to feel *very* strongly before she or he would say so to others directly. The group therefore decoded my message to read the same way, although I in fact did not feel very strongly at all.

This kind of confusion will necessarily accompany changes in behavior toward the feelings taboo. Each listener will decode messages in terms of his or her own scale of intensity (which happens all the time, anyway). Thus, managers who want to express themselves more freely will have to be willing to receive some overreactive responses from the others for a while, until they can develop a new language for the feelings area. If they stay with it, others may attempt to experiment as a result of this lead. Then, the group can shift to feelings and back to ideas without any great difficulty, just simply carrying out the business of dealing with whatever is true.

Most important, as with all taboos, the key is to open up feelings as an area so that they are not ruled out *in advance* as relevant or useful topics for discussion. The costs of the taboo in terms of problem-solving ability, sharing views on task performance, interpersonal vitality, and personal aliveness are too high to be worthwhile when there is an alternative mode of operation.[6]

NOTES

1. Sidney Jourard, *The Transparent Self,* New York: Van Nostrand/Insight, 1964, p. 169.

2. Edward E. Lawler, III, *Pay & Organizational Effectiveness: A Psychological View,* New York: McGraw-Hill, 1971, pp. 174–76, 256.

3. "BBC Censors Wilson Row Over Earnings," *The Guardian,* June 18, 1971.

4. Chris Argyris, *Personality and Organization,* New York: Harper & Brothers, 1957.

5. Chris Argyris, "Interpersonal Barriers to Decision-making," *Harvard Business Review,* **44,** 2, (March–April 1966): 87–88. Reprinted by permission.

6. For further ideas about reducing the suppression of feelings, see the article by Chris Argyris cited in note 5, as well as his book *Management and Organizational Development: The Path from xa to yb,* New York: McGraw-Hill, 1971.

QUESTIONS FOR DISCUSSION

1. Why do organizations spend so much money and time indoctrinating and socializing a new employee during the training process?
2. Does having the right attitude affect your advancement in most organizations?
3. At what point in the socialization process do you think that organizations *overstep* their bounds?
4. How does the reading by Fromm relate to the *Newsweek* reading?
5. How does the Army socialize the new recruit? What effect does it have on espirit de corp and morale?
6. Remember when you first entered college or graduate school? What socialization process did you undergo? If you are a member of a social group such as a fraternity, sorority, or eating club, what socialization process is used and what is its major purpose?
7. What effect do you think the socialization process has on productivity and satisfaction in the organization?
8. If you are active in a religious organization, what socialization process does that religious organization utilize, if any?
9. Are there any taboos in your college, university, or study group?

CHAPTER III
ENCOURAGING THEM TO STAY: GAINING LONG-TERM COMMITMENT

ORGANIZATIONAL SHOCK

- A commitment on the part of organizations to longevity and loyalty can be detrimental to the organization.
- Organizations use the principles of "faith" and "status" to gain psychological commitment to the organization.
- Many managers "drop out" of the organization and seek alternative life-styles because they cannot accept the requirements of longevity, faith, and status offered by the organization.
- Organizations seduce employees to accept a task assignment that will be detrimental to the employee's career.

One of the purposes of socialization mentioned in the last chapter was to get people to accept the norms and values of the work group and the organization. The second purpose of the indoctrination or socialization process obviously is to gain long-term commitment. Organizations are very concerned about turnover among their employees both at the entry and the managerial levels. Turnover is very costly and therefore loyalty, which is often defined as longevity, is often valued by organizations. In many cases, the shock you will experience is the discovery that this commitment to longevity and loyalty may be detrimental to the organization. Nevertheless, it seems to be very important for many organizations.

In the first article by Antony Jay, we see that one method by which organizations gain commitment is by leading employees to believe, in many cases rightfully, that they are doing something useful and worthwhile by enriching the lives of their fellow men and by virtue of their work with the corporation. In addition, they come to believe that the organization itself is doing good rather than harm to society. In order to gain this commitment, according to Jay, organizations like religious organizations use the concept of *faith* to gain long-term commitment among its employees.

In the second reading, by Michael Maccoby, we learn that some members of the organizations accept faith and status offered by the organization to such an extent that they *psychologically belong* to the organization. This, of course, is a shock experienced by most employees and it is what Maccoby calls the "company man" syndrome and what William Foot Whyte calls the "organization man" syndrome. According to Maccoby, company men are essential to the functioning of large corporations, but seem to function better at middle levels of management than at the top of the corporation. You will also note that in this reading Maccoby relates a "company man" to the socialization process described in the article by Fromm.

Faced with the option of becoming the company man and/or having experienced being a company man, many people believe that the acceptance of faith and the acceptance of the status symbols' importance leads to a distortion of reality when compared to a person's values system. This organizational shock has led to what the third reading of this section calls the "Great Male Dropout from the Work Ethic." This article from *Business Week* describes many formerly successful company men who have opted for a different life-style because, for them, the reality of the company man syndrome was based on an attitude toward work that they themselves could not accept.

In the last article by Lewicki we find a major dilemma faced by employees being described. Organizations often seduce employees, especially younger managers, into accepting assignments detrimental to the manager's career advancement.

RELIGION AND THE CORPORATION

ANTONY JAY

A corporation, like a state, needs a faith. Most people gain comfort from the feeling that they are in some way doing good, helping mankind, leaving the world a better place, serving a noble ideal; and a corporation which enables its employees to feel that they are doing all those things by virtue of their job is clearly on to a good thing. Just as soldiers fight much better for a great cause like Christianity or Liberty or Democracy than for the protection of trading interests, so insurance firms can put more pressure on salesmen who feel they are spreading protection and security and peace of mind among their fellow citizens than ones who simply believe they are being paid to increase the company's return on employed capital and the annual dividends of the shareholders. As Walter Bagehot says:*

> No orator ever made an impression by appealing to men as to their plainest physical wants, except when he could allege that those wants were caused by someone's tyranny. But thousands have made the greatest impression by appealing to some vague dream of glory, or empire, or nationality. The ruder sort of men—that is, men at *one* stage of rudeness—will sacrifice all they hope for, all they have, *themselves,* for what is called an idea—for some attraction which seems to transcend reality, which aspires to elevate men by an interest higher, deeper, wider than that of ordinary life.

In a simple sort of way, most corporations have a faith; most employees, if driven back on to their basic beliefs and prejudices, would say that they thought they were doing something useful and worthwhile in this general sense, that they were helping increase the health or comfort or happiness or richness of the lives of their fellow men by virtue of their work with the corporation, and that the corporation was in general a

Source: From Management and Machiavelli: An Inquiry into the Politics of Corporate Life by Antony Jay. Copyright © 1967 by Antony Jay. Reprinted by permission of Holt, Rinehart and Winston.

*Walter Bagehot, The English Constitution (London: Collins, 1963), p. 63.

force for good rather than harm in society. The great difference lies in the extent to which this personal feeling is exploited as the basis for the corporation religion.

Some corporations are extremely religious. They hold regular revivalist meetings at which rousing hymns are sung to the glory of the corporation and its products, and salesmen are encouraged to stand up and give passionate personal testimony about why they believe. There is a trenchant sermon from the preacher (the senior executive present) and a hate session against the deveil, the leading competitor. At the other end of the scale (which is also likely to be the other side of the Atlantic), the corporation regards religious observance as a personal and private matter and is only concerned that its staff should be believers in a fairly liberal sense. But in between there is a wide variety of religious practice and forms of religious observance: christenings (drinks to meet a new recruit to the department), funerals (farewell dinner, with speech-sermons, to retiring executives), regular services for corporate worship (departmental or regional or area meetings, with pep-talk sermon from the manager reaffirming points of faith or doctrine where there are signs of divergence or laxity), communion (meetings for senior management only, in which highly confidential facts from the board are passed to the confirmed but kept from the rest of the congregation), and from time to time convocation, when the top men from all over the world come together. Corporations which would never go to the extremes of hymn singing and emotional personal testimony may yet contain much stronger religious feeling and observances than is apparent from the outside.

One reason why this is necessary is to fight heresy. Nearly all corporations operate on certain working beliefs which cannot be proved, which is another name for faith. Newspapers have such beliefs about their readers, ("They want to be cheered up," or "They're not interested in a story that can't be told in 300 words"); shopkeepers, about their customers ("They'll always pay more for quality"); doctors, about their patients ("What they really come for is reassurance"); and all corporations, whether they are aware of it or not, have a number of such basic assumptions on which their success is founded. If these assumptions start to be questioned, then the roots of the corporation are threatened, and a group of young executives who started to act on different assumptions could destroy the whole concern. If a chain textile store built its reputation and success on the assumption that people really wanted durable, quality clothes, then a group who asserted that on the contrary they really wanted cheap clothes they could throw away after a month or two would undermine all the expertness, all the practices, all the training, all the customer loyalty and supplier standards built up over generations. For that reason the faith must be asserted and enforced. In corporation religions as in others, the heretic must be cast out not because of the probability that he is wrong but because of the possibility that he is right.

Doctrine, of course, is another matter; you can argue about doctrine. It is not axiomatic and fundamental, it has to do with practicalities, the best ways of achieving the objectives which have been determined in the light of faith. The same chain store might say as a point of doctrine that sales staff should always stress the durable, lasting qualities of the clothes they sold; but if it became apparent that this put customers off, that they did not like the idea of wearing the same dress for four years, then the doctrine could be changed. So long as the faith was upheld, so long as the quality remained high, it would be possible to stress the cut and color and other fashion points and play down the durability, just as the Christian church has varied the emphasis of its message over the centuries from the fear of hell to the love of God without altering the creed or rewriting the Bible.

But a religion needs more than faith and doctrine and corporate worship; it also needs a supreme being. It is the role the creative leader is cut out for. If he is successful over a long period of time, divinity will start to hedge him. Many corporations have, or have had, such a leader, to whom his own staff and employees have attributed mystical qualities. This charisma is not a quality born in the leader, it is constructed for him out of the need for an object of worship and reverence which exists in his staff coupled with the desire that the object of this worship should protect them from harm. Many leaders play up to it, and help to build their own myth. Montgomery was well aware that the glamorous publicity he received was a direct contribution to the high morale of the Eighth Army, but few corporations seem to realize the importance of a single, "divine" leader to the morale and religious fervor of their staff. Of course is has dangers too, but they are usually outweighed by the advantages. The point was once put to me with extreme perspicacity by the late Dunduza Chisiza, one of Dr. Hastings Banda's ministers in Malawi:

> All that our people can comprehend [he said] is a tribal chief. Therefore Banda must be a tribal chief and the rest of us no more than a council of elders, at least in their eyes. Malawi must be built round him and identified with him. All national feeling must center on him, all decisions must be represented as his. This means that we are creating, by building this Banda King-figure, something we cannot destroy. Moreover by making him a figure of adulation and worship, we increase the danger of his believing in his own myth. If this makes him intolerable, we are still stuck with the image we have created.

He also added that it would be wise not to underestimate the need for such a single leader-figure among the so-called civilized people of the West. To quote Bagehot again,* where he

*Ibid, p. 82.

talks of the need for a sovereign even though the cabinet is the instrument of government:

> The best reason why Monarchy is a strong government is, that it is an intelligible government. The mass of mankind understand it, and they hardly anywhere in the world understand any other. It is often said that men are ruled by their imaginations; but it would be truer to say they are governed by the weakness of their imaginations. The nature of a constitution, the action of an assembly, the play of parties, the unseen formation of a guiding opinion, are complex facts, difficult to know and easy to mistake. But the action of a single will, the fiat of a single mind, are easy ideas, anybody can make them out, and no one can ever forget them.

Not all corporations, of course, have a leader to whom divinity could be attached with even a remote appearance of credibility. All the same, a little success and the right sort of internal publicity can work wonders. Other corporations are too vast; but there is no reason why the head of Cadillac should not be put over to the Cadillac division as their divinity, rather than the president of General Motors. The priests of Apollo do not deny the divinity of Zeus. It is, incidentally, a question who the priests are: I suspect they are the personnel officers, exercising their care of souls and holding occasional confessionals with the faithful who have reached a spiritual crisis about whether they are in the right department or getting on fast enough, and who confide to them domestic problems and anxieties, which they would never admit in front of their closer colleagues. Compared with their counterparts in the Christian church, the corporation priests still have a lot to learn.

The strength of religion is never equal through the land: There are always some areas, some classes who need it more than others. In industry it is the sales force whose need is greatest. They go out on their own amongst the heathen, they are the corporation missionaries. Other members of the corporation see only each other—it is easy to be a good Catholic in the Vatican. But the salesman travels alone to a spiritual Limpopo with only the strength of his faith to sustain him. He meets men who laugh at his god and deride his priests with tales of missed delivery dates and unmet specifications. Indeed, selling is very close to religious conversion: Before you can start selling your own product, you have to convince the prospect that there is something wrong with his present state, that he is missing something marvelous or heading for disaster. Only when you have created real internal disquiet can you start to sell your goods or gods.

Also, for all that may be said about figures and facts and performances and specifications, there is still a strong emotional, irrational element in most purchases. Not just of detergents and deodorants, but—so the salesmen tell me—of computers and machine tools as well. And for this, the salesman's own shining faith can be an important factor in tipping the balance. That is why he so desperately needs to sell himself first—his belief is actually an important part of the product. He is in the position of Sir Thomas More. Whereas Galileo could recant, More could not; Galileo knew that whatever he said or signed, the earth would continue to orbit the sun, but More knew that his faith and martyrdom actually increased the strength of the Catholic Church. A salesman looking at a doubtful new product is like a priest receiving a new ruling on contraception or a Communist confronted with a change in the party line on China. There is a tremendously powerful need to believe, even though the intellect may resist. After all, it is likely to put the salesman in a very sensitive position: He must be loyal to the firm which pays him, and yet very often the man he will have to sell this new product to has become over the years a personal friend. If he has an urgent command to push this product which he knows is not right for his friend, what should he do? He is in the classic dilemma. It is no good saying that the long-term

interest of his firm will not be served by selling a customer the wrong product—unless he sells it, the firm may have no future at all.

However, it can be done: Frederick Dürrenmatt's parable play *The Visit* shows most persuasively how the offer of a million dollars or so enables the citizens of a small village to convince themselves that all considerations of ethics, morality, and common sense demand that they should—against their private, personal, selfish wishes, of course—strangle to death a man who had previously been the most popular person in the village. In the same way, the overriding need and desire to believe can usually compel belief against the protests of the intellect. The argument goes, "I may think it is a false doctrine (or crazy decision, or dud machine), but that is only my judgment. Am I going to be so arrogant as to set my unworthy judgment against that of all my superiors and the old man himself? And even if I am right, the cause, the faith, the firm needs the help of my belief to tide it over this difficulty, so that it can live on to fight for an object which transcends any single error. So I surrender my personal will to the overruling cause." It can be done, but the faith must be strong to compel it.

The other characteristic of most religions is a concept of ultimate reward and punishment which can be used to compel good conduct by hope or fear. The industrial religion also has a hereafter, but it starts at sixty or sixty-five instead of death. The promise of a comfortable, reasonably affluent retirement is the hope; the threat of nothing except a few dollars of savings and the old age pension is the fear. The pension scheme is often the instrument through which these hopes and fears are operated, the silver cord which binds the employee to his firm ever tighter as he gets older. His early hopes and dreams fade; gradually he realizes he is not going to climb as high as he once hoped, and retirement on a comfortable pension becomes the only real goal to aim for. "If you work for Procter & Gamble for ten years," said one of their former executives, "you wonder if you can afford to leave."* The fear of losing the pension becomes ever stronger as time passes, as the after-life gets nearer and fewer years of this one have to be endured. The fear of the sack is more than anything the fear of losing the pension, built up over so many years with such care, and without which the heaven of a comfortable bungalow with a garden by the sea becomes the hell of an old people's home. Before the comparatively recent idea of a retiring age, death was the only point after which anything nice could conceivably happen. Now it is sixty. And fortunately for those still working, their retired colleagues whom they visit (once) on a day trip to Elysium always say that everything is grand—to say anything else would be to admit that all those years had been wasted. And so the idea of a Valhalla persists. Just occasionally

*Vance Packard, *Pyramid Climbers,* (New York: McGraw-Hill, 1962), Chap. 1.

one of them will come back, ghostlike, to the old firm, revisiting the glimpses of the moon, and say he is bored and unhappy and only wishes he could come back and take his coat off and get down to work again. His haunted colleagues, obscurely troubled, will try and exorcise him with jocularity ("Nonsense, Charlie, you're having a whale of a time; we know!") but they never take the hint about the job. He discovers that Omar Khyyam was right:

And those that husbanded the golden grain
And those who flung it to the winds like rain
Alike to no such aureate earth are turned
As, buried once, men want dug up again.

Perhaps, at those farewell parties for retiring executives, his colleagues who subscribe so generously to the presentation clock or tankard or cigarette box should fork out a little bit extra for a bell, book, and candle—just to be on the safe side.

THE COMPANY MAN

MICHAEL MACCOBY

They are not the workers, nor are they the white-collar people in the usual, clerk sense of the word. These people only work for The Organization. The ones I am talking about belong to it as well. They are the ones of our middle class who have left home, spiritually as well as physically, to take the vows of organization life, and it is they who are the mind and soul of our great self-perpetuating institutions. Only a few are top managers or ever will be. In a system that makes such hazy terminology as "junior executive" psychologically necessary, they are the staff as much as the line, and most are destined to live poised in a middle area that still awaits a satisfactory euphemism. But they are the dominant members of our society nevertheless. They have not joined together into a recognizable elite—our country does not stand still long enough for that—But it is from their ranks that are coming most of the first and second echelons of our leadership, and it is their values which will set the American temper.*

William H. Whyte, Jr.

Surveying the corporate landscape of the fifties, Whyte recognized the company man as the emerging type. He could not predict that changing technology and markets would call forth a type of organizational leader who combined technical and business skills and was more oriented to risk-taking. Even so, the company man Whyte described is still the type most frequently found among the middle managers of the companies we studied.

On the whole, these managers accepted the categorization of company men but resented the overwhelmingly negative implications. Aware of their weaknesses, they also wanted credit for their contribution to the organization.

*William H. Whyte, Jr. *The Organization Man* (New York: Simon and Schuster, 1956), p. 3.

The idea that one is not an individualist touches a very sore spot in the American psyche.

Company man or not, we Americans still like to think of ourselves as an independent people, self-reliant, individualistic, and to a degree anarchistic. Compared to Europe, these traits still exist in the American character, but they were developed and reinforced by modes of work that have almost disappeared. The Republic was founded by farmers, craftsmen, proprietors, professionals, and entrepreneurs, and our form of democracy was rooted in the belief that there were enough independent Americans to stand up against demagogues and would-be dictators.

Of course, this view has always been exaggerated and romanticized. The slaves were not free, and the independence of many other Americans was antisocial. As with any other character trait, the meanings of "independence" vary according to the total character structure. For the crusty farmer or backwoodsman who rallied to the banner "Don't Tread on Me," independence meant stubbornness, suspiciousness, and uncooperativeness, as well as self-reliance. For the jungle fighters and hustlers, it meant being a lone wolf, free to exploit the suckers. As David Riesman pointed out in *The Lonely Crowd*, many nineteenth-century Americans appeared independent because they obeyed the internalized dictates of idealized parents, and were rigidly authoritarian and emotionally childish; their independence was bought at the expense of compulsive submission to the past.

The humanistic concept of independence implies following the dictates of conscience, as Ralph Waldo Emerson wrote, rather than submitting to either inner or external idols. But such creative independence needs roots in one's whole practice of life and usually in one's way of making a living. The traditional material basis of independence in American has been self-employment, ownership of property, or salable skills. The farmer, small shopkeeper, or craftsman could speak his mind, hold his ground, and even choose dignity over profit because he had no boss to worry about.* So attractive is the ideal of self-employment as a basis for independence that many corporate managers and engineers cling to the belief that the hardworking individual, with a little capital and a new idea, can make a go of it in business by himself, despite the evidence that this is seldom achieved. In the early nineteenth century, some 80 percent of all Americans were self-employed. By 1950, only 18 percent of all employed persons were self-employed, and this figure shrank to 14 percent in 1960 and 9 percent in 1970.† Furthermore, for every successful new business opened each year, eight or nine fail. The prevalent belief among corporate managers—that if one feels locked into an organization, it is due to lack of get up and go—has soothed the consciences of those who see no need to improve the quality of work. This same belief has in the past tranquilized workers who accept unfulfilling work because they hope someday to set up their own shops.

We should be learning how to establish the rights of managers and workers so as to develop a new basis of cooperative independence in the corporations based on mutual respect, equity, and democratic participation. Instead, we indulge in unreal daydreams of romantic independence, and they tend to support narcissistic fantasies, jungle-fighting

---

*Many small shopkeepers seek profit as the first priority, but this may in part be due to the extreme competition from chain stores, so that the small businessman must struggle to stay solvent. In less industrialized countries, such as Mexico, where there is less of such pressure, small shopkeepers sometimes take pleasure in refusing to sell their goods to rude or overbearing clients. Sometimes the attitude is allowed, by its justification of racial discrimination. However, it contrasts sharply with that of the employee of a large chain—such as Sears or Safeway—who is paid to maximize profit, not to exercise his sense of dignity.
†See Michael Maccoby and Katherine A. Tetzi, "Character and Work in America," in Philip Buenner and others, eds., *Exploring Contradictions: Political Economy in the Corporate State,* (New York: David McKay, 1974).

careerism, and game-playing. (For some people, independence means "I pursue any career without asking from or giving to others.") We even distort reality into this romantic mold. In an attempt to assimilate the heroic astronaut into the traditional image, schoolteachers compare him to earlier explorers, such as Columbus and Magellan. Although both twentieth-century astronaut and fifteenth-century seafarer share traits of competence and bravery, and faced the risks of sudden death, structurally they are poles apart. The early explorers were individualistic jungle fighters who overcame superstition, setting out in largely untested craft, with a fearful crew that needed to be kept in line, to confront unforeseen weather conditions and unknown cultures. There was no Mission Control back in Madrid. There was no backup system when Cortés burned his boats. In contrast, the astronauts were fine-tuned parts of a highly technological, intricate, and centrally controlled machine. The fewer the unknowns and the fewer decisions they had to make, the more successful the project for the team as a whole. They were in many ways similar to high-technology managers, and some, like Frank Borman, now president of Eastern Airlines, have gone on to lead corporations.

Company men are essential to the functioning of large corporations. They equate their personal interest with the corporation's long-term development and success. Company men believe they will benefit most if the company prospers, but their belief in the company may transcend self-interest. In the elite companies we studied, company men care about the corporation and its future development. As much as they are motivated by hope of success, they are also driven by fear and worry, for the corporate projects and the interpersonal relations around them, as well as their own careers. Separate from the corporation, company men feel insignificant and lost. As part of the organization, they have their spot at (or on) the cutting edge.

To rise to the top of the elite companies we studied requires many company-man qualities, though that is not enough. The typical company man—the functionary—can rise to middle management or a high-level staff position. But he lacks the risk-taking ability, toughness, detachment, confidence, self-control, and energy to reach the very top. (The managers told us that energy is extremely important for reaching the top. This is largely genetically determined, but not completely; energy is also generated by the fit between character and work, and conversely, internal conflict blocks energy.)

On the positive side, the belief of company men in something beyond themselves (the organization) may provide them with a sense of belonging, modesty, responsibility, and loyalty. On the negative side are their feelings of little self-worth and the persistent fear that they will lose their place. They are worriers. How are they doing? Are they falling behind? Do they understand what is going on? Can they believe the gamesmen who seem so sure of themselves? Will they be overtaken by brighter competitors?

Once I presented a seminar to a group of eight corporate company men of upper middle management and asked how many had anxiety dreams of arriving at an examination unprepared. (Failing the test for promotions.) Three hands went up. How many had dreams of being chased? (The competition catching up.) Five hands. How many had dreams of falling? (Losing one's position, failure.) Everyone's hand went up. Many company men told us dreams like this: "I dream I'm trying to run from something and not being able to move. Ending up at the end of a long, dark tunnel feeling totally insignificant." (Note that the speaker stops using the first person singular, I, and just uses gerunds, "not being," "ending," "feeling." The disappearing "I," the lost subject, is a common linguistic symptom of the centerless person.)

The typical company man is a functionary who accepts a bureaucratic role and expects to go no higher than middle management. He is likely to come from a large family (and an Irish-Catholic background), and he adapts to the corporation as if it were a new family where he must mediate among conflicting fraternal and paternal demands for the good of all. Self-sacrifice feels right to him and he descrbes love in terms of giving up self, submerging oneself in the other. (For example, "Love is the complete acceptance of the thought of another person and a desire to completely subject your wishes or desires in order to achieve the well-being of the other person or thing.") He enjoys serving others as the way to serve himself. (A typical company-man symbol expressed on the Rorschach—usually Card IX—is a coffeepot.)

In general, company men tend to be inside men who feel in an inhospitable environment outside the corporate culture. Although this makes them dependent on the corporation, it also heightens their sensitivity to the feelings, the emotional ups and downs, of the people around them, and to the politics of their bounded world. Corporate power centers are to them as baronies with territorial rights, and they are acutely aware of who belongs to whom and how far they can go before crossing a border. Because of this understanding, they contribute to forging alliances and making the treaties and compromises that are necessary to develop complex projects. Company men are suspicious of the craftsmen whose desire for perfection is uneconomical, and of the overzealous and tricky gamesmen who use people up and who in wanting so much to win, shift positions so easily and threaten the integrity and good name of the organization. In turn, craftsmen speak derisively of functionaries as "technical incompetents who are politically ambitious," and gamesmen call them "boy scouts," and often complain that if they would put as much effort into project success as they did into internal politics, everyone would be better off.

In bureaucracies less dynamic than high-technology corporations, many company men gain their sense of autonomy in a negative way, by sticking to the rules and resisting change.* This attitude may block progress but it also protects the organization against the gamesman's tendency to cut corners or the unprincipled manipulation of the jungle fighters who were unchecked in the Nixon Administration. *The Wall Street Journal,* in an editorial, commented that a few individuals emerged from the Watergate episode with their integrity intact; the *Journal* had a point when it argued that "the explanation seems to be that these officials had an unshakeable determination to defend their institutional interests, therefore they couldn't be persuaded to join in the Watergate circus. It's fashionable to ridicule the limited loyalties exhibited by organization men and bureaucratic institutions, and to disparage their preoccupations with minor improvements rather than sweeping reforms. Yet while such institutional inhibitions may be frustrating, they are also likely to be prudent."†

Company men function particularly well in the middle management of whatever size group they're in: project, division, or corporate level. They maintain the organization rather than setting the goals or doing the creative design work. As they move up to positions of direct line responsibility, they are often seen as trustworthy but unexciting leaders. Being trustworthy and responsible are their key terms (although they are more often conscientious than truly responsive to people). In normal times they negotiate between conflicting claims. It is they the organization turns to when it is a time for caution and retrenchment. But when strategic risks must be taken, or when it is necessary to spark the team to higher performance, they are replaced by tougher, less cautious types (like the gamesman). The same qualities that help company men to stabilize the corporate atmosphere also limit their rise.

*See Michel Crozier *The Bureaucratic Phenomenon* (Chicago: University of Chicago Press, 1964).
†*The Wall Street Journal,* April 4, 1974, p. 18.

Company men exemplify what Fromm has called the "marketing character." When they describe themselves, they seem to be trying to give the right impression, to sell themselves to the interviewer. It is as though they are constantly working on themselves in order to have the right kind of personality to fit the job. There is a movement in leading companies, General Electric a notable exmaple, to develop careful assessment techniques in order to reward competence and not merely the right image. Yet this attempt at a rational and fair procedure sometimes has the contrary result of putting more pressure on people to stay within the boundaries and not risk a bad evaluation. Company men's self-descriptions often sound as though they are trying to satisfy everyone's view of what they should be with the result that there is hardly any self to describe. A manager of a development project: "I'm just a little bit introverted, just a teeny bit. I've been accused of not bending my principles enough. Not that there is a definite company code. What's fair and so forth is the company code. You have to be aggressive. And sort out what's right and stick to it. You can't blow from side to side. The guys make me stay fair. The job requires real consideration. You have to consider the guys as well as the project." What started as a self-description ended up as a job description. He went on to say that the kind of people he most disliked working with are "those who have no concern for others, and are just concerned with themselves [the gamesmen] or the technology [the craftsmen]." His goal is to develop the project and protect the interests of his people. The winners and those overly concerned with technology and perfection are going to upset things if they are allowed to follow their egocentric paths. He added that the ideal manager is one who sacrifices his individual career for the company's needs.

In a similar way, another company man described himself in contrast to tougher, gamier managers as "humble, more reserved, more of the quiet thinker, wanting to analyze thoroughly before speaking or coming out with anything. Speaking my mind only when I know I'm right. I want to be a nice guy. It's difficult for me to take a hard-nosed attitude. Gradually becoming more hardnosed, but it's frustrating, my wanting to be a nice guy. It's an internal conflict. I'm a straight arrow as opposed to a wheeler-dealer. Dependable. Always follow through. Sometimes get focused on too many details. Sometimes have to force myself to stand back and look at the big picture, allowing subordinates to carry through the details. Really enjoy working with people, particularly the coordination of several groups on a common project. One of my strengths is more on organization, stabilizing controls and order in a chaotic situation. Many of my subordinates seem to thrive on chaotic situations, it's part of their being wheeler-dealers, they really enjoy dynamic situations."

This self-description gives me the feeling of constant self-comparison, self-monitoring, self-criticism, and analysis of interpersonal situations. Through their work, company men develop their sensitivity to people and organizational politics, but as Joseph Heller illustrates in his novel of an oversexed functionary, *Something Happened*,* this development may be one-sidedly careerist, at the expense of deeper personal development and relatedness. The quality of relations at work, while extensive and varied, is generally restricted to organizational roles without the regard and interest in each other that characterize a friendship which grows only gradually and bears fruit in real trust and mutual understanding. Company men, in general, tend rather to develop the routine graciousness and courteousness that allow them to avoid deeper encounters with themselves and others. Their careerist goals, their anxiety to constantly move ahead so as not to fall be-

*Joseph Heller, *Something Happened* (New York: Alfred A. Knopf, 1 74).

hind, leave little room for self-development or concern beyond what is necessary for performance.

They may agree that work satisfaction and the quality of life are worthwhile goals, but this receptivity rarely develops into a serious commitment to restructure the organization in order to stimulate the fullest possible human development of all workers and managers. Yet, if such a program were to be initiated from the top down, many company men would welcome it. And if they do not concern themselves with social conditions inside the company that directly affect their well-being, even less do they worry about the corporation's influence on the larger world.

Furthermore, company men overvalue the company in relationship to their family life, where, paradoxical as it may seem, they are less at home than the craftsmen. While craftsmen like Steward take outings with the family or organize family projects to build something, functionaries tend to go home looking for rest, peace, and quiet. For the craftsmen, family is equal to or more important than work, and they sometimes mention being a good husband and father as goals in life even before work; company men always mention work goals before family goals.

Although the company man's work tends to reinforce a responsible attitude to the organization and the project, it may also strengthen a negative syndrome of dependency; submissive surrender to the organization and to authority, sentimental idealization of those in power, a tendency to betray the self in order to gain security, comfort, and luxury.

Many functionaries have given in: they have surrendered and been swallowed by the company. In extreme cases, this total submission becomes masochism, in the sense described by Fromm in *Escape from Freedom.** The masochistic individual actually is satisfied to be

*Erich Fromm, *Escape from Freedom* (New York: Rinehart & Co., 1941).

humiliated. That is the only way he experiences a sense of belonging, feeling that while the dominant person (or in this case the representative of the powerful organization) is treating him the way he should be treated, the way he deserves, he is also accepted unconditionally.

Although submissiveness and idealization of the company turn out to be adaptive for the functionary, more extreme masochistic tendencies cripple the modern corporate manager at work as well as in his personal life.

A manager in a computer company sought psychotherapy because, at age forty, he was failing at both his work and his marriage. He had been unsuccessful in achieving three goals: to be a vice-president, to have a good relationship with his wife, and to become a warm human being. In fact, his work was falling to pieces because he was desperately trying to please all the people above him rather than understanding the business problems and resolving them. He was alternately bored and frightened by his beautiful wife, who, he said, didn't respect him because he wasn't a big success. In one dream, he saw her looking at him with contempt because he was taking orders from a black man. The black man was actually an employee whom he wanted to help, but he "knew" that his wife would consider him a worm because he put himself out for a black.

Beneath the self-hatred and fear, this man seemed to me to be a sensitive and receptive individual. As a young man he had been interested in religion and philosophy. He rejected an academic career or the church because he wanted to be rich and part of a glamorous elite company. He felt that he had sold himself to the devil, that he was damned. "I am afraid I feel nothing," he told me, "I am a hollow man," and his Rorschach responses described a world in which all impulses toward life and joy had been crushed by greed, decay, and evil.

This is an example of failure. What do the most successful company men feel about themselves?

Ron Goodwin, one of the most gifted and

idealistic men we interviewed, reached a high executive position in a large company but he faltered near the top because he did not understand the game well enough.

Goodwin was in his middle fifties, courtly, elegant, good-humored, receptive, and helpful. If he had not seemed a little too soft, he would have looked the part of a company president. In his forties, he thought he would at least become a corporate vice-president. At that time, he had risen rapidly through sales and marketing to become a general manager of a division, and he had successfully organized one of the company's overseas operations.

His success had been due to a combination of three factors. Goodwin understood how the product sold and why people bought it. He knew how to give the product glamour, and how to provide service. He could take a system and make you believe that your business life would become classier if you bought it, even though the price was much higher than that of other systems that less elegantly performed the same technical function.

Second, Goodwin's attitude of courtly deference to superiors and idealization of those in power flattered the corporate rulers and served him in the struggle for position.

Third, his sincere concern for peers and subordinates gained him their respect and affection.

Goodwin's goal was to combine Christian principles with corporate growth and profit, and "to have an effect on the world to promote understanding and more satisfaction and happiness by changing the company." He felt there was little he could do to change the world by himself, but by improving the company, he would better the world. How did Goodwin think the company could improve the world? It would not produce products before it was known whether or not they were good for humanity. The motto would be: if you can't forsee the results, don't build it. The company would also take a humanistic position on improving the quality of working and women's rights, and ending pollution, war, and racial injustice. How would the company determine these positions? By all the employees having a say.

Goodwin's managerial philosophy was that "responsibility and authority must be shared." He told me, "I believe in democracy with a strong recognition of its need for leadership and honest communication that can be understood by everyone."

But how would such a philosophy be put into effect within a giant multinational corporation? Goodwin was no one to organize or take part in a corporate revolution. His style was to flatter and persuade those in power. And they were not receptive to his idealistic views.

One of Goodwin's Rorschach responses expressed the contradiction and the lack of grounding for his goals. He saw fish, which he associated with the Christian faith, tied to a couple of court jesters teetering on the top of two docking spaceships. This symbolized his approach to corporate policy, an unstable combination of Christianity and the politics of the impotent courtier resting on technology in outer space. (The court fool tells the truth, but he is powerless.) He also expressed the contradiction between the principles of religion and power in the two historical figures he most admired. "Alexander the Great, he affected the future and was a great leader, but understood people and how to bring them together. And Jesus, he changed man without force, showed the power of working with people."

Goodwin wasn't tough enough to deal with the real challenges at the top. Nor was he radical enough either to organize an internal battle or leave the company. Instead, he was moved out of the mainstream. He was liked by the top executives, who appreciated his past marketing contributions, praised his humanism, but eased him out. In the meantime, he developed psychosomatic symptoms: depression, anxiety, restlessness, obsessive doubt, back troubles, and finally serious gastrointestinal difficulties.

Looking back at the top executives, now that he has left the company, Goodwin sees them as "people who don't like people—compassion is missing." In his own case, he told me, the traits that got in the way of success were his openness and spontaneity, idealism, generosity, and his critical questioning attitude to authority. He also felt that he lacked sufficient aggressiveness, tenacity, decisiveness, and energy to reach the top. He was not quite the right type.

THE GREAT MALE COP-OUT FROM THE WORK ETHIC

Business Week

When the mail-order company that employed him closed its regional operation, says a former $30,000-a-year suburban Philadelphia executive, "I found myself, at 45, in a situation where I could do anything I wanted." What he did was drop out of the labor force. He read books on male liberation, "found out where the clean socks came from," and became a house husband supported by his wife's earnings as a psychotherapist.

This man is one of a growing breed—males in the prime working years of 25 to 54 who have opted out of the job market. Some will probably reenter it sooner or later: young married students or men—many of them black—who are temporarily discouraged by today's high unemployment rate. But increasing numbers have apparently discovered that contemporary society offers a new government- and corporate-financed alternatives to working for a living, or that, like the Philadelphian, their place is in the home.

WORKING WIVES

Bureau of Labor Statistics figures tell the story. The percentage of prime-working-age men in the labor force was a stable 97% from 1950 through 1966. But from 1967 to 1976, it dropped from 96.6% to 94.2%. Put another way, the number of men outside the labor force grew 71% over the past nine years, in good times and bad, until now some 2.2 million neither hold nor seek jobs.

Their lot is cheerier than it would have been a decade ago. The disabled among them (a category that covers half of the 2.2 million) can more easily collect disability benefits under revised Social Security and other programs, and such benefits are generally higher now than they were in previous years. And the able rebels of this group can more freely cast off company bonds, thanks to a more supportive social atmosphere and, frequently, a working wife.

Not so coincidentally, the years of declining

male work-force participation were also years of rising participation for married women aged 20 to 54. Some 41.5% of married women worked in 1967 and some 52.4% in 1976. Among male work-force dropouts 25 to 34, 63% have wives who work. During the same decade, books such as *The Greening of America* expressed and inspired widespread questioning of the work ethic.

"I wouldn't go back to the corporate ulcer factory uner any circumstances," says Robert Huchingson, 53, a former vice-president of Falstaff Brewing Corp. in St. Louis. Huchingson has not looked for a job since Falstaff was sold in May, 1975. He remarks comfortably that his savings are "adequate," his wife teaches, and education for his four children is paid for. He enjoys writing short stories, although he has not yet sold one. "I'm perfectly satisfied that making money is not so all-important," Huchingson says.

RETIRING EARLY

"That attitude is growing," says an official of the National Council of Compensation Insurance in New York City, a national rate-setting organization. The council had to raise workers' compensation premiums by 17% last year, mostly because sick and disabled workers stay away from work longer than they formerly did. Rather than rush back to work, they seem willing to make do with benefits that are better than they used to be, although usually still well below their normal salaries.

This attitude toward work—expressed repeatedly by respondents to a *Business Week* survey and confirmed as widespread by experts in the field—casts a new light on the potential impact of proposed legislation moving the statutory retirement age from 65 to 70. Apparently headed for final passage in Congress soon, the bill has raised fears that a surge of working elderly would crowd younger workers onto the unemployment rolls.

But the 1967-to-1976 figures from the BLS

suggest that many men under 65 would take advantage of voluntary early retirement at the same time that some older men would work longer under the proposed law. The figures "indicate that a substantial number of men do not dread retirement but look forward to it, if they could just finance it," says Professor Herbert S. Parnes of the Center for Human Resource Research at Ohio State University.

Among all males, the downtrend in work-force participation was steepest for blacks, but this decline started long before 1967 and appears to be tied to the difficulty of finding jobs more than it is to anything else. Some black age groups have dropped as much as 20% in work-force participation since 1955, and the average decline among blacks since 1967 was 5.2%, to 88.5%.

Charles Benjamin, a black official of the Seattle-King County (Wash.) Manpower Consortium, notes that many blacks "just simply float around," living a hand-to-mouth existence. And John Hindman, a Social Security Administration official in Pittsburgh, lists some of the sources of such an existence: churches and the Salvation Army for food, public washrooms, and sometimes lodging—and even one Pittsburgh organization that gives as much as $14 weekly in spending money. But few would deliberately choose this way of life, Benjamin adds.

LIFETIME BENEFITS

The disabled face no such stark prospect, especially if they held jobs in the public sector or in unionized industries. A 27-year-old Los Angeles man who was employed as a custodian at a public college, for instance, injured his knee while lifting a garbage can last June. He collected temporary workers' compensation for several weeks, returned to work, and found the job painful. He has been receiving long-term benefits since Sept. 15 on the ground that his bad knee makes him permanently incapable of doing his job. He also collects enough additional money from the college's benefit program (a common fringe benefit among public institutions) to make up the difference between the disability check and his former paycheck. He visits the insurance carrier's doctor daily to verify that his knee still hurts. He is not sure he will ever work again.

Experts say that the longer a man stays off the job, the more likely he is to stay away permanently. William V. Deutermann Jr., a BLS demographer and a specialist in work-force dropouts, cites Census Bureau data showing that the proportion of men who say they will seek work within a year "drops sharply with increases in the period of inactivity."

Careless administration of workers' comp systems is partly to blame, says William Johnston, chairman of the Ohio Industrial Commission, a unit that sets policy for the state's workers' comp. "I've seen people under 35 being given lifetime benefits with no hope for anything else, and nothing left to do but drink beer and watch soap operas," he says. Some could go back to work, Johnston points out, if they received physical rehabilitation, but the program ought to begin no later than 12 weeks after illness or injury. "Unless you catch them by then, a compensation syndrome sets in," he says.

Some 70% of the Ohio cases are lower-back ailments—a widespread cause of disability. Notes Johnston: "Children and wives are always telling Dad not to lift or drive. So whether he has a long-term problem or not, he sure believes he does."

MATCHING SALARY

In addition to encouraging rehabilitation, Johnston seeks to guard against cheating by having two doctors examine each patient. As a result, the number of beneficiaries added to Ohio's permanent disability rolls has dropped from 300,500 in 1975 to 100,800 in 1976. This represents a payout of $93 million, compared with 1975's $186 million.

Even when cheating or a neglected rehabilitation program are not in question, though, disability payments do permit men who are marginally disabled to be selective about what work they will do. Jimmy R. Ulicnik, a 29-year-old postal worker in Houston, was injured 16 months ago when he swerved his post office jeep to avoid a car and overturned. His pelvic and internal injuries and his broken leg have healed, but he still cannot endure the rigors of "constant walking, getting in and out of the jeep, and carrying a mail pouch on my back," he says. He is now waiting for the post office to find him a desk job that he can perform without so much discomfort.

With his post office checks and compensation payments, Ulicnik clears the same $740 a month he earned before, losing only overtime and night-differential pay. His wife, Susan, works, too, although she was also on disability pay for six months when she slipped a spinal disc while moving her husband's wheelchair. They and their two children scrimped some during this period of double disability, but they still retain two cars, a mortgaged home, and investment property that, in another era, might have been sold off to keep Ulicnik from having to perform painful work.

For older workers, the combination of early retirement and disability pay can actually exceed salary, according to some employers. Says Alan Strohmaier, General Motors Corp.'s assistant director of unemployment and workers' compensation: "A large portion of workers retiring before 62 are getting some form of workers' comp." The $650 monthly pension for a 30-year veteran, together with a disability payment of $528, adds up to more than his former salary in some cases, he says.

MARGINAL EXISTENCE

The combination of pension and disability payments has spurred 80% of retirees at one Detroit-area plant to file for disability claims, Strohmaier says. At a similar plant, only 3% of retirees have filed for disability. So Strohmaier suspects that workers at the first plant are getting aggressive instruction on how to claim benefits.

The Big Three auto companies are prime victims of this formula, because United Auto Workers' pensions are among the best in the country. And Michigan disability law requires only that work aggravate a health problem to qualify a worker for benefits, not that it be the cause of the problem.

But aside from pensioners and older workers drawing disability benefits, more married students, other young husbands, and middle-aged men are staying home and letting their wives earn the paychecks. For example, a 31-year-old sales clerk in a Boston camera store quit his job last spring to take care of his nine-month-old daughter. He now does odd jobs and collects unemployment benefits—a common pattern among recent work-force dropouts. His wife is writing her doctoral thesis in anthropology and earns a small amount by tutoring.

Food stamps, family gifts, and a loan taken by his wife round out their income, so that the move involved no great change in lifestyle. "We had been living as students for 10 years," this man says, "which means we're really living a marginal existence." He reasons that his wife's doctorate will always outearn his bachelor's degree, and if there is to be only one breadwinner, he says, "I'll gladly defer."

STAYING HOME

Richard Ireland of Denver, also 31, has two master's degrees in education, but he has been content for the past five years to let his wife, a physician, earn the money while he stays home doing the cooking and washing. "If I ever do work, I will create the job," he says.

Ireland stresses that he enjoys working with people, but that a brief stint as a teacher soured him on institutions. "I'm not willing to play the politics of getting a job organized to deliver what I want it to," he says.

The ultimate self-described "house person," however, may be Allen B. Bentley, 32, who has not worked for more than six years. He quit his job as a warehouseman at Sears, Roebuck & Co.'s Los Angeles center in the summer of 1971 and moved in with his brother and sister-in-law in the San Francisco area while he hunted for a new job. "But I took the rest of the summer off, and when everyone else went back to work in the fall, I just didn't." He liked his new role so much that when his brother got divorced and moved out, Allen stayed on with his brother's ex-wife and her two children.

All of the support for Allen and the two children comes from his sister-in-law's salary as an $18,000-a-year special-program teacher at a Hayward (Calif.) elementary school. "It's definitely still work," says Bentley, describing his routine of seeing the kids off to school, cooking, cleaning, doing the laundry, shopping, and maintaining a $75,000 home. In fact, Bentley says, it is harder than his warehouseman's job because it is a 24-hour responsibility, with the male-oriented chores of fixing cars and chopping wood added to the domestic work. But the only time Bentley thinks about a regular job, he says, is around the end of the month, "when the money around here starts getting pretty thin."

OPTING OUT

Men such as Bentley, who are not on disability and not in school, constitute a third of all male nonworkers among both blacks and whites. Although the government disclaims any knowledge of their ways, lumping them simply as "others" in its statistics, the *Business Week* survey indicates that many are actually off-and-on workers. Sometimes the work is legal, such as carpentry, and sometimes—as one *Business Week* reporter discovered—it is illegal, such as selling drugs. Either way, men in this group work as unofficially and occasionally self-employed persons, thus evading labor-force statistics.

Bart Christner, for example, was earning

about $20,000 as a salesman of bakery equipment and supplies. He did not mind being on the road but hated returning to his home office in Pittsburgh. "It was a drag," he says. "Every day the same routine." So he quit in 1972 and has not had a steady job since.

Christner, 36, stays off welfare ("Welfare is only for poor people"), shares an apartment with a cousin, and supports himself by doing odd jobs in the building trades, often for friends. A small income from a marriage property settlement helps. If he really hustles, he can make $300 a month, he says, but he seldom pushes that hard.

Christner says he misses some of the things a salary could buy, but he adds quickly: "When I had the money, I wasn't happy. I didn't have the time to enjoy it." In the old days, he had three weeks' vacation; now he gets to Florida in the winter for a month or two.

"PLAYING BY EAR"

Arnold Amare, 43, resigned a $15,000-a-year job as a supervisor in a marine and electronics factory because the Madison (Conn.) executive found that as his salary increased, so did his blood pressure and the demands on his family time. Now most of the family income comes from his wife, a $17,000-a-year assistant professor at Southern Connecticut College in New Haven. Amare's wife also earns $2,000 as a Madison selectwoman. Amare adds to that by installing burglary and fire-detection systems "on a low-level, undemanding basis." He recently turned down two lucrative job offers. He prefers to be at home with his two sons and manage his wife's campaign.

In a few areas, work-force dropouts have begun to form a substantial percentage of the population. In the Florida Keys, an entire subculture of boat dwellers has abandoned regular work for a life of sailing, fishing, and odd-jobbing.

Two of the newest recruits are Will Adams, 38, and his wife Donna, 31, who are moored at Boot Key marina aboard a 22-foot sloop named Echoue (which means "run aground" in French). He has taken an unpaid leave of absence from a $13,500 job as a French professor at Lamar University in Beaumont, Tex., and she left a $6,000-a-year job at the college. He doubts whether he will return. "I'll just play it by ear and see," he says. "My only regret is that I didn't do it years ago."

SEDUCTION AND COMMITMENT IN THE ORGANIZATION

ROY J. LEWICKI

Definitions of commitment and research on the processes abound. A typical definition is presented by Lyman Porter and his colleagues: commitment is "a strong belief in and acceptance of the organization's goals and values, a willingness to exert considerable effort on behalf of the organization, and a strong desire to maintain membership in the organization." But one of the most troubling aspects of current definitions and research is that the commitment process is treated as a *rational* one. An individual's level of commitment to an organization has been viewed as though it were wholly determined by his or her own conscious choices and behavior, totally under his rational control, and totally subject to adjustment depending upon personal and environmental circumstances. Similarly, from the organization's perspective, the definitions and research expect that superiors and co-workers are constantly giving information to individuals about duties, performance, and "fit" with the organization, and constantly allowing the individual the choice and opportunity to adjust his commitment.

This approach to commitment does not square with the experience of many individuals in organizations. First, most organizations highly value commitment from their work force, believe that the best workers are the most committed workers, and attempt to create and maximize commitment wherever possible, rather than offer individuals free and open choices. Second, individuals do not make rational choices about their level of commitment. People do not say to themselves, when they take the job, "how committed am I going to be?" Nor do they always rationally adjust their commitment following significant positive or negative experiences. Instead, the process of becoming committed, staying committed, or becoming uncommitted, often appears to operate at another level of rationality, as a process that "happens" to individuals, rather than by virtue of conscious choice and decision making.

Source: Roy J. Lewicki, "Seduction and Commitment in the Organization." This article was especially written for this text, 1980. Reprinted by permission of author.

As an example, let us consider Frank and Janet Smith's decision to purchase a new house when Frank was transferred to Cleveland. Frank was offered the job by his company, but he really wasn't sure he was going to like it. He expected that the job would demand a lot out of him, including working nights and weekends. He wasn't sure that he could get along with his new boss, and enjoy the kind of open communication that the job required. Finally, Janet told him she really would rather have been transferred to Toledo instead, and didn't think she was going to like Cleveland. But they decided to try it anyway.

When it came time to make a decision about housing, Frank and Janet both knew that they preferred a house. They didn't want to rent an apartment, because they thought an apartment would probably be too small and inconvenient. So they had to either rent or buy a house. Now the "rational" approach to commitment would probably stress that since Frank and Janet's satisfaction with the new job and Cleveland is so uncertain, they ought to select housing that will be easy to move out of if they decide they don't like the new environment. The "pararational" approach to commitment (and the one they selected) argues, as they did, that "we won't really feel settled until we buy a house, and only then can we fairly determine whether we really like Cleveland and the job. And besides, if we like it, we won't have to move again from a rented house to our own." But once having made the decision to buy a house, the costs and inconveniences of selling it and moving again will discourage them from considering this possibility. Instead, Frank will probably try to adapt more to his job than he would if he rented an apartment, and Janet will probably exert more effort to try to find friends and activities that will allow her to enjoy her new life in Cleveland.

When asked about how organizations built commitment, most managers can only articulate the rational elements of the commitment process—interesting work, challenging work, satisfying work, finding the right individuals to match a particular job or workgroup. Yet these same managers are probably victims themselves of pararational commitment—a process they could not clearly describe, although they know that it works. The purpose here will be to explore the nature of this "hidden side" of organizational commitment—to find out what is "inside the black box" that effectively turns uncommitted into committed managers, perhaps (by their own admission) without their conscious intention to become so.

A DEFINITION OF "ORGANIZATIONAL SEDUCTION"

What is an appropriate descriptive phrase to describe the process by which organizations induce their members to become more committed, perhaps above and beyond the individual's choice about his proper level of commitment? "Seduction" has been chosen because it suggests the subtle, pararational nature of the influence process between individual and organization. A dictionary definition of "seduction" is helpful at this point:

1. To lead astray: entice away from duty or rectitude; corrupt
2. To induce (a woman to surrender) her chastity
3. To lead or draw away, as from principles, faith or allegiance
4. To win over; entice.

There are several key elements to this definition that should be noted. First, seduction is inducing an individual to make tempting choices and offering sufficient positive inducements to make the action justifiable. In a sexual relationship, one person may be seduced because of the attractiveness or flattery of the other; in an organizational relationship, the individual may be seduced because of the attractiveness or flattery of bosses or co-workers. Second, the influence process is one of enticement, not force; it involves the use of promises and opportunities, not threats or punishments. Third, the intention of the seducer may not only be to entice the individual into a particular course of action, but to draw the individual away from duty or principles. This is the particularly corrupting nature of seduction, since the choice alternatives for the victim are normally between allegiance to one's own values or morality, and the choices offered by the seducer. While we typically think of this form of persuasion in a perjorative sense—as the debasement of one's own values or ethics—any enticement away from principles could be labeled as seduction. A man who is persuaded by his girlfriend to take her out dancing may be as seduced by her influence as she would be if he had successfully convinced her to stay in his apartment and make love. While the later situation is typically labeled seduction, both processes fit the more formal elements of the definition.

Finally, a definition of seduction requires that the individual be given the *appearance of choice* to engage in the specified behavior. Although bombarded by flattery and promises, the victim is (theoretically) always free to reject temptation. Few individuals actually reject temptation, or are aware that the appearance of choice is really an appearance, while the choice option is seldom exercised. The most analagous situation would be one in which a child, offered a piece of candy, would say, "no thanks, it will rot my teeth." The importance of choice is *postdecisional*; by preserving the appearance of choice, individuals who may later regret their chosen alternative to be seduced have only themselves to blame. If they do blame the seducer, (he) can always argue that the victim was given a choice to resist the temptation. Legal, ethical, and moral challenges are easily dismissed on these grounds, since the apparent availability of choice to the victim at the time of decision absolves the seducer from responsibility for "coercing" the behavior.

HOW ORGANIZATIONS SEDUCE EMPLOYEES

Based on observations of organizations which have conducted successful seduction programs, the inducements on the following work dimensions are likely to be most important: (1) status, (2) an extremely pleasant work environment to satisfy all comfort needs, and (3) challenging, involving work that continually stimulates the individual but shapes his efforts toward greater loyalty to the organization that provided it. In elaborating upon nature of these phenomena, we will drawn upon direct quotes from the early chapters of John Dean's *Blind Ambition,* a rare and insightful perspective on organizational seduction that can serve as a lesson to all those who are potentially seducible by their organizations.

I. Status

> Everyone [on the White House Staff] jockeyed for a position close to the President's ear, and even an unseasoned observer could sense minute changes in status. Success and failure could be seen in the size, decor and location of offices. Anyone who moved to a smaller office was on the way down. If a carpenter, cabinetmaker or wallpaper hanger was busy in someone's office, this was a sure sign he was on the rise. Every day, workmen crawled over the White House complex like ants. Movers busied themselves with the continuous shuffling of furniture from one office to another as people moved in, up, down or out. We learned to read office changes as an index of the internal bureaucratic power struggles. The expense was irrelevant to Haldeman. "For Christ's sake," he once retorted when we discussed whether we should reveal such expenses, "this place is a national monument, and I can't help it if the last three Presidents let it go to hell." Actually, the costs had less to do with the fitness of the White House than with the need of its occupants to see tangible evidence of their prestige." (page 20)

In Dean's description of the White House milieu, status is both "absolute" in its attainment in this organization (e.g. working in a "national monument", working for the President of the United States), and "relative" with respect to Dean's specific position in the internal status hierarchy. Let us first consider the process of attaining membership in a high status organization.

A. Attainment of Status Seductive organizations are high status; the individual is motivated to *want* to be part of it before entry. High status, prestigious organizations are ones which are aspired to by able candidates, themselves desirous of success and all of the relevant benchmarks.

How is status or prestige created for an organization? Several ways are fairly common:

1. By virtue of its known and acknowledged position vis-a-vis their competitors for quality, innovation, or adherence to standards of excellence.
2. By virtue of the quality or standards of excellence adhered to *by its members,* whose *own status* may lend status to the organizations. For example, acknowledged scholars who have built professional reputations on the quality of their research, or on their service to professional organizations, will lend status to low status universities by virtue of being members of that system. In essence, observers reason that, "because Smith works for X organization, it must be a better place than I thought."
3. By virtue of the inherent difficulty of obtaining membership in such organizations. Status is also conferred when the demand for membership in an organization exceeds the supply of available positions, and when the standards for admission to organizational membership are allegedly made on the basis of screening procedures to determine "qualifications." These standards for admission need not be explicit, even if they are clearly used to

make selection decisions. Thus, acceptance to a Fulbright Fellowship Program is high status, not only because it requires superior academic ability but also some elusive, ambiguous evaluation of individual qualities that are difficult explicitly to describe or defend.

4. By virtue of the organization's known ability to confer upon its members benefits, opportunities, privileges or other "side-payments" that are not available to non-members.
5. By virtue of an organization's ability to "cultivate" past status, even if the current basis for status may have eroded. To retain a reputation of high status, organizations have to behave in ways consistent with high status, such as going through the procedures and "motions" that are spelled out in this paper. For example, certain academic institutions are able to maintain their image of high status because of their affluence, prestige among influential alumni, and ability to continually attract superior students, even though the quality of faculty members in many departments may be inferior to similar departments in less prestigious schools.

B. Conferring of Status—Initiation Rites and the "One of the Chosen Few" Induction John Dean describes his meeting with H. R. Haldeman and Richard Nixon at the San Clemente White House, to be "interviewed" for the job as Counsel to the President:

The meeting the next day in Haldeman's office had barely begun when his phone rang.

"Whoops", he said, bringing his feet down from his desk, "that's the President. Excuse me, this shouldn't take long."

Alone, I pondered my new intimacy with power. I had already been over-whelmed by the tension and the grandeur, and I knew everything I was feeling was a minute refraction of what touched the President himself. All of San Clemente, from the helicopters and the global communications to the breathless expressions of otherwise cynical men, reached to and from the President. Presidential pressure was everywhere, and the President was in the next room talking with Haldeman. I was delighted over the feel of my new title, Counsel to the President, when Haldeman came back and invited me to meet him.

Haldeman broke his trance: "Mr. President, I'd like you to meet John Dean."

"John," he said, "Bob has told me about your career as a lawyer and I want you to be my counsel." Then, almost as if he felt he had been too blunt, he quickly smiled and asked, "Would you like to be the counsel to the President?"

"Yes, Sir. It would be an honor." A tremble in my voice surely revealed my nervousness. (pages 10–11)

Membership or initiation rites serve a number of functions in organizations: to formally acknowledge and celebrate the acceptance of new members into a system, to formally delineate the time of membership, to indoctrinate new members in the norms, rules, and procedures of the group, and often, to provide a "test" situation to see if the individual is worthy of membership. In high status organizations practicing seduction, one purpose of membership rites is to impress upon new members that their individual status has been significantly enhanced by attaining organizational membership. "You are one of the chosen few. Out of (thousands) of well qualified and capable applicants from all over (the world), we have selected *you* as the best possible candidate. How does that make you feel?" Naturally, the answer is easy: flattered, embarrassed, recognized, indebted, obligatory. The seduction has begun.

A second function of membership rites is to extract from the individual specific commitments to become a member. The clearest example of this is evidenced in the Dean quote, when Nixon directly asks Dean: " 'John, . . . , Bob has told me about your career as a lawyer, and *I want you to be* my counsel.' Then, almost

as if he felt he had been too blunt, he quickly smiled and asked, '*Would you like to be* the counsel to the President'. 'Yes, sir', said Dean, '*It would be an honor*' " (emphasis mine). Not only do we have Dean publicly accepting the position of Counsel from Nixon, hence making a commitment to the position, but present is another element of seduction—*apparent choice*. Nixon rewords his original "mandate" so that Dean can respond to a "request" instead. What man would refuse such a tempting alternative? The seduction continues.

A third function of membership rites is to "reinstitute" the relative status relationship between initiate and system. Lest the initiate feel that his new membership allows him all rights and privileges in the organization, membership rites clarify the existence of internal status systems; the initiate has only entered on the bottom of a long and complex organizational ladder. While an initiate can boast to the world outside the organization that he is "one of the chosen few," *inside* the organization he is at the bottom of the status hierarchy. In this position, the initiate is maximally susceptible to influence by higher status members. This condition of "influencability," coupled with the feelings of *obligation* created by having been accepted to high status, (Dean's comment, "It would be an honor",) sets the stage for further seduction.

C. The Exploitation of Status—Normative Social Pressures and Individual Co-optation

Once he has become an "initiate" in a high status group, the new member usually searches for social cues to determine the ways he can be accepted by group members, and how he can "make it in the system." Individuals searching for these cues are sure to find them. Organizations often take great pains in socializing new members to the system, through training programs, communicating rules and expectations, and presenting strong role models for the individual to imitate. This broad, pervasive influence of groups on individuals has been called "normative social conformity" by one researcher. Low status members who aspire to improve their status will be subject to strong, pervasive pressures toward loyalty, conformity to group norms, and increased group commitment.

It is important to note that the *nature* of these norms will differ from group to group. For some groups, the norms will be entirely consistent with *individual, personal* success; that is, the norms communicate that the individual should behave in a way to maximize individual self-interest, to seek better positions in other organizations if the opportunities arise, and to feel "obligated" to maximize one's individual career success rather than the success of the particular organization. However, our experience in organizations, both corporate and academic, indicate that this is the *exception* rather than the rule. Most groups in organizations exert pressures on the individual to be *loyal* to the organization and *committed* to its specific goals and objectives, perhaps at the expense of the corruption of individual self-interests. We argue here that high status systems are prone to the following dispositions that impact upon new initiates:

1. *A disposition of arrogance,* generated by the continual affirmation of the group's power and status. When groups and organizations are continually acknowledged for their power and status, membership in them is actively sought by far more applicants than can be accommodated. As a consequence, the organization may develop arrogance and superiority that legitimizes asking for anything from anyone, and expecting to get it. Individuals or organizations can be powerful by acting powerful (giving orders, assuming control, being punitive for noncompliance with requests) or by looking powerful (arrangement of furniture, decor, personal dress). The process is best summarized by Russell Barnard, publisher of Harper's, in a collection of notes on the Watergate affair:

Corruption is the child of self-righteousness. Self-righteousness often springs from delusions of superiority. After all, if I consider myself a superior being, how can my understanding of morality be less than superior?

Superior people and power gravitate toward one another. . . . So if one someone comes along looking, talking and acting superior, he is likely to be given some power. This generally confirms in his mind that he *is* superior, so he looks for more power. After a while he is the head of something. Before long it dawns on him that he could demonstrate his superiority in more impressive ways (and, of course, acquire more power) if only he could get around some of the obstacles in his way—a law here or there or maybe an alleged ethic. These obstacles are not meant for him. They are to keep the inferior, soft-headed, sponge-fisted proles from running amok.

2. *A propensity to make risky decisions in areas of ethical, moral or legal questionability.*

Behavioral science research shows that groups, under certain conditions, make "riskier" decisions than individuals, and that the process is best described as a "polarization" of the initial attitudes of individual group members. Polarization can account for shifts in attitudes among juries, investment committees, or policymaking groups, who may collectively advocate a more extreme strategy than was initially favored by individual group members. Individuals engaging in discussion are likely to compare their own attitudes to those of other members, and to judge their own attitudes more favorably in light of the fact that others seem to agree. Favorable social comparison leads individuals to advocate their own position more strongly, in order to enhance one's own status in the group. Finally, listening to, as well as articulating, more polarized positions leads individuals to develop the facts and opinions to support these positions, and hence to come to believe what they have been verbally advocating. Research studies have shown that one of the most effective methods of attitude change is to have the individual publicly argue and defend the position he is to adopt. Publicly defending the organization's policies and decisions, or participating in the recruitment of new members, further serves to shape the individual's thinking toward the group mentality.

3. *An illusion that the group is invulnerable to possible negative consequences, and that their position is inherently moral.*

In describing the group dynamics that contributed to significant fiascos in United States foreign policy, Professor Irving Janis of Yale University cites the "illusion of invulnerability" as a factor in the willingness to engage in risky courses of action. The arrogance generated by power and status blinds actors to any possible negative consequences that could result from these actions. When negative consequences might be anticipated, their likelihood is denied. Moreover, the group also comes to believe that since they are worthy people, their decision must be worthy and moral. In the service of maintaining the group, it is appropriate to employ any strategy or tactic to defend the group from enemies and to maintain its superiority.

Group polarization, arrogance, invulnerability and inherent morality are processes that are common to high status groups interested in maintaining that status. As such, they exercise strong influence over their members for loyalty and allegiance to group objectives, and encourage the pursuit of any and all strategies necessary to achieve those objectives. Why do individuals allow themselves to be subjected to this process? Why does the individual allow his self-interest to be shaped by these normative social pressures, without recognizing the pressures and resisting them? There are several reasons: because he is desirous of being a part of a high status system, because effective normative pressures are often subtle and indiscernible in their slow but pervasive impact on individual values, and because the individual is consistently "cushioned" from any second thoughts he may have by a very comfortable environment. We will now describe the specific nature of this environmental cushion.

II. A Plentiful, Unlimited Supply of Hygienes—The Cushions That Protect Individuals in Their Fall from Grace

Why is it that managerial audiences are quick to see that negative KITA is *not* motivation, while they are almost unanimous in their judgment that positive KITA *is* motivation. It is because negative KITA is rape, and a positive KITA is seduction. But it is infinitely worse to be seduced than to be raped; the latter is an unfortunate occurrence, while the former signifies that you were a party to your own downfall. That is why positive KITA is so popular: it is a tradition; it is the American way. The organization does not have to kick you; you kick yourself. (Frederick Herzberg).

Frederick Herzberg's theory of motivation is one of the most popular in the managerial literature. He distinguishes two groups of factors that contribute to worker motivation: hygienes and motivators. Hygienes include various positive and negative techniques used by management to apply a "Kick in the A ____ " (KITA) to the worker, such as salary, better working conditions, titles, job security, improved relationships with supervisors and peers, and various company policies. When management applies these strategies to increase worker productivity or job satisfaction, he usually gets "movement" (i.e., worker compliance) in return, but not "motivation." "Motivators" are factors inherent in the job itself (variety, autonomy, challenge, complexity), achievement, recognition, responsibility, and opportunities for personal and organizational growth and development. When applied by management, these factors create internally induced motivation in the worker, rather than externally induced movement.

The research generated by this theory, and similar approaches to motivation, job enrichment, and the quality of life in the workplace has been monumental. Yet the researchers have shared the same blindness that Herzberg attributes to his managerial audiences. Researchers have been vitally concerned about individuals who are being raped by organizations—whose jobs are unfulfilling and unrewarding, whose satisfaction and productivity were low. But few researchers have been concerned with the individuals who are successfully applying KITA to themselves—being seduced—rather than being kicked by their organizations. These are the people who are actively involved in their own downfall.

Our major disagreement with Herzberg is that elaborate organizational strategies for applying positive KITA to its members is not designed to induce *motivation*, but to induce *obligation*. We will define this strategy as the process by which management supplies for its workers a PLentiful, Unlimited Supply of Hygienes (the PLUSH strategy). Their purpose is not to directly induce the individual to work harder, or more productively, but to surround him in an atmosphere of PLUSHness, minimizing any dissatisfaction with activities that may be compromising his self-interests or values. In essence, proper application of the PLUSH strategy makes the individual's life so comfortable that (a) material concerns are eliminated, (b) the individual feels a vague but distinct sense of indebtedness to the organization for all of these amenities, and (c) any thoughts about leaving the organization are immediately dismissed because one knows that things are "much tougher in the real world." Specific PLUSH tactics include:

—Spacious offices, usually carpeted and wood-paneled, with expensive furniture and decorations

—Unlimited budgets for photocopying, telephone, etc.

—Extremely prompt and efficient secretarial services

—Unlimited largess in travel budgets, and expense accounts

—"Apparent" flexibility of hours for reporting to work, and for lunch hours ("apparent" because the individual feels he has tremendous freedom, while probably in fact investing far more time than if he were on a fixed eight-hour day)

—Recreation facilities free to members, such as gymnasiums, tickets to athletic events or theatre, social and cultural opportunities, etc.

—Parking facilities within a three minute walk of the office, specifically reserved for high status members

—Liberal, unsupervised policies for using organization facilities and resources to conduct "personal" business—secretarial, photocopying, office supplies, etc.

—Stock options, retirement plans, and other techniques for "vesting" (committing?) the individual to the organization as tenure grows

—Other support services idiosyncratic to the profession and the organization, such as libraries, company cars, flexible working hours, computer services, etc.

III. The Individual Reaction—INWOAT

The seductive organization overwhelms the individual with splendor. It offers him membership in a high status system, and all of the individual status enhancement that comes from being a member of that system. It stresses that he is "one of the chosen few," a special unique individual who has made it into the ranks that many others aspire to but cannot attain. It puts him through a series of initiation rites which appear to offer him the opportunity to reject membership, but in fact are designed to elicit his commitment and loyalty to the system. It offers him a series of initially challenging and demanding tasks and assignments, increasing the attraction of the job while at the same time compromising his perspective and shaping him toward the organizations norms and values. Finally, it cushions the stress that may be induced by these challenging but subverting tasks by bathing him in a luxuriously comfortable environment that heightens his awareness of "how good I have it here," and "how much the benefits of this job outweigh a few liabilities."

In the context of inducements—contributions theory, the individual response is to feel overwhelmingly gratified—I'm Not Worthy of All This (INWOAT). The phenomena is one of holding the individual in a nearly perpetual state of awe during his early period in the organization. Wide-eyed and dazed by his own *actual, physical presence* in an organization that exceeds his fondest dreams, he responds with strong feelings of obligation and appreciation. This state of imbalance, with the individual feeling he "owes" the organization something for their flattery and generosity, sets the stage for the final act of organizational seduction.

IV. Co-optation of Cosmopolitanism and the Induction of Localism

The final state in the process or organizational seduction is to induce the individual to direct all of his efforts, bred out of obligation, to "repaying" the organization for its generosity and kindness to him. In essence, the organization and its primary agents become the target of commitment, although the individual's peers and colleagues, or the specific set of tasks and responsibilities that he performs (the job itself) may function as partially acceptable substitute targets.

Sociologist Alvin Gouldner, in a study of variations in an individual's selected "target" of commitment and identification, makes a critical distinction between individuals with "cosmopolitan" or "local" orientations. "Locals" were individuals who were strong in their loyalty to the particular organization that they worked for. These individuals used other individuals in

the same company as the basis for social comparison, and had low commitment to specific "professional" or occupational groups (e.g. professional academies, societies, fraternities, associations, etc.) "Cosmopolitans," on the other hand, were strong in thier professional and occupational groupings, compared themselves to other professionals who worked at similar jobs but for different organizations, and were low in their loyalty to the particular organization that employed them.

Gouldner suggests that most organizations value loyalty, because the most loyal and committed members are the most reliable, work the hardest for the institution, and perpetuate its values and standards. Yet loyalty is usually not a rewardable virtue in organizations, probably because it appears to others to be too nepotistic and unobjective. Hence, organizations maintain that they reward performance and competence instead. But loyalty is subtly rewarded nevertheless; the message gets propagated that, in exchange for a decreased cosmopolitan professional orientation, the individual will be suitably rewarded for his localistic orientation. These cross-pressures for "local" vs. "cosmopolitan" orientations are most easily seen in organizations which are largely composed of professionals—universities, law firms, medical centers, research and development departments, etc. In these environments, professional work is often neglected to serve the local organization. Professional ethics and standards are abdicated in order to help the local organization achieve respectable ends by not-so-respectable means. Personal aspirations are abandoned, and "remote duty assignments" are accepted in exchange for "better opportunities down the road." Some organizations are also notorious for reneging on these future commitments, arguing that they would never have agreed to such a thing, or that conditions have sufficiently changed so as to make the original commitment unfulfillable.

There are, therefore, three premises: (1) organizations desire loyalty and commitment from their members, (2) locals are the strongest forms of loyalty in the organization, and (3) cosmopolitans, while they may lend intangible "external status" to the organization, do little in the way of direct, noticeable contributions to fulfill the organization's view of the psychological contract. The conclusion is that organizations, consciously or subconsciously, exert strong pressures on their members to adopt a "local" orientation. The following strategies are commonly used to induce this orientation:

1. Isolate individuals from cosmopolitan cross-pressures. The more physically and spatially remote the organization is from other centers of professionals, the more difficult it will be for individuals to actively maintain cosmopolitan ties. Organizations located in small towns, in foreign countries, or in areas where travel is difficult due to weather, geography, or underdeveloped transportation systems, will have an easier time generating local loyalty because their organization is the "only game in town." Similar outcomes can be produced by making it difficult to communicate with the outside world, such as insufficient budget appropriations for telephone, correspondence, or professional travel.

2. Encourage interdisciplinary collaboration that will necessitate efforts to communicate with others from different disciplines in the same local environment. One way to keep cosmopolitans "down on the farm" is to require them to talk with others in their own environment, working more on interdisciplinary problems that on specific within-discipline problems. This will require them to invest large amounts of time learning to communicate and work on similar interests, all in the local environment. Should the teams develop such sophistication that they wish to begin to seek out other joint-teams in other environments (team cos-

mopolitanism), the organization can respond by changing the composition of the interdisciplinary teams, restructuring the problem, or other recycling techniques.

3. Keep resources sufficiently taut so that "cells" of latent cosmopolitans cannot develop. The organizational strategy used here is to encourage the "max-mix model" of organizational composition, so that every individual has some different background, orientation, or professional interest. To be avoided at all costs is the development of a subgroup of individuals, all with the same professional orientation or interests, who may be far more likely to develop an emergent "cosmopolitan" orientation as a result of their common professional backgrounds and interests.

    This is an insidious variable for organizations to control, since, the more successful they are, the more the demand for the organization's services will exceed its supply, and hence they are likely to grow to meet demand. A single individual in a professional discipline will no longer be able to meet the demands for required services. Extensive hiring to meet demand will introduce a number of similar individuals to an organization, who are likely to form a subgroup and begin to espouse cosmopolitan values. Some organizations have managed to resist this process by claiming that the quality and uniqueness of their success is in part determined by the current size of the organization—that "small is beautiful," that growth will shake the values of the current system, and that growth to meet demand will lead the organization to lose its unique niche in the marketplace. While this may be true, we will point out that it *is* an argument which serves to maintain the strength of localism and keep cosmopolitan values from undermining the environment.

4. Discourage lateral entry at the middle

and upper levels of the organization. Feelings of gratitude or satisfaction derived from recognition and praise by the organization are likely to increase the feelings of obligation and indebtedness to the organization (loyalty). Hence, organizational commitment and loyalty are strongly related to tenure with the organization. Moreover, the longer the senior group of employees goes unpenetrated by lateral entry of other seniors from different environments, the more localism they will display. This localistic inbreeding keeps cosmopolitan values and ideas from penetrating the senior group, and preserves the tradition of localistic Darwinism that only allows the best performers (read most loyal, committed, localistic) to enter the senior ranks.

5. Among the young impressionables, encourage the accumulation of a complex network of positive and rewarding experiences which become associated with organizational membership. Social events, personal friendships, and organizational rituals are some of the common ones. Pleasurable experiences, whether at work or merely because they are associated with a particular environment, are likely to lead to "halo effects" that will generalize to the organization. Many of these pleasurable experiences are a continuation of the PLentiful, Unlimited Supply of Hygienes (PLUSH) strategy.

6. Subvert the individual's desire to respond to cosmopolitan forces. Every individual thinks about leaving his organization; undersocialized locals think about leaving when they are dissatisfied with their work, or when they have recently been exposed to a group of cosmopolitans who painted an attractive picture of life in the outside world. Agents of organizations who are in charge of this subversion are traditionally skilled in a variety of persuasion factors,

typically designed to elicit (1) dissonance reduction ("things aren't as bad here as you think") (2) guilt, ("you owe us something after all we have done for you," or "you are irreplaceable"), (3) pride, ("you are an incredibly value asset, a unique individual in this unique environment"), or (4) fear, ("your stay in the organization has rendered you so unique that you would be unlikely to succeed anywhere else").

V. Critical Tests for Successful Seduction—Was the Operation Successful?

There are a number of test situations that will determine whether an organization seduction effort has been successful. From the organization's point of view, success is the ability to shape and then incorporate a dutifully loyal and committed new member into its ranks. From the individual's perspective, one may call it a case in which the operation was a success *because* the patient died—death being the extinction of all other values, principles or interests which are not in the service of the organization. The test situation that critically determines the magnitude of trace of organizational seduction is *persistence following failure.*

One of the most common tests for successful seduction is to determine if the individual continues to try harder in the face of failure. Doing so suggests that the individual has adapted a rather unique response to failure, since much research would indicate that failure *normally* leads individuals to feel dissatisfied with their job, decrease their commitment, invest less effort, and either try to change the organization or leave it. Persistence under failure, on the other hand, seems to suggest that the individual is induced to believe that increased efforts, or skills learned in the process of the previous failure, or a changed environment, will make success more likely in the future. Organizations which encourage persistence are usually doing so to cushion the blow of failure by helping the individual rationalize the failure rather than let it affect his self-esteem or commitment. In doing so, they are seducing the individual away from accurately perceiving the past situation, and instead contribute to forms of adaptation that preserve commitment and persistence in the future.

The tactics that organizations use to help individuals adapt to failure are clearly described from an insightful essay by sociologist Erving Goffman, "On Cooling the Mark Out." In this article, Goffman describes the process by which victims in exploitative relationships are "cooled out" to prevent them from publicly "squawking" or exposing the exploitation to public view, (and hence inhibiting the exploiter's ability to continue the process with other victims). Organizations have typically used a variety of these mechanisms to keep seduced victims from squawking:

a. Offering alternative status that lets the individual become something else, or do the same thing in another location: creating new status categories, new territories, new areas in which to accomplish the job. If appropriately played up, the individual can be made to feel like one of the chosen few for receiving this rare opportunity, while he is being cooled out at the same time. Additional PLUSHness may also be added to his job to reinstitute feelings of INWOAT—creating feelings in the individual that "I've failed in this organization, yet, these people are so nice to me. I still owe them something."

b. Offering another chance to aspire to the same status. Since failure usually occurs in complex task environments, individuals can be persuaded to believe that increased effort, or insights developed from previous failures, or changed environmental conditions, will increase the probability of success in the future.

c. Permitting the victim to "blow his stack," allowing a controlled venting of anger, so that the victim achieves some state of catharsis. Since many organizations do not permit the victim to express anger against the system, allowing this to happen (under the right conditions) may allow the mark to appreciate the opportunity to react directly to his seducer, and hence induce feelings of obligation for this opportunity—which will allow for further seduction. The *agent of the organization* who absorbs this blowoff is a key figure. Goffman suggests that it should be done by strong, powerful people who can tolerate the anger, while nonetheless conveying sympathy for the poor, frustrated mark. Many managers are incapable of performing this role, believing it is a demeaning and unnecessary part of their job. Hence, the task of absorbing the anger is given to sympathetic peers or personnel officers, whose specific job may be to cushion the blows and let the individual feel catharsis, hopefully minimizing his anger without allowing him to recognize the larger process of organizational control that persists.

d. Finally, Goffman suggests that in cases where the individual cannot be successfully cooled out, or where his usefulness to the organization has in fact ended, a process of collusion with the victim is desirable. Once again the process of *apparent (irrational) choice* operates. As Goffman puts it,

. . . the operator and the mark may enter into a tacit understanding according to which the mark agrees to act as if he were leaving of his own accord, and the operator agrees to preserve the illusion that this was the case. It is a form of bribery. In this way the mark may fail in his own eyes but prevent others from discovering the failure. The mark gives up his role and saves his face. The strategy is at work in the romantic custom of allowing a guilty officer to take his own life in a private way before it is taken from him publicly, and in the less romantic custom of allowing a person to resign for delicate reasons instead of firing him for indelicate ones. (page 378)

Requesting a resignation, helping the individual find a new job, writing a letter of recommendation that may be totally at odds with his performance appraisal, and cushioning the blows with severence pay or pensions are all means for collusively helping the individual out of the organization while letting him believe he is walking under his own control.

IMPLICATIONS FOR MANAGEMENT

The implications of this research for managers and organizations are profound. This paper proposed a blueprint for organizational seduction—a set of steps that can easily be followed by organizations in order to maximize individual loyalty and commitment. With suitable tailoring and fitting to the specifications of various organizations, it could easily be adapted as the basic foundation for shaping up new recruits to the service of the modern organization.

At the same time, many managers will recognize themselves as "victims" of this process in their own organizations, and react with the outrage that we would expect from anyone who discovers that he has been manipulated and seduced. So while the blueprints for the process are concisely described and potentially implementable, other managers who recognize the manipulation now going on in their own organizations are likely to "blow their stack" and "blow the organization's cover," calling the game for what it is.

One purpose of this paper, therefore, is *consciousness raising* about organizational manipulation and seduction. A critical test for the managers of organizational socialization programs is to ask the question, "is this what we are doing now?" While this question alone may produce some affirmative answers, a more

threatening—but important—process is to ask the same question to recent recruits in the organization. If the answers are even more affirmative, then the organization probably has a lot of capable individuals whose abilities and talents are being socialized out as they climb the hierarchy. In addition, there are probably a lot of angry, "sour grapes" individuals who didn't make it and are giving the organization a bad name in the outside world. The more that top management and new recruits can both point to the existence of specific seduction techniques and mechanisms, the more that organization needs to examine the consequences (and ethics) of its socialization program and its exploitation of human resources.

A second purpose of the paper is to caution those who may not *now* have a seductive socialization program for building loyalty and commitment, but who are thinking about implementing one based on this paper. Before designing and implementing any program to build loyalty and commitment, management *must* ask the question, *"would this program work if we explicitly told people what we were going to do and why we were going to do it?"* If the answer to the question, is "yes, it would still work", then the organization is proceeding with a program that has the informed choice and consent of the workforce about their ongoing level of commitment. The implicit psychological contract between the individual and the organization is made explicit, subject to scrutiny by both sides, and formally negotiated or discussed. If the answer to the question is "no, it would not work"—because recruits would feel angry and manipulated, and because they would never explicitly agree to the implicit contract we are seducing them into—then we have an immediate test for determining the viability of a seduction program. The more an organization is willing to use seductive commitment techniques, and rely on the dynamics of implicit psychological contracts, the more it is engaging in an exploitative process that corrupts valuable human capital and breaches the bounds of ethics in its conduct of employee relations.

A third and final purpose of this paper is to point out that *strategies of organizational seduction are probably not viable long run strategies for systems management.* Seduction may be a good way to attract qualified and capable individuals to the organization, and even a satisfactory way for getting them to share the organization's values and make productive contributions. But this paper has also shown that long-run seduction strategies can have serious consequences for organizations. The most seduced individuals rise in the upper ranks, contributing more loyalty and commitment to the organization than originality in thinking or problem solving. They tend to expect loyalty and commitment from the younger managers under them, hence imposing a confining corporate mentality on those further down the hierarchy. Meanwhile, those who have not made it into the higher ranks are either displaced to an organizational backwater, or leave

the organization angry and demean its status to the outside world. The long run impact, obviously, is that the quality of worklife in this organization, as well as the quality of the organization and its product vis-a-vis its competitors, is bound to decline and suffer. Once the pathology sets in, it is difficult to cure without dramatic repopulation and renewal of the organization at all levels.

If organizational seduction is truly a problem in the modern organization, then we should expect to hear screams of pain from all levels of management. For some it will be the pain that comes with the discovering of one's own seduction—and even the ways that one "allowed it" to happen. For others, it will be the pain that comes with the discovery of a subtle and perverse con game, or the angry denial that such games don't exist, or the defense that the game is necessary because "we've got to keep up with our competitors." Managers of seductive organizations ought to think hard about whether the game is worth the results.

1. Some people say that adherence to the work ethic in the United States is at an all-time low. Although this may vary from region to region and city to city, there does seem to be some grain of truth in this belief. How does this statement relate to the fact that for many people the organization indoctrinates them toward a work ethic that should lead to high rather than low productivity?

2. After reading the article by Jay on the religion in the corporation, do you agree that participation in many organizations including the college that you attend is based in part on faith? If so, in what ways?

3. Do you think it is wrong for organizations to differentiate among their employees based on status? In what ways have you seen this happen?

4. Why do you believe that the company man as described by Maccoby is more efficient at middle levels of management? Is it possible that the company man or woman is oversocialized to the extent that he or she is not a creative thinker?

5. What is your personal reaction to the nonemployed males described in the *Business Week* article? Can you think of methods that would allow the work ethic shared by these men to be compatible with the needs of organizations?

6. Do you believe that organizations seduce employees in order to gain long-term commitment? For example, do they often seduce employees to do what may not be in the best interest of their individual careers, but may be in the best interest of the organization at the time? Is it possible that the advancement opportunities of the employee suffers because of this seductive process? Can you think of examples?

CHAPTER IV
MOTIVATING THEM TO WORK

ORGANIZATIONAL SHOCKS

- Managers are often ill-prepared to deal with other people.
- Theories of work motivation taught in school, often aren't relevant to work settings because they deal with motivating one's self rather than motivating others.
- Organizations are often so efficiently organized as to be demoralizing.
- Performance appraisal systems in most organizations don't work, don't exist, or are rendered ineffective by other managerial actions.

One of the things we teach students in organizational behavior and other management courses is that managers are expected to influence the behavior and performance of subordinates. We know from various courses in psychology and organizational behavior that behavior is influenced by many things, including the attitudes, needs, and values held by a person being influenced. However, it is important for the manager to understand that he may not be able to control these variables directly but, instead, must influence whatever he or she can control directly. For example, managers can control directly *work involvement components,* such as physical surroundings, leadership style, and goal directions; *task design components* such as job scope, variety, decision autonomy, and job challenge; and *job consequence components* such as pay, feedback, and promotions.

This chapter presents several readings that describe how managers can effectively use motivational principles in the world of work. One of the shocks faced by managers, however, is that they are often ill-prepared to deal with other people. In most courses in organizational behavior and psychology we teach people how to understand themselves or understand what causes people to behave. We do very little to prepare them, however, for the fact that understanding and influencing other people is a much more difficult process than understanding one's own self.

In the first selection Robert Frost points out one of the most glaring organizational shocks experienced by managers and employees alike: Organizations are often so efficiently organized as to be demoralizing.

In the second selection by David McCullough from *Path Between the Seas,* we see how Colonel Goethals attempted to motivate his subordinates to build the Panama Canal. In the previous paragraphs we said that managers control three things directly: the work setting or climate, the task, and the consequences of the task. The previous director of the Panama Canal construction, John Stevens, had built a very positive work climate for his subordinates. Unfortunately, however, Mr. Stevens was not very good at getting the task accomplished. When Colonel Goethals took over, he was determined to make sure that the task was accomplished as quickly as possible. When he initially took charge, he correctly identified the major problem as being one of a poor task focus, but he failed to see the positive work climate. In his initial attempts he neglected to maintain the positive work climate and instead concentrated on building a positive task environment. In doing so, the work climate became negative and therefore productivity did not improve. As soon as he was able to identify this error he immediately began to work on the climate and the task and the productivity increased dramatically.

Another very important point to consider is the social aspect of performance evaluation. Before you can direct people and give them feedback about their performance you must be able to describe and measure their performance. One of the shocks experienced by many employees, especially new managers, is what is known as the vanishing performance appraisal. That is, either the items on which one is appraised are so general as to be meaningless, formal appraisals do not take place, or the period between performance reviews is so long that advancement is drastically slowed. One other organizational shock dealing with performance appraisal is the fact that in many companies, most managers are rated as outstanding or superior, which is the rating received by most of their colleagues. By doing this they are in effect not singled out or advanced, and often they receive a lower raise than they think they deserve based on their expectations, which have been generated from the high performance review. Often a person has conflicting performance objectives. One is to please the organization paying the salary and the second is to gain the respect of his or her peers. One way around this dilemma is to make sure that the performance evaluation is consumer-centered, product-centered, or application centered rather than process-oriented.

One of the most popular worker motivation programs in existence today is something known as *Organizational Development*. Organizational Development is based on a theory which states that the climate of the organization represents a set of properties of the work environment that is a major force in influencing the behavior of the employees on the job. Therefore, an improvement in the organizational climate would improve the motivation of employees to perform. The proponents of an improved climate contend that the traditional managerial system found in organizations breathes a climate of fear and mistrust that reduces management effectiveness. Therefore, programs that use such methods as team building, sensitivity training, and encounter groups unfreeze the negative climate and enhance the interpersonal relations. Once the interpersonal relationships are enhanced, then a supportive work climate can lead to better communication of organizational goals and standards and records for achieving these goals and standards.

A second popular work motivation program is one known as Job Enrichment or Task Design. In our next article by Irving Bluestone, the Vice-President of the United Auto Workers of America, we learn the history of organizational development and job enrichment for unionized employees around the world. The followup article to Mr. Bluestone's piece is an article from *Business Week* that talks about situations in which organizational development and job enrichment programs have not always worked.

In addition to improving the work climate and changing the task design, we said earlier that managers can also change the feedback system used in order to improve productivity. One of the most popular ways of doing this obviously is through pay. Unfortunately, as we have noted in the previous section, one of the taboos in an organization is any discussion about compensation. However, the motivational program called Merit Pay cannot work unless there are benchmarks against which people can measure their productivity. The last article in this section by Dale McConkey labels this paradox the "Jackass Effect in Management Compensation." Here he talks about the problem with making pay a motivator when secrecy is an overriding organizational socialization taboo.

DEPARTMENTAL

ROBERT FROST

An ant on the tablecloth
Ran into a dormant moth
Of many times his size.
He showed not the least surprise.
His business wasn't with such.
He gave it scarcely a touch,
And was off on his duty run.
Yet if he encountered one
Of the hive's enquiry squad
Whose work is to find out God
And the nature of time and space,
He would put him onto the case.
Ants are a curious race;
One crossing with hurried tread
The body of one of their dead
Isn't given a moment's arrest—
Seems not even impressed.
But he no doubt reports to any
With whom he crosses antennae,
And they no doubt report
To the higher up at court.
Then word goes forth in Formic:
'Death's come to Jerry McCormic,
Our selfless forager Jerry.
Will the special Janizary
Whose office it is to bury
The dead of the commissary
Go bring him home to his people.
Lay him in state on a sepal.
Wrap him for shroud in a petal.
Embalm him with ichor of nettle.
This is the word of your Queen.'
And presently on the scene
Appears a solemn mortician;
And taking formal position
With feelers calmly atwiddle,
Seizes the dead by the middle,
And heaving him high in air,
Carries him out of there.
No one stands round to stare.
It is nobody else's affair.

It couldn't be called ungentle.
But how thoroughly departmental.

Source: From *The Poetry of Robert Frost* edited by Edward Connery Lathem. Copyright © 1936 by Robert Frost. Copyright © 1964 by Lesley Frost Ballantine. Copyright © 1969 by Holt, Rinehart and Winston, Publishers. Reprinted by permission of Holt, Rinehart and Winston, Publishers.

PATH BETWEEN THE SEAS

DAVID McCULLOUGH

Source: From *Path Between the Seas* by David McCullough. Copyright 1977 by David McCullough. Reprinted by permission of Simon & Schuster, a Division of Gulf & Western Corporation.

The executive order had been signed at a meeting in the old de Lesseps' Palace at Cristobal on November 17, Roosevelt's last day on the Isthmus. [John] Stevens' authority, therefore, was not firmly fixed.

So it was both puzzling and extremely annoying to Roosevelt when, at the very moment he released his message, Stevens began making trouble. In Washington for a brief visit in December, Stevens was strangely irritable and caustic.

What went sour for Stevens is a mystery that Stevens chose never to explain. With the return of the dry season, the work was rolling ahead as never before. Excavation in Culebra Cut exceeded 500,000 cubic yards in January, more than double the best monthly record of the French. In February the figure was more than 600,000 cubic yards and Stevens' own popularity reached a new high.

Then on January 30, at Culebra, Stevens sent a letter to Roosevelt that reached the White House on February 12.

It was six pages in length and as devoid of cant or circumlocution as all his correspondence. It also revealed a very different man from the John Stevens of the previous year, an exhausted and embittered man. He complained of "enemies in the rear" and of the discomforts of being "continually subject to attack by a lot of people . . . that I would not wipe my boots on in the United States." While some "wise lawmakers" might think his salary excessive, he wanted it known that by staying on at Panama he was depriving himself of not less than $100,000 a year. His home life was disrupted; he was separated from his family much of the year. And at his age he had little enough time left "to enjoy the pleasures and comforts of a civilized life."

He wrote of the tremendous responsibility and strain put upon the man in his position, saying he doubted that he could bear up under them for another eight years. Technical problems were not the issue; it was "the immense amount of detail" one had to keep constantly in mind.

If there was to be glory attached to his role, he was uninterested. Nor in the final analysis did he see any special romance or meaning in the canal itself:

> The "honor" which is continually being held up as an incentive for being connected with this work, appeals to me but slightly. To me the canal is only a big ditch, and its great utility when completed, has never been so apparent to me, as it seems to be to others. Possibly I lack imagination. The work itself . . . on the whole, I do not like. . . . There has never been a day since my connection with this enterprise that I could not have gone back to the United States and occupied positions that to me, were far more satisfactory. Some of them, I would prefer to hold, if you will pardon my candor, then the Presidency of the United States.

This was the passage that settled his fate. The letter was not a formal resignation. He never said specifically that he wanted out, only that he was not "anxious to continue in service." He wanted a rest, and having assured Roosevelt of his high personal regard for him, he asked for his "calm and dispassionate" consideration of the matter.

A reporter who talked to someone who was with Roosevelt at the time Roosevelt received the letter wrote, "To say that the President was amazed at the tone and character of the communication is to describe the feelings mildly." The letter was sent immediately to Taft with a covering note: "Stevens must get out at once." Even if Stevens were to change his mind, it would make no difference "in view of the tone of his letter."

After a brief meeting with Taft, Roosevelt cabled Stevens that his resignation was accepted.

Taft again told Roosevelt that Major Goethals (who was about to become Lieutenant Colonel Goethals) was the best-equipped man for the job, so on the night of February 18 Goethals was summoned to the White house. The change, however, was kept secret until the twenty-sixth, when, with the announcement, Roosevelt issued his widely quoted declaration—a remark made as much for the benefit of the work force on the Isthmus as for the general public—that he would put the canal in the charge of "men who will stay on the job until I get tired of having them there, or till I say they may abandon it. I shall turn it over to the Army."

But in the same breath, according to the New York *Tribune,* he also remarked, "Then if the man in charge suffers from an enlarged cranium or his nerves go to the bad, I can order him north for his health and fill his place without confusion."

Stevens' primary tasks—the creation of a well-fed, well-housed, well-equipped, well-organized work force, the conception of a plan of attack—were over by 1907. As a railroad engineer he was inexperienced in the large-scale use of concrete; he knew very little about hydraulics; and these were the specialties of the Army engineers.

Stevens' two-fisted, independent spirit had been exactly what was needed. The critical situation in 1905 had demanded, as he later said, "a kind of politic 'roughneck,' who did not possess too deep a veneration for the vagaries of constituted authority." But ultimately the role called for a larger sense of mission than that.

For a long time now Roosevelt had spoken of building the canal as though it were a mighty battle in which the national honor was at stake, much as Ferdinand de Lesseps had so often spoken. Panama was a tumultuous assault for Progress, the only assault this most bellicose-sounding of American Presidents was ever to launch and lead. At the end of his last day at Cristobal, in an off-the-cuff speech to several hundred Americans, including John Stevens, he had said the canal was a larger, more important endeavor than anyone could as yet realize, and that by bringing it to successful completion they would stand like one of the famous armies of history. It was to be a long, arduous, uphill struggle, he said, one not unlike that of their fathers' in the Civil War. (His own two-month Cuban war would never have served as an example.)

> When your fathers were in the fighting, they thought a good deal of the fact that the blanket was too heavy by noon and not quite heavy enough by night, that the pork was not as good as it might be . . . and that they were not always satisfied with the way in which the regiments were led. . . . But when the war was done—when they came home, when they looked at what had been accomplished, all those things sank into insignificance, and the great fact remained that they had played their part like men among men; that they had borne themselves so that when people asked what they had done of worth in those great years all they had to say was that they had served decently and faithfully in the great armies. . . . I cannot overstate the intensity of the feeling I have . . . I feel that to each of you has come an opportunity such as is vouchsafed to but few in each generation. . . . Each man must have in him the feeling that, besides getting what he is rightfully entitled to for his work, that aside and above that must come the feeling of triumph at being associated in the work itself, must come the appreciation of what a tremendous work it is, of what a splendid opportunity is offered to any man who takes part in it.

By Roosevelt's lights, Stevens had failed in the most profound and fundamental sense, scarcely less than Wallace had. To Roosevelt the triumph was in the task itself, in taking the dare; the test was in the capacity to keep "pegging away," as he often stressed to his sons. Stevens was not merely giving up; Stevens saw it only as a "job"; there was no commitment of heart, not the slightest apparent sense of duty. To Roosevelt, Stevens was a commander abandoning his army.

He appears to have harbored no bitterness toward Stevens. ("You have done excellent work . . . and I am sorry to lose you," he wrote a few days after receiving Stevens' letter.) It was merely that if Stevens was the sort of man who looked upon the task as something to take or leave at will, then he was someone Roosevelt could quite readily do without and put from mind. In Roosevelt's long essay on the canal in his *Autobiography,* there would be no mention of John Stevens.

With the appointment of George Washington Goethals, Roosevelt's worries over the work at Panama came to an end. The canal would now be the "one-man proposition" John Stevens had called for, only the one man was to be an entirely different sort from Stevens.

For the man who now bore the burden of responsibility for [building the canal] the initial hurdle had been primarily personal and as difficult as anything in his experience.

Goethals' reception upon arrival had been pointedly cool. Plainly, neither he nor the Army was wanted by the rank and file of Americans on the job and everyone seemed eager to make a special point of Stevens' tremendous popularity. Thousands of signatures had been gathered for a petition urging Stevens to withdraw his resignation and stay. No one, it seemed, had anything but the strongest praise for him and all he had done. Never in his career, Goethals remarked, had he seen so much affection displayed for one man.

Stevens and Dr. Gorgas were at the pier the morning Goethals and Major Gaillard landed. No real reception had been arranged; nothing had even been done about a place for Goethals or Gaillard to stay. Stevens still occupied the official residence of the chief engineer, a new six-bedroom house at Culebra that was to be Goethals' once Stevens departed, but since Stevens "didn't seem inclined to take us into his house" (as Goethals wrote to his son George), the two officers had moved in with Gorgas at Ancon, where there was little privacy, not even a desk at which Goethals could work. His letters to his family those first weeks were written on his lap as he sat in a straight-backed chair in one of the bedrooms.

To add to the spirit of gloom, the *Star & Herald* openly deplored the prospect of military rule. Probably no workers would have to wear uniforms, the paper presumed, but neither should anyone be surprised if he had to answer roll call in the morning or salute his new superiors.

That the railroad men around Stevens had scant regard for Army engineers seemed also abundantly plain to Goethals. "Army engineers, as a rule, were said to be, from their very training dictatorial and many of them martinets," he would write, "and it was predicted that if they . . . were placed in charge of actual construction the canal project was doomed to failure." The Army men had only technical training, it was said; they had never "made a success as executive heads of great enterprises."

His own private estimate of the state of the work was entirely favorable. The difference between what he saw now and what he had seen in 1905, during the visit with Taft, was extraordinary. As he wrote to his son, "Mr. Stevens has done an amount of work for which he will never get any credit, or, if he gets any, will not get enough. . . ."

Several days passed before he was granted a more or less official welcome—a Saturday-night "smoker" given as much to entertain a party of visiting congressmen. John Stevens declined to attend and Goethals, at the head table, sat listening without expression as the toastmaster extolled Stevens at length and made several cutting remarks about the military. It was an evening he would never forget. With each mention of Stevens' name there was a resounding cheer, while the few obligatory references to Stevens' successor were met with silence. Goethals was furious at what he regarded as "slurs" on the Army, but kept still until it was his turn. He had come to the affair

not in uniform but in a white civilian suit. In fact, he had brought no uniforms to the Isthmus and never in the years to come would he be seen in one.

He was, he told the assembled guests, as appreciative as they of the work Stevens had accomplished and he had no intention of instigating a military regimen. "I am no longer a commander in the United States Army. I now consider that I am commanding the Army of Panama, and that the enemy we are going to combat is the Culebra Cut and the locks and dams at both ends of the Canal, and any man here on the work who does his duty will never have any cause to complain of militarism."

He took over from Stevens officially at midnight, March 31, 1907, and a week later Stevens sailed for home. One of the largest crowds ever seen on the Isthmus jammed the pier at Cristobal to see him off, everyone cheering, waving, and singing "Auld Lang Syne." Stevens was noticeably amazed and touched by the outpouring of affection. This time it was Goethals' turn not to attend.

Having none of Stevens' colorful mannerisms or easy way with people, Goethals impressed many at first as abrupt and arbitrary, a cold fish. The word *"goethals"* in Flemish, it was soon being said, meant "stiff neck."

He hated to have his picture taken. He found the visiting congressmen rude, tiresome, terribly time-consuming. Callers were "an awful nuisance." It was expected that he appear at every dance and social function at the Tivoli or the Culebra Club. He would "brace up" and go "out of a sense of duty" and spend the evening sitting on a porch listening to the music, waiting only for the time when he could politely withdraw.

Stevens' former secretary, having agreed to stay and help with the transition, suddenly resigned. William Bierd, the railroad boss, made a surprise announcement that he was retiring because of his health, but then Goethals learned that Bierd was taking a job with Stevens on the

New Haven Railroad. Frank Maltby decided no civilian engineer had a future any longer at Panama and so he too quit. Then the steam-shovel engineers, sensing the time was at last right for a show of strength, threatened to strike unless their demands were met. Goethals refused and they walked off the job. It was the first serious strike since the work had begun. Of sixty-eight shovels, only thirteen were still in operation. He recruited new crews.

Even the newly arrived Major Sibert was proving "cantankerous and hard to hold" in meetings. Mrs. Sibert, Goethals learned, was "disgusted" with the Panama weather.

From surviving letters written to his son George, then in his senior year at the Military Academy, it is apparent that he was also extremely lonely. Mrs. Goethals was still in Washington "doing society at a great rate"; another, younger son, Thomas, was at Harvard. He felt very out of touch, he wrote; there was not time even to read the paper. His sole source of amusement was the French butler, Benoit, who still spoke practically no English but went with the official residence at Culebra, Goethals being his seventh chief engineer.

The day began at first light. At 6:30, with Benoit standing stiffly in attendance, "the Colonel" had his breakfast—one peeled native orange stuck on the end of a fork, two eggs, bacon, one cup of coffee. By seven he had walked down to Culebra Station to catch either the No. 2, northbound at 7:10, or the No. 3, southbound at 7:19. The morning was spent inspecting the line. He carried a black umbrella and customarily wore white. Invariably he looked spotless; invariably he was smoking a cigarette.

Back at the house again, immediately upon finishing a light lunch, he would rest for half an hour, then walk to his large, square corner office on the first floor at the Administration Building. There he would receive people until dinner at seven. In the evening, unless otherwise engaged, he would return to the office to concentrate on his paper work until about ten.

To most observers he seemed wholly oblivious of his surroundings, intent only on his work. One employee, relaxing on his own porch one particularly beautiful moonlit evening, witnessed the following scene:

> There were only a few lights here and there in the Administration Building. One by one they went out, all except that in the old man's office. It was getting on toward ten when his window went dark. . . . A full moon, as big as a dining-room table, was hanging down about a foot and a half above the flagstaff—a gorgeous night. The old man came out and walked across the grass to his house. He didn't stop to look up at the moon; he just pegged along, his head a little forward, still thinking. And he hadn't been in his own house ten minutes before all the lights were out there. He'd turned in, getting ready to catch that early train. . . .

To his elder son, Goethals wrote that he was better off occupied, since there was nothing else to do. He confessed to working so hard that he would often end the day in a kind of daze. He was not the "clean-desk" man Stevens had been. His "IN" and "OUT" baskets were always jammed. Papers were piled wherever there was room on his desk—correspondence, folded maps, specifications, plans, half a dozen black notebooks, reports in heavy dark-blue bindings. The bit of clear desk surface he managed to maintain directly in front of him was soon peppered with cigarette burns.

He liked things on paper. If during his morning excursions along the line a department head or engineer urged some new approach or improvements, the inevitable response was "Write it down."

It was not in him to court popularity. He wanted loyalty first, not to him but to the work, that above all. He abhorred waste and inefficiency and he was determined to weed out incompetents. Nor was there ever to be any doubt as to his own authority. "What the Colonel said he meant," a steam-shovel engineer remembered. "What he asked for he got. It didn't take us long to find that out." Requests or directives from his office were not to be regarded as subjects for discussion. When the head of the Commissary Department, a popular and influential figure, informed Goethals that he would resign if Goethals persisted in certain changes in the purchasing procedure, Goethals at once informed him that his resignation was accepted and refused to listen when he came to retract the threat. "It will help bring the outfit into line," Goethals noted privately. "I can stand it if they can." He put Lieutenant Wood in as a replacement. ". . . I just put it up to him to make good . . ." he wrote.

"Executive ability," he observed on another occasion, "is nothing more or less than letting the other fellow do the work for you." But to some he gave every appearance of wishing only to dominate everything himself. Marie Gorgas, in particular, found him "grim, self-sufficing." He was much too abrupt for her liking. "His conversation and his manners, like his acts, had no finesse and no spirit of accommodation." She grew to dislike him heartily. Even Robert Wood, who admired his "iron will and terrific energy," found him "stern and unbending—you might say a typical Prussian. . . . I was his assistant for seven years," Wood recalled long afterward, "and I might say that everything in my life since has seemed comparatively easy."

But if the manner was occasionally severe, the standards demanding, he was invariably fair and gave to the job a dignity it had not had before. "I never knew him to be small about anything," recalled an electrical engineer named Richard Whitehead, who joined the force that same summer of 1907. Goethals knew how to pick men. He knew how to instill determination, to get people to want to measure up. He was not loved, not then or later, but he was impressive. And by late summer he had "the outfit in line."

"Another week of observation has confirmed my view . . . that the discontent and uneasiness which followed the departure of Stevens have nearly passed away . . ." wrote Joseph Bucklin Bishop to Theodore Roosevelt in mid-August. Undersized and grouchy-looking, with a little, pointed gray beard and a shiny bald head, Bishop was another new addition. He had been transferred from the Washington office on Roosevelt's orders and was to be at Goethals' side from then on, as secretary of the commission, ghost writer, policy adviser, alter ego. And not incidentally he was to feed confidential reports to the White House and how things were going.

Goethals, reported Bishop, was "worn and tired and says that he has had a veritable 'hell of a time,' but I believe he has won out. When I told him so, he said, 'Well, I don't know.' "

Mrs. Goethals had arrived and departed meantime. So his marriage, characterized years afterward by members of the family as "difficult," became still another topic for local speculation as the lights in his office burned on into the night.

At Bishop's suggestion, Goethals started a weekly newspaper, the *Canal Record,* the first such publication since de Lesseps' *Bulletin du Canal Interocéanique* and very similar in format. Goethals insisted that the paper be neither a rehash of news from the United States nor a means for trumpeting the reputation of anyone on the canal commission. Indeed, quite unlike the de Lesseps' paper, its editorial policy specifically forbade praise of any official. The objective was to provide the American force—as well as Congress—with an accurate, up-to-date picture of the progress being made, something hitherto unavailable in any form, as well as reports on social life within the Zone, ship sailings, sports, any activities "thought to be of general interest."

With Bishop as editor, the first edition appeared September 4, 1907. The style was direct and factual and so it would remain, except for occasional letters from employees. Still it was an amazing morale builder. It did for its readers much what *Stars and Stripes* would do for the A.E.F. in France. It brought the strung-out settlements in closer touch, made the Zone more of a community. In addition, it had an almost instant effect on productivity.

Bishop began publishing weekly excavation statistics for individual steam shovels and dredges, and at once a fierce rivalry resulted, the gain in output becoming apparent almost immediately. "It wasn't so hard before they began printing the *Canal Record*," a steam-shovel man explained to a writer for *The Saturday Evening Post*. "We were going along, doing what we thought was a fair day's work . . . [but then] away we went like a pack of idiots trying to get records for ourselves."

To give employees opportunity to air their grievances, Goethals next established his own court of appeal. Every Sunday morning, from about 7:30 until noon, he was at his desk to receive any and all who had what they believed to be a serious complaint or problem. He saw them personally, individually, on the basis of first come, first served, irrespective of rank, nationality, or color. By late 1907 there were thirty-two thousand people on the payroll, about eight thousand more than when he took over. By 1910 there would be nearly forty thousand. Yet once a week, beginning in the fall of 1907, any of these people—employees or dependents—could "see the Colonel" and speak their minds.

The scene was unique in the American experience, unique and memorable in the eyes of all who saw it. Jules Jusserand, the French ambassador, likened it to the court of justice held by Saint Louis beneath the oak at Vincennes. "One sees the Colonel at his best in these Sunday morning hours," wrote a reporter who had been greatly frustrated by what seemed a congenital inability on Goethals' part to talk about himself. "You see the immensely varied nature of the things and issues which are his concern. Engineering in the technical sense seems almost the least of them."

Some advance screening was done. Bishop saw the English-speaking workers, while the Italians, Spaniards, and other Europeans were seen by a multilingual interpreter, Giuseppe Garibaldi, grandson of the Italian liberator. And often these preliminary interviews were enough to resolve the problem—the mere process of free expression gave the needed relief—but if not, Goethals' door stood open.

On an average Sunday he saw perhaps a hundred people and very few appear to have gone away thinking they had been denied justice. They came to the front of the tall, barnlike Administration Building, entered a broad hallway hung with maps and blueprints and there waited their turn. Their complaints included everything from the serious to the trivial: harsh treatment by a foreman, misunderstanding about pay, failure to get a promotion, dislike of the food or quarters, insufficient furniture. He listened to appeals for special privileges and financial dispensation. One request was for the transfer of a particular steam-shovel engineer to a different division where a particular baseball team needed a pitcher. (The request was granted.) He was given constructive ideas regarding the work and was made party to the private quarrels between husbands and wives or families in adjoining apartments. By all accounts he was a patient listener.

Many complaints could be settled at once with a simple yes or no or by a brief note sent down the line. A serious situation of any complexity was promptly investigated. "He was a combination of father confessor and Day of Judgment," wrote Bishop. The vast majority who came before him were almost excessively respectful. Rarely would anyone challenge his authority and then to no avail. "If you decide against me, Colonel, I shall appeal," one man declared. "To whom?" Goethals asked.

Some of the remaining officials from the Stevens regime had expressed vehement disapproval when these Sunday sessions were first announced. Jackson Smith, of the Labor Department, had been especially exercised, since his own policy in past years had been to tell anyone who had a complaint to feel free to leave on the next ship. And this, apart from Smith's own rude manner, had been considered a perfectly appropriate policy. Stevens had been in full accord. The new approach was in fact wholly unorthodox by the standards of the day. In labor relations Goethals was way in advance of his time, and nothing that he did had so discernible an effect on the morale of the workers or their regard for him: "they were treated like human beings, not like brutes," Bishop recalled, "and they responded by giving the best service within their power."

In Goethals' own estimate, expressed privately many years afterward, it was thus that he won "control of the force," and control of the force was "the big, attractive thing of the job."

Within less than a year after Goethals took charge, several major changes were made in the basic plan of the canal, and with a sweeping reorganization, beginning in early 1908, he installed his own entirely new regime. The widespread impression was that the plan was firm, that this at last was the canal that was to be built, and that these were the men who would build it. The widespread impression was correct.

CREATING A NEW WORLD OF WORK

IRVING BLUESTONE[1]

A HISTORY OF ACHIEVEMENT

For free labor unions, improving the quality of working life is a daily, constant responsibility. Economic benefits such as higher wages or income and job security receive the publicity that goes with collective bargaining crises, but ensuring a decent workplace, enlarging the rights of workers on the job, creating greater job satisfaction, achieving for the worker the self-respect and fulfilment worthy of a human being command the attention of union leaders to an equal extent.

In November 1973 the American Assembly, Columbia University, brought together a representative group of prominent figures from management, labor, government and the academic world in a conference to discuss the changing world of work. An excerpt from its carefully prepared statement reads as follows:

> Unions have since their inception been seeking to "humanize" work. The current ideas of improving the quality of working life are basically an extension of this long-range goal. Unions have primarily sought and have achieved significant economic gains and have substantially increased job security. This should not obscure their long-term struggle for improvement in the quality of working life. . . .[2]

During the dark days of the great depression of the 1930s, the turbulent rise of industrial unionism in the United States was directed not only towards improving the workers' standard of living but, perhaps even more importantly, towards correcting intolerable conditions of work, blunting the authoritarianism of management and ensuring the worker a measure of dignity and self-respect on the job.

Just to read some modern labor contracts (collective agreements) concluded in the United States is to become acquainted with a

Source: Reprinted, by permission, from *International Labour Review,* Vol 115, No. 1, January–February 1977, pp. 1–10. Copyright + International Labour Organization 1977.
[1]Vice-President, International Union, United Automobile, Aerospace and Agricultural Implement Workers of America (UAW).

[2]Report of the 43rd American Assembly held at Arden House, Harriman, New York, 1–4 November 1973.

long list of workers' rights[3] on matters which before the advent of the unions were determined unilaterally by management. Thus lay-off and recall used to be matters for arbitrary decision by management, whereas today detailed seniority rules ensure fair treatment. In the past, again, a worker had to seek the foreman's favor in order to transfer to a more desirable job. Nowadays, transfer rights are specified in the labor contract. In pre-union days workers had no rights with regard to promotion. Practically every labor contract now contains detailed rules governing promotion opportunities. There are also provisions ensuring fair labor practices and prohibiting discrimination: labor contracts contained these provisions years before society decided on the need for legislation.

Furthermore, labor contracts protect against unfair disciplinary measures and dismissal. They contain extensive rules governing workers' rights with regard to production standards and the pace of work, and provide for paid rest breaks during working hours. There is protection against excessive overtime, but equal opportunity to work available overtime is also stipulated. Other provisions proscribe the contracting out of work where it would adversely affect the workers' job security. Nowadays, workers have the right to move with their jobs when work is transferred to another plant owned by the same company. They can also indicate shift preference and have rights with regard to the establishment of shift hours. They are entitled to leave of absence during periods of illness, or in order to improve their education, or to serve the community on a full-time basis. Protective clothing and equipment are provided by management free of charge.

Through their representatives, workers participate in the regulation of health and safety in the plant. In general it can be said that, as a result of union demands and shop-floor bargaining, tangible improvements in working conditions are made every day.

Not only have these and many other rights been gained, but their application is checked by representatives elected by the workers themselves. In addition, there is generally a grievance procedure, including final and binding arbitration, which provides an orderly basis for the resolution of disputes with management over the meaning, intent and implementation of the contract.

THE PERSISTENCE OF AUTHORITARIANISM

This by no means exhausts the list of workers' rights protected by contractual provisions. Despite this progress, however, life at work continues to be largely dominated by the employer, and the employee has only a limited opportunity to participate in the making of decisions concerning his job, and even less in the management of the enterprise. Workers have to struggle constantly to be heard, to influence decisions affecting their welfare and to participate in the decision-making process that affects their working life. Even with all the contractual provisions which have fundamentally altered the employer-employee relationship, the fact is that management retains authority over the methods, means and processes of production, relegating the worker substantially to the role of a machine-minding robot.

Picture the production worker employed in a typical factory. He leaves for work between 5 and 6 a.m., arrives at the factory, walks to his clock card, punches in and then proceeds to his work station. He has been told precisely what his task is, a task which has been broken down into several specific elements of work. He is instructed as to the order in which these work elements are to be performed, what tools to use, where his material is stacked, and within what time-span he must perform his task. He is allotted a specific area in which to do it. It must

---

[3]Not all the rights listed here are specified in all contracts in the United States.

be performed over and over again, each cycle within a fixed time established by stopwatch. His behavior is governed by an array of shop rules. Should he violate any of these instructions or rules he is subject to disciplinary measures. He is constantly under the watchful eye of supervisors, often even when he goes to the bathroom and during breaks. In moving assembly-line operations he cannot leave his work station until a relief worker is available to take over his job. After eight hours of this kind of repetitive work he leaves for home only to contemplate the next dreary day ahead of him.

Contrast this with his life outside. In a democratic society he is a citizen with broad rights of decision. With his vote he can help determine who his leaders will be, and turn them out of office as well. As a family man and a member of his community he participates in innumerable decisions affecting the life and the well-being of himself, his family, his fellow citizens and neighbors. In a large sense, he is master of his fate.

INTRODUCING DEMOCRACY AT THE WORKPLACE

Surely, then, the time has come for a society anchored in democratic principles to ensure that each individual at his place of work enjoys a measure of the dignity, self-respect and freedom which are his as a citizen. In his capacity as a worker he should be afforded an opportunity for self-expression and participation in the decisions that shape the quality of his working life.

In recent years increasing attention has been given to the contradiction between autocratic rule at the workplace and democratic rights in society. Whatever their motivation—for example increasing absenteeism, high labor turnover, declining product quality, the revolt of a younger, better-educated workforce against oppressive authority, etc.—more and more managements are coming to realize that life at

work must change. In the words of a former Chairman of General Motors: "We must improve working conditions and take boredom out of routine jobs. . . . We must increase an employe's satisfaction with his job, heighten pride of workmanship and, as far as feasible, involve the employe personally in decisions that relate directly to his job."[4]

Dozens of experiments and projects are being carried out with a view to finding answers to this problem both in Western Europe and in the United States. Each unique in its own way, whether established by law, as in the case of worker representation on corporate supervisory boards in certain countries, or unilaterally initiated by management, or conceived and implemented jointly and voluntarily by management and the unions. Most of the ideas applied to worker participation in the decision-making process in the United States are borrowed from Western Europe, especially Sweden and Norway. As always happens with borrowed innovations, however, they are being adapted to their new milieu and are acquiring a character of their own. By way of example, let us consider three cases.

AMERICAN WORKERS AT SAAB-SCANIA

In 1974 a worker exchange program was undertaken under the auspices of Cornell University whereby six UAW members employed in automobile engine assembly plants in the United States went to work at the Saab-Scania facility in Soejertaelje, Sweden. The primary purpose of the visit was to obtain first-hand experience of a new system of assembly which Saab-Scania had inaugurated some years earlier. Under this system a team of workers is responsible for the assembly of an entire automobile engine. All the workers are trained to

[4]Richard M. Gerstenberg in a speech at the Tax Foundation Dinner, New York, 6 December 1972.

perform all the operations required and assume their assignments in accordance with group decisions. This is in marked contrast to the production-line type of operation usual in engine assembly work, where workers are given a specific assignment involving a few rather simple tasks which they then perform repetitively and in prescribed sequence for the full eight-hour shift.

The American workers were briefed before leaving for Sweden and again after their arrival. They learned about the culture of the country and the differences in life-style which they were to experience. The Scania engine assembly system was explained to them. Altogether the program lasted four weeks, although the first week and a half had to be devoted essentially to briefings, training and learning the job. Normally, the training period alone lasts from five to six weeks.

The reports written upon their return indicated that, while deeply impressed with the excellence of the working conditions and the life-style in Sweden, most of the American workers were not altogether pleased with their work experience, although one worker in particular found that teamwork assembly was much more to her liking than the assembly-line operations to which she was accustomed in the United States. While the preparation of the American workers for their visit left something to be desired, and their subsequent report indicated that Saab was not fully prepared for their arrival, nevertheless the experience gained was on the whole both valuable and gratifying. In subsequent private interviews upon their return home, it became evident that much of their criticism of the Saab-Scania assembly operation related to one important point, namely that management took the initial policy decisions to change the work system and determined how the job was to be engineered, while the workers simply followed a basic format with a certain latitude to rotate assignments in assembling the entire engine. They also felt the work pace was faster than that to which they were accustomed.

Despite monthly union-management working committee meetings, it seemed to the American workers that the program was imposed from the top down, with the engineers and production supervisors making the ultimate decisions on the job design itself.

The American workers explained that they were accustomed to a strong and immediate union presence on the shop floor ready to challenge unfair treatment by management representatives. At Saab-Scania they felt that management was even more authoritative than in the United States, with the boss-worker relationship more pronounced. The consensus appeared to be that the group assembly concept, with workers having the freedom to decide such matters as job assignment and the operational procedures to be used, is on the whole more satisfying than the repetitive, monotonous assembly-line operation customary in the United States, and would be even more so if the work pace were less unrelenting and if the union's presence were felt more strongly and persistently on the shop-floor.

THE UAW-HARMAN INTERNATIONAL WORK IMPROVEMENT PROGRAM

What the UAW learned about successes and failures in this field both at Saab-Scania and at other factories in Norway and Sweden helped it in developing quality of working life programs in collaboration with managements in the United States. The program currently being undertaken at Harman Industries International in Bolivar, Tennessee, by the UAW and the company is a case in point. A major difference in approach is noticeable at Harman International in that decisions are made jointly by workers and management on the shop floor. No decisions are imposed from above, and the union is directly involved in all aspects of the program both on the job and in the meeting room.

The original idea of initiating a program to improve the quality of working life at this factory grew out of top-level discussions between the

UAW and the President of Harman International. Nevertheless, the scheme itself is operated entirely by those on the spot, with some third party assistance as explained below.

Early in the discussions the parties signed a special memorandum—a "shelter agreement" —which emphasizes the human rather than the productivity factor. Among other things it stipulates that:

> The purpose of the joint management-labor Work Improvement Program is to make work better and more satisfying for all employes, salaried and hourly, while maintaining the necessary productivity for job security. The purpose is not to increase productivity. . . .

The agreement contains guarantees which prohibit increasing the work pace or eliminating jobs by reason of the program.

The Director of the Harvard Project on Technology, Work and Character, a psychologist by profession, agreed to direct and supervise the program. He assigned staff to work on site guiding the program in close daily contact with the workers and their local union leaders on the one hand and the local management on the other.

After the program had been explained to the workers at a mass meeting in the plant, they voted in favor of its introduction. A working committee was formed consisting of five members appointed by management and five by the local union. This committee initiates projects within the framework of the program and provides over-all guidance. At first, groups of workers volunteered to take part in experiments in three departments. As these proved successful, other workers insisted on the program being applied to them also, and today the entire plant is participating.

Fundamental to the program is the promotion of democratic principles at the workplace, as spelt out in a letter the UAW sent to all members of the local union at Bolivar:

> We are taking this opportunity to discuss with you the nature and purpose of the experiments cur-

rently under way at your plant to improve the quality of worklife.

> First of all, what do we mean by a program "to improve the quality of worklife"? Isn't the union doing this all the time by negotiating higher wages and benefits and by concluding seniority, shift preference, transfer agreements and establishing many other rights for workers? Of course we are, for, as far as the UAW is concerned, advancing your standard of living and assuring more job security and rights in the plant are the hallmark of our union's effort and activity.

> But there is more involved in improving the quality of worklife. We are at that point in time where workers should have more to say about their job and how it should be run. They should participate in a meaningful way in making decisions about the job and the workplace—decisions which in the past were made pretty much exclusively by management.

> That's what the new program at your plant is all about—to set up a system in which workers make decisions affecting their jobs and workplace.

> Workers must not be automatons doing just as they are told and having no opportunity to make determinations of their own. . . . They must not be simply extensions of the machine or the assembly line; they must exercise some control over how they work. In the final analysis they must have the right to the dignity and self-respect on the job that they exercise outside the plant as citizens and human beings.

A survey carried out at the beginning of the program by means of a questionnaire and in-depth personal interviews generated considerable discussion among the workers and caused them to think over problems they encountered at work. Much of the program's orientation stems from the results of these in-depth interviews, which the interviewers described as follows:

> We interviewed a sample of 60 workers using a questionnaire with both open-ended and multiple choice questions. The interview lasted four hours and asked about work, values, life goals, physical and emotional problems. This included asking for material that could be used for psycho-analytical

interpretation of character, such as dreams and family relationships, as well as questions relating to feelings about authority. These interviews were subsequently analyzed in terms of character traits, leading first to a summary of traits shared by the majority of the factory workers (the social character) and second to subgroups, representing the different character types.

The program is now well under way, though it is not without its problems and there are still certain difficulties to be overcome. It may not of course violate the terms of the labor contract, but there is inevitably some overlapping. These problems are resolved on an ad hoc basis as they arise, on the clear understanding that matters involving collective bargaining are referred to the bargaining process and not the Work Improvement Program. The main thing, however, is that the workers and their union are part of the decision-making process on the shop floor. This is an effective expansion of democratic principles at the workplace.

Workers involved in the experiment may use their own discretion in solving problems related to their jobs. The program allows them to accumulate earned time, and this enables them to leave work early after completing their production assignment. Partly so as to make constructive use of the time thus earned, they have decided democratically to establish a "school" in which they study various subjects of their choice, including welding, time study, sewing and even business subjects such as accounting and pricing.

It is most important to note that this is not simply a job enrichment scheme in which production experts and engineers determine how jobs may be redesigned and enlarged and the workers merely follow instructions as they have done traditionally. The workers at Bolivar may and often do decide to enlarge their jobs, but that is their decision and they have the right to change it. The object of the program is to develop a system in which workers exercise a democratic right to make decisions regarding job design and layout, tools to be used, methods of production, etc. A point has now been reached where, after another year or so of outside assistance, the parties should be able to "go it alone." The social scientists will then leave the scene. It is to be hoped that the knowledge gained in the Bolivar experiment will enable them to initiate similar projects elsewhere.

Management gains from such a project in various ways, none of which is abhorrent to the workers or the union. Absenteeism and labor turnover decline. Product quality improves. The collective bargaining relationship develops into a more rational understanding of the other's problems. Workers' complaints are fewer and are resolved on the shop floor without the need to process them further. Moreover, the Bolivar management indicates that the program has already measurably improved the attitude and effectiveness of management staff, a major factor in the over-all improvement in the operation and administration of the plant.

The union and the workers gain by having more say in the management of the workplace without fear of putting themselves at a disadvantage as to either production requirements or job security. Work satisfaction is enhanced, and they also enjoy tangible rewards such as more free time and the educational program mentioned above.

Admittedly it is too early to speak of success or failure in achieving the ultimate goals. Nevertheless, it can truly be said that so far the program is proving its value. Management remains committed to it and the workers have reaffirmed their support by once again voting in its favor.

THE UAW-GENERAL MOTORS QUALITY OF WORKLIFE PROGRAM

Another approach is that adopted by the UAW and the General Motors Corporation in the United States. During the 1973 national contract negotiations with General Motors the UAW submitted a proposal whereby both sides would make a concerted effort to discuss, develop and implement programs for improving the quality of working life. In concluding the negotiations, General Motors sent the UAW a letter confirming its agreement to this idea.

The agreement drawn up between the parties particularly noted that they shared the belief that activity designed to improve the quality of working life would be to the advantage of the worker, the corporation and the consumer. A UAW-GM National Committee to Improve the Quality of Worklife was established with responsibility for overviewing the entire program. Among its tasks is the development of joint experiments and projects in this field with a view to enhancing worker participation in the decision-making process on the job. The Committee's functions are very broadly defined, leaving the parties considerable latitude to determine the direction their efforts will take. This is a wise approach, since they are entering a new and unexplored area of labor-management relations in the American automobile industry.

The basic issues involved in the adversarial relationship between management and labor remain largely unaffected, however. Collective bargaining continues to play a vital part, but projects to improve the quality of working life help to create a climate in which cool reason and judgment replace anger and emotion in working out solutions to controversial problems. They therefore have a beneficial effect on the total collective bargaining relationship.

The system works as follows. After full and careful consideration, the National Committee may decide to undertake a project in a particular plant. Apart from making this decision and giving over-all direction, the Committee leaves the actual initiation and implementation of the project to the local management and the local union, while nevertheless continuing to offer its assistance as needed. Representatives of

General Motors and of the National GM Department of the UAW visit the factory. In discussing with the local union shop committee the possibility of initiating a project the UAW representatives simply point out directions which might be taken and urge acceptance of the idea. Similarly, the Corporation representatives try to convince the local plant manager, who in turn must try to reduce the resistance of his superintendents and foremen. Being unfamiliar with this kind of innovative effort, both local management and the local union may have reservations about implementing the idea. Foremen, for instance, may view participation by the worker in the decision-making process as an erosion of their authority. It is of course very difficult to overcome habits of mind which have grown up over long periods during which foremen regarded workers as subservient to their orders. For their part, the local union and the workers are in many instances so accustomed to the adversarial relationship in which the supervisor makes decisions and the worker and his union contest them that they are reluctant to engage in an experiment which requires participation in the decision-making process on an equal basis.

Thus the first task of the National Committee's corporation and union representatives is to brush away the cobwebs of habit and tradition so that new approaches to old problems can be tried out. In some cases it may be desirable to undertake an employee opinion survey in a particular factory in order to identify and throw light on problems which are ripe for a solution.

When a project is initiated it may involve only a small number of volunteers who, after appropriate briefing, decide that they would like to participate. In some instances it may be desirable for an industrial psychologist to work with this group in order to create a suitable climate for the kind of worker participation it is proposed to institute. This implies working with supervisors as well as shop-floor workers, helping them to become better acquainted with one another, to understand one another's personalities and idiosyncrasies and at the same time to develop a sense of co-operation, as equals, in devising new ways of relating to one another and to the tasks which must be performed. The union committee man follows the development of the project closely and involves himself directly.

It is obviously too early to gauge the final result of this joint effort precisely. This is the first time in the United States that a major corporation and a major union have agreed to undertake a far-reaching endeavour of this type on a nation-wide basis. The first steps are naturally halting and cautious. A considerable amount of trial and testing will be necessary, for no one has all the answers and no two industrial situations are identical. If the program is successful, however, it could begin to alter intrinsically the shop-worn system of management-worker relations that has prevailed up to now and the philosophy underlying the concept of "scientific management." It could enhance the dignity of the worker on his job, involve him significantly in the decision-making process, increase opportunities for heightened job satisfaction, and generally initiate a movement towards greater democratization of the workplace.

This, of course, is the most optimistic view. Only time will tell whether it is justified. One thing is clear, namely that if the parties will embrace new concepts of worker participation seriously and affirmatively, the ingenuity of man in developing new and exciting approaches could well lead to a new and exciting quality of working life. Our modern technology is engineered by human beings and it can therefore be engineered to meet human needs.

SCEPTICISM AND PROGRESS

The joint union-management programs at Harman International and at General Motors are only two among many aimed at improving the quality of working life in the United States. Frequently they have their origin in on-going experimentation in Western Europe. Increasing interest in the movement makes it certain that it will continue to grow and develop in one form or another.

However, scepticism in both management and labor circles results in a "show me" attitude and a reluctance to embark on proejcts of this sort. Resistance on the part of management seems to stem from fear of an erosion of authority and a long and comfortable marriage to "scientific management" principles. Unions express concern that such programs are wolves in sheep's clothing, a gimmick to decoy the workers away from their loyalty to the union and make them even more pliant to the will of management. In the author's judgment, circumstances will cause this resistance to diminish in time. Through their unions the workers have already drastically reduced and traditional, autocratic type of managerial control over the worker and the workplace. The concept of workers' rights in the decision-making process has taken root. It will flower.

In the United States the thrust to improve the quality of working life will manifest itself in direct participation by workers in managing their jobs. Perhaps, in later years, it will spread to participation in managing the enterprise. The incontrovertible fact is that the democratic values of society—based on participation in the decision-making process—will be extended to the place of work. Democratizing work is an idea whose time has come.

STONEWALLING PLANT DEMOCRACY

BUSINESS WEEK

In the early 1970s, when everyone was talking about blue-collar blues and worker alienation, General Foods Corporation opened a dog-food plant in Topeka, Kansas, designed to be run with a minimum of supervision. Many functions normally the prerogative of management would be performed by the workers themselves. Workers would make job assignments, schedule coffee breaks, interview prospective employees, and even decide pay raises.

The plant was widely heralded as a model for the future, and General Foods claims that it still is. "Very successful" is the way J. W. Bevans, Jr., manager of organizational development for GF, describes the experiment. In fact, GF has applied a similar system at a second dog-food plant in Topeka and at a coffee plant in New Jersey. And it says it may eventually do the same at two plants in Mexico and among white-collar workers at its White Plains headquarters.

But management analysts and former employees tell a different story. And General Foods, which once encouraged publicity about the Topeka plant, now refuses to let reporters inside. Critics say that after the initial euphoria, the system, faced with indifference and outright hostility from some GF managers, has been eroding steadily.

"The system went to hell. It didn't work," says one former manager. Adds another ex-employee: "It was a mixed bag. Economically it was a success, but it became a power struggle. It was too threatening to too many people." He predicts that the plant will eventually switch to a traditional factory system. In fact, he says, the transition has already begun.

The problem has been not so much that the workers could not manage their own affairs as that some management and staff personnel saw their own positions threatened because the workers performed almost too well. One former employee says the system—built around a team concept—came squarely up against the company's bureaucracy. Lawyers, fearing reaction from the National Labor Relations Board, opposed the idea of allowing team members to vote on pay raises. Personnel managers objected because team members made hiring decisions. Engineers resented workers doing engineering work.

BALANCING ACT

Of course, having workers take on such duties was the whole idea. The process was an attempt "to balance the needs of the people with the needs of the business," says Bevans. GF had had problems with negative attitudes and low productivity in its Kankakee (Ill.) pet-food plant in the late 1960s and wanted to offset them at Topeka. Specific goals, says Bevans, included maximum machine utilization, minimum waste, low distribution costs, low productivity costs, and low absenteeism and turnover.

The system, designed by a GF task force working with Richard E. Walton, professor of business administration at Harvard University, eliminates layers of management and supervisory personnel and assigns three areas of responsibility—processing, packaging, and shipping, and office duties—to self-managing teams of workers. Each team on a shift has 7 to 14 members who share responsibility for a variety of tasks. The processing team, for instance, not only handles the actual pet-food manufacturing but also is responsible for unloading raw material and for equipment maintenance and quality control.

Working under the direction of a team leader, described as a "coach" rather than a foreman, team members rotate between dreary and meaningful jobs. Pay is geared to the number of tasks each individual masters. The teams make the necessary management decisions. GF even removed some of the status symbols of management that blue-collar workers resent. All employees use a common entrance, for instance, and there are no reserved parking spaces for management.

INSTABILITY

There is no question that the company has met many of its goals. Unit costs are 5 percent less than under a traditional factory system, Bevans estimates. This, says Walton, should amount to a saving of $1 million a year. Turnover is only 8 percent, and the plant went three years and eight months before its first lost-time accident. Even one who criticizes some aspects of the system, Lyman D. Ketchum, former manager of GF's pet-food operations and responsible for both the Kankakee and Topeka plants, says: "From the standpoint of humanistic working life and economic results, you can consider it a success."

But a former employee at the Topeka plant does not see it that way. "Creating a system is different from maintaining it," he says. "There were pressures almost from the inception, and not because the system didn't work. The basic reason was power. We flew in the face of corporate policy. People like stable states. This system has to be changing or it will die."

Change, of course, can be threatening in itself. "If you have a quality control manager who is successful, and along comes something very successful, he begins to wonder what's in it for him," says Ketchum. "Then there's the engineer who has been designing plants based on traditional principles. He gets anxious and perceives a threat. The controller wants someone from his fraternity in the system, and so on." As a result, Ketchum continues, "pressures come about. The system starts to be compartmentalized, and when you compartmentalize it, you degrade it." In other words, some management functions were again taken over by managers.

WEAKENED COMMITMENT?

Consequently, critics say, there has been a stiffening of the Topeka system, more job classifications, less participation, more supervision. GF has added seven management positions to the plant, including controller, plant engineering manager, and manufacturing services manager. GF says these were necessary because of a plant expansion. Last year, when GF geared up a plant adjacent to the first one to produce Cycle, a canned dog food, it introduced the Topeka process but deferred several elements of the system, including developmental training.

"This was interpreted by dry-plant members [at the first plant, which produces Gaines dog food] as evidence of a weakening of management commitment to the philosophy on which their own work system was based," writes Walton in a study of the plant prepared for a professional journal. He says the modifications contributed to the growing complacency and negative drift at Topeka. Walton and others have noticed a slight dip in quality, a buildup of minor problems because of fewer team meetings, and increased competition between shifts. Says one employee who left after two years: "There was too much competition because of jealousy between teams and team leaders."

Another problem area is pay. As the system was set up, team members voted on pay raises for fellow employees, which could be sticky. "You work with somebody for five years and get to be pretty good friends. It's a little tough to decide on a pay raise," says worker Rex Campbell. But that prerogative may be turning to management. A former manager claims that although workers still discuss one another's raises, the real decisions are made by management. GF declines comment.

More important, employees believe they ought to share financially in the system's success, an idea that has been backed by managers, though GF's headquarters is noncommittal. A bonus at Topeka could cause complications at other GF plants that do not happen to pay bonuses. "The personnel people don't like that," says a former manager. "It threatens them."

Workers also perceive that Topeka managers have suffered because of their involvement in the system. Along with Ketchum, now a management consultant, Edward R. Dulworth has left General Foods. He was plant manager until November 1975, and is now an executive with Tops Chewing Gum Inc. Two of three managers under him also left the company. Says one of them: "They saw we had created something the company couldn't handle, so they put their boys in. By being involved, I ruined my career at General Foods."

GF denies that anybody's career was hurt by the Topeka process. "They went to greener pastures," says a company spokesman. And Bevans defends the changes in the system when it was introduced outside the first Topeka plant. "You can't transplant the system whole," he says. "You take the important elements."

"THE BEST PLACE"

GF introduced the system in its Hoboken (N.J.) coffee plant two years ago to combat high production costs and the result was "significant," says Bevans. Pointing to plans to move the system into plants in Mexico and to headquarters in White Plains, he says: "We won't try to transplant it wholesale. We'll put it into the hands of local management so they can fashion it to meet their needs." But one critic scoffs: "The organization knows what happens to managers who innovate."

Such skepticism filters down to team members. "Every time you make a mistake, you wonder if White Plains thinks that maybe if we had a traditional system there wouldn't have been a mistake," says Campbell, the Topeka plant worker. Still, he adds: "It's the best place I ever worked."

That perhaps best sums up the Topeka experiment. While the system has not lived up to the goals of many of the managers involved, and while it seems to be deteriorating, it nevertheless has led to a productive working atmosphere and has met many of the goals set for it. The big question is whether it will renew itself or continue to erode, fulfilling the prediction of one manager that "the future of that plant is to conform to the company norm."

Professor Walton, summing up six years of the plant's operation, writes: "Never has the climate truly soured or even become neutral and indifferent." But he adds: "In my opinion, this will happen unless concerted effort is made to evolve the organization."

THE "JACKASS EFFECT" IN MANAGEMENT COMPENSATION

DALE D. McCONKEY

Parable: Once upon a time there was a dumb jackass standing knee-deep in a field of carrots contentedly munching away. A wise farmer wanted the jackass to pull a loaded wagon to another field but the jackass would not walk over to the wagon. So the wise farmer stood by the wagon and held up a bunch of carrots for the dumb jackass to see. But the dumb jackass continued to contentedly munch away on his own carrots.

Moral of story: Jackasses do not work for carrots.

Underlying the approach to managerial compensation followed by many companies is the implicit assumption that well-educated managers usually can be coaxed into doing that which even the dumb jackass will not do. But the majority of managers cannot be coaxed. This observation has led to the frequently espoused premise that managers do not work for money. The premise should be expanded to provide that managers do not work for money *when the jackass effect is inherent in a compensation plan.*

The jackass effect is present in any compensation plan when the plan is not formulated and administered in a manner which preserves and furthers the only two objectives of meaningful compensation. These objectives are, first, to promote and attain equity and, second, to motivate for better performance.

Equity is attained when a manager's compensation is based on the results he has achieved and is related to a comparison of these results with the results achieved by all other managers in his organization. The motivation objective requires that the manager be convinced that extra effort and achievement on his part will result in extra compensation. He must believe his efforts will be recognized and rewarded. The manager must know this in advance of expending the efforts—not after he takes the action.

THE JACKASS EFFECT IN PRACTICE

The jackass effect commonly assumes five forms in actual practice:

Source: From "The 'Jackass Effect' in Management Compensation," by Dale McConkey. Copyright, 1974, by the Foundation for the School of Business at Indiana University. Reprinted by permission of *Business Horizons.*

Compensation is on the wrong end of the action.

The manager's accountability is so nebulous that his performance cannot be measured.

An ineffective evaluation method is used.

The compensation plan acts to level all managers into a group rather than recognize variances in individual performance.

Compensation is separated from performance.

The Wrong End

Too often compensation plans are formulated in a manner that causes a manager to take some action and, then after the action is completed, someone determines how much the manager should be paid for the action. In this approach, compensation is treated almost solely as something which follows the action. It is not unlike an owner who tells a contractor to build a house and, after the house is completed, the owner tells the builder how much he will be paid.

Compensation cannot act as a motivating force unless its future impact is well known *prior* to the action. This prior knowledge, which the manager must carry with him while he is accomplishing the action, is the key to motivating him to better performance.

An excellent example of having compensation on the wrong end of the action is provided by a large Eastern food company. It has a "discretionary bonus" plan for its managers. Practice indicates that the word "discretionary" is used advisedly. At the end of each year, the president and a few of his advisors sit down and determine which of the managers will receive a bonus and how large each payment will be. There are no established eligibility criteria to decide which managers will receive payments, and there is no formula for determining how much each of the lucky ones will receive.

Surprises abound when payments are doled out each year. Managers are surprised at their selections, and the amount each receives is a surprise. The company's plan could be aptly labeled "The Surprise Approach to Compensation." Managers cannot be motivated when they have no advance knowledge of who will receive payments or on what basis the payments are calculated.

Measurement and Measuring Tool

Only one valid basis for rewarding manager exists—the quality of their performance. The jackass effect exacts its toll when accountability is delegated in a way that performance cannot be measured and when the measuring tool (managerial appraisal or evaluation) is not geared for judging the actual results.

Measurable accountability is not established when the traditional job description is used to delegate the accountability. Traditionally, rather feeble attempts were made to assign this accountability in the form of a job description. Too often, however, these job descriptions were overly general statements of activities which the managers should pursue. No emphasis was given to the specific results the managers should achieve. Usually, the descriptions required the managers to keep busy without specifying the end results of all the effort. Thus, the managers' accomplishments could not be measured with any degree of accuracy because there was no measuring scale.

Figure 1 provides an excellent illustration of a performance evaluation form which is commonly used and which does not measure how well the accountability has been carried out. It records only the superior's perception of the degree to which the subordinate possesses the personality traits which are listed on the form. There is no correlation with the actual results achieved and thus no basis for determining what compensation the manager should receive. This approach is usually adopted as a last resort when no measurable accountability has been fixed and there is nothing tangible to measure.

Figure 1 Example of Traditional Performance Evaluation Form

Factor	Excellent	Above Average	Average	Below Average	Poor
Degree of cost consciousness		X			
Grasp of function	X				
Initiative		X			
Decision-making ability	X				
Application	X				
Judgment		X			
Health	X				
Appearance	X				
Loyalty	X				
Gets along with people		X			
Develops subordinates			X		
Work habits		X			
Contribution to company's progress	X				
Potential for advancement		X			

Rated by

Reviewed by

The Great Leveler

Parable: Once upon a time there were six jackasses hitched to a wagon pulling a heavy load up a long steep hill. Two of the jackasses were not achievement oriented and decided to coast along and let the others do most of the pulling. Two others were relatively young and inexperienced, and had a difficult time pulling their share. One of the remaining two suffered from a slight hangover from consuming fermented barley the evening before. The sixth jackass did most of the work.

The wagon arrived at the top of the hill. The driver got down from his seat, patted each of the jackasses on the head, and gave six carrots to each. Prior to the next hill climb, the sixth jackass ran away.

Moral of the story: Never be the sixth jackass if everybody gets six carrots.

John Jones and Bill Smith are plant managers in the same company and each is currently earning $14,000 a year. The worth of their jobs has been evaluated by commonly accepted job evaluation techniques. The evaluations reveal that the Smith and Jones jobs are practically identical and, therefore, the following salary ranges have been established for both:

Salary Increase Schedule

Minimum	$12,000
Step 1	12,800
Step 2	13,700
Step 3	14,600
Step 4	15,600
Maximum	16,600

What happens under this plan if Jones contributes ten times as much as Smith during a particular year? What is the maximum increase in salary the outstanding producer can be granted over that of the other manager? Clearly, the maximum increase is $2,600 (the difference between their present salaries and the maximum of the range). In actual practice, it would be even less, probably $1,600 (the difference between Jones' present salary and Step 4). Thus, for making ten times the contribution of his counterpart, Jones receives only a routine merit increase. Such a small salary increase would be neither equitable to the high performance manager nor would it motivate him to continue his high performance.

Another problem resulting from utilizing only straight salaries is that every salary increase becomes a fixed cost and the manager will continue to receive it in the future regardless of the level of performance he maintains. To illustrate this point, take the above case in which the manager receives a salary increase of $1,600 for his outstanding performance. What happens next year when the manager's performance is only average? Usually, it is not advisable to reduce the salary of a manager. Thus, he will carry into future years a salary payment which he earned for his performance for only one year.

Obviously, the typical straight salary plan is not sufficiently dynamic and flexible to accommodate the differing circumstances which can and should exist in a management group. About the only way to achieve any flexibility in a straight salary plan—to recognize varying performance levels of managers—is to vary the amount and/or frequency of salary increases. Even this small amount of flexibility is not fully utilized by many organizations. As a result, it is usually advisable to add an incentive compensation plan to the salary plan. Incentive plans are discussed later in this article.

Compensation Separated From Performance

Parable: It came to pass that high unemployment among jackasses was visited upon the land, and the sixth jackass returned to climb the hill again. The hill was climbed and the driver said to the sixth jackass,

"Let's sit down and discuss your performance. We'll have an appraisal interview on how well you climbed the hill."

The sixth jackass wondered where his carrots were. Noting the puzzled, eager look on the sixth jackass' face, the driver explained that the purpose of the appraisal interview was to improve hill climbing. The carrots would be discussed at some time in the future. The sixth jackass ran away again.

Moral of the story: Never be the sixth jackass when it is not certain there is food at the top of the hill.

For years, the traditionalists have advocated that superior-subordinate discussions relative to the subordinate's performance should be clearly separated from any discussion concerning how much compensation the subordinate will receive for his performance.

The premise frequently advanced in favor of making the separation is that the injection of an emotional issue like compensation into a discussion on management development would cause the less attractive subject of development to be neglected. In principle, the argument sounds plausible. However, as a practical matter, it has yet to be demonstrated that the manager is ever able to forget compensation when his performance is being discussed. On the other hand, it has been repeatedly demonstrated that, no matter what is said during the performance interview, the manager is saying to himself, "Yeah, boss, I hear you talking, but what does it mean to my paycheck?"

Thus, attempts to omit the subject of compensation often have an effect the opposite of that intended. The deliberate skirting of the subject of compensation causes it to be spotlighted in the manager's mind; frustration and a lack of trust often result.

OVERCOMING THE JACKASS EFFECT

Major policy changes and decisions are necessary in most organizations if the jackass effect is to be overcome and if equity and motivation are to be built into managerial compensation. The magnitude and impact of these changes will bear a high degree of correlation with the extent to which the organization is mismanaging its compensation program.

Equitable compensation which truly motivates better managerial performance requires an integrated "building block" approach in which each of the following components or blocks is present in the right balance:

The establishment of clear-cut accountability which can be measured

The use of a measuring system (appraisal or evaluation) which effectively determines how well the accountability has been carried out

The adoption of a dynamic compensation plan which recognizes wide swings in managerial performance

The establishment of the greatest possible direct tie between performance and rewards.

The words "integrated" and "balance" are used advisedly because compensation must be practiced as a system of interrelated parts. Too often, compensation has been looked upon in the very narrow sense as comprising only the monetary payments; the other necessary components have been omitted or slighted. Effective compensation requires a broader perspective which views compensation as illustrated in Table 1.

If one or more of these components of the integrated system fail to play their proper roles, the system is damaged—equitable motivational compensation will suffer. For example, if measurable accountability has been established (Component 1) but the evaluation or appraisal methods (Component 2) are not sufficiently reliable to measure specific achievement against the accountability, there is no basis for rewarding the manager. Similarly, it is not possible to evaluate achievement unless measurable accountability has first been established.

Table 1
Components of Compensation

Component 1
Establishing measurable accountability

↓

Component 2
Measuring achievement accountability

↓

Component 3
Rewarding the achievement

↓

Component 4
Tying rewards to performance

Clear-Cut Accountability

The only true basis for compensating a manager is to first assign him accountability for achieving specific results. His accountability must be expressed in specific terms which can be measured later to determine how much and how well he accomplished his tasks.

The more effective compensation systems require that accountability be spelled out in the form of specific, measurable objectives which the manager must achieve during a particular target period. The following are specific measurable objectives for a general manager of an operating division for a particular year:

Achieve pretax profit of $5 million

Achieve sales of $60 million

Achieve a return on investment of 12 percent

Reduce average monthly inventory by 11 percent

Complete Phase 2 of management development program.

In this example, the vague, general nature of accountability has been avoided. Instead, the division manager's accountability is now expressed in specific, clear-cut terms which can be measured and used as the basis for meaningful compensation. These objectives will be used later to illustrate how the remaining parts of the compensation system are carried out.

Measuring Performance

Once clear-cut accountability has been established, the next step is to measure the extent to which the accountability was achieved—to evaluate managerial performance. Here again, the traditionalists failed to consider the system's nature of compensation. Because the accountability was vague and general, the traditionalists did not (and could not) follow a results-oriented approach to measuring, but fell back on evaluating the manager on the basis of effort expended. The traditional approach usually took the form of the previously described evaluation procedure which emphasized "personality traits."

Obviously, it all but completely ignores examination of the critical question of what specific accountability was delegated to the manager. This approach to evaluating performance must be eliminated if effective compensation is to be achieved.

Figure 2 is a good example of a results-oriented evaluation form. It incorporates specific measurable objectives for the division manager. In this approach, the manager's performance is measured against each of the objectives for which he was accountable during the preceding year. The culmination of this matching of performance against objectives serves as the basis for determining how much compensation he should receive. This approach is consistent with one of the cardinal rules of performance evaluation—that performance appraisal must be sufficiently valid so that the results may be used for compensation purposes.

Figure 2 Results-Oriented Performance Evaluation

Objectives (At beginning of year)	Results (At end of year)
Achieve pretax profit of $5 million	$ 6 million
Achieve sales of $60 million	$65 million
Achieve return on investment of 12 percent	13 percent
Reduce average monthly inventory by 11 percent	11 percent
Complete Phase 2 of management development program	Completed

Rewarding the Performance

Now that accountability has been established and performance on that accountability has been measured, the next step in the integrated system is to reward the performance in a way which promotes both equity and motivation.

While the importance of certain parts of a total compensation package such as stock options and pensions should not be minimized, they are not treated here because they are not directly related to individual performance. That is, the value of a stock option is not dependent upon individual performance but on how the investing public prices the stock, and all managers share equally in pension benefits. Two forms of compensation can and should be tied directly to individual managerial performance—salary and incentive payments.

Normally, direct compensation which is limited to salary payments is not sufficiently flexible and dynamic to recognize the wide swings or differences in performance among a group of managers. The cases of John Jones and Bill Smith, the two plant managers described earlier in this article, are vivid testimony to this premise.

Equity and motivation can best be served by utilizing both salary payments (fixed compensation) and incentive payments (variable compensation). With this approach, these direct payments can be viewed as resulting from two sources, salary payments and incentive payments.

Salary payments are rates paid for "holding down the job." The manager will always receive his salary, regardless of whether or not he receives incentive payments. The approaches and techniques for establishing salary rates are too well-known to dwell upon here. It will suffice to say that an enlightened compensation policy should provide for the payment of salaries based on the going rate for a particular managerial job based on a national average for that job. The rate should be examined at least annually to insure that it remains current.

Incentive payments are made, in addition to salary, on the basis of how well a job is accomplished. Because incentive payments are a variable form of compensation and are paid according to how well the manager performs, they provide the greatest possible opportunity to recognize any level of performance which the manager achieves (or fails to achieve). They permit compensation to be tied directly to performance on an individual basis.

If the manager's performance is below par, he receives no incentive payment—only his salary. If his performance exceeds par (his objectives), he receives above par incentive payments. For a year in which his performance was outstanding, he will receive commensurate incentive payments. All incentive payments are truly variable and based upon his varying levels of performance. An illustration of how the division general manager discussed earlier would be normally paid under an incentive plan follows.

The Weighting Problem The first requirement is to establish the relative weight of each of the manager's objectives *prior* to the beginning of the target year in which he is to carry out the objectives. Prior weighting of the objectives is critical; it places compensation on the beginning of the action. Only by making

known the future impact of compensation prior to the action can compensation exert an influence on the action as it occurs. In the instance of the division general manager, his objectives might be weighted as shown in Table 2.

The importance of the weighting of objectives cannot be overemphasized—nor should the difficulty be minimized. It is one of the more difficult chores in formulating an incentive compensation plan and one which has caused many organizations to avoid using incentive compensation in favor of less effective but easier to develop compensation approaches. One of management's top level responsibilities is to solve problems—not walk away from them.

As an illustration, how should the manager in the simplified example in Table 2 be evaluated and rewarded if he overachieves his profit objective? Or if he overachieves both his sales and profit objectives but fails to meet his objective for return on investment (ROI)? Or if he achieves all three objectives covering sales, profit, and ROI, but is able to do so because he completely neglected his inventory reduction and management development objectives?

Obviously, the compensation policy and plan must provide for evaluating the manager on his overall performance on both quantitative factors (effectiveness—were the objectives accomplished?) and qualitative factors (efficiency—how well were the objectives ac-

Table 2

Applying Point Weights to Objectives

Objectives	Possible Points
Achieve pretax profit of $5 million	50–100
Achieve sales of $60 million	30–80
Achieve return on investment of 12 percent	40–60
Reduce average monthly inventory by 11 percent	20–40
Complete Phase 2 of management development program	10–20

complished?). It would be self-deflating, for example, to evaluate a manager only on effectiveness (for example, he exceeded his sales objective by 15 percent) without also looking at his efficiency (achievement of the extra 15 percent by concentrating on easy sales of fast moving products with a high cost of goods sold but with low profit margins).

The balance must be preserved by clearly indicating in advance—through the step-by-step plans or programs which should always support major objectives—how and in what proportion the objectives will be achieved. Therefore, when the target period is over and the performance is being evaluated, it is possible to determine whether the manager used good planning to achieve his objectives or whether he achieved the objective through questionable management practices.

Another policy decision is to define "minimum" performance to qualify for extra compensation. Must all objectives be achieved? If not, which objectives must be, and in what proportion? Must an increase in the sales objective be accompanied by a corresponding increase in profit and return on investment?

The Normal Award As each of the points shown in Table 2 is translated into incentive payment dollars (using future accomplishment as the determining basis) the manager is provided with the option of determining at what level of accomplishment he wants to work during the target period, or, expressed differently, the amount of compensation he wishes to earn. It is possible to obtain this advance knowledge about objectives (and the effects on performance which it can help bring about) by using what is commonly referred to as the "normal award" for achievement of objectives. The normal award can be defined simply as the amount of incentive compensation (commonly expressed as a percentage of base salary) which a manager can expect to receive when he fully achieves his objectives. Table 3 portrays a

Table 3
Normal Awards at Various Salary Levels

Salary Level	Normal Award Percentage of Base Salary
$12,000	15%
20,000	20
30,000	25
40,000	30
50,000	35
—	—
100,000	50
—	—
200,000	65

normal award schedule for various levels of managers.

Obviously, the schedule or curve is constructed to increase the amount of the normal award at the higher levels of management. This reflects the greater potential of higher level managers to make a more substantial contribution to profits and to show greater responsibility for broader and more critical planning, decisions, and action.

Assume that the normal award for the division general manager is 35 percent of salary, and that his salary is $25,000. Two assumed levels of performance will be used to illustrate the compensation he would earn. In one case, he just achieves his objectives (par performance). In the second case, he exceeds his objectives (above par performance). The number of points he earns in both cases are shown in Table 4.

Following the "par" example used in Table 4, the division manager would receive 150 points for achieving his objectives. His normal incentive award at this point would be 35 percent of his salary, or $8,750. He would receive additional incentive compensation for the degree to which he achieves above par performance.

Once the normal award concept is adopted, the company must turn to a policy decision re-

Table 4
Points Earned at Various Performance Levels*

Objectives	Possible Points	Par		Above Par	
		Results	Points Earned	Results	Points Earned
$5 million profit	50–100	$5 million	50	$6 million	60
$60 million sales	30–80	$60 million	30	$65 million	33
12 percent ROI	40–60	12 percent	40	13 percent	44
Inventory reduction of 11 percent	20–40	11 percent	20	11 percent	20
Phase 2—management development program	10–20	Completed	10	Completed	10
Total			*150*		*167*

* In this example, the increased points are calculated on a one-to-one basis proportionate to the degree to which performance increased. Many companies accelerate the amount of the award at a higher rate once par performance has been achieved.

garding the amount of the reward for more than 100 percent achievement of objectives. This policy should provide at least a one-for-one reward for the degree to which the objectives are exceeded. Translated into an actual example, this policy might provide payments to the manager according to Table 5.

Table 5 may be extended indefinitely; its most important feature is that for every percentage increase by which the manager exceeds his objective, his incentive payment should be increased by at least a commensurate percentage. The amounts are expressed both as a percentage of salary and in absolute dollars,

Table 5
Rewards for More Than 100 Percent Objective Achievement

Percent of Objective Achievement	Incentive Payment Amount	
	As Percent of Base Salary	In Absolute Dollars
100	10	x dollars
110	20	2x dollars
120	30	3x dollars
130	40	4x dollars

since some companies relate incentive payments to the manager's salary and other companies establish absolute dollar levels which are not related to salaries. If all salaries have been established on an equitable basis, the former method is usually preferable, since it results in proportionately higher payments made to holders of higher level jobs.

Some companies limit maximum incentive payments to a certain percentage of salary. For example, the maximum payment a manager may receive is equal to 30 percent of his salary. Others use an open-ended method under which the amount of incentive payments is unlimited. The latter policy is more conducive to motivation because it emphasizes to the manager that his compensation is limited only by his accomplishments. The first policy does not provide the manager with real financial motivation to exceed his objectives by more than the point at which his compensation stops. However, for the first year or two of a new plan, to prevent incentive payments from running away while the plan and the objective-setting process are being "debugged" and refined, it may be well to establish a payment limitation. This limitation can be removed when the plan is operating effectively.

The Benefits The use of the weighting points and the normal award curve provide two major benefits to the manager—both of which bear heavily on equity and motivation. First, by knowing the weights prior to beginning the target year, he is able to calculate how many points he will earn at various levels of performance. For example, he knows that he will receive 30 points for achieving sales of $60 million (Table 4). If he desires to earn more points, he knows he must sell more than $60 million. He can make this decision prior to beginning his action for the target year. Second, he knows that his incentive compensation depends upon his own performance and that he has practically unlimited opportunity to earn additional compensation.

Neither time nor the purpose of this article permit the treatment here of the methods for establishing the total incentive fund for an organization as a whole or the methods for distributing portions of the total fund to various departments and divisions. It should be noted, however, that the total monies available for awarding an individual manager may be heavily influenced by the performance of the total company, his particular division or department, and, ultimately, by his own performance.

The Impact of Outside Factors

One of the more complex issues which must be considered when applying an incentive formula is how to handle the impact of outside factors over which the manager has no control. These outside factors can operate to enhance or impede his performance. For example, a few years ago a flu-like epidemic in the East caused a substantial and unanticipated demand for a leading brand of cough-drops. The sales manager for this product was able to greatly exceed his sales objective. This raised a question with respect to his incentive compensation. Should he receive additional compensation for the additional sales which did not result from his managing and planning but from factors outside of his control?

While there is not an easy or a perfect answer to this question, two general approaches are commonly followed. The first is to include a "windfall gain or loss" provision in the incentive plan. In this approach the manager's superior (and ultimately the incentive compensation committee comprised of outside directors) endeavors to isolate and evaluate the major factors which occurred and over which the manager had no control. The manager's incentive compensation may be adjusted according to this evaluation. A less desirable alternative is to consider only the results achieved without attempting to evaluate the "why." The manager's incentive sinks or swims according to the final tally.

The second approach is to evaluate the results achieved in light of the step-by-step plans developed by the manager to support his objectives. The purpose of this evaluation is to determine whether he planned (managed) his way to the results or whether he was just lucky. Evaluation of the planning process also permits an assessment of the impact of unfavorable outside events.

Regardless of which approach is used, the provisions and operations should be explained as completely as possible to all eligible managers before—not after—the target year begins.

Tying Compensation to Performance

If the equation "performance equals rewards" is to be valid, it is necessary to emphasize the interrelated nature of the two. This includes eliminating the arbitrary practice of separating performance appraisal interviews and compensation interviews. One of the traditional reasons advanced for making the separation goes to the heart of the old ineffective performance evaluation approach based on "personality traits." These were frequently used to justify just about any salary increase granted by a superior to a subordinate. For example, if a superior wanted to justify an increase for a subordinate, he would rate the subordinate as being excellent on all factors being rated. It was difficult to quarrel with the rating because it was not determined by objective results.

Thus, the traditionalists thought they could eliminate this stacking of the deck by separating the two interviews. However, any validity which this reasoning once enjoyed has now been negated by the increasing use of performance evaluation based on results. Measuring based on the specific results achieved makes it difficult to stack the deck to justify a whim or unjustified wish.

If performance is to truly equal rewards, increased emphasis should be devoted to discussing compensation as a natural and necessary part of the performance appraisal interview.

Parable: Once upon a time a farmer had six jackasses and a barn full of carrots which he kept under lock and key.

At the end of a day of wagon pulling, the farmer looked back over the day's performance of each jackass. To one of the jackasses he said, "You did an outstanding job; here are six carrots." To four of the others, he said, "Your performance was average; here are three carrots." To the remaining jackass he said, "You didn't pull your share of the load; here is one carrot."

Another day of wagon pulling dawned. The top jackass, having been properly rewarded, began the day in high spirits. The thoughts of the remaining jackasses were consumed with how they might earn more carrots through their efforts that day. The farmer had carrots available, but they had to be earned.

Moral of the story: Jackasses do work for carrots!

QUESTIONS FOR DISCUSSION

1. It has been noted that we are in the midst of a major work ethic crisis that has its roots in work that is designed more for robots than for mature adult human beings. Is this a recent phenomenon, given the fact that the poem by Robert Frost was written in the 1930's?

2. How would you rate the work climate, the task environment, and the feedback in the Panama Canal zone under Stevens' command? How would it change during the first year of Goethals command; and how would you rate it during the second year of Goethals command? What impact did these various dimensions have on productivity in building the Panama Canal?

3. Have you ever experienced the shock of being rated on performance dimensions which did not seem to relate to your job? Do you think this is a major problem in organizations? If so, why?

4. Do you think that Mr. Bluestone, who is a major union official, is typical of union leaders? One of the stereotypes of union leaders is that they are concerned with pay and are not that concerned about working conditions or increasing productivity. What is your feeling about unions and their interest in productivity and the quality of work life of people?

5. Put yourself in the situation described in the *Business Week* article. Would you prefer to work in a nontraditionally designed or a traditional designed work setting? Assuming you were the manager, which type of plant or work setting would you prefer?

CHAPTER V
THE UPWARD MOBILE ELITE

ORGANIZATIONAL SHOCKS

- Theories of motivation often don't apply to the world of work because they are based on the principle of upward mobility, which simply does not exist for the majority of employees in an organization.
- The cream does not always rise to the top.
- Often the upward mobile elite are born into their positions.

One of the problems with most theories of worker motivation taught in business schools today is that many of them deal only with people who have upward mobile potential. It is important for the student to realize that approximately 65% of the people in the United States and a similar proportion in most developed countries do not really have a great opportunity for mobility. In fact, the majority of these people will continue to hold approximately the same position throughout their lifetime. Therefore, this chapter and Chapter 6 are devoted to the differences between those people who have an upward mobile career curve and those whose career curve is presently flat.

In the first reading by Hall and Morgan, we learn about various career stages people pass through who have upward mobile experience. They present a model of career development that they recommend to managers as a method for increasing a manager's commitment and improving the organizational climate. In addition, this article describes how people in various stages of their careers react in their jobs and to others in the organization. From this article we can see that managers who are attempting to resolve conflict or increase motivation among employees would do well to respond to the various career stage needs of employees.

In the second article, Antony Jay discusses the controversial statement, "the cream always rises to the top." He points out that although there are many people who work exceptionally well within the organization, it is almost impossible for those at the top to know every one of them. This means that there are many men and women in the organization who have the talent to be at the top but are never recognized. One of the problems is whether or not you can get credit for your own work. Jay talks about methods for doing this and how you can differentiate the creative from the noncreative leader. One method by which a person may be able to get recognition when he feels that he is buried within the organization is through a method that Michael Maccoby calls "the gamesmen approach." He says that the modern gamesman is best defined as a person who loves chance and wants to influence its course. He therefore is willing to take a calculated risk and is fascinated by techniques and new methods. He sees a developing project, human relations, and his own career in terms of options and possibilities, as if they were a game. He is both cooperative and competitive, and while he appears to be a team player, he prefers to be a superstar.

The last article in this section about the upward mobile elite is taken from Joseph Heller's *Catch 22.* It is an excerpt from a chapter called "Major Major Major." Here we find that Major Major Major has been appointed a major in the Army because of his name rather than because of his skills. Often the upward mobile elite are born into their position. Whereas this may be less true today than it was prior to the industrial revolution, it still constitutes one of the major organizational shocks for many entering managers.

CAREER DEVELOPMENT AND PLANNING

DOUGLAS T. HALL
MARILYN A. MORGAN

Source: From "Career Development and Planning" by Douglas T. Hall and Marilyn A. Morgan in *Contemporary Problems in Personnel* edited by Hamner and Schmidt. Reprinted by permission of John Wiley and Sons, Inc. Copyright © 1977.

Organizations can only be as flexible, adaptive, and creative as the people they employ. People bring organizations to life. If organizations are to be effective, their people must perform effectively. Therefore, to improve the functioning of an organization, it is necessary to maximize the development and utilization of its human resources. This essay will explore one avenue for the improved utilization of human resources: career development and planning.

Why are careers important? Isn't the career the employee's own business—a private matter? Not really. For one thing, a person's career experiences and outcomes affect his or her performance, absenteeism, work quality, and turnover, all of which mean plus or minus dollars to the organization. For another, careers are a target for implementing equal employment opportunity. For many managers, in fact, career development and affirmative action are synonymous. For a third thing, one's work career is a major input to overall quality of life. People now have greater mobility and personal freedom than in the past, making it easier to achieve career fulfillment, which in turn puts more pressure on a person's employer to provide satisfying career opportunities. And, finally, given a sluggish, slow-growth economy, career opportunities have become more limited, making career planning more important if the person's career goals are to be met.

HUMAN DEVELOPMENT PROCESSES IN ORGANIZATIONS

The Career Success Cycle

Let's start at the beginning—with the individual. Our basic assumption is that people seek rewards and positive reinforcement from their work. These rewards can be extrinsic, such as a pay raise or a pat on the back, or intrinsic, such as a feeling of worthwhile accomplishment. We will further assume that work behavior which is rewarded will tend to be repeated.

133

Our third assumption is that whenever possible people attempt to increase their sense of self-esteem and avoid lowering their self-esteem. One way people can enhance their self-esteem is through the development of their competence, which is the ability to act successfully on one's environment (White, 1959).

Lewin (1936) and Argyris (1964) have described the conditions under which effective task performance will lead to increased self-esteem. For example, (1) if a woman sets a challenging goal for herself, and (2) the woman determines her own means of attaining that goal, and (3) if the goal is central to her self-concept, then she will experience *psychological success* upon attainment of that goal. This sense of personal success will lead to an increase in self-esteem. Since increased self-esteem is a powerful reinforcer, it will in turn lead to increased involvement in the task. This increased involvement will then lead the person to set additional goals in the same task area and to set higher levels of aspiration (Lewin, Dembo, Festinger, and Sears, 1944; Porter and Lawler, 1968).

Simply put, this theory suggests that success breeds success. This cycle of events can be self-reinforcing and can be generalized beyond simple tasks to people's careers. When a man experiences a success cycle at work, he may develop great enthusiasm for the career area represented by the successful activity. He may talk about "really finding himself" or being "turned on" by his work.

Research conducted at the General Electric Company illustrates how the career success cycle operates. In work planning and review sessions, employees who were given the most difficult goals (as opposed to either impossible or easy ones) showed the greatest gains in performance in later months (Stedry and Kay, 1962). People who participated in work planning and review sessions showed more positive work attitudes than people who received traditional performance appraisal sessions (in which

the focus was on evaluating the person's performance.) Key features of the work-planning sessions were self-appraisal, mutual goal setting, and collaborative problem solving on how to achieve future work goals (Kay and Hastman, 1966). Thus, in these GE studies, work performance and attitudes became more positive under two conditions necessary for psychological success; setting challenging self-relevant work goals, and independent effort in attaining work goals.

Career Stages: Changing Needs and Values

What Are Stages? Stages in human development are rather predictable, often stressful and trying (for the individual as well as others), and marked by potential for failure if mishandled.

A stage is a period of time in a person's life characterized by distinctive developmental tasks, concerns, needs, values, and activities. A stage is generally separated from the previous and subsequent stages by a role transition or status passage, and successful mastery of the developmental tasks at one stage is a necessary prerequisite to moving on to the following stage.

We tend to associate stages of development more with childhood than with adulthood. There are plenty of everyday terms available to describe life stages of children: "infancy," "childhood," "pre-teen," "adolescence," "high-schooler," "college student," and so forth. One reason for this is that there are more distinct statuses and status passages in childhood than in adulthood (starting grade school, becoming a teen-ager, getting a driver's license, graduating from high school, attaining legal age). The child's development is aided by the pacing which these clear passages provide.

The important passages and changes in adult life are harder to identify (Mills, 1970). Marriage and parenthood (and perhaps divorce) are often the last institutionalized role transitions a person moves through until retirement. Thus, the person must pace his or her development as an adult in terms of more subtle changes.

One guide for the pacing of adult development is the family and the life cycle of one's children. Since the passages of children are so clear, they can also serve to mark the parents'. In fact, an adult's development and social behavior may have more to do with the family life cycle than with his or her own age. As Cain has observed, "To be the father of a teen-age daughter elicits certain behavior patterns, whether the father be 30 or 70 years of age." (Cain, 1964, p. 289).

A second guide for pacing stages in adult development is the work career, which again may or may not be tied to age. As Hall has argued, "A lawyer or manager who is in the first permanent job following professional training (law school or business school) will probably be concerned about advancement and establish-ing a reputation among colleagues, whether he or she is 25 or 45" (Hall, 1976, p. 48). Let us examine the major career stages in some detail. (For an elaboration of the stages in adult development, the reader is referred to Gail Sheehy's [1974] *Passages*.)

A Model of Career Stages

Because the passages which mark adult life stages are less clear-cut than those of children, there is less agreement about just what are the main adult stages. However, enough work in different areas points in similar directions so that a sensitive composite model can be constructed (see Fig. 1.; this model draws from the work of Donald Super, Daniel Levinson and associates, Erik Erikson, and that of the first author).

Erik Erikson (1965) describes the adolescent exploratory period as a stage of identity formation. Through personal exploration at a time when the personal stakes are not too high, the

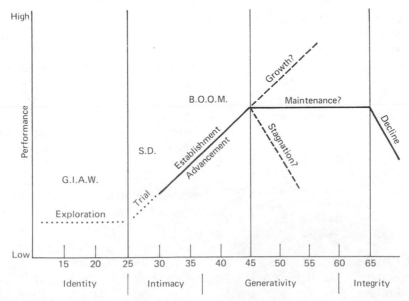

Figure 1. An Integrative Model of Career Stages (From Hall, 1976, p. 57).

person clarifies his or her self-concept and intentions for a future career. Levinson, Darrow, Klein, Levinson, and McKee (1974) refer to this period as "Getting Into the Adult World" (GIAW).

The most comprehensive statement of career stages comes from Donald Super (Super, 1957; Super and Bohn, 1970). Following a period of growth in childhood, the person goes through a period of *exploration,* in which self-examination, role tryouts, and occupational exploration take place. The final part of the exploration stage is a *trial* period, a time when a seemingly appropriate field has been selected, the person has found a beginning job, and is trying it out as a life work. This trial period may involve several job changes as the person attempts to find a good fit between his or her work interests, needs, and skills, on the one hand, and the demands and rewards of a particular job, on the other.

It is ironic that what is a trial period to the individual (a perfectly natural, necessary stage of human development) translates into high turnover for the organization. This high turnover occurs among new employees, and since turnover costs money (in testing, interviewing, training), organizations usually try to keep turnover as low as possible. To this extent, then, at this point in the employee's career, the goals of the organization and the developmental needs of the young employee are in conflict.

The next stage (between approximately ages 25 and 44) is termed *establishment* by Super:

Having found an appropriate field, effort is put forth to make a permanent place in it. There may be some trial early in this stage, with consequent shifting, but establishment may begin without trial, especially in the professions (Super et al., 1957, pp. 40–41).

Once the person has settled into a particular job or field, establishment consists of achievement, performance, and advancement. Levinson et al. (1974) refer to the start of this establishment period as "Settling Down" (SD), and to

the end of it, after one has severed ties with one's mentors, as "Becoming One's Own Man" (BOOM). In terms of general human development, Erikson calls this a stage of developing intimacy. By "intimacy," he means forming attachments and making commitments, to organizations and careers as well as to people (e.g., mates).

The forties mark the start of a *maintenance* stage, a mid-career plateau, according to Super: "Having made a place in the world of work, the concern is now to hold it. Little new ground is broken, but there is continuation along established lines" (Super et al., 1957, pp. 40–41). More recent writings, however, indicate that mid-career is not always the smooth plateau implied by Super. It can be a period of searching, reappraisal, depression, and redirection. Out of this mid-life, "crisis" can come either continuing growth, or stagnation and early decline, depending on how successful the person is in confronting and overcoming the developmental tasks of this period. In a similar vein, Erickson describes mid-life as a time for generativity, a concern for producing something meaningful to be felt for the next generation.

The passages into the trial and establishment periods are fairly easy to define. Trial often starts when the person leaves school and starts to work. Establishment begins after the person decides to stay in one career field or job. Midlife is harder to pinpoint. (In fact, we don't even have a good descriptive term to use for it; we have to fall back on a chronological referent, "mid-life.")

Rather than one single transition point marking mid-life, it seems to be triggered by a complex set of factors (from Hall, 1976):

Awareness of advancing age and awareness of death (the "psychology of turning 40").

Awareness of physical aging.

Leveling off of career advancement; the person knows how many career goals have or will be attained.

Search for new life goals.

Marked change in family relationships (e.g., teenaged children, a divorce).

Change in work relationships (e.g., now *you* are the boss, the S.O.B.)

Growing sense of obsolescence (as Satchel Paige put it, "Never look back; someone may be gaining on you").

Reduction in perceived occupational mobility.

These changes occur gradually, in contrast to earlier abrupt transitions such as college graduation or becoming a parent. Therefore, the person may experience vague, generalized discomfort and restlessness which cannot be explained or tied down to one simple causal factor. In this sense, mid-life may be more difficult to deal with than other stages because of its ambiguity, which in turn can aggravate its frustrations. Especially lucid popular descriptions of mid-life experiences are found in Sheehy's (1974) *Passages,* Persig's (1974) *Zen and the Art of Motorcycle Maintenance,* and Heller's (1974) *Something Happened.*

The final stage is termed *decline* by Super. Reacting to the unattractiveness of this term, Super, who had just retired himself, commented, "You can call it what you want—the Golden Years, the Sunshine Years, whatever. But I'm there; take my word for it, it's decline!" (Super, 1973, personal communication).

Erikson refers to this final period with a more pleasant term, "integrity," which is the feeling that the person is satisfied with his life, choices, and actions; he sees his life as having been meaningful and is willing to leave it as is. In terms of an organizational work career, this final stage involves the transition from membership to the organization to retirement and a new set of activities.

PEOPLE IN ORGANIZATIONAL CAREER SETTINGS

For individuals, career planning means identifying major career goals and interim objectives so that one becomes more than a manager of his or her own career. Similarly, the organization needs to assume the responsibility for facilitating self-management of careers by assisting the individual in planning expected progress through the organization. It seems, then, that the implications of career development are best expressed in terms of the importance of the *management* of careers. Such a perspective allows us to view career planning or development as an ongoing process designed to help both the individual and the organization.

Two factors—*job characteristics* and *work-force composition*—are critical in career planning. First, the nature of the jobs through which the manager progresses is crucial. Since the elements in the model of psychological success are challenging goals, effort, performance, psychological success, self-esteem, and involvement, the job itself is an important "trigger" to a positive success cycle. Jobs should be designed and selected on the basis of the degree to which they provide the necessary factors to better assure psychological success.

Second, the nature of the current work force has an impact on career development. What happens when "nontraditional" workers occupy these enriched jobs in organizations? The current work force has been expanded in the last decade to include women and members of minority groups. With these new members selected, the organization must work to plan their advancement within organizational settings. Similarly, we are seeing increasing numbers of dual career couples. The problems and opportunities created by such situations are beginning to be explored by organizations.

The Nature of the Job

The Initial Job   The importance of the first assignment is often underestimated. Research in the area of early job challenge suggests that employees who receive especially challenging job assignments early in their careers do better in later jobs (e.g., Berlew and Hall, 1956; Bray, Campbell, and Grant, 1974).

Too often managers are afraid to give new employees any real responsibility until they have adjusted to the new work situation and have demonstrated their capabilities. Consequently, the initial job most often involves being assigned to a training program of some sort, working on a small or easy project, or serving as an "assistant." The problem with the "prove yourself before we give you any responsibility" philosophy is its self-fulfilling nature. How can an organization identify the capabilities and potential of a new employee if they begin by placing severe limits on the opportunities to perform? Most people can complete successfully a simple task or project. New employees can usually perform well as an assistant when they are told exactly what to do. It is difficult, however, to identify the limitations of individuals in such controlled assignments. Similarly, the individual is not provided the opportunity to "stretch" or use many of the skills developed in the years of schooling. He or she will often feel frustrated or bored by the routine nature of initial assignments. Thus, when organizations give low initial challenge and responsibility to new employees, they are actually "developing" low performance standards.

If initial career experiences have a continuing impact on the development of a person's career, then the entry-level job assignment is a crucial aspect of an employee's overall career planning effort. Organizations should analyze entry-level jobs in order to provide a meaningful, challenging experience for their new members. It is not easy to make these jobs more challenging, but such long-term payoffs as performance, commitment, and involvement make the effort worthwhile.

Some organizations believe in an initial period of job rotation. Rotation which sends an employee through a series of short-term, meaningless positions where he or she is nothing more than an observer of different parts of the organization will not provide the new hire with the necessary amounts of job challenge. However, it seems reasonable to expect that an entry-level assignment which relies heavily upon *planned job rotation* will be able to reconcile competing problems created by the dual needs of initial job challenge and training. Planned job rotations rely upon a series of meaningful job moves during the first 6 to 12 months of the employee's career. This set of jobs should be selected to encourage the development of skills essential to future job performance. Planned job rotations are an efficient means of providing the employee with a variety of meaningful experiences in a short time, as well as the opportunity to "self-test" working in different settings as part of a career development plan.

The Individual's Career Path

The sequence of jobs through which an employee moves during a career constitutes his or her individual *career path* or *job history*. Research on the initial job assignment demonstrates the effect the first job has on the employee's overall growth and development. Consider the combined impact of a sequence of jobs on overall success over a 30- to 40-year career. Consider, for example, the potential paths to the job of store manager in a large retailing organization. The individual who moves through a series of jobs which provide him with increasing amounts of various job dimensions (e.g., challenge, variety, and functional area) will be better prepared to handle the responsibilities of store management because of it.

The career path or job history of an employee has a potentially stronger effect on overall development than any other experience or set of experiences in his or her career. A challenging job provides opportunities for varied experiences and skill development. Such experiences contribute to successful performance in the new job situation and are readily transferable to future situations. After performing well on a job, the employee has a better chance of moving on to another job which will provide opportunity for additional growth and development. Since most jobs have different characteristics, a variety of them encourages the development and use of varied skills. Movement through a variety of jobs increases the chances of career success, since performing well on one job will improve the chance of being assigned to a more demanding one. This means that a carefully planned sequence of job moves should be undertaken in an effort to assure levels of career success.

If job moves are to be used for growth and developmental purposes, care must be taken to use the career-planning process effectively. The following steps are important:

Selection of a Target Job The individual must consider his or her career aspirations within the organization. In some cases the target job is determined by the nature of the business. For example, in retailing, likely target jobs would be store manager and head buyer. Similarly, the target job is often determined by the nature of the profession. In the case of academia, for instance, the target job is most often full professor.

Identification of the Necessary Skills and Experiences Although it is difficult to get accurate, objective information with which to identify the skills and experiences necessary to successfully perform the target job, job descriptions and analyses are probably the best sources of evaluative information. Individuals employed by organizations which have implemented the Hay System[1] have a definite advantage in this area since the characteristics of each job have been measured and can be used as an indication of skill requirements.

Identification of the Necessary Sequence of Jobs The following guidelines are useful in considering the sequencing of planned job moves which will provide the required levels of experience and skill development:

1. Select jobs which provide changes which are large enough to "stretch" skills and capabilities, yet small enough to be manageable.

2. Consider lateral moves as well as promotions, since moves at the same level often provide opportunities for skill development (e.g., change in function).

3. Allow for enough time to master the job but not so long an assignment that the performance of the job becomes routine.

4. Consider jobs which complement or supplement, not those which duplicate previous experiences.

5. Provide alternative moves or sequences (i.e., a contingency plan), since it is unlikely that the normal demands of the organization will allow for all the scheduled moves exactly as planned.

The Nature of the Work Force: Nontraditional Employees

Women and Minorities Five or so years ago a major organizational concern was to attract women and minorities into professional and managerial positions. The literature was full of cases describing the types of discriminatory practices common to most organizations. While there is still a concern for recruitment and selection, another issue is how best to assure the successful performance and advancement of women and minorities in organizational settings. The following comment from *Business Week* offers evidence of this problem.

It took a decade of federal legislation, relentless agitation from the women's (and civil rights) movements, and seismic shifts in public opinion, but women (and minorities) are moving boldly into the mainstream of corporate management. The battle for equality in blue-collar and clerical jobs moved faster because bias was easier to prove. The far more complex struggle for equal status up the corporate ladder has taken longer and is far from over. But the big news is that women (and minorities) are making headway—slowly in the executive suite, faster at the lower rungs of middle management. (Nov. 24, 1975).

Career planning is recognized as an effective means of developing opportunities for minorities and women. Members of these groups need to plan their career moves very carefully in order to develop the necessary skills to assure successful performance in the more demanding jobs they will encounter as they move up the corporate ladder.

O'Leary (1974) identifies several factors which serve to inhibit the expression of upward occupational aspirations of women and could subsequently affect their overall career success: fear of failure, low self-esteem, sex role stereotypes, role conflicts, and the prevalence of the male managerial model. It is important that organizations consider these barriers to success in planning the career moves of women. Assignment to jobs which provide at least a minimal amount of support should be an important consideration. Support may take the form of good supervision, assignments which provide female peers or role models, and feedback on performance.

As with women's careers, careful career planning is important for the development of minorities. The challenge of integrating these employees into the workforce is an issue being addressed by most organizations. Hence, variables affecting the careers of women and minorities seem to be an important area for future research.

Dual Careers Dual career couples are those in which both husband and wife pursue a full-time career. As more married women enter the work force, dual careers are becoming increasingly important factors for career management, because it is difficult to relocate one partner if the other is unable or unwilling to move. When both husband and wife have full-time careers, career flexibility decreases and planning becomes more crucial. The problem of dual-career families is becoming increasingly common among young employees and must be dealt with by organizations.

For example, a large manufacturing firm in the Midwest recently experienced the following effects of a dual-career situation. A very promising and also married young attorney had been working in its legal department for five years. Not only was he well respected in his own department but he had caught the attention of the company president and had been identified as one of several "high-potential" employees. During the couple's stay in the Midwest, the wife worked toward a Ph.D. in psychology. Upon receiving this degree she was offered an academic position in a prestigious university on the East Coast. Recognizing that such a position would be a very good way to start his wife's academic career, her husband requested a transfer to the eastern division of the firm. The head of the legal department and the president refused to consider the request. This attorney is now working for a competitor in the competitor's New York office and his wife is teaching at the Eastern university.

This example suggests that the biggest problem created by dual-career situations is job transfers. A transfer to another location means that the working spouse must relocate, too. If both husband and wife are employed by the same organization, both career moves are within the control of one organization. In the much more frequent situations where employment is by different organizations, there is the risk of either losing employees when one spouse is transferred or of being asked to arrange a transfer to the same location. An article in *Business Week* (Aug. 23, 1976) stated that working wives were the most critical factor in the unwillingness to move of male executives.

Similar dual-career issues are found in recruiting employees. It is sometimes difficult to attract a person to an organization if its location does not provide career opportunities for the spouse. Organizations are often required to recruit both husband and wife, or to help find a job for the spouse. The point is that the spouse's career opportunities increasingly affect the recruitment and advancement of today's employees. The issue, however, has not yet been realized by many organizations, but it seems destined to become a crucial organizational problem. Consideration of the spouse's career must be made in he career planning and development efforts or the organization runs the risk of losing many good employees.

ORGANIZATIONAL MANAGEMENT OF CAREERS

What, then, can organizations do to manage employees' careers more effectively? We will now examine this critical, practical issue.

Stage-Specific Training

Much training in organizations is done across the board with large groups of employees. It may be aimed at all people at a particular job level or to all people about to enter a given job. This is reasonable. It is also reasonable that people in a given career stage—or people about to enter a given stage—may also need training in how to deal with the developmental tasks of that stage. Unfortunately, this sort of stage-specific training is rarely done. What would such training entail?

Assessing Stages   First, it is necessary to have a way to identify who is at a given career stage. The time at which people move through various stages varies with the occupation and with the organization. In most organizations there is usually some commonly accepted age at which advancement starts to level off. This could be taken as the start of mid-career. The trial period is easier to identify—people at this point are usually new employees in their first year or two. Establishment/advancement would probably span the second or third year of employment through the start of mid-career. Decline could be defined in terms of when people in the organization begin thinking about and preparing for retirement, perhaps five years before.

Once the stages have been defined, training needs can be identified. These can be broken down into two areas: task needs (dealing with job activities) and emotional needs (covering the feelings associated with career changes.) These needs are summarized in Table 1.

Trial Stage Needs   In the trial stage, the individual needs to be encouraged to spend some time in various job activities, but with enough time spent in each activity so that challenge and success can be experienced. Self-exploration, through career assessment and planning exercises, should also be encouraged. On the emotional side, the person should be pressed to begin making choices and settling in to an area of specialization. Even if the organization does not have a job-rotation training program, it would be a mistake to keep a young person in one function from the first day of employment without some opportunity to try some other areas.

Advancement Needs   In the establishment/advancement stage, job challenge is the critical need. The person needs to develop competence in some area of specialization. Technical training programs are especially important in this stage. A special effort should be made to develop creativity and innovation, since these qualities are usually at their peak in the early career years. After the person has developed specialized skills, the organization should avoid the temptation to keep the person in this area for too long. (Such a course is tempting because it would be a way of reaping a high

Table 1
Training Needs Within Career Stages[a]

Stage	Task Needs	Emotional Needs
Trial	1. Varied job activities 2. Self-exploration	1. Make preliminary job choices 2. Settling down
Establishment Advancement	1. Job challenge 2. Develop competence in a specialty area 3. Develop creativity and innovation 4. Rotate into new area after 3 to 5 years	1. Deal with rivalry and competition; face failures 2. Deal with work-family conflicts 3. Support 4. Autonomy
Mid-career	1. Technical updating 2. Develop skills in training and coaching others (younger employees) 3. Rotation into new job requiring new skills 4. Develop broader view of work and own role in organization	1. Express feelings about mid-life 2. Reorganize thinking about self in relation to work, family, community 3. Reduce self-indulgence and competitiveness
Late career	1. Plan for retirement 2. Shift from power role to one of consultation and guidance 3. Identify and develop successors 4. Begin activities outside the organization	1. Support and counseling to see one's work as a platform for others 2. Develop sense of identity in extraorganizational activities

[a] Adapted from Hall, 1976, p. 60.

return on the company's investments in the person's training, as, for example, when managers—especially sales managers—"capture" a good person and won't let that person advance.) After three to five years, the person should be moved into a new specialty, to prevent overspecialization and early obsolescence. On the emotional side, the advancing person needs to deal with strong feelings of rivalry and competition with peers. There may also be concerns about failure and about career-family conflicts which will call for opportunities to discuss them and emotional support from someone in the organization. Autonomy will be necessary to permit feelings of individual achievement and psychological success. An occasional "rap group" dealing with the stresses and conflict of expending high energy on success can be a beneficial way of dealing with these feelings.

Mid-Career Needs In mid-career, an individual's skills may need some updating if the person has not been rotated through new specialties at three- to five-year intervals earlier in the career. At this career point the person is doing less technical work and more administrative work. Harry Levinson (1969) posits that individuals should shift from being "quarterbacks" to "coaches" at this stage, and this calls for advanced training in human relations, communication, and management skills. Continued job rotation is still important to keep the person fresh and always learning. This is also a time when the person begins to identify more with the organization and can see his or her own work better in relation to the total organization's purposes. Seminars on company history, policies, and goals may be, ironically, better received by mid-career employees than by new employees, who usually get such material in their initial orientation sessions.

The emotional side of mid-career calls for an opportunity to talk with others about the feelings of mid-life (anguish, re-examination of goals, limited time, restlessness, etc.). It also helps to encourage or help employees to do some life planning and re-relate their work commitments to family, community, and other involvements. Since advancement is leveling off, there may be need to redirect competitive energies, perhaps into the vicarious success of aiding subordinates' careers.

Late Career Needs   In the decline stage, it is important to begin planning for retirement, since good planning leads to a good transition. This means, in a sense, starting the career cycle again, but now in the area of retirement activities (exploration, trial, establishment). After all, there is a *retirement career* to be planned for and managed, as well as the remaining work career. At the same time, the person must make arrangements to terminate the activities and responsibilities of the work career. This demands skills in identifying and developing successors, gradually involving successors in job activities and decisions. As the person plays a less active role in the organization, he or she can become more available as a source of consultation and organizational wisdom.

On the emotional side, there is a need to see how one's work has provided a foundation for the work of future generations of employees. There is a need to come to terms with one's overall work career and with the fact that it is ending. It is also important for the person to develop relationships and an identity outside the organization so that the end of employment is not seen as the end of his or her identity.

Why should an organization be concerned about the employee's planning for retirement? First, the late-career person can be a valuable resource in the development of younger employees *if* he has been well-treated by the organization and is thus motivated to be helpful. Furthermore, younger employees are more likely to make commitments of time, energy, and involvement to the organization if they see that the organization maintains its interest in the development of employees through their later career stages (i.e., ''If the organization treats pre-retirement employees well now, they'll probably treat me well, too'').

Changing the Work Environment

Some of the stage-specific training we have just discussed can be done off the job in training facilities. As mentioned earlier, however, there is much potential for career-developing training inherent in the nature of the work environment. Let us quickly run down the different facets of the work environment (employee, job itself, boss, organization structure, and personnel policies) to see how it can be redesigned to foster employee career growth.

Entry: Changing Employee Inputs
Young people just out of school and working on their first jobs often experience ''reality shock''—that is, a job which falls far short of their expectations for experiences such as challenge, responsibility, autonomy, and feedback. There are two ways to reduce this expectation versus reality gap: either improve the experience, or modify the expectations. One way to do the latter is for organizations to use *realistic job previews* (RJPs) in recruiting (Wanous, 1975). An RJP gives the negative features of a

job as well as its positive ones (e.g., a telephone operator's job has low variety and close supervision as well as good pay and security). Realistic job previews seem to result in subsequent lower turnover, and they do not appear to hurt recruiting success (Wanous, 1975).

Another way of providing more realistic job orientations is to give students more training in job-related skills in educational systems, such as business and professional schools. Better links between educators and employers (e.g., through job internships, field projects, executive-in-residence programs) will help on this score, too.

Finally, better selection methods can be used by employees to get a better fit between employee and job. This does not necessarily mean luring the brightest or best-educated candidates. One manufacturing firm in Connecticut sharply reduced its reject rate and employee turnover when it started hiring people in the second quartile—an ability level which fit the routine assembly jobs much better than hiring the highest-ability applicants.

Development Through the Job Itself

We have already heard about challenging initial jobs and career pathing as a way of building "stretching" experiences into the work environment. Employees should have several years to develop specialized competencies, but they should then be rotated into new activities every few years to prevent obsolescence. New job activities can force learning much more effectively than a whole string of university "up-date" courses.

Peer stimulation can be an excellent means of learning skills and positive work attitudes. Assigning the new employee to a work group or team of outstanding performers will pay dividends.

One of the largest areas of undeveloped potential for employee growth is feedback and performance appraisal. Feedback is essential in any kind of performance, and it is unfortunate that most of us "fly blind" on our jobs. We usually have to "read in" meaning to every subtle evaluative cue we receive from our bosses, and these inferences may be totally invalid. (That gruff "Hello!" this morning may have said more about his fight at home than about the report you turned in yesterday.) A simple, well-planned performance appraisal process (with a superior trained in how to do it) can be of the utmost value to the individual and the organization.

Finally, when you get good performance from an employee, don't let it pass unnoticed. As the work of many researchers shows, one of the simplest ways to increase the likelihood of occurrence of a behavior is to positively reinforce it. A word of recognition, a letter of congratulation, a pat on the back, a bonus—these are all ways to reward good performance and to encourage the performer to repeat it. Most of the time managers fail to respond to either good or poor performance—which in effect rewards poor performance and negatively reinforces good performance.

Changing the Superior's Role

To involve the boss in career development, give him or her the skills necessary to be a good career developer. Skills such as performance appraisal, feedback, counseling, job design, and career plotting are fairly easy to develop in two- or three-day training sessions. One of the big reasons managers don't do more about career development is that they lack the skills for it.

Another way to utilize the boss for employee development is to assign new employees to outstanding managers who will set high standards of expected performance. Research has shown that people tend to perform at whatever level is expected (Livingston, 1969), which casts the manager in the role of organizational Pygmalion. Often new employees are assigned to bosses on a random basis; more care in the job assignment process costs little and has a high payoff.

Changing Organization Structures   The design of the organization shows up in the "fingerprints" it puts on people. A functional organization produces (possibly narrow) functional specialists. A product organization trains people who are loyal to their product (perhaps at the expense of concern for the firm's other products). A matrix structure (in which people work on cross-functional product teams) can combine the best of both orientations. It also offers two directions for moving people—to a new product but in the same function, or vice versa—which makes a person branch out a bit while still staying to some extent in familiar territory.

One of the reasons more effort is not placed on employee development is that this activity is often not rewarded. And it is not rewarded because it is hard to measure. Human-resource accounting is a way of measuring an organization's investments in people and the resulting returns. Therefore, as more companies develop human-resource information systems, this change can make the payoff to a manager for employee development more tangible (Hall, Alexander, Goodale, and Livingstone, 1976).

A third area of activity for many organizations is career-planning services. These activities, designed specifically to stimulate career development, can range from very employee-oriented life planning (as at Continental Illinois Bank and The Travelers Insurance Companies, for example) through assessment center feedback (3M Company) to a combination of personal counseling, job design, and training bosses in career developing skills (AT&T). The range of these programs is wide, but though much activity is taking place, there is precious little evaluative research to help us separate the good from the godawful.

Changing Personnel Policies   The final aspect of the work environment which can be altered to stimulate career development is the area of personnel policies. For example, a policy of rotating managers through "people departments," such as personnel or organization development, can do as much to heighten line managers' sensitivity to employee development needs as can years of information campaigns. A policy of life-long job rotation, as we have said before, can counteract obsolescence and maintain employee flexibility.

Another policy which can aid development is lateral and downward job transfers. Lateral interfunctional transfers can be a way of developing new skills without promoting the person. (If economic and organizational growth slows, promotion opportunities will diminish accordingly, and other movement possibilities must be explored.)

More controversial is the idea of downward transfers. The option of moving employees down (even if only temporarily) immensely increases an organization's degrees of freedom. Two conditions are important in reducing an outcry against demotions: (1) a guarantee that no one will take a pay cut; and (2) a guarantee that anyone who is moved down will never lose his or her job (a form or organizational tenure). One organization started a downward transfer policy by deliberately moving down two key and obviously successful vice presidents in order to counter the belief that demotion means failure. The two VPs were assigned temporarily to "hot spots" in the organization, where they promptly shaped up ailing operations. The change also had the side effect of improving communications up to the other vice presidents. The antidemotion norm is a tough one to buck, however, and in many organizations the benefits will not be worth the cost. However, it is worth thinking the "unthinkable" and at least considering the possibility of downward moves. Because of the ambiguity in the structure of most organizations, whether a particular move is a promotion or a demotion is often the subject of debate anyway.

One way to reduce the risks of promotions or crossfunctional lateral moves is through fallback positions. A fallback position is identified before the transfer is made, and the organization and the employee agree in advance that if the transfer or promotion does not work out, the person will move to the fallback position with no stigma. This represents an acceptance by the organization that the transfer or promotion entails some risk, and that the company is prepared to share in the risk and help resolve any resulting problems. Companies such as Heublein, Proctor and Gamble, Continental Can, and Lehman Brothers have used fallback positions (*Business Week,* Sept, 28, 1974).

Another personnel innovation is organizational tenure. Using the university as a model, one Pennsylvania manufacturing company introduced a policy of evaluating new employees in two ways after their probationary periods. First, the standard retain-or-terminate decision was made. Then company management asked the question, "If we had to lay off 20 percent of our workforce because of economic setbacks, would this be a person we would let go (on the basis of performance)?" If the answer was yes, the person would still be offered the job, but feedback about being in the lowest 20 percent would be given. (Many of the low 20 percent employees stayed on, and the feedback improved performance for some, in which case the "contract" was revised.) The top 80 percent employees also received feedback and were given a form of tenure in the organization. The active ingredient in this system, of course, is the feedback, which is probably more important than the tenure itself.

A final important personnel policy area relates to the dual-career employee. As more women take up work careers (and assuming men continue to do so), and as long as men and women marry and/or live together, there will be increasing numbers of dual-career employees in organizations. If an organization sees it as the couple's responsibility to cope with the stresses of dual-career responsibilities, that organization runs the risk of losing—or fail-

ing to hire—talented, career-involved employees. A small interview survey conducted by Alison Martier, covering approximately 30 organizations in the Chicago area, identified the following policies for accommodating dual-career employees:

1. Recognition of the existence of problems in dual careers.
2. Help with relocation in the case of transfer of a spouse (or helping the spouse relocate if your employee is being transferred).
3. Flexible working hours (to facilitate child care).
4. Initiation of counseling for dual-career employees.
5. Family day-care centers.
6. Improved career planning and counseling.
7. A change in antinepotism rules (to make it easier for two members of the same family to work for the organization or perhaps the same unit in the organization.)

These are preliminary approaches because we are at a preliminary stage in the recognition of dual-career problems. As dual-career employees who are now relatively young and low in power in most organizations rise to higher levels, more pressure for solutions will be generated. For this reason, the dual-career issue has been called an "organizational time bomb" (Hall and Hall, 1976).

PLANNING FOR YOUR OWN CAREER

A summary of the ideas presented in the preceding section is given in Table 2. This section is based upon the work of Schein (1964), Hall (1976) and others. We'll be talking about *typical career experiences,* but of course each person's career is unique, so don't panic if you don't like what you read here. We want to discuss your expectations, the company's expectations, how its members may perceive you,

Table 2

Organizational Actions for Facilitating Career Development[a]

Entry: Changing Employee Inputs
1. Better links between school and work.
2. Training students in job-related skills.
3. Realistic job previews in recruiting.
4. Better selection for person-job fit.

Development Through the Job
1. Challenging initial jobs.
2. Periodic job rotation.
3. Colleague stimulation.
4. Frequent feedback and performance review.
5. Rewarding good performance.

Changing the Boss's Role
1. Make bosses career developers.
2. Train managers in job design and career planning.
3. Reward managers for employee development.

Changing Organizational Structures
1. Matrix organization structures.
2. Accounting for human resources.
3. Career planning services.

Changing Personnel Policies
1. Rotation of managers through "people departments."
2. Life-long job rotation.
3. Downward and lateral transfers.
4. Tenure.
5. Fallback positions for promoted employees.
6. Support for dual-career employees.

[a] Adapted from Hall, 1976, p. 177.

what you may experience in your first job, and how you can help yourself.

Your Expectations

If you're typical, from your first job you'll probably want opportunities for advancement, responsibility, interesting, meaningful and challenging work, a chance to use your skills and educational training, security, and good pay. (In a Doonesbury cartoon, when Mark told his father that he was expecting these qualities in his first job, his father's response was, "In short, you have no intention of getting a job!")

What The Company Will Expect of You

The company will expect you to have *competence* to get a job done—to identify problems and see them through to solutions. It will also expect you to *accept "organizational realities,"* that is, the need for stability and survival, informal power relationships, recognition of group loyalties, office politics, and the like. You will be expected to *generate and sell ideas*. This involves a wide range of human relations skills, such as translating technical solutions into practical, understandable terms, patiently overcoming resistance to change, and the ability to influence others. *Loyalty and commitment* may be important, especially in organizations with strong promotion-from-within policies. This loyalty may involve some sacrifice of parts of your personal life. *Personal integrity and strength* will also be highly valued as shown by your ability to stick to your own point of view without being a rebel, yet knowing how to compromise when necessary. Finally, the organization will look for your *ability to grow,* to assume responsibility and learn from mistakes (mistakes are expected, but not repeated mistakes).

How The Company Will Perceive You

How you are perceived naturally depends a lot on both you and the organization. The company may see you as overambitious and unrealistic in your expectations. You may seem too theoretical, too idealistic, or too naive and immature. You will probably lack experience. It may see you as too security-conscious and unwilling to take risks. You may have underdeveloped interpersonal skills, and you may have trouble selling your ideas. Overall, your boss and the organization may see you as a potentially *useful* resource, who must be broken in first ("house broken" in the words of some managers).

What You Will Experience

The most common complaint of new graduates is *lack of challenge*—that is, underutilization of your skills and training. (But remember: you're being trained for managerial jobs 5 to 15 years off, not just for the first assignment). Turnover is extremely high in the first year of employment, often around 50 percent. Because the actual job is so different from what you expected, you may experience reality shock.

To compound these problems, you may threaten your boss. Your starting pay may be uncomfortably closer to his or hers, yet you may be young enough to be your boss' daughter or son. And you'll be promoted above your present boss in a few years. And your boss may be a bit obsolete, threatened by your more recent skills and knowledge. And your boss may be going through a "mid-career crisis," and so forth.

You may get little or no feedback on your performance. You may have trouble creating your own challenges. And your company training may be inadequate (in many companies, training is just a sink-or-swim process).

What You Can Do

The organization you work for and chance events have a lot of control over your career, but that control is not absolute. *Develop some career goals* and *do some career planning.* Many universities have counseling centers which provide excellent career-planning services. A useful guide for self-management of careers is *What Color is Your Parachute?* by R. N. Bolles (1974).

Career maturity involves the following career competencies: self-appraisal, obtaining occupational information, problem-solving, plan-ning, and choosing goals. Try to develop these skills.

Try to get realistic information about any organizations from whom you have offers. Research has shown that people with good information (positive and negative) about the company are more satisfied and are less likely to quit.

If you have a choice of offers, go for the most challenging job. One of the best predictors of career success is the amount of challenge in your first job. In choosing your first job, challenge and potential for career growth should be more important than shorter-term considerations such as salary or location. If you are stretched and pushed toward excellence in your first job, you will be more successful later, and will have plenty of later offers with good salaries and locations.

Develop your communications and human relations skills. The most critical part of your job will be working with people, even if you are doing technical work.

Don't become overspecialized. It may be flattering to become the world's greatest expert on inflation accounting, but what happens to you when prices stabilize? To force yourself to keep learning and growing, move into a new area every three to five years. The time to begin fighting career obsolescence is now, when that obsolescence could be starting.

Finally, reassess your career periodically. Ask where you're headed and where you want to be, because the only way to get there from here, is to know where "there" is.

NOTE

1.   The Hay System is a method of evaluating jobs by relying on factors that are common to all jobs in varying degrees. The system provides useful information about certain characteristics of each job by considering factors such as accountability, problem-solving opportunities, and technical skill requirements, and compares jobs to determine which contain more of these factors than others.

REFERENCES

Argyris, C. *Integrating the Individual and the Organization.* New York: Wiley, 1964.

Berlew, D. E. and Hall, D. T. The socialization of managers: Effects of expectations on performance. *Administrative Science Quarterly,* 1966, *11,* 207–223.

Bolles, R. N. *What Color is Your Parachute? A Practical Manual for Job-Hunters and Career Changers.* Berkeley, Calif.: Ten Speed Press, 1974.

Bray, D. W., Campbell, R. J. and Grant, D. L. *Formative Years in Business: A Long Term AT&T Study of Managerial Lives.* New York: Wiley, 1974.

Cain, L. D., Jr. Life course and social structure. In R. Faris (ed.), *Handbook of Modern Sociology.* Chicago: Rand McNally, 1964.

Erikson, E. H. *Childhood and Society.* New York: Norton, 1963.

Goodale, J. G., Hall, D. T., and Rabinowitz, S. A test of an integrative model of job involvement. Working paper, York University, 1976.

Hall, D. T. A theoretical model of career subidentity development in organizational settings. *Organizational Behavior and Human Performance,* 1971, *6,* 50–76.

Hall, D. T. *Careers in Organizations.* Pacific Palisades, Calif.: Goodyear, 1976.

Hall, D. T. and Foster, L. W. Effects of goals, performance, and psychological success upon attitudes toward self, task, and career, *Academy of Management Journal,* 1977, in press.

Hall, D. T. and Hall, F. S. What's new in career management? *Organizational Dynamics,* 1976.

Hall, D. T. and Hall, F. S. The relationship between goals, performance, success, self-image, and involvement under different organization climates. *Journal of Vocational Behavior,* 1976, in press.

Hall, D. T., and Nougaim, K. E. An examination of Maslow's need hierarchy in an organizational setting. *Organizational Behavior and Human Performance,* 1968, *3,* 12–35.

Hall, D. T. and Schneider, B. *Organizational Climates and Careers: The Working Lives of Priests.* New York: Seminar (Academic) Press, 1973.

Hall, D. T., Alexander, M. O., Goodale, J. G., and Livingstone, J. L. How to make personnel decisions more productive. *Personnel,* 1976, *53,* 10–20.

Heller, J. *Something Happened.* New York: Ballantine Books, 1974.

Kay, E. and Hastman, R. *An Evaluation of Work Planning and Goal-Setting Discussions.* Crotonville, New York: Behavioral Research Service, General Electric Company, 1966.

Levinson, D. J., Darrow, C., Klein, E., Levinson, M., and McKee, B. The psychological development of men in early adulthood and the mid-life transition. In D. F. Hicks, A. Thomas, and M. Roff (eds.), *Life History Research in Psychopathology,* Vol. 3. Minneapolis: University of Minnesota Press, 1974.

Levinson, H. On being a middle-aged manager. *Harvard Business Review,* 1969, *47,* 51–60.

Lewin, K. The psychology of success and failure. *Occupations,* 1936, *14,* 926–930.

Lewin, K., Dembo, T., Festinger, L., and Sears, P. Level of aspiration. In J. McV. Hunt (ed.), *Personality and Behavior Disorders.* New York: Ronald Press, 1944.

Livingston, J. S. Pygmalion in management. *Harvard Business Review,* 1969, *47,* 81–89.

Managers move more but enjoy it less. *Business Week,* August 23, 1976, 19–20.

Mills, E. W. Career development in middle life. In W. Bartlett (ed.), *Evolving Religious Careers.* Washington, D.C.: Center for Applied Research in the Apostolate, 1970.

O'Leary, V. E. Some attitudinal barriers to occupational aspirations in women. *Psychological Bulletin,* 1974, *81,* 809–826.

Persig, R. M. *Zen and the Art of Motorcycle Maintenance: An Inquiry into Values.* New York: Bantam Books, 1974.

Porter, L. W. and Lawler, E. E., III. *Managerial Attitudes and Performance.* New York: Irwin-Dorsey 1968.

Schein, E. H. How to break in the college graduate. *Harvard Business Review,* 1964, *42,* 68–76.

Schein, E. H. The individual, the organization, and the career: A conceptual scheme. *Journal of Applied Behavioral Science,* 1971, *7,* 401–426.

Sheehy, G. *Passages: Predictable Crises of Adult Life.* New York: E. P. Dutton, 1974.

Stedry, A. and Key, E. *The Effects of Goal Difficulty on Performance.* Lynn, Mass.: Behavioral Research Service, General Electric Company, 1962.

Super, D. E. *The Psychology of Careers.* New York: Harper & Row, 1957.

Super, D. E. and Bohn, M. J., Jr. *Occupational Psychology*, Belmont, California: Wadsworth, 1970.

Super, D. E., Crites, J., Hummel, R., Moser, H., Overstreet, P., and Warnath, C. *Vocational Development: A Framework for Research*. New York: Teachers College Press, 1957.

Up the ladder, finally. *Business Week,* November 24, 1975, 58–68.

Wanous, J. P. Realistic job previews for organizational recruitment. *Personnel,* 1975, *52,* 50–60.

White, R. W. Motivation reconsidered: The concept of competence. *Psychological Review,* 1959, *66,* 297–323.

SPOT THE WINNER

ANTONY JAY

The cream always rises to the top. This happy domestic metaphor can be a great comfort to good corporation men, and the nearer they are to the top the more comforting they will find it. But not all corporations are milk bottles: Some (if we are to stay in the larder) can be jugs of salad dressing, in which the oil rises to the top and the vinegar stays at the bottom—even if the corporation would be better run by the vinegary executives than by the oily ones. It is, in fact, by no means inevitable that the best men will go to the top of the firm. And even if you pursue the milk metaphor, you will find that cream has another property as well as rising to the top. It also goes sour quickest.

Look inside a great corporation: There are hundreds, maybe thousands, of young or youngish men, who are managers or future managers. Most of them, no doubt, will be reasonably successful but probably only a handful have it in them to be creative leaders; and yet they are the ones on whom the future growth or decay of the corporation will one day depend. It is therefore of the utmost importance to be able to sort out the few potential winners from the greatest mass of intelligent, able, and efficient young men. It is also a great deal harder than it sounds.

The trouble, of course, lies in the numbers. There are so many that the chief executive or members of the board cannot possibly work with them all or get to know them all during their early years, and consequently they depend on the reports they get from the managers they work under. And regrettable as it may seem, the potential leader is often an uncomfortable, and sometimes a disagreeable, subordinate. It is possible that he is of higher caliber than the men he works under, which in itself is hard enough to bear; but he is also unlikely to conceal his perception of this truth, which they find almost unforgivable. When they describe him in formal reports or informal conversations as insolent, egocentric, and argumentative, they are likely to be speaking no less than the truth. They

151

will probably add that he is conceited or arrogant (the difference apparently being that if he thinks he is cleverer than you are, he is conceited, and if he knows he is, he is arrogant). Moreover, if he is already starting to see the corporation as a whole he is likely to question and criticize policies and decisions which have nothing to do with him or indeed with his immediate superiors, and this can be even more irritating since they find it harder to argue on unfamiliar territory. He is also likely to have extreme confidence in his own judgment, and this, while invaluable in a creative leader who needs to stimulate morale and enthusiasm among his team, is not a quality that superiors find endearing.

He is not even likely to be obedient—at least not all the time. He will take his own view about the instructions he receives, and will carry them out if he thinks they are reasonable; but if he thinks they are wrong it will be very difficult to make him comply, and go back and tell his own subordinates to do something which he does not believe in. Of course, this is always a problem for intermediate managers: You try to get a bad decision altered, fail, and then have to pass it on to your subordinates. Do you, out of loyalty to the organization, support the decision and let them think you are as stupid as all the rest of them? Or do you sell your superiors down the river, say they are a bunch of buffoons but nothing will convince them of their error, and retain the respect of those you have to lead? In the services it is somehow easier: You call them into your office, bark out, "C.O.'s instructions: All latrine doors to be painted in diagonal stripes of lilac and vermilion," and they salute and march off to the paint stores. Nobody says anything, but everybody understands. Perhaps you can get away with it in a totally repressive, autocratically run firm, but most firms allow a certain freedom of speech. What does the manager do then? His superiors are in no doubt: Having made his representations to them, he then accepts their decision and passes it on with all his personal authority behind it; when the outburst comes, he simply says "I'm sorry, but there are a great many other factors which you don't know about; I know it seems wrong, but you must take my word that it is the best decision in view of all the other considerations," or words to that effect. Alas, the embryo creative leader cannot be trusted to do the honorable thing. He is quite likely to tell his subordinates exactly what he thinks. Indeed he has probably already expressed his general opinions about what ought to be done so decisively that even if he said nothing they would know exactly what he thought.

The central dilemma is that in a junior management position there is only a certain amount of credit and good will that a man can get, and the more he gets from below the less he gets from above. If he does everything his superiors ask, and accepts all their rulings without demur, those superiors are likely to think him a first-class chap; but his subordinates, who find all their requests refused, their ideas rejected without discussion, rival departments growing at their expense, other people getting better facilities and more pay for less responsibility will think him a feeble, time-serving *apparatchik.* Conversely, if he quarrels with every unwelcome ruling, presses vigorously and repeatedly for extra scope and pay for his subordinates, and never takes no for an answer, then while his subordinates will think him splendid his superiors will find him a thorn in their flesh. And it seems to be characteristic of the creative leader that his personal loyalties are downward and not upward. His first loyalty is to his own ideas, his second to the people who he believes will help him realize them. Both these take a far higher priority than his superiors. Nor is he particularly loyal to the corporation as such; in so far as it enables him to achieve his objectives, he accepts and approves of it, but if it requires him to set his objectives on one side, to work as one member of a big team who are all working toward someone else's objective, then he is likely to lose interest and patience. The Prussian civil service lost a potentially excellent recruit for this reason: Bismarck explained the reason for his resignation (in his early twenties) in a letter to a cousin:

> Affairs and official service are utterly uncongenial to me; I should not think myself fortunate to become an official or even a minister of State; I deem it quite as respectable to grow corn as to write despatches, and in certain circumstances as more useful; I have more inclination to command than to obey. These are facts for which I can give no reason beyond my own tastes. . . . A Prussian official is like a player in an orchestra. No matter whether he be the first violin or the triangle, . . . he has to play his instrument as the needs of the concerted piece dictate. . . . But for my part, I want to play music such as I regard as good—or else not play at all.

Clearly a young graduate recruit to the corporation who makes it clear that he intends to play such music as he regards as good, or else not play at all, is not likely to get the best personal report of his group. Equally clearly, not many of his temperament would have turned out to be Bismarcks; but if none of them get through then the possibility of finding any potential Bismarcks is excluded.

Another reason why the potential creative leader is likely to antagonize his superiors is that he is, almost by definition, a bad courtier. One of the constant preoccupations of courtiers is to try and be identified with all successful projects and no unsuccessful ones. Much of their time and ingenuity is spent hedging bets, devising forms of words which will cover them against all eventualities ("Other things being equal, this should work out well—so long as we can be sure that other things will stay equal"). If the enterprise fails, you will find they all advised against it, tried to stop it, warned that this would happen; if it succeeds, you will equally find that each of them was the one behind it from the

start, the one who tilted the balance in its favor, the one who stuck by it when others were weakening. The creative leader is not good at this game: He will have expressed himself far too forcibly on one side or the other from the start, and while if it succeeds he will be one of the many to share the credit, if he fails he will be the only one left with the blame.

Another not very appealing characteristic of the creative leader is that he does not assume that his superiors will make the right decision on questions he refers to them. From time to time, therefore, he will make decisions on his own initiative because he suspects that if he refers them to his superiors, they will decide wrongly. Alternatively he will somehow manage not to see a memo giving him instructions he does not want to follow. "Turning a blind eye" has come to mean deliberately not noticing the misdemeanors of subordinates, but at the Battle of Copenhagen, where the phrase originated, Nelson was the subordinate going out on a limb, ignoring the instruction to break off the engagement issued by Sir Hyde Parker, his superior officer, and risking the most almighty row if he had failed. There is no defense in the event of failure in such a situation, and only grudging forgiveness for success, so it takes considerable self-confidence or a very steady nerve. Even if he turns out to have saved his superiors from disaster, they will not think it was the most lovable way to do it.

For all these reasons, there is a danger that the few potential creative leaders may not rise like cream but be kept down like vinegar—which indeed they resemble more closely. It is only too possible that their immediate superiors will dislike and resent them, report adversely on them, and promote the docile, obedient, easy young executives instead. And of course arrogant, egocentric, argumentative behavior is not in itself a guarantee of high potential—the exceptional ability has to be there as well. Rough diamonds can turn out to be rough paste. But it does take considerable wisdom on the part of the senior executive to realize that because this man is difficult to work over, he is not necessarily difficult to work under, and that the unlovable qualities may yet be of greater value to the corporation than the smooth charm of his complaisant contemporaries; and that arrogance, stubbornness, and insubordination are only self-confidence, determination, and initiative with a coating of disapproval. And yet often it is only through his immediate superiors that the top management of the firm receive their reports. It is rather like nurses in a hospital, who are reported on by the ward sister; certainly her report is essential, but there is another additional standard of judgment, namely, the patient's. It is by no means impossible for the best nurse from the patient's point of view to be the worst from the sister's point of view, and vice versa. The sister's ideal may keep everything tidy and sterile, always be swift, efficient, and punctual, and leave the patients frightened, depressed, and unhappy; the other may keep the whole ward cheerful and contented, but give them the wrong drugs from time to time. The point is that both these judgments are relevant, while the former is the only one that will be passed on. In the same way there is often another view of the young creative leader which may never be made known.

The solution adopted by some military commanders—certainly General Horrocks*—is to establish the practice whereby the man directly responsible for the job reports to the commander, the chief executive; not on routine matters, but when there is an emergency, when the pressure is on, or when important plans are being formulated or results analyzed. It may mean only two conversations a week, of fifteen

minutes each, with junior officers or managers, but that is still meeting a hundred a year; and not socially, on good behavior, but operationally, under testing conditions in which lucidity, intelligence, knowledge, judgment, and independence are all called on. Horrocks always invited the man's superior officer to be present if he wished, to show that it was not a going-behind-the-back operation. The advantage is not just a chance for the chief executive to make up his own mind about the quality of the younger managers, but also to get authentic information and appraisals and proposals directly from the man who generated them and not filtered through number of barons and courtiers.

It is harder to know just how the young potential leader himself should behave toward a superior who is likely to block his proposals, reject his ideas, and frustrate his plans. The only practical advice I know of was intended for a rather different situation, namely, what you should do if you are walking in the jungle and you meet a lion. If you turn and run, it will chase you by instinct; if you move toward it and corner it, it will leap at your throat out of fear. What you must do is advance on it steadily and confidently, but make sure to leave it a way out, a line of retreat. Then as you get too near for comfort it will turn around and slink away. In other words, however, bitter his row with his superior, he must always leave him a way open to consent without climbing down: he must keep back a significant fact or an alternative proposal or a reasonable modification until his superior realizes the strength of determinations he is up against, just as Kennedy did in the Cuban missile crisis. Then, when the lion starts to look around for a track through the jungle, the escape route is ready for him to slink down.

*Conversation with the author.

THE GAMESMAN

MICHAEL MACCOBY

*The whole life of an American is passed like a game of chance, a revolutionary crisis, or a battle. As the same causes are continually in operation throughout the country, they ultimately impart an irresistible impulse to the national character.**

Alexis de Tocqueville

Studying Americans in the 1830s, Tocqueville questioned why the American shipping industry was able to navigate at a lower rate than those of the Europeans. The reason was not that they had cheaper ships or paid less for labor. American ships cost almost as much to build as European vessels, and pay for the American sailor was higher. "How does it happen, then, that the Americans sail their vessels at a cheaper rate than we can ours?" Tocqueville asked. "I am of the opinion that the true cause of their superiority must not be sought for in physical advantages, but that it is wholly attributable to moral and intellectual qualities."†

Tocqueville went on to focus on those aspects of the American character that impelled crews to take greater risks and try new methods in order to triumph over competitors, and he saw the American spirit infused by the spirit of a game. Inventiveness, flexibility, and the love of novelty gave America its advantage in an industry where success depended on technology, interdependence, and competitiveness.‡

*Alexis de Tocqueville, *Democracy in America* (New York: Vintage Books, 1958), p. 443.
†*Ibid.,* p. 441.
‡Francis J. Grund, a German visitor around the same time, was also impressed by the spirit of American business:

> There is, probably, no people on earth with whom business constitutes pleasure, and industry amusement, in an equal degree with the inhabitants of the United States of America. Active occupation is not only the principle source of their happiness, and the foundation of their national greatness, but they are absolutely wretched without it, and instead of the *"dolce far niente,"* know but the *horrors* of idleness. Business is the very soul of an American: he pursues it, not as a means of procuring for himself and his family the necessary comforts of life, but as the fountain of all human

During the late nineteenth and early twentieth centuries, although the gamesman streak was never absent from the American character, the gamesman took a minor role in large organizations, which were run by autocratic jungle fighters like Carnegie and Frick. In the organizational world of the 1950s, the gamesman was too independent and irreverent to reach the top of the largest corporations.

But increasingly this trait in the American character has proved adaptive to the changing markets and technology. The modern gamesman fits the leadership needs of organizations based on:

1. Competition—internal, national, international.
2. Innovation—continual creation of new products or projects to gain an advantage over the competition.
3. Interdependent teams—experts who must discover, develop, and market the product.
4. Fast-moving flexibility—the need to meet changing schedules and deadlines, requiring a manager who can motivate a team of craftsmen and company men to move at a faster pace.

These factors also describe modern political teams, which increasingly are also led by gamesmen.

Although most gamesmen have elements of the craftsman, the jungle fighter, and the company man, none of the others shares their unique qualities. Whereas gamesmen increasingly set the organizational style of flexibility, individuality, and risk-taking, other types imitate

them but do not share their zest for this kind of life.

The modern gamesman is best defined as a person who loves change and wants to influence its course. He likes to take calculated risks and is fascinated by technique and new methods. He sees a developing project, human relations, and his own career in terms of options and possibilities, as if they were a game. His character is a collection of near paradoxes understood in terms of its adaptation to the organization requirements. He is cooperative but competitive; detached and playful but compulsively driven to succeed; a team player but a would-be superstar; a team leader but often a rebel against bureaucratic hierarchy; fair and unprejudiced but contemptuous of weakness; tough and dominating but not destructive. Unlike other business types, he is energized to compete not because he wants to build an empire, not for riches, but rather for fame, glory, the exhilaration of running his team and of gaining victories. His main goal is to be known as a winner, and his deepest fear is to be labeled a loser.

The games of business are both sociologically and psychologically different from other forms of play. In early childhood, play has the function of both expressing exuberance and mastering reality in the realm of freedom. In *Beyond the Pleasure Principle,* Freud described an example of an infant making a toy appear and disappear in order to master the recurrent trauma of the mother leaving him.* By the age of six or seven, many children's games, like hide-and-seek, have a new psychological function. They symbolize the struggle with authority, represented by the "it," or central person, who tries to limit the child's freedom. Children must learn to band together to free themselves from the authority. At this time, as Jean Piaget has pointed out, rules of reciprocity develop as an

---

felicity; and shows as much enthusiastic ardor in his application to it as any crusader ever evinced for the conquest of the Holy Land, or the followers of Mohammed for the spreading of the Koran.
　—Francis J. Grund, *The Americans in Their Moral, Social, and Political Relations* (Boston: Marsh, Capen & Lyon, 1837), p. 202.

*Sigmund Freud, *Beyond the Pleasure Principle* (London: Hogarth Press, 1922).

integral part of the game. Fair play becomes a basis for democratic moral judgments.†

As the child grows older, play takes two distinct paths. One is the disciplined development of spontaneous creative activity, which leads to the theological ideal of activity for its own sake, done out of love of beauty and wisdom. Examples are dancing, skiing, sailing, woodworking, etc. The most creative person is the "grave-merry" individual, writes the Jesuit Hugo Rahner, who "kicks the world away from him with the airy grace of a dancer, and yet at the same time, presses it to his heart.‡ In this sense of creativity, the ideal of making work into play is a noble adolescent dream, and we admire the scientists, artists, and craftsmen who come close to making it a reality. Thus, a group of leading American scientists in the middle nineteenth century called themselves the "Lazzaroni," after a society of Italian workmen whose goal was to make work into play.

If in fact scientists or artists fall short of the mark and are sometimes moved by baser motives, at least one can conceive of their work as disciplined play, although often science is in fact a more competitive activity. In the business world, there is less playfulness of this sort; the businessman generally wins at another's expense. In American folklore, Tom Sawyer was a prototypic gamesman-manager who motivated others to do his work for him, manipulating them, but at the same time making the boring work seem enjoyable.

The other type of play is the competitive game, which ranges from friendly tests of skill to warlike extremes of combat, where total aggressiveness is limited only by rules and penalties and the boundaries of time and space. In these games, there are plays, but little creative play carried out in the spirit of freedom. Although big business resembles aggressive-

competitive games in many ways, it cannot be classified as a game, since it is not limited in time and space, and fashions realities that determine our daily life.

Yet business increasingly takes the form of interrelated games—the money game, the marketing game, the R & D game—all requiring specialized players. "What's your game?" has become a substitute for "What do you do?" On the higher levels, the corporate manager must respond to constant challenge having to do with new products, financing, descisions about production, labor costs, etc. Many businessmen can make sense of this crisis-style world only in gamelike metaphors. They will speak of the "game plan," of making "the big play." They will say, "We're going to have to punt now" or "Let's try an end around and see if we can corner a few more yards of the market." They will test out a new man by "giving him the ball and letting him run with it." Indeed, this language is increasingly the vocabulary of corporate business.

In the most dynamic corporations, managerial meetings have a locker-room atmosphere, where discussion of game strategy is punctuated with detached, mildly sadistic humor, employed by the superior to keep the inferior in his place. These little put-downs, which may be deeply resented by craftsmen or dignified company men, can be called "homeopathic doses of humiliation" necessary to maintain a minimum of hierarchy, to show who is boss, without having to humiliate the subordinate definitively by, for example, having him eat in another dining room or calling his boss "Mister Jones" rather than "Jack." Women who have reached top corporate positions have said that getting used to such joking is one of the hardest hurdles. Learning to accept ego punctures without being permanently deflated may be something acquired in team sports, and those who respond best are those who have played team sports seriously and can adopt the gamelike attitude.

†See Jean Piaget, *The Moral Judgment of the Child* (London: Kegan Paul, Trench, Trubner & Co., 1932).
‡Hugo Rahner, *Man at Play* (New York: Herder & Herder, 1967), p. 9.

One female executive on the way up told us how she fought back. Kidded about her short skirts, she put a shapely leg up on the table and asked her challenger whether he saw anything wrong with it. Although such a comeback to a superior is unusual, her gamy spirit won her points from the other gamesmen.

The semiconductor components industry is an example of an industry run by cool and daring gamesmen. Here we find executives who are highly imaginative gamblers. Like the auto parts maker, they sell vast quantities of their product (one company president called them "jellybeans") to relatively few customers, mainly those making computers, TV's, and radios (200 customers account for 70 percent of the business, according to this president). This produces fierce competition and pressure to lower price. Unlike the auto parts industry, here innovative craftsmen are the key to success, since the semiconductor component can be improved through research and development, and the customers can easily test them to determine which is the best for the price. On the basis of the test, customers will buy vast batches or none at all. The top executive must constantly weigh two variables that determine success or disaster. One is the level of design sophistication and the other is the capacity to produce large numbers of components. The overly cautious company man might produce an inferior component too hurriedly in order to have a product to sell, while the more scientifically oriented craftsman, driven by the hope of creating the ultimate design, might hold off developing production facilities until too late.

A spirit of intense competition for high stakes pervades the whole industry and is experienced on all levels. I asked the president of one semiconductor company what kind of people succeeded at this work and he said, "The competition is fierce; it's unbelievable. It has attracted an enormous number of bright people, but it's like Truman's kitchen, there are many dropouts and crack-ups."

It is common knowledge in the electronics industry that the components people are a special breed of gamesman. As if they did not have enough excitement at work, they tend to enjoy playing poker or tennis, games in which they beat others by capitalizing on their weaknesses. And they discuss one another in "game" terms, measuring their opponents as John Kennedy probably did when he saw himself up against Khrushchev or Castro. They say, "He tends to bluff in this kind of situation" or "He's going to think he'll get a scientific advantage here and so he's not going to produce in time, and I'm going to cut in here and zap him."

This spirit exists only in part because the industry is a young one and most of the top people know one another; the small, mass-produced technology and the specialized competitive market intensify it. In computer companies, where product lead times are greater and the customers' decisions are not made solely on the basis of cost and technical performance—programming, servicing, etc., are also important—the nature of the competitive struggle is considerably more relaxed. In some giant companies, the internal competition between project groups may be even greater than that with other companies.

In all the companies we studied, the spirit of competition prevails, sparked by either real survival conditions or by the executives' view of the expanding world market in which the company must either continue to grow or lose its position and eventually its profits. The gamesman's character also feeds competition. Even to enter the world of advanced technology, it is necessary to be competitive. But we have seen that the competitive urge is very different for each of the four character types. The following table summarizes these differences and the meaning of competitive behavior. Each type is motivated or energized differently, the craftsman by interest and pleasure in building and bettering the standard; the jungle fighter by his drive for power over others to escape being

Roots of Competition

Character Type	Craftsman	Jungle Fighter	Company Man	Gamesman
Typical meanings of competition	Drive to build the best Competition vs. self· and the materials	Kill or be killed Dominate or be dominated	Climb or fall Competition as price for secure position	Win or lose Triumph or humiliation
Source of psychic energy for competitive drive	Interest in work, goal of perfection, pleasure in building something better	Lust for power and pleasure in crushing opponent, fear of annihilation Wish to be the only one at the top	Fear of failure, desire for approval by authority	The contest, new plays, new options, pleasure in controlling the play

crushed by them; the company man by fear of failure and wish for approval; and the gamesman by glory and the need to be in control.

The gamesman's emotional attitude has meshed perfectly with the corporation's need for managers who could be turned on by the new technical challenges of the post-sputnik era and who could also excite others. More than any other types, gamesmen told us that the ability to dramatize ideas and to stimulate or activate others were among the most important abilities for their work. Charles L. Hughes, former industrial relations manager of Texas Instruments, wrote a book in the mid-sixties called *Goal Setting.** He pointed out that extensive research showed that the kind of people who were most successful in the high-technology corporation were those "compulsively and habitually seeking to win." Speaking to older-style bosses and organization men who might be put off by the gamesman, Hughes astutely observed an advantage to the corporation in that the compulsive winner's main goal was not to become rich, but to win. For the gamesman, a high salary is important mainly because this is the way the game is scored, and he doesn't want to fall behind the others. He sees his salary not in absolute terms of be-

*Charles L. Hughes, *Goal Setting* (New York: American Management Assn., 1965).

coming rich, but in comparative terms of staying ahead of others in his peer group.

The gamesman is not easily evaluated by traditional moral categories. In contrast to the authoritarian boss of the past, he tends to be unbigoted, nonideological, and liberal. He believes that everybody who is good should be allowed to play, and that race, sex, religion, or anything else has no bearing besides contributing to the team. Nor is he hostile. ("Nastiness and vindictiveness mean that person has already shown himself a loser," one gamesman told us.) Unlike the jungle fighter, he takes no pleasure in another man's defeat. But this does not imply that he is sensitive to others' feelings or sympathetic about their special needs. He is not compassionate, but he is fair. He is open to new ideas, but he lacks convictions.

Since he is so concerned about winning, the gamesman tends to evaluate co-workers almost exclusively in terms of what they can do for the team. Unlike softer or more loyal company men, he is ready to replace a player as soon as he feels that person weakens the team. "The word 'loyalty' is too emotional," said one gamesman, "and empathy or generosity get in the way of work." Nor does he share the jungle fighter's need for accomplices.

Although he may try to spark the "deadwood," the gamesman believes he is being democratic by giving others a "fair" chance to play the game. If a person, due to his background or temperament, never has a fair chance to compete against those gamesmen who are quicker and more driven, that means he belongs to an inferior class. The gamesman tends to classify people as winners or losers.

Many gamesmen operate well while young managers, but fail to resolve middle-age and middle-management crises. The ones who do reach the top are those able to renounce adolescent rebelliousness and become at least to some extent believers in the organization.

The typical gamesman's mid-career crisis exposes the weaknesses in his character. His strengths are those of adolescence; he is playful, industrious, fair, enthusiastic, and open to new ideas. He has the adolescent's yearning for independence and ideals, but the problem of facing his limitations. More dependent on both others and the organization than he admits, the gamesman fears feeling trapped. He wants to maintain an illusion of limitless options, and that limits his capacity for personal intimacy and social commitment.

This is one reason why imaginative gamesmen tend to create a new reality, less limiting than normal, everyday reality. Like many adolescents, they seem to crave a more romantic, fast-paced, semifantasy life, and this need puts them in danger of losing touch with reality and of unconsciously lying. The most successful gamesmen keep this need under control and are able to distinguish between the game and reality, but even so, in boring meetings they sometimes imagine that they are really somewhere else—at a briefing for an air-bombing mission, or in a hideout where the detested manager who is speaking is really a Mafia chieftain whom the games will someday rub out.

Even such a gifted gamesman as Henry Kissinger imagines himself in an unreal, romantic fantasy. Ignoring the fact that he never travels without an entourage of his aides and the press, he tells an interviewer that he is like "the cowboy entering a city or village alone on his horse.

Without even a pistol maybe, because he doesn't go in for shooting."*

At their worst moments gamesmen are unrealistic, manipulative, and compulsive workoholics. Their hyped-up activity hides doubt about who they are and where they are going. Their ability to escape allows them to avoid unpleasant realities. When they let down, they are faced with feelings that make them feel powerless. The most compulsive players must be "turned on," energized by competitive pressures. Deprived of challenge at work, they are bored and slightly depressed. Life is meaningless outside the game, and they tend to sit around watching TV or drinking too much. But once the game is on, once they feel they are in the Super Bowl or one-on-one against another star, they come to life, think hard, and are cool. While other character types found in the corporation, such as the craftsmen or the more security-seeking company men, find such high-pressure competition enervating and counterproductive, for the gamesmen it is the elixir of life.

The gamesmen's yearnings for autonomy and their fear of being controlled contribute to a common midcareer uneasiness. Even the most successful gamesmen feel a kind of self-contempt that they are giving in, that they are performing for others rather than developing their own goals. A number of gamesmen respond ingeniously. Impatient with red tape and unwilling to be boxed in, some try to skirt authority to create their own organizations within the larger company.

Fred Gordon is thirty-six years old and manages four thousand people in a division of a multinational corporation. His goal is to have power. "I experience power," he said, "as not being pushed around by the company; it's a kind of freedom. Also, I can tell others what to do and set the direction and the strategy and the tone." As a young marketing manager,

---

*"Kissinger: Interview," ed. by O. Fallaci, *New Republic*, 167:17–22, December 16, 1972.

Gordon figured out that the way to the top was to get a relationship with a powerful customer to use against the company. "You need a very big customer who is always in trouble and demands changes from the company," he said. "That way you automatically have power in the company, and with the customer too. I like to keep my options open."

Gamesmen like Gordon try to create their own antibureaucratic teams, but in gaining their "autonomy," they may threaten the whole organization. Another such gamesman succeeded in forming his own "semi-autonomous" team, but his superiors complained that he was trying to set up his own barony and was making it more difficult to develop a more rational company-wide policy.

One gamesman near the top of a huge corporation has a recurrent dream in which he is a fugitive being chased by a powerful organization like the FBI or the CIA. But, in the dream, he knows he is secretly working for the organization, although those hunting him do not know it. He is testing the organization, its capacity to catch even the most resourceful individualists. He told me that he would leave the company if he didn't feel he could leave it any time he wished and make a good living elsewhere.

Such gamesmen are unable to resolve the conflict between their wish for total independence and their ambition to run the organizational team, which means satisfying their superiors and developing the team. They may create a successful project and even energize a whole company for a while, but over the long pull, some lack the patience and commitment to people and principles necessary to maintain a dynamic organization.

Bedazzled by the perpetually adolescent charm of the gamesman and sympathetic to his struggle against less attractive bureaucrats, our society romanticizes him. One might say that although we have no heroes because we have lost faith in our leaders, the gamesman is our favorite anti-hero. In the most popular motion picture of 1974, *The Sting,* two playful gamesmen, Johnny Hooker and Henry Gondoroff (played by Robert Redford and Paul Newman), confuse and conquer Doyle Lonnegan, the hated boss of a large gangster organization, dazzling him with a fake reality created by the fast-moving teamwork of many specialists using technology and sleight of hand. Like a modern morality play, *The Sting* presents the gamesman versus the old-style jungle fighter who built the organization. In this modern morality play, boyish and unprejudiced (black and white work together), informal gamesmen have the audience's full support because they are fighting killers. One quickly forgets that they started the trouble by ripping off the organization. Even though the master gamesman, Newman, is shown as bored and hung over when there is no action, one also tends to forget that these "heroes" are amoral, manipulative confidence men, lonely hustlers who drift apart after the game is over.

The fatal danger for gamesmen is to be trapped in perpetual adolescence, never outgrowing the self-centered compulsion to score, never confronting their deep boredom with life when it is not a game, never developing a sense of meaning that requires more of them and allows others to trust them.

An old and tiring gamesman is a pathetic figure, especially after he has lost a few contests, and with them, his confidence. Once his youth, vigor, and even the thrill in winning are lost, he becomes depressed and goalless, questioning the purpose of his life. No longer energized by the team struggle and unable to dedicate himself to something he believes in beyond himself, which might be the corporation or alternatively the larger society, he finds himself starkly alone. His attitude has kept him from deep friendship and intimacy. Nor has he sufficiently developed abilities that would strengthen the self, so that he might gain satisfaction from understanding (science) or creating (invention, art). In contrast to such aging gamesmen, there are seventy-year-old craftsmen whose goal in life is not winning, but making something better, and who are still energetic and interested in new ideas, although retired from the corporation.

Lundberg is now forty-six. Seven years ago, he was on top, the manager of a project that gained great profits for his corporation. He was a winner. Tall and blond, with an air of command, he had come to the company from the air force, where he was a pilot. Speaking of the past, he said, "I never wanted security; I felt we were all good race horses and we'd be allowed to run. I wanted to be part of the winning team. The corporation had begun to take off. It was wide open." Now, he has failed twice, and has been given a staff position with vague responsibilities. His superiors worry about what to do with him. He has become an alcoholic. His conversation was depressed. "I don't fear death now," he said, "but I fear discomfort. Hard knocks grind your ego down. There is a lot of pain there too. We sure had an ego then, partly because we were young."

Mitchell is still at the top at age forty, but is starting to worry about the future. Despite his success, he feels a failure. "I am considering whether all this is worth it. I started thinking about this four or five years ago. Before, I never thought about it. I feel a lack of joy. I don't see where all this is leading to." I asked him whether he felt his life lacked meaning. "Yes, it is running full tilt without direction. I'd like to do something that would make me *happy*. But I'm too lazy to do anything about it. I'd like to go fishing, but I'd probably go crazy in retirement. This environment is continually in a crisis mode. It's all high-speed. You can't talk about trivia. It turns me off when my wife wants to chatter. It's stupid when you think about it; what else can you do but listen."

Those who avoid middle-aged disintegration are the ones who have committed themselves to something beyond just winning games.

At the age of fifty, John Price, a gamesman with a company man's quasi-religious identification with the organization, became chief executive of the corporation where Ron Goodwin had failed to reach the top. Goodwin, we saw, was too idealistic and mild to achieve his aims. Unlike Price, he did not understand the game, its rules and boundaries, strategy and tactics. In his relation to authority, Goodwin was a courtier, while Price was more like a knight who had joined the Round Table.

Price told me his strength was solving problems with others: "I have the ability to participate in a group in a harmonious manner which does not completely sublimate the ego. This is one of the most helpful qualities for a complex business. No one ever knows everything. An executive needs to be able to assess people and to be able to listen to what they say and evaluate it."

In contrast to Goodwin's warmth, enthusiasm, and idealism, the key term to describe Price's personality might be *controlled sensitivity*. Price does not waste a word. He can turn himself off and on. Even when detached, his radarlike sensitivity scans the emotional horizon. Whereas Goodwin believed he could change the world by humanizing the company, Price was convinced that the company already represents the best there is. Although he was modest about his own role, he felt deeply about the company, and his eyes watered when he talked about it. "What is central here," he told me, "is the idea that what we are doing is not only technologically important but socially important. We have a belief that we are inherently the best. We have a belief in excellence to support that. We are all very committed here. We don't see the end of this. The good we produce will probably reach a plateau someday, but we have a commitment to *growth*."

I remarked that there seemed to be a kind of religious feeling among top management, and he said, "There *is* a religious fervor here. It is the belief in what we are doing. We are doing much more than selling soap. We are at the cutting edge of society."

John Price was not opposed to humanizing the corporation or the world, and he respected those who undertook that mission. But it was not his. He was sympathetic to greater employee participation in decision making. "But I've tried very hard to see if there is anything more than rhetoric in this, and I feel it is not very practical except at the very low levels where people should have more of a say in determining how they work."

I asked him what he thought about the other issues that were so important to Goodwin. "A lot of it is very theoretical," he said. "It doesn't recognize the practical problems. Perhaps these issues are really way ahead of their time in relation to our sociological progress. Maybe if we were more affluent, we could worry about the social costs of the products we are making. Today we live in a competitive world."

Yet Price was open to change and was excited by it. He was proud that his sons had opposed the war, that they had sought more exploratory, less routinized education at their Ivy League colleges, and that his wife, a high school teacher, supported women's liberation. He saw the company like himself, responsive to new and reasonable social needs, just as it responded so effectively to changes in consumer demands.

What motivates Price? Not one simple motive. Like other executives, he said he wants a high income and financial independence, but unlike jungle fighters, there are limits to his ambitions, which are republican rather than imperial. He is also motivated by the game itself. Unless there is a contest, he said he gets too relaxed. "Everything is competitive here," he went on, and his Rorschach responses indicated that he is sparked, energized by the competition. He played football in high school and intramural sports in college. He loves puzzles and problem-solving, and welcomes the variety of problems at work. He likes to be where the action is, at the center.

Price is also motivated by the fear of failure.

"I have always felt I must either move up the ladder or quit," he said. Besides the need for constant success, here is another theme common to the gamesman. He wants to believe he could leave if he did not make the top, but he knows he must keep on being promoted to keep his place as a respected member of the company. Unlike the functionary, he is too proud to accept a secure but humble place. His pride is maintained both by the respect of peers and by a sense (or illusion) of independence which compensates for unconscious feelings of being like an insignificant insect or small animal scurrying for food (images expressed by Price on the Rorschach).

I asked another gamesman, a corporate vice-president, to describe himself and he said, "I have a strong need to succeed. And a very strong need to be accepted by people. I feel some insecurity and self-doubt about how competent I am. I want to play the game if I can win and gain respect. If not, you don't want to play that game at all. You'd rather play one you can win." I asked if there was anything more important than winning. "Winning is really not it—it's not the right thing to say. It's really the need for respect from my peers. I'd rather be a highly respected Number Two than a poorly respected Number One." (You gain respect because you execute the plays and you are concerned about the total organization.)

As a child, Price dreamt anxiously of falling off bridges and of being chased, dreams of failure and competition. More recently, he dreamt of a spinning top. He asked me what it might mean, and I suggested that he was like a top which had to stay in constant motion, if he let up and relaxed, he would fall over. He agreed, adding, "I can't even take a vacation."

The dream might symbolize both the gamesman's psychic need for action and the corporation's demand that he keep moving to stay "on top."

Gamesmen like Price, who have reached the very top, take pride in their problem-solving abilities and coolness under stress (control) rather than their power (*machismo*).* They do not try to be glamorous. (In contrast to younger gamesmen on their way up with young and glamorous secretaries, the executive type invariably picks a plain, no-nonsense type.) The more adolescent gamesman still fantasies power and glory, and does not have the company man's belief in the organization. Although his passion to win may be enough to motivate a project team by offering others the chance to be winners with him, it does not serve to direct a giant corporation, to inspire thousands of employees, or to inspire confidence in bankers and large stockholders.

Gamesmen like Price are more independent and aggressive than the company men. I have asked them what they mean when they describe a successful manager as "tough," because while they seem to me detached, they also appear sensitive about hurting anyone's feelings. They lack the jungle fighter's willingess to destroy competitors or even to fire incompetents. (The executives of elite corporations hardly ever fire someone, unless they believe he is harming the company.) The toughness seems to be within the rules of the game. One top executive told me, "A tough guy genuinely induces fear in others. He has an aura of power, of being right. It is a strength of character, a winning attitude. Most people are backed off by it. You experience his inner violence."

Being tough in this sense is necessary to become a winner. Perhaps another reason why executives become tough and even subtly sadistic is because they have to accept constant humiliations. Their toughness is self-protective and their controlled meanness is a form of compensation, to reassure themselves that they have not been totally emasculated by the corporation.

The Rorschach responses of executives suggested that one of their most repressed feelings is humiliation at having to perform for others—from parents and teachers in childhood to the admired superiors at work—to be vulnerable and judged by them no matter how much the corporate policy emphasizes "respect for the individual." For example, on Card II, a corporate vice-president first saw two performing elephants, symbolizing strong and proud animals that have been trained and humbled. His next response was running tears of blood, symbolizing sadness, impotence, powerlessness, followed by rocket exhaust and flames, symbolizing phallic resistance, anger, hardening. He agreed with me that this represented the experience of castration and that it had led to compensatory toughness. Unlike the farmer or craftsman, the manager always remains in some way the schoolboy who is being judged on his performance. In this regard, it is interesting that the executive almost invariably mentions one of his superiors among the people he most admires, even when he complains about the man's treatment of him ("but if he weren't tough, we would not be where we

---

*Dr. Ignacio Millán reports a dream of a Mexican manager of a multinational company in which he attacks a tall, blond European or American chief of the company who is sleeping beside him. In the dream the Mexican takes up a huge hammer. He recalled, "I raise the hammer with both arms, and I strike the head of the stranger with all my strength. Despite my tremendous effort, something unbelievable happens. When the hammer reaches his head, it hardly touches him. It only wakes him up. I feel terribly afraid and anguished. The foreigner looks at me steadily and without words orders me to hold his penis. I do it . . . His penis is flaccid. I strike it and his testicles with my fists, again and again. I feel furious and I see they are disintegrating but that there is no blood, and the man keeps on staring at me without showing any pain or emotion."

Besides expressing the repressed fury and humiliation the Mexican feels toward his foreign masters, the dream also revealed his experience of a totally different character type. The Mexican found that the executive's power is in his head. The Mexican's primitive force could not damage this, but only aroused the executive and provoked his retaliation. Forced to submit and humiliate himself, the Mexican tried to fight on a genital, animal level. Maybe he could triumph as a *macho* "Latin lover." But he discovered that the executive did not even need his penis and testicles. The executive could not be hurt at that level, and with this realization the Mexican woke up terrified.

are"). Rather than submit abjectly, he identifies with the aggressor.

Of course, in another sense, so-called "toughness" may really mean the courage to act on one's knowledge, in contrast to the soft-hearted alternative, which merely avoids having to take a stand. For example, a company-man executive saw that one of his managers lacked the technical knowledge and capacity to handle his job. Instead of stepping in right away, putting it straight to the manager and together working out a solution, probably a different assignment, the "nice guy" executive ignored the problem, telling himself he was giving the manager another chance. When the latter inevitably failed, he ended up with a negative report and a painful experience that could have been avoided if the executive had been "tougher."

The gamesman saves himself from the company man's surrender by emphasizing toughness and placing his primary value on fine-tuned self-control. By controlling himself so successfully and maintaining control over the organization, he begins to enjoy control for its own sake. The brain becomes the overwhelmingly dominant organ of potency. Others are judged also on their powers of control. Can they laugh at the hierarchical put-down without taking it personally? Can they take defeat as well as victory without losing their cool? Can they play the game, take the pressure, even when the results are unclear for long periods? Can they sublimate themselves harmoniously when need be and take over to analyze the problem and motivate others when that is needed? Can they communicate clearly? If so, they have succeeded in making themselves valuable and fine-tuned instruments.

Aristotle defined self-control as moderation and balance for the sake of healthy enjoyment of life. "Consequently, the appetitive element of a self-controlled man must be in harmony with the guidance of reason. For the aim of both his appetite and his reason is to do what is noble.

The appetite of a self-controlled man is directed at the right objects, in the right way, and at the right time; and this is what reason prescribes."*

Executive gamesmen would agree with Aristotle, but in their case, control has become as much an end as a means. Their own testimony, confirmed by the Rorschach responses, shows that the cost is dampened passion, emotional castration, and depression. More dependent on the organization than they realize for their life's meaning, their efforts at self-development make them valuable tools for the company. Outside the company, they have little social function or individual purpose. More than anyone else, they have exploited themselves.

John Price is a typical example of the gamesmen we interviewed who are taking over large corporations. Like most of them, he is a first son and Protestant. He attended an elite Ivy League graduate school, although he received his B.A. at a large state university, and he served as an officer in the Navy.

His whole life is organized to further his career.

Like most who reach the top, his wife is, in his terms, "flexible and supportive." He went on to say, "It is very unusual for someone to get ahead in the corporate world if his wife does not support him. They seldom get to the very top. People at the very top generally have very attractive wives who are respected. They are the kind of people others want to emulate."

Usually, the wives of these top executives are as intelligent, as energetic, and as competent at any activity they take on as their husbands are. They also spend time sitting on committees and performing civic duties that enhance both their own image and the corporation's as socially responsible. The most successful marriages are based on mutual respect for accomplishment.

The executive wives we interviewed were

*Aristotle, *Nicomachean Ethics,* (Indianapolis-New York: Bobbs-Merrill, 1962), Book: 3:11, p. 81.

also just as oriented to success as their husbands, although this was not always their view of themselves. In one case, a gamesman executive told me that while he was competitive and analytical, his wife was emotional, compassionate, and intuitive. Later, when he was telling me about their leisure activities, he mentioned tennis. I asked if they played together. "No," he answered with some embarrassment. Remembering that he had been a college quarterback, I was not surprised; she probably was not good enough for him. "No," he corrected me. "She won't play with me. She was nationally ranked." On meeting his wife, I discovered she was every bit as intelligent, analytical, and competitive as her executive husband. Forced to take the time to raise very small children, she was looking forward to when she could develop her own career.

Another executive wife's earliest memory was "I was not allowed to be leader of the line in the first grade and I was totally furious." She, too, saw herself as more oriented to the emotional than her husband, but it was a matter of degree and complementarity. There was enough difference between his tougher, controlled sensitivity and her more spontaneous subjectivity to create an exciting polarity; they both respected each other and enjoyed mutual criticism. Both were leaders who moved inevitably to the top of the organizations they joined. Neither was very sociable; they had few friends and spent most of their time together and with their children (taking trips, playing sports, and competitive games—cards, Monopoly).

The executive wives we interviewed are women who like men. Most of them enjoyed close relationships with fathers who also liked them. Although they support the women's movement for equal rights, they disapprove of the "extremists" who hate men or practice lesbianism. They feel at home in a world dominated by men, and they admire their husbands.

The implicit marital contract between these women and their husbands is to become successful corporate models and to live a gracious, comfortable (though not opulent) life, with opportunities for travel and stimulating contact in the larger world of the successful (scientists, artists, politicians).

In bringing up their children, they encourage those traits and talents that will best prepare them to be winners like their parents. A gamesman executive's wife stated that her "number-one goal is to have a happy home so my husband and children have a springboard for success." Her husband told me that he feels a responsibility to push his children to succeed and achieve. This worked well with an older son who took after his father and was successful in sports, sciences, and school politics, but not with a more receptive, affectionate, and artistic younger son. With him, the father felt powerless and the boy escaped into compulsive eating and TV watching (his father countered by bringing home a TV camera and suggesting his son become a director).

Because this executive could not understand that his son was not motivated by problem-solving and winning, he was ready to conclude that the boy had no motivation. "I worry about him and I fear failure as a father," he told me. "I worry what people will think and what he will think." His wife also worried, but she more wisely decided that the son would be happier in a less performance-oriented culture. She said, "Unfortunately, a family can't be the best environment for all types of children."

The gamesman's attitude and talents fit the needs of the modern corporations, where his character has been developed. The gamesman qualities help him respond to constant changes in markets, methods, and technology. Since he is stimulated by the give-and-take of argument and the challenge of competition, he is less likely than more authoritarian jungle fighters or insecure company men to surround himself with yes men. He enjoys the give-and-take, the cooperative-competitive problem-solving, the trial by combat to assess good ideas and select comers.

So long as the corporation's relative standing

is not threatened, the gamesman chief executive will favor programs that make the corporation more attractive to the brightest young people, and that will likely provide more chance for initiative and individual challenge. But here as elsewhere he will wait to respond to pressures. (One progressive top executive said that he was disappointed that the young engineers and managers entering the corporation in the late sixties did not demand more internal democracy and corporate social responsibility. But since they did not, the pressure for change was minimal.)

The gamesman will not initiate social programs that leave his company in an unfavorable competitive position. Nor will he pass up a chance for a big win in the market. He will trade anywhere he can, whether or not he approves of the regimes. (While older-style ideological managers and labor leaders criticize the Government for détente with the Soviet Union and China that they believe strengthens them and weakens us, the new high-technology executives complain that empty ideology and bureaucratic confusion prevent increased trade, which they maintain will liberalize the Communists.)

The gamesman will pollute the environment, even when he privately supports environmentalists, unless the law is such that each corporation must clean up its mess and none is penalized for being cleaner than the others. He will produce and advertise anything he can sell unless food and drug laws or other legislation stops him.

Even when he believes that the Government spends too much on weapons, he will make them. Even though he values privacy and is outraged by illegal intrusion of the state in the individual's affairs, he will build the technology that makes this possible. (A gamesman told me that his corporation had tried to build a new automated retail store system without hidden TV cameras to check employees as well as customers. Despite his distaste, his corporation had to build in the spying technology to remain competitive.)

But the new type of executive is ready and willing to play by the rules. One told me, "I like the game to be defined. Our main ability is that we know how to win at this game of business. Society can make any rules it wants, as long as they are clear-cut, the same for everyone. We can win at any game society can invent."*

Given our socioeconomic system, with its stimulation of greed, its orientation to control and predictability, its valuation of power and prestige above justice and creative human development, these fair-minded gamesmen may be as good as we can expect from corporate leaders.

*Note the testimony of Dr. C. Lester Hogan, Vice-Chairman of the Board of Fairchild Camera and Instrument Corporation, before the Subcommittee on Multinational Corporations of the Senate Foreign Relations Committee, July 22, 1974, p. 3.

> But Fairchild has found it difficult to obtain a clear understanding of the government's position on the transfer of technology—particularly semiconductor technology—to Eastern Europe. This absence of a clear definition of policy has been especially disappointing to Fairchild in light of its 15-month effort aimed at working with the government on a particular export license application, which was recently denied, involving a proposed transfer of semiconductor technology to Poland for use in consumer products.
>
> In matters of East-West trade, Fairchild has been and remains willing and eager to play by the "rules of the game" as determined by this country's policymakers. But it would certainly like to find out what those rules are.

MAJOR MAJOR MAJOR MAJOR

JOSEPH HELLER

Source: From *Catch 22* by Joseph Heller. Copyright ©
1955, 1961 by Joseph Heller. Reprinted by permission of
Simon & Shuster, a division of Gulf & Western Corporation.

Major Major Major Major had had a difficult time
from the start.

Like Miniver Cheevy, he had been born too
late—exactly thirty-six hours too late for the
physical well-being of his mother, a gentle, ailing woman who, after a full day and a half's
agony in the rigors of childbirth, was depleted
of all resolve to pursue further the argument
over the new child's name. In the hospital corridor, her husband moved ahead with the un-
smiling determination of somone who knew
what he was about. Major Major's father was a
towering, gaunt man in heavy shoes and a
black woolen suit. He filled out the birth certifi-
cate without faltering, betraying no emotion at
all as he handed the completed form to the floor
nurse. The nurse took it from him without comment and padded out of sight. He watched her
go, wondering what she had on underneath.

Back in the ward, he found his wife lying
vanquished beneath the blankets like a desic-
cated old vegetable, wrinkled, dry and white,
her enfeebled tissues absolutely still. Her bed
was at the very end of the ward, near a cracked
window thickened with grime. Rain splashed
from a moiling sky and the day was dreary and
cold. In other parts of the hospital chalky
people with aged, blue lips were dying on time.
The man stood erect beside the bed and gazed
down at the woman a long time.

"I have named the boy Caleb," he announced to her finally in a soft voice. "In accordance with your wishes." The woman made no
answer, and slowly the man smiled. He had
planned it all perfectly, for his wife was asleep
and would never know that he had lied to her as
she lay on her sickbed in the poor ward of the
county hospital.

From this meager beginning had sprung the
ineffectual squadron commander who was now
spending the better part of each working day in
Pianosa forging Washington Irving's name to official documents. Major Major forged diligently
with his left hand to elude identification, insulated against intrusion by his own undesired au-

thority and camouflaged in his false mustache and dark glasses as an additional safeguard against detection by anyone chancing to peer in through the dowdy celluloid window from which some thief had carved out a slice. In between these two low points of his birth and his success lay thirty-one dismal years of loneliness and frustration.

Major Major had been born too late and too mediocre. Some men are born mediocre, some men achieve mediocrity, and some men have mediocrity thrust upon them. With Major Major it had been all three. Even among men lacking all distinction he inevitably stood out as a man lacking more distinction than all the rest, and people who met him were always impressed by how unimpressive he was.

Major Major had three strikes on him from the beginning—his mother, his father and Henry Fonda, to whom he bore a sickly resemblance almost from the moment of his birth. Long before he even suspected who Henry Fonda was, he found himself the subject of unflattering comparisons everywhere he went. Total strangers saw fit to deprecate him, with the result that he was stricken early with a guilty fear of people and an obsequious impulse to apologize to society for the fact that he was not Henry Fonda. It was not an easy task for him to go through life looking something like Henry Fonda, but he never once thought of quitting, having inherited his perseverance from his father, a lanky man with a good sense of humor.

Major Major's father was a sober God-fearing man whose idea of a good job was to lie about his age. He was a long-limbed farmer, a God-fearing, freedom-loving, law-abiding rugged individualist who held that federal aid to anyone but farmers was creeping socialism. He advocated thrift and hard work and disapproved of loose women who turned him down. His speciality was alfalfa, and he made a good thing out of not growing any. The government paid him well for every bushel of alfalfa he did not grow. The more alfalfa he did not grow, the

more money the government gave him, and he spent every penny he didn't earn on new land to increase the amount of alfalfa he did not produce. Major Major's father worked without rest at not growing alfalfa. On long winter evenings he remained indoors and did not mend harness, and he sprang out of bed at the crack of noon every day just to make certain that the chores would not be done. He invested in land wisely and soon was not growing more alfalfa than any other man in the country. Neighbors sought him out for advice on all subjects, for he had made much money and was therefore wise. "As ye sow, so shall ye reap," he counseled one and all, and everyone said, "Amen."

Major Major's father was an outspoken champion of economy in government, provided it did not interfere with the sacred duty of government to pay farmers as much as they could get for all the alfalfa they produced that no one else wanted or for not producing any alfalfa at all. He was a proud and independent man who was opposed to unemployment insurance and never hesitated to whine, whimper, wheedle, and extort for as much as he could get from whomever he could. He was a devout man whose pulpit was everywhere.

"The Lord gave us good farmers two strong hands so that we could take as much as we could grab with both of them," he preached with ardor on the courthouse step or in front of the A & P as he waited for the bad-tempered gum-chewing young cashier he was after to step outside and give him a nasty look. "If the Lord didn't want us to take as much as we could get," he preached, "He wouldn't have given us two good hands to take it with." And the others murmured, "Amen."

Major Major's father had a Calvinist's faith in predestination and could perceive distinctly how everyone's misfortune but his own were expressions of God's will. He smoked cigarettes and drank whiskey, and he thrived on good wit and stimulating intellectual conversation, particularly his own when he was lying about his age or telling that good one about God and his wife's difficulties in delivering Major Major. The good one about God and his wife's difficulties had to do with the fact that it had taken God only six days to produce the whole world, whereas his wife had spent a full day and a half in labor just to produce Major Major. A lesser man might have wavered that day in the hospital corridor, a weaker man might have compromised on such excellent substitutes as Drum Major, Minor Major, Sergeant Major, or C. Sharp Major, but Major Major's father had waited fourteen years for just such an opportunity, and he was not a person to waste it. Major Major's father had a good joke about opportunity. "Opportunity only knocks once in this world," he would say. Major Major's father repeated this good joke at every opportunity.

Being born with a sickly resemblance to Henry Fonda was the first of a long series of practical jokes of which destiny was to make Major Major the unhappy victim throughout his joyless life. Being born Major Major Major was the second. The fact that he had been born Major Major Major was a secret known only to his father. Not until Major Major was enrolling in kindergarten was the discovery of his real name made, and then the effects were disastrous. The news killed his mother, who just lost her will to live and wasted away and died, which was just fine with his father, who had decided to marry the bad-tempered girl at the A & P if he had to and who had not been optimistic about his chances of getting his wife off the land without paying her some money or flogging her.

On Major Major himself the consequences were only slightly less severe. It was a harsh and stunning realization that was forced upon him at so tender an age, the realization that he was not, as he had always been led to believe, Caleb Major, but instead was some total stranger named Major Major Major about whom he knew absolutely nothing and about whom nobody else had ever heard before. What

playmates he had withdrew from him and never returned, disposed, as they were, to distrust all strangers, especially one who had already deceived them by pretending to be someone they had known for years. Nobody would have anything to do with him. He began to drop things and to trip. He had a shy and hopeful manner in each new contact, and he was always disappointed. Because he needed a friend so desperately, he never found one. He grew awkwardly into a tall, strange, dreamy boy with fragile eyes and a very delicate mouth whose tentative, groping smile collapsed instantly into hurt disorder at every fresh rebuff.

He was polite to his elders, who disliked him. Whatever his elders told him to do, he did. They told him to look before he leaped, and he always looked before he leaped. They told him never to put off until the next day what he could do the day before, and he never did. He was told to honor his father and his mother, and he honored his father and his mother. He was told that he should not kill, and he did not kill, until he got into the Army. Then he was told to kill, and he killed. He turned the other cheek on every occasion and always did unto others exactly as he would have had others do unto him. When he gave to charity, his left hand never knew what his right hand was doing. He never once took the name of the Lord his God in vain, committed adultery, or coveted his neighbor's ass. In fact, he loved his neighbor and never even bore false witness against him. Major Major's elders disliked him because he was such a flagrant nonconformist.

Since he had nothing better to do well in, he did well in school. At the state university he took his studies so seriously that he was suspected by the homosexuals of being a Communist and suspected by the Communists of being a homosexual. He majored in English history, which was a mistake.

"*English* history!" roared the silver-maned senior Senator from his state indignantly. "What's the matter with American history?

American history is as good as any history in the world!''

Major Major switched immediately to American literature, but not before the F.B.I. had opened a file on him. There were six people and a Scotch terrier inhabiting the remote farmhouse Major Major called home, and five of them and the Scotch terrier turned out to be agents for the F.B.I. Soon they had enough derogatory information on Major Major to do whatever they wanted to with him. The only thing they could find to do with him, however, was take him into the Army as a private and make him a major four days later so that Congressmen with nothing else on their minds could go trotting back and forth through the streets of Washington, D.C., chanting, ''Who promoted Major Major? Who promoted Major Major?''

Actually, Major Major had been promoted by an I.B.M. machine with a sense of humor almost as keen as his father's. When war broke out, he was still docile and compliant. They told him to enlist and he enlisted. They told him to apply for aviation cadet training, and he applied for aviation cadet training, and the very next night found himself standing barefoot in icy mud at three o'clock in the morning before a tough and belligerent sergeant from the Southwest who told them he could beat hell out of any man in his outfit and was ready to prove it. The recruits in his squadron had all been shaken roughly awake only minutes before by the sergeant's corporals and told to assemble in front of the administration tent. It was still raining on Major Major. They fell into ranks in the civilian clothes they had brought into the Army with them three days before. Those who had lingered to put shoes and socks on were sent back to their cold, wet, dark tents to remove them, and they were all barefoot in the mud as the sergeant ran his stony eyes over their faces and told them he could beat hell out of any man in his outfit. No one was inclined to dispute him.

Major Major's unexpected promotion to major the next day plunged the belligerent sergeant into a bottomless gloom, for he was no longer able to boast that he could beat hell out of any man in his outfit. He brooded for hours in his tent like Saul, receiving no visitors, while his elite guard of corporals stood discouraged watch outside. At three o'clock in the morning he found his solution, and Major Major and the other recruits were again shaken roughly awake and ordered to assemble barefoot in the drizzly glare of the administration tent, where the sergeant was already waiting, his fists clenched on his hips cockily, so eager to speak that he could hardly wait for them to arrive.

''Me and Major Major,'' he boasted, in the same tough, clipped tones of the night before, ''can beat hell out of any man in my outfit.''

The officers in the base took action on the Major Major problem later that same day. How could they cope with a major like Major Major? To demean him personally would be to demean all other officers of equal or lesser rank. To treat him with courtesy, on the other hand, was unthinkable. Fortunately, Major Major had applied for aviation cadet training. Orders transferring him away were sent to the mimeograph room late in the afternoon and at three o'clock in the morning Major Major was again shaken roughly awake, bidden Godspeed by the sergeant and placed aboard a plane heading west.

Lieutenant Scheisskopf turned white as a sheet when Major Major reported to him in California with bare feet and mud-caked toes. Major Major had taken it for granted that he was being shaken roughly awake again to stand barefoot in the mud and had left his shoes and socks in the tent. The civilian clothing in which he reported for duty to Lieutenant Scheisskopf was rumpled and dirty. Lieutenant Scheisskopf, who had not yet made his reputation as a parader, shuddered violently at the picture Major Major would make marching barefoot in his squadron that coming Sunday.

''Go to the hospital quickly'' he mumbled, when he had recovered sufficiently to speak, "and tell them you're sick. Stay their until your allowance for uniforms catches up with you and you have some money to buy some clothes. And some shoes. Buy some shoes."

"Yes, sir."

"I don't think you have to call me 'sir,' sir," Lieutenant Scheisskopf pointed out. "You outrank me."

"Yes, sir. I may outrank you, sir, but you're still my commanding officer."

"Yes, sir, that's right," Lieutenant Scheisskopf agreed. "You may outrank me, sir, but I'm still your commanding officer. So you better do what I tell you, sir, or you'll get into trouble. Go to the hospital and tell them you're sick, sir. Stay there until your uniform allowance catches up with you and you have some money to buy some uniforms."

"Yes, sir."

"And some shoes, sir. Buy some shoes the first chance you get, sir."

"Yes, sir. I will, sir."

"Thank you, sir."

Life in cadet school for Major Major was no different than life had been for him all along. Whoever he was with always wanted him to be with someone else. His instructors gave him preferred treatment at every stage in order to push him along quickly and be rid of him. In almost no time he had his pilot's wings and found himself overseas, where things began suddenly to improve. All his life, Major Major had longed for but one thing, to be absorbed, and in Pianosa, for a while, he finally was. Rank meant little to the men on combat duty, and relations between officers and enlisted men were relaxed and informal. Men whose names he didn't even know said "Hi" and invited him to go swimming or play basketball. His ripest hours were spent in the day-long basketball games no one gave a damn about winning. Score was never kept, and the number of players might vary from one to thirty-five. Major Major had never played basketball or any other game before, but his great, bobbing height and rapturous enthusiasm helped make up for his innate clumsiness and lack of experience. Major Major found true happiness there on the lopsided basketball court with the officers and enlisted men who were almost his friends. If there were no winners, there were no losers, and Major Major enjoyed every gamboling moment right up till the day Colonel Cathcart roared up in his jeep after Major Duluth was killed and made it impossible for him ever to enjoy playing basketball there again.

"You're the new squadron commander," Colonel Cathcart had shouted rudely across the railroad ditch to him. "But don't think it means anything, becuase it doesn't. All it means is that you're the new squadron commander."

Colonel Cathcart had nursed an implacable grudge against Major Major for a long time. A superfluous major on his rolls meant an untidy table of organization and gave ammunition to the men at Twenty-seventh Air Force Headquarters who Colonel Cathcart was positive were his enemies and rivals. Colonel Cathcart had been praying for just some stroke of good luck, like Major Duluth's death. He had been plagued by one extra major; he now had an opening for one major. He appointed Major Major squadron commander and roared away in his jeep as abruptly as he had come.

For Major Major, it meant the end of the game. His face flushed with discomfort, and he was rooted to the spot in disbelief as the rain clouds gathered about him again. When he turned to his teammates, he encountered a reef of curious, reflective faces all gazing at him woodenly with morose and inscrutable animosity. He shivered with shame. When the game resumed, it was not good any longer. When he dribbled, no one tried to stop him; when he called for a pass, whoever had the ball passed it; and when he missed a basket, no one raced him for the rebound. The only voice was his own. The next day was the same, and the day after that he did not come back.

Almost on cue, everyone in the squadron

stopped talking to him and started staring at him. He walked through life self-conscious with downcast eyes and burning cheeks, the object of contempt, envy, suspicion, resentment and malicious innuendo everywhere he went. People who had hardly noticed his resemblance to Henry Fonda before now never ceased discussing it, and there were even those who hinted sinisterly that Major Major had been elevated to squadron commander because he resembled Henry Fonda. Captain Black, who had aspired to the position himself, maintained that Major Major really was Henry Fonda but was too chickenshit to admit it.

Major Major floundered bewilderedly from one embarrassing catastrophe to another. Without consulting him, Sergeant Towser had his belongings moved into the roomy trailer Major Duluth had occupied alone, and when Major Major came rushing breathlessly into the orderly room to report the theft of his things, the young corporal there scared him half out of his wits by leaping to his feet and shouting *"Attention!"* the moment he appeared. Major Major snapped to attention with all the rest in the orderly room, wondering what important personage had entered behind him. Minutes passed in rigid silence, and the whole lot of them might have stood there at attention till doomsday if Major Danby had not dropped by from Group to congratulate Major Major twenty minutes later and put them all at ease.

Major Major fared even more lamentably at the mess hall, where Milo, his face fluttery with smiles, was waiting to usher him proudly to a small table he had set up in front and decorated with an embroidered tablecloth and a nosegay of posies in a pink cut-glass vase. Major Major hung back with horror, but he was not bold enough to resist with all the others watching. Even Havemeyer had lifted his head from his plate to gape at him with his heavy, pendulous jaw. Major Major submitted meekly to Milo's tugging and cowered in disgrace at his private table throughout the whole meal. The food was

ashes in his mouth, but he swallowed every mouthful rather than risk offending any of the men connected with its preparation. Alone with Milo later, Major Major felt protest stir for the first time and said he would prefer to continue eating with the other officers. Milo told him it wouldn't work.

"I don't see what there is to work," Major Major argued. "Nothing ever happened before."

"You were never the squadron commander before."

"Major Duluth was the squadron commander and he always ate at the same table with the rest of the men."

"It was different with Major Duluth, sir."

"In what way was it different with Major Duluth?"

"I wish you wouldn't ask me that, sir," said Milo.

"Is it because I look like Henry Fonda?" Major Major mustered the courage to demand.

"Some people say you *are* Henry Fonda," Milo answered.

"Well, I'm not Henry Fonda," Major Major exclaimed, in a voice quavering with exasperation. "And I don't look the least bit like him. And even if I do look like Henry Fonda, what difference does that make?"

"It doesn't make any difference. That's what I'm trying to tell you, sir. It's just not the same with you as it was with Major Duluth."

And it just wasn't the same, for when Major Major, at the next meal, stepped from the food counter to sit with the others at the regular tables, he was frozen in his tracks by the impenetrable wall of antagonism thrown up by their faces and stood petrified with his tray quivering in his hands until Milo glided forward wordlessly to rescue him, by leading him tamely to his private table. Major Major gave up after that and always ate at his table alone with his back to the others. He was certain they resented him because he seemed too good to eat with them now that he was squadron commander. There was never any conversation in the mess tent when Major Major was present. He was conscious that other officers tried to avoid eating at the same time, and everyone was greatly relieved when he stopped coming there altogether and began taking his meals in his trailer.

Major Major began forging Washington Irving's name to official documents the day after the first C.I.D. man showed up to interrogate him about somebody at the hospital who had been doing it and gave him the idea. He had been bored and dissatisfied in his new position. He had been made squadron commander but had no idea what he was supposed to do as squadron commander, unless all he was supposed to do was forge Washington Irving's name to official documents and listen to the isolated clinks and thumps of Major —— de Coverley's horeshoes falling to the ground outside the window of his small office in the rear of the orderly-room tent. He was hounded incessantly by an impression of vital duties left unfulfilled and waited in vain for his responsibilities to overtake him. He seldom went out unless it was absolutely necessary, for he could not get used to being stared at. Occasionally, the monotony was broken by some officer or enlisted man Sergeant Towser referred to him on some matter that Major Major was unable to cope with and referred right back to Sergeant Towser for sensible disposition. Whatever he was supposed to get done as squadron commander apparently was getting done without any assistance from him. He grew moody and depressed. At times he thought seriously of going with all his sorrows to see the chaplain, but the chaplain seemed so overburdened with miseries of his own that Major Major shrank from adding to his troubles. Besides, he was not quite sure if chaplains were for squadron commanders.

He had never been quite sure about Major —— de Coverley, either, who, when he was not away renting apartments or kidnapping foreign laborers, had nothing more pressing to do than pitch horseshoes. Major Major often paid strict attention to the horseshoes falling softly against the earth or riding down around the small steel pegs in the ground. He peeked out at Major —— de Coverley for hours and marveled that someone so august had nothing more important to do. He was often tempted to join Major —— de Coverley, but pitching horseshoes all day long seemed almost as dull as signing "Major Major Major" to official documents, and Major —— de Coverley's countenance was so forbidding that Major Major was in awe of approaching him.

Major Major wondered about his relationship to Major —— de Coverley and about Major —— de Coverley's relationship to him. He knew that Major —— de Coverley was his executive officer, but he did not know what that meant, and he could not decide whether in Major —— de Coverley he was blessed with a lenient superior or cursed with a delinquent subordinate. He did not want to ask Sergeant Towser, of whom he was secretly afraid, and there was no one else he could ask, least of all Major —— de Coverley. Few people ever dared approach Major —— de Coverley about anything and the only officer foolish enough to pitch one of his horsehoes was stricken the very next day with the worst case of Pianosan crud that Gus or Wes or even Doc Daneeka had ever seen or even heard about. Everyone was positive the disease had been inflicted upon the poor officer in retribution by Major —— de Coverley, although no one was sure how.

Most of the official documents that came to Major Major's desk did not concern him at all. The vast majority consisted of allusions to prior communications which Major Major had never seen or heard of. There was never any need to look them up, for the instructions were invariably to disregard. In the space of a single productive minute, therefore, he might endorse twenty separate documents each advising him to pay absolutely no attention to any of the others. From General Peckem's office on the mainland came prolix bulletins each day headed by such cheery homilies as "Procrastination is the Thief of Time" and "Cleanliness is Next to Godliness."

General Peckem's communications about cleanliness and procrastination made Major Major feel like a filthy procrastinator, and he always got those out of the way as quickly as he could. The only official documents that interested him were those occasional ones pertaining to the unfortunate second lieutenant who had been killed on the mission over Orvieto less than two hours after he arrived on Pianosa and whose partly unpacked belongings were still in Yossarian's tent. Since the unfortuante lieutenant had reported to the operations tent instead of to the orderly room, Sergeant Towser had decided that it would be safest to report him as never having reported to the squadron at all, and the occasional documents relating to him dealt with the fact that he seemed to have vanished into thin air, which, in one way, was exactly what did happen to him. In the long run, Major Major was grateful for the official documents that came to his desk, for sitting in his office signing them all day long was a lot better than sitting in his office all day long not signing them. They gave him something to do.

Inevitably, every document he signed came back with a fresh page added for a new signature by him after intervals of from two to ten days. They were always much thicker than formerly, for in between the sheet bearing his last endorsement and the sheet added for his new endorsement were the sheets bearing the most recent endorsements of all the other officers in scattered locations who were also occupied in signing their names to that same official document. Major Major grew despondent as he watched simple communications swell prodigiously into huge manuscripts. No matter how many times he signed one, it always came back for still another signature, and he began to despair of ever being free of any of them. One day—it was the day after the C.I.D. man's first visit—Major Major signed Washington Irving's name to one of the documents instead of his own, just to see how it would feel. He liked it. He liked it so much that for the rest of that afternoon he did the same with all the official documents. It was an act of impulsive frivolity and rebellion for which he knew afterward he would be punished severely. The next morning he entered his office in trepidation and waited to see what would happen. Nothing happened.

He had sinned, and it was good, for none of the documents on which he had signed Washington Irving's name ever came back. Here, at last, was progress, and Major Major threw himself into his new career with uninhibited gusto. Signing Washington Irving's name to official documents was not much of a career, perhaps, for it was less monotonous than signing "Major Major Major." When Washington Irving did grow monotonous, he could reverse the order and sign Irving Washington until that grew monotonous. And he *was* getting something done, for none of the documents signed with either of these names ever came back to the squadron.

1. At what stage are you in your own career cycle? Can you recognize in your own cycle the four stages discussed by Hall and Morgan?

2. Why do you think that the mid-career crisis for managers has been described as male menopause? Have you known anyone who has undergone this big career crisis?

3. Do you believe that Jay is right that the potential creative leader could be so resented by a superior that he is kept from being promoted?

4. According to Michael Maccoby in the *Gamesmen,* part of the success in an organization is due to being able to take risks and also to bring attention to oneself in a positive manner. How do you separate risk-taking from ability? Do you believe that a person who is a bigger risk-taker tends to end up at the head of a corporation or do you believe that ability accounts for a person's success?

5. In this chapter we have discussed the importance of ability, risk-taking, creativity, and luck. In the article by Heller, for example, luck seems to be a major reason for Major Major Major's success. How much in real life do you think is due to luck in organizations?

6. It turns out that Major Major Major was very bored in his job and therefore started doing things in order to increase his arousal level. Do you believe that middle-level managers as well as blue collar employees can have job boredom problems?

CHAPTER VI
THE NONUPWARD MOBILES: ARE THEY SECOND CLASS CITIZENS?

ORGANIZATIONAL SHOCKS

- Because of the low self-image nonupward mobiles receive from their job settings, they tend to identify more with activities outside the organization than activities within the organization.
- Nonupward mobiles often have no opportunity for escape from their jobs.
- Being entrapped by the organization in a nonupward, dependent job causes high group cohesiveness among workers who share a common fate. These employees often adopt through withdrawal, withholding performance, or sabotage.

As briefly mentioned in the last chapter, most of the theories of organizational behavior motivation are based on the assumption of potential for upward mobility. Unfortunately, these theories are of limited use to people who are not upward mobile, that is, people who have flat career curves, in a Hall and Morgan sense. Partly this is because their expectations are not long-term expectations and, in many cases, their self-image is not completely tied to the organization. Often they have had to base their self-image on their family, their friends, and their social activities, since these activities give them the greatest chance for improvement and development. Also it is partly because in a social context we tend to pigeonhole people according to the jobs they possess. For this reason, the blue collar and nonupward mobile white collar employees are typically placed in a different social status than are upward mobile professional, technical, and managerial employees.

These differences can be seen in the selection of readings in this chapter. For example, in the first reading by Joanne Greenberg called "Rites of Passage", we see how a man who wanted to share food with those on welfare is treated by state employees. Notice that he is treated by these employees based on the way he is dressed and appears. They automatically assume that he is there to receive welfare rather than to relieve the needs of those who are on welfare. Also notice how inflexible the bureaucratic system is and think back to the readings by Frost and others.

The second article by David Jenkins points out an interesting but controversial point. One of the major problems with the nonupward mobile employee is that the individual employee has no feeling of ownership toward the product produced or the service being offered. Many workers experience a real shock when they realize there is little chance for escape. This is shown not only in the article by David Jenkins but again in the exposé by Rick King. One of the results apparently of being trapped in a boring, repetitive job from which there is little chance to escape is the group cohesiveness that forms among workers who share a common fate. Employees in many cases learn to adapt by psychologically withdrawing, through sabotage, and through other means.

RITES OF PASSAGE

JOANNE GREENBERG

It was a bright green day. Big trees on the side streets were raining seeds and the wind stirred in its second sleep. A long flatbed truck came rattling down one of the streets and stopped by the new steel, chrome, and glass building. The building's lines were so "functional" it made Cephas wonder if anyone actually worked in it. Then he saw some women going in. Good.

He checked his appearance by hitching up to the rearview mirror. He was wearing a clean white shirt and a bow tie and his thin gray hair had been slicked down with water. When he was sure he was presentable, he got down out of the cab of the truck, dusted himself off, and began to walk slowly toward the building.

It had been many years, perhaps they had moved. No, there was the sign: BOONE COUNTY DEPARTMENT OF PUBLIC WELFARE. The last time he had been here the building had been a temporary shed and people had been lined up outside waiting for the relief trucks to come. That had been in 1934 in the winter. His father had been proud of holding out until '34.

Cephas stopped and looked at the building again. Some secretaries came out, laughing and talking. They didn't look at him, being used to seeing people who came hesitantly to their offices to acknowledge failure in life.

Cephas checked himself again in the big glass door and then went in. There was a large booth with a woman behind it and eight or nine rows of benches facing it. People were sitting quietly, staring at nothing waiting. To the right there were a series of chutes with numbers over them. Cephas went up to the booth.

"Take a number," the woman said without looking at him.

"Ma'am?"

"You take a number and wait your turn. We'll call you."

He took one of the plastic number cards. It said 15. He sat down and waited.

"Five," the woman called. A heavy woman got up slowly and went to the booth and then to one of the chutes.

179

Cephas waited. Minutes were born, ripened, aged, and died without issue.

"Number six." Around him the springtime asthmatics whistled and gasped in their season. He looked at the cracks in his fingers.

"Number seven." An hour went by, another. He was afraid to go out and check his truck lest the line speed up and he lose his place.

"Number thirteen," the woman called. . . .

They came to his number at last and he went up to the desk, gave back the plastic card, and was directed to his chute. Another woman was there at another desk. She took his name, Cephas Ribble, and his age, sixty-eight.

Had he been given aid before?

Yes.

Had he been on General Assistance, Aid to the Needy, Disabled or Tuberculosis Aid?

"It was what they called Relief."

"But under what category was it?"

"It was for people that was off their farms or else didn't have nothin' to eat. They called it goin' on the county.' It was back in nineteen and thirty-four. We held out 'till thirty-four."

"I see. . . . Now you are applying for the old-age pension?"

He said he wasn't.

"Are you married, Mr. Ribble?" She sighed.

"Never had the pleasure," he said.

"Are you without funds, in emergency status?"

He said he wasn't.

"Then take this card and go to Room Eleven, to your left." She pressed a little light or something and he felt the people shifting their weight behind him. Number 16, he supposed. He made his way to Room Eleven.

The lady there was nice; he could see it right off. She told him about the different requirements for what they called "Aid," and then she had him sign some forms: permission to inquire into his bank account, acceptance of surplus or donated food, release of medical information,

and several others. Then she said sympathetically, "In what way are you disabled?"

He thought about all the ways a man might be disabled and checked each one off. It was a proud moment, a man sixty-eight without one thing in the world to complain of in his health.

"I ain't disabled no way. I am pleased you asked me, though. A man don't take time to be grateful for things like his health. If the shoe don't pinch, you don't take notice, do you?" He sat back, contented. Then he realized that the sun was getting hotter, and what with everything in the truck, he'd better get on.

The woman had put down her ball-point pen. "Mr. Ribble, if you aren't disabled or without funds, what kind of aid do you want?" A shadow of irritation crossed her face.

"No aid at all," he said. "It's about somethin' different." He tried to hold down his excitement. This was his special day, a day for which he had waited for over a decade, but it was no use bragging and playing the boy, so he said no more.

The woman was very annoyed. "Then why didn't you tell the worker at the desk?"

"She didn't give me no chance, ma'am, an' neither did that other lady. I bet you don't have many repair men comin' in here to fix things— not above once, anyway except them gets paid by the hour."

"Well, Mr. Ribble, what is it you want?" She heard the noise of co-workers leaving or returning on their cofffee breaks. She sighed and began to drum her fingers, but Cephas wasn't aware of her impatience. He was beginning back in 1934. Good God, she thought, he's senile. She knew that she would have to listen to all of it in his time, in his way.

"Thirty-four cleaned us out—cleaned us bare. You wonder how *farmers* could go hungry. I don't know, but we did. After the drought hit, there was nothin' to do but come to town an' sign up on the County. Twice a month my pa would come in an' bring back food. Sometimes

I came with him. I seen them lines of hungry men just standin' out there like they was pole-axed an' hadn't fallen yet. I tell you, them days was pitiful, *pitiful.* He glanced at her and then smiled. "I'm glad to see you done good since—a new buildin' an' all. Yes, you come right up." He looked around with approval at the progress they had made.

"Mr. Ribble. . . .?"

He returned. "See, we taken the Relief, but we never got to tell nobody the good it done for us. After that year, things got a little better, and soon we was on toward bein' a payin' farm again. In forty-six we built us a new house—every convenience—an' in fifty-two we got some of them automated units for cattle care. Two years ago we dug out of debt, an' last year, I knew it was time to think about my plan for real. It was time to thank the Welfare."

"Mr. Ribble, thanks are not necessary—_____"

"Don't you mind, ma'am, you just get your men an' come with me."

"I beg your pardon. . . ."

"I don't just talk, ma'am. I act. You just bring your men."

Mr. Morrissey had come back from his coffee break and was standing in the hall.

The woman signaled him with her eyes as she followed Cephas Ribble, now walking proud and sure out the door to this truck. Mr. Morrissey sighed and followed, wondering why he was always around when somebody needed to make a madness plain. Why did it never happen to McFarland?

Cephas reached into his pocket and both of the welfare people thought *Gun.* He took out a piece of paper and turned to them as they stood transfixed and pale, thinking of death. "I got it all here, all of what's in the truck. Get your men, ma'am, no use wastin' time. It's all in the truck and if it don't get unloaded soon, it's gonna spoil."

"What is this *about,* Mr. Ribble?"

"My gift, ma'am, my donation. I'm giving the Relief four hundred chickens, thirty barrels of tomatoes, thirty barrels of apricots—I figured, for variety. Don't you think the apricots was a good idea—ten barrels Eyetalian beans, six firkins of butter. . . . Ma'am, you better get the chickens out—it don't do to keep 'em in the sun. I thought about milk, so I give two cans—that's a hundred gallons of milk in case there's hungry babies."

They were dumbfounded. Cephas could see that. He wanted to tell them that it wasn't a case of trying to be big. He'd figured that everybody gave when they could. He'd even signed a form right there in the office about promising to accept donated food and clothing. Their amazement at his gift embarrassed him. Then he realized that it was probably the only way they could thank him—by making a fuss. People on the State payroll must have to walk a pretty narrow line. They'd have to be on the lookout for people taking advantage. That was it. It was deep work, that Welfare—mighty deep work.

"What are we supposed to do with all that food?" Mr. Morrissey asked.

Cephas knew that the man was just making sure that it wasn't a bribe. "Why, give it to the poor. Call 'em in and let 'em get it. You can have your men unload it right now, an' I'd do it quick if I was you. Like I said, it won't be long 'till it starts to turn in all this heat."

Mr. Morrissey tried to explain that modern welfare methods were different than those in 1934. Even then, the food had been U.S. surplus, not privately donated. It had come from government warehouses.

Cephas spoke of the stupidity and waste of Government in Farming, and rained invective on the Soil Bank.

Mr. Morrissey tried again to make his point. "We don't *give* out any food. There hasn't been any food *donated* since nineteen sixteen!"

No doubt of it, these Welfare people had to

be awful careful. Cephas nodded. "The others do what they can—don't blame 'em if it don't seem like much," he said sympathetically. "I signed that slip in there about the donated food, so there must be a lot of donated food."

"It's an old law," Morrissey argued tiredly. "It's one of the old Poor Laws that never got taken off the books."

" 'An here you folks are followin' it, right to-day," Cephas mused. "It must make you mighty proud."

"Mr. Ribble, *we have no place to store all this!*"

Cephas found his throat tightening with happiness. He had come in humility, waited all morning just so he could show his small gratitude and be gone, and everyone was thunderstruck at the plenty. "Mister," he said. "I pay my taxes without complainin', but I never knowed how hard you people was workin' for your money. You got to guard against every kind of bribes an' invitations to break the law; you got to find ways to get this food to the poor people so fast, you can't even store it! By God, Mister, you make me proud to be an American!"

A policeman had stopped by the truck and was tranquilly writing a ticket. Cephas excused himself modestly and strode off to defend his situation. The two Welfare workers stood staring after him as he engaged the officer.

It was, after all, State Law that food could be donated. Were there no loading camps, no men attending them? Had the department no parking place for donors? The policeman began to look at the two stunned bearers of the State's trust. He had stopped writing.

"Could that truck fit in the workers' parking lot?" Morrissey murmured.

"What are we going to do with it all?" Mrs. Traphagen whimpered.

"All those chickens—four hundred chickens!"

Mrs. Traphagen sighed. "The poor will never stand for it."

"First things first." Mr. Morrissey decided, and he went to confront the policeman.

Cephas' truck in the workers' parking lot blocked all their cars. As a consequence, the aid applications of eight families were held pending investigation. Six discharged inmates of the State hospital remained incarcerated for a week longer pending home checkups. Thirty-seven women washed floors and children's faces in the expectation of home visits which did not come about. A Veneral Disease meeting at the Midtown Hotel was one speaker short, and high-school students who had been scheduled to hear a lecture entitled "Social Work, Career of Tomorrow," remained unedified. Applicants who came to apply for aid that afternoon were turned away. There was no trade in little plastic cards and the hive of offices were empty. But the people of the Boone County Department of Public Welfare were not idle. It was only that the action had moved from the desks and files and chutes to the workers' parking lot and into the hands of its glad tyrant, Cephas Ribble.

All afternoon Cephas lifted huge baskets of apricots and tomatoes into the arms of the Welfare workers. All afternoon they went from his truck to their cars, carrying baskets, or with chickens festooned limply over their arms. When they complained to Mr. Unger, the head of the department, he waved them off. Were they to go to every home and deliver the food? He said he didn't care—they were to get rid of it. Were big families to get the same amount as small families? He said that the stuff was political dynamite and that all he wanted was to be rid of it before anybody noticed.

Cephas, from the back of his flat-bed, was a titan. He lifted, smiling and loaded with a strong hand. He never stopped to rest or take a drink. The truck steamed in the hot spring light, but he was living at height, unbothered by the heat, or the closeness, or the increasing rankness of his chickens. Of course he saw that the Welfare people weren't dressed for loading food. They were dressed for church, looked like. It was deep work, very deep, working for the State. You had to set a good example. You had to dress up and talk very educated so as to give the poor a moral uplift. You had to be honest. A poor man could lie; Cephas had been poor himself, so he knew, but it must be a torment to deal with people free to lie and not be able to do it yourself.

By three thirty the truck had been unloaded and Cephas was free to go home and take up his daily life again. He shook hands with the director and the case-work supervisor, the head bookkeeper and the statistician. To them he presented his itemized list, with weights carefully noted and items given the market value as of yesterday, in case they needed it for their records. Then he carefully turned the truck out of the parking lot, waved good-bye to the sweating group, nosed into the sluggish mass of afternoon traffic, and began to head home.

A cacophony of high-pitched voices erupted in the lot behind him.

"I've got three mothers of drop-outs to visit!"

"What am I going to *do* with all this stuff?"

"Who do we give this to?. ... My people won't take the Lady Bountiful bit!"

"Does it count on their food allowance? Do we go down Vandalia and hand out apricots to every kid we see?"

"I don't have the time!"

"Which families get it?"

"Do we take the value off next month's check?"

"It's hopeless to try to distribute this fairly." the supervisor said.

"It will cost us close to a thousand dollars to distribute it at all," the statistician said.

"It would cost us close to two thousand dollars to alter next month's checks," the bookkeeper said, "and the law specifies that we

have to take extra income-in-kind off the monthly allowance."

"If I were you," the director said, "I would take all this home and eat it, and not let anyone know about it."

"Mr. Morrissey!" Mrs. Traphagen's face paled away the red of her exertion, "that is fraud! You know as well as I do what would happen if it got out that we had diverted Welfare Commodities to our own use! Can you imagine what the Major would say? The Governor? The State Department of Health? The HEW, The National Association of Social Workers?!" She had begun to tremble and the two chickens that were hanging limply over her arm nodded to each other with slow decrum, their eyes closed righteously against the thought.

Cars began to clot the exit of the parking lot. The air was redolent.

But many of the workers didn't take the food home. The wolf of hunger was patient in shadowing the poor, even in summer, even on Welfare. As the afternoon wore on, apricots began to appear in the hands of children from Sixteenth and Vandala Street all the way to the Boulevard. Tomatoes flamed briefly on the windowsills of the Negro ghetto between Fourteenth and Kirk, and on one block, there was a chicken in every pot.

The complaints began early the next day. Sixteen Negroes called the Major's Committee on Racial Harmony, claiming that chickens, fruit, and vegetables had been given to the White Disadvantaged, while they had received tomatoes, half of them rotten. A rumor began that the food had been impregnated with contraceptive medicine to test on the poor and that three people had died from it. The Health Department denied this, but its word was not believed.

There were eighteen calls at the Department of Welfare protesting a tomato fight which had taken place on Fourteenth and Vandala, in which passers-by had been pelted with tomatoes. The callers demanded that the families of those involved be stricken from the Welfare roles as Relief cheaters, encouraging waste and damaging the moral fiber of working people.

Eighteen mothers on the Aid to Dependent Children program picketed the Governor's mansion, carrying placards that read: *Hope, Not Handouts* and *Jobs, Not Charity.*

Sixty-eight welfare clients called to say that they had received no food at all and demanded equal service. When they heard that the Vandalia Street mothers were picketing, a group of them went down as counter-pickets. Words were exchanged between the two groups and a riot ensued in which sixteen people were hospitalized for injuries, including six members of the city's riot squad. Seven of the leaders were arrested and jailed pending investigation. The FBI was called into the case in the evening to ascertain if the riot was Communist-inspired.

At ten o'clock the Mayor appeared on TV with a plea for reason and patience. He stated that the riot was a reflection of the general decline in American morals and a lack of respect for the law. He ordered a six-man commission to be set up to hear testimony and make recommendations. A political opponent demanded a thorough investigation of the county Welfare System, the War on Poverty, and the local university's radicals.

The following day, Mrs. Traphagen was unable to go to work at the Welfare office, having been badly scalded on the hand while canning a bushel of apricots.

Cephas Ribble remembered everyone at the Welfare Office in his prayers. After work, he would think about the day he had spent in the city, and of his various triumphs, the surprise and wonder on the faces of the workers, the open awe of the lady who had said, "You don't need to thank us." How everyone had dropped the work they were doing, and ran to unload the truck. It had been a wonderful day. He had given his plenty unto the poor, the plenty and nourishment of his own farm. He rose refreshed to do his work, marveling at the meaning and grandeur with which his chores were suddenly invested.

"By God," he said, as he checked the chickens and noted their need for more calcium in the feed, "a man has his good to do. I'm gonna do it every year. I'm gonna have a day for the poor. Yessir, every year." And he smiled genially on the chickens, the outbuildings, and the ripening fields of a generous land.

WORK—IT WILL MAKE YOU UGLY

DAVID JENKINS

If we seek more precise information on just what is wrong with work under industrial capitalism, there is an abundance of discouraging data provided by critics.

The most penetrating commentary is still that of Karl Marx. His special contribution was the concept of "alienation" of the worker under industrial capitalism.

It should be emphasized that the notion of alienation need not merely be a vague and indefinable feeling of discontent (a "rather general *Weltschmertz*," as one Marxist philosopher derisively describes some writing on the subject). There is a good deal of discussion about the alienation of various groups in society, as if it were a kind of mysterious epidemic that might strike at any time and for which there is no known cure, but the alienation of the worker is quite tangible.

According to Marx, the capitalist "appropriates" the result of the worker's labor, and therefore "the worker is related to the *product* of his labor as to an alien object." The worker is also, in part because of the division of labor under industrialism, alienated from the work and, eventually, from life: "In his work . . . he does not affirm himself but denies himself, does not feel content but unhappy, does not develop freely his physical and mental energy but mortifies his body and ruins his mind. The worker . . . is at home when he is not working, and when he is working he is not at home. His labor is therefore not voluntary, but coerced; it is *forced labor*. It is therefore not the satisfaction of a need; it is merely a *means* to satisfy needs external to it. Its alien character emerges clearly in the fact that as soon as no physical or other compulsion exists, labor is shunned like the plague."

Marx believed that alienation derived directly from the existence of private property, and that "the emancipation of the workers" could only occur with "the emancipation of society from private property." The logical connection was so tight, he argued, that "the overthrow of the existing state of society by the communist revolution . . . and the abolition of private property" would automatically bring about "the liberation of each single individual."

Marx's analysis breaks down at this critical point: the importance of ownership. Numerous studies have shown that the average employee is relatively untroubled by the fact that his company may or may not be owned by absentee landlords (and is largely uninterested in the question). Moreover, experience in both the East and the West indicates that a shift in ownership from private to state (or vice versa) or even to a labor union has no automatic connection with a decrease in alienation. Some of the most spectacular labor disputes in, for example, France, Britain, and Sweden have occurred at state-owned enterprises. This does not mean that ownership cannot have, under special circumstances, an importance to the workers, but the connection is by no means necessary.

Nevertheless, Marx's recognition of the basic problem, and many of his observations were, and still are, perceptive. For example, he considered the possibility of combating alienation through raising workers' wages. He erred in thinking that this was impossible under capitalism (an "anomaly," he said), but he was correct in predicting that, if by some chance it could occur, it would not alone restore to the worker his "human status and dignity"—a view that has been amply confirmed by the premium-priced but nonetheless dehumanizing methods of scientific management.

Modern investigations of alienation support in part the outlines of Marx's thought. Robert Blauner, in his book *Alienation and Freedom,* offers a definition based on recent sociological studies: "Alienation exists when workers are unable to control their immediate work processes, to develop a sense of purpose and function which connects their jobs to the overall organization of production, to belong to integrated industrial communities, and when they fail to become involved in the activity of work as

a mode of personal self-expression." He isolates four ingredients of alienation: (1) powerlessness (regarding ownership of the enterprise, general management policies, employment conditions, and the immediate work process); (2) meaninglessness (with respect to the character of the product worked on as well as the scope of the product or the production process); (3) isolation (the social aspect of work); and (4) self-estrangement ("depersonalized detachment," including boredom, which can lead to "absence of personal growth").

As thus broken down, alienation is inherent in industrial capitalism and its customary concomitants—pyramidal, bureaucratic management patterns and advanced, Taylorized technology, which divide and subdivide work into minute, monotonous elements.

This breaking up of work into tiny subtasks is more or less involved in all of Blauner's categories of alienation and has received considerable attention by other students of the subject. French social philosopher Georges Friedmann's aptly titled book *Le Travail en Miettes* (literally, "work in crumbs") analyzed in detail the effects of such work. Adam Smith saw quite early the "stupidity and ignorance" produced in workers by the first efforts along this line; Marx, in turn, attacked the "stupidity, cretinism" generated by the system.

As Friedmann shows, the progress of compartmentalization of work has been steady, and has long since reached alarming proportions. He cites, as a rather tame example, but all the more appalling for that, a wine-bottling facility where one worker "whose job is, all day long, all week long, all year long, to place on the bottle a label. . . . But she only places it on the neck. It is one of her colleagues, her neighbor on the line, who glues it down." As he points out, such work is designed for "mental cripples."

It is not only philosophers and sociologists who have noticed the grimness of this type of work; workers themselves are painfully aware of the problems. The context most famous for its creation of alienating work conditions is the assembly line—and especially the automobile assembly line. Its fame is understandable, since it contains all the worst and most degrading aspects of modern work. It is completely authoritarian; few of the jobs require any intelligence whatever; the average worker has virtually no freedom to make even the smallest decision of his own; most see only a small part of the total production process (in many assembly-line operations, workers have scarcely any idea of what they are working on); the work is deadening because it is split up into tiny elements and because the worker is completely subjected to the machine. It is in automobile plants that the money-instrumental attitude to work has reached its highest refinement (it is no accident that auto workers are, in most countries, among the highest paid of any group possessing comparable low-level skills).

No doubt few auto workers have read Marx, and thus might not be supposed to know that they are alienated, but the overwhelming majority of them dislike intensely the repetitive, boring nature of their jobs—in the Walker and Guest study, *The Man on the Assembly Line,* about 90 percent—and the relatively high wages, though welcome, do not make the work any easier to bear. Moreover, their spontaneous comments confirm their alertness to the defects of their Sisyphus-like work: "The assembly line is no place to work, I can tell you. There is nothing more discouraging than having a barrel beside you with 10,000 bolts in it and using them all up. Then you get another barrel with another 10,000 bolts, and you know that every one of those 10,000 bolts has to be picked up and put in exactly the same place as the last 10,000 bolts." "It's not a matter of pace. It's the monotony. It's not good for you to get so bored. I do the same thing day after day; it's just an everlasting grind." "The job gets so sickening—day in and day out plugging in ignition wires. I get through with one motor, turn

around, and there's another motor staring me in the face. It's sickening." Almost all the workers interviewed in the Walker and Guest study wanted to transfer to other jobs, not to improve their "economic or social status," but to "get away from the line." The most sought-after jobs were those involving challenge, variety, and some intelligence, such as those of maintenance man and "utility man" (a worker who fills in wherever needed and who thus must learn a multitude of jobs).

But for most workers, there are few chances for escape. Despite the pleasant Horatio Alger mythology in American business, the average worker's chances of rising into management ranks are almost nil. There is a widespread dream of setting up one's own business, but there is also a widespread consciousness that it is only a dream: "If I could be my own boss," remarked one worker, "or work myself up to that position, I'd leave. Otherwise, I might as well stay where I am." Walker and Guest stress the all-pervasive character of the line: "This is one of the most important effects of mass production methods of industrial organization. . . . The immediate world of the auto assembler is the factor. It is still becoming possible to rise in that world and even out of it, but each year it is becoming more difficult."

Or, as the French philosopher Simone Weil described the impact on a worker: "From one day to the next, he becomes a mere supplement to the machine, a little less than a 'thing.' . . . Most workers at this moment in their lives experience the feeling of no longer existing."

One critical fact in all this is often overlooked: Rigidly authoritarian work environments not only affect an individual's attitude toward his job; they can also poison his entire life. As a student poster displayed in Paris during the 1968 revolt put it with admirable conciseness: "Work—It Will Make You Ugly."

Work is by far the dominant activity in most people's lives, and it would be surprising if it did not have a profound influence on one's entire existence. Workers subjected to the modern industrial-capitalist world tend to become "stupid and ignorant" not only on the job, but off it as well.

Various aspects of this situation have been apparent for some time. In 1927, B. Zeigarnik investigated the deleterious effects of the sub-division of work into small units where each worker performs only a part of the task and none has an over-all view of the whole. Zeigarnik compared reactions of workers to jobs that they carried through to fulfillment with others on which they performed only a part. He found that, when asked to describe the tasks, the workers remembered the interrupted jobs about twice as fast as the others. Friedmann comments: "When a task is completed, it is easy to forget. On the other hand, when it is not completed, it weighs on the mind and can even derange one's mentality." A Swedish survey on the subject concludes: "Work which gives limited opportunities for independent control, meaningfulness, and self-actualization tend to lead to weaker and more passive behavior in other contexts of life as well—such as social relations, involvement in social activities, and the like."

Further light is shed by Arthur Kornhauser's study in the 1950s of the mental health of auto workers. Mental health, as defined by Kornhauser, is "an overall balanced relationship to the world which permits a person to maintain realistic, positive belief in himself and his purposeful activities," which he breaks down into six components: manifest anxiety, self-esteem, hostility, sociability and friendship, over-all satisfaction with life, and personal morale.

Kornhauser found a striking correlation between the type of job held and the individual's mental health. The impact of repetitive, non-skilled jobs is unmistakable. When the jobs are classified in a descending scale, ranging from highly skilled to unskilled, the workers holding these jobs tend to rank on a downward-sloping mental health pattern. The lowest-grade workers rate lowest on the scale of mental health, and they have fewer friends and have less satisfactory family relationships. On the other hand, those with higher mental health "resort less to passive, 'escapist' activities like television . . . and drinking at bars; and they devote more time to reading."

This poisonous character of low-grade work was observed some years ago by Georges Friedmann, who noted that assembly line work tended to disorient workers outside of work, "to stimulate aggressive impulses, through which the personality seeks to assert itself in a brutal manner in the use of stimulants of all sorts—gambling, alcohol, habits of conspicuous consumption, brutal amusements such as 'stock cars' and mass spectacles of so-called 'sports' such as boxing, wrestling, and horror and crime films." Stanley Parker, a British sociologist, found that persons more involved in their jobs, as shown by their opportunities to use many of their abilities in their work, were more likely to belong to outside organizations than those who used few of their abilities (78 percent against 57 percent) and also were more apt to spend free time reading or studying (25 percent against 9 percent). He concludes: "Non-involvement in work seems more likely to discourage than to facilitate involvement in leisure."

It is not only personal life and social relationships that suffer from dehumanizing work patterns, but also workers' views of society as a whole, which become warped and degraded. Among Kornhauser's more disturbing findings was a general antisocial attitude among industrial workers. They were seen to possess markedly primitive attitudes toward racial integration and to harbor great admiration for strict authority. And workers in low-grade jobs tended to be especially outstanding on these points.

In today's world, we have been so thoroughly indoctrinated with the money-instrumental attitude toward work—that an adequate wage has top priority and that the work itself is not supposed to make any real sense—that there is a constant, automatic effort to repress any feelings that might conflict with these principles. It scarcely ever occurs to us to question the mind-killing nature of monotonous, authoritarian work environments. That does not mean the feelings do not exist; they are there, just below the surface. In probing to learn workers' real attitudes, Kornhauser (and other researchers) found that by far the most important aspect of a job for most workers was the opportunity it provided to use one's thinking powers. Despite everything, a deeply rooted anti-authoritarianism survives throughout long years of repression in a harshly authoritarian structure. The brainwashing is so complete that workers almost never voluntarily mentioned this subject in discussing their jobs, yet many showed immediate enthusiasm when it was brought to their attention. Other job characteristics—pay, job security, and physical working conditions (which have traditionally received, and still do receive, the main attention of both management and labor)—were outranked by the opportunity the work offers for "use of the worker's abilities and for associated feelings of interest, sense of accomplishment, personal growth, and self-respect." The chance for the worker to use his own abilities is precisely the feature that has been carefully filtered out of most jobs.

It is worth pointing out that there are parallels between the alienation suffered by industrial workers and mental states that are generally considered to be more alarming. The detachment of the worker form his work is similar to the detachment in the schizoid condition described by R. D. Laing. The individual subjected to the strain of "a threatening experience from which there is no physical escape" develops an elaborate protective mechanism, "he becomes a mental observer, who looks on, detached and impassive, at what his body is doing or what is being done to his body." For that person, "the world is a prison without bars, a concentration camp without barbed wire." Instead of experiencing reality directly, he develops a "false" self as a buffer for the real world, while the real self retires to an "inner" position of unexposed safety. All of life seems full of "futility, meaninglessness, and purposelessness," since it is not, in fact, being directly experienced. The real self is completely blocked, barred from any spontaneous expressions or real freedom of action, and totally sterile. "In the absence of a spontaneous natural, creative relationship with the world which is free from anxiety, the 'inner self' thus develops an overall sense of inner impoverishment, which is expressed in complaints of the emptiness, deadness, coldness, dryness, impotence, desolation, worthlessness of the inner life.

Laing's description of the depths of the schizoid state at its worst are remarkably similar to the descriptions of industrial capitalist work at its worst.

Though we have been discussing the authoritarian work atmosphere under capitalism, it should be made clear that it is also present in that "other" system, the one in force in the Soviet Union—which the French businessman-philosopher Marcel Loichot terms "monocapitalism," as contrasted to the Western "oligocapitalism."

That is to say, it is present insofar as one is able to judge. According to the original Marxist dogma, alienation was to disappear with the abolition of private ownership of the means of production. This principle has been a bit modified by more recent Soviet Marxists, though the official line still holds that the type of subhuman work we have been discussing is somehow different under the Soviet system. Foreign researchers are not exactly welcome to see for themselves how this works out, and most reports by the Soviets themselves seem suspiciously one-sided. For example, the abolition of the division between intellectual and manual labor is not only claimed to have taken place, but it is even written into law, and official spokesmen are not anxious to dispute the law. E. Kapustin, director of the Moscow Scientific Research Institute for Labor, at a congress on workers' participation held in Geneva in 1970, revealed that workers are not only vigorously participating in management, but his scientific studies "prove the advantages of socialism over capitalism."

Nevertheless, there are grounds for suspecting that work alienation in the Soviet Union is roughly as severe as it is in the West. It could scarcely be otherwise, since the Soviet industrial apparatus has been largely copied from the Western model.

This was not the original idea. In 1917, Lenin said: "It is perfectly possible . . . immediately, within 24 hours after the overthrow of the capitalists and the bureaucrats, to replace them in control of production and distribution, in the business of control of labor and products by the armed workers, by whole people in arms." A central weapon in Lenin's seizure of power was the slogan "all power to the Workers' and Soldiers' Councils," and workers' councils were in fact given full control of factories by a decree shortly after the revolution of November 1917. This did not last long.

Even though the period of "workers' control" was rather brief, many historians argue, as does Olga A. Narkiewicz, that the workers were "in many cases . . . running the nationalized factories quite efficiently." There are a number of documented case histories of factories that prospered under the management of the workers' councils. It is true that over-all industrial production fell, but this was in large part due to the chaos caused by the civil war, raw material shortages, disruption of communications, and deliberate sabotage by the former capitalist owners. Nevertheless, Lenin quickly turned his attention to the liquidation of workers' control. His official reasoning was the claimed inefficiency of the councils, but he was doubtless also conscious of the possible threat to the cen-

tralized state if the councils should grow too strong. In any case, there was no real chance to judge the effectiveness of the councils, since they lasted only about a year. By early 1919 "workers' control" was being replaced by "workers' management," which, in practice, turned out to be only a euphemism for a tightly disciplined militaristic management system.

There was obviously, perhaps because of the general admiration of Western production methods and eagerness to imitate these methods, a "capitalistic" disinclination to believe that workers could accept responsibility or could make any worthwhile contributions in industry. Mrs. Narkiewicz regards the ending of workers' control as a grievous failure to capitalize on the workers' good will, and avers that this failure created lasting antagonism among workers and "contributed in a great measure to the many ills from which Soviet industry suffers even today." By 1918, Lenin was developing a fulsome admiration for Frederick Taylor. Though he described Taylor's scientific management as an example of "the refined brutality of bourgeois exploitation," he also saw it as one of the "up-to-date achievements of capitalism," and urged: "We must organize in Russia the study and teaching of the Taylor system and systematically try it out and adapt it to our own ends." A management "class" was soon under development, differing in no great respect from that in the West.

The mythology has been carefully maintained, however. By the 1930s, according to Friedmann, work that was identical to that done in capitalist countries somehow "took on an entirely different significance and psychological coloration for the Soviet worker, influenced by 'socialist emulation,' working in an enterprise belonging to the collectivity and whose profits he knows go to the collectivity."

But even though it is different, it is the same. A fascinating collection of essays by Soviet work experts illuminates the point. A study by Zdravomsylov and Yadov on attitudes to work produces very much the same results as similar studies made in the West. By far the most important aspect of a job is the degree to which it offers an opportunity to use one's abilities, exercise one's thinking powers, and makes one's own decisions. The authors note: "The employment of one's intellectual facilities in the course of work, regardless of vocational distinctions, was shown to be the prime incentive for the young workers interviewed." So influential is this factor, say the authors, that the main target in education of young workers "should be to give greater play to the worker's initiative." But nowhere is there any indication that this type of work is any more common in the Soviet Union than in capitalist countries, nor that less inspiring types of work have been eliminated in the USSR.

Other essays in the same anthology suggest that a principal concern of work specialists in the USSR is very much the same as those in the West—that is, to further refine authoritarian work environments along Tayloristic lines. D. A. Oshanin, an enthusiastic admirer of Pavlov, calls for more efforts to control the worker's movements and reactions in detail, and thus make him a more efficient appendage to the machine, through carefully controlled stimuli: "The effectiveness of various mental functions, such as perception of signal stimuli of different modalities and sensory characteristics, loudness, brightness, color, shape, etc., could then be taken directly into account by designers of automatic systems."

Scattered evidence indicate that this process is causing troubles very similar to those in the West. One report described a group of highly educated young people in a Krasnoyarsk engine repair shop. They were complaining about, among other things, the petty autocracy of the foreman, who refused to give them any scope for developing new ideas. Because of the rapid growth in the numbers of trained people planned for the future, the report observes: "Situations like this are likely to become more

and more typical," and it cites an ominous warning from *Izvestia* that the managers were "clashing with the spirit of the times, and this spirit you can neither sack nor remove to another job."

At the moment, the USSR would seem to be marked by an extremely authoritarian work philosophy. Work historian Reinhard Bendix wrote a few years ago regarding the head of an enterprise: "The authority of the Director is absolute within the enterprise. He is charged with responsibility for the fulfillment of the plan and he is given the powers necessary to accomplish that end."

And developments do not seem to be for the better. A new labor law put into effect in the USSR in July 1970 (replacing the one from 1922) spells out in great detail the autocratic structure that is to prevail. It lays down as a central principle an admonition lifted from St. Paul: "He who does not work, neither shall he eat."

The main objective of work, according to the law, is "promoting labor productivity, efficiency in social production." The means for achieving this end is "strengthening labor discipline, gradually transforming labor for the common weal into the prime vital need of each able-bodied citizen." One of the fifteen chapters of the law is devoted to this subject, specifying, among other things, "it is the duty of the factory workers and office employees to work honestly and conscientiously to observe labor discipline, to carry out the orders of the administration promptly and accurately, to raise labor productivity, to improve the quality of the products, observe the requirements of the production techniques. . . ." Although workers who follow these strict rules stand a chance of getting a bonus or even a "listing in the Book of Honor or the Roll of Honor," there is nothing in the law about efforts to eliminate alienation or the promotion of employee participation in management. It may be true, as E. Kapustin claims, that working conditions in the USSR "prove the advantages of socialism over capitalism," but the evidence is not especially convincing.

Despite all the gloomy evidence of the effects of work under modern conditions, it is important to realize that not all jobs in a single industry are alike and that not all industries are alike. In this respect, Robert Blauner's analysis of conditions in four different industries is illuminating. The industries are: printing (a close cousin to traditional crafts), textiles (a highly mechanized, "machine-tending" industry), automobiles (the hard-driving, fast-paced assembly line), and chemicals (representing the newer, highly automated process industries).

Printing is characterized by a "nonalienating relation" to work, largely because the workers have a large degree of control over their own work. They use their skills and their intelligence to a high degree, make many of their own decisions, and they suffer to a minimum from interference by petty superiors. Interestingly enough, this unusual state of affairs is in large part the creation of a powerful union, which has taken care to preserve the almost "medieval" freedom of the workers. Blauner comments: "When work provides opportunities for control, meaning, and self-expression, it becomes an end in itself, rather than simply a means to live. For printers . . . satisfactions are largely intrinsic, related to the nature of the work itself, rather than extrinsic, or concerned with aspects of the job beyond the actual work."

In the textile industry, the situation is precisely the opposite. Despite the obvious presence of "objectively alienating conditions" in an industry marked by "organizational backwardness," the actual presence of alienation is minimal. This is strictly attributable to extrinsic factors—a low educational level, a high percentage of women workers (whose main interest is outside work), and tightly knit social patterns connecting the community to the work place. Moreover, Blauner observes: "The

traditional-oriented workers in the industry have few aspirations for work with control, challenge, and growth potential, and are therefore not greatly frustrated by the absence of these qualities."

The worker in the automobile industry, as is apparent from other studies, suffers greatly from alienation—perhaps more so than in any other industry.

When we look at the worker in the chemicals industry, we are confronted with an entirely new phenomenon. The further automatization of production does not lead to a further rise in alienation—quite the contrary. The number of workers employed in a chemical plant is small relative to the capital employed. Their work is neither physically demanding nor precisely paced, and consists primarily of keeping watch on a rather large number of controls. It is thus varied and flexible. In an emergency, it places high demands on quick thinking and ability to react. These workers are mostly nonalienated, and they enjoy a high degree of satisfaction and pride in their work.

The appearance of this type of work—and this type of worker—in the latest phase of industrial capitalism might be regarded as the sure cure for all the ills of alienation.

Indeed, Blauner suggests that the direction of industrial development is to some extent taking care of the problem. He argues that, as the character of industry moves from (1) a traditional craft structure to (2) a medium degree of mechanization to (3) a high degree of automation, the extent of worker alienation traces "a course that could be charted on a graph by means of the inverted U-curve—that is, through a bleak stage of "deskillization" in mechanization and then to a phase of higher demands on intelligence and responsibility in fully automated processes. This type of work, Blauner says, should increase steadily in importance.

But as we veer along this U-curve, a change is taking place. The worker in the chemicals process industry is not the craft worker who is engaged in a free, creative activity. What is required "in place of the *able workman*," Blauner notes, is a *"reliable employee."* Because this worker tends to be "luke-warm to unions and loyal to his employer, the blue-collar employee in the continuous-process industries may be a worker 'organization man' in the making." Many observers would object that this is scarcely progress, the "organization man" being a prominent example of the crushed, conformist individual under industrial capitalism.

And many experts do not agree that this evolution toward non-alienating jobs is at all inevitable as more production processes are automated. Some newly created jobs do call for more alertness and sharper skills, but in many cases the "deskilling" process continues. Paul Blumberg, after examining the evidence, observes: "Those who believe that complex automated machinery demands increased skill of the machine operator have simply not thought the matter through thoroughly."

A major effect of the automating of industry is, of course, the gradual reduction in the percentage of the workforce accounted for by manufacturing employees, and a corresponding growth in the importance of white-collar and other commercial and clerical jobs. It might be thought that such jobs are immune to alienation; this is not so, and is becoming steadily less so. Traditionally, office work is thought of as more elegant and prestigious than blue-collar work, but this belief is largely based on rather hollow status considerations. C. Wright Mills writes: "The alienating conditions of modern work now include the salaried employees as well as the wage-workers. There are few, if any, features of wage-work . . . that do not also characterize at least some white-collar work." Anyone who has ever worked in an office can recognize the familiar gloom described by Theodore Roethke's lines:

I have known the inexorable sadness of pencils,
Neat in their boxes, dolor of pad and paperweight. . . .
Ritual of multigraph, paper-clip, comma,
Endless duplication of lives and objects. . . .

Indeed, some of the most poignant descriptions of work in an overpoweringly authoritative atmosphere have been of office work—ranging from Gogol's timid civil servants and Melville's "Bartleby the Scrivener" to more recent tales of executive suites and gray flannel suits and *New Yorker*-type tales of middle executives in a state of despair.

White-collar and service work environments have been steadily degraded, with the growth of importance of these sectors and the refinement of management techniques, developed primarily for use in manufacturing, applied to other types of work. One report points out: "The scientific management theory has been successful in the entire industrialized world and is being applied today by most managers and industrial engineers, more or less to the letter. It would be a gross error to assume that this management philosophy has become obsolete. . . . Quite the contrary, it appears that scientific management principles, which were originally developed for industrial organizations, are now spreading to all other areas, such as offices, hospitals, and government administrations." One consultant firm active in applying precise work-measurement and work-planning techniques to office work claims to be able to break down office work to their minutest details with the help of "massive tables prepared over the years to calculate 'target times' for performing clerical jobs." Among other things, the tables show "the time it takes to prepare a first-class mailing label (24 seconds) or make a phone call (slightly over 25 seconds to notify someone that a duplicating order is ready) to the time required for a telephone-company draftsman to draw up a street conduit system 1,220 feet long (one hour)."

As a result of the refinements of dehumanizing management techniques, white-collar workers have been rapidly catching up with blue-collar workers in terms of alienation. In a 1969 survey of worker attitudes made by the Survey Research Center at the University of Michigan for the Department of Labor, 13 percent of white-collar workers expressed negative attitudes toward work, not a great deal under the 17 percent figure for blue-collar workers. More significantly, in the under-thirty age groups, the percentage of those in the two groups harboring negative feelings toward work was identical: 24 percent.

And white-collar alienation does not know any upper limits. P. C. Jersild, a Swedish novelist and psychiatrist, has written: "Even a white-collar worker who is pressured to the point of a bleeding ulcer by his boss can feel the threat to his existence—even if the process takes place on a wall-to-wall carpet." Erich Fromm notes: "The managerial elite . . . are just as much appendages of the machines as those whom they command. They are just as alienated, or perhaps more so, just as anxious, or perhaps more so, as the worker in one of their factories." This has, in fact, been empirically confirmed. An astonishing report on "management discontent" published by the American Management Association pinpointed "an increasing condition of alienation" among executives, and three out of four managers polled believed the situation was getting worse. The reasons are identical to those behind the bluecollar discontent: "a decreasing sense of personal reward and personal achievement" arising from "the highly bureaucratic and authoritarian structure" of the modern corporation, preventing the average executive from "making the decisions he feels his position entitles him to make; they are made for him. . . ." So deeply unhappy are managers that 18 percent would consider joining a "managers' union," and this

figure rises to 50 percent in the under-thirty groups. The authors warn of "the possibility of a revolt in the ranks of supervisory and middle management.

Regardless of the fact that many jobs, if not most, are "objectively alienating," according to studies of sociologists and other scientists, the large majority of workers, when asked directly, profess themselves to be satisfied with their work. Is not this fact, observed in numerous studies, rather embarrassing for anyone seeking to stress the importance of alienation?

No.

In the first place, the existence of deep discontent among a sizable minority of the population would seem in itself adequate justification for attacking the problems. In the 1969 study made for the Department of Labor, some 15 percent of workers were found to express "negative attitudes toward work," and the percentage was far higher for some groups; for black workers under thirty it was 37 percent. Though this is a minority of all workers, it would seem a minority of sizable proportions.

In addition, the situation is deteriorating under the pressures of rising education and other influences that work to increase worker aspirations. Einar Thorsrud, a Norwegian work psychologist, explained to me that this was a powerful impetus behind the Norwegian drive for industiral democracy: "We saw that people were getting more and more general education, but 'scientific management' was making jobs more and more simple. Why were we taking the trouble to educate people? It was apparent that something was wrong."

Obviously, the effects of brain-numbing work on a worker without much brains is not especially noticeable. But as the basics change, so do the consequences. This is clearly shown in Blauner's studies. "The more education a person has received," he writes, "the greater the need for control and creativity." He shows that alienation in southern textile mills tends to be lower than one might expect, due to factors of education and other characteristics affecting aspirations: "Because of their relative lack of education and aspiration, southerners are less likely to find routine work monotonous than northerners . . . the question of aspiration is paramount."

This is a critical point in the United States. Though the U.S. educational system is frequently attacked, a larger number of Americans get a good education than is the case in Europe. One British analysis of OECD data concluded that "the really striking difference between the United States and the rest of the world is that more people are better educated on their side of the Atlantic than on ours," and offered this as one reason for the higher U.S. standard of living. In 1965, there were 28.6 university students per 1000 population in the United States—two to three times the figures in European countries.

These rising standards of education are colliding head-on with jobs that are less and less demanding, in increasingly authoritarian climates. Workers are acquiring more and more brainpower and less and less opportunity to use it.

And what might happen to aspirations if the general population should become aware of the fact that work need not be so alienating, that job atmospheres need not be so uniformly poisonous, that there are viable alternatives to strict authoritarianism in work organizations? Up to now, workers have been generally willing to accept the conventional wisdoms about work without too much question. The person who cannot adapt and who suffers every minute of his job in more or less dignified silence is often apt to blame himself for his shortcomings. That work could be, or should be, something other than mere punishment or drudgery is not a possibility that most workers have ever been confronted with, even on the most theoretical level. It would thus hardly ever occur to the average worker to question the natural painfulness of

work. But a low level of aspirations does not mean that work is not having its under-the-surface paralyzing effects. It also does not mean that aspirations will not rise—as they almost certainly will. If and when there appears a general awareness of the tragic wrongs being perpetrated in contemporary work organizations, and of the readily available means for righting the wrongs, the effects could be explosive.

Economic progress is also transforming worker expectations. In the early days of the Industrial Revolution, the money-instrumental view of work was not all that unreasonable, since the desire to stay alive was paramount, and the role of work in helping to achieve that desire outranked any other characteristics it might have had. Obviously, this is no longer true in industrialized countries, and it will doubtless have an increasingly great effect on worker expectations.

The distaste for work is so grave and so widespread that one intriguing question arises quite naturally: is work necessary?

In examining the average man's disdain for work, Freud wrote about the fortunate man who "knows how to heighten sufficiently his capacity for obtaining pleasure from mental and intellectual work. . . . The weak point of this method, however, is that it is not generally applicable; it is only available to the few." Proceeding from this point of view, theorists sometimes speak of a future utopia in which the business of work would be handled by a handful of individuals, while the remainder could be free to enjoy "life"—meaning an absence of work.

But it will very likely be more practical to reform work than to do away with it, as work appears to be a "natural" and, indeed, essential part of life. Peter Drucker has written: "Individual dignity and fulfillment in an industrial society can only be given in and through work." But this does not apply only to industrial societies. A report on the Abkhasians in the

USSR, who make up a society only slightly industrialized, and who commonly live to 120 years and more, notes the great emphasis this culture places on work: "An Abkhasian is never 'retired,' a status unknown in Abkhasian thinking. From the beginning of life until its end, he does what he is capable of doing because both he and those around him consider work vital to life." Evidently, the efforts to provide useful work geared to the physical capacities of individuals is of great benefit: "Both the Soviet medical profession and the Abkhasians agree that their work habits have a great deal to do with their longevity." And, obviously, Americans compare poorly in this respect: "Even as adults, only a small percentage of Americans have the privilege of feeling that their work is essential or important."

Even in other societies, opportunities to work are frequently seized by people who are generally supposed to be not interested in work at all. Philips Lamp in the Netherlands has built production facilities especially designed to provide work to retired persons who do not want to remain idle. In Florence, after the 1966 flood, hundreds of young people, usually assumed to be interested only in pop music and other such amusements, turned up as volunteers to wade through the mud to help repair the damage. In Denmark, in summer "free communities" provided for young people to "do their thing," the authorities take care to provide opportunities for satisfying work, such as restoring Viking towers, which the young people themselves manage.

The most important human need satisfied by work is the need for the creative accomplishment of some task in a relatively free atmosphere, together with some recognition of the accomplishment. As Antoine de St.-Exupéry wrote: "One becomes a man by challenging an obstacle." Or as Adam Smith put it, the worker yearns "to exert his understanding or to exercise his invention in finding out expedients for removing difficulties." In more scientific descriptions, researchers differ somewhat on details, but they agree on the general outlines. For example, the work psychologists Lawler and Hackman specify four elements in jobs which, if all are present, will positively affect job satisfaction as well as quality of performance: variety, autonomy, task identity (the execution of a "whole" piece of work), and feedback (a return of information to the individual on his performance).

These characteristics are not so very different from those of many other human activities. We noted earlier that, in primitive societies, there is no real division between work and leisure, and the perception of work as a separate phenomenon is a relatively recent innovation. If it is practicable to reorganize work to accord more closely with man's needs, it should be possible to break down the sharp division between work and leisure and to see the two as existing along a continuum, both presenting similar, though not necessarily precisely identical, characteristics. Stanley Parker observes that "whether these two spheres need to be as separate as they are for most people today is debatable."

Studied from this point of view, work can be seen to be a more "natural" activity than is sometimes believed. The child psychologist Erik Erikson speaks of "a sense of industry" as a key stage in a child's development: "His ego boundaries include his tools and skills: the work principle teaches him the pleasure of work completion by steady attention and persevering diligence." "Pleasure" may seem an odd word to apply to work, considering work's low repute today, but it is not, in its essentials, all that different from play. The Dutch thinker Huizinga, in his study of play, lists the need to "accomplish" as a central element in play: "all want to achieve something difficult, to succeed, to end a tension." The work-play relation is distorted and obscured, of course, by the grotesque ways in which work is organized. Scott Myers gives a provocative illustration of the distortion in considering the consequences of reorganizing a game of bowling; "Hiding the pins from the bowler by hanging a drape halfway down the alley. . . . Having a 'supervisor' give the bowler an opinion of how well he is doing—along with some 'constructive criticism.' . . . Changing the rules of the game . . . without involving the bowler in the change process, or even telling him why the changes were made. . . . Preventing social interaction among bowlers. . . . Giving most of the credit and recognition to the supervisor for performance of the bowlers under his supervision. . . . Keeping bowlers on the job by threat of job security or by paying them enough money to make the 'time' in the bowling alley worth their while." It would be surprising if a bowling establishment restructured along such lines would enjoy much business, yet this is precisely the way most work organizations are set up—and managers frequently wonder why the interest of employess is at a low level.

The key point would seem to be the way an activity is organized, rather than the type of activity. In the eighteenth century, Elector Max Emanuel of Bavaria, who entertained a strong feeling for the common man, ordered a small lathe constructed for himself, so that he might learn to operate it and thereby acquire an insight into the thought-processes and problems of the ordinary worker. He did in fact develop some facility with the thing, and in time was able to turn out candlesticks and the like with fair skill. But he neglected to realize that his voluntary toil in the sumptuous rococo surroundings of his Nymphenburg Palace could scarcely tell him much about the average worker's feelings. Artistic creation is generally considered to be in its nature nonalienating, but one wonders if the employees of the Douven factory at Leopoldsburg, Belgium—which turns out six thousand handpainted pictures a week on an assembly-line basis—are any less alienated than workers in any other kind of factory. And even the most creative work contains traces of drudgery. Bertrand Russell's *Principia Mathematica* is considered to be one of the great intellectual achievements of all time, yet he recalled that, once he got the basic theories worked out in his head, writing the book was a purely "mechanical job" at which he labored "ten to twelve hours a day for about eight months." And on the other side, washroom attendants and such workers are sometimes found to be astonishingly pleased with their jobs. British industrial psychologist J. A. C. Brown cited the case of a lavatory cleaner who became highly insulted when she was asked to clean ovens—it seems that the lavatory cleaner's job in that particular factory carried especially high status, since the occupant enjoyed a great deal of autonomy and freedom, "had charge of certain materials such as soap and toilet rolls, and had the authority to move out other workers when she considered that they had been talking or smoking too long."

This fact is all the more striking if we consider the automobile industry. There is scarcely an activity more engrossing and attractive to young men than tinkering with automobiles; yet the designers of auto plants have performed the considerable achievement of transforming this fascinating activity into the world's most hated work place. The mother of one of the young rebels at the Lordstown GM plant explained her son's reaction: "One thing, Tony is not lazy. He'll take your car apart and put it together any day. Ever since he's been in high school we haven't had to worry about car trouble. . . . And I'm not lazy either. I love to cook. But supposing they gave me a job just cracking eggs with bowls moving past on a line. Pretty soon I'd get to the point where I'd wish the next egg was rotten just to spoil their whole cake."

One large difficulty with insisting on a terminological division between work and leisure is that they cannot be separated in real life. As we have seen, there is a powerful interaction between the two, and experience in work—both positive and negative—will inevitably and powerfully affect other spheres of a person's life.

This central importance of work is increasingly recognized. David Riesman, when he wrote *The Lonely Crowd* in 1951, theorized that, so rapid was the advance of automation and so hopeless the situation of work, that "the meaning of life" should best be "sought in the creative use of leisure." But he later (1965) changed his mind and declared that work was so central to man's life that it could not be neglected. But neither could it be left in its present state: "What I am asking for now is hardly less than reorganizing work itself so that man can live humanely on as well as off the job."

It thus appears that, for better or worse, work is here to stay—and that we had better make our peace with it.

What, then, should be done about work?

The most obvious answer and the most popular is: nothing. There is a widespread feeling that the problems, if ignored with sufficient intensity, will somehow disappear; that the classes of society involved are not worthy of all that much attention; or that it would be generally fruitless to try to work on such problems. There is a surprisingly common belief that life is inevitably and unavoidably full of suffering—as Sophocles put it: "Not to be born, is past all prizing, best."

Moreover, so immense do the problems appear that some of these observers who have studied them most closely have the most pessimistic views of their susceptibility to cure. Arthur Kornhauser concludes his depressing study of the mental dangers of modern industrial processes with the very frank opinion that, from a practical point of view, nothing much can be done about it. He offers, as his best suggestion, that workers might get more "zest" out of their lives if they were "to join with their fellows in efforts to build a better world."

As it happens, there do exist solutions, and there is overwhelming evidence that they work. And they revolve around a rather simple equation: If the problems arise mainly from an excessively authoritarian structure, which leads to endless division and subdivision of tasks and deprives the worker of his decision-making abilities, then the obvious cure is to reverse the process, abolish the authoritarian patterns, and give the worker's intelligence back to him—that is, the replacement of autocracy by democracy.

This is, of course, an oversimplification. Working out the actual equation can be quite complicated. But the general principle would seem demonstrably valid, as most of the rest of this book will strive to make clear.

That does not mean that there are not enormous difficulties involved. One of the most serious is the existence of long-established thinking patterns, the strength of which no sane person would underestimate. The most obvious barrier of this type is the resistance of management to change in the established power relationships (about which we will have more to say later), but it is worth noting that another hindrance to democracy—and linked, in a way, to the first—is the fear of freedom among more subordinate persons. This seemingly odd phenomenon was noticed by Rousseau, who pointed out: "Man is born free, and everywhere he is in chains." Unfreedom, he said, becomes a habit: "Slaves lose everything in their chains, even including the desire to be rid of them; they love their servitude. . . ."

That people should enjoy servitude, especially in a world full of fervent defense of freedom at all points along the political-economic spectrum, can appear peculiar, but there is a great deal of *willingness* in the acceptance of degrading work conditions—even if the process is a largely unconscious one.

It is likely that this is one of the strengths of the modern work system. Individuals can be seen to cling to an outmoded authoritarian system in order to protect themselves from the unknown dangers that freedom might hold. Erich Fromm, in *Escape from Freedom,* holds that this situation arose with industrial capitalism, which, supported by the work-oriented philosophies of Luther and Calvin, succeeded in giving the human being all the necessary elements needed for freedom—except freedom itself. Having failed to master the new set of circumstances, man instead acquired a "feeling of individual insignificance and powerlessness."

In attempting to resolve the problems thus created, one escape is to "fuse one's self with somebody or something outside oneself in order to acquire the strength which the individual self is lacking." This masochism is connected with a "desire to get rid of the individual self" and thereby to rid oneself of gnawing doubts about oneself. By seeking pain, the individual attempts to get rid of everything that is involved with his real self. But he never thereby overcomes his isolation and powerlessness—indeed, they only increase—and he thus never gets what he has been trying "to pay for: inner peace and tranquility."

To come back to the other side of the authoritarian pattern—the managers—we see that it is only a variation on the same theme. Fromm notes that the sadist and the masochist are victims of the same basic disease, and they attempt to combat it through basically similar approaches: gaining power over another, or submitting to another's power, and thus merging with the other and escaping from one's insignificant self. "Both the masochistic and sadistic strivings tend to help the individual to escape his unbearable feelings of aloneness and powerlessness." These methods are ultimately unsatisfactory, but they do accomplish one thing: They get rid of "the burden of freedom." This leads to "the authoritarian character"—the admiration for and love of involvement with power, on both sides of the equation; such a person "admires authority and tends to submit to it, but at the same time he wants to be an authority himself and have others submit to him."

This argument helps illuminate a paradox: Why should workers so often support the myths of the authoritarian structure in which they are enmeshed—that is to say, the ideology of industrial capitalism, the superiority of the profit motive, and the virtues of ambition and hard work—even though they do not stand the slightest chance of ever benefiting from such abstractions? One can gain a kind of inner strength by submitting to the system, however apparent its injustices.

Nevertheless, the desire for democracy remains strong. Says Fromm: "The drive for freedom inherent in human nature, while it can be corrupted and suppressed, tends to assert itself again and again."

As noted earlier, it is surprising that industrial democracy has made so little progress in America, which possesses a democratic ideology. Yet the principles involved are, basically, the same as those applying in the political field. Thomas Jefferson wrote: "The general spread of the light of science has already laid open to every view the palpable truth, that the mass of mankind has not been born with saddles on their backs, nor a favored few booted and spurred, ready to ride them legitimately, by the grace of God."

Despite the obvious parallels, the connection between industrial democracy and political democracy is rarely discussed. One of the few political thinkers to insist on it was G.D.H. Cole, the British democratic socialist, who attacked the idea of collectivist-bureaucratic control along with capitalist-bureaucratic control. Democracy in industry, was, he argued, an essential element of full citizenship democracy in society as a whole, and he spoke of "giving to the workers responsibility and control, in short freedom to express their personality in the work is their way of serving the community. . . . Political democracy must be completed by democracy in the workshop." More recently, Carole Pateman, a political science thinker, has made very much the same point in a theory of "participatory democracy." The exclusion of so important a sphere as industry from an over-all democratic system is scarcely logical, she says, and most probably damaging to the efficient functioning of the system. All important elements of a society must be included in a democratic whole. "The most important area is industry," she writes. "If individuals are to exercise the maximum amount of control over their own lives and environment then authority structures in these areas must be so organized that they can participate in decision making." She concludes that the "authority structure" of a person's work environment can have a deciding influence on his political opinions, and she suggests that increased democracy in industry could have a larger social impact: "Experience of a participatory authority structure might also be effective in diminishing tendencies toward nondemocratic attitudes in the individual."

This observation accords with findings regarding the disturbingly antisocial attitudes among blue-collar workers engaged in assembly-line jobs, which can very probably help to explain the puzzling surge of antidemocratic views among workers in the United States in recent years.

Many theories of industrial democracy have been advanced, and many forms have been tried—some good, some not so good. But the efforts made so far have great lessons for the future. Elements of various systems can prove worthwhile in constructing even more satisfactory systems—or, as one should more democratically put it, in creating conditions under which individuals involved in systems can themselves construct them. Even the failures can be instructive. There is no intention here to make an exhaustive survey of this area, but we can usefully look at some of the attempts that have been made to satisfy what in our modern world is a basic human feeling—the desire for democracy.

IN THE SANDING BOOTH AT FORD

RICK KING

It's a cold, windy morning in January 1974. The recession is getting worse, and manufacturing plants all over the San Francisco Bay area are laying off. A steel plant has closed. International Harvester and Raytheon have laid off a shift. But the Milpitas Ford plant is hiring a swing shift to make more Pintos and Mustangs. It is the only plant in the United States actively hiring.

I'm 24, unemployed, and trying to avoid going to law school. At 6:30 there are already 20 people in line. By the time the office opens at 8:00, the line has tripled in size. Most of the applicants are black or Chicano and half are women.

It is the same mix you see in unemployment offices. Men in platform shoes and construction boots, Coors beer tank tops and neatly ironed, flowered shirts. The only difference is that all the women wear pants, as if to point out that they are ready for manual labor. Everyone waits patiently. Already there are six applications for every place. The pay is over $5 an hour (by 1976 it will be over $6). No one talks.

At 9:00 I am sitting across from my interviewer, a black in his middle thirties. I notice his Boalt Law School ring and then look into his eyes. I promise myself I won't look down until he does. We stare at each other through the whole interview. I point out that I will do anything to get the job; stand in line again, fill out another application. He is impressed by my enthusiasm and assures me that one application is enough.

"Usually, we like people to stand outside longer," he confides, adjusting his tie. "If it rains and people stay in line, we think that's a good sign. Shows they really want the job." For the first and only time, I look away and then back to see if he is serious. He is.

Three months later, I take a physical and am ready to work. Another 14 days and I am sitting at a seminar table with 20 other new hires. Five are women. Our group leader from Labor Relations, who looks like Rocky Marciano, is passing out forms; medical insurance forms for Detroit and the union local. He advises that we

Source: Reprinted by permission from *The Washington Monthly.* Copyright 1976 by The Washington Monthly Co., 1611 Connecticut Ave N.W. Washington, D.C. 20009.

take Blue Cross instead of Kaiser health insurance. All 20 of us dutifully follow his advice.

I look around the table. Most of the women are big, and everybody is healthy. There is none of the fat that would distinguish 20 randomly chosen Americans. I am one of the few who is not married. There is only one man over 30. He has worked previously making Mack trucks.

We watch a movie, "Don't Paint It Like Disneyland." The film consists of interviews with Ford workers at River Rouge. The message is clear: the work is hard but the pay is good. Our group leader turns off the projector and announces that he worked on the line for ten years.

"If you don't have any guts, you'll quit the first day. I almost did. And you'll want to quit, I promise you that." I became convinced that if this behemoth almost quit, I'll never last five minutes.

"You're going to hate that job so bad during the first few weeks. You're going to hate Ford, this plant, your foreman. If you get through the first week, you have a chance."

He pauses and drops his voice. "But folks, let's face it. There's no place in the country, no place in the world, that's going to hire people like you, without any skills, and pay them over $5 an hour." I look at the man next to me, a young Chicano in an army jacket with Sanchez stenciled over the left pocket. He raises his eyes in an expression of resignation and agreement.

Carefully we put on our safety glasses, file out of the room, and walk through a door that says "Safety Equipment Required Beyond This Point." Moving from the quiet of the office, we are assaulted by a noise level like that of an airport runway. Everywhere there are cars of all different colors, lines of cars moving in different directions. Cars extend as far as can be seen.

We follow the group leader through the plant, respectful and wide-eyed as if in a cathedral for the first time. Conveyor belts hanging from the

ceiling carry tires and parts. People hurry by in blue overalls or aprons. The foremen's neat shirts, ties, and slacks are a stark contrast. Everyone wears a watch.

Within the confusion I notice a few specific jobs. A young woman with a huge afro jams gas nozzles into cars as they pass by. Two men grab tires off a rack, bounce them on the floor, deftly catch them, secure them to each car, and bolt them tight.

As we walk workers stare at us and grin. Many are yelling. My ears gradually adjust to the din. "Don't do it," the workers are yelling. "You'll be sorry." I grin at the people pointing at us and realize that we new hires are the only ones wearing safety glasses.

Eight hours later, I drive home despondent. My hands are bleeding and I feel like an idiot. I am supposed to be a block sander. Unfortunately, I am only able to do about one-fifth of the work assigned me. Lew, who is teaching me the job, assures me that it is all right. "You'll learn," he says. "Don't worry. At least you hustle. As long as you kill yourself for them, they'll keep you." I arrive home, drink two beers, eat a steak, and go to bed four hours early.

THE CLOSER YOU LOOK . . .

Within a few weeks, everything is more familiar. I drive to work with Denny, a block sander who was hired on the same day I was. We pass by alternating orchards, factories, trailer parks, and billboards. WHAT IS A BULLFROG? asks one. The answer is Smirnoff and lime. Just before you get to the plant, the Galaxy bar is full of people trying out bullfrogs before work. Similarly, the liquor stores do a rush business on beer. Many cars pulling into the plant parking lot give off the odor of marijuana.

The executive parking lot is uniformly populated by late model Fords. The employees lot is crowded with '56 Chevies, Toyotas, Datsuns and some exquisite, hand-painted motorcycles. People who have worked at both GM and Ford say that GM puts a little extra time into building its cars.

A huge banner over the employees' entrance proclaims, "The closer you look, the better we look."

Before work I walk slowly toward the time clock, relishing the few moments of freedom. If there's time, I wander around the plant. Under one roof, it has a floor space of ten football fields. The roof is two stories high. In some places the assembly line goes up in the air or crisscrosses over itself. A private railroad brings in parts from the Midwest and divides the plant in half. On the west side, cars are made. On the east, small pickup trucks.

A few minutes before 4:30, I clock in, drink two cartons of chocolate milk for energy, go to the bathroom (no chance again until break), hop over two lines, and walk into the booth. I work in the paint department in an enclosed booth. The cars enter and exit through a narrow opening at either end. Our job is to sand the car smooth before it receives its final coat of colored paint.

The booth is hazy with dust from the shift before. The primer coat is lead-based and I wear a surgeon's mask that I bought in San Francisco. Ford provides masks, but they are uncomfortable. Art, who works across from me, uses the mask I give him. Denny, next to me, doesn't; it makes it too hard to breathe.

I hold a ten-pound air sander in my right hand and a handful of sandpaper in my left. My responsibility is the right-hand half of the trunk, roof, and hood. I open the passenger door and sand quickly inside with the sandpaper in my left hand. Then I sand the whole surface area with the air sander. Any large metal burrs or blobs of paint have to be removed with a scraper I carry in my apron pocket. The many paint runs, grease spots, or specks of dirt have to be ground down to bare metal and smoothed out. Also, the small grill in front of the windshield has to be sanded over three times. Since the line speed is usually between 55 and 58 cars

per hour, I have to perform my job within 67 seconds.

After a few months, the work is routine. I've learned which parts of the job I can skip when I get tired. One day, however, a Frederick Taylor efficiency expert appears with a stopwatch and lurks behind pillars hoping we won't notice him. Even the foreman, Stan, hates him. If the expert thinks fewer workers are needed, the responsibility for enforcing an increased workload falls on Stan.

The word is quickly spread and the whole line slows down. Jobs that a worker used to be able to finish with a few seconds to spare suddenly become unbearable. In our case the acting is to no avail. Two people are taken out of the booth and the four remaining are given extra work. In addition to my normal job, I now have to sand around the tail and headlights, and help Denny, in front of me, with the sides.

COPING

The four of us adjust. The work is always physically exhausting, like playing a game of football or soccer. But the real punishment is the inevitability of the line. I want to take a walk, go to the bathroom, have a Mr. Goodbar. It doesn't matter. There's always another car.

Someone shows me a *Newsweek* article with a picture of an autoworker playing a guitar while the line rolls by. The implication is that the work is so easy it's possible to take time off to play a little blues. I have to plan ahead to get a drink of water: five seconds to the fountain, five seconds for the drink, five seconds back into the booth.

The monotony of the line binds us together. Small gaps, usually a few car lengths, happen almost every day. We constantly peer down the line to see if any are coming. The big hope is that a gap won't appear during your break.

Occasionally, the line breaks down. This is what we all wait for. The plant is turned upside down. Foremen in ties appear from nowhere and furiously try to figure out what has happened. It is the only time they do physical work. At the same time, we stand around grinning and give specious advice. For once, Ford is paying us to do nothing.

Yet, such moments are rare. Within the booth, we rely on each other for entertainment. We yell at each other or speculate about whether we'll go home early. Ron and Denny trade statistics from the *Guinness Book of World Records*. We invent a form of basketball using a trashcan as a basket and play fast games during gaps. The other three constantly exchange cigarettes. We tell each other about our lives before we joined Ford.

The booth is our world. Because we have to see any spots on the plant, the booth is white and brightly lit by neon lights. It is three car lengths long and 15 feet wide. The booth is enclosed to prevent the dust from escaping. There is a coating of dust on everything. The noise of the sanders makes it necessary to shout to be heard.

While working, although we may be immersed in our own thoughts, there is always an unconscious awareness of the other three. Unused to repetitive work, I am the most absentminded. Once, I find my foot caught on the line. The next car is proceeding normally and will run over my foot in a few seconds. I scream. Instantaneously, without need for explanation, Ron, Denny, and Art snap out of their private thoughts. They push the moving car back up the line and then free my foot. The whole incident takes five seconds.

I also have the least capacity to endure the frustration. One day, hating myself and hating Ford, I smash my $150 sander into a hunk of twisted metal. I look up at my friends. They are amazed. To steal from Ford or to sabotage a car is understandable. But to destroy a tool is simply childish.

Our reliefman, who studied four years to be a Jesuit, gives me another sander. He switches parts among a few old sanders and is able to disguise the fact that my sander was ever destroyed. What I have done is no big deal, just odd.

YOU DIE IN LITTLE WAYS

Sabotage against the cars themselves is common. As a matter of course, we used to force the trunks closed in a way that ensured the cars couldn't be painted properly. But most sabotage takes place in the trim department, where dashboards, mirrors, inside panels, windows, and extras are installed. Because so many items are installed in this section, it is difficult to trace the saboteur. Every day, mirrors are smashed and quarter panels are ripped. The art lies in sabotaging in a way that is not immediately discovered. As work is done further down the line, it becomes progressively more difficult to repair the original problem. Another form of sabotage is to ignore work. There is a legendary trim worker whose job is to install six screws. He never puts in more than four.

Sometimes the results are artistic. For a week, cars would periodically come down our line with a huge, sculpted penis where the gear shift was to be installed. Workers came from all over the plant to look at these wonders. Gradually they grew larger and larger until the last was at least four feet long. Then they mysteriously ceased.

Usually the day passes with few such diversions. After conversation has lost its appeal, one slips inevitably, reluctantly, into daydreams. Ron mostly dreams about sex. Art hears music. Denny builds and rebuilds fantasy motorcycles or thinks of his ex-girlfriend and their little girl. I imagine going to South America and learning Spanish.

The fantasies on the line are replaced by nightmares of the line slowly devouring them or of falling further and further behind. One friend installs dream quarter panels into his girlfriend's back. She wakes him up, but the minute he falls asleep, he starts all over again.

Faced with the daytime prospect of working on 400 cars, it's nice to have a little artificial energy. The plant seems to be fueled by "crossroads"—little white benzedrine pills with a cross imprinted on them.

Speed is sold openly, when it's available. Dealers walk through the plant on a half-hour break and sell 20 bags. Sections of the line buy a couple of $5 or $10 bags and split them up over a week. However, there is never enough to fill the demand.

One day the painters in the booth next to us drop acid. Luis, who has two kids and a condominium on time, paints sitting down, can't talk, and skips lunch. The pass rate on their paint jobs is normal.

Drugs, no matter how strong, provide no anesthesia for certain conditions. The ventilation in the paint booth never seems to work too well. The painters complain of being unable to breathe and of getting headaches. One day they carry Luis out of their booth unconscious. He has been overcome by the paint fumes.

Another time, Denny comes back from his break and announces a big gap coming up. Half an hour later, when the gap arrives, we hear there has been a walkout in the arc welding booth. "Just a little labor problem," mutters our foreman. "I don't know any more about it than you do. "I start to walk over to Body. "Got to keep to the area, Rick," Stan tells me. "General foreman wants it that way."

A taper comes back from break and says the welders are back at work. It was something about gloves and safety equipment, but she isn't sure. Three hours later, another rumor arrives. This time the welders have walked out of the plant. The four of us in the booth look at each other. We let two cars go by.

What was happening? Why had they walked out? If we joined them, would we be the only ones leaving the plant? "I'll do it if you do it." "I'll do it if *you* do it." Ron's wife has just had a baby. Art is getting married in a week. We start working again. You die in little ways.

WHY THE WELDERS WALKED OUT

The arc welders who walked out had been trained together in a federally financed manpower program in San Jose. They had been hired directly from the program. By the time they got to Ford, they already knew and trusted each other. Arc welding is one of the dirtiest, most painful jobs in the plant. The torches and general heat in Body Section combine to make the area like an oven. At the same time, the welders have to wear bulky protective clothing. Despite protective gloves, welders' arms are crisscrossed with scars from the sparks thrown up by their torches.

Their foreman, Becker, had been brought from St. Louis, where a Mercury shift had been laid off. Discipline in the St. Louis plant is reputed to be the tightest in the Ford organization. In the summer it gets so hot that workers have to tie wet towels around their heads to keep from overheating. One time, St. Louis workers stayed on the line with a foot of water on the floor. California employees shake their heads in disbelief when they hear such stories.

Becker thought his young California workers were chicken. They kept asking for replacements of the long gloves that protected their arms. He wouldn't provide them; they're expensive and he wanted to make them last longer. The welders called their union rep. He told them things would be all right.

Becker continued to supervise their work. They asked for the gloves again. "They're coming." Everybody knows that safety equipment is kept in lockers close to the work area. Becker was playing with them. They stopped work.

Instantly, they were surrounded by UAW representatives, Labor Relations department bigwigs, and foremen. They demanded that the foreman be transferred and that they get their gloves. The gloves were produced. It was promised that the foreman would be replaced during lunch.

When the welders came back from lunch, the

foreman was still there. One welder put down his tools and started walking out. Another later told me, "Hell, I didn't want to walk out right then. But when he's walking out of the plant, what can you do?" They all walked out.

Ten welders and two other workers left the plant. They were all fired. The UAW assured them that the problem was being handled. But nothing happened. Some of the welders appeared at the plant gates and passed out leaflets asking people to come to the next union meeting. A few days later, the company rehired three of the welders who were not considered "ringleaders." Anybody passing out leaflets was, of course, a ringleader.

At the union meeting it took two of the three hours and a challenge to the chair to bring up the question of the arc welders. A member of the International happened to be at the meeting and counseled against any type of action. Someone was finally able to move that the Union put out an informational leaflet about the incident. Union official after union official warned that a leaflet would upset the delicate balance of negotiations. When asked what negotiations, they replied that they could not say.

People who supported the welders were baited as college agitators (as indeed some were). When it came to a vote, all the workers from the line voted unsuccessfully for the welders. Almost all the UAW officials voted against them.

UNITED AGAINST WORKERS

Ford won the battle of attrition. Without the support of the union, unable to muster a significant following inside the plant, the welders became increasingly discouraged. Gradually, Ford hired back the welders who had lost heart, the ones who stopped passing out leaflets at the plant gates. In the end, only the two or three most militant welders kept passing out leaflets

and trying to organize legal help. They were never rehired.

What makes the assembly line work efficiently is fear, not engineering. There have been no significant technological breakthroughs since Henry Ford first designed the line. The system is based on forcing men and women to produce as much per minute as possible. Once inside the factory, the fear system is immediately apparent. Every problem becomes a crisis, because it threatens to disrupt the smooth flow of the line.

Each department (Body, Paint, Trim, Chassis, and Pre-Delivery) has a quota to meet. In Paint, for example, 75 percent of the cars are supposed to pass inspection. Because the departments are competitive, there is a reluctance to admit mistakes. When a department supervisor has a problem he can't solve, he often just hides it.

Before the cars come to us to be sanded, they are dipped in an ionized paint solution called "E" coat. This coat of paint actually penetrates the metal and prevents rust. One day we noticed there was no E coat on the cars. We called Stan and he went to talk to the department supervisor.

A few minutes later Stan returned and told us to keep sanding. I counted at least 75 cars that passed without any E coat. The supervisor made sure they were duly inspected and passed. Once outside the paint section, the paint job would never be inspected again. Most people on the line estimated that the cars would rust out within a year. "They'll ship 'em to Boston and blame it on the rock salt," was the general prognosis.

If the department supervisor is displeased with a foreman under him, he will do anything to frighten him into performing better. Brutal tonguelashing is common. Foremen work under the constant threat of being returned to the line (foremen cannot be fired, they have the opportunity to start over as workers). While ulcers are a common problem among foremen, heart attacks are also frequent. Many new foremen quit in disgust and go back to the line.

The ones who remain are the most brutal and competitive. Strangely enough, their drive to extract the utmost from the workers carries over to the machines, which are used until they break. Obviously, it would be cheaper to replace them as they wear out, but the mentality doesn't allow it.

If management is harsh, at least it doesn't pretend to help you. But the union does, and some of the worst contempt is reserved for union officials. UAW stands for United Against Workers, a friend tells me.

Typically, union officials seem more at home with Labor Relations executives than with workers. The atmosphere is one of smoke-filled back rooms and secret bargains. It is hard to find a union official in the plant. When you have a problem, you have to telephone and then wait for your representative. Sometimes he comes and sometimes he doesn't.

Of course, all locals are different. Local 560 can be characterized by my own representative, who spent ten minutes one day delineating the problems of the auto industry to me. The root of the problem, he explained, is that workers are lazy. If people would just come to work faithfully and work a little harder, we'd all be better off.

A few years ago, someone was killed in Body Section. A piece of machinery fell on him. The story is that the chairman of the Health and Safety Committee presented his regular report at the next meeting a few weeks later. He didn't mention the dead man. When asked why not, he pointed out that the man hadn't filed a grievance. Consequently, he couldn't investigate the problem.

STAYING HUMAN

From what I've said, working at Ford must seem like a circle in Hell. That's mostly the way I re-member it. The work is trivial and the conditions poor. Intense discipline is combined with poor planning. The UAW, one of the most liberal unions in the country, constantly proves itself unresponsive to workers' needs. Aside from a few isolated ex-student revolutionaries, there are no political movements.

Each worker seemingly stands alone. Some want to work for a few years and then go to school. Most want to last 30 years and retire with a full pension. As Jerry, our reliefman, says, "I may have been born here, but I'm not going to die here."

But the atmosphere is not one of total defeat. Among workers there is a strong, unstated feeling of trust. It manifests itself in little ways. On a break, a complete stranger will tell you about his deepest marital problems or his feelings of despair, simply because you too are wearing overalls. After five minutes, he'll look at his watch, wave goodbye, and rush back to the job.

Although opposition to Ford is not organized, it is constant. Militancy on an individual level is high. Overly tough foremen find their work sabotaged and are subject to continual verbal harassment. Efficiency experts are forced to hide while doing their inspections. Workers are united in one thing—hating Ford.

Still, 30 years is a very long time. Sabotage helps relieve frustration, but without some type of political context it becomes an empty gesture. So, the worker settles into a slow, cynical wait for retirement. After all, it's a steady job.

During the wait, there remains the dignity of not joining management. There is a clear distinction between exploiter and exploited. The refusal to become one of the exploiters is the constant, steadfast expression of humanity in the face of Ford's regime.

One of my clearest memories of Ford is walking down the chassis line one afternoon. One part of the line runs above the workers who assemble the undercarriage. All day they stand in a narrow concrete trench working on the cars passing over their heads. They have no room to move around and can't see anything.

I hear a strange noise suddenly, like the beat of jungle drums in a Tarzan movie. It gathers force and grows louder, drowning out the sound of the rest of the plant.

Every worker beneath the line is beating on the bottom of the cars with his wrenches. All around, above ground, people laugh and walk in rhythm to the percussion.

Sometimes, on the line, I fantasize about that sound, and the rhythm spreads and spreads.

QUESTIONS FOR DISCUSSION

1. Do you think it is possible that these four readings overstate the alienation problem among blue collar and nonupward mobile white collar employees? Interview 10 employees with these characteristics and ask them to describe the world of work as they see it.

2. Read Studs Terkel's book entitled *Working.* In this book almost all of the interviews are done with people who feel some alienation with work. Do you think that this is an unbiased sample?

3. How would you modify the theories of motivation that you have studied in management and organizational behavior courses if you recognize that a subset of the work force perceives work in the manner described in these articles?

4. Write a position paper proving that the points in these articles are not typical. For example, you might start by looking at the national surveys on worker satisfaction and on the reports from the health education and welfare department called *Work in America* (MIT Press, 1971).

5. When you have had jobs or activities in which you were bored but felt trapped, how did you psychologically adjust?

CHAPTER VII

INDIVIDUAL AND GROUP DIFFERENCES IN THE ORGANIZATION

ORGANIZATIONAL SHOCKS

- Motivation theory teaches us to treat people as individuals, whereas society insists that we consider group characteristics such as race and sex.
- Contrary to what we teach about motivation, managers are really expected to motivate groups of people rather than individuals.
- Every action on the part of a manager toward one person in a group affects every other member of the group.
- Competition within a group reduces group productivity.

In the chapter on work motivation we discussed that there are many variables that influence an individual's productivity and job satisfaction. Some of these variables are directly influenced by managers, such as task design, organizational climate, and feedback. Others, however, are influenced by the individual makeup of a person and group differences among various groups of people. This becomes evident in this selection of readings. For example, in the first reading by Bem and Bem, we learn that women and men are different in part because women are educated and socialized differently than men. Thus we see that socialization does not take place the first day you enter the work force but often takes place the first day you enter the world. For example, when a female is born it is customary to use the color pink for announcements, parties, and so forth; and for a male child blue is used. From there socialization expands into many other forms. This reading examines the controversy surrounding this socialization process.

Although the constitution and the courts have attempted to insure that women and minorities are not discriminated against, organizations must be careful to treat all people equally, including white males. Thus it seems that organizational leaders are truly caught in the middle. They are socialized to believe one thing about various groups, they are told to treat people equally, but because of the disproportionately low number of women and especially minorities in managerial ranks, they have been given pressure both internally and externally to increase these numbers at a rapid rate. In doing so, they have perhaps overlooked an equally qualified white male. When this occurs we see they are again caught in the middle. This of course seems to be a Catch-22 of individual differences. One of the organizational shocks of being a manager, of course, is learning how the external environment teaches you to treat people *equally,* whereas the theories of motivation that we teach in organizational behavior tells us to treat people *equitably.*

The next reading, on workaholism show how certain individuals tend to shun the need for rest or recreation and engage in their occupations as if it were their total life. According to this article, in some cases workaholism becomes less healthy for the individual and the organization than one might suppose. Workaholics are not necessarily found only in top management positions, but at all levels in the organization. This might explain why men and women who are not upward mobiles continue to work and produce at a high rate even when group sanctions are such that high productivity is punished.

The next article by Donald F. Roy called "Banana Time" talks about how groups set quotas for workers in order that the balance of power between management and employees can be maintained. This is a classic article and is as relevant today as it was when it was written in 1960.

The last article by Tuckman is an intriguing article about how group cohesiveness develops over time. If you have ever watched a sports team develop each year or seen a fraternity or sorority during rush you can see the obvious parallels between those processes and this discussion. The same is true with any organization. The makeup of groups is always changing and the groups are finding themselves in one of four stages of development. The point of this article is that for a group to be most effective it must be in the *performing* stage.

HOMOGENIZING THE AMERICAN WOMAN: THE POWER OF AN UNCONSCIOUS IDEOLOGY

SANDRA BEM AND DARYL BEM*

In the beginning God created the heaven and the earth . . . And God said, Let us make man in our image, after our likeness; and let him have dominion over the fish of the sea, and over the fowl of the air, and over the cattle, and over all the earth . . . And the rib, which the Lord God had taken from man, made he a woman and brought her unto the man . . . And the Lord God said unto the woman, What is this that thou has done? And the woman said, The serpent beguiled me, and I did eat . . . Unto the woman God said, I will greatly multiply thy sorrow and thy conception; in sorrow thou shalt bring forth children; and thy desire shall be to thy husband, and he shall rule over thee (Gen. 1, 2, 3).

There is a moral to that story. St. Paul spells it out even more clearly.

For a man . . . is the image and glory of God; but the woman is the glory of man. For the man is not of the woman, but the woman of the man. Neither was the man created for the woman, but the woman for the man (1 Cor. 11).

Let the women learn in silence with all subjection. But I suffer not a woman to teach, nor to usurp authority over the man, but to be in silence. For Adam was first formed and then Eve. And Adam was not deceived, but the woman, being deceived, was in the transgression. Notwithstanding, she shall be saved in childbearing, if they continue in faith and charity and holiness with sobriety (1 Tim. 2).

Now one should not assume that only Christians have this kind of rich heritage of ideology about women. So consider now, the morning prayer of the Orthodox Jew:

Blessed art Thou, oh Lord our God, King of the Universe, that I was not born a gentile.

Blessed art Thou, oh Lord our God, King of the Universe, that I was not born a slave.

Blessed art Thou, oh Lord our God, King of the Universe, that I was not born a woman.

*Order of authorship determined by the flip of a coin.
Source: From *Beliefs, Attitudes and Human Affairs* by Sandra L. Bem and Daryl J. Bem. Copyright 1972 by Sandra L. Bem and Daryl J. Bem. Reprinted by permission of the authors.

Or, consider the Koran, the sacred text of Islam:

> Men are superior to women on account of the qualities in which God has given them preeminence.

Because they think they sense a decline in feminine "faith, charity, and holiness with sobriety," many people today jump to the conclusion that the ideology expressed in these passages is a relic of the past. Not so, of course. It has simply been obscured by an egalitarian veneer, and the same ideology has now become unconscious. That is, we remain unaware of it because alternative beliefs and attitudes about women, until very recently, have gone unimagined. We are very much like the fish who is unaware of the fact that his environment is wet. After all, what else could it be? Such is the nature of all unconscious ideologies in a society. Such, in particular, is the nature of America's ideology about women.

What we should like to do in this paper is to discuss today's version of this same ideology.

When a baby is born, it is difficult to predict what he will be doing 25 years later. We can't say whether he will be an artist, a doctor, a lawyer, a college professor, or a bricklayer, because he will be permitted to develop and fulfill his own unique potential—particularly, of course, if he happens to be white and middle class. But if that same newborn child happens to be a girl, we can predict with almost complete confidence how she is likely to be spending her time some 25 years later. Why can we do that? Because her individuality doesn't have to be considered. Her individuality is irrelevant. Time studies have shown that she will spend the equivalent of a full working day, 7.1 hours, in preparing meals, cleaning house, laundering, mending, shopping and doing other household tasks. In other words, 43% of her waking time will be spent in activity that would command an hourly wage on the open market well below the federally set minimum for menial industrial work.

Of course, the point really is not how little she would earn if she did these things in someone else's home. She will be doing them in her own home for free. The point is that this use of time is virtually the same for homemakers with college degrees and for homemakers with less than a grade school education, for women married to professional men and for women married to blue-collar workers. Actually, that's understating it slightly. What the time study really showed was that college-educated women spend slightly *more* time cleaning their houses than their less-educated counterparts!

Of course, it is not simply the full-time homemaker whose unique identity has been rendered largely irrelevant. Of the 31 million women who work outside the home in our society, 78% end up in dead-end jobs as clerical workers, service workers, factory workers, or sales clerks, compared to a comparable figure of 40% for men. Only 15% of all women workers in our society are classified by the Labor Department as professional or technical workers, and even this figure is misleading—for the single, poorly-paid occupation of non-college teacher absorbs half of these women, and the occupation of nurse absorbs an additional quarter. In other words, the two jobs of teacher and nurse absorb three-quarters of all women classified in our society as technical or professional. That means, then, that fewer than 5% of all professional women—fewer than 1% of all women workers—fill those positions which to most Americans connote "professional": Physician, lawyer, engineer, scientist, college professor, journalist, writer, and so forth.

Even an I.Q. in the genius range does not guarantee that a woman's unique potential will find expression. There was a famous study of over 1300 boys and girls whose I.Q.'s average 151 (Terman & Oden, 1959). When the study began in the early 1900's, these highly gifted youngsters were only ten years old, and their careers have been followed ever since. Where are they today? 86% of the men have now achieved prominence in professional and managerial occupations. In contrast, only a minority of the women were even employed. Of those who were, 37% were nurses, librarians, social workers, and non-college teachers. An additional 26% were secretaries, stenographers, bookkeepers, and office workers! Only 11% entered the higher professions of law, medicine, college teaching, engineering, science, economics, and the like. And even at age 44, well after all their children had gone to school, 61% of these highly gifted women remained full-time homemakers. Talent, education, ability, interests, motivations: all irrelevant. In our society, being female uniquely qualifies an individual for domestic work—either by itself or in conjunction with typing, teaching, nursing, or (most often) unskilled labor. It is this homogenization of America's women which is the major consequence of our society's sex-role ideology.

It is true, of course, that most women have several hours of leisure time every day. And it is here, we are often told, that each woman can express her unique identity. Thus, politically interested women can join the League of Women Voters. Women with humane interests can become part-time Gray Ladies. Women who love music can raise money for the symphony. Protestant women play Canasta; Jewish women play Mah Jongg; brighter women of all denominations and faculty wives play bridge.

But politically interested *men* serve in legislatures. *Men* with humane interests become physicians or clinical psychologists. *Men* who love music play in the symphony. In other words, why should a woman's unique identity determine only the periphery of her life rather than its central core?

Why? Why nurse rather than physician, secretary rather than executive, stewardess rather than pilot? Why faculty wife rather than faculty?

Why doctor's mother rather than doctor? There are three basic answers to this question: (1) Discrimination; (2) Sex-role conditioning; and (3) The presumed incompatibility of family and career.

DISCRIMINATION

In 1968, the median income of full-time women workers was approximately $4500. The comparable figure for men was $3000 higher. Moreover, the gap is widening. Ten years ago, women earned 64% of what men did; that percentage has now shrunk to 58%. Today, a female college graduate working full-time can expect to earn less per year than a male high school dropout.

There are two reasons for this pay differential. First, in every category of occupation, women are employed in the lesser-skilled, lower-paid positions. Even in the clerical field, where 73% of the workers are women, females are relegated to the lowest status positions and hence earn only 65% of what male clerical workers earn. The second reason for this pay differential is discrimination in its purest form: unequal pay for equal work. According to a survey of 206 companies in 1970, female college graduates were offered jobs which paid $43 per month less than those offered to their male counterparts in the same college major.

New laws should begin to correct both of these situations. The Equal Pay Act of 1963 prohibits employers from discriminating on the basis of sex in the payment of wages for equal work. In a landmark ruling on May 18, 1970, the U.S. Supreme Court ordered that $250,000 in back pay be paid to women employed by a single New Jersey glass company. This decision followed a two-year court battle by the Labor Department after it found that the company was paying men selector-packers 21.5 cents more per hour than women doing the same work. In a similar case, the Eighth Circuit Court of Appeals ordered a major can company to pay more than $100.000 in back wages to women doing equal work. According to the Labor Department, an estimated $17 million is owed to women in back pay. Since that estimate was made, a 1972 amendment extended the Act to cover executive, administrative and professional employees as well.

But to enjoy equal pay, women must also have access to equal jobs. Title VII of the 1964 Civil Rights Act prohibits discrimination in employment on the basis of race, color, religion, national origin—and sex. Although the sex provision was treated as a joke at the time (and was originally introduced by a Southern Congressman in an attempt to defeat the bill), the Equal Employment Opportunities Commission discovered in its first year of operation that 40% or more of the complaints warranting investigation charged discrimination on the basis of sex (Bird, 1969).

Title VII has served as one of the most effective instruments in helping to achieve sex equality in the world of work. According to a report by the E.E.O.C., nearly 6,000 charges of sex discrimination were filed with that agency in 1971 alone, a 62% increase over the previous year.

But the most significant legislative breakthrough in the area of sex equality was the passage of the Equal Rights Amendment by both houses of Congress in 1972. The ERA simply states that "Equality of rights under the law shall not be denied or abridged by the United States or by any state on account of sex." This amendment has been introduced into every session of Congress since 1923, and its passage now is clearly an indication of the changing role of the American woman. All of the various ramifications are hard to predict, but it is clear that it will have profound consequences in private as well as public life.

Many Americans assume that the recent drive for equality between the sexes is primarily for the benefit of the middle-class woman who wants to seek self-fulfillment in a professional career. But in many ways, it is the woman in more modest circumstances, the woman who *must* work for economic reasons, who stands to benefit most from the removal of discriminatory barriers. It is *she* who is hardest hit by unequal pay; it is *she* who so desperately needs adequate day-care facilities; it is *her* job which is often dead-ended while her male colleagues in the factory get trained and promoted into the skilled craft jobs. And if both she and her husband work at unfulfilling jobs eight hours a day just to make an adequate income, it is still *she* who carries the additional burden of domestic chores when they return home.

We think it is important to emphasize these points at the outset, for we have chosen to focus our remarks in this particular paper on those fortunate men and women who can afford the luxury of pursuing self-fulfillment through the world of work and career. But every societal reform advocated by the new feminist movement, whether it be the Equal Rights Amendment, the establishment of child-care centers, or basic changes in America's sex-role ideology, will affect the lives of men and women in every economic circumstance. Nevertheless, it is still economic discrimination which hits hardest at the largest group of women, and it is here that the drive for equality can be most successfully launched with legislative and judicial tools.

SEX/ROLE CONDITIONING

But even if all discrimination were to end tomorrow, nothing very drastic would change. For job discrimination is only part of the problem. It does impede women who choose to become lawyers or managers or physicians. But it does not, by itself, help us to understand why so many women "choose" to be secretaries or nurses rather than executives or physicians; why only 3% of 9th grade girls as compared to 25% of the boys "choose" careers in science or engineering; or why 63% of America's married women "choose" not to work at all. It certainly doesn't explain those young women whose vision of the future includes only marriage, children, and living happily ever after; who may, at some point, "choose" to take a job, but who almost never "choose" to pursue a career. Discrimination frustrates choices already made. Something more pernicious perverts the motivation to choose.

That "something" is an unconscious ideology about the nature of the female sex, an ideology which constricts the emerging self-image of the female child and the nature of her aspirations from the very beginning; an ideology which leads even those Americans who agree that a black skin should not uniquely qualify *its* owner for a janitorial or domestic service to act as if the possession of a uterus uniquely qualifies *its* owner for precisely such service.

Consider, for example, the 1968 student rebellion at Columbia University. Students from the radical Left took over some administration buildings in the name of equalitarian ideals which they accused the university of flouting. Here were the most militant spokesmen one could hope to find in the cause of equalitarian ideals. But no sooner had they occupied the buildings than the male militants blandly turned to their sisters-in-arms and assigned them the task of preparing the food, while they—the menfolk—would presumably plan future strategy. The reply these males received was the reply that they deserved—we will leave that to your imagination—and the fact that domestic tasks behind the barricades were desegregated across the sex line that day is an everlasting tribute to the class consciousness of these ladies of the Left. And it was really on that day that the campus women's liberation movement got its start—when radical women finally realized that they were never going to get to make revolution, only coffee.

But these conscious co-eds are not typical, for the unconscious assumptions about a woman's "natural" talents (or lack of them) are at least as prevalent among women as they are among men. A psychologist named Philip Goldberg (1968) demonstrated this by asking female college students to rate a number of professional articles from each of six fields. The articles were collated into two equal sets of booklets, and the names of the authors were changed so that the identical article was attributed to a male author (e.g., John T. McKay) in one booklet and to a female author (e.g., Joan T. McKay) in the other booklet. Each student was asked to read the articles in her booklet and to rate them for value, competence, persuasiveness, writing style, and so forth.

As he had anticipated, Goldberg found that the identical article received significantly lower ratings when it was attributed to a female author than when it was attributed to a male author. He had predicted this result for articles from professional fields generally considered the province of men, like law or city planning, but to his surprise, these women also downgraded articles from the fields of dietetics and elementary school education when they were attributed to female authors. In other words, these students rated the male authors as better at everything, agreeing with Aristotle that "we should regard the female nature as afflicted with a natural defectiveness." Such is the nature of America's unconscious ideology about women.

When does this ideology begin to affect the life of a young girl? Research now tells us that from the day a newborn child is dressed in pink, she is given "special" treatment. Perhaps because they are thought to be more fragile, six-month-old infant girls are actually touched, spoken to, and hovered over more by their mothers while they are playing than are infant boys (Goldberg & Lewis, 1969). One study even showed that when mothers and babies are still in the hospital, mothers smile at, talk to, and touch their female infants more than their male infants at two days of age (Thoman, Leiderman, & Olson, 1972). Differential treatment can't begin much earlier than that.

As children begin to read, the storybook characters become the images and the models that little boys and little girls aspire to become. What kind of role does the female play in the world of children's literature? The fact is that there aren't even very many females in that world. One survey (Fisher, 1970) found that five times as many males as females appear in the titles of children's books; the fantasy world of Doctor Seuss is almost entirely male; and even animals and machines are represented as male. When females do appear, they are noteworthy primarily for what they do *not* do. They do not drive cars, and they seldom even ride bicycles. In one story in which a girl does ride a bicycle, it's a two-seater. Guess where the girl is seated! Boys in these stories climb trees and fish and roll in the leaves and skate. Girls watch, fall down, and get dizzy. Girls are never doctors, and although they may be nurses or librarians or teachers, they are never principals. There seemed to be only one children's book about mothers who work, and it concludes that what mothers love "best of all" is "being your very own Mommy and coming home to you." And although this is no doubt true of many daddies as well, no book about working fathers has ever found it necessary to apologize for working in quite the same way.

As children grow older, more explicit sex-role training is introduced. Boys are encouraged to take more of an interest in mathematics and science. Boys, not girls, are usually given chemistry sets and microscopes for Christmas. Moreover, all children quickly learn that mommy is proud to be a moron when it comes to math and science, whereas daddy is a little ashamed if he doesn't know all about such things. When a young boy returns from school all excited about biology, he is almost certain to be encouraged to think of becoming a physician. A girl with similar enthusiasm is usually told that she might want to consider nurse's training later on, so she can have "an interesting job to fall back upon in case—God forbid—she ever needs to support herself." A very different kind of encouragement. And any girl who doggedly persists in her enthusiasm for science is likely to find her parents as horrified by the prospect of a permanent love affair with physics as they would be either by the prospect of an interracial marriage or, horror of horrors, no marriage at all. Indeed, our graduate women report that their families seem convinced that the menopause must come at age 23.

These socialization practices take their toll. When they apply for college, boys and girls are about equal on verbal aptitude tests, but boys score significantly higher on mathematical aptitude tests—about 60 points higher on the College Board Exams, for example (Brown, 1965). Moreover, for those who are convinced that this is due to female hormones, it is relevant to know that girls improve their mathematical performance if the problems are simply reqorded so that they deal with cooking and gardening, even though the abstract reasoning required for solution remains exactly the same (Milton, 1958). That's not hormones! Clearly, what has been undermined is not a woman's mathematical ability, but rather her confidence in that ability.

But these effects in mathematics and science are only part of the story. The most conspicuous outcome of all is that the majority of America's women become full-time homemakers. And of those who do work, nearly 80% end up in dead-end jobs as clerical workers, service workers, factory workers or sales clerks. Again, it is this "homogenization" of America's women which is the major consequence of America's sex-role ideology.

The important point is not that the role of homemaker is necessarily inferior, but rather that our society is managing to consign a large segment of its population to the role of homemaker—either with or without a dead-end job—solely on the basis of sex just as inexorably as it has in the past consigned the individual with a black skin to the role of janitor or domestic. The important point is that in spite of their unique identities, the majority of American women end up in virtually the *same* role.

The socialization of the American male has closed off certain options for him, too. Men are discouraged from developing certain desirable traits such as tenderness and sensitivity, just as surely as women are discouraged from being assertive and, alas, "too bright." Young boys are encouraged to be incompetent at cooking and certainly child care, just as surely as young girls are urged to be incompetent at math and science. The elimination of sex-role stereotyping implies that each individual would be encouraged to "do his own thing." Men and women would no longer be stereotyped by society's definitions of masculine and feminine. If sensitivity, emotionality, and warmth are desirable *human* characteristics, then they are desirable for men as well as for women. If independence, assertiveness, and serious intellectual commitment are desirable *human* characteristics, they are desirable for women as well as for men. Thus, we are not implying that men have all the goodies and that women can obtain self-fulfillment by acting like men. That is hardly the utopia implied by today's feminist movement. Rather, we envision a society which raises its children so flexibly and with sufficient respect for the integrity of individual uniqueness that some men might emerge with the motivation, the ability, and the opportunity to stay home and raise children without bearing the stigma of being peculiar. Indeed, if homemaking is as glamorous as women's magazines and television commercials would have us believe, then man, too, should have that option. And even if homemaking isn't all that glamorous, it would probably still be more fulfilling for some men than the jobs in which they now find themselves forced because of their role as breadwinner. Thus, it is true that a man's options are also limited by our society's

sex-role ideology, but as the "predictability test" reveals, it is still the women in our society whose identity is rendered irrelevant by America's socialization practices.

FURTHER PSYCHOLOGICAL BARRIERS

But what of the woman who arrives at age 21 still motivated to be challenged and fulfilled by a growing career? Is she free to choose a career if she cares to do so? Or is there something standing even in her way?

There is. Even the woman who has managed to finesse society's attempt to rob her of her career motivations is likely to find herself blocked by society's trump card: the feeling that one cannot have a career and be a successful woman simultaneously. A competent and motivated woman is thus caught in a double-bind which few men have ever faced. She must worry not only about failure, but also about success.

This conflict was strikingly revealed in a study which required college women to complete the following story: "After first-term finals, Anne finds herself at the top of her medical-school class" (Horner, 1969). The stories were then examined for concern about the negative consequences of success. The women in this study all had high intellectual ability and histories of academic success. They were the very women who could have successful careers. And yet, over two-thirds of their stories revealed a clearcut inability to cope with the concept of a feminine, yet career-oriented, woman.

The most common "fear-of-success" stories showed fears of social rejection as a result of success. The woman in this group showed anxiety about becoming unpopular, unmarriageable, and lonely:

Anne starts proclaiming her surprise and joy. Her fellow classmates are so disgusted with her behavior that they jump on her in a body and beat her. She is maimed for life.

Anne is an acne-faced bookworm . . . She studies twelve hours a day, and lives at home to save money. "Well, it certainly paid off. All the Friday and Saturday nights without dates, fun—I'll be the best woman doctor alive." And yet a twinge of sadness comes through—she wonders what she really has . . .

Anne doesn't want to be number one in her class . . . She feels she shouldn't rank so high because of social reasons. She drops to ninth and then marries the boy who graduates numer one.

In the second "fear-of-success" category were stories in which the women seemed concerned about definitions of womanhood. These stories expressed guilt and despair over success and doubts about their femininity and normality:

Unfortunately Anne no longer feels so certain that she really wants to be a doctor. She is worried about herself and wonders if perhaps she is not normal . . . Anne decides not to continue with her medical work but to take courses that have a deeper personal meaning to her.

Anne feels guilty . . . She will finally have a nervous breakdown and quit medical school and marry a successful young doctor.

A third group of stories could not even face up to the conflict between having a career and being a woman. These stories simply denied the possibility that any woman could be so successful:

Anne is a code name for a nonexistent person created by a group of med students. They take turns writing for Anne . . .

Anne is really happy she's on top, though Tom is higher than she—though that's as it should be. Anne doesn't mind Tom winning.

Anne is talking to her counselor. Conselor says she will make a fine nurse.

By way of contrast, here is a typical story written not about Anne, but about John:

John has worked very hard and his long hours of study have paid off . . . He is thinking about his girl, Cheri, whom he will marry at the end of med school. He realizes he can give her all the things she desires after he becomes established. He will go on in med school and be successful in the long run.

Nevertheless, there were a few women in the study who welcomed the prospect of success:

Anne is quite a lady—not only is she top academically, but she is liked and admired by her fellow students—quite a trick in a man-dominated field. She is brilliant—but she is also a woman. She will continue to be at or near the top. And . . . always a lady.

Hopefully the day is approaching when as many "Anne" stories as "John" stories will have happy endings. But notice that even this story finds it necessary to affirm repeatedly that femininity is not necessarily destroyed by accomplishment. One would never encounter a comparable story written about John who, although brilliant and at the top of his class, is "still a man, still a man, still a man."

It seems unlikely that anyone in our society would view these "fear-of-success" stories as portraits of mental health. But even our concept of mental health has been distorted by America's sex-role stereotypes. Here we must indict our own profession of psychology. A recent survey of seventy-nine clinically-trained psychologists, psychiatrists, and social workers, both male and female, revealed a double standard of mental health (Broverman, Broverman, Clarkson, Rosenkrantz, & Vogel, 1970). That is, even professional clinicians have two different concepts of mental health, one for men and one for women; and these concepts parallel the sex-role stereotypes prevalent in our society. Thus, according to these clinicians, a woman is to be regarded as healthier and more mature if she is: more submissive, less independent, less adventurous, more easily influenced, less aggressive, less competitive, more excitable in minor crises, more susceptible to hurt feelings, more emotional, more conceited about her appearance, less objective, and more antagonistic toward math and science! But this was the very same description which these clinicians used to characterize an unhealthy, immature man or an unhealthy, immature adult (sex unspecified)! The equation is clear: Mature woman equals immature adult.

Given this concept of a mature woman, is it any wonder that few women ever aspire toward challenging and fulfilling careers? In order to have a career, a woman will probably need to become relatively more dominant, independent, adventurous, aggressive, competitive, and objective, and relatively less excitable, emotional and conceited than our ideal of femininity requires. If she were a man (or an adult, sex unspecified), these would all be considered positive traits. But because she is a woman, these same traits will bring her disapproval. She must then either be strong enough to have her "femininity" questioned; or she must behave in the prescribed feminine manner and accept second-class status, as an adult and as a professional.

And, of course, should a woman faced with this conflict seek professional help, hoping to summon the strength she will need to pursue her career goals, the advice she is likely to receive will be of virtually no use. For, as this study reveals, even professional counselors have been contaminated by the sex-role ideology.

It is frequently argued that a 21-year-old woman is perfectly free to choose a career if she cares to do so. No one is standing in her way. But this argument conveniently overlooks the fact that our society has spent 20 years carefully marking the woman's ballot for her, and so it has nothing to lose in that 21st year by pretending to let her cast it for the alternative of her choice. Society has controlled not her alternatives (although discrimination does do that), but more importantly, it has controlled her motivation to choose any but one of those alternatives. The so-called "freedom-to-choose" is illusory, and it cannot be invoked to justify a society which controls the woman's motivation to choose.

BIOLOGICAL CONSIDERATIONS

Up to this point, we have argued that the differing life patterns of men and women in our society can be chiefly accounted for by cultural conditioning. The most common counter argument to this view, of course, is the biological one. The biological argument suggests that there may really be inborn differences between men and women in, say, independence or mathematical ability. Or that there may be biological factors beyond the fact that women can become pregnant and nurse children which uniquely dictate that they, but not men, should stay home all day and shun serious outside commitment. What this argument suggests is that maybe female hormones really are responsible somehow. One difficulty with this argument, of course, is that female hormones would have to be different in the Soviet Union, where one-third of the engineers and 75% of the physicians are women (Dodge, 1966). In America, by way of contrast, women constitute less than 1% of the engineers and only 7% of the physicians. Female physiology *is* different, and it may account for some of the psychological differences between the sexes, but America's sex-role ideology still seems primarily responsible for the fact that so few women emerge from childhood with the motivation to seek out any role beyond the one that our society dictates.

But even if there really were biological differences between the sexes along these lines, the biological argument would still be irrelevant. The reason can best be illustrated with an analogy.

Suppose that every black American boy were to be socialized to become a jazz musician on the assumption that he has a "natural" talent in that direction; or suppose that parents and counselors should subtly discourage him from other pursuits because it is considered "inappropriate" for black men to become physicians or physicists. Most Americans would disapprove. But suppose that it *could* be demonstrated that black Americans, *on the average,* did possess an inborn better sense of rhythm than white Americans. Would *that* justify ignoring the unique characteristics of a *particular* black youngster from the very beginning and specifically socializing him to become a musician? We don't think so. Similarly, as long as a woman's socialization does not nurture her uniqueness, but treats her only as a member of a group on the basis of some assumed *average* characteristic, she will not be prepared to realize her own potential in the way that the values of individuality and self-fulfillment imply that she should.

THE PRESUMED INCOMPATIBILITY OF FAMILY AND CAREER

If we were to ask the average American woman why she is not pursuing a full-time career, she would probably not say that discrimination had discouraged her; nor would she be likely to recognize the pervasive effects of her own sex-role conditioning. What she probably would say is that a career, no matter how desirable, is simply incompatible with the role of wife and mother.

As recently as the turn of the century, and in less technological societies today, this incom-

patibility between career and family was, in fact, decisive. Women died in their forties and they were pregnant or nuring during most of their adult lives. Moreover, the work that a less technological society requires places a premium on mobility and physical strength, neither of which a pregnant woman has a great deal of. Thus, the historical division of labor between the sexes—the man away at work and the woman at home with the children—was a biological necessity. Today it is not.

Today, the work that our technological society requires is primarily mental in nature; women have virtually complete control over their reproductive lives; and most important of all, the average American women now lives to age 74 and has her last child before age 30. This means that by the time a woman is 35 or so, her children all have more important things to do with their daytime hours than to spend them entertaining some adult woman who has nothing fulfilling to do during the entire second half of her life span.

But social forms have a way of outliving the necessities which gave rise to them. And today's female adolescent continues to plan for a 19th century life style in a 20th century world. A Gallup poll has found that young women give no thought whatever to life after forty (Gallup & Hill, 1962). They plan to graduate from high school, perhaps go to college, and then get married. Period!

THE WOMAN AS WIFE

At some level, of course, this kind of planning is "realistic." Because most women do grow up to be wives and mothers, and because, for many women, this means that they will be leaving the labor force during the child-rearing years, a career is not really feasible. After all, a career involves long-term commitment and perhaps some sacrifice on the part of the family. Furthermore, as every "successful" woman knows, a wife's appropriate role is to encourage her husband in *his* career. The "good" wife puts her husband through school, endures the family's early financial difficulties without a whimper, and, if her husband's career should suddenly dictate a move to another city, she sees to it that the transition is accomplished as painlessly as possible. The good wife is selfless. And to be seriously concerned about one's own career is selfish—if one is female, that is. With these kinds of constraints imposed upon the work life of the married woman, perhaps it would be "unrealistic" for her to seriously aspire toward a career rather than a job.

There is some evidence of discontent among these "selfless" women, however. A 1962 Gallup poll (Gallup & Hill, 1962) revealed that only 10% of American women would want their daughters to live their lives the way they did. These mothers wanted their daughters to get more education and to marry later. And a 1970 study of women married to top Chicago-area business and professional men (Ringo, 1970) revealed that if these women could live their lives over again, they would pursue careers.

Accordingly, the traditional conception of the husband-wife relationship is now being challenged, not so much because of this widespread discontent among older, married women, but because it violates two of the most basic values of today's college generation. These values concern personal growth, on the one hand, and interpersonal relationships on the other. The first of these emphasizes the individuality and self-fulfillment; the second stresses openness, honesty, and equality in all human relationships.

Because they see the traditional male-female relationship as incompatible with these basic values, today's young people are experimenting with alternatives to the traditional marriage pattern. Although a few are testing out ideas like communal living, most seem to be searching for satisfactory modifications of the husband-wife relationship, either in or out of the context of marriage. An increasing number of young people claim to be seeking fully equalita-

rian relationships and they cite examples like the following:

> Both my wife and I earned college degrees in our respective disciplines. I turned down a superior job offer in Oregon and accepted a slightly less desirable position in New York where my wife would have more opportunities for part-time work in her specialty. Although I would have preferred to live in a suburb, we purchased a home near my wife's job so that she could have an office at home where she would be when the children returned from school. Because my wife earns a good salary, she can easily afford to pay a housekeeper to do her major household chores. My wife and I share all other tasks around the house equally. For example; she cooks the meals, but I do the laundry for her and help her with many of her other household tasks.

Without questioning the basic happiness of such a marriage or its appropriateness for many couples, we can legitimately ask if such a marriage is, in fact, an instance of interpersonal equality. Have all the hidden assumptions about the woman's "natural" role really been eliminated? Have our visionary students really exorcised the traditional ideology as they claim? There is a very simple test. If the marriage is truly equalitarian, then its description should retain the same flavor and tone even if the roles of the husband and wife were to be reversed:

> Both my husband and I earned college degrees in our respective disciplines. I turned down a superior job offer in Oregon and accepted a slightly less desirable position in New York where my husband would have more opportunities for part-time work in his specialty. Although I would have preferred to live in a suburb, we purchased a home near my husband's job so that he could have an office at home where he would be when the children returned from school. Because my husband earns a good salary, he can easily afford to pay a housekeeper to do his major household chores. My husband and I share all other tasks

around the house equally. For example, he cooks the meals, but I do the laundry for him and help him with many of his other household tasks.

Somehow it sounds different, and yet only the pronouns have been changed to protect the powerful! Certainly no one would ever mistake the marriage *just* described as equalitarian or even very desirable, and thus it becomes apparent that the ideology about the woman's "natural" place unconsciously permeates the entire fabric of such "pseudo-equalitarian" marriages. It is true the wife gains some measure of equality when she can have a career rather than have a job and when her career can influence the final place of residence. But why is it the unquestioned assumption that the husband's career solely determines the initial set of alternatives that are to be considered? Why is it the wife who automatically seeks the part-time position? Why is it *her* housekeeper rather than *their* housekeeper? Why *her* household tasks? And so forth throughout the entire relationship.

The important point is not that such marriages are bad or that their basic assumptions of inequality produce unhappy, frustrated women. Quite the contrary. It is the very happiness of the wives in such marriages that reveals society's smashing success in socializing its women. It is a measure of the distance our society must yet traverse toward the goal of full equality that such marriages are widely characterized as utopian and fully equalitarian. It is a mark of how well the women has been kept in her place that the husband in such a marriage is almost always idolized by women, including his wife. Why? Because he "permits her" to squeeze a career into the interstices of their marriage as long as his own career is not unduly inconvenienced. Thus is the white man blessed for exercising his power benignly while his "natural" right to that power forever remains unquestioned. Such is the subtlety of America's ideology about women.

In fact, however, even these "benign" in-

equities are now being challenged. More and more young couples really are entering marriages of full equality, marriages in which both partners pursue careers or outside commitments which carry equal weight when all important decisions are to be made, marriages in which both husband and wife accept some compromise in the growth of their respective careers for their mutual partnership. Certainly such marriages have more tactical difficulties than more traditional ones: It is simply more difficult to coordinate two independent lives rather than one-and-a-half. The point is that it is not possible to predict ahead of time *on the basis of sex,* who will be doing the compromising at any given point of decision.

It should be clear that the man or woman who places career above all else ought not to enter an equalitarian marriage. The man would do better to marry a traditional wife, a wife who will make whatever sacrifices his career necessitates. The woman who places career above all else would do better—in our present society—to remain single. For an equalitarian marriage is not designed for extra efficiency, but for double fulfillment.

THE WOMAN AS MOTHER

In all marriages, whether traditional, pseudo-equalitarian or fully equalitarian, the real question surrounding a mother's career will probably continue to be the well-being of the children. All parents want to be certain that they are doing the very best for their children and that they are not depriving them in any important way, either materially or psychologically. What this has meant recently in most families that could afford it was that mother would devote herself to the children on a full-time basis. Women have been convinced—by their mothers and by the so-called experts—that there is something wrong with them if they even want to do otherwise.

For example, according to Dr. Spock (1963),

any woman who finds full-time motherhood un-fulfilling is showing "a residue of difficult rela-tionships in her own childhood." If a vacation doesn't solve the problem, then she is probably having emotional problems which can be re-lieved "through regular counseling in a family social agency, or if severe, through psychiatric treatment . . . Any mother of a pre-school child who is considering a job should discuss the issues with a social worker before making her decision." The message is clear: If you don't feel that your two-year-old is a stimulating, full-time, companion, than you are probably neurotic.

In fact, research does not support the view that children suffer in any way when mother works. Although it came as a surprise to most researchers in the area, maternal employment in and of itself does not seem to have any nega-tive effects on the children; and part-time work actually seems to benefit the children. Children of working mothers are no more likely than chil-dren of non-working mothers to be delinquent or nervous or withdrawn or anti-social; they are no more likely to show neurotic symptoms; they are no more likely to perform poorly in school; and they are no more likely to feel deprived of their mothers' love. Daughters of working mothers are more likely to want to work them-selves, and, when asked to name the one woman in the world that they most admire, daughters of working mothers are more likely to name their own mothers! (Nye & Hoffman, 1963). This is one finding that we wish every working woman in America could hear, be-cause the other thing that is true of almost every working mother is that she *thinks* she is hurting her children and she feels guilty. In fact, re-search has shown that the worst mothers are those who would like to work, but who stay home out of a sense of duty (Yarrow, Scott, de Leeuw, & Heinig, 1962). The major conclusion from all the research is really this: What matters is the quality of a mother's relationship with her children, not the time of day it happens to be administered. This conclusion should come as

no surprise; successful fathers have been demonstrating it for years. Some fathers are great, some fathers stink, and they're all at work at least eight hours a day.

Similarly, it is true that the quality of substitute care that children receive while their parents are at work also matters. Young children do need security, and research has shown that it is not good to have a constant turnover of parent-substitutes, a rapid succession of changing baby-sitters or housekeepers (Mac-coby, 1958). Clearly, this is why the establish-ment of child care centers is vitally important at the moment. This is why virtually every woman's group in the country, no matter how conserva-tive or how radical, is in agreement on this one issue: that child care centers ought to be avail-able to those who need them.

Once again, it is relevant to emphasize that child care centers, like the other reforms advo-cated, are not merely for the benefit of middle-class women who wish to pursue professional careers. Of the 31 million women in the labor force, nearly 40% of them are working mothers. In 1960, mothers constituted more than one-third of the total woman labor force. In March, 1971, more than 1 out of 3 working mothers (4.3 million of them) had children under 6 years of age, and about half of these had children under 3 years of age. And most of these women in the labor force—like most men—work because they cannot afford to do otherwise. Moreover, they cannot currently deduct the full costs of child care as a business expense as the execu-tive can often deduct an expensive car. At the moment, the majority of these working women must simply 'make do' with whatever child care arrangements they can manage. Only 6% of their children under 6 years of age currently receive group care in child care centers. *This* is why child-care centers are a central issue of the new feminist movement. This is why they are not just an additional luxury for the middle-class family with a woman who wants to pursue a professional career.

But even the woman who is educationally

and economically in a position to pursue a career must feel free to utilize these alternative arrangements for child care. For once again, America's sex-role ideology intrudes. Many people still assume that if a woman wants a full-time career, then children must be unimportant to her. But of course, no one makes this assumption about her husband. No one assumes that a father's interest in his career necessarily precludes a deep and abiding affection for his children or a vital interest in their development. Once again, America applies a double standard of judgment. Suppose that a father of small children suddenly lost his wife. No matter how much he loved his children, no one would expect him to sacrifice his career in order to stay home with them on a full-time basis—even if he had an independent source of income. No one would charge him with selfishness or lack of parental feeling if he sought professional care for his children during the day.

It is here that full equality between husband and wife assumes its ultimate importance. The fully equalitarian marriage abolishes this double standard and extends the same freedom to the mother. The equalitarian marriage provides the framework for both husband and wife to pursue careers which are challenging and fulfilling and, at the same time, to participate equally in the pleasures and responsibilities of childrearing. Indeed, it is the equalitarian marriage which has the potential for giving children the love and concern of two parents rather than one. And it is the equalitarian marriage which has the most potential for giving parents the challenge and fulfillment of two worlds—family and career—rather than one.

In addition to providing this potential for equalized child care, a truly equalitarian marriage embraces a more general division of labor which satisfies what we like to call "the roommate test." That is, the labor is divided just as it is when two men or two women room together in college or set up a bachelor apartment together. Errands and domestic chores are as-signed by preference, agreement, flipping a coin, alternated, given to hired help, or—perhaps most often the case—left undone.

It is significant that today's young people, so many of whom live precisely this way prior to marriage, find this kind of arrangement within marriage so foreign to their thinking. Consider an analogy. Suppose that a white male college student decided to room or set up a bachelor apartment with a black male friend. Surely the typical white student would not blithely assume that his black roommate was to handle all the domestic chores. Nor would his conscience allow him to do so even in the unlikely event that his roommate would say: "No, that's okay. I like doing housework. I'd be happy to do it." We suspect that the typical white student would still not be comfortable if he took advantage of this offer because he and America have finally realized that he would be taking advantage of the fact that such a roommate had been socialized by our society to be "happy" with such obvious inequity. But change this hypothetical black roommate to a female marriage partner, and somehow the student's conscience goes to sleep. At most it is quickly tranquilized by the comforting thought that "she is happiest when she is ironing for her loved one." Such is the power of an unconscious ideology.

Of course, it may well be that she *is* happiest when she is ironing for her loved one.

Such, indeed, is the power of an unconscious ideology.

REFERENCES

Bird, C. *Born female: the high cost of keeping women down.* New York: Pocket Books, 1969.

Broverman, I.K., Broverman, D.M., Clarkson, F. E., Rosenkrantz, P.S., & Vogel, S.R. Sex-role stereotypes and clinical judgments of mental health. *Journal of Consulting and Clinical Psychology,* 1970, *34,* 1–7.

Brown, R. *Social psychology.* New York: Free Press, 1965.

Dodge, N.D. *Women in the Soviet economy.* Baltimore: Johns Hopkins press, 1966.

Fisher, E. The second sex, junior division. *The New York Times Book Review,* May, 1970.

Gallup, G., & Hill, E. The American woman. *The Saturday Evening Post,* Dec. 22, 1962, pp. 15–32.

Goldberg, P. Are women prejudiced against women? *Transaction,* April, 1968, *5,* 28–30.

Goldberg, S., & Lewis, M. Play behavior in the year-old infant: early sex differences. *Child Development,* 1969, *40,* 21–31.

Horner, M.S. Fail: bright women. *Psychology Today,* November, 1969.

Maccoby, E.E. Effects upon children on their mothers' outside employment. In *Work in the lives of married women.* New York: Columbia University Press, 1958.

Milton, G.A. Sex differences in problem solving as a function of role appropriateness of the problem content. *Psychological Reports,* 1959, *5,* 705–708.

Nye, F.I., & Hoffman, L.W. *The employed mother in America.* Chicago: Rand McNally, 1963.

Ringo, M. The well-placed wife. Unpublished manuscript, John Paisios & Associates, 332 South Michigan Ave., Chicago, Illinois 60604.

Spock, B. Should mothers work? *Ladies' Home Journal,* February, 1963.

Terman, L.M., & Oden, M.H. *Genetic studies of genius, V. The gifted group at mid-life: Thirty-five years' follow-up of the superior child.* Stanford, California: Stanford University Press, 1959.

Thoman, E.B., Leiderman, P.H., & Olson, J.P. Neonate-mother interaction during breast feeding. *Developmental Psychology,* 1972, *6,* 110–118.

U.S. Department of Labor, Wage and Labor Standards Administration, Women's Bureau. Fact sheet on the earnings gap, February, 1970.

U.S. Department of Labor, Wage and Labor Standards Administration, Women's Bureau. *Handbook on women workers,* 1969. Bulletin 294.

Yarrow, M.R., Scott, P., de Leeuw, L., & Heinig, D. Child-rearing in families of working and nonworking mothers. *Sociometry,* 1962, *25,* 122–140.

WORKAHOLICS: THIS LAND OF OURS HAS TO HAVE THEM

WAYNE OATES

Source: From pages 14–19 in *Confessions of a Workaholic: The Facts About Work Addiction* by Wayne Oates (World Publishing Company). Copyright © 1971 by Wayne Oates. Reprinted by permission of Harper and Row, Inc.

WORKAHOLISM: THE ORGANIZATION MAN'S NECESSITY

The organizational life of business, industry, or the church tends to call for the workaholic. One asks whether this syndrome of effort-riddenness is not spawned by a bureaucratic culture. There are certain identifiable cultural factors in alcoholic addiction and drug addiction which produce an "alcoholic culture" or a "drug culture," and my point here is that this is true of work addiction also. One kind of person that an organization must have is the man or woman who has *no* value that is not subordinated by the "good of the organization." He idolizes his outfit. If he celebrates his wedding anniversary, he feels he has to do it in such a way as to be good public relations for the organization. If he takes a vacation, it must be used in a way to make progress for the company, the school, or the plant.

Furthermore, this man does not work a given number of hours. He is always on call for the company. As William H. Whyte describes him and his kind, "they are never at leisure [even] when they are at leisure." This person is one who "is so completely involved in his work that he cannot distinguish between work and the rest of his life—and he is happy that he cannot."* This is rarely a salaried man who works so many days a month and year for his income, nor the nine-to-five man who when he finishes his daily stint forgets about work until his shift comes up again. This is a person who works around the clock. Let us take a look at his typical day.

He awakens at a specific time each morning without being called or without an alarm. He lies in bed for a few minutes and arranges in his mind every known detail of the schedule for that day. He ritualistically dresses and eats breakfast. He then moves through a day in which every moment is scheduled, except the time of

The Organization Man (New York: Doubleday, 1957), p. 164.

leaving the office. At the end of the day—usually after everyone else has gone home—he never heads for home until he has gathered materials for work at night. He eats his dinner, and his work is the main topic of the conversation at the table. He then retreats to his workroom to make the best of the remaining hours of the day. He retires and spends the time just before he drops off to sleep in trying once again to solve the problems that defied solution during the day, rehearsing accounts of conflicts he has had with other people during the day, and experiencing considerable anxiety about the amount of work he has to do the next day, week, or month.

I recall a businessman telling me of an experience which changed his whole life. He decided that he was going to quit taking work home at night. He first did so by staying at the office until he finished, gradually reducing the length of time he stayed at the office. Then he disciplined himself to have all his work done by 5:30 p.m. He tells of the first evening he went home when the rest of the office force did. He stood outside the office building and watched each one go by on his way home. Then he went through an "almost physical agony" as he resisted the temptation to go back upstairs to work or to get his briefcase to take work home. He finally made a break for home and has neither worked late nor taken work home since.

My central point in this section is: the organization *needs* a few workaholics to prosper as an organization. Culture as we have it calls for this kind of devotee to his work—workaholics who live by a sweephand watch and dream of ways to give more time than twenty-four hours each day.

WORKAHOLISM IN THE NINE-TO-FIVE MAN

The impression I have left thus far would seem to suggest that the work addict is an upper-middle-class and lower-upper-class phenomenon. He is not. The recent concern about "law and order" has called attention to the wages of policemen and firemen. Because of their relatively low pay these persons are forced to take additional jobs as security policemen, night watchmen, fire wardens, etc., for private companies in order to supplement their income.

The same need is felt also by public school teachers, and even university and college professors. I recently found one schoolteacher who worked in the evenings as a motel clerk, a job in which he could be paid extra and still have time to grade papers and prepare for classes the next day. During the Christmas holidays, he, being overweight served as a Santa Claus in a nearby department store. These are persons with fixed-hour schedules who nevertheless moonlight in order to make additional money.

At first, the basic factor in overwork by people on fixed-schedule jobs seems to be purely financial. They need to make more money, which is not forthcoming from the public budgets out of which their initial salaries are paid. Usually they are in types of work where labor unions, and thus strikes for higher wages, etc., are taboo. Consequently, the need for more income can only be met by taking extra work. On the surface, this seems to be *the* reason for moonlighting. However, closer inspection reveals other more subtle factors.

One of them is social prestige. These persons want their families to have what other families have, notably education. They and their wives both work in order to send their children to college. They themselves had to work long hours in order to get a college education. They do not want their sons and daughters to have to work as they did but to be able to give *all* their time to study. They want to have two cars so their wives can get around as they wish and so the children can have "wheels." They want to move to a better neighborhood so their children will have a chance to better themselves through the prestige of the kinds of friends they associate with, and marry.

As we probe underneath these social factors, we find the element of competition. In the Ten Commandments, we are told not to be covetous, but tradition approves all forms of competition. The ambiguous condition of the workaholic is that he works hard to get the things and the place in society that other men envy. At the same time he isolates himself from the very people whose approval he thinks he can get by outdoing them. The salty brine of competition is exciting to swim in, cooling to the skin as one revels in it, but does not satisfy the thirst for companionship and communion with others. As Samuel Johnson said in 1775, "That is the happiest conversation where there is no competition, no vanity, but a calm, quiet interchange of sentiments."

As we probe underneath the competitive factor, we find other causes of overwork. We find men who no longer can *see* the results of their labors. Even the assembly worker on the line does not *see* the total design of what he is doing. He has to assume that by doing his particular operation he has accomplished a great deal. The assembly line has removed the artisan from our culture, rarely today can one man in business for himself create enough pieces of furniture, jewelry, pottery, etc., to earn a living by direct sale of what he produces. There is a poignancy in the situation of a man who cannot invest his identity in the *substantive things he produces* rather than in the intangible of money. He has trouble communicating to his family the *worthwhileness* of what he is doing because he cannot show them the fruits of his hands except in the form of money. He cannot teach them his skill, but can only prove his manhood by bringing money home. It is little wonder that he seeks to work more and more in order to bring more and more money home. Yet all he gets as his reward is loneliness. Money creates a mythology of power in his family's mind; it also isolates him from them. He cannot easily teach his own children how to work, or communicate with his wife about what *his* work is really like. Little

wonder that he solves the problem by returning to work! When he is gone and at work, he feels that they understand a *little.* When he is at home with *nothing to do,* they have no place for him because they have organized their lives on the assumption of his absence.

AGE AND WORKAHOLISM

One of the things that our culture is doing for us and to us at the same time is enabling us to live longer. Even a full generation ago retirement for people of certain social classes was unknown. Social security has changed all this.

The middle-aged person approaching retirement begins to feel the pangs of his workaholism just when he has earned enough money to have the right to a certain amount of leisure because he doesn't know how to use that leisure. Also, unwillingness to spend money for recreational or creative purposes may actually express the fear of spending money without doing a sufficient amount of work to punish oneself for it. For example, one doctor told me that when he went on vacation he always borrowed the money because he would have to punish himself with work to pay it back, and this was just penance for the pleasure of not working!

The middle-aged person, furthermore, often feels the need to redouble his efforts in order to get ready for retirement. He continues to do repetitious tasks in order to have something in reserve for a "rainy day." He then may become severely depressed. Fortunately, excellent methods of treatment for "middle-aged depressions" are available, and a professional person can be of real assistance to someone who is suffering in this way. They have the "know-how" to help him decide things he hitherto has had no support in deciding. They can even intervene directly and decide a few things for him, such as specific changes in his work habits. Thus, although middle-aged depression is very painful, it can often lead the middle-aged work addict to do what he should have done in the first place without becoming depressed and feeling guilty about it: interrupt his routine of work, do something for a while that he really enjoys doing, and stop driving himself like a slave.

Today culture has created the possibility of more leisure time for us through a shorter work week. As a people, we have more of this world's goods at an earlier age. We are lengthening life; we can retire. Yet we have not escaped the compulsion about work that defies external efforts to make life easier. We have not found the answer to the covetousness that makes men compete with each other in their work all out of proportion to their needs. We have not found the secret of rest in the midst of plenty, renewal in the midst of work, and companionship in the atmosphere of loneliness that tarrying too long at the job produces. Our culture produces the workaholic. We need to attend to the nature of a society that needs such slaves to work, and at the same time to struggle against our individual compulsions to work.

BANANA TIME—JOB SATISFACTION AND INFORMAL INTERACTION

DONALD F. ROY

This paper undertakes description and exploratory analysis of the social interaction which took place within a small work group of factory machine operatives during a two-month period of participant observation. The factual and ideational materials which it presents lie at an intersection of two lines of research interest and should, in their dual bearing, contribute to both. Since the operatives were engaged in work which involved the repetition of very simple operations over an extra-long workday, six days a week, they were faced with the problem of dealing with a formidable "beast of monotony." Revelation of how the group utilized its resources to combat the "beast" should merit the attention of those who are seeking solution to the practical problem of job satisfaction, or employee morale. It should also provide insights for those who are trying to penetrate the mysteries of the small group.

Convergence of these two lines of interest is, of course, no new thing. Among the host of writers and researchers who have suggested connections between "group" and "joy in work" are Walker and Guest, observers of social interaction on the automobile assembly line.[1] They quote assembly line workers as saying, "We have a lot of fun and talk all the time,"[2] and, "If it weren't for the talking and fooling, you'd go nuts."[3]

My account of how one group of machine operators kept from "going nuts" in a situation of monotonous work activity attempts to lay bare the issues of interaction which made up the content of their adjustment. The talking, fun, and fooling which provided solution to the elemental problem of "psychological survival" will be described according to their embodiment in intra-group relations. In addition, an unusual opportunity for close observation of behavior involved in the maintenance of group equilibrium was afforded by the fortuitous introduction of a "natural experiment." My unwitting injection of explosive materials into the stream of interac-

Source: Reproduced by permission of the Society for Applied Anthropology from Human Organization, Vol. 18(4), 1960.

tion resulted in sudden, but temporary, loss of group interaction.

My fellow operatives and I spent our long days of simple repetitive work in relative isolation from other employees of the factory. Our line of machines was sealed off from other work areas of the plant by the four walls of the clicking room. The one door of this room was usually closed. Even when it was kept open, during periods of hot weather, the consequences were not social; it opened on an uninhabited storage room of the shipping department. Not even the sound of work activity going on elsewhere in the factory carried to this isolated work place. There were occasional contacts with "outside" employees, usually on matters connected with the work; but, with the exception of the daily calls of one fellow who came to pick up finished materials for the next step in processing, such visits were sporadic and infrequent.

Moreover, face-to-face contact with members of the managerial hierarchy were few and far between. No one bearing the title of foreman ever came around. The only company official who showed himself more than once during the two month observation period was the plant superintendent. Evidently overloaded with supervisory duties and production problems which kept him busy elsewhere, he managed to pay his respects every week or two. His visits were in the nature of short, businesslike, but friendly exchanges. Otherwise he confined his observable communications with the group to occasional utilization of a public address system. During the two-month period, the company president and the chief chemist paid one friendly call apiece. One man, who may or may not have been of managerial status, was seen on various occasions lurking about in a manner which excited suspicion. Although no observable consequences accrued from the peculiar visitations of this silent fellow, it was assumed that he was some sort of efficiency expert, and he was referred to as "The Snooper."

As far as our work group was concerned, this was truly a situation of laissez-faire management. There was no interference from staff experts, no hounding by time-study engineers or personnel men hot on the scent of efficiency or good human relations. Nor were there any signs of industrial democracy in the form of safety, recreational, or production committees. There was an international union, and there was a highly publicized union-management cooperation program; but actual international processes of cooperation were carried in somewhere beyond my range of observation and without participation of members of any work group. Furthermore, these union-management get-togethers had no determinable connection with the problem of "toughing out" a twelve-hour day at monotonous work.

Our work group was thus not only abandoned to its own resources for creating job satisfaction, but left without that basic reservoir of ill-will toward management which can sometimes be counted on to stimulate the development of interesting activities to occupy hand and brain. Lacking was the challenge of intergroup conflict, that perennial source of creative experience to fill the otherwise empty hours of meaningless work routine.[4]

The clicking machines were housed in a room approximately thirty by twenty-four feet. They were four in number, set in a row, and so arranged along one wall that the busy operator could, merely by raising his head from his work, freshen his reveries with a glance through one of three large barrel windows. To the rear of one of the end machines sat a long cutting table; here the operators cut up rolls of plastic materials into small sheets manageable for further processing at the clickers. Behind the machine at the opposite end of the line sat another table which was intermittently the work station of a female employee who performed sundry scissors operations of a more intricate nature on raincoat parts. Boxed in on all sides by shelves and stocks of materials, this latter locus of work appeared a cell within a cell.

The clickers were of the genus punching machines; of mechanical construction similar to that of the better-known punch presses, their leading features were hammer and block. The hammer, or punching head, was approximately eight inches by twelve inches at its flat striking surface. The descent upon the block was initially forced by the operator, who exerted pressure on a handle attached to the side of the hammer head. A few inches of travel downward established electrical connection for a sharp, power-driven blow. The hammer also traveled, by manual guidance, in a horizontal plane to and from, and in an arc around, the central column of the machine. Thus the operator, up to the point of establishing electrical connections for the sudden and irrevocable downward thrust, had flexibility in maneuvering his instrument over the larger surface of the block. The latter, approximately twenty-four inches wide, eighteen inches deep, and ten inches thick, was made, like a butcher's block, of inlaid hardwood; it was set in the machine at a convenient waist height. On it the operator placed his materials, one sheet at a time if leather, stacks of sheets if plastic, to be cut with steel dies of assorted sizes and shapes. The particular die in use would be moved, by hand, from spot to spot over the materials each time a cut was made; less frequently, materials would be shifted on the block as the operator saw need for each adjustment.

Introduction to the new job, with its relatively simple machine skills and work routines, was accomplished with what proved to be, in my experience, an all-time minimum of job training. The clicking machines assigned to one was situated at one end of the row. Here the superintendent and one of the operators gave a few brief demonstrations, accompanied by bits of advice which included a warning to keep hands clear of the descending hammer. After a short practice period, at the end of which the superintendent expressed satisfaction with progress and potentialities, I was left to develop my learning curve with no other supervision than that afforded by members of the work group. Further advice and assistance did come, from time to time, from my fellow operatives, sometimes upon request, sometimes unsolicited.

THE WORK GROUP

Absorbed at first in three related goals of improving my clicking skill, increasing my rate of output, and keeping my left hand unclicked, I paid little attention to my fellow operatives save to observe that they were friendly, middle-aged, foreign-born, full of advice, and very talkative. Their names, according to the way they addressed each other, were George, Ike, and Sammy.[5] George, a stocky fellow in his late fifties, operated the machine at the opposite end of the line; he, I later discovered, had emigrated in early youth from a county in Southeastern Europe. Ike, stationed at George's left, was tall, slender, in his early fifties, and Jewish; he had come from Eastern Europe in his youth. Sammy, number three man in line, and my neighbor, was heavy set, in his late fifties, and Jewish; he had escaped from a country in Eastern Europe just before Hitler's legions had moved in. All three men had been downwardly mobile as to occupation in recent years. George and Sammy had been proprietors of small businesses, the former had been "wiped out" when his uninsured establishment burned down; the latter had been entrepreneuring on a small scale before he left all behind him to flee the Germans. According to his account, Ike had left a highly skilled trade which he had practiced for years in Chicago.

I discovered also that the clicker line represented a ranking system in descending order from George to myself. George not only had top seniority for the group, but functioned as a sort of leadman. His superior status was marked in the fact that he received five cents more per hour than the other clickermen, put in the longest workday, made daily contact, outside the workroom, with the superintendent on work matters which concerned the entire line, and communicated to the rest of us the directives which he received. The narrow margin of superordination was seen in the fact that directives were always relayed in the superintendent's name; they were on the order of, "You'd better let that go now, and get on the green. Joe says they're running low on the fifth floor," or, "Joe says he wants two boxes of the 3-die today." The narrow margin was also seen in the fact that the superintendent would communicate directly with his operatives over the public address system; and, on occasion, Ike or Sammy would leave the workroom to confer with him for decisions or advice in regard to work orders.

Ike was next to George in seniority, then Sammy. I was, of course, low man on the totem pole. Other indices to status differentiation lay in informal interaction, to be described later.

With one exception, job status tended to be matched by length of workday. George worked a thirteen-hour day, from 7 A.M. to 8:30 P.M. Ike worked eleven hours, from 7 A.M. to 6:30 P.M; occasionally he worked until 7 to 7:30 for an eleven and a half- or a twelve-hour day. Sammy put in a nine-hour day, from 8 A.M. to 5:30 P.M. My twelve hours spanned from 8 A.M. to 8:30 P.M. We had a half hour for lunch, from 12 to 12:30.

The female who worked at the secluded table behind George's machine put in a regular plant-wide eight-hour shift from 8 to 4:30. Two women held this job during the period of my employment; Mable was succeeded by Baby. Both were Negroes, and in their late twenties.

A fifth clicker operator, an Arabian *emigré* called Boo, worked a night shift by himself. He usually arrived about 7 P.M. to take over Ike's machine.

THE WORK

It was evident to me, before my first workday drew to a weary close, that my clicking career was going to be a grim process of fighting the clock, the particular timepiece in this situation being an old-fashioned alarm clock which ticked away on a shelf near George's machine. I had struggled through many dreary rounds with the minutes and hours during the various phases of my industrial experience, but never had I been confronted with such a dismal combination of working conditions as the extra-long workday, the infinitesimal cerebral excitation, and the extreme limitation of physical movement. The contrast with a recent stint in the California oil fields was striking. This was no eight-hour day of racing hither and yon over desert and foothills with a rollicking crew of "roustabouts" on a variety of repair missions at oil wells, pipe lines, and storage tanks. Here there were no afternoon dallyings to search the sands for horned toads, tarantulas, and rattlesnakes, or to climb old wooden derricks for raven's nests, with an eye out, of course, for the tell-tale streak of dust in the distance which gave ample warning of the approach of the boss. This was standing all day in one spot beside three old codgers in a dingy room looking out through barred windows at the bare walls of a brick warehouse, leg movements largely restricted to the shifting of body weight from one foot to the other, hand and arm movements confined, for the most part to a simple repetitive sequence of place the die, —— punch the clicker, —— place the die, —— punch the clicker, and intellectual activity reduced to computing the hours to quitting time. It is true that from time to time a fresh stack of sheets would have to be substituted for the clicked-out old one, but the stack would have been prepared by someone else, and the exchange would be only a minute or two in the making. Now and then a box of finished work would have to be moved back out of the way, and an empty box brought up, but the moving back and the bringing up involved only a step or two. And there was the half hour for lunch, and occasional trips to the lavatory or the drinking fountain to break up the day into digestible parts. But after each momentary respite, hammer and die were moving again: click, ——— move die, ——— click, ——— move die.

Before the end of the first day, Monotomy was joined by his twin brother, Fatigue. I got tired. My legs ached, and my feet hurt. Early in the afternoon I discovered a tall stool and moved it up to my machine to "take the load off my feet." But the superintendent dropped in to see how I was "doing" and promptly informed me that "we don't sit down on this job." My reverie toyed with the idea of quitting the job and looking for other work.

The next day was the same: the monotony of the work, the tired legs and sore feet and thoughts of quitting.

THE GAME OF WORK

In discussing the factory operative's struggle to "cling to the remnants of joy in work," Henri de Man makes the general observations that "it is psychologically impossible to deprive any kind of work of all its positive emotional elements, "that the worker will find *some* meaning in any activity assigned to him, a "certain scope for initiative which can satisfy after a fashion the instinct for play and the creative impulse," that "even in the Taylor system there is found luxury of self-determination."[6] De Man cites the case of one worker who wrapped 13,000 incandescent bulbs a day; she found her outlet for creative impulse, her self-determination, her meaning in work by varying her wrapping movements a little from time to time.

So did I search for *some* meaning in my continuous mincing of plastic sheets into small ovals, fingers, and trapezoids. The richness of possibility for creative expression previously discovered in my experience with the "Taylor system"[8] did not reveal itself here. There was no piecework, so no piecework game. There was no conflict with management, so no war game. But, like the light bulb wrapper, I did find a "certain scope for initiative," and out of this slight freedom to vary activity, I developed a game of work.

The game developed was quite simple, so elementary in fact, that its playing was reminiscent of rainy-day preoccupations in childhood, when attention could be centered by the hour on colored bits of things of assorted sizes and shapes. But this adult activity was not mere pottering and piddling, what it lacked in the earlier imaginative content, it made up for in clean-cut structure. Fundamentally involved were: (a) variation in color of the materials cut, (b) variation in shape of the dies used, and (c) a process called "scraping the block." The basic procedure which ordered the particular combination of components employed could be stated in the form: "As soon as I do so many of these, I'll get to do those." If, for example, production scheduled for the day featured small, rectangular strips in three colors, the game might go: "As soon as I finish a thousand of the green ones, I'll click some brown ones." And, with success in attaining the objective of working with brown materials, a new goal of "I'll get to do the white ones" might be set. Or the new goal might involve switching dies.

Scraping the block made the game more interesting by adding to the number of possible variations in its playing; and what was perhaps more important, provided the only substantial reward, save for going to the lavatory or getting a drink of water, on days when work with one die and one color of material was scheduled. As a physical operation, scraping the block was fairly simple; it involved application of a coarse file to the upper surface of the block to remove roughness and unevenness resulting from the wear and tear of die penetration. But, as part of the intellectual and emotional content of the game of work, it should be in itself a source of variation in activity. The upper left-hand corner of the block could be chewed up in the clicking of 1,000 white trapezoid pieces, then scraped. Next, the upper right-hand corner, and so on until the entire block had been worked over. Then, on the next round of scraping by quadrants, there was the possibility of a change of color or die to green trapezoid or white oval pieces.

Thus the game of work might be described as a continuous sequence of short-range production goals with achievement rewards in the form of activity change. The superiority of this relatively complex and self-determined system over the technically simple and outside-controlled job satisfaction injections experienced by Milner at the beginner's table in a shop of the feather industry should be immediately apparent:

> Twice a day our work was completely changed to break the monotony. First Jennie would give us feathers of a brilliant green, then bright orange or a light blue or black. The "ohs" and "ahs" that came from the girls at each change was proof enough that this was an effective way of breaking the monotony of the tedious work.

But a hasty conclusion that I was having lots of fun playing my clicking game should be avoided. These games were not as interesting in the experiencing as they might seem to be from the telling. Emotional tone of the activity was low, and intellectual currents weak. Such rewards as scraping the block or "getting to do the blue ones" were not very exciting, and the stretches of repetitive movement involved in achieving them were long enough to permit lapses into obsessive reverie. Henri de Man speaks of "clinging to the remnants of joy in work," and this situation represented just that. How tenacious the clinging was, how long I could have "stuck it out" with my remnants, was never determined. Before the first week was out this adjustment to the work situation was complicated by other developments. The game of

work continued, but in a different context. Its influence became decidedly subordinated to, if not completely overshadowed by, another source of job satisfaction.

INFORMAL SOCIAL ACTIVITY OF THE WORK GROUP: TIMES AND THEMES

The change came about when I began to take serious note of the social activity going on around me; my attentiveness to this activity came with growing involvement in it. What I heard at first, before I started to listen, was a stream of disconnected bits of communication which did not make much sense. Foreign accents were strong and referents were not joined to coherent contexts of meaning. It was just "jabbering." What I saw at first, before I began to observe, was occasional flurries of horseplay so simple and unvarying in pattern and so childish in quality that they made no strong bid for attention. For example, Ike would regularly switch off the power of Sammy's machine whenever Sammy made a trip to the lavatory or the drinking fountain. Correlatively, Sammy invariably fell victim to the plot by making an attempt to operate his clicking hammer after returning to the shop. And, as the simple pattern went, this blind stumbling into the trap was always followed by indignation and reproach from Sammy; smirking satisfaction from Ike, and mild paternal scolding from George. My interest in this procedure was at first confined to wondering when Ike would weary of his tedious joke or when Sammy would learn to check his power switch before trying the hammer.

But, as I began to pay closer attention, as I began to develop familiarity with the communication system, the disconnected became connected, the nonsense made sense, the obscure became clear, and the silly actually funny. And, as the content of the interaction took on more and more meaning, the interaction began to reveal structure. There were "times" and "themes," and roles to serve their enaction. The interaction had subtleties, and I began to savor and appreciate them. I started to record what hitherto had seemed unimportant.

Times

This emerging awareness of structure and meaning included recognition that the long day's grind was broken by interruptions of a kind other than the formally instituted or idiosyncratically developed disjunctions in work routine previously described. These additional interruptions appeared in daily repetition in an ordered series of informal interactions. They were, in part, but only in part and in very rough comparison, similar to those common fractures of the production process known as the coffee break, the coke break, and the cigarette break. Their distinction lay in frequency of occurrence and in brevity. As phases of the daily series, they occurred almost hourly, and so short were they in duration that they disrupted work activity only slightly. Their significance lay not so much in their function as rest pauses, although it cannot be denied that physical refreshment was involved. Nor did their chief importance lie in the accentuation of progress points in the passage of time, although they could perform that function far more strikingly than the hour hand on the dull face of George's alarm clock. If the daily series of interruptions be likened to a clock, then the comparison might best be made with a special kind of cuckoo clock, one with a cuckoo which can provide variation in its announcements and can create such an interest in them that the intervening minutes become filled with intellectual content. The major significance of the interactional interruption lay in such a carryover of interest. The physical interplay which momentarily halted work activity would initiate verbal exchanges and thought processes to occupy group members until the next interruption. The group interaction thus not only marked off the time; they gave it content and hurried it along.

Most of the breaks in the daily series were designated as "times" in the parlance of the clicker operators, and they featured the consumption of food or drink of one sort or another. There was coffee time, peach time, banana time, fish time, coke time, and, of course, lunch time. Other interruptions, which formed part of the series but were not verbally recognized as times, were window time, pickup time, and the staggered quitting times of Sammy and Ike. These latter unnamed times did not involve the partaking of refreshments.

My attention was first drawn to this times business during my first week of employment when I was encouraged to join in the sharing of two peaches. It was Sammy who provided the peaches; he drew them from his lunch box after making the announcement, "Peach time!" On this first occasion I refused the proffered fruit, but thereafter regularly consumed my half peach. Sammy continued to provide the peaches and to make the "Peach time!" announcement, although there were days when Ike would remind him that it was peach time, urging him to hurry up with the mid-morning snack. Ike invariably complained about the quality of the fruit, and his complaints fed the fires of continued banter between peach donor and critical recipient. I did find the fruit a bit on the scrubby side but felt, before I achieved insight into the function of peach time, that Ike was showing poor manners by looking a gift horse in the mouth. I wondered why Sammy continued to share his peaches with such an ingrate.

Banana time followed peach time by approximately an hour. Sammy again provided the refreshments, namely, one banana. There was, however, no fourway sharing of Sammy's banana. Ike would gulp it down by himself after surreptitiously extracting it from Sammy's lunch box, kept on a shelf behind Sammy's work station. Each morning, after making the snatch, Ike would call out, "Banana time!" and proceed to down his prize while Sammy made futile protests and denunciations. George would join in with mild remonstrances, sometimes scolding Sammy for making so much fuss. The banana was one which Sammy brought for his own consumption at lunch time; he never did get to eat his banana, but kept bringing one for his lunch. At first this daily theft startled and amazed me. Then I grew to look forward to the daily seizure and the verbal interaction which followed.

Window time came next. It followed banana time as a regular consequence of Ike's castigation by the indignant Sammy. After "taking" repeated references to himself as a person badly lacking in morality and character, Ike would "finally" retaliate by opening the window which faced Sammy's machine, to let the "cold air" blow in on Sammy. The slandering which would, in its echolalic repetition, wear down Ike's patience and forbearance usually took the form of the invidious comparison: "George is a good daddy! Ike is a bad man! A very bad man!" Opening the window would take a little time to accomplish and would involve a great deal of verbal interplay between Ike and Sammy, both before and after the event. Ike would threaten, make feints toward the window, then finally open it. Sammy would protest, argue, and make claims that the air blowing in on him would give him a cold; he would eventually have to leave his machine to close the window. Sometimes the weather was slightly chilly, and the draft from the window unpleasant, but cool or hot, windy or still, window time arrived each day. (I assume that it was originally a cold season development.) George's part in this interplay, in spite of the "good daddy" laudations, was to encourage Ike in his window work. He would stress the tonic values of fresh air and chide Sammy for his unappreciativeness.

Following window time came lunch time, a formally designated half-hour for the midday repast and rest break. At this time, informal interaction would feature exchanges between Ike and George. The former would start eating his lunch a few minutes before noon, and the latter, in his role as straw boss, would censure him for malobservance of the rules. Ike's off-beat lun-

cheon usually involved a previous tampering with George's alarm clock. Ike would set the clock ahead a few minutes in order to maintain his eating schedule without detection, and George would discover these small daylight saving changes.

The first "time" interruption of the day I did not share. It occurred soon after I arrived on the job, at eight o'clock. George and Ike would share a small pot of coffee brewed on George's hot plate.

Pickup time, fish time, and coke time came in the afternoon. I name it pickup time to represent the official visit of the man who made daily calls to cart away boxes of clicked materials. The arrival of the pickup man, a Negro, was always a noisy one, like the arrival of a daily passenger train in an isolated small town. Interaction attained a quick peak of intensity to crowd into a few minutes all communications, necessary and otherwise. Exchanges invariably included loud depreciations by the pickup man of the amount of work accomplished in the clicking department during the preceding twenty-four hours. Such scoffing would be on the order of "Is that all you've got done? What do you boys do all day?" These devaluations would be countered with allusions to the "soft job" enjoyed by the pickup man. During the course of the exchanges news items would be dropped, some of serious import, such as reports of accomplished or impending layoffs in the various plants of the company, or of gains or losses in orders for company products. Most of the news items, however, involved bits of information on plant employees told in a light vein. Information relayed by the clicker operators was usually told about each other, mainly in the form of summaries of the most recent kidding sequences. Some of this material was repetitive, carried over from day to day. Sammy would be the butt of most of this newscasting, although he would make occasional counter-reports on Ike and George. An invariable part of the interactional content of pickup time was Ike's introduction of the pickup man to George. "Meet Mr. Papeatis!" Ike would say in mock solemnity and dignity. Each day the pickup man "met" Mr. Papeatis, to the obvious irritation of the latter. Another pickup time invariably would bring Baby (or Mabel) into the interaction. George would always issue the loud warning to the pickup man: "Now I want you to stay away from Baby! She's Henry's girl!" Henry was a burly Negro with a booming bass voice who made infrequent trips to the clicking room with lift-truck loads of materials. He was reputedly quite a ladies' man among the colored population of the factory. George's warning to "Stay away from Baby!" was issued to every Negro who entered the shop. Baby's only part in this was to laugh at the horseplay.

About mid-afternoon came fish time. George and Ike would stop work for a few minutes to consume some sort of pickled fish which Ike provided. Neither Sammy nor I partook of this nourishment, nor were we invited. For this omission I was grateful; the fish, brought in a newspaper and with head and tail intact, produced a reverse effect on my appetite. George and Ike seemed to share a great liking for fish. Each Friday night, as a regular ritual, they would enjoy a fish dinner together at a nearby restaurant. On these nights, Ike would work until 8:30 and leave the plant with George.

Coke time came late in the afternoon, and was an occasion for total participation. The four of us took turns in buying the drinks and in making the trip for them to a fourth floor vending machine. Through George's manipulation of the situation, it eventually became my daily chore to go after the cokes; the straw boss had noted that I made a much faster trip to the fourth floor and back than Sammy or Ike.

Sammy left the plant at 5:30, and Ike ordinarily retired from the scene an hour and a half later. These quitting times were not marked by any distinctive interaction save the one regular exchange between Sammy and George over the former's "early washup." Sammy's ten-dency was to crowd his washing up toward five o'clock, and it was George's concern to keep it from further creeping advance. After Ike's departure came Boo's arrival. Boo's was a striking personality productive of a change in topics of conversation to fill in the last hour of the long workday.

Themes

To put flesh, so to speak, on this interactional frame of "times," my work group had developed various "themes" of verbal interplay which had become standardized in their repetition. These topics of conversation ranged in quality from an extreme of nonsensical chatter to another extreme of serious discourse. Unlike the times, these themes flowed one into the other in no particular sequence of predictability. Serious conversation could suddenly melt into horseplay, and vice versa. In the middle of a serious discussion on the high cost of living, Ike might drop a weight behind the easily startled Sammy, who hit him over the head with a dusty paper sack. Interaction would immediately drop to a low comedy exchange of slaps, threats, guffaws, and disapprobations which would invariably include a ten-minute echolalia of "Ike is a bad man, a very bad man! George is a good daddy, a very fine man!" Or, on the other hand, a stream of such invidious comparisons as followed a surreptitious switching-off of Sammy's machine by the playful Ike might merge suddenly into a discussion of the pros and cons of saving for one's funeral.

"Kidding themes" were usually started by George or Ike, and Sammy was usually the butt of the joke. Sometimes Ike would have to "take it," seldom George. One favorite kidding theme involved Sammy's alleged receipt of $100 a month from his son. The points stressed were that Sammy did not have to work long hours, or did not have to work at all, because he had a son to support him. George would always point out that he sent money to his daughter; she did not send money to him. Sammy received occasional calls from his wife, and his claim that these calls were requests to shop for groceries on the way home were greeted with feigned disbelief. Sammy was ribbed for being closely watched, bossed, and henpecked by his wife, and the expression "Are you man or mouse?" became an echolalic utterance, used both in and out of the original context.

Ike, who shared his machine and the work scheduled for it with Boo, the night operator, came in for constant invidious comparison on the subject of output. The socially isolated Boo, who chose work rather than sleep on his lonely night shift, kept up a high level of performance, and George never tired of pointing this out to Ike. It so happened that Boo, an Arabian Moslem from Palestine, had no use for Jews in general; and Ike, who was Jewish, had no use for Boo in particular. Whenever George would extol Boo's previous night's production, Ike would try to turn the conversation into a general discussion on the need for educating the Arabs. George, never permitting the development of serious discussion on this topic, would repeat a smirking warning, "You watch out for Boo! He's got a long knife!"

The "poom poom" theme was one that caused no sting. It would come up several times a day to be enjoyed as unbarbed fun by the three older clicker operators. Ike was usually the one to raise the question, "How many times you go poom poom last night?" The person questioned usually replied with claims of being "too old for poom poom." If this theme did develop a goat, it was I. When it was pointed out that I was a younger man, this provided further grist for the poom poom mill. I soon grew weary of this poom poom business, so dear to the hearts of the three old satyrs, and, knowing where the conversation would inevitably lead, winced whenever Ike brought up the subject. . . .

Series themes included the relating of major misfortunes suffered in the past by group members. George referred again and again to the loss, by fire, of his business establishment. Ike's chief complaints centered around a chronically ill wife who had undergone various operations and periods of hospital care. Ike spoke with discouragement of the expenses attendant upon hiring a housekeeper for himself and his children; he referred with disappointment and disgust to a teen-age son, an inept lad who "couldn't even fix his own lunch. He couldn't even make himself a sandwich!" Sammy's reminiscences centered on the loss of a flourishing business when he had to flee Europe ahead of Nazi invasion.

But all serious topics were not tales of woe. One favorite serious theme which was optimistic in tone could be called either "Danelly's future" or "getting Danelly a better job." It was known that I had been attending "college," the magic door to opportunity, although my specific course of study remained somewhat obscure. Suggestions poured forth on good lines of work to get into, and these suggestions were backed with accounts of friends, and friends of friends, who had made good via the academic route. My answer to the expected question, "Why are you working here?" always stressed the "lots of overtime" feature, and this explanation seemed to suffice for short-range goals.

There was one theme of especially solemn import, the "professor theme." This theme might also be termed "George's daughter's marriage theme"; for the recent marriage of George's only child was inextricably bound up with George's connection with higher learning. The daughter had married the son of a professor who instructed in one of the local colleges. This professor theme was not in the strictest sense a conversation piece; when the subject came up, George did all the talking. The two Jewish operatives remained silent as they listened with deep respect, if not actual awe, to George's accounts of the Big Wedding which, including the wedding pictures, entailed an expense of $1,000. It was monologue, but there was listening, there was communication, the sacred communication of a temple, when George told of going for Sunday afternoon walks on the Midway with the professor, or of joining the professor for a Sunday dinner. Whenever he spoke of the professor, his daughter, the wedding, or even of the new son-in-law, who remained for the most part in the background, a sort of incidental like the wedding cake, George was complete master of the interaction. His manner, in speaking to the rank-and-file of clicker operators, was indeed that of master deigning to notice his underlings. I came to the conclusion that it was the professor connection, not the straw-boss-ship or the extra nickel an hour, which provided the fount of George's superior status in the group.

If the professor theme may be regarded as the cream of verbal interaction, the "chatter themes" should be classed as the dregs. The chatter themes were hardly themes at all; perhaps they should be labelled "verbal states," or "oral autisms." Some were of doubtful status as communication; they were like the howl or cry of an animal responding to its own physiological state. They were exclamations, ejaculations, snatches of song or doggerel, talkings-to-onself, mutterings. Their classification as themes would rest on their repetitive character. They were echolalic utterances, repeated over and over. An already mentioned example would be Sammy's repetition of "George is a good daddy, a very fine man! Ike is a bad man, a very bad man!" Also, Sammy's repetition of "Don't bother me! Can't you see I'm busy? I'm a very busy man!" for ten minutes after Ike had dropped a weight behind him would fit the classification. Ike would shout "Mamariba!" at intervals between repetition of bits of verse, such as:

Mama on the bed,
Papa on the floor,
Baby in the crib
Says giver some more!

Sometimes the three operators would pick up one of these simple chatterings in a short of chorus. "Are you man or mouse? I ask you, are you man or mouse?" was a favorite of this type.

So initial discouragement with the meagerness of social interaction I now recognized as due to lack of observation. The interaction was there, in constant flow. It captured attention and held interest to make the long day pass. The twelve hours of "click,———move die,———click,———move die" became as easy to endure as eight hours of varied activity in the oil fields or eight hours of playing the piecework game in a machine shop. The "beast of boredom" was gentled to the harmlessness of a kitten.

BLACK FRIDAY: DISINTEGRATION OF THE GROUP

But all this was before "Black Friday." Events of that dark day shattered the edifice of interaction, its framework of times and mosaic of themes, and reduced the work situation to a state of social automization and machine-tending drugery. The explosive element was introduced deliberately, but without prevision of its consequences.

On Black Friday, Sammy was not present, he was on vacation. There was no peach time that morning, of course, and no banana time. But George and Ike held their coffee time, as usual, and a steady flow of themes was filling the morning quite adequately. It seemed like a normal day in the making, at least one which was going to meet the somewhat reduced expectations created by Sammy's absence.

Suddenly I was possessed of an inspiration for modification of the professor theme. When the idea struck, I was working at Sammy's machine, clicking out leather parts for billfolds. It was not difficult to get the attention of close neighbor Ike to suggest *sotto voce,* "Why don't you tell him you saw the professor teaching in a barber college on Madison Street? . . . Make it near Halsted Street."

Ike thought this one over for a few minutes, and caught the vision of its possibilities. After an interval of steady application to his clicking, he informed the unsuspecting George of his near West Side discovery; he had seen the professor busy at his instructing in a barber college in the lower reaches of Hobohemia.

George reacted to this announcement with stony silence. The burden of questioning Ike for further details on his discovery fell upon me. Ike had not elaborated his story very much before we realized that the show was not going over. George kept getting redder in the face, and more tight-lipped; he slammed into his clicking with increased vigor. I made one last weak attempt to keep the play on the road by remarking that barber colleges paid pretty well. George turned to hiss at me, "You'll have to go to Kankakee with Ike!" I dropped the subject. Ike whispered to me, "George is sore!"

George was indeed sore. He didn't say another word the rest of the morning. There was no conversation at lunchtime, nor was their any after lunch. A pall of silence had fallen over the clicker room. Fish time fell a casualty. George did not touch the coke I brought for him. A very long, very dreary afternoon dragged on. Finally, after Ike left for home, George broke the silence to reveal his feelings to me:

> Ike acts like a five-year-old, not a man! He doesn't even have the respect of the niggers. But he's got to act like a man around here! He's always fooling around! I'm going to stop that! I'm going to show him his place! . . . Jews will ruin you, if you let them. I don't care if he sings, but the first time he mentions my name, I'm going to shut him up! It's always "Meet Mr. Papeadis! George is a good daddy!" And all that. He's paid to work! If he doesn't work, I'm going to tell Joe! [The superintendent.]

Then came a succession of dismal workdays devoid of times and barren of themes. Ike did not sing, nor did he recite bawdy verse. The shop songbird was caught in the grip of icy winter. What meager communication there was took a sequence of patterns which proved interesting only in retrospect.

For three days, George would not speak to Ike. Ike made several weak attempts to break the wall of silence which George had put between them, but George did not respond; it was as if he did not hear. George would speak to me, on infrequent occasions, and so would Ike. They did not speak to each other.

On the third day George advised me of his new communication policy, designed for dealing with Ike, and for Sammy, too, when the latter returned to work. Interaction was now on a "strictly business" basis, with emphasis to be placed on raising the level of shop output. The effect of this new policy on production remained indeterminate. Before the fourth day had ended, George got carried away by his narrowed interests to the point of making sarcastic remarks about the poor work performances of the absent Sammy. Although addressed to me, these caustic depreciations were obviously for the benefit of Ike. Later in the day Ike spoke to me, for George's benefit, of Sammy's outstanding ability to turn out billfold parts. For the next four days, the prevailing silence of the shop was occasionally broken by either harsh criticism or fulsome praise of Sammy's outstanding workmanship. I did not risk replying to other impeachment of panegyric for fear of involvement in further situational deteriorations.

Twelve-hour days were creeping again at snail's pace. The strictly business communications were of no help, and the sporadic bursts of distaste or enthusiasm for Sammy's clicking ability helped very little. With the return of boredom, came a return of fatigue. My legs tired as the afternoons dragged on, and I became engaged in conscious efforts to rest one by shifting my weight to the other. I would pause in my work to stare through the barred windows at the grimy brick wall across the alley; and, turning my head, I would notice that Ike was staring at the wall too. George would do very little work after Ike left the shop at night. He would sit in a chair and complain of weariness and sore feet.

In desperation, I fell back on my game of work, my blues and greens and white, my ovals and trapezoids, and my scraping the block. I came to surpass Boo, the energetic night worker, in volume of output. George referred to me as a "day Boo" (day-shift Boo) and suggested that I "keep" Sammy's machine. I managed to avoid this promotion, and consequent estrangement with Sammy, by pleading attachment to my own machine.

When Sammy returned to work, discovery of the cleavage between George and Ike left him stunned. "They were the best of friends!" he said to me in bewilderment.

George now offered Sammy direct, savage criticism of his work. For several days the good-natured Sammy endured these verbal aggressions without losing his temper, but when George shouted at him "You work like a preacher!" Sammy became very angry, indeed. I had a few anxious moments when I thought that the two old friends were going to come to blows.

Then, thirteen days after Black Friday, came an abrupt change in the pattern of interaction. George and Ike spoke to each again, in friendly conversation:

I noticed Ike talking to George after lunch. The two had newspapers of fish at George's cabinet. Ike was excited; he said, "I'll pull up a chair!" The two ate for ten minutes. . . . It seems that they went up to the 22nd Street Exchange together during lunch period to cash pay checks.

That afternoon Ike and Sammy started to play again, and Ike burst once more into song. Old themes reappeared as suddenly as the desert flowers in spring. At first, George managed to maintain some show of the dignity of superordination. When Ike started to sing snatches of "You Are My Sunshine," George suggested that he get "more production." Then Ike backed up George in pressuring Sammy for more production. Sammy turned this exhortation into low comedy by calling Ike a "slave driver" and by shouting over and over again, "Don't bother me! I'm a busy man!" On one occasion, as if almost overcome with joy and excitement, Sammy cried out, "Don't bother me! I'll tell Rothman! [the company president] I'll tell the union! Don't mention my name! I hate you!"

I knew that George was definitely back into the spirit of the thing when he called to Sammy, "Are you man or mouse?" He kept up the "man or mouse" chatter for some time.

George was for a time reluctant to accept fruit when it was offered to him, and he did not make a final capitulation to coke time until five days after renewal of the fun and fooling. Strictly speaking, there never was a return to banana time, peach time, or window time. However, the sharing and snitching of fruit did go on once more, and the window in front of Sammy's machine played a more prominent part than ever in the renaissance of horseplay in the clicker room. In fact, the "rush to the window" became an integral part of increasingly complex themes and repeated sequences of interaction. This window rushing became especially bound up with new developments which featured what may be termed the "anal gesture."[10] Introduced by Ike, and given backing by an enthusiastic, very playful George, the anal gesture became a key component of fun and fooling during the remaining weeks of my stay in the shop:

Ike broke wind, and put his head in his hand on the block as Sammy grabbed a rod and made a mock rush to open the window. He beat Ike on the head, and George threw some water on him, playfully. In came the Negro head of the Leather Department; he remarked jokingly that we should take out the machines and make a playroom out of the shop.

Of course, George's demand for greater production was metamorphized into horseplay. His shout of "Production please!" became a chatter theme to accompany the varied antics of Ike and Sammy.

The professor theme was dropped completely. George never again mentioned his Sunday walks on the Midway with the professor.

CONCLUSIONS

Speculative assessment of the possible significance of my observations on information interaction in the clicking room may be set forth in a series of general statements.

Practical Application

First, in regard to possible practical applications to problems of industrial management, these observations seem to support the generally accepted notion that one key source of job satisfaction lies in the informal interaction shared by members of a work group. In the clicking-room situation the spontaneous development of a patterned combination of horseplay, serious conversation, and frequent sharing of food and drink reduced the monotony of simple, repetitive operations to the point where a regular schedule of long work days became livable. This kind of group interplay may be termed "consumatory" in the sense indicated by Dewey, when he makes a basic distinction between "instrumental" and "consumatory" communication.[11] The enjoyment of communication "for its own sake" as "mere sociabilities," as "free, aimless social intercourse," brings job satisfaction, at least job endurance, to work situations largely bereft of creative experience.

In regard to another managerial concern, employee productivity, any appraisal of the influence of group interaction upon clicking-room output could be no more than roughly impressionistic. I obtained no evidence to warrant a claim that banana time, or any of its accompaniments in consumatory interaction, boosted production. To the contrary, my diary recordings express an occasional perlexity in the form of "How does this company manage to stay in business?" However, I did not obtain sufficient evidence to indicate that, under the prevailing conditions of laissez-faire management, the output of our group would have been more impressive if the playful cavorting of three middle-aged gentlemen about the barred windows had never been. As far as achievement of managerial goals is concerned, the most that could be suggested is that leavening the deadly boredom of individualized work routines with a concurrent flow of group festivities had a negative effect on turnover. I left the group, with sad reluctance, under the pressure of strong urgings to accept a research fellowship which would involve no factory toil. My fellow clickers stayed with their machines to carry on their labors in the spirit of banana time.

Theoretical Considerations

Secondly, possible contribution to ongoing sociological inquiry into the behavior of small groups, in general, and factory work groups, in particular, may lie in one or more of the following ideational products of my clicking-room experience:

1. In their day-long confinement together in a small room spatially and socially isolated from other work areas of the factory the Clicking Department employees found themselves ecologically situated for development of a "natural" group. Such a development did take place; from worker intercommunications did emerge the full-blown sociocultural system of consumatory interactions which I came to share, observe, and record in the process of my socialization.

2. These interactions had a content which could be abstracted from the total existential flow of observable doings and sayings for labelling and objective consideration. That is, they represented a distinctive sub-culture, with its recurring patterns of reciprocal influencings which I have described as times and themes.

3. From these interactions may also be abstracted a social structure of statuses and roles. This structure may be discerned in the carrying out of the various informal activities which provide the content of the sub-culture of the group. The times and themes were performed with a system of the sub-culture of the group. The times and themes were performed with a system of roles which formed a sort of pecking hierarchy. Horseplay had its initiators and its victims, its amplifiers and its chorus; kidding had its attackers and attacked, its least attacked and its most attacked, its ready acceptors of attack and its strong resistors of attack. The fun went on with the participation of all, but within the controlling frame of status, a matter of who can say or do what to whom and get away with it.

4. In both the cultural content and the social structure of clicker group interaction could be seen the permeation of influences which flowed from the various multiple group memberships of the participants. Past and present "other-group" experiences in anticipated "outside" social connections provided significant materials for the building of themes and for the establishment and maintenance of status and role relationships. The impact of reference group affiliations on clicking-room interaction was notably revealed in the sacred, status-conferring expression of the professor theme. This impact was brought into very sharp focus in developments which followed my attempt to degrade the topic, and correlatively, to demote George.

5. Stability of the clicking-room social system was never threatened by immediate outside pressures. Ours was not an instrumental group, subject to disintegration in a losing struggle against environmental obstacles or oppositions. It was not striving for corporate goals; nor was it faced with the enmity of other groups. It was strictly a consumatory group, devoted to the maintenance of patterns of self-entertainment. Under existing conditions, disruption of unity could come only from within.

Potential for breakdown were endemic in the interpersonal interactions involved in conducting the group's activities. Patterns of fun and fooling had developed within a matrix of frustration. Tensions born of long hours of relatively meaningless work were released in the mock aggressions of horseplay. In the recurrent attack, defense, and counterattack there continually lurked the possibility that words or gestures harmless in conscious intent might cross the subtle boundary of accepted, playful aggression to be perceived as real assault. While such an occurrence might incur displeasure no more lasting than necessary for the quick clarification or creation of kidding norms, it might also spark a charge of hostility sufficient to disorganize the group.

A contributory potential for breakdown from within lay in the dissimilar "other group" experiences of the operators. These other-group affiliations and identifications could provide differences which could make maintenance of consensus in regard to kidding norms a hazardous process of trial and error adjustment.

6. The risk involved in this trial and error determination of consensus on fun and fooling in a touchy situation of frustration—mock aggression—was made evident when I attempted to introduce alterations in the professor theme. The group disintegrated, *instanter.* That is, there was an abrupt cessation of the interaction which constituted our groupness. Although both George and I were solidly linked in other-group affiliations with the higher learning, there was not enough agreement in our attitudes toward university professors to prevent the interactional development which shattered our factory play group. George perceived my offered alterations as a real attack, and he responded with strong hostility directed against Ike, the perceived assailant, and Sammy, a fellow traveler.

My innovations, if accepted, would have lowered the tone of the sacred professor theme, if not to "Stay Away From Baby" ribaldry, then at least to the verbal slapstick level of "finding Danelly an apartment." Such a downgrading of George's reference group would, in turn, have downgraded George. His status in the shop group hinged largely upon his claimed relations with the professor.

7. Integration of our group was fully restored after a series of changes in the patterning and quality of clicking-room interaction. It might be said that reintegration took place *in* these changes, that the series was a progressive one of step-by-step improvement in relations, that re-equilibration was in process during the three weeks that passed between initial

communication collapse and complete return to "normal" interaction.

The cycle of loss and recovery of equilibrium may be crudely charted according to the following sequence of phases: (a) the stony silence of "not speaking"; (b) the confining of communication to formal matters connected with work routines; (c) the return of informal give-and-take in the form of harshly sarcastic kidding, mainly on the subject of work performance, addressed to a neutral go-between for the "benefit" of the object of aggression; (d) highly emotional direct attack, and counter-attack, in the form of criticism and defense of work performance; (e) a sudden rapprochement expressed in serious, dignified, but friendly conversation; (f) return to informal interaction in the form of mutually enjoyed mock aggression; (g) return to informal interaction in the form of regular patterns of sharing food and drink.

The group had disintegrated when George withdrew from participation and, since the rest of us were at all times ready for rapprochement, reintegration was dependent upon his "return." Therefore, each change of phase in interaction on the road to recovery could be said to represent an increment of return on George's part. Or, conversely, each phase could represent an increment of reacceptance of punished deviants. Perhaps more generally applicable description of a variety of reunion situations would be conceptualization of the phase changes as increments of reassociation without an atomistic differentiation of the "movements" of individuals.

8. To point out that George played a key role in this particular case of re-equilibrium is not to suggest that the homeostatic controls of a social system

may be located in a type of role or in a patterning of role relationships. Such controls could be but partially described in terms of human interaction; they would be functional to the total configuration of conditions within the field of influence. The automatic controls of a mechanical system operate as such only under certain achieved and controlled conditions. The human body recovers from disease when conditions for such homeostasis are "right." The clicking-room group regained equilibrium under certain undetermined conditions. One of a number of other possible outcomes could have developed had conditions not been favorable for recovery.

For purposes of illustration, and from reflection on the case, I would consider the following as possibly necessary conditions for reintegration of our group: (a) Continued monotony of work operations; (b) Continued lack of a comparatively adequate substitute for the fun and fooling release from work tensions; (c) Inability of the operatives to escape from the work situation or from each other, within the work situation. George could not fire Ike or Sammy or remove them from his presence, and it would have been difficult for the three middle-aged men to find other jobs if they were to quit the shop. Shop space was small, and the machines close together. Like a submarine crew, they had to "live together"; (d) Lack of conflicting definitions of the situation after Ike's perception of Geroge's reaction to the "barber college" attack. George's anger and his punishment of the offenders was perceived as justified; (e) Lack of introduction of new issues or causes which might have carried justification for new attacks and counter-attacks, thus leading interaction

into a spiral of conflict and crystallization of conflict norms. For instance, had George reported his offenders to the superintendent for their poor work performance; had he, in his anger, committed some offense which would have led to reporting of a grievance to local union officials; had he made his anti-Semitic remarks in the presence of Ike or Sammy, or had I relayed these remarks to them; had I tried to "take over" Sammy's machine, as George had urged; then the interactional outcome might have been permanent disintegration of the group.

9. Whether or not the particular patterning of interactional change previously noted is somehow typical of a "re-equilibration process" is not a major question here. My purpose in discriminating the seven changes is primarily to suggest that re-equilibration, when it does occur, may be described in observable phases and that the emergence of each succeeding phase should be dependent upon the configuration of conditions of the preceding one. Alternative eventual outcomes may change in their probabilities, as the phases succeed each other, just as prognosis for recovery in sickness may change as the disease situation changes.

10. Finally, discrimination of phase changes in social process may have practical as well as scientific value. Trained and skillful administrators might follow the practice in medicine of introducing aids to re-equilibration when diagnosis shows that they are needed.

NOTES

1. Charles R. Walker and Robert H. Guest, *The Man on the Assembly Line,* Harvard University Press, Cambridge, 1952.

2. *Ibid.,* p. 77.

3. *Ibid.*, p. 68.

4. Donald F. Roy, "Work Satisfaction and Social Reward in Quota Achievement: An Analysis of Peacework Incentive," *American Sociological Review,* 18 (Oct., 1953), 507–14.

5. All names used are fictitious.

6. Henri de Man, *The Psychology of Socialism,* Henry Holt and Company, New York, 1927, pp. 80–81.

7. *Ibid.*, p. 81.

8. Roy, *op. cit.*

9. Lucille Milner, *Education of An American Liberal,* Horizon Press, New York, 1954, p. 97.

10. I have been puzzled to note widespread appreciation of this gesture in the "consumatory" communication of the working men of this nation. For the present I leave it to clinical psychologists to account for the nature and pervasiveness of this social bond.

11. John Dewey, *Experience and Nature,* Open Court Publishing Co., Chicago, 1925, pp. 202–206.

DEVELOPMENTAL SEQUENCE IN SMALL GROUPS

BRUCE W. TUCKMAN

The purpose of this article is to review the literature dealing with the developmental sequence in small groups, to evaluate this literature as a body, to extrapolate general concepts about group development, and to suggest fruitful areas for further research.

Within the studies reviewed, an attempt will be made to distinguish between *interpersonal* stages of group development and *task* behaviors exhibited in the group. The contention is that any group, regardless of setting, must address itself to the successful completion of a task. At the same time, and often through the same behaviors, group members will be relating to one another interpersonally. The pattern of *interpersonal relationships* is referred to as *group structure* and is interpreted as the interpersonal configuration and interpersonal behaviors of the group at a point in time, that is, the way the members act and relate to one another as persons. The content of interaction as related to the task at hand is referred to as *task activity.* The proposed distinction between the group as a social entity and the group as a task entity is similar to the distinction between the task-oriented functions of groups and the social-emotional-integrative functions of groups, both of which occur as simultaneous aspects of group functioning (Bales, 1953; Coffey, 1952; Deutsch, 1949; Jennings, 1947).

PROPOSED DEVELOPMENTAL SEQUENCE

The following model is offered as a conceptualization of changes in group behavior, in both social and task realms, across all group settings, over time. It represents a set of hypotheses reflecting the author's biases and the perception of trends in the studies reviewed which become considerably more apparent when these studies are viewed in the light of the model. The model of development stages presented below is not suggested for primary use as an organizational vehicle, although it serves that function here. Rather, it is a conceptual statement suggested by the data presented and subject to further test.

In the realm of group structure the first hypothesized stage of the model is labeled as *testing and dependence.* The term "testing" refers to an attempt by group members to discover what interpersonal behaviors are acceptable in the group, based on the reactions of the therapist or trainer (where one is present) and on the reactions of the other group members. Coincident to discovering the boundaries of the situation by testing, one relates to the therapist, trainer, some powerful group member, or existing norms and structures in a dependent way. One looks to this person, persons, or standards for guidance and support in this new and unstructured situation.

The first stage of task-activity development is labeled as *orientation to the task,* in which group members attempt to identify the task in terms of its relevant parameters and the manner in which the group experience will be used to accomplish the task. The group must decide upon the type of information they will need in dealing with the task, and how this information is to be obtained. In orienting to the task, one is essentially defining it by discovering its "ground rules." Thus, orientation in general characterizes behavior in both interpersonal and task realms during this stage. It is to be emphasized that orientation is a general class of behavior which cuts across settings; the specifics of orientation, that is, what one must orient to and how, will be setting-specific.

The second phase in the development of group structure is labeled as *intragroup conflict.* Group members become hostile toward one another and toward a therapist or trainer as a means of expressing their individuality and resisting the formation of group structure. Interaction is uneven and "infighting" is common. The lack of unity is an outstanding feature of this phase. There are characteristic key issues that polarize the group and boil down to the conflict over progression into the "unknown" of inter-

personal relations or regression to the security of earlier dependence.

Emotional response to task demands is identified as the second stage of task-activity development. Group members react emotionally to the task as a form of resistance to the demands of the task on the individual, that is, the discrepancy between the individual's personal orientation and that demanded by the task. This task stage will be most evident when the task has as its goal self-understanding and self-change, namely, the therapy and training-group tasks, and will be considerably less visible in groups working on interpersonal realms, emotionality in response to a discrepancy characterizes this stage. However, the source of the discrepancy is different in the different realms.

The third group structure phase is labeled as the *development of group cohesion.* Group members accept the group and accept the idiosyncracies of fellow members. The group becomes an entity by virtue of its acceptance by the members, their desire to maintain and perpetuate it, and the establishment of new group-generated norms to insure the group's existence. Harmony is of maximum importance, and task conflicts are avoided to insure harmony.

The third stage of task activity development is labeled as *the open exchange of relevant interpretations.* In the therapy-and training-group context, this takes the form of discussing oneself and other group members, since self and other personal characteristics are the basic task inputs. In the laboratory-task context, exchanged interpretations take the form of opinions. In all cases one sees information being acted on so that alternative interpretations of the information can be arrived at. The openness to other group members is characteristic in both realms during this stage.

The fourth and final developmental phase of group structure is labeled as *functional role-relatedness.* The group, which was established as an entity during the preceding phase, can now become a problem-solving instrument. It does this by directing itself to members as objects, since the subjective relationship between members has already been established. Members can now adopt and play roles that will enhance the task activities of the group, since they have learned to relate to one another as social entities in the preceding stage. Role structure is not an issue but an instrument which can now be directed at the task. The group becomes a "sounding board" on which the task is "played."

In task-activity development, the fourth and final stage is identified as the *emergence of solutions.* It is here that we observe constructive attempts at successful task completion. In the therapy- and training-group context, these solutions are more specifically *insight* into personal and interpersonal processes and constructive self-change, while in the laboratory-group context the solutions are more intellectual and impersonal. Here, as in the three preceding stages, there is no essential correspondence between group structural and task realms over time. In both realms the emphasis is on constructive action, and the realms come together so that energy previously invested in the structural realm can be devoted to the task.

The next section presents a review of relevant studies separated according to setting. The observations within each study are separated according to stage of development and realm.

STAGES OF DEVELOPMENT IN NATURAL AND LABORATORY GROUPS

Stage 1

Group Structure: Testing and Dependence Modlin and Faris (1956), studying an interdisciplinary professional group, identify an initial stage of *structuralization,* in which members are dependent upon roles developed outside of the group, well-established traditions, and a fixed hierarchy of responsibility.

Schroder and Harvey (1963) describe an initial stage of *absolutistic dependency,* featuring the emergence of a status hierarchy and rigid norms which reduce ambiguity and foster dependence and submission.

Theodorson (1953) observed a tendency initially for only one leader to emerge and for group members to categorize one another so that they could define the situation and reduce ambiguity.

Schutz (1958) sees the group dealing initially with problems of *inclusion*—to join or not to join, to commit oneself or not. The group concern, thus, is boundary problems, and the behavior of members is individually centered. This description is somewhat suggestive of testing.

Task Activity: Orientation Bales and Strodtbeck (1951) and Bales (1953), using Bales' (1950) interaction-process categories, discovered that leaderless laboratory groups begin by placing major emphasis on problems of *orientation* (as reflected in Bales' categories: "asks for orientation" and "gives orientation"). This orientation serves to define the boundaries of the task (i.e., what is to be done) and the approach that is to be used in dealing with the task (i.e., how it is to be accomplished).

Stage 2

Group Structure: Intragroup Hostility Modlin and Faris (1956) describe unrest characterized by friction and disharmony as the second stage, while Shroder and Harvey (1963) identify a second stage of *negative independence* featuring rebellion, opposition, and conflict. In this stage the greater emphasis is on autonomy and individual rights. Theodorson (1953) observed more friction, disharmony, and animosity early in the group life than during later periods.

Schutz (1958) postulates a second stage in which the group deals with problems of *control.*

This entails a leadership struggle in which individual members compete to establish their place in hierarchy culminating in resolution.

In the task area, the stage of *emotional response to task demands* is not delineated, presumably due to the impersonal and nonthreatening nature of the task in these settings. When the task does not deal with the self at a penetrating level, extreme emotionality in the task areas is not expected.

Stage 3

Group Structure: Development of Group Cohesion Modlin and Faris (1956) identify change as the third stage, characterized by the formation of the concept of the group as a functioning unit and the emergence of a team "dialect." Schroder and Harvey (1963) refer to Stage 3 as *conditional dependence,* featuring a group concern with integration and an emphasis on mutuality and the maintenance of interpersonal relationships.

Theodorson (1953) observed the following group tendencies over time (i.e., tending to occur later as opposed to earlier in group development): (a) discovering what is common to the members and developing a within-group "parochialism"; (b) the growth of an interlocking network of friendship; (c) role independence; (d) mutual involvement and identification between members with a concommitant increase in harmony and solidarity; and (e) the establishment of group norms for dealing with such areas as discipline.

Schutz (1958) postulated a third stage wherein problems of *affection* are dealt with. Characteristic of this stage are emotional integration, pairing, and the resolution of intimacy problems.

Task Activity: Expression of Opinions

Bales and Strodtbeck (1951) and Bales (1953) observed that the orientation phase was followed by a period in which major emphasis was placed on problems of *evaluation* (as reflected by categories: "asks for opinion" and "gives opinion"). "Evaluation" as a descriptor of the exchange of opinions appears to be comparable to the third task stage in therapy- and training-group development which was heretofore labeled as "discussing oneself and others." Because the therapy and training tasks are personal ones, task opinions must involve self and others. When the task is an impersonal one, the content of task opinions varies accordingly.

Step 4

Group Structure: Funcional Role-Relatedness Modlin and Faris (1956) identify integration as the fourth and final stage in which structure is internalized and the group philosophy becomes pragmatic, that is, the unified-group approach is applied to the task.

Schroder and Harvey (1963) postulate a final stage of *positive interdependence,* characterized by simultaneous autonomy and mutuality (i.e., the members can operate in any combination, or as a unit), and an emphasis on task achievement which is superordinate to social structure.

Theodorson (1953) sees the group as developing into a subculture over time, along with the development of member responsibility to the group.

Schutz (1958) does not identify a fourth state; rather, he sees his three postulated stages in continually cycling over time.

Task Activity: Emergence of Solution The third and final phase observed by Bales and Strodtbeck (1951) and Bales (1953) is one in which major emphasis is placed on problems in *control* (as reflected by categories: "asks for suggestion" and "gives suggestion"). The purpose of suggestions is to offer solutions to the task based on information gathered and evaluated in previous developmental periods. This then represents an analogue to final stages in therapy- and training-group task development where the emergence of insight yields solutions to personal problems.

These authors do not identify a period of task development in laboratory groups comparable to the second task stage in therapy- and training-group development which features the expression of emotional material. Again, because therapy and training tasks are personal ones, this will be reflected in the content of discussion, specifically by the manifestation of resistance prior to dealing with the personal task at a level of confidence and honesty. This task stage does not appear to be quite relevant in laboratory discussion groups, and its existence has not been reported by Bales and Strodtbeck (1951) or Bales (1953).

Philp and Dunphy (1959) have further substantiated the findings of Bales and Strodtbeck (1951) and Bales (1953) by observing the same phase-movement pattern in groups working on a different type of discussion problem. Furthermore, Philp and Dunphy (1959) present evidence which indicates that sex of the participants does not affect the pattern of phase movements.

Finally, Smith (1960) has observed that experimental groups show early concentration on matters not related to the task, and, only later in the development sequence, concentrate on task-relevant activities. Again, this finding suggests a strong similarity between task development in laboratory groups and in therapy and training groups, since, in the latter settings, constructive task-relevant activity appears only late in the developmental sequence.

Discussion

In order to isolate those concepts common to the various studies reviewed (across settings), a developmental model was proposed. This model was aimed at serving a conceptual function as well as an integrative and organizational one. The model will be summarized here.

Groups initially concern themselves with orientation accomplished primarily through testing. Such testing serves to identify the boundaries of both interpersonal and task behaviors. Coincident with testing in the interpersonal realm is the establishment of dependency relationships with leaders, other group members, or preexisting standards. It may be said that orientation, testing, and dependence constitute the group process of *forming*.

The second point in the sequence is characterized by conflict and polarization around interpersonal issues, with concomitant emotional responding in the task sphere. These behaviors serve as resistance to group influence and task requirements and may be labeled as *storming*.

Resistance is overcome in the third stage in which ingroup feeling and cohesiveness develop, new standards evolve, and new roles are adopted. In the task realm, intimate, personal opinions are expressed. Thus, we have the stage of *norming*.

Finally, the group attains the fourth and final stage in which interpersonal structure becomes the tool of task activities. Roles become flexible and functional, and group energy is channeled into the task. Structural issues have been resolved, and structure can now become supportive of task performance. This stage can be labeled as *performing*.

Although the model was largely induced from the literature, it would seem to withstand the test of common sense as well as being consistent with developmental theory and findings in other areas. It is not unreasonable to expect "newness" of the group to be greeted by orienting behavior and resultant unsureness and insecurity overcome through dependence on an authority figure, as proposed in the model. Such orienting responses and dependence on authority are characteristic of the infant during the first year (Ilg & Ames, 1955), the young child when first apprehending rules (Piaget, 1932), and the patient when first entering psychotherapy (Rotter, 1954).

After the "newness" of the group has "worn off," the members react to both the imposition of the group and the task emotionally and negatively, and pose a threat to further development. This proposal is mirrored by the rebelliousness of the young child following his "obedient" stages (Ilg & Ames, 1955; Levy, 1955).

Such emotionality, if overcome, is followed by a sense of "pulling together" in the group and being more sensitive to one another. This sensitivity to others is mirrored in the development of the child (Ilg & Ames, 1955; Piaget, 1932) and represents an essential aspect of the socialization process (Mead, 1934).

Finally, the group becomes a functional instrument for dealing with the task. Interpersonal problems lie in the group's "past," and its present can be devoted to realistic appraisal of and attempt at solutions to the task on hand. This interdependence and "marriage to reality" is characteristic of the "mature" human being (Erikson, 1950; Fromm, 1941) and the "mature" 9-year-old child (Ilg & Ames, 1955).

REFERENCES

Bales, R. F. *Interaction process analysis: A method for the study of small groups.* Cambridge, Mass.: Addison-Wesley, 1950.

Bales R. F. The equilibrium problem in small groups. In T. Parson, R. F. Bales, & E. A. Shils, *Working papers in the theory of action.* Glencoe, Ill.: Free Press, 1953, Pp. 111–161.

Bales, R. F. & Strodtbeck, F. L. Phases in group problem-solving. *Journal of Abnormal and Social Psychology,* 1951, *46,* 465–495.

Coffey, H. S. Socio and psyche group process: Integrative concepts. *Journal of Social Issues,* 1952, *8,* 65–74.

Deutsch, M. A. A theory of cooperation and competition. *Human Relations,* 1949, *2,* 129–152.

Erikson, E. H. *Childhood and society,* New York: Norton, 1950, Pp. 213–220.

Fromm, E. *Escape from freedom.* New York: Rinehart, 1941.

Ilg, Frances, L. & Ames, Louise B. *Child behavior.* New York: Harper, 1955.

Jennings, Helen H. Sociometric differentiation of the psychegroup and sociogroup. *Sociometry,* 1947, *10,* 71–79.

Levy, D.M. Oppositional syndromes and oppositional behavior. In P. H. Hoch & J. Zubin (Eds.), *Psychopathology of childhood.* New York: Grune & Stratton, 1955, Pp. 204–226.

Mead, G. H. *Self, mind and society.* Chicago: Univer. Chicago Press, 1934.

Modlin, H. C. & Faris, Mildred. Group adaption and integration in psychiatric team practice. *Psychiatry,* 1956, *19,* 97–103.

Philp, H., & Dunphy, D. Developmental trends in small groups. *Sociometry,* 1959, *22,* 162–174.

Piaget, J. *The moral judgement of the child.* New York: Harcourt Brace, 1932.

Rotter, J. B. *Social learning and clinical psychology.* New York: Prentice-Hall, 1954.

Shroder, H. M., & Harvey, O. J. Conceptual organization and group structure. In O. J. Harvey (Ed.), *Motivation and social interaction,* New York: Ronald Press, 1963. Pp. 134–166.

Schutz, W. F. *FIRO: A three-dimensional theory of interpersonal behavior.* New York: Rinehart, 1958, Pp. 168–188.

Smith, Anthony J. A developmental study of group processes. *Journal of Genetic Psychology,* 1960, *97,* 29–39.

Theodorson, G. A. Elements in the progressive development of small groups. *Social Forces,* 1953, *31,* 311–320.

1. Does a manager have to be a "good judge of people" to be effective? Why or why not?
2. Were males and females socialized differently in your family? How might you change this process, if at all, when raising your own children?
3. Have you known any workaholics? Have they succeeded more rapidly than people who seem to have a different balance between work, family, and social activities? How would you rate yourself?
4. If you were manager of a group that was in the banana time syndrome, how would you manage it? How would theories of motivation help you to break any group norm of low productivity?
5. Is socialization of new members to groups crucial for the group survival? How do outside enemies affect group cohesiveness?
6. Think about two similar groups such as study groups, basketball teams, and so forth, who are at a different stage of development. What impact has this had on cohesiveness and group productivity? Is there a difference in physically being a member of an organization or group and psychologically being a member of an organization or group? For example, when you first entered this university or graduate school program were you psychologically as well as physically and mentally committed? At what point did you become psychologically committed? Has that made a difference on your outlook?

CHAPTER VIII
CULTURAL DIFFERENCES IN ORGANIZATIONS

ORGANIZATIONAL SHOCKS

- Work ethic among fellow managers is often low.

- Professional, technical, and managerial employees often feel alienated from work or the organization in which they work.
  Productivity per man hour is lower in the United States than in many other developed countries.

- Group rewards are more important motivators of performance than are individual rewards in many cultures.

- Work motivation theories as taught in the United States culture are often not transferable to other cultures.

Just as individual differences have an impact on employee's work motivation so do the individual's cultural background and cultural environment exert an influence. The readings in this chapter point out how different cultures in Europe and Asia impact on work and employees perceptions of work. Many aspects of these various environments might be applicable to the United States and Canadian work place.

In earlier readings we observed that upward mobile managers often feel trapped (remember Major Major Major Major). In Europe this is also true, but now the European manager is calling for unionization. These middle managers feel they are the most vulnerable employees in an organization because in a cost-cutting situation they are expendable, whereas employees in top management position are not. To protect themselves they are beginning to unionize.

In the next article we learn that Japan has a different philosophy about layoffs. Seniority and lifetime employment has not been detrimental to productivity. In fact, Japan's productivity measured in output per man-hour is one of the highest in the free world.

The reader should note, however, there are cultural differences within Asia. Mainland China with 800,000,000 people has its own view of work. Whereas Japan, Europe, and the United States are capital intensive, China is labor intensive. In Chinese society, motivation is maintained by a fostering of group rewards instead of material individual rewards. However, changes are taking place in China because of its rapid industrialization, and many of the Western cultural norms may soon have an impact on its ethic. One of the organizational shocks faced by many young managers is the realization that the United States system is not the only way, and in many cases may not be the best way for all people, when measured in terms of productivity per man-hour or longevity of the work force.

EUROPEAN EXECUTIVES: "UNION NOW"

JEAN ROSS-SKINNER

They might have been agents *provocateurs* bent on foreign intrigue. Actually, though, the two men who met one dark rainy night last March near the waterfront of the ancient Netherlands town of Dordrecht were a couple of Dutch business executives. One was Jan van Leeuwen, a sales manager at giant Unilever; the other a senior engineer with E.I. du Pont's Dutch subsidiary. Over steins of pale golden lager in an old raftered pub, they talked long and animatedly, taking copious notes and poring over documents. Several hours later, the two men nodded agreement, shook hands and walked out into the rain-drenched streets of Dordrecht.

What the intent negotiators accomplished that night would have been considered a European impossibility only a scant few years ago—the creation of a new union of middle-management executives in Dutch industry. For on top of his Unilever sales job, van Leeuwen is a vice president of the Netherland Central Union for Higher Personnel (NCHP) and his moonlighting mission is to establish company-based unions of executives throughout Holland. As a result of that clandestine conference, he told *Dun's* last month, "We formally established the du Pont de Nemours (Nederland) Association of Higher Personnel. Out of a potential 300 members, we already have 125 signed up."

Unlike American middle managers, who talk a lot about job disenchantment ("The Revolt of the Middle Managers—Phase Two," *March 1973*), Europe's second-echelon executives are doing something about their grievances as they flock to join rapidly expanding middle-management unions. In effect, they are European industry's new militants, rushing to the business barricades in double-breasted suits.

Executive unions have been part of European industry since the Forties. But only in the past few years of increased militancy has the middle-management labor movement become

Source: Reprinted with special permission of *Dun's Review;* April 1974. Copyright 1974 by Dun & Bradstreet Publications Corporation.

sufficiently broad to cause waves of apprehension in executive suites from Stockholm to Rome.

The unions are strongest in Sweden, where about one-half of all middle managers are unionized, and in Holland, where some 40% are dues-paying members. In France and Germany, the unions have signed up about one out of ten middle managers, while in Britain, which has enough trouble trying to mollify miners let alone executives, the movement has only recently sprung to life.

Following the common market concept, moreover, the middle-management unions are finding strength in bigness. Most national unions have grouped together in the International Confederations of Executive Staffs (ICES), which serves as a combination listening post and lobby for its several hundred thousand members across the Continent. With offices and full-time staffs in Paris, Geneva and Brussels, ICES acts as a clearing house for information on executive benefits and pressures European governments and the EEC Commission for legislation favorable to middle managers.

At first glance, perhaps, it would seem that the European cry of "Union Now" is being heard in the wrong place. Most European middle managers may earn less and pay higher taxes than their American counterparts, but they enjoy considerably greater security and are cushioned by their companies against a variety of future shocks. Pensions are vested early and are often as high as 75%–80% of final salary, compared with the U.S. norm of around 50%. In a number of countries, executives are entitled by law to immediate 100% vesting in their pension rights, which are even inflation-proofed by being tied to cost-of-living indexes. When a retired European executive dies, his widow can expect to receive 50% to 70% of her husband's pension; in the U.S. she would get only a modest lump sum. And in Belgium and Italy, the executive who is laid off after fifteen years of service is assuaged with severance pay amounting to three years' salary, a lot more than his opposite number in the U.S. could expect.

ODD MAN OUT?

Why, then, the urge to unionize? Basically, the European middle manager, like his American counterpart, worries that he is fast becoming industry's odd man out, squeezed from the top by management's cost-cutting limitations on his salary growth and from below by the growing demands of increasingly militant blue-collar trade unions. The European middle manager fears that the once poles-apart difference between his salary and that of rank-and-file company employees is narrowing to the point that his very status and prestige are at stake. At the same time, of course, inflation has slowed the growth of his purchasing power. "In West Germany," says Jeurgen Borgwardt, general secretary of the Union der Leitenden Angestellten (ULA), the German executives' union, "some managers have actually suffered a fall in their real purchasing power."

But money is by no means the only issue. The discontent of the middle managers cuts much deeper than that. Demanding a voice in the way their companies are run, they see unionism as a base from which they can insist on dialogue with top management. Declares Louis Bouan, president of France's executive union Centre National des Jeunes Cadres, and a consultant with the Metra group in Paris: "French middle managers carry out company policy, but they have no say in the framing of it. Their frustration is pushing them to unionism."

German executives are particularly vociferous in demanding a bigger say in company affairs. They see themselves as an emerging third force powerful enough to play a major independent role in shaping corporate policy. Just recently, for example, they won a limited right to representation on the supervisory boards that appoint the top managers of all large German companies. Explains Jeurgen Borgwardt, "Sometimes employers make short-sighted decisions with short-term profits in mind. Or they ignore the company's impact on the public. At the other extreme, the workers have been pushing for excessively high wage demands. We believe our interests are most closely aligned with the long-term health of the company itself. And," adds Borgwardt determinedly, "we want a say in how it is run."

Nevertheless, executive unionism is growing fastest in those countries where changing company fortunes and policies appear to threaten the status of middle managers. Across Europe, in fact, executive unionists consider their first goal to be the improvement of job security and direct aid to those middle managers who, through no fault of their own, are marked "redundant" (a European synonym for "expendable"). In Sweden, for instance, the brisk surge in membership in SACO, the union that represents most of the 50% of Swedish executives who have organized closely parallels the recent climb in managerial redundancies.

To lighten the burden of the laid-off executive, SACO and the Swedish Employers' Confederation set up a joint fund three years ago that finances a nationwide executive placement agency and provides free retraining to executives over forty. And SACO itself has a special fund that pays luckless managers who are separated from bankrupt companies without severance pay about 80% of their former salaries for up to 300 working days.

When multiple redundancies threaten, SACO negotiators move in and negotiate with management, often winning reprieves for many a middle manager who could not survive alone. Says an official of the Swedish Association of Graduate Engineers, a SACO affiliate representing executives with economic and engineering backgrounds: "When a company tells us it must dismiss, say, 150 executives, we often find that we can cut the number of dismissals to seventy or less by persuading the company to move men into other divisions and to retrain others."

In Britain, the Staff Association of Britain's Cadbury Schweppes was little more than a cozy company club until the chocolate maker and beverage bottler merged in 1969 and began furloughing middle executives as a fillip to efficiency. Now more than 500 of Cadbury Schweppes' 750 middle managers belong to the company's executive union. "Even senior managers, who had been pretty complacent, have joined," reports union chief Gilbert Drake, a controller in the confectionery division. "They saw the virtue of having an organization the company would listen to."

Similarly, the house executive union at giant Imperial Chemical Industries was launched in 1971 as a defensive move against a new cost-cutting program designed to whittle down the work force. Says a key organizer for the ICI Staff Association: "We did not dispute the fact that the company was overmanned. But we felt that because executives were unorganized, they were bearing the brunt of the cutbacks."

Even at the Common market level, the International Confederation of Executive Staffs, the federation representing most European executive unions, pushes for special assistance from the EEC Social Fund for executives thrown out of work by shutdowns and mergers in depressed areas. Explains Martinus Vermeer, an insurance executive who is a vice president of Holland's NCHP: "Because of their specialization, these men have difficulty finding new jobs. We think the Social Fund should help by providing them with free retraining and paying older redundant executives a percentage of their pay on a reducing scale."

FLACK FROM LABOR

As might be expected when two salesmen work the same territory, the rise of executive unionism in Europe has led to bitter acrimony between middle-management organizers and the established labor unions. The labor unions maintain that they should be the representatives of executives, who are, after all, company employees. They also charge that house executive unions are the creatures of top management and are designed only to preserve differentials between base pay and other benefits—a barb that in many cases is not far from the mark.

In some cases, the conflict with labor has also helped swell executive union ranks. In Holland, for instance, membership in the NCHP doubled last year. The increase was directly fueled by an agreement between government, industry and the workers' union to clamp a ceiling on the total cost of wage agreements. When the blue-collar unions lobbied to increase their share of pay increases and diminish that of managers, Dutch executives saw red and rushed to join the union. Says President Henk van der Schalie of the NCHP, a onetime senior economist at Philips Lamp: "A lot of senior managers who thought they were too important to organize suddenly realized they did not count for anything and needed better protection."

A growing force in Dutch industry, the NCHP's structure, it methods and many of its goals are broadly similar to those of other executive unions throughout Europe. A federation that offers common ground to all executives up to—but excluding—board level, the NCHP membership roster includes 3,500 individual executives, associations of managers in such industries as banking and textiles, and 75 company-based unions. The NCHP has organized at such big Dutch names as Philips Lamp, Unilever, KLM, Fokker, DAF and Hoogo-vens Steel, and at important U.S. subsidiaries like those of General Electric, Mobil Oil, Cincinnati Milacron, Merck, Sharp and Dohme and now, thanks to Jan van Leeuwen's mission to Dordrecht, du Pont.

With member managers paying annual dues of $30 a head, last year's 100% increase in membership has enabled the burgeoning NCHP to move into a twelve-room modern office suite in downtown Utrecht and staff it with fifteen full-time employees. Under President van der Schalie and Manager Paul Labohm, another former Philips executive who turned to executive unionism because of frustrations on the job, the NCHP has succeeded in getting the managements of most Dutch companies to sit down and discuss their differences. Even on that informal basis, considerable progress has been made in middle management's impact on long-term planning. For one thing, the unions have persuaded a number of companies to project their executive needs ahead five years and more, a trend that will help guide undergraduates into the most needed skills.

But the NCHP is after a lot more than that. "We want knowledge," says Labohm. "We want to know what executives are being paid in all companies. And we want a role in deciding salary levels and differentials. The federation's goal is nothing less than collective-bargaining agreements with companies throughout Dutch industry, and with contracts binding on both sides."

What's more, van der Schalie sees success at hand. "Within the next few weeks," he predicts, "the first companies will give in, starting with AKZO [the big Dutch textile manufacturer]."

To achieve its aims, the NCHP trots out all the tools of traditional labor unions. It pressures individual companies, industry groups and the national employer's federation, prods the Ministry of Social Affairs and lobbies politicians of all parties. One thing the executive union has going for it that the trade unions do not is an alumni of highly placed Dutch business executives who have graduated out of middle-management ranks and are highly sympathetic to NCHP aims.

Even the ultimate weapon of labor—the strike—is kept fully primed. "We would be reluctant to use it," allows courtly Martinus Vermeer, "and there are better methods. But if, for example, industry gave in to the workers' unions and executive salaries actually fell, then we would certainly strike."

At the moment, a rise in real executive income does not seem to be in the cards. "We are fighting more to preserve what we have," Vermeer admits. "Our backs are to the wall." But the federation is compaigning to improve the middle manager's lot in a number of ways.

Among the current demands on van der Schalie's list: "time for time" (extra time off for executives who work overly long hours); protection of the rights of senior staff people who develop patents; compulsory pension funds for all sizable companies plus the executives' right to appoint half the pension fund trustees; and the creation of a new state-run job agency geared to placing redundant executives. The NCHP recently scored a breakthrough in another goal: salary adjustments for all executives to offset the eroding effects of inflation. It persuaded one reluctant U.S. subsidiary to introduce the plan, not just for junior staff members, but for senior executives as well.

MANAGEMENT HOSTILITY

But the permissive attitude of Dutch companies toward executive unions is far from universal. Corporate attitudes range from wary neutrality to outright hostility. Possibly because blue-collar unions have been putting on the pressure, Britain's Imperial Chemical Industries, for example, has steadfastly refused to recognize the ICI Staff Association as a negotiating body.

Yet even that may come if, as seems likely, the executive union wins official standing under Britain's Industrial Relations Act.

According to Belgian Jean Defer, joint secretary general of ICES, the big European federation, U.S. subsidiaries are among the least receptive to executive unions, at least at first. While "many soon grasp the advantages of a continuing dialogue with their executive ranks," Defer allows, he says that others remain staunchly opposed to a concept that could have dangerous repercussions back in the U.S.

Particularly in Germany, says ULA organizer Jeurgen Borgwardt, "many U.S. companies are very shortsighted and fight our organization. They think their executives are only interested in higher remuneration and won't talk to them. They should wake up and recognize the social realities in Germany."

Ford of Europe, for one, rejects any suggestion that the company is anti-union, but questions whether corporate executives ought to engage in collective bargaining. While Ford regularly deals with white-collar unions that include lower echelon managers, it steadfastly refuses to have any truck with organized senior executives. Declares Vice President Walter Haynes: "It is our view that above a certain level our executives are members of management, and to be a member of a union as well is a contradiction in terms. We are not willing to discuss this type of union."

The attitude certainly reflects the views of American parent companies back home, where, despite rumblings of middle-management discontent, no groundswell for executive unions has yet developed. But in Europe, the idea has not only come, but seems here to stay. Conceivably, an economic boom in the late 1970s could alleviate middle-management fears of redundancy, take the pressure off mounting demands for more pay and perks and stem the growth of executive union membership. But most of the managers who are signing up with unions today for purely defensive reasons see a much wider potential for their organized strength in the future.

"There is a spirit among middle managers now," says Holland's Henk van der Schalie, "a realization that we should continue to increase our power. For example, when we approached the executives at AKZO a short time ago, we found that those men had not really thought about organizing before. But when they heard what we were doing, 92% of them favored organizing. Their immediate reaction was, "Yes, that's right. That's what we want.' "

MANAGEMENT CAN LEARN FROM JAPAN

JOHN DIEBOLD

Rather surprisingly, the Japanese business system is now plainly outperforming the American business system in some of the most important respects. Successful American firms may want to learn variants of Japanese methods. Without suggesting that we need a Commodore Perry in reverse, it is time to start a debate about which ones to learn.

The two most distinctive and most-frequently-derided features of the Japanese system are: lifetime employment (*sushin koyo*) for nearly all the white-collar and many of the permanent blue-collar workers in big corporations in Japan, and payment by age and length of service (*nenki jorestu seido*). It is fashionable and polite to say that the Japanese are changing the system, but they are changing it much less than many commentators like to suppose. The status and pride of life of a Japanese employee, therefore, still usually depend almost wholly on the automatic factor, his length of service. (He is "Mr. Noyamura, a university graduate who has been an executive with the firm since 1953.") His status is not tied to his present nominal job as "executive vice-president in charge of marketing circular widgets in Southeast Asia." As a result, he is not always fighting mainly for the maximum budget for marketing circular widgets. And he is not personally insulted if technological change and market experience signal that sales of circular widgets in Southeast Asia should be run down.

Americans have always assumed that this Japanese system would have four main bad results, in mounting order of importance:

- Lifetime employment in Japan, it was assumed, would inhibit firms from efficiently trimming payrolls in times of cyclical recession. This is true, but in a modern industrial country, with problems of labor unions, personnel relations, and redundancy pay, it does not matter. Modern corporations are not going to succeed if they are the sort that

Source: Reprinted from the September 29, 1973 issue of *Business Week* by special permission, © 1973 by McGraw-Hill, Inc., New York, N.Y. 10020. All rights reserved.

expect to have to dismiss workers in large numbers during each small downswing.

- Lifetime employment was supposed to make it likely that Japanese firms whose products became technologically obsolete would hang on to making those products with too large labor forces instead of changing step with the times. This has proved to be the opposite of the truth. In an American corporation, changes are likely at some early or late stage to be delayed because they will cut across the interests of some senior and respected executive who is in charge of producing or marketing existing products in the established way. The Japanese system, making one's status depend on length of service instead of on the continued relative importance of one's present job, puts fewer human barriers in the way of diversification.

- The biggest disadvantage of the Japanese system was supposed to be that payment and status by seniority, instead of by achievement, would rob Japanese executives of the incentive to dare and to take risks and even to work. This fear has certainly proved the opposite of the truth. Nearly all Japanese executives (and an extraordinary number of ordinary Japanese shop-floor workers) plainly feel a massive group urge to see their company emulate and beat all competitors. In part, this is a normal pecuniary urge, because if you work in a successful company you will get bigger group bonuses and better group fringe benefits. But in even larger part, it is because the sense of belonging to a proudly successful company is more fun than in belonging to an unsuccessful one. It is common in America to crack jokes at such spectacles as the Matsushita workers singing each morning their company hymn, "Grow Matsushita, grow, grow, grow." But a team

feeling that hymns advance a corporate entity in this way is likely to lead to dynamism and innovation. By contrast, there are positive stagnationist dangers in the equally mystic, though sometimes unadmitted, feelings that commonly develop in American business: group pride in belonging to some craft that ought to be superseded gradually by technological advance, pride in the traditional products which can become obsolescent, attachment to some outdated way of doing things.

- Americans have always liked to believe that Japanese firms are likely to get nowhere because so much of their decision-making is arrived at by consensus, in fairly large meetings where nobody seems willing to show that he is disagreeing too sharply with anybody else. In fact, however, it has become apparent that, in our more competitively hierarchical business establishments in the West, some American and even more European corporations are now very bad at securing adequate participation by middle and lower management in the decision process. The Japanese system whereby everybody pretends politely that he is agreeing with everybody else, even when he is plainly saying something quite different, has to some degree been turned into a rather sophisticated form of middle management communication and even participation. A bright junior Japanese executive who is very keen on some particular innovative idea may now be able to push it through more easily than a junior executive in an American firm. Nobody above him will be afraid that success in this venture will allow the young man to get ahead of himself in the rat race.

As a result of all this, I now suspect the Japanese business system may outperform the American business system in the following fields: making investment decisions that require long lead times and rather lengthy payback periods (e.g., 20-year periods when no American executive expects to be with the same firm, but most 35-year-old Japanese do); introducing very innovative and retraining methods (including much more scientifically programmed and computer-based instruction, which is going to become very important); taking advantage of some, though not all, of the other opportunities that in the next decades will be produced by the computer revolution.

In addition, the Japanese may enjoy a very general advantage in approaching the increasing number of problems where initiatives, even by single companies, should be multiple instead of stereotyped. The Japanese approach to establishing their equivalent of multinational corporations, for instance, may be successfully eclectic and multivariantly adapted to political conditions in each host country.

I find this a rather frightening list.

The question is: How can American business adopt some of the advantages which have proved to attach to the Japanese system, but do so in a gentle progression and while retaining the advantages of our own system? My feeling is that the main problems can be identified under three heads:

1. **Pains of change.** Remember the story of the Australian aborigine who was given a new boomerang, and killed himself trying to throw the old one away? We have a hierarchical system in most of our big American corporations now, with elements of rat race built into it instead of the Japanese *nenko* system. This can only be changed gradually, but the crucial need is that corporations should regard it as proper that their initiatives should be multiple, instead of each initiative being regarded as most strictly within Mr. So-and-So's province. It may be increasingly important that organization charts, prefer-ably rather untidy ones, be drawn with this in mind, that words like "unacceptable intrusion" become forbidden, that the biggest black mark against a departmental head should be when his subordinates are not themselves sponsoring and urging new initiatives (including the airing of some with which he disagrees).

2. **New products and investment.** Japan's real GNP has expanded by 10% to 15% in many years. The annual growth in production by its most successful corporations has often been over 25%. A company on that sort of growth path introduces much of its machinery and many of its products brand-new eveey year. Big Japanese firms, therefore, have large numbers of people wholly engaged in the task of bringing in new projects, and they are now more practiced at it than anybody else. It is no good saying just that American corporations ought to put more people on to the task of planning innovations. What is needed is some change in our business system so that interest in innovation becomes more lively and diffuse. One way toward this may be to make the executives increasingly into participatory entrepreneurs. When there is some proposed new product which the firm has decided—on a narrow balance of advantage—not to make, it might often be worth asking whether anybody in the firm would like to make it himself as an entrepreneurial venture in partnership with the firm. The corporation, having judged the quality of the employee who is bidding to start the venture, would specify the size of the stake it is itself willing to risk (distribution facilities, office space, research material, and probably a stated willingness to take the executive back into his place in the corporate hierarchy if the venture fails). It will be argued that this is not the Japanese system. It isn't, but it would be an American-style

move in the direction of achieving the same results.

3. **Corporate loyalty.** The ordinary Japanese makes most of his friends through his work, he is happiest when he is with them, and this has extraordinary consequences. Many (perhaps most) Japanese foolishly do not take the full annual holiday to which they are entitled, and they admirably feel a sense of enjoyment with each achievement of their firm. Here again, it is not possible to establish this feeling in American corporations simply by organizational restructuring. (Anyway, it is not in all respects desirable to do so.) But, as only one example of paternalism, middle-grade Japanese executives generally regard it as their job to watch out whether any of their employees look lonely or unhappy. While such concern could easily become vulgarly intrusive, it also could be a sophisticated form of personnel relations.

There are many other aspects of the Japanese business system that deserve study and some thought in the West. They include the generally supportive relations between the Japanese bureaucracy and Japanese business. They include the emphasis Japanese trading houses put on understanding the distribution systems employed abroad. They include the capability for constant retraining that springs from the lifetime employment system.

They include many adverse factors as well. Japanese companies are often often overstaffed, and they make disgracefully little use of the talents of women; Japan's internal distribution system is most inefficient, and the subcontracting system is sometimes loaded murderously in favor of big business; small Japanese businesses are influenced too much by nepotism; and too many Japanese businessmen engage in very wasteful high living on business expenses. A notable shortcoming is that Japanese decision-making is ineffective in crisis situations—for example, in reacting to the yen problem. But nobody is suggesting America should copy the worst features of the Japanese system. We should just start thinking very carefully about the features that have succeeded, and how we could emulate some of them.

QUESTIONS FOR DISCUSSION

1. How do organizational behavior theories, especially work motivation theories, apply to the culture of Japan, China, and Western Europe? How are these theories to be modified if they were to be applied in these cultures?

2. Do you believe that work motivation theories are changing in other parts of the world because of the United States' approach or do you think our theories of how to motivate people may change because of other countries' approaches?

3. Suppose in this country we had lifetime employment guarantees, seniority was a major factor in upward mobility, and managers could unionize. What impact would this have on our social and economic system, and in your view would this be an improvement or a detriment to our capitalistic society?

CHAPTER IX

DESIGNING A STYLE OF LEADERSHIP FOR TODAY'S ORGANIZATION

ORGANIZATIONAL SHOCKS

- The theories of leadership that you discussed in college courses have very little application in the world of work.
- Leadership effectiveness is based on the success of the subordinates.
- Leaders must be two-faced to be successful.
- Where you sit in an organization determines your attitude about issues.

One of the most popular topics for management education programs is leadership. However, the future manager should be prepared for the shock that we really don't know as much about leadership as we would like. Much of the theory dealing with leadership deals with ways to measure leadership style and very little tells us how we can develop good leadership traits in individuals. This section has six readings in which each of the leaders in question discover a various rule or technique of leadership that seems to be effective. The first reading by Jennings discusses why there are few great leaders, and why those who do appear seem to be a mix of the princes, heroes, and supermen. Jennings points out that if we were able to accommodate the superman leader, we must restructure and reorganize the work environment to accommodate the leader.

In the second reading Don Quixote gives advice to Sancho Panza, who is about to set out to govern an island. Based on what he has learned from his own experiences in life, Don Quixote describes the characteristics he thinks determines the effective leader. If you think back to the article by David McCullough from *Path Between the Seas,* one wonders what advice Teddy Roosevelt gave to Colonel Goethals. Did you see a parallel in these two readings?

The next article is from Mark Twain's classic *Tom Sawyer.* In this selection Tom is duping his friends into doing his work. If we think of leadership as getting work done through other people, then you have to admit that Tom Sawyer was a classic leader. Not only were his friends willing to do the work but they were willing to do what was generally considered an alienated task with great enthusiasm. If you think back to Jennings' original article, one of the things he says a leader must do is to reduce alienation by praising performance.

The next two readings in this chapter are descriptions of two leaders from the recent past. The first article is about Mayor Richard J. Daley of Chicago. Anyone who has lived or visited Chicago knows that Mayor Daley ran a tight ship but one that was very efficient and effective for its citizens. In this reading we learn some of the secrets he used to maintain order and also to increase productivity among city officials. The second reading is about the leadership style of Coach Vince Lombardi. It talks about how he used love, fear, and avoided hatred in maintaining leadership. It points out that leadership has to be made through follower effectiveness not through leadership style. The last article by Miles points out two crucial points rarely discussed in academic settings. Leaders often must be "two-faced" to be successful and attitudes and opinions change among leaders depending on where they are in the organization.

REBIRTH OF THE LEADER

EUGENE E. JENNINGS

Source: From *An Anatomy of Leadership Princes, Heroes, & Supermen* by Eugene Jennings. Published by McGraw-Hill Book Company. Copyright © 1972 by Eugene Jennings. Reprinted by permission of author.

Our faith in personal, conspicuous leadership is being threatened today largely because life appears fully organized and predetermined. Real beginnings do not appear to be as easily made as they once were. It has become exeedingly difficult for us to believe that we can master our destiny, when at the same time we feel deeply interdependent with a foreign and unsympathetic world. How can executives run their organizations that are so closely tied to other organizations that are beyond their orbit of influence and control? Real beginnings and real possibilities have receded into the background as their already vastly overorganized life rambles on, seemingly out of control of their personal powers. They feel more and more insufficient. It is this feeling of powerlessness that contributes greatly to their growing tendency to become submerged in the anonymity of huge organization, to escape from the responsibility of personal leadership, to become an age without heroes.

However, the actual nature of this escape from leadership may be something different from the many interpretations of the American scene. The picture conveyed by Whyte's organization man, by Kerr's treatise concerning the end of the independent man, by Fromm's description of the typical western man as automaton conformist, or lastly, by Riesman's description of the other-directed man, does not provide a concise and adequate understanding of what many executives are actually like today and the major problems that they face.

The fact of the matter is that after an era of tremendous heroic, thrustful activity which transformed our emerging society into one huge factory capable of producing undreamed of material wealth, there is creeping over the American business scene a kind of conservatism in which change and progress are still expounded but only the kind that represents the established and on-going direction and character of the organization. Now, of course, this is quite an unusual and unexpected condition in the light of our dynamic, creative past. But this conservatism is even more fascinating when we consider that it is a form of power seeking.

THE PROBLEM: WHO AM I?

Herein lies the problem. The individual attracted to the top of our business hierarchy is just as ambitious for success, status, and power perhaps even more so, than his predecessor. But the augmented "too bigness" and "out-of-handedness" of the frame of reference cast by his huge organizations prohibits personally ordering a change of character or direction in the creative image of one who feels personally responsible. This means that the executive is no more for the organization than he was in the past. He is simply for himself, but the ambiguity of his organization life has today made it terribly difficult for him to see the difference. He finds it impossible to think of himself without thinking of the function his organized role prescribes for him. He is for himself, but is at a loss as to what his "self" really is.

In other words, he is no longer able to operate as satisfactorily and effectively by means of his own inner resources as his predecessors. Because he is being overcome by the rapidity with which his managerial framework is expanding, his self-determining facilities are gradually but surely being annihilated. Being less able to tap his own productive resources, he must rely increasingly upon external resources. These external resources upon which he depends include the authority that comes formally and impersonally with his position in the hierarchy, the prestige that is associated with his function, the formal knowledge that his "expertese" conveys, the group forces that he has learned to rely heavily upon, and the status symbols that show success and fitness such as carpeted floors, executive-shaped desks, and daily filled water decanters. But more importantly, he increasingly relies upon the imperatives of his organizational functions and the traditions or commonly accepted purposes and practices of his firm to make up for his growing lack of self-directedness. This is truly what we mean by the term "all too executive."

It is possible that the complexity and size of the modern organization have not really exceeded the ability of one individual to give it direction and character, but rather that the typical executive uses up so much of his psychological energy controlling his feelings of inadequacy and powerlessness that the full realization of his capacity for heroic leadership has been arrested. In other words, the typical executive has not grown psychologically in proportion to the increase in the number and complexity of stimuli stirred up by modern organization. He finds himself psychologically unable to handle these massive stimuli in a fresh and spontaneous manner, and so forces onto them a preconceived mental organization which brings them into the sphere of familiarity but does not do justice to their unique qualities. Although this may severely limit the range of his management capacity and make necessary more executives, more decision-making groups, and the use of other external resources in order to operate a given enterprise effectively, it also deprives him of spontaneity and greater realization of the unique present. An inhibiting mechanism develops that provides the executive with a restricted impression of what can be changed and to what extent. He becomes thereby abstracted from the real opportunities for leadership.

THE EXECUTIVE FACE

If we translate this new conservatism into our own terminology, we may say that the executive who aspires to the top is more and more becoming a prince who lacks the hero's sense of purpose or historical opportunity. Nevertheless, he tries to appear heroic, partly because the cultural stereotypes requires it of him. We previously described his condition by saying that he is a prince who wears a hero's halo. Now, his disguise would not be so bad if some kind of heroic action resulted from the executive's drive for success, but unfortunately, all too often the direction of the organization continues in a straight line after the change of executives. In fact, this lack of change is one of the tip-offs to the dominant presence of this new type of power seeker. Today all too many executives merely add their dots to a series of dots reflecting the evolving histories of their organizations. Under the ethic of finishing the unfinished task started by his great predecessors, this type of executive receives the advantages and benefits of the prince's power seeking without incurring the risk of the hero's attempt at major innovation. In short, he seeks success and personal advantage but does not have a sense of purpose or historical opportunity.

The illusive and masquerading feature of all of this is that the organization typically continues to get bigger. Someone usually gets credit for the growth partly because giving credit is a strong habit carried over from our heroic past. The mania for bigness is, however, a perfect example of how many executive's today fit into an on-going direction and character of their organizations in such a manner that they merely midwife the enterprises through what are actually predetermined courses. There is no change from the normal or expected pattern of growth as a consequence of his personal efforts, but rather only a continued increase in size and complexity under the illusion of heroic leadership.

It simply is not fair for the executive under these circumstances to be given the title of a leader since change is really not change after all. Change that occurs in the direction of the normal and expected is certainly not innovation in its true essence and it certainly cannot engender the degree of risk that is the differentiating feature between the leader and the executive.

In other words, power is a disruptive and

reformative—a creative—tool in the care of a leader. The power of one who acts as an executive is a sustaining and maintaining—a conservative—tool. Because many executives today do not have a strong creative opportunity or sense of purpose but have the same drive for power as their predecessors, we may say that they are potential leaders who suffer from arrested development. To know what causes their development to be arrested is one of the most important steps that they must take to solve their problem.

THE RISK REDUCER

But before we attempt to summarize the factors of this arrested development, it will be useful to note the major implication of this condition at present. An individual who has a strong drive for power, but who does not have a strong purpose to which he can attach that drive, would necessarily appear more power seeking than he might actually be. There is, of course, a lot to be said for the argument that his power drive may tend to increase in the absence of an objective goal that will give it form and sanction. But in either case, the very "nakedness" of his power seeking would seem to prompt him to inhibit it, which in turn brings on a psychological condition whereby it becomes even more difficult to develop heroic thrust. If we keep in mind, then, that the problem of many executives today is that they must appear to be thrusting and aggressive while at the same time not appear to be too power seeking, we have in capsule the essence of what they are trying to do. In other words, how to extricate themselves from these paradoxical demands is indeed the key to their success today.

One reason why all too few executives wish to have power to accomplish great and noble things is that the power struggle involves considerable personal risk. To remove the risk one must, of course, make permanent his power. But in making his power permanent he cannot make it apparent, for in making his drive for power too apparent he necessarily makes enemies of both those who are equally driven by the same urge and those who abhor the evil effects that power brings to both the organization and the personality of the individual himself. Implementing the power drive subtly and silently is a delicate skill that separates the power elite from the more common contenders. As a matter of fact, knowing how to play the power game well is far more the basis of determining who gets what, where, and when, than knowing the more narrowly encompassing skills and techniques of administrators. The latter can be mastered in a relatively short period of time, given the right training and experience. Incomparably more difficult to learn are the rules of acquiring through subtle means the necessary power with which to control others. It is for this reason that many executives fail to achieve the power necessary to affect major changes.

We might note that the price of failure is often more than forfeiture of the gains won by the attempt at leadership. This penalty often includes the loss of executive position. So the accepted pattern of many executives has become to gain power and make it permanent by not personally causing or sponsoring major innovations. For them it is safer to use power as a conservative force than as a creative force. Consequently, this kind of executive is not only as interested in gaining power as was his predecessor, but he is today incomparably more skilled in gaining and maintaining his power than in knowing and using his power for creative purposes.

The executive who makes the mistake of emerging into the fierce light of daring leadership is apt to become caught in dilemmas his talents are inadequate for resolving. No prince worthy of the name will struggle to meet standards beyond his capabilities. This is asking for unnecessary risk, sacrifice, and possible failure.

Furthermore, a major innovation is something that requires time to work itself out. Even if the program goes on to achieve success in heroic proportions, the executive could be knocked off because of an errant move in the interim. Anyone who takes long chances will find that the averages are against him. This we found to be an axiom of political experience. Major changes set loose unknown forces that gather a momentum of their own and smash through to results unwanted by anyone, including the executive. Consequently, it is far wiser to sponser many minor changes that only appear to be tests of ability although they must, of course, be beneficial to the organization, and many executives are becoming aware of this fact.

THE PRINCE'S MINUET

One favorite technique of many executives today is to place the responsibility for major changes in the hands of groups and thus shield themselves from the responsibility of complete failure. The idea here is to delegate to the "responsible group" those problems that are of major significance. By this means the executive assumes more "individual responsibility" for the more numerous minor innovations with the thought that many minor innovations will give heroic stature more than one major change, especially one that hazards failure or is cushioned by group responsibility. In effect, the strategy is to become cumulatively heroic through acts that are so integrated as to compound themselves. This we found to be Caesar's simulation played in a modern key, or we might say is the prince's minuet in F (foxy) Flat.

It may be argued that this new conservatism is made possible partly by large bureaucratic organizations wherein decisions must be increasingly made by the group method. Since the group is generally more conservative than the individual, the executive naturally becomes less radical and creative. Then, too, the increasing use of group meetings both formal and informal has forced out into the open the good intentions of the executive. As long as the executives could personally and privately deal with his superiors, subordinates, and peers, he did not have to reveal or fear to reveal his intentions toward power. He received ethical justification under the code of enlightened self-interest. But the convening of a group makes it imperative for the ambitious executive to manifest the most noble intentions simply because a group has a moral quality that is not found in the members taken separately. All good princes today know that in such quasipublic gatherings as conferences, committees, and even informal meetings, one must never be anything less than noble and moral, and above all, never appear too eager or overtly ambitious. The revealed ambition of an executive is grossly magnified by the ratio of the number of group members who witness the accidental droppings of his disguise. This means that in group meetings the executive today must hide his apparent need and drive for power by not being radically different, or at least not standing pat on a radical program. He knows that sponsoring a terribly different idea automatically forces him to draw upon the total power resources available to him. This just is never done today.

THE LIMITED OFFENSIVE

Therefore, for many the mark of the successful executive today is that he never uses the full potential of his personality. Of course, no one ever uses the full potential of his personalty, but we are concerned here with the fact that many executives use increasingly less. This lack of self-directedness shows up in his interpersonal relations. He is calm, but engaging, argumentative at times but not disagreeable, alert but not too trusting. He approaches people easily but also he is able to move out when he gets involved. The word is "heavy" when he talks about the conversations he seeks to avoid. When caught unavoidably in a "heavy" he has

the skill to work problems through to a convenient and acceptable solution, but in those cases his personality is invariably engaged on behalf of calming the disturbances, restoring the equilibrium, and thwarting accusations of being "difficult."

In all cases, blows of lethal and total effectiveness must never be swung, even in the form of words. It is far better to succeed a little bit than to destroy the opposition completely, which always brings trouble· later because of bitterness and recrimination. Pleasantries can never remove the pain of a grievous offense. This kind of executive believes strictly in a limited offensive with maximum opportunity for numerous engage-disengage sequences that will persuade but not offend. Above all, he must not make apparent his resources as an individual apart from his position, because of the tendency to impute ambition to the individual who shows personal talents that are not directly identified with the accepted norms and practices of his function and position. In other words, there is a tendency to confuse the individual with his formal rank and function in the hierarchy.

Many executives generally have no grand design, no mission, no great plan calling for change and progress. It is the true hero who has a grand design, which is reflected by a chainlike sequence of relevant and integrated events that serve as stepping stones. Of course, the grand design may not be easily deciphered until it is completed. Contrariwise, the prince lets each situation dictate to him his special set of techniques and plans of action. He sees no overall strategy except that which reflects the on-going and established interests of the various claimant groups involved in his organization. This allows him maximum flexibility without the personal risks of long range programs.

Anyone familiar with modern massive organization knows that there are too few today who have a sense of mission and too many who want merely the power available to them as executives in high offices. It is difficult for the typical executive to have a deep and disturbing sense of mission when he is so specialized and boxed in by bureaucratic formulas that he cannot rise above the trivia to see what is ahead, above, and behind. But if he suffers from "administrivia," he more importantly suffers from annihilation of all privacy.

Heroic leadership requires not so much a determination to out-maneuver the other fellow, but an ability to anticipate the effects of action now in progress and to devise plans that will be essentially preventive rather than remedial. But who is doing the thinking? Telephone any executive during business hours and you will probably be told that he is "at a meeting," for he spends most of his time "in conference." The executive has a genius for cluttering up his day and many have somehow managed to persuade themselves that they are too busy to think, to read, to look back, and to see into the future. Being busy is more than a national passion as some believe, and it is more than an excuse; it is a means of escape. The real question concerning the opportunity for heroic leadership is not the time or lack of it that is provided for thought, but the value that is placed on thought. The business world has always been action oriented, but lately what little thought has existed has been largely sacrificed to meetings where thinking is done in haste and geared to specific problems at hand, to say nothing about the power tactics that consume vast amounts of intellectual and emotional energy.

THE HERO OF THE FUTURE

We now arrive at the heart of the matter. The hero of the future will be that individual with the great mission to overcome the mass feeling of alienation and self-inadequacy. He will recognize that this struggle starts not with his community, nor even with his principal organization, but rather it starts with *himself*. He puts his own house in order; he gradually and diligently de-

velops the necessary values, courage, and self-control whereby he can successfully become identified with, but not absorbed by, his organization. He disciplines himself to wholeness and from this newly acquired inner strength he dominates the pressures of his organization and leads the people about him. In this way power over others comes to him because he is inwardly a superior person. The emergence of this hero, who is admittedly a rare gift to any organization or society, will by the changes he helps bring about prepare the way for other executives to become better leaders.

There are many executives today who are on "crusades" to restore the uncommon man, bring back the independent spirit, destroy the organization man, and revive the Titan's inner-directed conscience. They write books, give speeches, appear in only the most proper public gatherings and social circles, associate with the elites of their choice, buy and in some cases read the best literature, and identify with the most sophisticated of authors. If it were not for the fact that they are so noisy and public about this build-up we would actually think of them as somewhat sincere. Contrarily, we cannot help but believe that this eagerness to appear to be something akin to our superior person is really the attempt to assure themselves that they are what they are not.

Great care must be taken by the executive in his effort to overcome his feeling of alienation. If the skills required to prevent his absorption by his organization do not increase as rapidly as his involvement, he may end up more alienated than he is already in spite of his good intentions to the contrary.

It is in line with good hero theory that only a few will be able to recapture the will to lead. Of course, it never has been absolutely extinct, but the point is that these few promising executives need to be encouraged or they will find that their way back to conspicuous leadership will be too strenuous for them and they will have a fate similar to that of the late Robert Young.

Some may believe that everything must be done, every available resource must be used to help develop the promising executive into a superior type of person. The danger of this advice is that the appearance of a hero or even a prince with the hero's sense of historical purpose cannot be well planned and predicted. This, however, makes it all the more imperative that we should do certain things that are within our power to create a conducive atmosphere for the reappearance of the man of exceptional talent.

THE RETURN OF RARITY

We have seen that great leaders are, among other things, a rare, delicate, and variable mixture of the qualities of the prince, the hero, and the superman, and therefore, it is impossible to determine who the future leaders will be. Any attempt at scientific selection will produce a contemptible arrogance resulting from a lack of awareness of the limitations of technical kinds of identification and selection. Attempts to determine exactly the traits of a leader have resulted in complete failure. In spite of this we all have a crude but amazingly efficient sensitivity to the essence of leadership and to the existence of great leaders. We can recognize them even though their characteristics cannot be scientifically measured. The tendency today is to deny these rare men any psychological room, let alone social status and organizational prestige. We have tried in this book to present some of the characteristics by which we can identify heroic leaders, but these traits were only roughly described because words can only approximate the emotional quality with which we identify our heroes. To be sure the actual worship of heroes today has acquired a grotesque posture as seen in current biographical literature. But the essential spark is still there in the minds and hearts of many people and needs only to be rekindled.

In other words, it is not that we cannot recognize our heroes but rather that we no longer value them as highly as we once did. Therefore, scientific tests should definitely be discouraged so that our eminently more superior powers of observation and intuition can once again help us to find and to raise to our highest positions men of rare and exceptional leadership potential. In this way talent and ability will be brought into line with position, all of which will help, but of course not guarantee, a return to heroic leadership.

THE THOUGHTFUL MAN

Recommendations as to how to structure and reorganize for the rebirth of leadership could become so demanding and pervasive that the tendency to rely too heavily upon organization to eliminate the organization man could move us one notch back rather than one notch forward. All suggestions to help bring about a superior man in our organization should be tempered by judicious concern for the extreme fallacy of organizing to return to independence. We must be careful to place our reliance upon the individual to find his way to psychological recovery and not upon the forces inherent in the group and organization.

With this due caution, there is still another recommendation reflected in our concept of the superman. This recommendation concerns the value we place upon thought, that is, private deliberation resulting from a well-disciplined use of one's intellectual reserves. Each executive who shows promise of heroic leadership should be allowed ample opportunity to think. Perhaps once every five or seven years he should be given a year off with pay so that he can read and study and perhaps even write. When it is possible to organize his time and responsibilities he should be given time off to think, to get away from his office, and to become aware of the broader possibilities found in studying literature, philosophy, art, and the social sciences. Under proper and well-conceived circumstances this effort will not be an escape from leadership responsibilities, although this is a distinct danger. However, this program can be effective only with men who are willing and able to make major innovations and assume great responsibility and risks and who will profit from getting out and seeing a broader or higher purpose to which their organizations and themselves may become devoted. A vigorous emphasis on the value of the thoughtful man will allow a leadership to come forth that will be devoted to great and noble missions, not out of compulsive needs but out of choice that comes from inner wisdom.

Of course, finding ways to give the promising executive this opportunity to develop his intellectual resources will require a change in present-day values. The direction and character of the typical business organization will have to be changed since the man of action has heretofore been its standard breed. While we wait for some great innovator to show us the way toward the major innovation, there are some small things we can do ourselves. Most important among these is to reverse our tendency to walk into offices and homes, and backyards for that matter, because of an overpowering need to have friends and acquaintances. We can afford to be hard on ourselves and others who want not privacy but companionship. A good brother's keeper is one who helps the other person to suffer a little by leaving him alone and unengaged because this will in the long run help him to struggle and perhaps find himself.

But whatever opportunities are made available for the executive to develop his intellectual essence he should be twice as energetic to use his own free time for this purpose. Instead of playing some sport when he feels anxious and powerless he should spend his time more productively in meditation, thought, study, and perhaps even artistic accomplishments that will bring him the intellectual energy and discipline necessary to come into a more meaningful relationship with his organization. No doubt not all men are willing to sacrifice their leisure time and

others will be heard arguing tritely that physical exercise is necessary because it is relaxing. This may be true for many but it is questionable as to whether physical exercise in any way disciplines and gives effectiveness to one's efforts at heroic leadership. Many an executive has enhanced his feelings of alienation and powerlessness unwittingly by ascribing to the argument that physical rather than intellectual energy is needed.

Human progress occurs to a great extent through the intellectual efforts of its great men. Leadership might well be viewed as thought in command, while action and implementation might be the limitations imposed upon the individual who does not have or cannot use superior intellectual resources. It is fitting that we started this book and now we end it with this emphasis on the value of deliberation. Displacing or eliminating this great resource will assuredly reduce our opportunity and potentiality for change and progress.

CONCLUSION

In conclusion, ours is a society whose chief characteristic is a lost sense of self-direction as seen in the tendency to escape from leadership responsibility. The challenge is to revive the individual's unique powers of innovation and his courage to assume and sustain great risks. To be sure, there are many recommendations that could be made to this end, but because the purpose of this book is to diagnose our problem today, we have highlighted only a few. They include denial of the value of extraorganizational effort, resistance to the responsible group trend, respect for a man's privacy, faith in men of rare ability, and giving highest value to that talent reflected in thoughtful deliberation.

In spite of what we do to prepare the way for this hero, we cannot be sure that what we do will bring forth a figure who is superior or ideal. The great man is always to some extent a reflection of the times. With feelings of alienation and powerlessness building up in an already overly organized life, a major crisis in the form of an economic catastrophe or a war with communism may be just the situation necessary to produce a collective regression in the form of dictatorship. It could well be a fascist dictatorship if the executive suffers from alienation as acutely as we imagine he does in our more pessimistic moments.

Millions of Frenchmen flocked to Napoleon's lethal banner to escape the dreadful monotony of making another million collar buttons in a factory system considerably less mechanized than ours is today.[1] Hitler fed on the anxiety of the German middle class which had been deeply aroused by their perceived threat of monopolistic capitalism. In both cases anxiety and alienation were such that the people involved were moved to a state of panic that could be quieted only by submission to powerful leaders and by domination over those who were less powerful than they.[2] In addition to the problems of work monotony and economic monopoly, we have the problem of organizational impersonality or perhaps even tyranny. We may well ask to what great man's banner will we flock and will he be a prince, a hero, or a superman. We can be certain that among other things, he will be a rare and delicate mixture of these three but this does not assure us as to what this blend will actually be.

---

[1] I am indebted to Will Durant, *The Story of Philosophy,* Simon and Schuster, 1953, for his illuminating discussion on these points.

[2] See Erich Fromm, *Escape from Freedom,* Rinehart, 1941, for a fuller discussion of this point.

OF THE ADVICE WHICH DON QUIXOTE GAVE SANCHO PANZA BEFORE THE LATTER SET OUT TO GOVERN HIS ISLAND, WITH OTHER WELL-CONSIDERED MATTERS.

CERVANTES

The duke and duchess were so well pleased with the successful and amusing outcome of the adventure of the Distressed One that they made up their minds to continue with the jest, seeing what a suitable subject they had when it came to accepting the imaginary for the real. Accordingly, having instructed their servants and vassals as to how to behave toward Sancho in the governorship of his promised island, they informed the squire the next day (which was the one following Clavileño's flight) that he was to make ready to go and assume his gubernatorial duties, as his islanders were waiting for him as for the showers of May. Sancho made a low bow.

"Ever since I dropped down from Heaven," he said, "ever since I looked at the earth from up there and saw how little it is, I am not as anxious to be a governor as I was once upon a time. What greatness is there in ruling over a grain of mustard, or imperial dignity and power in governing half a dozen human beings the size of hazelnuts? For there did not seem to me to be any more than that. If your Lordship would be pleased to give me a little bit of Heaven, even if it was no more than half a league, I'd rather have it than the biggest island in the world."

"See here, friend Sancho," replied the duke, "I cannot give anyone a bit of Heaven, even if it were a piece no bigger than your fingernail. It is reserved for God alone to grant such grace and favors as that. What I can give, I do give you; and that is an island, perfect in every respect, tight and well proportioned and exceedingly fertile, where, if you know how to make use of your opportunities, you may contrive to gain Heaven's riches along with those of earth."

"Very well, then," said Sancho, "let the island come, and I'll do my best to be such a governor that, in spite of all the rascals, I'll go straight to Heaven. It's not out of greed that I want to quit my humble station or better myself; it is because I wish to see what it's like to be a governor."

Source: From *The Portable Cervantes,* translated and edited by Samuel Putnam. Copyright 1949, copyright © 1949, 1950, 1951 by The Viking Press Inc. Reprinted by permission of Viking Penguin, Inc.

"Once you try it, Sancho," the duke warned him, "you will be eating your hands off after it, so sweet a thing it is to give orders and be obeyed. You may be sure than when your master gets to be an emperor—as he undoubtedly will, the way things are going for him now—no one will be able to take that office away from him without a struggle, and he will be sick at heart over all the time he lost in not being one."

"Sir," said Sancho, "in my opinion, it is a good thing to be the one to give the orders, if only to a herd of cattle."

"Let them bury me with you, Sancho," said the duke, "if you do not know everything, and I only hope you will be such a governor as your wit seems to promise. But let us leave the matter there. Remember, it is tomorrow that you go to assume the governorship of your island, and this afternoon they will fit you out with the proper apparel and all the other things needed for your departure."

"Let them clothe me any way they like," replied the squire, "for however I go dressed, I'll still be Sancho Panza."

"That is true enough," agreed the duke, "but clothes must be suited to one's rank or dignity. It would not be well, for example, for a jurisconsult to wear the garb of a soldier, or a soldier that of a priest. You, Sancho, will go glad partly as a man of learning and partly as a captain, for in the island that I am bestowing on you arms and letters are equally necessary."

"I don't know much about letters," said Sancho; "in fact, I don't even know my ABC's; but to be a good governor, it's enough for me to be able to remember the Christus. As to arms, I'll handle those that they give me till I drop, and God help me from then on."

"With so good a memory as that," observed the duke, "Sancho cannot go wrong."

At this point Don Quixote came up and, upon hearing that Sancho was to leave so soon for his government, with the duke's permission, took him by the hand and led him to his room, with the intention of advising him as to how he was to conduct himself in office. Having entered the room and closed the door, he almost forced Sancho to sit down beside him, and then, very calmly, he began speaking as follows:

"Sancho, my friend, I thank Heaven with all my heart that good Fortune should have come your way before I have met with her. I had counted upon my luck to enable me to pay you for your services, but here am I at the beginning of my adventures while you, ahead of time and contrary to all reasonable expectation, are seeing your desires fulfilled. Some there be that count upon bribery, importunity, begging, early rising, entreaties, and pertinacity, and still do not attain what they seek; and then some other will come along and, without knowing the why or wherefore of it all, will find himself in the place and office that so many covet. Here it is that the common saying fits in well, to the effect that there is good luck and bad luck in all the strivings of men. You to my mind are beyond any doubt a blockhead, you neither rise with the sun nor keep nightly vigil, you are not industrious, and yet, as a result of the mere breath of knight-errantry that has been breathed upon you, you find yourself without more ado the governor of an island, as if it were nothing at all.

"I say all this, Sancho, in order that you may not attribute to your own merits the favor you have received. Rather, you should give thanks to Heaven for its beneficence, and, after that, to the great profession of knight-errantry for the potentialities inherent in it. Having, then, disposed your heart to believe what I have said to you, be attentive, my son, to this your Cato, who would counsel you and be the guiding star that leads you to a safe harbor as you set forth upon the storm-tossed sea that is now about to engulf you; for office and high trusts are nothing other than a deep abyss of trouble and confusion.

"First of all, my son, you are to fear God; for therein lies wisdom, and, being wise, you cannot go astray in anything. And in the second place, you are to bear in mind who you are and seek to know yourself, which is the most difficult knowledge to acquire that can be imagined. Knowing yourself, you will not be puffed up, like the frog that sought to make himself as big as the ox. Do this, and the memory of the fact that you once herded pigs in your own country will come to serve as the ugly feet to the tail of your folly."

"That is true," said Sancho, "but it was when I was a lad. Afterward, as a young fellow, it was geese, not pigs, that I guarded. But I can't see what all this has to do with the case. Not all those that govern come from the race of kings."

"You are right," replied Don Quixote, "and for that very reason those who are not of noble origin should be suave and mild in fulfilling the grave duties of their office. In this way they will be able to free themselves of that malicious gossiping to which no station in life is immune. Look to humility for your lineage, Sancho, and do not be ashamed to say that you come of peasant stock, for when it is seen that you do not blush for it, no one will try to make you do so. Pride yourself more on being a good man and humble than on being a haughty sinner. The number of persons of lowly birth who have gone up to the highest pontifical and imperial posts is beyond counting; by way of proving the truth of this, I could give you so many examples that it would tire you to listen to them.

"Remember, Sancho, that if you employ virtue as your means and pride yourself on virtuous deeds, you will have no cause to envy the means possessed by princes and noble lords; for blood is inherited but virtue is acquired, and virtue by itself alone has a worth that blood does not have. This being the case, as indeed it is, if perchance one of your relatives should come to your island to visit you, do not neglect or offend him, but rather receive, welcome, and entertain him. By so doing, you will be pleasing Heaven, which does not like anyone to despite what it hath wrought, and at the same time you will be acting in accordance with the laws of your own better nature.

"Should you bring your wife to be with you—and it is not well for those in government to be long without their womenfolk—teach and instruct her and smooth down her native roughness; for all that a wise governor may acquire, a foolish and boorish wife may well squander and lose for him. In case you become a widower (a thing that may happen), by virtue of your office look for a better consort. Do not take one to serve you merely as a hook and fishing rod or as a friar's hood for the receiving of alms, for, of a truth I tell you, all that the judge's wife receives her husband will have to account for on Judgment Day, when he will have to make in death a fourfold payment for things that in life meant nothing to him.

"Never be guided by arbitrary law, which finds favor only with the ignorant who plume themselves on their cleverness. Let the tears of the poor find more compassion in you, but not more justice, than the testimony of the rich. Seek to uncover the truth amid the promises and gifts of the man of wealth as amid the sobs and pleadings of the poverty-stricken. When it is a question of equity, do not bring all the rigor of the law to bear upon the delinquent, for the fame of the stern judge is no greater than that of the merciful one. If the rod of justice is to be bent, let it not be by the weight of a gift but by that of mercy. When you come to judge the case of someone who is your enemy, put aside all thought of the wrong he has done you and think only of the truth. Let not passion blind you where another's rights are concerned, for the mistakes you make will be irremediable, or only to be remedied at the expense of your good name and fortune.

"If some beautiful woman came to you seeking justice, take your eyes from her tears, listen not to her moans, but consider slowly and deliberately the substance of her petition, unless you would have your reason drowned in her weeping and your integrity swept away by her sighs. Abuse not by words the one upon whom punishment must be inflicted; for the pain of the punishment itself is enough without the addition of insults. When a guilty man comes under your jurisdiction, remember that he is but a wretched creature, subject to the inclinations of our depraved human nature, and insofar as you may be able to do so without wrong to the other side, show yourself clement and merciful; for while the attributes of God are all equal, that of mercy shines brighter in our eyes than does that of justice.

"If you observe these rules and precepts, Sancho, your days will be long, your fame will be eternal, rewards will be heaped upon you, indescribable happiness shall be yours, you will be able to marry off your children as you like, your children and your grandchildren will have titles to their names, you will live in peace with all men, and in your last days death will come to you amid a ripe and tranquil old age, and the gentle, loving hands of your great-grandchildren will tenderly close your eyes.

"What I have said to you thus far has been in the nature of instructions for the adornment of your soul. Listen now to those that will serve you where your body is concerned."

TOM SAWYER, MASTER WHITE-WASHER

MARK TWAIN

Saturday morning was come, and all the summer world was bright and fresh and brimming with life. There was a song in every heart; and if the heart was young, the music issued at the lips. There was cheer in every face and a spring in every step. The locust trees were in bloom and the fragrance of the blossoms filled the air. Cardiff Hill, beyond the village and above it, was green with vegetation, and it lay just far enough away to seem a Delectable Land, dreamy, reposeful, and inviting.

Tom appeared on the sidewalk with a bucket of whitewash and a long-handled brush. He surveyed the fence, and all gladness left him and a deep melancholy settled down upon his spirit. Thirty years of board fence nine feet high. Life to him seemed hollow, and existence but a burden. Sighing, he dipped his brush and passed it along the topmost plank; repeated the operation; did it again; compared the insignificant whitewashed streak with the far-reaching continent of unwhitewashed fence, and sat down on a tree-box discouraged. Jim came skipping out at the gate with a tin pail, and singing "Buffalo Gals." Bringing water from the town pump had always been hateful work in Tom's eyes before, but now it did not strike him so. He remembered that there was company at the pump. White, mulatto, and Negro boys and girls were always there waiting their turns, resting, trading playthings, quarreling, fighting, skylarking. And he remembered that although the pump was only a hundred and fifty yards off, Jim never got back with a bucket of water under an hour—and even then somebody generally had to go after him. Tom said:

"Say, Jim, I'll fetch the water if you'll whitewash some."

Jim shook his head and said:

"Can't, Mars Tom. Ole missis, she tole me I got to go an' git dis water an' not stop foolin' roun' wid anybody. She say she spec' Mars Tom gwine to ax me to whitewash, an' so she tole me go 'long an' 'tend to my own business—she 'lowed *she'd* tend to de whitewashin'."

Source: Tom Sawyer, Master White-Washer, by Mark Twain, John C. Winston Publishers, Chicago, 1931, 10–16.

"Oh, never you mind what she said, Jim. That's the way she always talks. Gimme the bucket—I won't be gone only a minute. *She* won't ever know."

"Oh, I dasn't, Mars Tom. Ole missis, she'd take an' tar de head off'n me. 'Deed she would."

"*She!* She never licks anybody—whacks 'em over the head with her thimble—and who cares for that, I'd like to know? She talks awful, but talk don't hurt—anyways it don't if she don't cry. Jim, I'll give you a marvel. I'll give you a white alley!"

Jim began to waver.

"White alley, Jim! And it's a bully taw."

"My! Dat's a mighty gay marvel, *I* tell you! But, Mars Tom, I's powerful 'fraid ole missis—"

"And besides, if you will, I'll show you my sore toe."

Jim was only human—this attraction was too much for him. He put down his pail, took the white alley, and bent over the toe with absorbing interest while the bandage was being unwound. In another moment he was flying down the street with his pail and a tingling rear, Tom was whitewashing with vigor, and Aunt Polly was retiring from the field with a slipper in her hand and triumph in her eye.

But Tom's energy did not last. He began to think of the fun he had planned for this day, and his sorrows multiplied. Soon the free boys would come tripping along on all sorts of delicious expeditions, and they would make a world of fun of him for having to work—the very thought of it burnt him like fire. He got out his worldly wealth and examined it—bits of toys, marbles, and trash; enough to buy an exchange of *work*, maybe, but not half enough to buy so much as half an hour of pure freedom. So he returned his straightened means to his pocket, and gave up the idea of trying to buy the boys. At this dark and hopeless moment an inspiration burst upon him! Nothing less than a great, magnificent inspiration.

He took up his brush and went tranquilly to work. Ben Rogers hove in sight presently—the very boy, of all boys, whose ridicule he had been dreading. Ben's gait was the hop-skip-and-jump—proof enough that his heart was light and his anticipations high. He was eating an apple, and giving a long, melodious whoop, at intervals, followed by a deep-toned ding-dong-dong, ding-dong-dong, for he was personating a steamboat. As he drew near, he slackened speed, took the middle of the street, leaned far over to starboard and rounded to ponderously and with laborious pomp and circumstance—for he was personating the *Big Missouri,* and considered himself to be drawing nine feet of water. He was boat and captain, and engine-bells combined, so he had to imagine himself standing on his own hurricane deck, giving the orders and executing them:

"Stop her, sir! Ting-a-ling-ling!" The headway ran almost out and he drew up slowly toward the sidewalk.

"Ship up to back! Ting-a-ling-ling!" His arms straightened and stiffened down his sides.

"Set her back on the stabboard! Ting-a-ling-ling! Chow! ch-chow-wow! Chow!" His right hand, meantime, describing stately circles—for it was representing a forty-foot wheel.

"Let her go back on the labboard! Ting-a-ling-ling! Chow-ch-chow-chow!" The left hand began to describe circles.

"Stop the stabboard! Ting-a-ling-ling! Stop the labboard! Come ahead on the stabboard! Stop her! Let your outside turn over slow! Ting-a-ling-ling! Chow-ow-ow! Get out that headline! *Lively* now! Come—out with your spring-line—what're you about there! Take a turn round that stump with the bight of it! Stand by that stage, now—let her go! Done with the engines, sir! Ting-a-ling-ling! *Sh't! s'h't! sh't!*" (Trying the gauge-cocks.)

Tom went on whitewashing—paid no attention to the steamboat. Ben stared a moment and then said:

"Hi-*yi! You're* up a stump, ain't you?"

No answer. Tom surveyed his last touch with the eye of an artist; then he gave his brush another gentle sweep and surveyed the result as before. Ben ranged up alongside of him.

Tom's mouth watered for the apple, but he stuck to his work. Ben said:

"Hello, old chap, you got to work, hey?"

Tom wheeled suddenly and said:

"Why it's you, Ben! I warn't noticing."

Say—*I'm* going in a-swimming, *I* am. Don't you wish you could? But of course you'd druther *work*—wouldn't you? Course you would!"

Tom contemplated the boy a bit, and said:

"What do you call work?"

"Why, ain't *that* work?"

Tom resumed his whitewashing and answered carelessly:

"Well, maybe it is, and maybe it ain't. All I know is, it suits Tom Sawyer."

"Oh, come, now, you don't mean to let on that you *like* it?"

The brush continued to move.

"Like it? Well, I don't see why I oughtn't to like it. Does a boy get a chance to whitewash a fence every day?"

That put the thing in a new light. Ben stopped nibbling his apple. Tom swept his brush daintily back and forth—stepped back to note the effect—added a touch here and there— criticized the effect again—Ben watching every move and getting more and more interested, more and more absorbed. Presently he said:

"Say, Tom, let *me* whitewash a little."

Tom considered, was about to consent; but he altered his mind:

"No—no—I reckon it wouldn't hardly do, Ben. You see, Aunt Polly's awful particular about this fence—right here on the street, you know—but if it was the back fence I wouldn't mind and *she* wouldn't. Yes, she's awful particular about this fence; it's got to be done very careful; I reckon there ain't one boy in a thousand, maybe two thousand, that can do it the way it's got to be done."

"No—is that so? Oh, come, now—lemme just try. Only just a little—I'd let *you,* if you was me, Tom."

"Ben, I'd like to, honest injun; but Aunt Polly—well, Jim wanted to do it, but she

wouldn't let him; Sid wanted to do it, and she wouldn't let Sid. Now don't you see how I'm fixed? If you was to tackle this fence and anything was to happen to it—"

"Oh, shucks, I'll be just as careful. Now lemme try. Say—I'll give you the core of my apple."

"Well, here—. No, Ben, now don't. I'm afeared—"

"I'll give you *all* of it!"

Tom gave up the brush with reluctance in his face but alacrity in his heart. And while the late steamer, *Big Missouri,* worked and sweated in the sun, the retired artist sat on a barrel in the shade close by, dangled his legs, munched his apple, and planned the slaughter of more innocents. There was no lack of material; boys happened along every little while; they came to jeer, but remained to whitewash. By the time Ben was fagged out, Tom had traded the next chance to Billy Fisher for a kite in good repair; and when *he* played out, Johnny Miller bought in for a dead rat and a string to swing it with— and so on, and so on, hour after hour. And when the middle of the afternoon came, from being a poor, poverty-stricken boy in the morning, Tom was literally rolling in wealth. He had beside the things before mentioned, twelve marbles, part of a jews-harp, a piece of blue bottle-glass to look through, a spool cannon, a key that wouldn't unlock anything, a fragment of chalk, a glass stopper of a decanter, a tin soldier, a couple of tadpoles, six firecrackers, a kitten with only one eye, a brass doorknob, a dog collar—but no dog—the handle of a knife, four pieces of orange peel, and a dilapidated old window sash.

He had a nice, good, idle time all the while—plenty of company—and the fence had three coats of whitewash on it! If he hadn't run out of whitewash, he would have bankrupted every boy in the village.

Tom said to himself that it was not such a hollow world, after all. He had discovered a great law of human action, without knowing it—namely, that in order to make a man or a boy covet a thing, it is only necessary to make the thing difficult to attain. If he had been a great and wise philosopher, like the writer of this book, he would now have comprehended that Work consists of whatever a body is *obliged* to do, and that Play consists of whatever a body is not obliged to do. And this would help him to understand why constructing artificial flowers or performing on a treadmill is work, while rolling tenpins or climbing Mont Blanc is only amuse-ment. There are wealthy gentlemen in England who drive four-horse passenger coaches twenty or thirty miles on a daily line in the summer, because the privilege costs them considerable money; but if they were offered wages for the service, that would turn it into work and then they would resign.

The boy mused a while over the substantial change which had taken place in his worldly circumstances, and then wended toward headquarters to report.

BOSS: RICHARD J. DALEY OF CHICAGO

MIKE ROYKO

If there is a council meeting, everybody marches downstairs at a few minutes before ten. Bush and the department heads and personal aides form a proud parade. The meeting begins when the seat of the mayor's pants touches the council president's chair, placed beneath the great seal of the city of Chicago and above the heads of the aldermen, who sit in a semi-bowl auditorium.

It is his council, and in all the years it has never once defied him as a body. Keane manages it for him, and most of its members do what they are told. In other eras, the aldermen ran the city and plundered it. In his boyhood they were so constantly on the prowl that they were known as "the Gray Wolves." His council is known as "the Rubber Stamp."

He looks down at them, bestowing a nod or a benign smile on a few favorites, and they smile back gratefully. He seldom nods or smiles at the small minority of white and black independents. The independents anger him more than the Republicans do, because they accuse him of racism, fascism, and of being a dictator. The Republicans bluster about loafing payrollers, crumbling gutters, inflated budgets—traditional, comfortable accusations that don't stir the blood.

That is what Keane is for. When the minority goes on the attack, Keane himself, or one of the administration aldermen he has groomed for the purpose, will rise and answer the criticism by shouting that the critic is a fool, a hypocrite, ignorant, and misguided. Until his death, one alderman could be expected to leap to his feet at every meeting and cry, "God bless our mayor, the greatest mayor in the world."

But sometimes Keane and his trained orators can't shout down the minority, so Daley has to do it himself. If provoked, he'll break into a rambling, ranting speech, waving his arms, shaking his fists, defending his judgment, defending his administration, always with the familiar "It is easy to criticize . . . to find fault . . . but where are your programs . . . where are your ideas . . ."

If that doesn't shut off the critics, he will declare them to be out of order, threaten to have the sergeant at arms force them into their seats, and invoke *Robert's Rules of Order,* which, in the heat of debate, he once described as "the greatest book ever written."

All else failing, he will look toward a glass booth above the spectator's balcony and make a gesture known only to the man in the booth who operates the sound system that controls the microphones on each alderman's desk. The man in the booth will touch a switch and the offending critic's microphone will go dead and stay dead until he sinks into his chair and closes his mouth.

The meetings are seldom peaceful and orderly. The slightest criticism touches off shrill rebuttal, leading to louder criticism and finally an embarrassingly wild and vicious free-for-all. It can't be true, because Daley is a man who speaks highly of law and order, but sometimes it appears that he enjoys the chaos, and he seldom moves to end it until it has raged out of control.

Every word of criticism must be answered, every complaint must be disproved, every insult must be returned in kind. He doesn't take anything from anybody. While Daley was mediating negotiations between white trade unions and black groups who wanted the unions to accept blacks, a young militant angrily rejected one of his suggestions and concluded, "Up your ass!" Daley leaped to his feet and answered, "And up yours too." Would John Lindsay have become so involved?

Independent aldermen have been known to come up with a good idea, such as providing food for the city's hungry, or starting day-care centers for children of ghetto women who want to work; Daley will acknowledge it, but in his own way. He'll let Keane appropriate the idea and rewrite and resubmit it as an administration measure. That way, the independent has the satisfaction of seeing his idea reach fruition and the administration has more glory. But most of the independents' proposals are sent to a special subcommittee that exists solely to allow their unwelcome ideas to die.

The council meetings seldom last beyond the lunch hour. Aldermen have much to do. Many are lawyers and have thriving practices, because Chicagoans know that a dumb lawyer who is an alderman can often perform greater legal miracles than a smart lawyer who isn't. . . .

The afternoon work moves with never a minute wasted. The engineers and planners come with their reports on public works projects. Something is always being built, concrete being poured, steel being riveted, contractors being enriched.

"When will it be completed?" he asks.

"Early February."

"It would be a good thing for the people if it could be completed by the end of October."

The engineers say it can be done, but it will mean putting on extra shifts, night work, overtime pay, a much higher cost than was planned.

"It would be a good thing for the people if it could be completed by the end of October."

Of course it would be a good thing for the people. It would also be a good thing for the Democratic candidates who are seeking election in early November to go out and cut a ribbon for a new expressway or a water filtration plant or, if nothing else is handy, another wing at the O'Hare terminal. What ribbons do their opponents cut?

The engineers and planners understand, and they set about getting it finished by October.

On a good afternoon, there will be no neighborhood organizations to see him, because if they get to Daley, it means they have been up the ladder of government and nobody has been able to solve their problem. And that usually means a conflict between the people and somebody else, such as a politician or a business, whom his aides don't want to ruffle. There are many things his department heads can't do. They can't cross swords with ward bosses or politically heavy businessmen. They can't make important decisions. Some can't even make petty decisions. He runs City Hall like a small family business and keeps everybody on a short rein. They do only that which they know is safe and that which he tells them to do. So many things that should logically be solved several rungs below finally come to him.

Because of this, he has many requests from neighborhood people. And when a group is admitted to his office, most of them nervous and wide-eyed, he knows who they are, their leaders, their strength in the community. They have already been checked out by somebody. He must know everything. He doesn't like to be surprised. Just as he knows the name of every new worker, he must know what is going on in the various city offices. If the head of the office doesn't tell him, he has somebody there who will. In the office of other elected officials, he has trusted persons who will keep him informed. Out in the neighborhoods his precinct captains are reporting to the ward committeemen, and they in turn are reporting to him.

His police department's intelligence-gathering division gets bigger and bigger, its network of infiltrators, informers, and spies creating massive files on dissenters, street gangs, political enemies, newsmen, radicals, liberals, and anybody else who might be working against him. If one of his aides or hand-picked officeholders is shacking up with a woman, he will know it. And if that man is married and a Catholic, his political career will wither and die. That is the greatest sin of all. You can make money under the table and move ahead, but you are forbidden to make secretaries under the sheets. He has dumped several party members for violating his personal moral standards. If something is leaked to the press, the bigmouth will be tracked down and punished. Scandals aren't public scandals if you get there before your enemies do.

So when the people come in, he knows what they want and whether it is possible. Not that it means they will get it. That often depends on how they act.

He will come out from behind his desk all

smiles and handshakes and charm. Then he returns to his chair and sits very straight, hands folded on his immaculate desk, serious and attentive. To one side will be somebody from the appropriate city department.

Now it's up to the group. If they are respectful, he will express sympathy, ask encouraging questions, and finally tell them that everything possible will be done. And after they leave, he may say, "Take care of it." With that command, the royal seal, anything is possible, anybody's toes can be stepped on.

But if they are pushy, antagonistic, demanding instead of imploring, or bold enough to be critical of him, to tell him how he should do his job, to blame him for their problem, he will rub his hands together, harder and harder. In a long, difficult meeting, his hands will get raw. His voice gets lower, softer, and the corners of his mouth will turn down. At this point, those who know him will back off. They know what's next. But the unfamiliar, the militant, will mistake his lowered voice and nervousness for weakness. Then he'll blow, and it comes in a frantic roar:

"I want *you* to tell *me* what to do. *You* come up with the answers. *You* come up with the program. Are we perfect? Are *you* perfect? We all make mistakes. We all have faults. It's easy to criticize. It's easy to find fault. But *you* tell me what to do. This problem is all over the city. We didn't create these problems. We don't want them. But we are doing what we can. *You* tell me how to solve them. *You* give me a program." All of which leaves the petitioners dumb, since most people don't walk around with urban programs in their pockets. It can also leave them right back where they started.

They leave and the favor seekers come in. Half of the people he sees want a favor. They plead for promotions, something for their sons, a chance to do some business with the city, to get somebody in City Hall off their backs, a chance to return from political exile, a boon. They won't get an answer right there and then. It will be considered and he'll let them know. Later, sometimes much later, when he has considered the alternatives and the benefits, word will get back to them. Yes or no. Success or failure. Life or death.

Some jobseekers come directly to him. Complete outsiders, meaning those with no family or political connections, will be sent to see their ward committeemen. That is protocol, and that is what he did to the tall young black man who came to see him a few years ago, bearing a letter from the governor of North Carolina, who wrote that the young black man was a rising political prospect in his state. Daley told him to see his ward committeeman, and if he did some precinct work, rang doorbells, hustled up some votes, there might be a government job for him. Maybe something like taking coins in a tollway booth. The Rev. Jesse Jackson, now the city's leading black civil rights leader, still hasn't stopped smarting over that.

Others come asking him to resolve a problem. He is the city's leading labor mediator and has prevented the kind of strikes that have crippled New York. His father was a union man, and he comes from a union neighborhood, and many of the union leaders were his boyhood friends. He knows what they want. And if it is in the city's treasury, they will get it. If it isn't there, he'll promise to find it. He has ended a teacher's strike by promising that the state legislature would find funds for them, which surprised the Republicans in Springfield, as well as put them on the spot. He is an effective mediator with the management side of labor disputes, because they respect his judgment, and because there are few industries that do not need some favors from City Hall. . . .

COACH: A SEASON WITH LOMBARDI

TOM DOWLING

Three days after I arrived in camp, the Redskins were to fly to Tamp, Florida, for a nationally televised Saturday-night game with the Detroit Lions. It would be the nation's first glimpse of the Lombardi Redskins, and the practice that Friday hardly seemed auspicious for its viewing pleasure. Running back Gerry Allen ran a sideline pattern, muffed the catch, and punched his palm in frustration. Lombardi came out of the backfield and paced off the route of the pattern, showing Allen where to make his cut, pointing down at the spot on the turf like a master indicating to his puppy where the newspaper was. Allen tried again, and instead of running the square-out Lombardi had just ordered, did a little button-hook. Lombardi was aghast. "That's just the opposite of what I told you," he said, his voice jagged with anger. "Someone was on me," Allen replied in a reedy voice. Lombardi sucked in some air and opened his mouth as if to explode. Then he suddenly stopped, blowing the air back out, apparently recalling some arcane instruction that gave Allen the option of changing his pass route. "That's right," he mused and then let out a big laugh. "Hey, that's right. That's good. Atta way to think in there, Gerry."

The team moved over to the regular gridiron, and the press corps ambled over to the stands. Presently we were joined by Marie Lombardi. She had never missed a game played by a Lombardi-coached team, was something of a self-styled den mother on the away game flights, and had driven up from Washington to ride to Tampa on the chartered team flight. She is a slender woman in her early fifties, rather attractive with blond hair, angular features, and an ironic shrug and voice. The only times I saw her during the season were at games or on the way to them, and there was always the sense that she regarded those football weekends as more of an obligation than a pleasure.

As she sat down with us in the stands, she lit a cigarette and showed around a charm bracelet with gold footballs hanging from it. She explained that two of the golden pigskins were for Lombardi's high-school championships, two from his coaching days at Fordham, two from Army-Navy games, and the rest for Green Bay Championships. "I had to take some of the high-school footballs off," she said. "It got too heavy."

"Yes, when you win so many championships it gets vulgar," one of the reporters said.

She laughed and shook the bracelet. "There's a stone in here that's loose in its setting," she said. "I have to put cotton-batting in there to keep it from rattling. The noise drives him crazy." She seemed to take immense pleasure in this last revelation, as if savoring the knowledge that she held the key to her husband's sanity, could pluck out the piece of cotton if he got out of hand. As I came to know her better, however, I learned that the ironic manner she assumed when talking about Lombardi was pure smokescreen. At bottom she was ferociously loyal to her husband, and was a skilled infighter on his behalf. In the end it seemed to me that the Lombardis had achieved that rare American ambition, a happy marriage. On the face of it Lombardi did not seem to be the easiest man in the world to live with. Certainly I never heard even the most admiring Redskin express the hope that his daughter would grow up to marry a man like Coach. And yet, there it was: Lombardi had married a nice woman, and they seemed happy together.

Down on the field Lombardi grabbed a running back by the shoulder pads. "Goddamn it, can't you remember," he said. "That's not the way you shift. One, two, three," he roared, marching the man three steps.

Marie shrugged.

"Goddamn it, that's the worst running I've ever seen," he yelled a few plays later. "We're going to stay out here until four o'clock this afternoon."

"Hey, Marie, give us a tip," a reporter asked. "We going to make that plane on time?"

"Sure," she said.

A hearse at the head of a long cortege of cars came down the road along the side of the practice field. Mrs. Lombardi looked at the funeral procession, exhaled a long jet of cigarette smoke, and said, "Do you think they'll stop to watch practice?"

"That's the way the deceased would have wanted it," I said.

"Well if they do," she dead-panned, "I hope Vin stops swearing."

The Lions game was another disaster. The Redskins drew first blood on a 15-yard Gogolak field goal. Then the Lions marched 80 yards for a touchdown. The Redskins ended the first half with an 80-yard scoring drive of their own, capped by a 25-yard Jurgensen-to-Jerry Smith touchdown pass. The Redskins added another field goal, this one, a 34-yarder, early in the third period, then tried for another. It was blocked, and Lion cornerback, Lem Barney scooped up the loose ball and went down the side line for a touchdown. The Lions added another score after a long drive, climaxed by a 24-yard pass to Mel Farr in the end zone. Then, with time running out, Redskin strong safety Brig Owens intercepted a pass that set up a touchdown run by Gerry Allen a few plays later. It was then Lions 21, Redskins 20, and that was the way it ended a few minutes later after the Redskin on-side kick failed. It had been a sloppily played game and a costly one for the Redskins. Free safety Tommy Brown suffered a shoulder separation, running back Bob Brunet got a concussion, and defensive end Jim Norton had his ankle fractured when teammate Carl Kammerer fell on top of him. It was to be a costly game for Charlie Gogolak as well. Lombardi was suspicious of soccer-style kickers, "sidewinders" as he called them, and felt that their trajectory was too low. He decided to deactivate Gogolak and to try rookie placekicker, Curt Knight, in the next two exhibition games. "Our kicking game," he explained, "is the laughing-stock of the league."

Lombardi, I was told, had delivered a

ripsnorting phillipic in the clubhouse after the Lions game. On the plane he had doubled up with the chest pressure that assaults him after a loss, seething with agony as intense as that of any out-of-shape 270-pounder at grass drills. After his recovery he asked for a flight manifest and drew up a team depth chart on the back of the paper. He then turned the manifest right-side up and cut the squad on the spot, placing an "X" beside the unlucky names.

Nonetheless, it is an injustice to Lombardi to pretend that he is all excoriation and hot rage on the gridiron, in the clubhouse, and on the team plane. He is a man who yields to the pull of his emotions, but if he is often angry, he is also often cheerful. The difference is that the first mood is more noticeable than the second. His gift is for intensity rather than blandness, and he had trouble coming to terms with that fact about himself. Nothing pained him more deeply than the impression in the land that he was the meanest man in football, a profane, heartless despot tyrannizing youngsters with peach-fuzz on their faces. He blamed the press for creating this image, and he thought that writers pandered to the public need for more of it. What he overlooked was the nature of fame, which feeds on its possessor's strongest, most dramatic characteristics. And while Lombardi had ridden the crest of pro football's wave, had become one of the most dominating personalities in the pantheon of the American Dream, he was still a man who had been shaped by the obscurity of his own past, those days in St. Cecilia Prep, Fordham, and West Point. No one had noticed him then, and that must have grated, for he was surely a man who yearned for the sort of recognition that Red Blaik enjoyed. When Blaik had been a national figure in the 1940's and early 1950's, football had been cocooned in the illusion of moral uplift. Coaches were pictured as saintly men who beamed encouragement to their charges, taught them the good clean virtues of the American Way. The harshness of the coaching vocabulary, the violence of football,

its unremitting pressure on fragile human vessels—this was all shrouded from view. Now football was a big business and all that had changed. No one was prepared to regard Lombardi as a saintly, gentle man. They saw him as a ruthless business tycoon who got ahead because he was tough and brooked no obstacles. Indeed, it was this toughness that delighted the Lombardi supporters out in Middle America. The country needed more screamers, more no-nonsense men.

I once asked Lombardi who his favorite sportswriters were. He thought a while and then said that most of them were dead. It was a lament like that of an aged literary man surveying the current titles from Grove Press and wondering what had happened to authors like Arnold Bennett, Hugh Walpole, and Galsworthy, fellows you could read aloud to the family after dinner.

Lombardi did not like the press then, because as Spiro Agnew pointed out, it had a tendency to dwell on bad news. The reporters led their stories with an account of the scream that punctuated a busted play rather than the unobtrusive pat on the rump that followed a well-executed one. In addition, he distrusted writers because he feared that in their need to say something every day, they would push back the boundaries football had erected to keep the public ignorant of the game's real nature. "You see too damn much," he had told one Washington reporter, who had noticed a shift of personnel in the first-string defensive unit at practice. In a nutshell, they saw too much and they asked too many questions.

Coming to Washington had exacerbated the problem. When Lombardi went to Green Bay in 1959 he was a nonentity nationally, but in Washington great things were expected of him, and soon. Like it or not, he was Vince Lombardi, and the news media were going to tell the country he was still the same old Coach everyone had heard about. So Lombardi had been under pressure to produce from the moment he had stepped up to the nest of microphones in the Sheraton-Carlton Hotel back in February, and the pressure had started to build from the moment the grass drills had begun on July 10. Lombardi was a great believer in pressure, in submerging yourself in it until you mastered it, but there was one difference now. In Washington, he was working with ballplayers he did not know and who did not know him, except to hold him in awe because of what they had heard and read. In Green Bay he had had a team that was used to him and that had proved able to thrive on an extra turn of pressure each year. The pressure he exerted in Green Bay had been an evolutionary process, a decade in the making. But to have picked up in Washington where he had left off in Green Bay would have been a revolutionary change for the Redskins, a departure so radical as to risk the destruction of the team. For the secret of pressure was knowing when to stop, and the 1969 Redskins had a lower tolerance for it than the 1967 Packers had had. The question was, would Lombardi recognize this, realize that he was starting all over again from scratch as in 1959, not just picking up the 1967 reins again after a year on the side lines. The doubt that surrounded that proposition was the nature of the pressure that faced the Redskins. They ran the risk of being broken. The nature of the pressure that faced Lombardi was that he could never go back to 1959. His legend would never permit it.

In 1959 Lombardi took over the Packers and said he would have a championship in five years. People scoffed at him. In 1969 if he had said he expected a championship in five years, people would have scoffed once more, but for different reasons. Five years for a championship? Hell, Otto could have done better than that. Five years? What are we paying him all that money for if that's the best he can do? Is he Vince Lombardi, or isn't he?

Yes, Lombardi was in something of a bind. He had, in the words of the sports clichés, put it on the line, hung it all out. Time and personnel were not on his side. He had not inherited a young and malleable team, as he had in Green Bay. Trades had taken away his top draft choices for 1968 and 1969. He expected the press to remind the public of that, to acquaint them with the length of the odds, and he was annoyed when they didn't, but continued to dwell on the forthcoming *annus mirabilis*. Moreover, the handful of established Redskin stars was not, on the face of it, Lombardi-style players who blended with his system. Jurgensen was not a ball-control quarterback, not a leader; Jerry Smith was too light to provide blocking strength at tight end; Charley Taylor was too loose, too erratic a catcher for the dependability the Lombardi passing game required. Chris Hamburger was too light and too much of a free-lance operator to give the Lombardi precision linebacking coverage on the outside. Among the stars, only Len Hauss at center seemed to have the credentials for Lombardi football; he was tough and quick, like Jim Ringo, a little underweight for a pro lineman, but a 110 percenter.

Bobby Mitchell had not been a 1968 regular, but he was unquestionably one of the great athletes in NFL history. Like Charley Taylor, Mitchell was a gamebreaker, but a man who made a spectacular catch one play and dropped the ball all alone in the end zone the next; he lacked the consistency that Lombardi had always sought in his receivers, and he was getting old as well.

Sam Huff was the quintessential Lombardi player, but he had sat out a season and had even been in physical decline during his last two playing years in 1966 and 1967.

It was harder to assess the adaptability of the 1968 Redskin regulars. Although there were some good ballplayers among them, they lacked star identity and the strongly marked personal characteristics that would indicate how well they would mesh with the Lombardi system.

In the aggregate, the Redskins were a team largely composed of low draft choices, free agents, and veterans acquired from other teams, sometimes at prohibitively high prices. It was a team that had a history of folding, of swooning at the last moment. in 1967, five games had been lost or tied in approximately the final minute of play; in 1968, the team went downhill from the opening kickoff. Was it a team that had been under too much pressure, or too little? Under the right sort of pressure or the wrong? Lombardi didn't know, and he once told me, "The most important thing a coach needs is the knowledge that his team can or can't play under pressure. If it can't you need new players; if it can, you can make do with average ones." From the start, then, he was determined to put the team under more pressure than they were used to, or at least a different kind of pressure—Lombardi pressure. It was both a mental and a physical process: it was physical in the relentless grind of conditioning at training camp and the need to play in spite of injury and exhaustion; it was mental in the humiliation of harassment and screaming, the ever-present threat of being cut, traded, or waived, and the insistence that there was only one right way to do something.

"To stay or not to stay, that was the question of training camp for most people," Vince Promuto told me. "Sometimes it takes more character to walk out than to stay on." Promuto was not speaking for himself, because he was determined to stay, to make Lombardi respect him, just as he respected Lombardi; there was almost a touch of the aspiring Mafioso in Promuto's hunger to gain that respect. Like Lombardi, Promuto was a poor Italian boy from New York City. He had won a football scholarship to Holy Cross and was playing his tenth year as the starting Redskin guard. He felt strongly that football had made a vast difference in his life, had allowed him to go to college, to make a decent living, and to see him through law school in the off-season. This sense of indebt-

edness was fortified by periodic trips to his boyhood neighborhood, where men he had grown up with were engaged in lives of petty crime and menial drudgery. He once told me he had run into an old teen-age pal in the Bronx who had just been sentenced to two years in jail for stealing a car. "Gee, that's too bad," he told the man. "Ahhh, don't worry about it, Vinnie," the friend had replied, "nothing to it. I can do two years standing on my ear." Promuto described the exchange and shook his head with its square jaw and features as strongly etched as a pop-art painting of Mr. America. These two years in the stir might have been his own fate without football, he was clearly thinking, and he smiled, thinking that he would have accepted them with something of his friend's bravura. The Lombardi training camp was then something he figured he could do standing on one ear, for it was the ethic of his youth that winning respect was the name of the game.

"I'd heard Lombardi practiced for an hour and a half," he said. "Well, I've practiced for two and a half hours in my day and I could make the trip. I figured I was a tough sonofabitch and nobody was going to get me down. That first day in Carlisle I found I was wrong. I was ready to say uncle. Lombardi don't stop until everybody gets bushed. And you weren't used to him, you never knew how much longer he'd make you do those damn ups-and-downs. You'd lie on the ground and say, 'This guy's a madman, he'll never stop,' and within fifteen minutes you were bushed, frightened to exhaustion, and you had to do the next one hour and fifteen minutes on courage alone. This is his idea of getting you ready for the fourth quarter. Not even the Chinese could do so well at breaking you that first week. And I was trying so hard to look good, to show a great coach that I could play for him that I burned myself out, lost twenty pounds, and was actually down to 230 and I hadn't weighed that since college.

"Well, I lasted it out, got some of my weight back and just as I started to feel real good, a halfback ran into my left knee and it swelled up with water the day before the Buffalo game and I knew I'd have to play that way and I did. After the game he comes up to me and says, 'How do you feel, Vincent?' I said, 'I'm all right, Coach.' He says, 'Atta way to talk.' I said, 'That's the name of the game; you got to play when you're hurt.' Jesus, you should have seen him light up. He says, 'Atta way to go, Vincent, atta way to go.'

"Well, playing in Buffalo set me back a month. My knee got so bad I could hardly walk. Then I broke three ribs and separated my shoulder. But it was the knee that bothered me. What you need in this game is your legs. Shoulders and ribs, they hurt when you get hit there again, but you don't need them to do your job. There are a lot of big people walking around the earth, and the value of a pro ballplayer over a big guy walking around is the pro can play hurt.

"I'll tell you, most people play the game because they want to be heroes. Sure they do. I do. You play it to be recognized, for one, by a man you respect, like Lombardi. And you play it so you can see it in yourself. The greatest moment for me is when you walk into the locker room after you've won, and you've had a good day personally. You're beat up and bruised, but you don't feel hurt. And you get a couple of minutes sitting in front of your locker before you say the team prayer, and you're sitting there saying, 'Hey, I'm a bitch. I'm really something.'

"Well, I had some days like that this year, and I got to be pretty biased in favor of Lombardi and his system. I'll tell you why. Because I learned not to be afraid of him. If you play for him because he gets to you out of fear, then there's a defect in Lombardi's system, because the minute you're not with him anymore, you'll fizzle out. You see, some guys feel they're only doing what he wants them to do to keep from being yelled at. They're losers. You have to make one more step and see that it's not him that's making you play better football, but yourself. That's a feeling worth having."

But if Promuto had found the Lombardi system a cause to believe in, there were other players I liked and admired who challenged the whole philosophical underpinning of the Lombardi method. And they were not losers, either. One of them told me, "He says if he sees forty ballplayers playing to the best of their ability he's satisfied. Maybe, but if they do, it's because they're afraid. He motivates through fear. It's a terrible feeling to know you're afraid of the man you work for, terrible. When I think personally of what I have gone through this year! The hell you go through making the team, and it was hell. And then the fear of having that taken away from you. The statements he makes when you're hurt, like if you don't play for me hurt I'll get rid of you. I've heard him tell that to people. Hell, he's told it to me. When you've got a family, is that right to be told you're fired because you're hurt? You ask yourself, would he really do something like that? I think he would. And this is why his theory of winning has to be questioned, because of the man you become, because of the man the coaches, like Lombardi, become. He's trying to be the father image. He's tough, he's mean, and he's hard, and then sometimes he'll do a decent thing, something that's more than fair. Yes, he's capable of that too. More so than most people in this business. But in the end it comes down to winning and losing, and I ask myself, is that fatherhood? Well, I have a kid and I don't want to be that kind of father.

"You know, I was talking to some guys I knew on the Packers before training camp began, and they laughed at me and said, 'Hey, you're going to get that dirty bastard,' and 'When he gets ahold of you guys he's going to have your tongue hanging out.' They were all laughing, you know. With glee! Yet you'd think they'd really want him back, would miss him, but they didn't seem to. Maybe human nature doesn't want to win all that bad. You accept things more than you really want them. You accept being the champions of the world, but when the man who made you champions is gone, it's a tremendous relief.

"So I said to these Packers, 'Okay, why'd you guys have the 6–7–1 season last year?' And they said because Lombardi wasn't here. Hell, maybe that's just an excuse they used because they got outplayed. Ballplayers will alibi you forever. But they seemed like they believed it, like they knew Lombardi's going was why they lost. I tell you, you lean on a guy like Lombardi. He *is* the reason. You take him out, and the motivation, the control, the drive is all gone. He walks into the training room and says, 'Nobody's hurt, get the hell out of here,' and everybody limps out.

"He can get it out of you. He can win anywhere, providing he has just halfway decent ballplayers. But the trouble is, if you do win with Lombardi, you have the feeling you, the *team,* didn't do it. HE did it. Hell, he told us to our face in Carlisle. 'All I need is bodies, gentlemen.' Well dammit, I like to play this game. I feel like when I have a good day, that's me who's had a piece of winning."

As this particular ballplayer talked in my living room, my wife sat in a chair listening. A stranger to professional sports, she asked a question that certainly had not occurred to me.

"Is it possible," she asked, "that Lombardi is capable of arousing such hatred that the team would want to humiliate him so badly they'd welcome defeat?"

The player thought for a while and said, "This is true."

"In that case," my wife said, "you have to believe in Lombardi. You have to try and believe in him, anyway. It's such a thin line he's drawing that if you step over it, you'll ruin yourselves as well as him."

"Yes," the player laughed, "he's got you, doesn't he? There's no way out of it."

So the Lombardi pressure elicited different reactions. Both of these players had gotten through training camp, had made the forty-man roster, but they judged things differently.

There was, I thought, great risk in such divergence, for Lombardi was trying to make a team, and his notion of a team, as I understood it, was a group of forty men united in a common purpose and outlook who submitted their will to the larger demands of Lombardi-type football. It was hard to know whether frightened men and questioning men fitted into that scheme. It was too early to tell, in any case. And I supposed that, from Lombardi's standpoint, he didn't care whether he had doubters and detracters, for in the end they would either show they could play football for him or would be eliminated.

MILES'S SIX OTHER MAXIMS OF MANAGEMENT

RUFUS E. MILES, JR.

Source: Reprinted, by permission of the publisher, from *Organizational Dynamics,* Summer 1979, © 1979 by AMACOM, a division of American Management Associations. All rights reserved.

"A manager's authority should equal responsibility; otherwise, he cannot fairly be held accountable for the success or failure of his organization." So goes an old maxim of management, now obsolete, if it ever was valid, but still mouthed by people whose administrative acquisitiveness exceeds their managerial wisdom. The plain fact is that in any large organization it is impossible to give managers authority equal to their responsibility.

It is time to stow this old adage away in the archives or curiosity shop of administrative historians and replace it with one that will help, rather than hinder, managers who have not yet reached their level of incompetence. Here is a suggested substitute: "The responsibility of every manager exceeds his authority, and if he tries to increase his authority to equal his responsibility he is likely to diminish both"—otherwise known as Miles's Second Maxim of Management.

The responsibility of every manager is to get things done—as effectively, economically, and expeditiously as could reasonably be expected of a first-rate manager. But no manager should demand or expect to have all necessary organizational resources, as well as full authority over policies and personnel, under his personal command.

We are talking about managers who have superiors, as most managers do. Each such manager is placed in charge of a unit that fits into a larger context. Within this context, power and authority are virtually certain to be distributed in such a way that various specialized units are set up to assist the chief executive in arriving at certain types of policy decisions that will be broadly applicable to subordinate units, or to provide services that are believed to be furnished more economically on a centralized than on a decentralized basis.

Most managers cannot be given total control over pay levels for their subordinates, the procedure for hiring and firing personnel, or the location of offices and plants. They do not have full control over their contracting procedures or the design of their accounting and control systems. In respect to these and other control and service functions, such as management auditing and various types of research, a centralized organizational design may be selected by top management. Subordinate managers with large areas of responsibility may chafe under some aspects of this organizational arrangement, but with rare exceptions, they are better off accepting it and demonstrating that they can make this system work.

The contrasting management styles of three men with whom I was associated will help illuminate the purpose of this maxim. The first was a former mayor of a smallish Midwestern city who was given a Presidential appointment to a high position (on paper) within the Department of Health, Education, and Welfare (HEW). One of the first things he asked for when he assumed office was a "job description" enumerating his responsibilities and authority. He quickly concluded that the assigned responsibilities considerably exceeded his delegated authority, an indisputable conclusion. Thereupon, he informed the Secretary that in order to do what was expected of him, he should have transferred to him certain organizational units that he perceived to be essential to the discharge of his responsibilities.

The Secretary said he would think the matter over and get back to him. After pretending to do so, he denied the request. The Secretary had spotted him immediately as a man who did not understand how to exercise power and influence without having a written document to record for any skeptics the source and extent of his authority. Having had no hand in picking the man, the Secretary decided to test him out before expanding any formal delegation of power to him. From the standpoint of the new appointee, the attempt to increase his authority proved a gross tactical error from which he never recovered. The Secretary's rebuff got him off on the wrong foot, and he never learned how

to get things done under the constraints he faced. Power flowed around him as water flows around a large rock in a fast-flowing stream.

In sharp contrast, a talented career bureau chief carefully cultivated the skills of working with key people not under his organizational command to enlist their aid in getting his job done. He had a knack for making staff people in the Office of the Secretary and even, to some degree in the General Services Administration and the Civil Service Commission, feel as though they were his associates in a great enterprise that involved the delivery of services to the American people. He had the extraordinary capacity to convey the idea that it would enhance their reputations if they demonstrated that they could do something in an unusually flexible or rapid manner. Nobody thought about comparative ranks or power, except in unusual circumstances, when agreement by open and candid discussion could not be achieved—something that happened rarely.

Ninety percent of the time the efforts were collaborative rather than adversarial. He was gracious to the secretaries and staff assistants of the officials with whom he worked—never condescending or demanding. He was the perfect embodiment of a man who understood how to discharge his responsibility without trying to enhance his technical authority or enlarge his empire. I say "technical" authority because his real authority, measured in influence terms, kept growing and growing.

Still a third example, this time of a somewhat lower-level manager, provides an insight into how a smart manager can extend his capacity to get things done in an imaginative way. This midlevel manager concentrated a greater amount of effort than anybody in the department on recruiting first-rate talent for his organization. He personally visited universities and colleges where he had identified first-rate professors who encouraged some of their best students—those who seemed more like activists than scholars—to seek careers in government. He found young men and women who looked like the managers and executives of the future. He hired as many of these top students as his budget would allow, and steered others to sister units of the larger organization, thereby pleasing the professors, the students, and his associates.

As might be expected, his own staff soon became known as "comers," and other managers from all over the department sought out and hired these able young people at higher grades and pay rates than his budget would allow. One day I overheard someone say to him, "Steve, how can you stand having the rest of the department steal you blind the way they do?" His reply was revealing:

Oh, you don't understand—I have scads of young friends and helpers throughout the department as a result of this process. Time and time again, I need the aid of people outside this organization to get things done, and I have a marvelous network of people whom I have recruited, trained, and helped, to whom I can turn for assistance. Mayor Daley once said that the art of politics is the art of putting people under obligation to you. The arts of politics and public administration aren't all that different. Besides which, I enjoy the process of finding and encouraging smart young people to begin their careers here and then seeing them move up.

These latter two career managers had learned—and sought to teach their subordinates—how to get things done. They understood that trying to gain authority to equal one's responsibility inevitably stamps you as an empire builder, and nothing is more likely to hinder your effectiveness—in any organization.

RELUCTANCE TO DELEGATE

"Managers at any level think they can make better decisions than either their superiors or their subordinates. Most managers therefore seek maximum delegations from their superiors and make minimum delegations to their subordi-

nates." This is Miles's Third Maxim of Management. Like Mile's Law—"Where you stand depends on where you sit"—it is the statement of a strong behavioral tendency within organizations, a mode of behavior that a smart manager will seek to guard against in himself. It is a tendency that deserves to be thought about, particularly by people who are in the early stages of developing their own managerial styles.

Two high officials of HEW, one of whom succeeded the other, managed with dramatically different approaches to delegation—and with dramatically different results. The first was reluctant to delegate anything significant; the second preferred to delegate whenever possible. The first official spent long hours, working virtually every evening and weekend, either alone or in what one wiseacre dubbed "endless group grope sessions," surrounded by frustrated advisers. Problems queued up at his door for decisions and subordinates tore their hair because they could not get answers to any but the most urgent and high-priority issues—and sometimes not even these. Anything that could be deferred was pushed back. Consequently, many decisions that might have seemed good if they had been timely were badly tarnished by the time they were issued.

It was like the freshness of spring after a harsh winter when this official was replaced by a natural-born delegator. Morale rose rapidly. Decisions got made because they had been delegated to the right level for handling. The top manager was almost always available on short notice in case a subordinate had a crisis or other problem of sufficient importance to warrant the top manager's attention. The productivity of the organization (judged subjectively because its products were neither comparable with one another nor countable) shot up along with its morale. And, best of all, when a subordinate's decision turned sour, the top manager was the first to assume responsibility and take the heat.

Most good managers have a high degree of

Miles's Law and Six Other Maxims of Management

Law: Where you stand depends on where you sit.

Maxim 2.   The responsibility of every manager exceeds his authority, and if he tries to increase his authority to equal his responsibility, he is likely to diminish both.

Maxim 3:   Managers at any level think they can make better decisions than either their superiors or their subordinates; most managers therefore seek maximum delegations from their superiors and make minimum delegations to their subordinates.

Maxim 4:   Serving more than one master is neither improper nor unusually difficult if the servant can get a prompt resolution when the masters disagree.

Maxim 5:   Since managers are usually better talkers than listeners, subordinates need courage and tenacity to make their bosses hear what they do not want to hear.

Maxim 6:   Being two-faced—one face for superiors and one for subordinates—is not a vice but a virtue for a program manager if he or she presents his or her two faces openly and candidly.

Maxim 7:   Dissatisfaction with services tends to rise rapidly when the provider of the services becomes bureaucratically bigger, more remote, and less flexible, even if costs are somewhat lower.

Source: Rufus E. Miles, Jr. "The Origin and Meaning of Miles' Law," *Public Administration Review,* September—October, 1978, p. 403. Miles' Law is fully explained in this article.

---

self-confidence. They should have. Some overdo it, of course, but self-doubt is out of place in a manager. It is hardly surprising, therefore, that managers do tend to think they can make better decisions in respect to any matter within their purview than can their superiors, especially when they feel they have more intimate knowledge of the issues under consideration. Since they don't have full knowledge of some of the factors their superiors have to take into account, however, and since their superiors don't always feel at liberty to disclose all these factors, midlevel managers (or even higher-level ones) may chafe under the reins that hold them in check. Many ask for latitude to make more key decisions than they are permitted to make. The subordinate managers may be absolutely right. Their superiors may, in fact, be victims of this maxim, making too few delegations. The primary lesson of this maxim is that every manager should examine his own delegations to see whether he is doing the same thing to his subordinates that he believes his superior is doing to him—not trusting them sufficiently to make good decisions.

Three principal elements come into play in developing a set of subordinates to whom the delegation of decisions can confidently be made. The first is obvious: Get good people. The second is somewhat less self-evident: Share as fully as possible with subordinates all relevant information in the possession of the superior that will help the subordinate make a good decision. In fact, lean over backward in being generous in sharing information that may have a bearing on the key decisions of subordinates. Many errors are made by managers because of factors their bosses should have told them but didn't. The third is the least well appreciated: You should expect your subordinates to make mistakes, and you should shoulder the blame when they do.

Freedom to make good decisions also means freedom to make bad decisions. Nobody yet has devised a system under which a delegation can be controlled in such a way that only good decisions will be made. Many have tried it, but all have failed. Either you make up your mind that you, as a manager, will have a certain tolerance for decisions made in a way that you would not make them, or you make no important delegations at all. And one bad mistake should not cause you to blow a subordinate out of the water if his record has otherwise been good. This is often harder advice to follow in a public agency that operates in a fishbowl atmosphere than in a private business, but it is important in both arenas. Everyone learns by a combination of successes and failures, and all must have the freedom to learn from both kinds of experience if they are to develop into effective and wise managers.

In the public arena, especially, political appointees with an expected tenure of perhaps two or three years in which to make a name for themselves may be especially reluctant to entrust decision making to subordinates in respect to any matter they think is "sensitive"— meaning something the news media would pounce on. This jitteriness is conveyed by emotional osmosis throughout the organization, causing many program managers two or three layers down from the agency head to behave the same way. Such circumstances "separate the men from the boys." Mature managers continue to behave maturely and go on developing their subordinates through delegation and by acting as a heat shield when mistakes are made.

SERVING MORE THAN ONE MASTER

This brings us to Miles's Fourth Maxim of Management: "Serving more than one master is neither improper nor unusually difficult if the servant can get a prompt decision when the masters disagree." This maxim is an explicit contradiction of a biblical saying adduced years ago by the high priests of the "line and staff" principle of management to sanctify it. They drew organization charts that showed who were the line officers and who were the staff officers and made sure that each was always shown to report to a single superior; that every line officer reported to a higher-echelon line office, never to a staff officer; and that every head of a staff officer reported to a superior line officer, never to a staff officer at a higher echelon. That is the way organization charts are still drawn, generally speaking. But that is not the way things work.

First, let us take a moment to delve into the history of the idea that "no man can serve two masters." The assertion comes directly from the Sermon on the Mount (*Matthew* 6, verse 24) wherein Jesus is quoted as saying, "No man can serve two masters: for either he will hate the one and love the other; or else he will hold to the one and despise the other. Ye cannot serve God and mammon." Upon close examination, it seems clear that what Jesus intended was to focus attention on the supreme importance of devotion to God. Later, in response to a question, Jesus answered, "Render unto Caesar that which is Caesar's and unto God that which is God's." This seems to nullify any simplistic interpretation of the unmodified statement that "No man can serve two masters."

We learn from the time we are small children to serve two masters—our mothers and our fathers. If they are wise, parents handle their relations with their children in such a way that their instructions do not conflict. They are careful to see their children cannot play them off against each other in getting what they want. As long as parents and children behave that way, serving two masters is neither improper nor unusually difficult. At age five or six, a child goes off to school and begins to serve a third master—the schoolteacher. Later, he or she learns to serve the football or the basketball coach or to obey the traffic officer or an employer or an Internal Revenue Service agent. All this is done without much difficulty, as long as each behaves himself or herself and no uncertainty derives from conflicting instructions.

Undoubtedly, the great stimulus to the idea that within large organizations each person should report to a single, clearly designated superior came from the military. That is where the line-and-staff concept was hatched. Battlefield operations were where it made the greatest amount of sense. In a rifle squad or on a ship, where commands must be followed quickly and precisely, multiple directives, with the potential for conflict, would be intolerable. If it is good for the military, and sanctified by the Sermon on the Mount, who could question it as, a sound principle to guide management in general? No wonder it has retained its standing even though it is universally ignored in practice—except, of course, when people draw organization charts.

What actually happens in practice? Anybody who has ever been part of a large organization knows that almost everybody above the journeyman level learns to accept instructions from multiple sources. Line officers accept and follow instructions both from their line superiors and from staff offices at a higher echelon, as long as they believe that the staff officers are carrying out the explicit or implicit bidding of their common superior. Staff officers sometimes take instructions from their line superiors and sometimes from staff officers at the next higher echelon. Any line officer who insisted he would follow instructions only if they came directly and explictly from his line superior would quickly find himself in the gravest of difficulty. Thereafter, he would find his promotional opportunities either cut off or sharply limited. For the fact is that executives need to have the flexibility of getting decisions carried out either by line or staff subordinates, depending on circumstances.

When the general counsel of an organization concludes that a course of action proposed by a unit of the organization would be illegal, he is generally authorized to tell the manager of the unit his conclusion and, in effect, order him not to proceed with it. The general counsel need not send his advice to the chief executive and have the chief executive issue the formal instructions not to proceed. If the director of personnel finds that the personnel policies of the organization are being violated, he is usually authorized to instruct the violators to take corrective action. He does not have to bother the chief executive in order to get the corrective action taken. If the chief executive decides to create a task force chaired by one of his top staff officers with the idea of hammering out a new policy on an important subject, the staff officer does not have to ask his superior's permission every time he wants to call a meeting, or whenever he wants to make a committee assignment to an important line officer serving on the task force. It is clearly understood by all that this is the way things work.

In government more than in business, high executives find themselves at the narrow neck of the hourglass in terms of the number of superiors and subordinates they have. The superiors may not be superiors in a technical sense, but they clearly are tantamount to superiors in a practical sense. The Secretary of a department finds that to be effective he must consult and, in varying degrees, be responsive to numerous superiors—staff officers in the Office of Management and Budget, in the White House, and in the Office of Personnel Management; members and staff of the Senate and the House of Representatives; and officials of special interest groups and influential private citizens—to help him achieve his goals. Many a successful manager in private business has been importuned to try his hand at a high-level appointment in government, only to find that its lack of structure at the top levels and its premium on previous broad acquaintance with the nation's political movers and shakers makes his proven business management skills seems of low utility. Some make the transition effectively, but others return rather quickly to the world they know and in which they feel secure.

When subordinate officials and managers take their direction from multiple sources, it is imperative for top management to minimize conflicting signals, but some conflict is inevitable. When it occurs, it is essential to have a clearly understood method for getting a single decision promptly. A subordinate manager or official should have a clear obligation to identify a conflict to his line superior and ask to have it resolved. It is then the duty of the higher line official to identify the source of the trouble and eliminate the conflict. Except in emergency situations, responsible managers who are faced with conflicting directives should certainly not use the conflict as an excuse for doing nothing. Moreover, it should not serve as a justification for substituting their own judgment as to what policy to follow without allowing higher officials to become aware of the conflict and straighten it out.

The basic line-and-staff principles of organization are far from obsolete, but they must be modified to incorporate the flexibilities described above.

QUARANTINING THE BEARER OF BAD TIDINGS

Who the first king was who ordered the bearer of bad tidings beheaded is not known, but his influence has persisted down through the centuries to the bureaucratic potentates of today. One modern-day capsule description of this behavior pattern is Miles's Fifth Maxim of Management: "Since most managers are better talkers than listeners, subordinates need both persistence and courage to make their bosses hear what they do not want to hear."

Most management bigwigs abhor bad news if it's likely to be interpreted by their superiors and the general public as reflecting on their performance. Their first reaction is likely to be disbelief. The reporter of the bad news must have gotten his facts wrong. He is sent back to see if there aren't other facts that would make the situation look better and to recheck the first report. Back it comes with more verification and no offsetting good news. The next reaction is: Get another reporter—this one must surely be biased in favor of gloom. Then, they ask themselves how to cover up the bad news and postpone the evil day when it will all come out. They seek, too, to figure out how to put the best possible face on it when it does come out. If the reporter of bad news keeps wanting to make a clean breast of things and change policies, he risks being treated as if he had the bubonic plague.

It is not easy for the reporter of unfavorable developments to have a calm and rational dialog about how to cut one's losses. Those who sought during the Vietnam War to lay out the facts, cold turkey, and have them considered by higher-echelon officials learned how hard it is to get facts considered fairly and honestly when they don't fit the preconceived ideas of committed officials. Vietnam was the most dramatic and disastrous example of this human failing in recent decades, but a similar scenario is played out again and gain in more inconspicuous ways in peacetime operations of large organizations.

One can imagine that something like this must have happened when Firestone had to recall its steel-belted "500" radial tires in 1978 at a horrendous cost to the company. It seems likely that earlier reports of tire failure, if they had been heeded promptly and carefully, would have resulted in a much more rapid recognition and correction of the problem. This is true of various faulty design features of American automobiles that have led to massive recalls in recent years. It is also true of certain components of military weapons systems.

Within government, some of these bearers of embarrassing information have "gone public" when they could not dissuade their superiors from purusing courses of action they considered to be wrongheaded, biased toward a poor product or grossly wasteful. They are known as "whistle-blowers." They are an acute source of discomfort to their superiors. Not surprisingly, they are rarely promoted thereafter and are likely to be shunted off to jobs where they will have the least possible potential for causing further embarrassment. Yet some of them stubbornly persist in a frigid atmosphere. One cannot help but marvel at the extraordinary fortitude of the most outstanding whistle-blowers, especially those who seem from various accounts to have a great deal of right on their side and who keep battling powerful hierarchies. Ernest Fitzgerald, whistle-blower on the cost overruns of the Air Force's C-5A, is a classic example of the breed. He got under the skin of his superiors all the way up to and including President Nixon, who ordered that he be beheaded, occupationally speaking. Fortunately, he has proved himself more durable than Nixon, occupationally speaking.

This fifth maxim—about the tendency of managers to be deficient listeners—carries an implicit message: Managers should carefully cultivate the habit and the art of being good listeners if they are to become first-rate managers. Ideally, they should be as receptive to bad news as they are to good news. This is asking a good deal. Perhaps it would be sufficient to be three-fourths as receptive to bad news as to glad tidings.

A VIRTUOUS WAY OF BEING TWO-FACED

Being "two-faced" has a strongly negative connotation—so negative, in fact, that many people seem to believe they cannot properly present different faces to different people or groups and still retain their integrity. I deliberately chose to use this pejorative term in Miles's Sixth Maxim of Management in order to dramatize its legitimacy under various circumstances. Here is the maxim: "Being two-faced—one face for superiors and one for subordinates—is not a vice but a virtue for a program manager, if he presents his two faces openly and candidly."

This is a corollary of Miles's Law, which says: "Where you stand depends on where you sit." When a person changes his position organizationally, according to Miles's law, his responsibilities—and perspective—change so that what he thought was valid when he occupied one position seems suddenly to lose its validity when looked at from another angle. A simple illustration of that principle was an incident that occurred when Frank Pace, Director of the Bureau of Budget under President Truman, was appointed Secretary of the Army in 1950. He promptly appealed to the new Director of the Bureau to overturn a decision he had made just before leaving his position as Director of the Bureau of the Budget, a decision that he suddenly considered to be adverse to the interests of the Army. Each person within a government or business hierarchy sees matters from a different perspective, none of which can be characterized as purely objective. Correspondingly, being two-faced in a nonpejorative sense is part of the business of understanding and *representing different perspectives while holding a single position.*

Each manager within a hierarchy has multiple roles. The most difficult, however, especially in the context of government, is to be the spokesperson for top management in explaining decisions that are contrary to the judgments they have argued for in the decision-making process. Yet the capacity to be an advocate for policies in which one does not fully concur is an essential part of being an effective team player and program manager. The difficulty of performing such an advocacy role will obviously vary greatly, depending on how strongly one feels about a position defended originally. Another influential element is how much one respects the final decision and the decision makers who made it. In the extreme, an individual may choose to resign or seek to be transferred rather than have to be the spokesperson for a policy with which he strongly disagrees. But, short of that extreme, he has an obligation to put the best face on the decision he possibly can. In doing so, he is placing the ethic of organizational loyalty above total personal integrity.

Lawyers have an easier time behaving in this manner than most others because of their training to represent the interests of their clients.

The ethics of "followership" are worth considering, as well, particularly as part of the effective functioning of government agencies. Three paragraphs from "Administrative Adaptability to Political Change" (*Public Administration Review,* September, 1965) are worth quoting here:

> Administrative loyalty, important at all levels, has a peculiarly important quality and significance where top career people are directly responsible to key political appointees. Here the career people are the program experts with knowledge of the evolution of program policies. They must explain the underlying rationale for policies, be open-minded in respect to new ideas, and be imaginative in adapting ideas [of] conceivable utility.

> Still, career people must be vigorous opponents of change they believe to be deeply destructive to the program, even when it is proposed and supported by the highest officials of an Administration. But such opposition always must be voiced directly and privately to the superior after careful consideration of the superior's proposal. A Secretary is badly served when he does not obtain the best thinking of his career staff, no matter how contrary it may be to his own. If a top career man believes that proposed policy would have serious adverse effects upon the program he administers, it would be the very reverse of administrative loyalty to acquiesce meekly. Vigorous exchange of views between the political and the career people is the only way political appointees can properly test the soundness of their thinking and prepare themselves against external crit-

icism. Such debates may not occur unless initiated by the career people. When they do occur, it is likely that the elements of the ongoing program most worth saving will be saved. The proposal which emerges is more likely to be one which the bureau chief can support. He will better understand the thinking of his superiors and be better prepared to enlist support for it.

> When a considered decision has been reached by the responsible political appointee, it is the clear duty of the career official to do his level best to make the newly decided policy work. He must put the best possible face on such a policy when explaining it to Congress, to his external constituency, and to his own subordinates, even though he may have argued vigorously against its adoption. If he cannot do this, he no longer belongs in his position. If he returns to his career associates and says that he defended the traditional institutional views but the well meaning but ignorant new crowd overruled him, if he makes no conscientious attempt to interpret and defend the rationale of their decision, he is guilty of administrative deloyalty. Nothing can more rapidly accomplish the demoralization and decline of an organization.

When I assert that being "two-faced" is not a vice but a virtue for a program manager under the conditions I have described, I mean that organizational chaos would result if program managers were unable to become the advocates for the decisions of their superiors. Avoiding organizational self-destruction has to be regarded as a behavioral norm of high importance—I didn't say of the highest importance. The behavioral norm of highest importance in organization life is adherence to the total code of ethics developed by the thoughtful individual—including the obligation to resign from an organization when circumstances make that the only clear alternative that would preserve the essential integrity and life-shaping ethical code of the individual.

Some such decisions are painful, especially when an individual has no contingency plan that will make resignation a realistic option. Everyone who operates in an environment in which he finds decisions being made that are deeply distasteful to him needs to establish firmly a sticking point beyond which he will not be subtly pressured or unsubtly dragged. He must also have a thoughtful plan of action that can be put into effect if worse comes to worst. Otherwise, his self-respect may be insidiously eroded. Such contingency planning requires a strong sense of self-confidence and a readiness to take a reasonable degree of personal risk.

Least defensible, in terms of personal integrity and long-range effectiveness, is to convey the impression to one's superiors of accepting a decision against which one has argued and then failing to carry it out as directed.

THE HAZARD OF CENTRALIZED SERVICES

The last of Miles's Seven Maxims of Management may well be the most important from the standpoint of efficiency and economy. It is: "Dissatisfaction with services tends to rise rapidly when the provider of the services becomes bureaucratically bigger, more remote, and less flexible, even if costs are somewhat lower." This maxim says to managers, especially to top executives: "Don't accept, without extremely careful consideration, the recommendation of a feasibility study that tells you that you can save x dollar by centralizing any particular service." (This maxim also applies to services to the public, but in this context it is focused on administrative support services necessary for the efficient operation of any organization.)

Within the Department of Health, Education, and Welfare, and its predecessor, the Federal Security Agency, library services became centralized in 1947. This structural reorganization was a major reason for the Commissioner of Education's resignation in 1948. It also was the subject of a classic case study of the controversy. I observed the fight from the vantage point of the Bureau of the Budget.

At the time, I wondered whether the management analysts who conducted the feasibility study realized or took into account the dissatisfaction costs of taking the Office of Education's library away from it and putting it under the Office of the Administrator of the Federal Security Agency. So far as I could discover, they did not. Emotions ran so high that, when this decision was added to other provocations, the Commissioner of Education and an assistant commissioner resigned.

One of the principal motivations of the designers of the plan was to consolidate the libraries of the Federal Security Agency in order to overcome the separatist feeling and behavior of the major units of the agency. The goal was to bring them into the agency "family." In this it failed utterly. In fact, it backfired. The staff of the Office of Education felt that the office had been dragooned into this organizational arrangement. The consolidation only embittered them toward their parent agency, a result no one had sought.

After the Federal Security Agency was converted to the Department of Health, Education, and Welfare in 1953, I became its Director of Administration, and later Assistant Secretary for Administration. For 12 years, the consolidated library was one of my numerous management responsibilities. I became increasingly convinced that it was a grave error to have removed the Office of Education library from HEW's jurisdiction.

The Office of Education was never happy with the services that it received. From its standpoint, the Office of the Secretary neither understood their needs nor sought to obtain enough funds to meet them from Congress. Library services for a subordinate unit of the department were unavoidably of much lower priority than were other needs of the Office of the Secretary. This sharp contrast in perspective and priorities is especially evident in a political context, where the centralized services come under an official who is inescapably oriented toward the priorities of his politically appointed superior. The time horizon of such political appointees is extremely likely to be short.

Subordinate units that depend on centralized services are inclined to feel that if they had the control of their share of the funds, they could do a better job of providing the services than a central service agency can. Whether or not this is true, both the officials of the subordinate units and the users of the services are very likely to believe it, and this is important. The services are more likely to be flexibly responsive when under the control of subordinate units, even if not demonstrably more economical.

At any given level of service, the level of dissatisfaction rises rapidly as the opportunity to control the levels, types, and flexibility of service is taken out of the hands of the subordinate unit and moved to a higher and more remote organizational level. Therefore, before centralizing services at a high level of management, it is vital to make certain—or as certain as reasonably possible—that the services will be *markedly better,* and not just equally good or slightly better and somewhat or slightly cheaper.

Some years ago, it was proposed that the General Services Administration set up a group of regional computer services that would serve all the federal agencies in each region. Each department and agency would have been required to buy computer time from the GSA regional centers, and few exceptions would have been permitted. Fortunately, the proposal was defeated. I can think of nothing that would result in a more intense level of user dissatisfaction than such an arrangement. Fortunately, too, the advances in computer technology in the last ten or fifteen years have relaxed the comparative advantage that was thought to come from the centralization of such services. Small computers, organizationally and physically located close to the users, have the capacity to render rapid and flexible service at an economical

cost. This is one of the most important triumphs for decentralized support services in the last generation or two.

Library and computer services, used here as examples, are but two of a substantial list of support services to which this maxim applies. The list includes accounting services, personnel services of various kinds, payrolling, procurement, printing and duplicating, and space management. This is an area to which a series of good management research studies should be directed. The hidden costs in lost time and low morale should be identified and estimated when services are remote and inflexible. All sorts of devices are resorted to when support services become distant and impersonal. Resourceful individuals figure out ways to outfox the system by supplementing some of the centralized services with their own close-to-home services. Much more needs to be learned about this subject.

BE YOUR OWN MAXIMIZER

These maxims were unsystematically developed from especially memorable encounters with reality. There are scores more members of both the public administration and business administration communities have on the tips of their tongeus or in the recesses of their minds. Many of these have been stated, but too few have been sufficiently explained, illustrated, and shared with colleagues. If you have some good maxims that could help debunk a few more of the myths of management that seem to muddle the minds of managers, why not become your own "maximizer"? This should consternate the economists and add another pleasurable and nonquantifiable dimension to the peculiarly polysemous profession of public administration as well as the more pecuniarily prestigious profession of private management.

QUESTIONS FOR DISCUSSION

1. How do theories of leadership that you have studied in management and organizational behavior classes relate to these six readings?

2. Take one of the theories of leaderships you have discussed in this class (for example, Ohio State, University of Michigan, Managerial Grid, 3-D, reciprocal causation, decision making) and do a profile on Sancho Panza, Tom Sawyer, Richard Daley, and Vince Lombardi. How do these leaders differ and how are they similar? What conclusions can you draw about your findings?

3. How does the advice Don Quixote gave Sancho Panza relate to the Panama Canal situation *(Path Between the Seas)*?

4. In your study group describe the strengths and weaknesses of a successful leader of today. Are there any similarities between this leader and the four people described in this chapter?

CHAPTER X
ENCOURAGING THEM TO LEAVE: THE REAL SHOCK

ORGANIZATIONAL SHOCKS

- It is hard to motivate a younger employee when older employees continue to hold on to the key jobs.
- Age is held against an employee in an organization. Either he is too old or too young for the job.
- It is almost impossible to fire someone for low productivity.
- It is easy to fire someone for a lack of loyalty.

Unlike the Japanese culture described in an earlier reading, in the United States, Canadian, and European cultures, we learn at a very young age that after a person reaches a certain age, usually around 65, their usefulness to the organization in the world of work diminishes quite rapidly. In addition, they tend to hold down slots that younger employees would like to have and need for motivational purposes. Therefore, in our country we have typically retired people at somewhere between the age of 55 and 70. When a person approaches this period, (remember the article by Hall and Morgan on career development), they begin to realize the shock that they soon will be pressured to retire from the world of work. The shock for the young employee in many cases, comes when they realize that top level jobs are being held by people who are between the ages of 40 and 50, which means that their chances of getting that job are reduced drastically.

The four readings in this chapter point up several of the conflicting problems surrounding this phenomenon. The first reading is a short excerpt from Kurt Vonnegut's book entitled *Cat's Cradle*. In this short excerpt, he says that it is almost impossible to force people out for low productivity. This is sad, of course, because the only way one can make room for people is by forcing them out because of age. That is, we can either force people out because of too much service (retirement) or too little service (low seniority) even though the principles of motivation tell us we should force people out because of productivity.

The next reading by Arthur Miller from *Death of a Salesman* talks about what happens when Willie Loman is forced out because of age even though his productivity is exemplary. The forcing out of Willie Loman was like sentencing him to death, as you will see.

The next article talks about the revolt of the older people in this country toward this forced classification of incompetence. One of the main repercussions of this movement to extend the retirement age has been that many older employees have gained self-esteem and respect, and their contribution in terms of productivity has improved. The last article by Ewing discusses how organizations punish dissidents and disloyal employees.

BICYCLES FOR AFGHANISTAN

KURT VONNEGUT, JR.

"Christ, back in Chicago, we don't make bicycles any more. It's all human relations now. The eggheads sit around trying to figure out new ways for everybody to be happy. Nobody can get fired, no matter what; and if someones does accidentally make a bicycle, the union accuses us of cruel and inhuman practices and the government confiscates the bicycle for back taxes and gives it to a blind man in Afghanistan."

"And you think things will be better in San Lorenzo?"

"I know damn well they will be. The people down there are poor enough and scared enough and ignorant enough to have some common sense!"

Source: From "Bicycles for Afghanistan" excerpted from the book *Cat's Cradle* by Kurt Vonnegut, Jr. Reprinted by permission of Delacorte Press, Seymour Lawrence.

DEATH OF A SALESMAN

ARTHUR MILLER

From the right, Willy Loman, the Salesman, en-ters, carrying two large sample cases. The flute plays on. He hears but is not aware of it. He is past sixty years of age, dressed quietly. Even as he crosses the stage to the doorway of the house, his exhaustion is apparent. He unlocks the door, comes into the kitchen, and thankfully lets his burden down, feeling the soreness of his palms. A word-sigh escapes his lips—it might be "Oh, boy, oh, boy." He closes the door, then carries his cases out into the living-room, through the draped kitchen doorway.

Linda, his wife, has stirred in her bed at the right. She gets out and puts on a robe, listening. Most often jovial, she has developed an iron repression of her exceptions to Willy's behavior—she more than loves him, she ad-mires him, as though his mercurial nature, his temper, his massive dreams and little cruelties, served her only as sharp reminders of the turbu-lent longings within him, longings which she shares but lacks the temperament to utter and follow to their end.

Linda, *hearing Willy outside the bedroom, calls with some trepidation:* Willy!

Willy: It's all right. I came back.

Linda: Why? What happened? *Slight pause,* Did something happen, Willy?

Willy: No, nothing happened.

Linda: You didn't smash the car, did you?

Willy, *with casual irritation:* I said nothing happened. Didn't you hear me?

Linda: Don't you feel well?

Willy: I'm tired to the death. *The flute has faded away. He sits on the bed beside her, a little numb.* I couldn't make it. I just couldn't make it, Linda.

Linda, *very carefully, delicately:* Where were you all day? You look terrible.

Willy: I got as far as a little above Yonkers. I stopped for a cup of coffee. Maybe it was the coffee.

Source: From *Death of a Salesman* by Arthur Miller. Copyright 1949. Copyright renewed 1977 by Arthur Miller. Reprinted by permission of Viking Penguin Press.

Linda: What?

Willy, *after a pause:* I suddenly couldn't drive any more. The car kept going off onto the shoulder, y'know?

Linda, *helpfully:* Oh. Maybe it was the steering again. I don't think Angelo knows the Studebaker.

Willy: No, it's me, it's me. Suddenly I realize I'm goin' sixty miles an hour and I don't remember the last five minutes. I'm—I can't seem to—keep my mind to it.

Linda: Maybe it's your glasses. You never went for your new glasses.

Willy: No, I see everything. I came back ten miles an hour. It took me nearly four hours from Yonkers.

Linda, *resigned:* Well, you'll just have to take a rest, Willy, you can't continue this way.

Willy: I just got back from Florida.

Linda: But you didn't rest your mind. Your mind is overactive, and the mind is what counts, dear.

Willy: I'll start out in the morning. Maybe I'll feel better in the morning. *She is taking off his shoes.* These goddam arch supports are killing me.

Linda: Take an aspirin. Should I get you an aspirin? It'll soothe you.

Willy, *with wonder:* I was driving along, you understand? And I was fine. I was even observing the scenery. You can imagine, me looking at scenery, on the road every week of my life. But it's so beautiful up there, Linda, the trees are so thick, and the sun is warm. I opened the windshield and just let the warm air bathe over me. And then all of a sudden I'm goin' off the road! I'm tellin' ya, I absolutely forgot I was driving. If I'd gone the other way over the white line I might've killed somebody. So I went on again—and five minutes later I'm dreamin' again, and I nearly—*He presses two fingers against his eyes.* I have such thoughts, I have such strange thoughts.

Linda: Willy, dear. Talk to them again. There's no reason why you can't work in New York.

Willy: They don't need me in New York. I'm the New England man. I'm vital in New England.

Linda: But you're sixty years old. They can't expect you to keep traveling every week.

Willy: I'll have to send a wire to Portland. I'm supposed to see Brown and Morrison tomorrow morning at ten o'clock to show the line. Goddammit, I could sell them! *He starts putting on his jacket.*

Linda, *taking the jacket from him:* Why don't you go down to the place tomorrow and tell Howard you've simply got to work in New York? You're too accommodating, dear.

Willy: If old man Wagner was alive I'd a been in charge of New York now! That man was a prince; he was a masterful man. But that boy of his, that Howard, he don't appreciate. When I went north the first time, the Wagner Company didn't know where New England was!

Linda: Why don't you tell those things to Howard, dear?

Willy, *encouraged:* I will, I definitely will. Is there any cheese?

Linda: I'll make you a sandwich.

Willy: No, go to sleep. I'll take some milk. I'll be up right away. . . .

[*Editor's note:* The scene shifts to Howard Wagner's office the following day.]

Willy: Pst! Pst!

Howard: Hello, Willy, come in.

Willy: Like to have a little talk with you, Howard.

Howard: Sorry to keep you waiting. I'll be with you in a minute.

Willy: What's that, Howard?

Howard: Didn't you ever see one of these? Wire recorder.

Willy: Oh. Can we talk a minute?

Howard: Records things. Just got delivery

yesterday. Been driving me crazy, the most terrific machine I ever saw in my life. I was up all night with it.

Willy: What do you do with it?

Howard: I bought it for dictation, but you can do anything with it. Listen to this. I had it home last night. Listen to what I picked up. The first one is my daughter. Get this. *He flicks the switch and "Roll out the Barrel" is heard being whistled.* Listen to that kid whistle.

Willy: That is lifelike, isn't it?

Howard: Seven years old. Get that tone.

Willy: Ts, ts. Like to ask a little favor if you . . .

The whistling breaks off, and the voice of Howard's daughter is heard.

His Daughter: "Now you, Daddy."

Howard: She's crazy for me! *Again the same song is whistled.* That's me! Ha! *He winks.*

Willy: You're very good!

The whistling breaks off again. The machine runs silent for a moment.

Howard: Sh! Get this now, this is my son.

His Son: "The capital of Alabama is Montgomery; the capital of Arizona is Phoenix; the capital of Arkansas is Little Rock; the capital of California is Sacramento . . ." *and on, and on.*

Howard, *holding up five fingers:*   Five years old, Willy!

Willy: He'll make an announcer some day!

His Son, *continuing:*   "The capital . . ."

Howard: Get that—alphabetical order! *The machine breaks off suddenly.* Wait a minute. The maid kicked the plug out.

Willy: It certainly is a—

Howard: Sh, for God's sake!

His Son: "It's nine o'clock, Bulova watch time. So I have to go to sleep."

Willy: That really is—

Howard: Wait a minute! The next is my wife. *They wait.*

Howard's voice: "Go on, say something." *Pause.* "Well, you gonna talk?"

His Wife: "I can't think of anything."

Howard's Voice: "Well, talk—it's turning."

His Wife, *shyly, beaten:*   "Hello." *Silence.* "Oh, Howard, I can't talk into this . . ."

Howard, *snapping the machine off:*   That was my wife.

Willy: That is a wonderful machine. Can we—

Howard: I tell you, Willy, I'm gonna take my camera, and my bandsaw, and all my hobbies, and out they go. This is the most fascinating relaxation I ever found.

Willy: I think I'll get one myself.

Howard: Sure, they're only a hundred and a half. You can't do without it. Supposing you wanna hear Jack Benny, see? But you can't be at home at that hour. So you tell the maid to turn the radio on when Jack Benny comes on, and this automatically goes on with the radio . . .

Willy: And when you come home you . . .

Howard: You can come home twelve o'clock, one o'clock, any time you like, and you get yourself a Coke and sit yourself down, throw the switch, and there's Jack Benny's program in the middle of the night!

Willy: I'm definitely going to get one. Because lots of time I'm on the road, and I think to myself, what I must be missing on the radio!

Howard: Don't you have a radio in the car?

Willy: Well, yeah, but who ever thinks of turning it on?

Howard: Say, aren't you supposed to be in Boston?

Willy: That's what I want to talk to you about, Howard. You got a minute? *He draws a chair in from the wing.*

Howard: What happened? What're you doing here?

Willy: Well . . .

Howard: You didn't crack up again, did you?

Willy: Oh, no. No . . .

Howard: Geez, you had me worried there for a minute. What's the trouble?

Willy: Well, tell you the truth, Howard. I've come to the decision that I'd rather not travel any more.

Howard: Not travel! Well, what'll you do?

Willy: Remember, Christmas time, when you had the party here? You said you'd try to think of some spot for me here in town.

Howard: With us?

Willy: Well, sure.

Howard: Oh, yeah, yeah. I remember. Well, I couldn't think of anything for you, Willy.

Willy: I tell ya, Howard. The kids are all grown up, y'know. I don't need much any more. If I could take home—well, sixty-five dollars a week, I could swing it.

Howard: Yeah, but Willy, see I—

Willy: I tell ya why, Howard. Speaking frankly and between the two of us, y'know—I'm just a little tired.

Howard: Oh, I could understand that, Willy. But you're a road man, Willy, and we do a road business. We've only got a half-dozen sales-men on the floor here.

Willy: God knows, Howard, I never asked a favor of any man. But I was with the firm when your father used to carry you in here in his arms.

Howard: I know that, Willy, but—

Willy: Your father came to me the day you were born and asked me what I thought of the name of Howard, may he rest in peace.

Howard: I appreciate that, Willy, but there just is no spot here for you. If I had a spot I'd slam you right in, but I just don't have a single solitary spot.

He looks for his lighter. Willy has picked it up and gives it to him. Pause.

Willy, *with increasing anger:* Howard, all I need to set my table is fifty dollars a week.

Howard: But where am I going to put you, kid?

Willy: Look, it isn't a question of whether I can sell merchandise, is it?

Howard: No, but it's a business, kid, and everybody's gotta pull his own weight.

Willy, *desperately:* Just let me tell you a story, Howard—

Howard: 'Cause you gotta admit, business is business.

Willy, *angrily:* Business is definitely business, but just listen for a minute. You don't un-derstand this. When I was a boy—eighteen, nineteen—I was already on the road. And there was a question in my mind as to whether selling had a future for me. Because in those days I had a yearning to go to Alaska. See, there were three gold strikes in one month in Alaska, and I felt like going out. Just for the ride, you might say.

Howard, *barely interested:* Don't say.

Willy: Oh, yeah, my father lived many years in Alaska. He was an adventurous man. We've got quite a little streak of self-reliance in our family. I thought I'd go out with my older brother and try to locate him, and maybe settle in the North with the old man. And I was almost decided to go, when I met a salesman in the Parker House. His name was Dave Singleman. And he was eighty-four years old, and he'd drummed mer-chandise in thirty-one states. And old Dave, he'd go up to his room, y'understand, put on his green velvet slippers—I'll never forget—and pick up his phone and call the buyers, and without ever leaving his room, at the age of eighty-four, he made his living. And when I saw that, I realized that selling was the greatest career a man could want. 'Cause what could be more satisfying than to be able to go, at the age of eighty-four, into twenty or thirty different cities, and pick up a phone, and be remem-bered and loved and helped by so many dif-ferent people? Do you know? when he died—

and by the way he died the death of a salesman, in his green velvet slippers in the smoker of the New York, New Haven and Hartford, going into Boston—when he died, hundreds of salesmen and buyers were at his funeral. Things were sad on a lotta trains for months after that. *He stands up. Howard has not looked at him.* In those days there was personality in it, Howard. There was respect, and comradeship, and gratitude in it. Today, it's all cut and dried, and there's no chance for bringing friendship to bear—or personality. You see what I mean? They don't know me any more.

Howard, *moving away, to the right:* That's just the thing, Willy.

Willy: If I had forty dollars a week—that's all I'd need. Forty dollars, Howard.

Howard: Kid, I can't take blood from a stone, I—

Willy, *desperation is on him now:* Howard, the year Al Smith was nominated, your father came to me and—

Howard, *starting to go off:* I've got to see some people, kid.

Willy, *stopping him:* I'm talking about your father! There were promises made across this desk! You mustn't tell me you've got people to see—I put thirty-four years into this firm, Howard, and now I can't pay my insurance! You can't eat the orange and throw the peel away—a man is not a piece of fruit! *After a pause:* Now pay attention. Your father—in 1928 I had a big year. I averaged a hundred and seventy dollars a week in commissions.

Howard, *impatiently:* Now, Willy, you never averaged—

Willy, *banging his hand on the desk:* I averaged a hundred and seventy dollars a week in the year of 1928! And your father came to me—or rather, I was in the office here—it was right over this desk—and he put his hand on my shoulder—

Howard, *getting up:* You'll have to excuse me, Willy, I gotta see some people. Pull yourself together. *Going out:* I'll be back in a little while.

On Howard's exit, the light on his chair grows very bright and strange.

Willy: Pull myself together! What the hell did I say to him? My God, I was yelling at him! How could I! *Willy breaks off, staring at the light, which occupies the chair, animating it. He approaches this chair, standing across the desk from it.* Frank, Frank, don't you remember what you told me that time? How you put your hand on my shoulder, and Frank . . . *He leans on the desk and as he speaks the dead man's name he accidentally switches on the recorder, and instantly*

Howard's Son: ". . . of New York is Albany. The capital of Ohio is Cincinnati, the capital of Rhode Island is . . ." *The recitation continues.*

Willy, *leaping away with fright, shouting:* Ha! Howard! Howard! Howard!

Howard, *rushing in:* What happened?

Willy, *pointing at the machine, which continues nasally, childishly, with the capital cities:* Shut it off! Shut it off!

Howard, *pulling the plug out:* Look, Willy . . .

Willy, *pressing his hands to his eyes:* I gotta get myself some coffee. I'll get some coffee . . .

Willy starts to walk out. Howard stops him.

Howard, *rolling up the cord:* Willy, look . . .

Willy: I'll go to Boston.

Howard: Willy, you can't go to Boston for us.

Willy: Why can't I go?

Howard: I don't want you to represent us. I've been meaning to tell you for a long time now.

Willy: Howard, are you firing me?

Howard: I think you need a good long rest, Willy.

Willy: Howard—

Howard: And when you feel better, come back, and we'll see if we can work something out.

Willy: But I gotta earn money, Howard. I'm in no position to—

Howard: Where are your sons? Why don't your sons give you a hand?

Willy: They're working on a very big deal.

Howard: This is no time for false pride, Willy. You go to your sons and you tell them that you're tired. You've got two great boys, haven't you?

Willy: Oh, no question, no question, but in the meantime . . .

Howard: Then that's that, heh?

Willy: All right, I'll go to Boston tomorrow.

Howard: No, no.

Willy: I can't throw myself on my sons. I'm not a cripple!

Howard: Look, kid, I'm busy this morning.

Willy, *grasping Howard's arm:* Howard, you've got to let me go to Boston!

Howard, *hard, keeping himself under control:* I've got a line of people to see this morning. Sit down, take five minutes, and pull yourself together, and then go home, will ya? I need the office, Willy. *He starts to go, turns, remembering the recorder, starts to push off the table holding the recorder.* Oh, yeah. Whenever you can this week, stop by and drop off the samples. You'll feel better, Willy, and then come back and we'll talk. Pull yourself together, kid, there's people outside. . . .

REQUIEM

[*Editor's note:* Biff & Charley are Willy's sons.]

Charley: It's getting dark, Linda.

Linda doesn't react. She stares at the grave.

Biff: How about it, Mom? Better get some rest, heh? They'll be closing the gate soon.

Linda makes no move. Pause.

Happy, *deeply angered:* He had no right to do that. There was no necessity for it. We would've helped him.

Charley, *grunting:* Hmmm.

Biff: Come along, Mom.

Linda: Why didn't anybody come?

Charley: It was a very nice funeral.

Linda: But where are all the people he knew? Maybe they blame him.

Charley: Naa. It's a rough world, Linda. They wouldn't blame him.

Linda: I can't understand it. At this time, especially. First time in thirty-five years we were just about free and clear. He only needed a little salary. He was even finished with the dentist.

Charley: No man only needs a little salary.

Linda: I can't understand it.

Biff: There were a lot of nice days. When he'd come home from a trip; or on Sundays, making the stoop; finishing the cellar; putting on the new porch; when he built the extra bathroom; and put up the garage. You know something, Charley, there's more of him in that front stoop than in all the sales he ever made.

Charley: Yeah. He was a happy man with a batch of cement.

Linda: He was so wonderful with his hands.

Biff: He had the wrong dreams. All, all, wrong.

Happy, *almost ready to fight Biff:* Don't say that!

Biff: He never knew who he was.

Charley, *stopping Happy's movement and reply. To Biff:* Nobody dast blame this man. You don't understand: Willy was a salesman. And for a salesman, there is no rock bottom to the life. He don't put a bolt to a nut, he don't tell you the law or give you medicine. He's a man way out there in the blue, riding on a smile and a shoeshine. And when they start not smiling back—that's an earthquake. And then you get yourself a couple of spots on your hat, and you're finished. Nobody dast blame this man. A salesman is got to dream, boy. It comes with the territory.

Biff: Charley, the man didn't know who he was.

Happy, *infuriated:* Don't say that!

Biff: Why don't you come with me, Happy?

Happy: I'm not licked that easily. I'm staying right in this city, and I'm gonna beat this racket! *He looks at Biff, his chin set.* The Loman Brothers!

Biff: I know who I am, kid.

Happy: All right, boy. I'm gonna show you and everybody else that Willy Lowman did not die in vain. He had a good dream. It's the only dream you can have—to come out number one man. He fought it out here, and this is where I'm gonna win it for him.

Biff, *with a hopeless glance at Happy, bends toward his mother:* Let's go, Mom.

Linda: I'll be with you in a minute. Go on. Charley. *He hesitates.* I want to, just for a minute. I never had a chance to say good-bye.

Charley moves away, followed by Happy. Biff remains a slight distance up and left of Linda.

She sits there, summoning herself. The flute begins, not far away, playing behind her speech.

Linda: Forgive me, dear. I can't cry. I don't know what it is, but I can't cry. I don't understand it. Why did you ever do that? Help me, Willy, I can't cry. It seems to me that you're just on another trip. I keep expecting you. Willy, dear, I can't cry. Why did you do it? I search and search and I search, and I can't understand it, Willy. I made the last payment on the house today. Today, dear. And there'll be nobody home. *A sob rises in her throat.* We're free and clear. *Sobbing more fully, released:* We're free. *Biff comes slowly toward her.* We're free . . . We're free . . .

Only the music of the flute is left on the darkening stage as over the house the hard towers of the apartment buildings rise into sharp focus, and

The Curtain Falls

NOW, THE REVOLT OF THE OLD
A Winning Fight for the Right To Go On Working

TIME

It might as well have been a vote for motherhood or apple pie or sunshine. There were no opposing speeches, dissent was muttered only in the safety of the cloakroom, and the final floor vote was a whopping 359 to 4. Yet the bill that breezed through the U.S. House of Representatives may be the session's most important piece of legislation, with ramifications no one can foresee. It extends the mandatory retirement age from 65 to 70 in private industry and removes it altogether for federal employees. Said the bill's sponsor, Florida Democrat Claude Lepper, 77: "At long last, we will have eliminated ageism as we have previously eliminated sexism and racism as a basis for discrimination in this country, and we will be putting a new emphasis on human rights."

A potent combination of sentiment, shrewdness and pure political muscle whisked the bill through the House, and it seems destined to pass the Senate as well, either at the end of this session or early next year. Indeed, Senator Jacob Javits, 73, is preparing an amendment that would completely phase out manatory retirement over a five-year period. This abrupt, stunning legislative success is the hallmark of another revolt in America, this time by the aged. The 1960s was the decade of aroused youth; the 1970s may well belong to their grandparents. Some 23 million Americans, about 10% of the population, are 65 or over. Numbers alone give them political clout, because they vote more consistently than younger groups. In addition, they have begun to organize with all the skill and determination of other embattled minorities. Such burgeoning pressure groups as the Gray Panthers, the National Council on the Aging, the National Association of Retired Federal Employees and the National Council of Senior Citizens have given their political representatives little respite. Foremost among their goals has been the fight for the right to work.

The Protestant work ethic is alive and more than well among older Americans. Study after

Source: Reprinted by permission from *Time, The Weekly Newsmagazine:* © Time, Inc., 1977.

study has shown what many oldsters feel in their bones: without employment, their lives go blank. They become listless and preoccupied with their frailties, real or imagined. There is a disproportionate death rate among those forced to retire, and 25% of all known suicides are committed by people over 65. Beyond that, years of substantial inflation have eroded their pensions and kept many of them from enjoying the often illusory, but highly touted leisure pursuits of their allegedly golden years. Says Joseph Schwartz, who retired after 27 years as a Chicago schoolteacher, then retired once again as a park supervisor and is looking for a job now: "Above all, you must work. You have to be active mentally as well as physically. If you're not, what good is living?"

Until recently in America, old people did not have much trouble living up to that philosophy. Work and age had not been severed. In colonial times, elderly people were fewer, but they held the best jobs. Nor did they budge from their posts until death or ill health forced them out. In 17th century New England, 90% of the ministers and magistrates died in office. People showed their respect for age—and power—by attempting to look older than they were. They powdered their hair and wore the severely cut clothing of the aged. Gradually, this esteem for the ancients was undermined by notions of liberty and equality that in part stemmed from the French Revolution. The prerogatives of age were swept away. At the end of the 18th century, the first American mandatory retirement laws were enacted in New York State.

The financial disabilities of old age were first recognized as a serious social problem by German Chancellor Otto von Bismarck, who initiated the social security pension system in 1884. He arbitrarily set the age for receiving benefits at 65, and his model has been followed ever since in much of the Western world. The same age for receiving benefits—and therefore being a candidate for forced retirement—was enshrined in the U.S. Social Security system

when it was established in 1935, and was copied in almost all the private pension plans that mushroomed after World War II. Yet in Bismarck's time, only a small percentage of the population lived to 65: life expectancy at birth was about 37 years. Today's advances in health and medicine have produced a virtual army of robust over-65 unemployed. Future medical breakthroughs will swell these ranks even more. Sooner or later, the work demands of the aged would have to be heard—and in the U.S., it appears to be sooner.

Modification or elimination of mandatory retirement is an idea that has arrived with a rush, catching almost everybody off guard. Concedes a U.S. Labor Department official: "The prospect of more old folks working hit us this month like a bolt from the blue, and quite honestly, we don't know how this is going to affect problems like chronic youth unemploymet, sex discrimination and shifting consumer patterns. Nobody knows. Warns Brookings Institution Economist John Palmer: "It's incredible that Congress would be moving so fast to replace one retirement system with a new one we know so little about."

Reactions vary from complacent to fearful. "The legislation just won't have a major impact on this country," says James Schulz of Brandeis University's School of Advanced Studies in Social Welfare. "After all, the main questions involved are those of equity and rights, not economics." Schulz estimates that less than 10% of Americans approaching 65 are affected by mandatory retirement. "When you get down to hard numbers," he says, "we're talking about thousands of people, not millions." The Senate Commiteee on Human Resources believes that 200,000 people, or two-tenths of 1% of the labor force, would choose to work beyond 65. But a 1974 Louis Harris survey indicates that one-third of those aged 65 to 69 would go to work at least part-time if they were given the opportunity. That would add up to a shocking 2.8 million people, which would raise the current 7% unemployment rate to roughly 10%, since the over-65 worker would theoretically be taking a job from somebody.

The fact that the Pepper bill was passed so overwhelmingly by the House does not mean it has a similar percentage of support off Capital Hill. Debates about it are just beginning to build, and views are sharply divided. Opponents and proponents have marshaled contradictory sets of ideas and statistics to support radically different points of view.

Those who believe that the impact of the new legislation will be limited are encouraged by the continuing trend toward early retirement. It is a paradox that while some older people are battling for the right to work, others are stopping work as soon as they can. At General Motors, the average retirement age is 58, even though the mandatory retirement age is 68 for blue-collar hourly workers, 65 for white-collar salaried employees. Only 11% of GM's salaried workers stay on the job long enough to reach mandatory retirement, and a mere 2% of the blue-collar workers. The experience of some other large companies is similar. Only 20% of Exxon's employees wait until 65 to retire, and only 33% at General Foods Corp.

However, these statistics do not reflect the number of retired people who reentered the labor force by getting new jobs from which they may not want to be dislodged at 65. Nor do they show how many retire early in time to get a second job because they know that option will not be open to them if they wait too long. If the forced retirement date were postponed to 70 or completely removed, they might behave differently.

Much depends on the type of job. A blue-collar worker who has labored for 30 years at a grimy, bone-wearying task on an assembly line may welcome retirement with the enthusiasm of a sweepstakes winner. Says Nelson Cruikshank, chairman of the Federal Council on Aging: "If you talk to the black laundry worker about the 'privilege' of continuing to work after

65, she'll spit in your eye. The auto workers' slogan epitomizes this: '30 and out.' " But people in more sedentary or fulfilling occupations, including most levels of management, may be inclined to linger. The U.S. Foreign Service offers an example. Last June a U.S. district court struck down mandatory retirement at 60 for those in the service as unconstitutional. While the decision is being appealed to the Supreme Court, 40% of the people scheduled for retirement have chosen to keep working.

What concerns economists the most is that if too many oldsters decide to stay on the job, the effect on the youth labor market will be severe. The 17.5% unemployment rate for U.S. youth is already a grave concern. "Some people make real sacrifices to get an education and then find there are no jobs," says Robert Geraughty, 58, who retired this year from Southwestern Bell. "Talk about rights, what about the rights of the young?"

Belatedly, the Pepper bill, which would go into effect six months after it became law, is arousing serious alarm among businessmen. A survey released this summer by William M. Mercer Inc., a New York consulting firm on employee benefits, shows that 65% of the 400 business executives polled favor mandatory retirement at 65. Says George Skoglund, executive vice president for personnel at Bank of America: "The underlying problem is that these laws constitute more and more regulation, more of Government looking on and telling us how to manage. It is another one of those things that cause us to lose options." An analysis made by Sears, Roebuck indicates that if one-third of its 433,000 employees continue to work after 65, some 20,000 job changes will be prevented over a five-year period, and its hiring rate will be reduced by 7%.

The new law is expected to clog the channels of promotion; tired old blood will not get a proper infusion of fresh corpuscles. "Each year," says Skoglund, "we hire about 150 hard-charging, fire-eating M.B.A.s who want to become president of the company the next year. What will they do if senior people decide to stay on?" Adds Thomas Egliht, manager of personnel relations at Shell Oil Co. in Houston: "If you put your finger on the key concern today, it is turnover at senior levels. We find value in bringing in new perspectives, ideas and points of view with younger people in top jobs earlier. If the new law affects this, we'll lose something of importance."

It is not only a question of bringing new people in but of getting deadwood out. Mandatory retirement has spared businesses some difficult decision making. No matter how good or bad a worker may be, at a certain age he goes, and that's the end of it. But now even the most paternalistic company may feel compelled to rate much more sternly the performance of older employees. Such performance evaluations are subjective at best and open to rebuttal. Says Madeleine Hemmings, director of employee benefits for the National Association of Manufacturers: "That's going to make for a very uncomfortable workplace. We'll have to keep records and document the mistakes people make. We'll have to do that to protect ourselves." This may not be such a draconian change, however, since many companies keep such records as a matter of course. Corporations envision innumerable lawsuits being brought by older people who are fired for cause. Executives might be put in the position of having to go to court to belittle an employee who had served the company competently and faithfully for many years.

If compulsory retirement is a traumatic experience for a worker, perhaps no less trying would be a situation in which he is downgraded at the office for a decade or more. Many companies already exert subtle and not so subtle pressure on older people to get them to retire. Says Detroit Attorney V. Paul Donnelly, who specializes in age-discrimination cases involving white-collar workers: "If they are going to do you in by age 53 and make you worthless, in-

creasing the retirement age is not the answer. I believe it means nothing."

Much of the U.S. pension system, hammered out over years of onerous labor negotiations, will have to be reviewed. This is the reason, initially at least, the AFL-CIO opposed changing the retirement age. The unions have fattened pensions and won other concessions by trading off such payments against a mandatory retirement age. Now, if people work past 65, actual pension costs will decrease. But salary costs will rise, since older workers are generally the highest paid, More will have to be budgeted for health insurance. John Bragg, president of the Life Insurance Co. of Georgia, speculates that a full pension might well be denied workers until they reached 70. Anyone who wanted to retire before that age would have to leave with less.

Educators are as worried about the Pepper bill as businessmen. The prospect at the university level is that a comfortably tenured faculty, whose work is not subject to any kind of review, will stay on forever, regardless of competence. This change could not come at a worse time, since the number of teaching jobs is shrinking. Says Robben W. Fleming, president of the University of Michigan: "We're creating a missing generation that doesn't have a chance in the academic world. The department heads say they are not going to have many openings for the next ten years. That's disastrous. They need stimulating young people to challenge them."

Universities also complain that the Pepper bill would hamper their efforts to comply with affirmative-action programs for hiring women and minorities. Says Dartmouth President John G. Kemeny: "It seems patently unfair to give one desirable social goal precedence over another program of immense social importance." Sudden intense lobbying by educators may pay off. The Senate Human Resources Committee approved an amendment late last week that would keep the mandatory retirement age at 65 for tenured college professors and public school teachers.

Most of the world would find America's revolt of the aged hard to understand. Abroad, 65 remains the most common retirement age, and people are still fighting the battle to leave the job earlier with fatter pensions. There are exceptions. In Japan, where age is revered, employers are being pressured to raise the mandatory retirement age in the private sector from 55 to 60. In the Soviet Union, oldsters are encouraged to stay on the job because there is an acute labor shortage. But in most countries, unemployment is a significant problem and older workers are being pushed to retire to make room for younger people. India is considering lowering its mandatory retirement age from 58 to 55. In Kenya, where not one person out of 14 has a job, youngsters are demanding that the compulsory retirement age be dropped to 50 or 45. Retirement however, is more pleasant in Kenya than it used to be. Says a clerk who is being pensioned off at 70 by a Nairobi law firm: "I can live in peace and comfort until I die. Less than a century ago, it was the custom of my people to carry old, sick men from their huts into the bush to be eaten alive by hyenas."

Many Americans are optimistic about what more older workers would bring to the economy, business and academic life. They are confident that the aged can be absorbed into the work force without undue strain. California Governor Jerry Brown signed legislation in September outlawing mandatory retirement in both the state government and the private sector. California thus became the 14th state to pass laws limiting compulsory retirement on grounds of age. Says Brown: "The more human talent that is used and the more people's minds and bodies contribute to the society, the more work is created. People should not be viewed as liabilities and jobs as finite quantities." Indeed, some economists believe that the oldsters will be needed in the U.S. work force. Demographic studies show that the number of youths starting

work is going to decrease in the next few years to the point that there will be a labor shortage in blue-collar occupations by the mid-1980s. By 1985, the 16-to-24 age group will decline to 15% of the total population and constitute 21.9% of the labor force. Those who are 65 or over will account for 11.7% of the population, but if the mandatory retirement age is not raised, they will make up a mere 2.7% of the work force. Obviously, there will be a large pool of elderly people to draw upon.

The oldtimers can also reduce the "piggyback problem": too few productive workers supporting too many nonproductive people. By staying at work, the older people would provide some relief for the overburdened, near-bankrupt Social Security system. Otherwise, that tax load could become intolerable. At present there are 30 Social Security beneficiaries for every 100 workers; early in the next century it is expected that there will be 52 recipients for every 100 workers. But Social Security officials caution against expecting more than a "minor" impact on the system from having the old work longer.

There are examples of companies that do not have mandatory retirement and are having no problems with that policy. Some even make a special effort to hire people over 65. John D. MacArthur, 80, chairman of the board of Bankers Life and Casualty Co. in Chicago, eliminated mandatory retirement for his company when he was still in his 40s. He has no regrets. About 4% of his 12,000 employees are 65 or over, and the company says they perform just as well as, if not better than, their juniors. "The forgetfulness of a younger person is called absent-mindedness," says Gerald L. Maguire, director of corporate services for Bankers Life. "But when a person 70 years old forgets, it is called senility. However, we are tough about requiring a good day's work. We don't think the senior citizens want to be crutched in any special way."

Tektronix Inc., an electronics firm in Oregon

and the state's largest private employer, allows all its 15,900 workers to pick their own date of retirement, provided they are doing a satisfactory job. "We don't make generalized assumptions about age and its effect on productivity," says Susan Stone, director of communications. "We try to focus on the employee and his manager rather than set hard and fast rules. It's a pay-for-performance situation. We have people over 65 doing a heck of a job, no matter where we put them." Texas Refinery, a petroleum-products manufacturer in Fort Worth, prefers to hire older people. Says Bob Phillips, assistant personnel director: "We couldn't operate as efficiently without our over-65-year-olds. The mature salesman has the patience to stay with a customer until he's sold." That is borne out by studies conducted by the National Council on Aging. Says its director of preretirement planning, Edmund W. Fitzpatrick: "Every indication we have to date shows that workers over 65 have less absenteeism and suffer fewer accidents than those, say, in the 30-to-40 age group."

Oldsters have proved capable not only of routine work but of quite demanding tasks as well. International Executive Service Corps was started in 1964 to give retired executives employment as business advisers in developing countries, where the living is not usually easy. In these prickly circumstances, the outcast executives have thrived. They have served on 5,000 projects in 62 different countries. "Age is no factor," says Saul Eisenberg, volunteer recruiter. One man went to Zaire to advise on marketing procedures when he was 82. So far only one executive has had to come home because of a physical disability. "Older people can take the rigors that anybody can," says Eisenberg.

Joan Allen, coordinator of training and education for the Davis Institute for the Care and Study of the Aging in Denver, believes that old age can be a state of mind. "Persons begin to perceive themselves as not as healthy as before, and the self-fulfilling prophecy is very real." Charles Whipple, 63, ombudsman at the Boston *Globe*, feels that mandatory retirement creates employees in its own image. "I've seen a number of employees who, if it weren't for approaching retirement, would continue to be loyal and efficient workers. Because of it, they have lapsed into premature senility. They walk around like zombies just waiting for the day they retire." Younger people behave differently toward the man soon to retire, thinks Whipple. "They no longer respect him, and sadly, he does not respect himself."

On the job as well as in the family, many experts think that older people are needed to balance youth and occasionally to act as a corrective force. Says Molly Freeman, a San Francisco sociologist who is doing research on aging: "By segregating old people and branding them useless, we deprive the young and middle-aged of role models. They do not witness the lives of older people who are active, useful and needed. Instead, they see empty, wasted lives and come to believe this is how things inevitably end."

In her 22 years as director of the U.S. Passport Office, Frances Knight, 72, who retired last summer, complains that she has witnessed all too many "enthusiastic and inexperienced Government officials initiating programs that have proved to be ineffective and even disastrous. To discard the type of practical experience and the intimate knowledge which calls a halt to making repeated errors in judgment is foolishness. Our Government is unconsciously wasteful in its discarding of past experience, of its own history."

Like it or not, American institutions are going to have to come to terms with the aged, and there are ways of coping that involve intergenerational compromise. Robert N. Butler, director of the National Institute on Aging and author of a highly regarded book on aging, *Why Survive?*, sees a "real possibility of replacing mandatory retirement with flexible, functional retirement." The growing diversity of work schedules provides an opportunity for making use of older employees, especially on a part-time basis. One example: stores are staying open longer on weekdays and weekends, and they need help. Automotive companies, as well as many other industries, complain about mounting absenteeism. Older people could work on Mondays and Fridays, when so many other employees fail to show up. Throughout the educational system, teachers over 65 might be allowed to stay on the job with half pay and some pension. With the money that is saved, a younger man could be hired to share the duties. In the executive suite, turnover in top jobs could be assured by putting strict time limits on the positions. At the end of his tenure, the executive leaves the job but not the company. If his new post is not so rewarding as the old one, it is still—in the opinion of the experts—far better than no job at all.

A greater variety of second careers could be made available to those who leave a job. California Senator S.I. Hayakawa, 71, who favors mandatory retirement (he retired from San Francisco State College in 1973) sees politics as a good new career for the aged. By then ambition, at least of an opportunistic sort, is spent, he says. "When you are 65, you have proven yourself or you have not. It does not matter any more. We are no longer on the make." For Hayakawa, politics is much like scuba diving, which he has just taken up. "It is scary, but extremely exhilarating," he says. "If you have ceased to be ready to face the frightening, then you become old. We weren't put on earth to behave like barnacles."

Ellsworth Bunker, 83, who also supports mandatory retirement, retired as director of the National Sugar Refining Co. at 56, and since then he has devoted himself to public service as an ambassador to various trouble spots, including Viet Nam. He has now successfully negotiated—along with Sol Linowitz—a new Panama Canal treaty. Explains Bunker: "I don't think there is any age limitation on a person's usefulness. It depends entirely on the individual." At 71, Averell Harriman negotiated the atomic test-ban treaty with the Soviet Union. At 85, he continues to offer sage counsel to the less experienced Carter Administration.

American is renowned as a society of leisure pursuits with the time to indulge in them. But if there is anything old people have learned—often to their sorrow—leisure is not enough. "Work is life" is an equation that was defined by philosophers and intuited by all human beings long before the work ethic was invented. "Idleness is the death of a living man," said the 17th century British prelate Jeremy Taylor. Work is an anodyne for the inevitability of death, says contemporary Sociologist Daniel Bell. For Sigmund Freud, work was a means of binding an individual to reality and his community. Governor Brown reports that while institutions in his state generally favored keeping compulsory retirement, individuals opposed it. One company sent literature that urged him to veto the legislation eliminating mandatory retirement; attached to the pamphlets was a note from the company's lobbyist saying that he personally supported the measure. There is much to be said for the positions of both individuals and institutions, and even more to be said for their finding common ground.

HOW BUREAUCRATS DEAL WITH DISSIDENTS

DAVID EWING

Recently, the Carter administration introduced some long-awaited reforms in the Civil Service. A new agency, the Merit System Protection Board, independent from Civil Service operations, would hear appeals from civil servants who believed themselves victims of scabrous treatment.

Alas, however, the bureaucrats know all the moves; they are accomplished in destroying any attack on their prerogatives and can dispatch any civil servant with grace and aplomb.

Codification of these techniques is due largely to Alan May, field director in 1968 of the large Republican vote-getting in northern California. After the election, he was rewarded with a job on the Nixon inauguration committee and then in the Department of Health, Education and Welfare, where he concentrated on personnel problems.

It was there, in 1972, that he concocted a manual for the guidance of administrators of federal agencies frustrated by recalcitrant subordinates. May's manual tells the harassed administrator how to dispatch an "unresponsive" agency employee, the quixotic individual who feels obliged to discourage or even publicize wrongdoing, to criticize waste or to decline an immoral directive.

May's manual demonstrates that, while it may be necessary to comply with the letter of Civil Service regulations, it is quite unnecessary to comply with the spirit of these impractical rules. It carefully describes, for instance, the sort of transfer which is a promotion according to the regulations, but one which will force the pariah to resign.

May has left a manual which grows in usefulness and fecundity. Here are a few of the suppressive techniques which agency administrators may use without jeopardy.

1. PUT THEM IN BROWN SHOES

Although government agencies were once cursed with the idealism of their employees, it is now known that unruly subalterns can be ma-

Source: Reprinted by permission of David W. Ewing and Julian Bach Literary Agency, Incorporated.

nipulated. Their weakness lies in their inability to suffer reassignment to tasks where their talents are wasted.

An example of brilliant execution of the proper technique comes from the Food and Drug Administration. In 1970 the FDA hired Dr. Carol Kennedy. A crusader for children's safety, she felt deeply about protecting children from exposure to unnecessary risks of new drugs. Soon she became critical of her superiors, who in their wisdom were less worried by these risks than she, especially when a drug company was pressing them to approve a new medication.

Although Kennedy's work was commended for technical excellence, it soom became obvious that, like Dolly in E.M. Forster's "Howard's End," she was a good little girl but a little bit of her went a long way. Her superiors deftly transferred her to another division and assigned her to a task she had no interest in. Unable to tolerate the feeling of being a pair of brown shoes while the rest of the world was a tuxedo, she resigned.

One agency official I know, who considers himself the very model of a modern manager, says he accepts the sinner's resignation with words like "profound regret" and "your leaving will be a loss to us all." He may even send a handwritten note of best wishes to the dissident at the farewell lunch. In his manual, May magnanimously suggests that an award might be handed to the vanquished critic.

2. MAKE THEM FLIES IN AMBER

Unfortunately, not all capable dissenters are young and idealistic. Because of age or family obligations, some feel committed to serve out their careers in the agency. Since the accursed Civil Service regulations maintain that these retainers cannot be fired after years of loyal service—a protection that is scorned in private business—the only reasonable solution is to muffle them.

For 12 years the FDA made remarkably

clumsy attempts to fire John Nestor, a physician whose cautious approach to the approval of new drugs irritated top management. (Suppression of dissidence is as delicate a business as French cooking and brain surgery. When it succeeds, it is spectacular, but when it fails it is ghastly.) By 1972 it was too late under Civil Service rules to force Nestor to resign. Thus the FDA, as Howard Cosell might say, "applied true brilliance." It transfixed the nettlesome Nestor in an obscure division where he could bother no one.

A team investigating such harassment failed to see the wisdom of this strategy. They stated: "The payment of a substantial federal salary for almost no work is intolerable." The observation, of course, is not merely naive but false. The payment of a $36,000 salary is perfectly tolerable to Nestor's former superiors, who now go their happy, prophylactic way without criticism. They needn't sign his paychecks: the taxpayer does.

3. ELIMINATE THE JOB

In the agency executive's bag of tricks, this one is unusual in its directness. To exorcise the truculent spirit, simply abolish the job. Thus when Paulette L. Barnes, after being promised a promotion in the Environmental Protection Agency, resisted the sexual advances of her boss, management declared the position she had held superfluous. Unfortunately, Barnes resisted, and took the EPA to court; in a moment of weak judicial resolve, the local U.S. Court of Appeals decided in her favor. Nonetheless, wise officials know that few troublemakers will share Barnes' determination.

4. STONEWALL THEM

A more prolonged strategy, but fiendishly clever in the right situation, is to void the evidence that might support the critic's charges. For questioning the purchasing practices of the Department of Defense at a supply center in

Columbus, Ohio, Ralph Applegate, a 15-year veteran of the department, was charged with insubordination and later fired. When members of Congress sought to learn the facts about the case, the agency refused to release the information. When Applegate appealed his discharge in 1976, a judge on the review board who requested some vital transcripts was rebuffed, and to this day the transcripts remain with the department.

The federal official with a sense of humor can exploit a similar but more witty technique: reprimand the critic; let him or her go to the expense of hiring an attorney and suffer the agonies of a long wait for a formal hearing; then, a few days before the scheduled hearing, when the dissident is tense with anticipation, suddenly and for no announced reason withdraw the charges. The top wags at the FDA used this droll method to check Dr. Alice Campbell, who had protested the safety of a new antidepressant drug being approved by the agency.

Campbell had been thoughtless and ill-mannered enough to present an unfavorable review of the drug and write a report on its clinical toxicity. In the spring of 1973, her superior handed her an official letter of reprimand. When she asked him about the letter, he refused to discuss the charges, an act that, though required by personnel procedure in the bureaucracy, we shall overlook here. After she hired an attorney and filed a formal grievance, a hearing was scheduled for Sept. 28. Two days before the hearing, the superior rescinded his letter of reprimand and the hearing was canceled. The distraught Campbell asked, "What about the $1,500 I spent on my lawyer's fee?" Personnel officials answered sadly that she had no recourse.

Wiser for the experience, she left the FDA the following summer.

5. MAKE THEM COME UNBUTTONED

For officials who are amenable to delays and confusion, this technique—imported from Russia—is the solution of choice. An example comes from Foggy Bottom.

According to information released by the State Department last fall, a young black, Walter J. Thomas, filed a racial discrimination complaint while serving in the Peace Corps. Later he had the temerity to apply for a position in the Foreign Service. After passing his physical, his earlier indiscretion caught up with him: He was ordered to take the exam again. During the second exam the doctor harassed him with so many questions that he flunked for "hypertension, hyperuricemia, elevated fasting blood sugar," and other impairments. The case is being reviewed, but at last report Mr. Thomas was "broke, disillusioned and suspicious."

One agency official put it this way: "First we drive the dissident crazy. Then we tell people not to listen to him because he's crazy."

6. ICE THE PUCK

An agency resentful of an employee's criticisms can cut the dissident's budget, transfer his secretary, close his office without warning and refuse to grant further promotions. The current record for professional stasis is held by John Coplin, a supervisor employed by the Department of Agriculture. He was rising fast through the departmental hierarchy until he revealed some unethical practices in Philadelphia in 1955; in the 24 years since, he has served without a promotion.

7. IMITATE MUSHROOM FARMING

Sophisticated agency officials have discerned in the cultivation of mushrooms a lesson in management. Mushrooms are grown in cool, dark caves in a rich, nitrogenous soil and, when they grow to size, are harvested. Similarly, officials can keep the potential dissident in the dark, embed him im manure and, as soon as he sticks his head up, cut it off.

The General Services Administration employed this technique to singular advantage in

1975. Robert Tucker, a young electrical engineer, was assigned to investigate construction contracts in Boston but was not informed of the GSA's own practice of illegal favoritism in contract awards. When he did discover the improprieties and presented his data to the FBI, he was fired. A little later, another GSA investigator, Robert Sullivan, uncovered the story and shared it with the Boston Globe. He, too, promptly suffered the fate of a mushroom.

Last year Sullivan and Tucker got their jobs back as a result of an unfortunate hitch. Sullivan had brought suit against the GSA. In the pretrial hearing in Boston, the judge informed the government that it didn't have much of a case. Obviously the judge understood neither the new etiquette nor the requirements of a smoothly functioning bureaucracy. The GSA was forced to settle out of court in order to avert a worse loss and bad publicity.

QUESTIONS FOR DISCUSSION

1. Do you agree with the statement made in the introduction to this chapter that it is almost impossible to terminate employees except for too much or too little seniority?

2. What impact did the social security system have on the expansion of the retirement age?

3. If all states pass a law stating that no employee can be forced to retire at any age, what impact will this have on motivation and productivity in our society?

4. The Japanese system focuses on the older employee rather than the younger employee. Why has this emphasis worked so well?

5. When you seek your next job, will the age of the senior management have any impact on your selection? As a group, survey five to ten senior managers between the ages of 60 to 65 and see how they view retirement. Compare this to five or six interviews with similar people who have retired in the past four or five years. Is the *Death of a Salesman* phenomenon present?

6. How prevalent do you think the lack of freedom discussed by Ewing is in organization?

CHAPTER XI
THE SOCIAL ETHICS OF ORGANIZATIONAL BEHAVIOR

ORGANIZATIONAL SHOCKS

- A little knowledge about the psychology and sociology of organizational behavior can be dangerous.
- Organizations don't punish people who lie or cheat; they punish people who embarrass the organization by getting caught.
- Managers are often expected to lie to protect the organization.

In courses about organizational behavior and management we often teach potential managers how to motivate, influence, manipulate, and change employees for the purpose of increasing productivity. We talk, for example, about group decision-making, leadership, cohesiveness, personality, self-insight, and other useful psychological and sociological phenomena. One of the things we often failed to do, however, is to talk about the social ethics of organizational behavior principles. One of the shocks that many managers experience is that they are ill-prepared to motivate other people because they have not had relevant courses in management and organizational behavior (and therefore this is a popular topic for senior management executive development programs). Another shock comes from those people who have studied it but find out that it may or may not work. However, a little knowledge *can* be dangerous because it may work only in certain very limited situations. It also may backfire on you.

The four readings in this chapter deal with leadership situations where a question of social ethics appeared. The first reading by Janis describes the group of phenomenon called "groupthink," which influenced the escalation of the Vietnam War. If you think about this in relation to the chapter on group, individual, and cultural differences you will see the powerful impact that others have on leaders in the decision-making capacity.

The second reading by Max Ways from *Fortune* uses Watergate as a case study of management. He talks about how Watergate really was a situation where mismanagement was the biggest crime. Part of this dealt with the selection of people, part of this dealt with interpersonal relations, and part of this dealt with the overriding need for group cohesiveness. This reading in combination with the one by Janis should give managers and leaders a feel for the interactive effect of the leader and his or her group on organizational outcome.

The third reading concerning the Air Force A-7D brake scandal presents a similar problem. In this case, a senior level employee of the B. F. Goodrich Company made a mistake and refused to admit it; therefore it snowballed into a major scandal. By the time all senior management became aware of the problem, it probably was too late to correct this mistake so they compounded it by supporting the person who had supposedly presented false results.

The fourth article in this chapter talks about corporate morality as an organizational phenomenon. This article by James Waters takes the three situations, similar to the ones we have discussed previously and talks about ways managers can use principles of organizational behavior to overcome the shock that many people will experience when the organization asks them to make statements and decisions that they feel are ethically wrong.

ESCALATION OF THE VIETNAM WAR: HOW COULD IT HAPPEN?

IRVING L. JANIS

All observers agree that a stable group of policy advisers met regularly with President Johnson to deliberate on what to do about the war in Vietnam. Fragmentary evidence now at hand gives some clues about how and why the group's policy of escalating the war was so assiduously pursued during the period from 1964 through 1967. The escalation decisions were made despite strong warnings from intelligence experts within the United States government, as well as from leaders of the United Nations, from practically all of America's allies, and from influential sectors of the American public. Even if the members of Johnson's advisory group were willing to pay a high price to attain their economic and political objectives in Vietnam, they apparently ignored until too late the mounting signs that their decisions to escalate the war were having devastating political repercussions within the United States, and that these repercussions were threatening to destroy the President's chances of being reelected. Accounts in the Pentagon Papers about the group's meetings and private statements made by individual members expose what seem to be gross miscalculations and blatant symptoms of groupthink. The evidence now available is far from complete, and conclusions will have to be drawn quite tentatively. Nevertheless, it is worthwhile to grapple with the main questions that need to be answered to discover if the groupthink hypothesis applies to these recent, notoriously ill-conceived decisions.

WHAT NEEDS TO BE EXPLAINED?

More than a mere exercise in the psychological analysis of recent foreign policy decisions, showing how group dynamics may have influenced America's Vietnam policy may help us to understand how conscientious statesmen could ignore the impressive voices of so many reputable Americans concerning the immorality as well as the adverse political consequences of their military actions. Perhaps even more important, an analysis of the shared illusions of Johnson's inner circle may give us insights that help explain how such men could still the inner voices of their own consciences. As Ithiel Pool, one of the few American professors of political science who supported the Johnson administration's basic Vietnam policy, points out: "It is hard to understand how intelligent men could believe that aerial bombardment, harassment and interdiction artillery fire, defoliation, and population displacement could be effective means to win a population, or how moral men could believe them appropriate means of action among the population we are defending." After all, the policy-makers in the Johnson administration were sincere democrats who prided themselves on their humanitarian outlook. How could they justify their decisions to authorize search-and-destroy missions, fire-free zones, and the use of "whatever violent means are necessary to destroy the enemy's sanctuaries"—all of which set the stage, the normative background, for the Mylai massacre and other acts of violence by the United States military forces against Vietnamese villagers?

The most thorough analysis of the Johnson administration's Vietnam War decisions is in the Department of Defense's study known as the Pentagon Papers, which was declassified and published in twelve volumes by the United States government in 1971, after *The New York Times* and other newspapers had revealed the main contents to the American public. In restrained but unambiguous terms, the historians and political analysts who prepared this secret study call attention time and again to the poor quality of the decision-making procedures used by the policy-makers who met regularly with President Johnson. They emphasize in particular the group's failure to canvass the full range of alternative courses of action and their superficial assessment of the pros and cons of the military recommendations under consideration during 1964 and 1965. For example, at a major strategy meeting on September 7, 1964, ac-

cording to the Department of Defense analysts, "a rather narrow range of proposals was up for consideration." Neil Sheehan, in *The New York Times* book on the Pentagon Papers, adds that "the study indicates no effort on the part of the President and his most trusted advisers to reshape their policy along the lines of . . . [the] analysis" prepared jointly by experts from the three leading intelligence agencies of the government toward the end of 1964. According to that analysis, bombing North Vietnam had little chance of breaking the will of Hanoi. The vital decision made on February 13, 1965, to launch the previously planned air strikes against North Vietnam, the Defense Department study states, "seems to have resulted *as much from the lack of alternative proposals as from any compelling logic in their favor.*"

After leaving the government, Bill Moyers, an articulare member of Johnson's in-group, admitted: "With but rare exceptions we always seemed to be calculating the short-term consequences of each alternative at every step of the [policy-making] process, but not the long-term consequences. And with each succeeding short-range consequence we became more deeply a prisoner of the process."

Who were the prisoners and why couldn't they escape?

PRESIDENT JOHNSON'S INNER CIRCLE

During the Johnson administration the major Vietnam decisions were made by a small inner circle of government officials, most of whom remained for a few years and then were replaced, one at a time. In addition to the President, the in-group included Special White House Assistant McGeorge Bundy (later replaced by Walt Rostow), Secretary of Defense Robert McNamara (replaced during the last year of the Johnson administration by Clark Clifford), and Secretary of State Dean Rusk (who managed to remain in Johnson's advisory group from the bitter beginning to the bitter end). For several years Press Secretary Bill Moyers and Undersecretary of State George Ball also participated in the meetings. The group also included General Earl Wheeler, chairman of the Joint Chiefs of Staff from 1964 on, and Richard Helms, director of the Central Intelligence Agency from 1966 on.

President Johnson consulted this small group on all major policy decisions concerning the Vietnam War. Although most individual members of the inner circle were replaced before the Johnson administration came to an end, "its work was distinctively continuous because new men joined it only infrequently and always one at a time." The members sometimes called themselves "the Tuesday Lunch Group," and others have referred to the group as "the Tuesday Cabinet." At their Tuesday noon meetings, the members deliberated about the next steps to be taken in the Vietnam War and often dealt with purely military matters, such as the targets in North Vietnam to be bombed next.

Before discussing symptoms of groupthink, we must consider whether Johnson's inner circle was unified by bonds of mutual friendship and loyalty, an essential precondition for the emergence of the groupthink syndrome. Some journalists depict Lyndon B. Johnson as an extraordinarily aggressive and insensitive leader, who made such excessive and humiliating demands on everyone who came in frequent contact with him that he was cordially disliked, if not hated. With these alleged attributes in mind, we are led to wonder if perhaps the apparent unity of Johnson's inner circle was simply superficial conformity and polite deference out of a sense of expediency, with each member inwardly feeling quite detached from the leader and perhaps from the group as a whole. But if this were the case, it was not detected by Chester Cooper, J. Townsend Hoopes, Bill Moyer, James Thomson, Jr., and other observers in the Johnson administration who were in contact with members of the inner circle. Rather, the picture we get from those who observed from close at hand is that the group was highly cohesive.

Most explicit on this point is Henry Graff, who had the opportunity to conduct private interviews with President Johnson and with each of his principal advisers on four different occasions between mid-1965 and the end of 1968. Graff was repeatedly impressed by what appeared to him to be genuine friendship and mutual support among the members of the Tuesday Cabinet, which he felt characterized the group up until early 1968. Later in 1968 he noted a tone of querulousness in the comments the men made about the mounting barrage of criticisms directed against Johnson's war policy, as the increasingly obvious signs of its failure began to take their toll. But before that final phase, according to Graff:

> The men of the Tuesday Cabinet were loyal to each other, with a devotion compounded of mutual respect and common adversity. They soon learned, as all congenial committeemen learn, to listen selectively and to talk harmoniously even when in disagreement. Familiarity with one another's minds became an asset as well as a handicap in the years they conferred and labored. And their facility with words (laced with the Pentagonese all spoke so fluently) made the sessions memorable for the participants week in and week out.

Even in early 1968, when outstanding officials like Deputy Secretary of Defense Paul Nitze were submitting their resignations and it was hard to avoid bickering within the inner circle about whether the Vietnam War policy could be salvaged, Graff was still impressed by the "loyalty with which the men around the President defended him and the decisions they had helped him reach, regardless of any private misgivings they may have increasingly entertained." During the preceding year or two, as the members "felt increasingly beleaguered," Graff surmises, "they turned toward one another for reassurance" and became "natural friends" of their chief. He adds that the Tuesday Cabinet exerted an extraordinarily powerful influence over its leader, perhaps more than any other presidential advisory group in American history.

Bill Moyers, from his personal observation as a member of Johnson's inner circle, has corroborated Graff's conclusion that the group was highly cohesive. Directly in line with the groupthink hypothesis, Moyers mentions the concurrence-seeking tendency of the members as part of his explanation for the lack of critical debate about Vietnam War policies:

> one of the significant problems in the Kennedy and Johnson Administrations was that the men who handled national security affairs became too close, too personally fond of each other. They tended to conduct the affairs of state almost as if they were a gentlemen's club, and the great decisions were often made in that warm camaraderie of a small board of directors deciding what the club's dues are going to be for the members next year. . . . So you often dance around the final hard decision which would set you against . . . men who are very close to you, and you tend to reach a consensus.

According to the Pentagon Papers, the escalation of the air war was planned secretly during the election campaign in the fall of 1964. The decision to authorize the first phase of the plan was made one month *after* Johnson's election victory; the decision to authorize the second phase was made only about two months later. In this period the administration did not need to be very concerned about the prospects of defeat of its program in Congress, and the next election was a long way off. The landslide victory itself must have shown the astute political minds in Washington that the failure of Goldwater's aggressive anti-Communist campaign meant that at least for the time being there was little realistic basis for worry about the power of the right-wing Republicans to mobilize public

support. Yet precisely during the months when the election victory was still fresh in mind President Johnson and his advisers made the major decisions to authorize the Rolling Thunder program.

Tom Wicker, *New York Times* associate editor and columnist, reports that he was informed by several officials close to the President in 1964 that the same type of elated self-confidence that had pervaded the thinking of Kennedy's in-group prior to the Bay of Pigs fiasco was reexperienced following the 1964 election victory, at the time Johnson and his advisers committed themselves to escalating the air war in Vietnam:

> Several officials who were close to Johnson at that time . . . recall the sheer *ebullience* of the moment. One of them had also served Kennedy and remembers the same *sense of omnipotence* in the White House in early 1961. . . . [He said,] *"We thought we had the golden touch. It was just like that with Johnson after sixty-four."*

These observations, if accurate, suggest that when Johnson and his principal advisers were deliberating about the escalation decisions, they shared a staunch faith that somehow everything would come out right, despite all the gloomy predictions in the intelligence reports prepared by their underlings.

MAJOR SOURCES OF ERROR

James Thomson, Jr., a historian who was a member of McGeorge Bundy's staff in the White House, has attempted to explain the poor quality of the escalation decisions, which he calls "Lyndon Johnson's slow-motion Bay of Pigs." He addresses himself to the paradox that although the members of the policy-making group had all the attributes of well-qualified ad well-intentioned leaders—sound training, high ability, and humanitarian ideals—they persistently ignored the major consequences of practically all their Vietnam War policy decisions.

They repeatedly gave in to pressures for a military rather than a diplomatic or political solution; they took little account of the destructive impact of their policies on the Vietnamese people, whom they were supposedly helping; they badly bungled or sabotaged every opportunity to negotiate disengagement of the United States from Vietnam. What could cause a group of responsible policy-makers to persist in a course of action that was producing so much suffering to the people of Vietnam and so much havoc within their own nation?

In attempting to answer this question, Thomson discusses a large number of causal factors. Some are historical and political considerations, such as institutional constraints in the State Department against sponsoring policies that could be construed as "soft on communism" in the Far East; these were the legacy of America's Asia policy of the 1950s. Thomson also points out that the policy advisory group was insulated from political expertise in the government and, as the Vietnam decisions progressively involved more and more military force, it was essential for the policy-makers to consult more and more with military experts, who almost always proposed escalating the war. Still, being exposed to strong pressures from the military establishment should not necessarily cause high-level civilians who preside over their country's foreign policy to move consistently in the direction of military escalation. Surely hardheaded policy-makers in the Johnson administration could raise critical questions, insist on full political briefings, assess the unfortunate consequences of military escalation, and work out alternative ways of settling the problems of United States involvement in Vietnam.

What happened to the critical evaluators, the doubters, the dissenters? Thomson answers this crucial question, again on the basis of his personal observations and experiences within the White House, by citing a number of psychological factors that he believes influenced decision-making by the group of men who shaped America's Vietnam policy. He lists about two dozen specific factors, which can be classified into six major categories: (1) excessive time pressures, (2) bureaucratic detachment, (3) stereotyped views of Communists and Orientals, (4) overcommitment to defeating the enemy, (5) domestication of dissenters, and (6) avoidance of opposing views. I shall try to show how Thomson's seemingly diverse points may be brought together into a single psychological explanation by giving an interpretation in terms of the groupthink hypothesis.

APPLYING THE GROUPTHINK HYPOTHESIS

Because we do not yet have well-authenticated details of the way the President and his inner circle carried out their policy deliberations from 1964 to 1968, the available observations must be used mainly to point up the new questions that need to be answered in order to determine whether the groupthink hypothesis offers at least a partial explanation of the ill-fated escalation decisions made by the Johnson administration. Thomson's account of the defective ways Johnson's in-group arrived at its Vietnam policy decisions are fairly well corroborated by other inside observers (Cooper, Hoopes, and Moyers) and hint at small-group processes. But neither Thomson nor any other observer explicitly discusses any aspect of group dynamics (except for the few sentences quoted from Bill Moyers concerning the group's tendency to seek consensus instead of debating the issues). Thomson confines his discussion to two different types of causes, both of which may have played an important role in the Vietnam escalation policy. One type involves the sociological features of the large organization—the social patterns and pressures that arise in a government bureaucracy. The other type pertains to individual psychology, focusing on the way the individual decision-maker reacts to the tasks and pressures imposed upon him. Do these two types of causal factors tell the whole story?

The groupthink hypothesis, when added to the sociological and the individual psychological factors, may contribute a more complete explanation and may help us understand how and why the various patterns of behavior described by Thomson became dominant reactions. The groupthink hypothesis can encompass the psychological factors he discusses but points to a different source of trouble from that of explanations focusing either on the bureaucratic organization or on the individual. Rather than assuming that each policy-maker is responding to the demands of the bureaucracy and to other pressures in his own way and that it so happens that each of them ends up by becoming detached, biased, overcommitted to his past decisions and prone to ignore challenging intelligence reports, we shall pursue the possibility that the commonality of the responses of the key policy-makers may arise from their interaction in a small group, which generates norms that all the members strive to live up to.

EFFECTS OF STRESS ON GROUP COHESIVENESS

The first factor derived from Thomson's analysis—excessive time pressure—is likely to affect the mental efficiency of any individual, whether he is functioning alone or in a group. Time pressure is, of course, one of the sources of stress that besets any group of executives in a crisis, especially if the members are required to take prompt action when they are confronted with contradictory political pressures from many different interested parties. Whenever a decision has to be made that vitally affects the security of his nation, the government executive is likely to undergo a variety of severe stresses. He realizes that a great deal is at stake for his country and for the rest of the world and that it also may be a crucial moment in his personal

career. If he chooses the wrong course of action, he may lose his status, face public humiliation, and suffer a profound loss of self-esteem. These political and personal threats can have a cumulative effect, especially when the decision-maker is under constant time pressure and has little opportunity to study even the most important proposals. (Washington bureaucrats quipped that the reason McNamara looked so good, in comparison to the others who participated in the White House meetings, was that the long drive from the Pentagon gave him eight extra minutes to do his homework in the back of his limousine.) All members of a government policy-making group share these common sources of stress whenever they have to make an important foreign policy decision. Even if the President alone is officially responsible, each of his close advisers knows that if the group makes a serious error and the prestige of the administration is badly damaged, every member may in one way or another be held accountable. Any member of the inner circle might become a scapegoat and be pilloried by investigating committees or the news media. The members of Johnson's advisory group were subjected to a mounting spiral of severe stress as the threats of public humiliation and loss of prestige gradually began to materialize.

Field studies of infantry platoons, air crews, and disaster control teams bear out the findings of social psychological experiments with college students that show that external sources of stress produce a heightened need for affiliation. In times of crisis, a natural tendency arises among the harassed members of a preestablished group to meet together more often and to communicate more than ever with each other, to find out what the others know about the dangers confronting them, to exchange ideas about how the threats might best be dealt with, and to gain reassurance. The heightened need for affiliation, which leads to greater dependency upon one's primary work group and increased motivation to adhere to the group's norms, can have beneficial effects on morale and stress tolerance. But the increase in group cohesiveness will have adverse effects if it leads, as the groupthink hypothesis predicts, to an increase in concurrence-seeking at the expense of critical thinking. An executive committee like Johnson's Tuesday Lunch Group would be expected to show both the positive and the negative effects of increased cohesiveness during periods of crisis.

We can view the excessive time pressures described by Thomson as a causal factor that adversely affects the quality of the policy-makers' decisions in at least two different ways. First, overwork and fatigue generally impair each decision-maker's mental efficiency and judgment, interfering with his ability to concentrate on complicated discussions, to absorb new information, and to use his imagination to anticipate the future consequences of alternative courses of action. (This is a matter of individual psychology and is the aspect emphasized by Thomson.) The additional aspect to be considered is this: Excessive time pressure is a source of stress that, along with the even more severe sources of stress that generally arise in a crisis, will have the effect of inducing a policy-making group to become more cohesive and more likely to indulge in groupthink. Thus, in order to pursue the groupthink hypothesis, we are led to raise this question: *Did the members of Johnson's advisory group display signs of an increase in group cohesiveness and a corresponding increase in manifestations of concurrence-seeking during crisis periods, when they had relatively little time off from their jobs?* We shall return to this question shortly.

EFFECTS OF COMMITMENT TO PRIOR GROUP DECISIONS

Bureaucratic detachment and stereotyped views of Communists and Asians involve attitudes that affect the deliberations preceding each new decision. From the beginning, most members of Johnson's inner circle probably shared similar ideological viewpoints on basic issues of foreign policy and domestic politics. However, all of them probably did not start with the same attitude of detachment toward the human suffering inflicted by the war and the same unsophisticated stereotypes concerning world communism and the peoples of the Orient. As a historian, Thomson was shocked to realize the extent to which crudely propagandistic conceptions entered the group's plans and policy statements. He indicates that Johnson's inner circle uncritically accepted the domino theory, which simplistically assumes that all Asian countries will act alike, so that if the Communists were permitted to gain control over one country in the Far East, all neighboring countries would promptly become vulnerable and fall under Communist domination. As for the Vietcong and the North Vietnamese, the dominant stereotypes made these "Communist enemies" into the embodiment of evil and thus legitimized the destruction of countless human lives and the burning of villages. In support of Thomson's analysis, psychologist Ralph K. White has shown how consistently the public statements of Johnson, Rusk, McNamara, and others in the Tuesday Lunch Group reveal the pervasiveness of the policy-maker's black-and-white picture of the Vietnam War, which always contrasts an image of the diabolical opponents with an image of the invariably moral and virile American government.

When Johnson's Tuesday Lunch Group was formed, some members probably held these attitudes strongly and others probably had somewhat different views. In the course of interaction, the former may have influenced the latter. For example, as Thomson suggests, the few members who had spent many years participating in military planning conferences at the Pentagon may have introduced to the rest of the group a detached dehumanizing attitude toward the Vietnam War, using the euphemistic vocabulary of "body counts," "surgical air strikes," and "pacification." The members of the group who began with a more humanistic way of thinking and talking about the evils of war may have followed the lead of the military men. But why would the members holding detached attitudes succeed in getting the others to adopt their dehumanizing outlook? Why not the other way around?

One of the main psychological assumptions underlying the groupthink hypothesis is that when a policy-making group becomes highly cohesive, a homogenization of viewpoints takes place, helping the group to preserve its unity by enabling all the members to continue to support the decisions to which the group has become committed. When one of the main norms is being committed to pursuing a war policy, as in this case, we expect that commitment will be bolstered by subsidiary norms that reduce disputes and disharmony within the group. In this context, detachment toward the use of military means and dehumanization of the victims of war, as well as negative stereotypes of the enemy, have functional value for a group committed to military escalation. Sharing such attitudes tends to minimize the likelihood that any member will challenge the group's policy by raising moral and humanitarian considerations, which would stimulate bickering, recriminations, and discord. It follows from the same psychological assumption that if the same group were to commit itself to a nonviolent peace-seeking course of action, a reverse trend would appear: The members who personally think in terms of moral and humanitarian values would no longer suppress such considerations but, rather, would take the lead in setting a new fashion for using a humanizing vocabulary that bolsters the new group norm.

Additional historical evidence is obviously needed in order to pursue the suggestion that the attitude of detachment toward the victims of war and the stereotyped conceptions of the North Vietnamese Communists expressed by Johnson's Tuesday Lunch Group might be interpreted as symptoms of groupthink. Among the main questions to be answered are those having to do with when, in the sequence of decisions, these adverse attitudes were manifested by most or all members of the group. *Were attitudes of detachment and stereotyped views of Communists and Asians expressed relatively rarely by members of the in-group before their first major decisions to escalate the war? Does the emergence of a dehumanizing vocabulary and stereotyped terms in the group's discussions fit the pattern of a subsidiary group norm that follows the militaristic decisions the members had previously agreed upon?*

Overcommitment to defeating the enemy—another factor described by Thomson—involves a well-known human weakness that makes it hard for anyone to correct the errors he has made in the past. The men in Johnson's inner circle, according to Thomson, ultimately convinced themselves that the Vietnam War was of crucial significance for America's future—a conviction that grew directly out of their own explanations and justifications. It became essential to the policy-makers to continue the costly and unpopular war, Thomson surmises, because they had *said* it was essential. Instead of reevaluating their policy in response to clear-cut setbacks, their energetic proselytizing led them to engage in "rhetorical escalation" that matched the military escalation, deepening their commitment to military victory rather than a political solution through negotiation with the government of North Vietnam. The members of Johnson's inner circle, according to another inside observer, remained "united both in their conviction about the rightness of present policy and the fact that all were implicated in the major [escalation] decisions since 1964."

We know that most individuals become heavily ego-involved in maintaining their commitment to any important decision for which they feel at least partly responsible. Once a decision-maker has publicly announced the course of action he has selected, he is inclined to avoid looking at evidence of the unfavorable consequences. He tries to reinterpret setbacks as victories, to invent new arguments to convince himself and others that he made the right decision, clinging stubbornly to unsuccessful policies long after everyone else can see that a change is needed. Each policy-maker, whether he has made the crucial decisions by himself or as a member of a group, is thus motivated to perpetuate his past errors—provided, of course, that his nose is not rubbed in inescapable evidence.

Like attitudes of detachment and derogatory stereotypes, the tendency to recommit oneself to prior decisions can be greatly augmented by social pressures that arise within a cohesive group. From time to time, setbacks induce a policy-maker to doubt the wisdom of past decisions in which he has participated. But what a man does about his doubts, if he is a member of an in-group of policy-makers, depends in large part on the norms of the group. If the members agree that loyalty to their group and its goals requires rigorous support of the group's primary commitment to open-minded scrutiny of new evidence and willingness to admit errors (as in a group committed to the ideals of scientific research), the usual psychological tendency to recommit themselves to their past decisions after a setback can give way to a careful reappraisal of the wisdom of their past judgments. The group norm in such a case inclines them to compare their policy with alternative courses of action and may lead them to reverse their earlier decisions. On the other hand, if, as often happens, the members feel that loyalty to the group requires unwavering support of the group's past policy decisions, the usual psychological tendency to bolster past commitments is reinforced. Following a series of escalation decisions, every member is likely to insist that the same old military drumbeat is the right one and that sooner or later everyone who matters will want to be in step with it.

Did President Johnson's group of policy-makers show signs of adhering to a norm requiring the members to continue supporting the group's past escalation decisions? Many of the characteristics mentioned by Thomson and other observers suggest a positive answer. In elaborating on the group's commitment to its past decisions, Thomson describes the group's tendency to evolve a set of shared rationalizations to justify the militant Vietnam policy. He mentions a closely related symptom that also carries a strong taint of groupthink—mutual agreement to rewrite recent history in a way that would justify the Vietnam escalation policy:

> another result of Vietnam decision-making has been *the abuse and distortion of history*. Vietnamese, Southeast Asian, and Far Eastern history has been rewritten by our policy-makers, and their spokesmen, to conform with the alleged necessity of our presence in Vietnam. Highly dubious analogies from our experience elsewhere—the "Munich" sellout and "containment" from Europe, the Malayan insurgency and the Korean War from Asia—have been imported in order to justify our actions. And more recent events have been fitted to the Procrustean bed of Vietnam. Most notably, the change of power in Indonesia in 1965–1966 has been ascribed to our Vietnam presence; and virtually all progress in the Pacific region—the rise of regionalism, new forms of cooperation, the mounting growth rates—has been similarly exploited. The Indonesian allegation is undoubtedly false (I tried to prove it, during six months of careful investigation in the White House, and had to confess failure); the regional allegation is patently unprovable in either direction.

We cannot avoid recollecting how the bureaucrats in Orwell's *1984* rewrote their own history and were able to make their new versions quite acceptable to those who remembered what really happened by requiring all loyal followers of Big Brother to practice "doublethink"—knowing and at the same time not knowing the truth. How did the policy-makers in the Johnson administration handle this problem within their own ranks? *Were the insiders who could not accept the new rationalized version of East Asian history silenced by the rest of the group?*

CONFORMITY PRESSURES

Similar questions need to be answered about the way in which the policy-makers handled the "loyal opposition," the government officials, Vietnam experts, and Congressmen who were arguing in favor of the alternative policy of negotiating a peace settlement. Did the members of Johnson's policy-making group consider the eminent members of their own political party who advocated alternative policies to be transmitters of potentially important ideas about how the problems of Vietnam might be solved? Or *did they gravitate toward the groupthink view that advocates of a negotiated peace were disloyal and had to be kept out of their high counsel? Did they privately brand the leading doves as despicable "isolationists" who were a threat to American security?*

We can see from the foregoing questions that from the standpoint of a groupthink interpretation, the phenomena resulting from the group's commitment to its past policy decisions include the remaining types of factors extracted from Thomson's analysis—domestication of dissenters and avoidance of opposing views from critics inside and outside the government. Both of these may be manifestations of a group process involving a constant striving for homogeneous beliefs and judgments among all members of the in-group, in line with their past commitments. Striving for consensus, which helps the members achieve a sense of group unity and esprit de corps, is, of course, the psychological basis for all the symptoms of groupthink.

We learn from Thomson that during the Johnson administration everyone in the hierarchy, including every senior official, was subjected to conformity pressures, which took the form of making those who openly questioned the escalation policy the butt of an ominous epithet: "I am afraid he's losing his effectiveness." This "effectiveness trap"—the threat of being branded a "has been" and losing access to the seats of power—inclines its victims to suppress or tone down their criticisms. In a more subtle way, it makes any member who starts to voice his misgivings ready to retreat to a seemingly acquiescent position in the presence of quizzical facial expressions and crisp retorts from perturbed associates and superiors.

Thomson also informs us that during Johnson's administration, whenever members of the in-group began to express doubts—as some of them certainly did—they were treated in a rather standardized way that effectively "domesticated" them through subtle social pressures. The dissenter was made to feel at home, providing he lived up to two restrictions: first, that he did not voice his doubts to outsiders and thus play into the hands of the opposition; and second, that he kept his criticisms within the bounds of acceptable deviation, not challenging any of the fundamental assumptions of the group's prior commitments. One "domesticated dissenter" was Bill Moyers, a close adviser of President Johnson. When Moyers arrived at a meeting, Thomson tells us, the President greeted him with, "Well, here comes Mr. Stop-the-Bombing." Undersecretary of State George Ball, who became a critic of the escalation decisions, was similarly domesticated for a time and became known as "the inhouse devil's advocate on Vietnam." From time to time he was encouraged to "speak his piece . . . and there was minimal unpleasantness." The upshot, Thomson says, was that "the club remained intact."

From the standpoint of reducing tension and bolstering morale within "the club," the subtle domestication process may work well, both for the dissenter and for the rest of the group. The nonconformist can feel that he is still accepted as a member in good standing. Unaware of the extent to which he is being influenced by the majority, he has the illusion that he is free to speak his mind. If on occasion he goes too far, he is warned about his deviation in an affectionate or joking way and is reminded only indirectly of his potentially precarious status by the labels the others give him ("Mr. Stop-the-Bombing," "our favorite dove."). The others in the group, as Thomson says, feel satisfied about giving full consideration to the opposing position and can even pat themselves on the back for being so democratic about tolerating open dissent. Nevertheless, the domesticated dissenter repeatedly gets the message that there is only a very small piece of critical territory he can tread safely and still remain a member in good standing. He knows that if he is not careful he will reach the boundary beyond which he risks being branded as having lost his "effectiveness."

In this connection, we wonder why two of the domesticated dissenters within Johnson's in-group—George Ball and Bill Moyers—unexpectedly resigned from their posts and left Washington in 1966. A similar question arises about the departure of McGeorge Bundy in 1967 and Robert McNamara in 1968. Did these men leave for purely personal reasons that had nothing to do with their criticisms of the escalation policy? Were they perhaps fired by President Johnson—without the consent of his other advisers—because he was dissatisfied with their work or because he was offended by their criticisms? *Or was the departure of any of these formerly domesticated dissenters a result of a group process, involving collective pressures from most or all other members of the in-group because of violation of a group norm—the taboo against challenging the war policies to*

which the group had previously committed itself? If the evidence points to an affirmative answer to the last question, indicating that one or more of the dissenters became casualties of group pressures, we shall have some strong support for the groupthink hypothesis.

These are not rhetorical questions. Several alternative hypotheses could account for the departure of the domesticated dissenters. The groupthink hypothesis, though one plausible explanation, cannot yet be evaluated as being more valid than (for example) the possibility that the President got rid of these men not as the leader acting on behalf of the group but solely on his own initiative, without the support of the majority of his close advisers. It is even conceivable that the inner circle was split into factions and that a coalition of (for example) the Joint Chiefs of Staff and Walt Rostow won the support of the President at the expense of an opposing faction that was pushing for deescalation. We cannot expect to be in a position to evaluate the applicability of the groupthink hypothesis to the handling of dissenters among Johnson's advisers until more candid observations become available from the men who left the group and from the core insiders such as Johnson, Rusk, Rostow, Wheeler, and Helms. Even more valuable would be detailed minutes of their meetings, specifying who said what about each of the issues raised by the domesticated dissenters. In the meantime; we have to make do with the observations already at hand.

THE WAYS OF A TRANSGRESSOR: EXIT ROBERT McNAMARA

Fortunately, a detailed account has been published of how Secretary of Defense McNamara was precipitously removed from his position as the second most powerful member of the Johnson administration. The story comes from Townsend Hoopes, whose position as undersecretary of the Air Force brought him in frequent contact with McNamara during the Secretary's last months in office. Hoopes was in a position to make firsthand observations of events at the Pentagon, but, regrettably, he does not inform us about his sources of information concerning what McNamara and others said at high-level meetings of the President's advisory group, in which the undersecretary was not a participant. If Hoopes' statements prove to be accurate, we shall be led to conclude that McNamara was a domesticated dissenter who, despite desperate attempts to remain a loyal member of Johnson's team, was eliminated from the government because his repeated efforts to bring about a policy change in the direction of deescalation of the Vietnam War could not be tolerated by what Hoopes calls the "gathering of homogeneous hawks."

In the spring of 1967, according to Hoopes, the inner group of advisers was nearly unanimous in supporting the Vietnam War policy, the one dissenter being McNamara. The book on the Pentagon Papers prepared by *The New York Times* contains a considerable amount of documentary evidence of McNamara's dissent:

> Mr. McNamara's disillusionment with the war has been reported previously, but the depth of his dissent from established policy is fully documented for the first time in the Pentagon study, which he commissioned on June 17, 1967.
>
> The study details how this turnabout by Mr. McNamara—originally a leading advocate of the bombing policy and, in 1965, a confident believer that American intervention would bring the Vietcong insurgency under control—opened a deep policy rift in the Johnson Administration.
>
> The study does not specifically say, however, that his break with established policy led President Johnson to nominate him on November 28, 1967, as president of the World Bank and to replace him as Secretary of Defense.

There are many indications that throughout the spring of 1967 McNamara went through considerable turmoil after he had concluded that the others in the group were wrong in assuming that the North Vietnamese could be bombed into coming to the negotiating table. According to some reports, supposedly originating with his wife, he was "at war with himself" and up half the night trying to decide what he ought to do.

A highly revealing episode occurred shortly after McNamara had presented some impressive facts about the ineffectiveness of the bombings to a Senate investigating committee. President Johnson was displeased by McNamara's statement and made bitter comments about his giving this information to the Senators. The President complained to one Senator, "that military genius, McNamara, has gone dovish on me." To someone on his staff in the White House, the President spoke more heatedly, accusing the Secretary of Defense of playing right into the hands of the enemy, on the grounds that his statement would increase Hanoi's bargaining power. "Venting his annoyance to a member of his staff, he drew the analogy of a man trying to sell his house, while one of the sons of the family went to the prospective buyer to point out that there were leaks in the basement." This line of thought strongly suggests that in his own mind Johnson regarded his ingroup of policy advisers as a family and its leading dissident member as an irresponsible son who was sabotaging the family's interests. Underlying this revealing imagery seem to be two implicit assumptions that epitomize groupthink: We are a good group, so any deceitful acts we perpetrate are fully justified. Anyone in the group who is unwilling to distort the truth to help us is disloyal.

Hoopes describes how with each passing month McNamara was gradually eased out of his powerful position, finding himself less and less welcome at the White House, until finally he was removed from his high office in "a fast shuffle" by the President, who was "confident that he would go quietly and suffer the indignity in silence." Once McNamara was removed from the group, Hoopes concludes, the members could once again enjoy complete unity and relatively undisturbed confidence in the soundness of their war policy. During the months following McNamara's nonvoluntary departure, increasing numbers of intelligence specialists and other experts were urging a reappraisal on the basis of new evidence following the surprise Tet offensive by the supposedly defeated Vietcong in early 1968. But, according to Hoopes, the in-group, having become temporarily homogeneous once again, avoided calling them in for consultation and apparently did not study their reports.

The members' sense of confidence may have been maintained for a time by Rostow's effective mindguarding, which went far beyond the call of duty. Hoopes claims that during the last year of Johnson's administration, as discontent with the Vietnam War was growing throughout America and even within the military bureaucracy, Rostow cleverly screened the inflow of information and used his power to keep dissident experts away from the White House. This had the intended effect of preventing the President and some of his advisers from becoming fully aware of the extent of disaffection with the war and of the grounds for it. The group managed to discount all the strong pressures from prestigious members of their own political party and even from former members of the White House group (such as McGeorge Bundy) until after a new member of the Tuesday Lunch Group—Clark Clifford, who replaced McNamara as Secretary of Defense—unexpectedly became convinced of the soundness of the deescalation position. (Clifford had been brought in as a dependable hawk who would restore unity to the group). Relatively unhampered by loyalties to the old group, Clifford reported to Hoopes and the rest of his revitalized staff at the Pentagon that at the daily meetings on Vietnam in the White House he was outnumbered 8 to 1. But Clifford fought hard and well, according to Hoopes. During this period other

powerful influences may also have been at work to induce Secretary of State Rusk and others in the group to take account, belatedly, of the numerous persuasive reasons for modifying their policy. The transformation culminated in the unprecedented speech from the White House on March 31, 1968, when, with tears in his eyes, President Johnson announced that he was deescalating the war in Vietnam and would not seek reelection.

If Hoopes' account of the way McNamara and other nonconformists were dealt with is corroborated by subsequent testimony from other observers and by documentary records, we shall have strong evidence that at least during the last half of 1967, the failure of Johnson's in-group to take account of the growing signs that its Vietnam policy required drastic revision was a product of groupthink. The hypothesis leads us to ask questions about other symptoms of groupthink, such as striving for unanimous agreement and willingness to take serious risks on the basis of a shared illusion of invulnerability.

UNANIMITY WITHIN THE GROUP

In the Pentagon Papers, the Department of Defense analysts say that "from the September [1964] meeting forward, there was little basic disagreement among the principals [the term the study uses for the senior policy-makers] on the need for military operations against the North." Lyndon B. Johnson, however, says in his memoirs that sometimes there were marked disagreements among his advisers. But the instances he describes seem limited to periods when more than one member of the group was proposing a temporary halt in the bombing as a move toward peace. For example, at a meeting on December 18, 1965, when McNamara, Rusk, and Bundy argued for a bombing pause in order to pursue Soviet Ambassador Dobrynin's proposal for diplomatic discussions with Hanoi, the military men and others gave opposing arguments that were "equally persuasive," according to Johnson, and it was "another of those 51–49 decisions that . . . keep [the President] awake late at night." In contrast, Johnson emphasizes the unanimous agreement of the group in his descriptions of six meetings at which major escalation decisions were recommended—on September 9, 1964; February 6 and 8, 1965; July 27, 1965; January 31, 1966; and September 28, 1967. On the last of these dates, for example, the issue was whether to speed deployment of American troops to Vietnam, as requested by General Westmoreland. Johnson's only comment is, "All my advisers agreed that we should carry out this acceleration."

Henry Graff, when interviewing members of the Tuesday Lunch Group, was impressed by the repeated emphasis on unanimity expressed by each of them. George Ball, when asked in 1966 about his opposition to bombing North Vietnam, took pains to affirm his basic agreement with the rest of the group. "The one thing we have to do," Ball resolutely told Graff, "is to win this damned war." He added that until the commitment of a large number of troops was made six months earlier, other options may have been open, but now "there is no longer any useful argument to be made about current policies." Ball seems to have become so domesticated at the time of the interview that we can hardly believe he was still a dissenter.

Confidence in ultimate victory despite repeated setbacks and failures was another theme in the interviews. For example, in January 1968 Rostow told his fellow-historian with complete certainty, "History will salute us." On this point, Graff's interviews bear out an admission made by Bill Moyers after he had resigned from his post in the White House: "There was a confidence," Moyers said, "it was never bragged about, it was just there—a residue, perhaps of the confrontation over the missiles in Cuba—that when the chips were really down, the other people would fold."

OVERLOOKING THE RISKS

The Department of Defense study, in disagreement with Ellsberg's claim that the administration was never optimistic when major escalation decisions were made, indicates that the members of the policy-making group were overoptimistic about defeating North Vietnam by means of bombing raids during 1964 and early 1965. In the book on the Pentagon Papers published by *The New York Times,* Neil Sheehan's summary of the Defense Department study states that in November 1964 the air war against North Vietnam was expected "to last two to six months during which Hanoi was apparently expected to yield." Despite momentary periods of pessimism and gloom about setbacks, according to Chester Cooper, a great deal of overoptimism was manifested from 1964 up until the last several months of the Johnson administration:

> The optimistic predictions that flowered from time to time . . . reflected genuinely held beliefs. While occasional doubts crossed the minds of some, perhaps all [senior policy-makers] the conviction that war would end "soon" and favorably was clutched to the breast like a child's security blanket. Views to the contrary were not favorably received. . . . We thought we could handle Vietnam without any noticeable effect on our economy or society. . . .
>
> Because the war was likely to be over "soon," there was also a reluctance to make any substantial changes in the bureaucratic structure. There would be no special institutional arrangements for staffing the war, for implementing or following up decisions.

We know, of course, that Johnson's Tuesday Lunch Group did not have a carefree attitude about the dangers of extending the Vietnam War to the point where China or Russia might become directly involved. During certain periods, especially before 1966, the members were so keenly aware of the vulnerability of America's forces in Vietnam and of the possible fall of the government of South Vietnam that they wanted to avoid engaging in peace negotiations for fear of having little or no bargaining power. The members of the group continued to be aware of the precariousness of South Vietnam's cooperation with America's anti-Communist efforts throughout the entire Johnson administration. Thus it certainly cannot be said that they maintained grossly overoptimistic illusions about the overall security of the American military enterprise in Vietnam. Yet at times there may have been a more limited type of illusion that inclined the policy-makers to be willing to take long-shot gambles. Many observations suggest that the group experienced some temporary lapses in realism about the grave material, political, and moral risks of escalation. The lapses were caused by shared illusions that "everything will go our way, none of the dangers will seriously affect us."

Observations bearing directly on the risky decisions made by Johnson's Tuesday Lunch Group during 1966 are reported by David Kraslow and Stuart Loory, two well-known journalists who made a careful study of the public record of the Vietnam War and interviewed more than forty United States officials who knew something about the inside story. In their account of what went on behind the scenes when Johnson's Tuesday Lunch Group was making its crucial decisions, we can identify many clear indications of a sense of unwarranted complacency about the ultimate success of the group's chosen policy. If their account proves to be substantially verified by subsequent historical analysis, it will raise a number of additional questions concerning the role of groupthink in the policy-makers' willingness to take extreme risks with regard to provoking an all-out war with China and Russia, presumably on the basis of a shared assumption that events were bound to come out the way they hoped.

Throughout 1966 the Tuesday Lunch Group was primarily concerned about selecting bombing targets in North Vietnam. Kraslow and Loory describe how the group attempted to evaluate every proposed target by following a special procedure, which the members felt would enable them to take account of all the relevant criteria:

> As a result of all the staff work in the Pentagon and at the State Department, the authorization requests for each target were reduced to a single sheet of paper—a kind of report card—on which the suggested strikes were described in summary. Each individual sheet contained a checklist for four items:
> 1. The military advantage of striking the proposed target.
> 2. The risk of American aircraft and pilots in a raid.
> 3. The danger that the strike might widen the war by forcing other countries into the fighting.
> 4. The danger of heavy civilian casualties.
> At the Tuesday lunch, President Johnson and his advisers worked over each of the target sheets like schoolteachers grading examination papers. Each of the men graded each of the targets in the four categories.
>
> The decisions were made on the basis of averaged-out grades. . . .
>
> In this manner the President and his principal advisers, working over a lunch table in the White House, showed their intense concern with individual road junctions, clusters of trucks and structures down to small buildings in a land thousands of miles away. Their obvious concern lent great weight to the contention that never has more care been taken in making sure that limited war-making objectives were not being exceeded.

Did the group's ritualistic adherence to a standardized procedure for selecting targets induce the members to feel justified in their destructive way of dealing with the Vietnamese people? After all, the danger of heavy civilian casualties from United States air attacks was being taken into account on their checklists. Did they allow the averaging to obscure the fact that they were giving the greatest weight to military objectives, with relatively little regard for humanitarian considerations or for political effects that could have serious consequences for United States national security? *Did the members of the group share the illusion that they were being vigilant about all aspects of United States policy in Vietnam, while confining their efforts almost solely to the routines of selecting bombing targets?*

The great need for vigilance, of course, derived from the danger that a bombing attack would provoke Russia or China to transform the Vietnam War into the third world war. Although this risk was on the members' checklist, on at least one occasion, according to Kraslow and Loory, this consideration was given less importance than the supposed advantages of striking the target. In the late spring of 1966, the Tuesday Lunch Group authorized, for the first time, the bombing of the large petroleum-storage depot in the Hanoi-Haiphong area, even though the members were informed that Soviet ships were located dangerously close to the target area in the harbor at Haiphong. The rationale for this risky decision was that the bombing might push the government of North Vietnam to begin negotiations under conditions favorable to the United States. Throughout the spring of 1966, American government officials had repeatedly tried to find out if the enemy was ready to work out a peace settlement. Ambassador Lodge reported from Saigon that he had some indications that the bombing raids and supply difficulties were creating a strong desire in Hanoi for peace talks. With this information in mind and with full awareness that Soviet ships might accidentally be sunk, the Tuesday Lunch Group decided that the time was ripe for a severe blow in the vicinity of the enemy's major harbor. This decision must have involved much more than mere wishful thinking about the ultimate military and political success of bombing North Vietnam. If Kraslow and Loory are reporting accurately, all members of the group knew the venture was precarious and could bring America to the brink of war with the Soviet Union. The Defense Department analysts who prepared the Pentagon Papers say that the execution message sent to the commander in chief of Pacific forces was "a remarkable document, attesting in detail to the political sensitivity of the strikes."

If the air attack was so politically sensitive, why was it authorized in the first place? *Was this decision to carry out the bombing raid (despite the risk of provoking the Soviet Union to enter the war) based on a flimsy sense of invulnerability shared by the members of the group while they were conferring?*

We are not informed about how complacent or perturbed the members felt when they were making the decision, but we are told that subsequently the leading participant, when he was alone, became deeply agitated as he thought about the riskiness of the decision. President Johnson on the night the raid was to be executed (June 29, 1966) was too upset to sleep.

> For months afterward, President Johnson would tell occasional visitors how he worried that night that the raids would somehow go wrong and an errant bomb would strike a Soviet ship in Haiphong harbor and start World War III.
>
> He worried so much that his daughter, Luci, returning home from a date with her fiance, Pat Nugent, urged the President to pray. She . . . urged her father to seek solace in the [Catholic] church [to which she belonged]. . . . At 10:30 P.M. a waiting Dominican monk saw two black limousines drive up to the entrance of the neo-Gothic building. The President, Mrs. Johnson, Luci and Nugent stepped out of one car; a detail of Secret Service men, from the other.
>
> The entire group entered the dim, empty church. The presidential party dropped to its knees and prayed silently.
>
> Back in the White House, the President remained awake most of the night, awaiting the final reports on the raids. At 4:30 A.M., satisfied that no great mishap had occurred, he went to sleep.

Did the President's anxiety about the risks arise only when he was alone, when the members of the group were not available to reassure

*him about the dangerous action they had col-
lectively authorized? During the day or so preceding the scheduled bombing (when it could
have been called off) did he set aside his deep
concerns about the danger of provoking the
outbreak of World War III out of a sense of
commitment to the group? Did he abstain from
using his presidential powers to cancel the
dangerous mission or to call another meeting of*
the group to reconsider the decision because
he felt that any move toward reversal might be
regarded as a violation of the group's taboo
against raising doubts about his prior decisions? Unfortunately, Lyndon B. Johnson is less
than candid in his memoirs, *The Vantage Point*.
He makes no mention of the episode. Perhaps
these questions will be answered later in a more
revealing biography.

WATERGATE AS A CASE STUDY IN MANAGEMENT

MAX WAYS

Watergate will not become, as some of those hurt by it have suggested, a mere footnote in history. For generations ahead, political scientists, lawyers, and moralists will be sorting out this jumble of facts, quasi-facts, confessions, lies, and accusations. Since it involves organized activity, Watergate can also be approached as a study in management.

The prime measure of management is effectiveness—when expressed as a relation of benefit to cost. Although neither benefits nor costs need be monetary, effectiveness is a frankly pragmatic test, separated from larger considerations of legality and morality. Speaking managerially, one gang of assasins may be judged "better" than a rival gang. One monastery may be judged "better" than another although both pursue high ends with equal ardor. A well-run gang of assassins may even be "better"—managerially—than a sloppy monastery.

That kind of statement does not imply that management in real life has nothing to do with morality. Like any other specialized approach, a managerial analysis is incapable of expressing the whole truth about a messy mass of phenomena from which the material under study has been selected. A look at Watergate as management, then, is not meant to evade or supersede judgments made from political or legal or moral viewpoints. On the contrary, a management analysis may throw some peripheral light on larger issues, and vice versa.

AN EXECUTIVE'S NIGHTMARE

Managerially, Watergate is an obvious disaster area. Its participants—whoever they may be assumed to be—incurred "costs" so much larger than "benefits" that it would be hard to think of an organized peacetime operation with an effectiveness rating farther on the wrong side of zero. Bad luck will not begin to explain the Watergate calamity. No matter which of

Source: From "Watergate as a Case Study in Management" by Max Ways, in *Fortune Magazine*. Reprinted by permission of *Fortune Magazine;* © 1973 Time Inc.

many possible assumptions is adopted about how much Nixon knew at what "points in time," Watergate from its start to the present reeks of mismanagement.

Especially conspicuous are defects in the lifeblood of organizations: accurate communication. . . . The assumption that Nixon knew as little as he says he did, represents a manager's nightmare: the wishes (or presumed wishes) of the chief executive are magnified and distorted as they move down through his hierarchy to the plane of action; on the other hand, information about what is actually going on is diminished as it moves toward the chief executive. The well-known management malady called constipated feedback seems to have been especially severe in the White House during the period of the cover-up when the President, on his own version of events, was isolated from both the activities of his aides and from rising public concern.

No doubt the universal managerial problem of communication is particularly difficult in the White House, where awe of presidential power can foster both overkill in efforts to serve and undue reticence in reporting unpleasant information. Such tendencies must be countered by presidential vigilance. After all, the essence of any President's job is to stay in touch with the people. The main function of his staff is to help him do that. When the staff became more of a barrier than a conduit, failure in a central responsibility occurred.

AN OVERCAPITALIZED ENTERPRISE

But this is only one of a hundred managerial flaws that can be identified in the Watergate record. Organizational objectives were ill selected and ill defined. Choice of people, that key management function, was poor, not so much in terms of their over-all quality but rather in the casting for the particular roles they played, somewhere a personnel manual must exist that warns against slotting the likes of

Liddy, Hunt, and Dean in the operational spots they came to occupy. Coordination was weak. Cooperators, who needed to communicate, didn't. The enterprise was so overcapitalized that money was recklessly sloshed around in a way that facilitated detection. The burglaries were overmanned; nobody can argue with the judgment of the former New York cop, Anthony Ulasewicz, that professionals "would not have walked in with an army." Indeed, analysis of Watergate can be discouraged or misled by the very richness of its pathology. So many people at so many levels in and around the White House made so many different kinds of mistakes that the observer is first tempted to say that this was the stupidest lot of managers ever assembled.

That lazy hypothesis is demolished by the plain fact that neither Richard Nixon nor the men around him are stupid—managerially or otherwise. Nixon is believed by some shrewd observers of government to be the most management-minded of recent Presidents. Those who viewed the parade of witnesses before the Ervin committee knew they were listening to intelligent men. Management analysis of Watergate, then, must turn upon the question of why officials, whose ability ranged from average to very high, made so many mistakes.

Much of the answer must lie in the ambience of the group, the cognitive and emotional patterns that permeated and shaped its organizational style. Such a collective atmosphere is not necessarily the exact sum of the attitudes, ideas, suppositions, desires, and values of the individuals who make up the group. Every organization has its own character, its own way of acting and reacting, and this quality powerfully colors what its members feel, think, say, and do within the organization. We will dig around in some Watergate material, starting at the bottom with the burglaries themselves, in an attempt to find the poisoned spring from which so much error flowed.

Hindsight makes it perfectly clear that nobody in or around the White House should have dabbled in burglary. But one of the attributes of management is supposed to be foresight. The quality of the decision to embark upon burglary must be appraised on the basis of what the deciders knew—or could have known—at the time of decision. The question may be cast in a strictly managerial form, leaving aside consideration of legality and morality: should an organization, not usually in the burglary business, diversify its activites in that direction?

THE BASIC ECONOMY OF BURGLARY

Superficially, the prospect may seem inviting, just as people who pay restaurant checks are often seduced into believing that the restauranteur has an automatic and infallible surplus of benefits over costs. (A little research would show that more than half of new restaurants fail within a year.) White House staffers (no career burglars among them) were, like most of us, victims or potential victims of burglary. From that viewpoint, the burglar's profit seems easy and assured. Again, a little research into the burglary industry would have disclosed a repellent picture.

Though the number of burglaries in the U.S. is high and rising (2,345,000 in 1972), the curve of growth has been flattening out—and no wonder. Total cost to the victims was an impressive $722 million (or $308 per job). But burglars, because of the severe markdown traditional in thieves' markets, do not gain nearly as much as their victims lose. The actual take is probably closer to $200 per job, and this often has to be split among two or more perpetrators.

In the vast majority of burglaries, operating costs are so low as to be negligible. But risks, which are costs *in posse,* are formidable. While an individual netting $150 per job would have to commit fifty burglaries a year to achieve a modest income of $7,500 (tax-free, to be sure), the basic risk statistics of the industry indicate that one burglary in every five ends up with an arrest. Among adults arrested, half of those charged with burglary are convicted. Consequent unemployment and other costs reinforce the conclusion that burglary is not an activity that commends itself to mature and prudent people. No doubt that explains why half of all those arrested for burglary are under eighteen years old; the other half includes a high proportion of drug addicts, school dropouts, and persons otherwise disadvantaged and/or disturbed.

TARGET SELECTION: POOR

As every manager knows, attractive "special situations" sometimes appear in even those industries that are statistically most bleak. In the case of the Watergate sequence of burglaries, we have to ask whether the specific rewards that could reasonably be expected were so great or the specific risks so low as to overbalance the general probability that shows burglary to be a game for losers.

The sad truth is that the Watergate burglaries were "special situations" only in a negative sense: their prospective rewards were lower and their operating costs and contingent costs (risks) were both very much higher than in the modal U.S. burglary. The highest expectable benefit that could have been gained from the break-in at the office of Daniel Ellsberg's psychiatrist would have been a file containing otherwise unobtainable personal information about him, information that might have been used (although it isn't clear how) to discredit him or to stop leaks. None of the White House deciders paused to note: (1) that the Pentagon papers case turned on legal and political issues to which Ellsberg's personality and motives were largely irrelevant; (2) that knowledge of Ellsberg's emotional make-up would not have contributed to solving the general problem of Washington leaks, which derive from many different kinds of people, few of whom bear a psychological resemblance to Ellsberg; (3) that since Ellsberg is not a notably secretive man, lots of personal information about him, for what it was worth, could have been gathered, free of risk, around Harvard Yard, around the Pentagon, and around the Rand Corp. From the burglary at the psychiatrist's office that promised such meager rewards, the burglars got, in fact, precisely nothing.

Nevertheless, the same team with some unhelpful additions was retooled to break into the Democratic National Committee. Once again, target selection was deplorable. Here the main mission was to bug the phone of Lawrence O'Brien, a man of probity and circumspection, two qualities often found together—although some barefoot moralizers insist virtue has no need of prudence. Public officials and politicians have been wary of telephones ever since 1876 when Alexander Graham Bell, demonstrating his gadget in Philadelphia, unwittingly startled the visiting Emperor of Brazil. An O'Brien friend says: "If you had a verbatim transcript of every telephone conversation Larry has engaged in since he was nineteen years old, you wouldn't have enough to embarrass him." In short, the break-in at the Watergate office building had an expectable reward very close to zero.

THE PREVALENCE OF OGRES

These footless ventures would remain forever incomprehensible unless we turned to the beliefs and emotional patterns of the participants. These attitudes were shaped in part by the general ambience that enveloped the White House and the Committee to Re-elect the President, and that ambience included a lot of fear, suspicion, and hostility. Although the word "paranoia," used by many people, is too strong, it is correct to say that a high level of self-pity influenced the style of the Nixon White House.

The seeds of this attitude were sown long before Watergate. Self-pity was evident, though excusable, in many of Nixon's periods of adver-

sity, and it had not melted away in the warm sun of ambition fulfilled. The public utterances of President Nixon, and those he encouraged Vice President Agnew to make in the early years of their first terms, often contained a strong theme of complaint against the unfairness of adversaries. The internal atmosphere of the White House was even more marked by this air of hostility and suspicion toward such outside bodies as Congress, the federal bureaucracy, and the press. All Presidents have had adversaries, but no other White House institutionalized its hostility by keeping, as Nixon's did, an "enemies list."

The U.S. organizes its political life, as well as its business life, through competition. Not only do we have competing parties, but government has many separate elements that are simultaneously in cooperation and competition with one another. Among the people themselves we don't expect—and don't want—a placid homogeneity of outlook and aims. In our kind of pluralist politics, a degree of combativeness, an awareness of adversaries, is inevitable and constructive. But there's a line, blurred but real, beyond which a normal self-assertion in the face of opposition can move over into either arrogance or self-pity.

Many business managers have seen in their own sphere examples of the damage that can be done when this blurred line is crossed. It is desirable, for instance, that a sales force be on its toes, alert to spot and to counter moves by its opposition. A given sales force can become too proud of its competitive ability and be made vulnerable by overconfidence. Or it can become demoralized by the pressure of competition. A sensitive executive would worry if his salesmen were constantly telling him and one another about the perfidy of their competitors, dwelling on their dirty tricks, exaggerating their unfairness. In that ambience his own salesmen would have a built-in excuse for poor performance, or they might goad themselves into foolish and imprudent acts.

The nearest business equivalent of the Watergate folly was the great electrical price-fixing conspiracy uncovered in 1962. The question that then ran through the business world was: how could experienced executives in well-run companies do anything so stupid? Much of the answer lay in the ambience of the conspirators. They felt overpressured—by their bosses, by rising costs, by government regulations they considered unfair. One executive in the industry, trying to explain his colleagues' gross misjudgment, told a *Fortune* reporter at the time that the conspirators did what they did because they were "distressed men."

The distress, of course, was not visible in their objective condition of opulence and success. The distress was in their minds. So, too, powerful men in the White House came to think of themselves as inhabitants of a beleaguered and distressed city, surrounded by enemies whose strength and malice they exaggerated. An intense will to win, coupled with the belief that the situation is desperate, can release a lot of energizing adrenalin. If it goes too far, such a state of mind can also trigger reckless misjudgments. Whom the gods would destroy they first make unduly sorry for themselves.

A SURPLUS OF SINCERITY

Nixon's White House, of course, was not the first to overstress the power and menace of its adversaries. Franklin Roosevelt had depicted himself as standing, along with the weak, against the "economic royalists" who, he implied, were really in charge of the country. This tactic was so brilliantly successful that all subsequent Presidents have flirted with it. But in Roosevelt's underdog posture there was always a saving measure of insincerity. He never really believed his histrionic pretense that the dragons he opposed were all that monstrous. Nor did the men around him, cheerfully manipulating the reins of power, lose themselves in the dramatic myth he had created. Nixon's aides, unfortunately, seem to have let the role of victim capture their hearts and minds.

In a culture that prizes justice, fears power, and roots for underdogs, the temptation to cast oneself as a victim is ever present. The average American, when looking privately at his own situation, resists this temptation rather effectively; he knows—most of the time—that he is not doing too badly. But in any public discourse or in any capacity where he represents others, the contemporary American tends toward donning the victim's robe.

Listening to the speeches of businessmen, with their frequent emphasis on the abuse of government and labor-union power, an observer may worry lest their self-pity blind them to the ever expanding scope of action that beckons to business. Spokesmen for blacks or women can express real grievances in terms so extravagant that their followers will not perceive actual opportunities; the result can be stagnation or angry, self-destructive action. This unhappy pattern even extends to sports. One September night this year in Baltimore the managers of both baseball teams were thrown out of the same game for protesting too raucously against the injustice of the umpires. Passionate complaint is the almost unvarying tone of those man-in-the-street interviews cherished by producers of TV news programs. If Americans ever became, in fact, as sorry for themselves as they sound in public discourse, the country as a whole might begin to act as foolishly as the "distressed" men who blindly stumbled into Watergate.

Nixon early recognized the danger in protest run wild. It was he who laudably set out to "bring us together" and admonished us to "lower our voices." One of the deepest ironies of Watergate is the public demoralization that has occurred because the Nixon White House got carried away by its own agonized indignation toward the "unfairness" of its adversaries. The public in 1973 would never have had occasion to "wallow in Watergate" (as the President expressed it) had not the White House, years before, wallowed in self-pity.

ARISTOTLE WOULD UNDERSTAND

Watergate is often referred to as a "tragedy," as indeed it is in the sense that it blasted lives and caused suffering. But Watergate imitates in may other ways the structure of classic tragedy as Aristotle described it. The action of the plot, he said, proceeds from a "flaw" *(hamartia).* This may be either a defect of knowledge (e.g., Oedipus didn't know that his wife, Jocasta, was his mother) or an emotional imbalance (e.g., Medea, filled with woe-is-me, overreacted to Jason's infidelity by killing their children). Sometimes the tragic flaw is a mingling of cognitive and emotional imperfections.

From the flaw emerges *hubris,* which has long been translated as pride or arrogance. But recent scholarship pushes toward a different understanding of *hubris.* Walter Kaufmann in *Tragedy and Philosophy* argues persuasively that *hubris* refers to the quality of the action that proceeds from the flaw; it is not the internal flaw itself. Greek writers used the word *hubris* in referring to rivers that overflow their banks. They applied *hubris* to armies that run riot, indulging in wanton behavior, or to anything—human, animal, vegetable, or inanimate—that rankly transgresses the usual order of its nature.

In the Watergate case, the flaw obviously was not pride, which scorns to slink about by night in other people's offices. If we think of self-pity as the tragic flaw in Watergate, then all the wild imprudence of the consequent actions, the *hubris,* becomes less baffling. The literary analogy may illuminate details of a problem in management analysis.

Act I, Scene I occurs in the summer of 1971, in the ruler's room of state. He is giving urgent orders to members of his staff. The precise content of his instruction is not known to us, but its tone and general import are clear. His government is bedeviled by leaks of information to a press deemed hostile. He invokes his highest responsibility, that in respect to the national security, as he tells them he wants his government sealed against leaks.

So far, there is nothing irrational about the ruler's attitude or the gist of his instruction. Leaks are no trivial matter. They can impair national security—and some have done so. More often they are devices employed by a government official to support a policy he favors, to hurt a rival, or advance his own career. Such leaks sow distrust among officials, inhibit frank discussion, and demoralize government. Now, publication of the Pentagon Papers, a veritable Niagara of a leak, requires drastic and immediate remedy.

At first the plumbers' unit interprets its responsibility in a normal and harmless way. Its members start to carry out a staff assignment to needle the chiefs of line departments and the regular investigatory agencies into greater vigilance against leaks. But progress, if any, is too slow. At this point, the tragic flaw in the spiritual ambience of the White House group begins to manifest itself.

In and around the plumbers' unit, deviation from organizational normality takes two forms. The atmosphere of a besieged city overmotivates the staffers involved. They wish so intensely to succeed in their assigned task that restraints of ordinary prudence drop away. The second manifestation of the flaw is more specifically managerial: they transform a staff function into a line operation. They decide that they themselves will gather the evidence that will retard leaks.

Their master, the President, deploys under his hand the largest, most expensive, and most professional array of investigatory agencies this side of the Soviet border. Yet these agencies are bypassed when the plumbers' unit decides to go into clandestine operations—which is no woods for babes. Neither Egil Krogh nor David Young, who headed the plumbers, had relevant experience in this line of work. Their immediate superior, John Ehrlichman, had no investigatory experience. Liddy, who had worked for the FBI, and Hunt, who had worked for the CIA, did have relevant experience. But many instances are known where individuals can render valuable service within a large professionalized organization and yet be helpless or harmful when working without professional supervision and organized support. In the plumbers' unit, Liddy and Hunt plainly lacked the competence, restraint, and judgment to be found (one hopes) in the organizations that had previously girdled their exuberance.

A former aide to a different President believes that all White House staffs, becoming impatient with the regular line agencies of government, are from time to time tempted to get into operations themselves. They hardly ever do so, however, partly because of what he called "the danger of involving the President." He was talking about possible interventions far less dangerous to the presidential reputation than burglary. Why, then, was the Nixon White House so incautiously willing to bypass the regular agencies and place its honor in the hands of people who knew so little about what they were doing?

SHOULD BUREAUCRATS OBEY?

The decision was almost certainly influenced by an attitude of distrust toward the whole federal bureaucracy. This was one of the areas where members of the Nixon circle felt most sorry for themselves. One expert on government structure remembers a long meeting of Nixon staff men at San Clemente devoted to the question of how to make the bureaucracy more obedient.

A familiar management problem is involved here, as anybody knows who has taken over the top spot in a corporation, or a division, or even a small office. He is likely to have found there men and women who took their own responsibilities seriously and who are entrenched by their specialized competence. A wise executive does not try to command the servile obedience of such people. His responsibility for coordinating their efforts and changing the over-all direction of the organization can only be achieved through the patient arts of leadership. He has to talk, to listen, to persuade and be persuaded.

But from the first the Nixon inner circle seems to have misunderstood the nature of the difficulty. It saw bureaucratic resistance as arising from political philosophy. No doubt, most civil servants are Democrats and maybe even "liberals." But this is not as important a truth as the Nixon people thought it. Presidents Kennedy and Johnson also had trouble with the bureaucracy. A Nixon official who has been most effective in his leadership of civil servants is Secretary of the Treasury George Shultz, whose own political philosophy happens to be most remote from the presumed liberalism of the bureaucrats. Shultz talks and listens to his experts. Shultz does not withdraw into injured and persecuted silence because they won't obey him. In short, Shultz follows a pattern widespread among managers of corporations who anticipate resistance from their experts. They do not perceive it as disloyalty or hostility. They know that dealing with such resistance is just what they are hired to do.

WHEN THE BIG SCENE WAS BUNGLED

But the Nixon Administration, with some distinguished exceptions, had never been notable for strong, independent personalities, secure enough to listen to the experts below and speak candidly to the chief above. The White House staff, the citadel of the beleaguered city, seems to have been chosen more for its zeal to protect the boss than for ability to serve him with information and argument. This criterion owed part of its origin to the tragic flaw, and it resulted in disaster at a crucial decision time.

Classic tragedy moves toward a point of

"recognition," the scene where the flaw in all its horror is revealed to the audience and the dramatis personae. In the Watergate sequence, that point was reached in the summer of 1972 after the arrests, after the disclosure that large sums of money had been "laundered" in Mexico. Clearly, these were no ordinary burglars. They had backing at high levels.

If at that point the President or his former Attorney General had publicly recognized that a serious error had occurred, Watergate would never have grown to anything approaching its ultimate proportions. Such a public recognition would have been painful, but it almost certainly would not have cost Nixon either the election or the respect of several millions of Americans who lost confidence in him this year.

Nixon and the men around him bungled the recognition scene. Or to put the same thought in business terms, they failed to face the hard decision to cut their losses. Exactly what went on in the White House in the year following June, 1972, is still far from clear. But on any assumption about those months, there was serious managerial trouble in two big areas: personnel and communications.

In the most unlikely case, that Nixon knew exactly what was going on at every step, he was picking the wrong people to do the wrong things. On the much more likely assumption that Nixon didn't know much about the cover-up efforts, then those who were involved in it badly needed some coordinator—and they needed one with more authority, prudence, experience, and fiber than John Dean.

As a group, the White House staff contained too few men of the caliber and courage to make Nixon face the situation that the public, Nixon's audience, had long since recognized. On one version of events, it was not until April 15, 1973, that anybody told Nixon just how bad the situation was and what immediate steps he had to take. That messenger was Henry Petersen, not a member of Nixon's staff but one of the despised careerists, who had never spoken to the President until he stood before him in tennis shoes and old clothes on a Sunday afternoon and finally got the bad news across.

Nixon understands organizational information systems better, perhaps, than any previous President. But he showed in the Watergate sequence no sign that he grasped the most important fact about such systems: they are all far short of perfect. A prudent executive keeps testing his organization's ability to tell him what he needs to know about its own activities. A classical management story on this point goes back to 1924 and its hero is Alfred P. Sloan. In the spring of that year General Motors plants were turning our cars much faster than salesmen were getting rid of them. The established channels of information failed to bring this bad news to corporate headquarters. Corporate calamity was averted only because Sloan visited dealers in St. Louis, Kansas City, and Los Angeles, and himself counted the cars that had piled up in their lots. Nixon, on his version of what happened during the cover-up, never got down to personal investigation of widely published reports of what was being done in his name.

THE PRESS *IS* UNFAIR

It is quite possible that Nixon simply did not believe what the media were reporting concerning the cover-up because he had grown so accustomed to considering himself the victim of a press hostile to him.

The press is unfair to Nixon in a sense more fundamental than he knows. It has been unfair to all recent Presidents. It is unfair to businessmen, labor leaders, and everybody else responsible for carrying out action in a world whose complexity makes for dull writing. The inadequacy of the press in explaining to the public actual working of government processes may be one of the most serious defects in contemporary democracy. Compared to this problem, the additional fact that many influential journalists don't much like Richard Nixon pales toward insignificance.

The Nixon White House diminishes its chances of constructive coverage by its attitude of pained withdrawal from the media. The exceptions demonstrate this general point. Henry Kissinger, who talks frequently and (relatively) frankly with reporters, manages to get through the media to the public. Nixon himself, on the rare occasions when he endures face-to-face contact with the media, handles press conferences with verve. His San Clemente press conference of August 22 was one of the few effective White House moves in the long Watergate sequence.

Nixon's relations with Congress also have that hurt and withdrawn look. Before he came to office, Congress was already becoming restless under what many of its members considered the undue power of the executive branch. Nixon was bound to have trouble with Congress, no matter what its political coloration might have been. But Nixon seems to have taken congressional opposition as a personal affront. In its day-to-day contact with individual Congressmen, the Nixon White House has been less active, less persuasively communicative than previous Administrations, including Eisenhower's. In public Nixon has, as a President must, often summarized what was wrong about the record of Congress and what was right about his own record. But in his relations with Congress he has not, as they say in Seville, worked close to the bull.

WHY WE REMEMBER HANNIBAL

Deplorable tendencies in Congress, in the bureaucracy, and in the media are easier to denounce than to overcome. A President, nevertheless, will be appraised by how much headway he makes against such objective difficulties. Hannibal is remembered for actually crossing the Alps, not for whatever Carthaginian maledictions that he, frustrated in Gaul, might have hurled at the "unfair" gradients confronting him.

The flaw that mars Nixon's style in domestic affairs becomes the more glaring when it is limned against his foreign-policy successes. In dealing with Red China and the Soviet Union he has brilliantly demonstrated that he can rise above self-pity. He has studied these offshore adversaries so long and so intently that he can handle the problems they represent much more cooly, objectively, and effectively than he handles the onshore problems represented by Daniel Ellsberg or Larry O'Brien or the federal bureaucracy or the *Washington Post*. Nixon isn't thrown off stride by Peking's or Moscow's "dirty tricks." It never seems to occur to him that Brezhnev or Mao is "unfair." He manages his relations with them like a manager, not with the mien of a wounded deer.

Excessive self-pity is, of course, an emotional and moral flaw. It is often found entwined with an inaccurate cognitive picture of reality. Individuals or groups marked by such a flaw may be handicapped in practical affairs, even in those activities that are put in such specialized pigeonholes as politics or economics or management.

Machiavelli taught the world that politics, for instance, has rules of success that are independent of moral strictures. But he never taught that men who act in politics are to be considered unbound by moral law. Twenty years ago Professor Charles Singleton in a memorable lecture called "The Perspective of Art" pointed to a passage in Machiavelli's *Discourses* as a corrective to the popular view of what the Florentine believed. Machiavelli, in one of those typical passages about what a ruler must do to grasp and hold power, gives an example of some morally horrible but politically effective policies carried out by Philip of Macedon. Then Machiavelli says: "Doubtless these means are

THE SOCIAL ETHICS OF ORGANIZATIONAL BEHAVIOR **361**

cruel and destructive of all civilized life, and neither Christian nor human, and should be avoided by everyone."

Now that politics is clearly recognized as an independent art, any practitioner faces a double hurdle. What he does must be good as politics, but must not be bad as morals. The point is even clearer in the relation of morals to economics. When Alfred Sloan, in the example given above, learned that unsold cars were piling up, he shut down the production lines. As a compassionate man, he regretted the consequent unemployment and suffering. But in the economic circumstances his decision was not immoral. On the contrary, once he knew the facts any other decision would have been economically, managerially, and morally irresponsible.

Allen Dulles, when he was head of the CIA, once told a group of journalists that anyone entering upon his job must leave all moral considerations outside the door. This dangerous proposition is an example of the vulgar misreading of the Machiavellian view. The head of the CIA works in circumstances that ordinary citizens do not encounter. Circumstances change cases, and the head of the CIA may morally do things which an ordinary citizen would have no compelling occasion and no moral right to do. But the head of the CIA must nevertheless weigh the morality of any such act by whatever standards are appropriate to the circumstances.

John Ehrlichman in his testimony indicated that he could think of circumstances involving, say, the threat of nuclear attack, in which a President could justifiably order a burglary. But does this mean that a President, by invoking the name of national security, can order *any* burglary? A weighing of circumstances becomes critical in government morality, as indeed it is in private morality. It is not only managerially shocking but morally shocking that so serious an offense as the Beverly Hills break-in was undertaken in circumstances that did not come within miles of requiring it.

MELANCHOLY EXAMPLE

The moral standards of political life are, indeed, often more strict than those of private life. "Dirty tricks" that may be merely tasteless in undergraduate elections are seriously offensive when plotted by people on a White House staff. All that useless Dick-Tuckery revealed by the Ervin committee is one of the most appalling aspects of the Watergate disclosures. Another, and more melancholy, example is brought to mind by Spiro Agnew's resignation. Many people may not regard an ordinary citizen's failure to report taxable income as one of the graver moral offenses. But when a Vice President of the United States is exposed as having done that, we are all—quite logically—horrified.

In the Watergate sequence, self-pity blinded the participants to dangers that were political, managerial, legal, and moral. As their retribution unfolds, the rest of us may from time to time ask whether our own legitimate resentment against our share of the injustices that all men experience might not be making us so sorry for ourselves that we mismanage our practical affairs.

AIR FORCE A-7D BRAKE PROBLEM

Mr. VANDIVIER. In the early part of 1967, the B. F. Goodrich Wheel & Brake Plant at Troy, Ohio, received an order from the Ling-Temco-Vought Co. of Dallas, Tex., to supply wheels and brakes for the A−7D aircraft, built by LTV for the Air Force.

The tests on the wheels and brakes were to be conducted in accordance with the requirements of military specification Mil−W−5013G as prepared and issued by the U.S. Air Force and to the requirements set forth by LTV Specification Document 204−16−37D.

The wheels were successfully tested to the specified requirements, but the brake, manufactured by Goodrich under BEG part No. 2−1162−3, was unable to meet the required tests.

The laboratory tests specified for the brake were divided into two categories: dynamic brake tests and static brake tests.

The dynamic brake tests basically consisted of 45 simulated normal energy stops, 5 overload energy stops and one worn-brake maximum energy stop, sometimes called a rejected take-off, or RTO.

These simulated stops were to be conducted on one brake assembly with no change in brake lining to be allowed during the test.

In addition, a maximum energy brake stop (or RTO) was to be conducted on a brake containing new linings and still another series of tests called a turnaround capability test was to be performed.

The turnaround capability test consisted of a series of taxis, simulated takeoffs, flight periods and landings, and time schedule for the turnaround test was supplied by LTV to coincide with conditions under which the A−7D brake might operate on a typical mission.

Generally speaking, the brake successfully passed all the static brakes tests, but the brake could not and did not pass any of the dynamic tests I have just described with the exception of the new brake maximum energy stop.

During the first few attempts to qualify the brake to the dynamic tests, the brake ran out of

Source: From the Hearing before the Subcommittee on Economy in Government of the Joint Economic Committee of the Congress of the United States, Ninety-first Congress, August 13, 1969.

362

lining material after a few stops had been completed and the tests were terminated. Attempts were made to secure a lining material that would hold up during the grueling 51-stop test, but to no avail.

Although I had been aware for several months that great difficulty was being experienced with the A−7D brake, it was not until April 11, 1968, almost a full year after qualification testing had begun, that I became aware of how these tests were being conducted.

The 13th attempt at qualification was being conducted under B. F. Goodrich Internal Test No. T-1867.

On the morning of April 11, Richard Gloor, who was the test engineer assigned to the A−7D project, came to me and told me he had discovered that some time during the previous 24 hours, instrumentation used to record brake pressure had *deliberately* been miscalibrated so that while the instrumentation showed that a pressure of 1,000 pounds per square inch had been used to conduct brake stops No. 46 and 47 (two overload energy stops) 1,100 p.s.i. had actually been applied to the brakes. Maximum pressure available on the A−7D is 1,000 p.s.i.

Mr. Gloor further told me he had questioned instrumentation personnel about the miscalibration and had been told they were asked to do so by Searle Lawson, a design engineer on the A−7D.

Chairman PROXMIRE. Is this the gentleman who is with you now, Mr. Vandivier?

Mr. VANDIVIER. That is correct. I subsequently questioned Lawson who admitted he had ordered the instruments miscalibrated at the direction of a superior.

Upon examining the log sheets kept by laboratory personnel I found that other violations of the test specifications had occurred.

For example, after some of the overload stops, the brake had been disassembled and the three stators or stationary members of the brake had been taken to the plant toolroom for rework and during an earlier part of the test, the position of elements within the brake had been reversed in order to more evenly distribute the lining wear.

Additionally, instead of braking the dynamometer to a complete stop as required by military specifications, pressure was released when the wheel and brake speed had decelerated to 10 miles per hour.

The reason for this, I was later told, was that the brakes were experiencing severe vibrations near the end of the stops, causing excessive lining wear and general deterioration of the brake.

All of these incidents were in clear violation of military specifications and general industry practice.

I reported these violations to the test lab supervisor. Mr. Ralph Gretzinger, who reprimanded instrumentation personnel and stated that under no circumstance would intentional miscalibration of instruments be tolerated.

As for the other discrepancies noted in test procedures, he said he was aware they were happening but that as far as he was concerned the tests could not, in view of the way they were being conducted, be classified as qualification tests.

Later that same day, the worn-brake, maximum energy stop was conducted on the brake. The brake was landed at a speed of 161 m.p.h. and the pressure was applied. The dynamometer rolled a distance 16,800 *feet* before coming to rest. The elapsed stopping time was 141 seconds. By computation, this stop time shows the aircraft would have traveled over 3 miles before stopping.

Within a few days, a typewritten copy of the test logs of test T−1867 was sent to LTV in order to assure LTV that a qualified brake was almost ready for delivery.

Virtually every entry in this so-called copy of the test logs was drastically altered. As an example, the stop time for the worn brake maximum energy stop was changed from 141 seconds to a mere 46.8 seconds.

On May 2, 1968 the 14th attempt to qualify the brakes was begun, and Mr. Lawson told me that he had been informed by both Mr. Robert Sink, project manager at Goodrich—I am sorry, Mr. Sink is project manager—and Mr. Russell Van Horn, projects manager at Goodrich, that "Regardless of what the brake does on test, we're going to qualify it."

Chairman PROXMIRE. What was that?

Mr. VANDIVIER. The statement was, "Regardless of what the brake does on test, we're going to qualify it."

He also said that the latest instructions he had received were to the effect that if the data from this latest test turned out worse than did test T−1867, then we would write our report based on T−1867.

Chairman PROXMIRE. The statement was made by whom?

Mr. VANDIVIER. Mr. Lawson told me this statement was made to him by Mr. Robert Sink, projects manager and Mr. Russell Van Horn, project manager.

During this latest and final attempt to qualify the four rotor brake, the same illegal procedures were used as had been used on attempt No. 13. Again after 30 stops had been completed, the positions of the friction members of the brake were reversed in order to more evenly distribute wear.

After each stop, the wheel was removed from the brake and the accumulated dust was blown out.

During each stop, pressure was released when the deceleration had reached 10 miles per hour.

By these and other irregular procedures the brake was nursed along until the 45 normal energy stops had been completed but by this time the friction surfaces of the brakes were almost bare, that is, there was virtually no lining left on the brake.

This lack of lining material introduced another problem.

The pistons which actuate the brake by forcing the friction surfaces together were almost at the end of their allowable travel and it was feared that during the overload stops the pistons might actually pop out of their sockets within the brake, allowing brake fluid to spray the hot surfaces, resulting in fire.

Therefore, a metal spacer was inserted in the brake between the pressure plate and the piston housing.

This spacer served to make up for the lack of friction material and to keep the pistons in place.

In order to provide room for the spacer, the adjuster assemblies were removed from the brake.

The five overload stops were conducted without the adjuster assemblies and with the spacer in place.

After stop number 48—the third overload stop—temperatures in the brake were so high that the fuse plug, a safety device which allows air to escape from the tire to prevent blowout, melted and allowed the tire to deflate.

The same thing happened after stop number 49—the fourth overload stop. Both of these occurrences were highly irregular and in direct conflict with the performance criteria of the military requirements.

Chairman PROXMIRE. I understand you have a picture of this that might help us see it.

Mr. VANDIVIER. Yes.

Mr. PROXMIRE. Do you want to show that to us now?

Mr. VANDIVIER. I was going to show it here just a little bit later.

Chairman PROXMIRE. Go ahead.

Mr. VANDIVIER. For the worn brake maximum energy stop the adjusters were replaced in the brake and a different spacer was used between the pressure plate and the piston housing.

Now I have a copy, a picture of this brake just before it went on the maximum energy test, and here you may see at the top is the additional spacer that has been added in order to get sufficient braking action on the brake.

Chairman PROXMIRE. Who took that picture?

Mr. VANDIVIER. That was taken with a Polaroid camera. I am not sure ———

Chairman PROXMIRE. I think it is only fair to the

committee, Mr. Conable and the committee, to ask you about it later. You go ahead and we will ask questions.

Mr. VANDIVIER. All right.

In addition to these highly questionable practices, a turnaround capability test, or simulated mission test, was conducted incorrectly due to a human error. When the error was later discovered, no corrections were made.

While these tests were being conducted, I was asked by Mr. Lawson to begin writing a qualification report for the brake. I flatly refused and told Mr. Gretzinger, the lab supervisor, who was my superior, that I could not write such a report because the brake had not been qualified.

He agreed and he said that no one in the laboratory was going to issue such a report unless a brake was actually qualified in accordance with the specification and using standard operating procedures.

He said that he would speak to his own supervisor, the manager of the technical services section, Mr. Russell Line, and get the matter settled at once.

He consulted Mr. Line and assured me that both had concurred in the decision not to write a qualification report.

I explained to Lawson that I had been told not to write the report, and that the only way such a report could be written was to falsify test data.

Mr. Lawson said he was well aware of what was required, but that he had been ordered to get a report written, regardless of how or what had to be done.

He stated if I would not write the report he would have to, and he asked if I would help him gather the test data and draw up the various engineering curves and graphic displays which are normally included in a report.

I asked Mr. Gretzinger, my superior, if this was all right and he agreed as long as I was only assisting in the preparation of the data, it would be permissible.

Both Lawson and I worked on the elaborate curves and logs in the report for nearly a month.

During this time we both frankly discussed the moral aspects of what we were doing and we agreed that our actions were unethical and probably illegal.

Several times during that month I discussed the A−7D testing with Mr. Line, and asked him to consult his superiors in Akron, in order to prevent a false qualification report from being issued.

Mr. Line declined to do so and advised me that it would be wise to just do my work and keep quiet.

I told him of the extensive irregularities during testing and suggested that the brake was actually dangerous and if allowed to be installed on an aircraft, might cause an accident.

Mr. Line said he thought I was worrying too much about things which did not really concern me and advised me to just "do what you're told."

About the first of June ———

Chairman PROXMIRE. You skipped one line here.

Mr. VANDIVIER. Yes.

Chairman PROXMIRE. You said "I asked him"

———

Mr. VANDIVIER. Yes. I asked Mr. Line if his conscience would hurt him if such a thing caused the death of a pilot and this is when he replied I was worrying about too many things that did not concern me and advised me to "do what you're told."

About the first of June 1968, Mr. Gretzinger asked if I were finished with the graphic data and said he had been advised by the Chief engineer, Mr. H. C. Sunderman, that when the data was finished it was to be delivered to him—Sunderman—and he would instruct someone in the engineering department to actually write the report.

Accordingly, when I had finished with the data, I gave it to Mr. Gretzinger who immediately took it from the room. Within a few minutes, he was back and was obviously angry.

He said that Mr. Sunderman had told him no one in the engineering department had time to write the report and that we would have to do it ourselves.

At this point, Mr. Line came into the room demanding to know "What the hell is going on." Mr. Gretzinger explained the situation again and said he would not allow such a report to be issued by the lab.

Mr. Line then turned to me and said he was "sick of hearing about this damned report. Write the —— thing and shut up about it."

Chairman PROXMIRE. Let me ask you, you had this in quotes. Did you make a note of this at the time?

Mr. VANDIVIER. Yes.

Chairman PROXMIRE. Do you have your notes with you?

Mr. VANDIVIER. No. I have notes with me, yes. I am not sure if I have this note or not, but I have notes with me.

Chairman PROXMIRE. All right.

Mr. VANDIVIER. When he had left, Mr. Gretzinger and I discussed the position we were in and Mr. Gretzinger said that we both should have resigned a long time ago. He added that there was little to do now except write the report.

Accordingly, I wrote the report, but in the conclusion, I stated that the brake had "not" met either the intent or the requirements of the specifications and was therefore "not" qualified.

When the final report was typewritten and ready for publication, the two "nots" in the conclusion had been eliminated, thereby changing the entire meaning of the conclusion.

I would like to point out at this time the various discrepancies between the military standards and procedures and the qualification tests actually conducted:

1. Brake pressure was cut on all stops at 10 miles per hour and the wheel allowed to coast to a stop.
2. The five overload stops were conducted with a spacer between the pressure plate and the piston housing.

3. The lining carriers used for the test were specially made with an additional 0.030 of an inch lining material. This was done to assure sufficient lining material on the carriers.
4. Stators in the brake were physically reversed after stop 30 and remained in these positions throughout the test.

Mr. Chairman, the next two sentences of my printed statement contain a typographical error, words have been omitted and I would like to insert those in at this time.

5. The worn brake RTO was conducted with an additional pressure plate between the original pressure plate and piston housing. This was done because allowable piston travel had been exceeded and without the additional pressure plate the brakes could not have been applied.
6. Prior to the worn brake RTO (maximum energy stop), the inside diameter of the lining carriers was increased by 0.120 of an inch to alleviate the severe shrinkage of the lining carriers on the torque tube caused by overheating.
7. On stops 48 and 49 (overload stops 3 and 4) the fuse plug eutectic material—material designed to melt at a specified temperature—melted, allowing the tire to deflate.
8. The torque plate and keyway inserts for the wheel had their drive surfaces chromeplated, because of extreme wear. This was not a production process on this brake.
9. Before the start of the tests and at teardowns the keyway inserts were sprayed with molybdenum disulfate (a lubricant).
10. After every stop the wheel and tire assembly were removed from the brake, the brake was blown out with high-velocity air and the keyway inserts and heat shield were wiped clean.

11. After stops Nos. 10, 20, 30, 40, 45, and 50 the brake was disassembled and the expansion slots in the lining carriers were cleaned of excess lining material and opened. Excess materials removed from between the segments in the rotors and the lugs and links on the rotors were cleaned and radiused by machining processes. This in a sense is equivalent to a minor overhaul in the brake linings.

In addition there were at least four other major irregularities in the test procedure.

These, gentlemen, are only irregularities which occurred during the testing. As for the report itself more than 80 false entries were made in the body of the report and in the logs.

Many, many of the elaborate engineering curves attached to the report were complete and total fabrications, based not on what had actually occurred, but on information which would fool both LTV and the Air Force.

I have already mentioned that the turn-around capability test which was supposed to determine what temperatures might be experienced by the brake during a typical flight mission, had been misconducted through a human error on the part of the test lab operator.

Rather than rerun this very important test, which would have taken only some 6 hours to complete, it was decided to manufacture the data.

This we did, and the result was some very convincing graphic curves. These curves were supposed to demonstrate to LTV and the Air Force exactly what the temperatures in the brakes had been during each minute of the simulated mission.

They were completely false and based only on data which would be acceptable to the customers.

I could spend the entire day here discussing the various elaborate falsifications that went into this report but I feel that, by now, the picture is clear.

The report was finally issued on June 5, 1968, and almost immediately, flight tests on the brake were begun at Edwards Air Force Base in California.

Mr. Lawson was sent by Goodrich to witness these tests and when he returned, he described various mishaps which had occurred during the flight tests and he expressed the opinion to me that the brake was dangerous.

That same afternoon, I contacted my attorney and after describing the situation to him, asked for his advice.

He advised me that, while I was technically not guilty of committing a fraud, I was certainly part of a conspiracy to defraud.

He further suggested a meeting with U.S. Attorney Roger Makely in Dayton, Ohio.

I agreed to this and my attorney said he would arrange an appointment with the Federal attorney.

I discussed my attorney's appraisal of our situation with Mr. Lawson, but I did not, at this time, tell him of the forthcoming visit with Mr. Makely.

Mr. Lawson said he would like to consult with my attorney and I agreed to arrange this.

Shortly thereafter, Mr. Lawson, went to the Dallas offices of LTV and, while he was gone, my attorney called and said that, upon advice of the U.S. attorney, he had arranged an interview with the Dayton office of the FBI.

I related the details of the A–7D qualification to Mr. Joseph Hathaway, of the FBI.

He asked if I could get Mr. Lawson to confirm my story and I replied that I felt Mr. Lawson would surely do this.

Upon Mr. Lawson's return from Dallas, I asked him if he still wished to consult my attorney and he answered "I most certainly do."

Mr. Lawson and I went to the attorney's office, and Mr. Lawson was persuaded to speak to the FBI.

I wish to emphasize that at no time prior to Mr. Lawson's decision to speak to the FBI was he aware that I had already done so. His decision and mine were both the result of our individual actions.

Mr. Lawson related his own story to Mr. Hathaway, who advised us to keep our jobs and to tell no one that we had been to see him. I might add here that he advised us that an investigation would be made.

About this time the Air Force demanded that Goodrich produce its raw data from the tests.

This Goodrich refused to do, claiming that the raw data was proprietary information.

Goodrich management decided that, since pressure was being applied by the Air Force, a conference should be arranged with LTV management and engineering staff.

A preconference meeting was set for Goodrich personnel in order to go over the questionable points in the report.

On Saturday, July 27, 1968, Mr. Robert Sink, Mr. Lawson, Mr. John Warren—A—7D project engineer—and I met and went over the discrepant items contained in the qualification report.

Each point was discussed at great length and a list of approximately 40 separate discrepancies was compiled.

These, we were told by Mr. Sink, would be revealed to LTV personnel the following week.

However, by the time of the meeting with LTV, only a few days later, the list of discrepancies had been cut by Mr. Sink from 43 items to a mere three.

Mr. Chairman, during this meeting Mr. Lawson took from the blackboard at the Goodrich conference room word for word listing of all these discrepancies. This contains the 43 items I have just mentioned.

I would like to enter this into the record, and also enter the subsequent list of three major discrepancies which later came out of this meeting.

Chairman PROXMIRE. Do you have copies of those documents?

Mr. VANDIVIER. Yes, I do have.

Mr. VANDIVIER. The following 2-month period was one of a constant running battle with LTV and the Air Force, during which time the Air Force refused final approval of the qualification report and demanded a confrontation with Goodrich about supplying raw data.

On October 8, another meeting was held, again with Mr. Sink, Mr. Lawson, Mr. Warren, and myself present.

This was only 1 day prior to a meeting with Air Force personnel and Mr. Sink said he had called the meeting "so that we are all coordinated and tell the same story."

Mr. Sink said that LTV personnel would be present at the meeting with the Air Force and our policy would be to "Let LTV carry the ball." Mr. Sink appeared to be especially concerned because Mr. Bruce Tremblay, the Air Force engineeer most intimate with A—7D brake would be present at the meeting and it was felt at B. F. Goodrich that Mr. Tremblay was already suspicious.

Mr. Sink warned us that "Mr. Tremblay will probably be at his antagonistic best."

He added that the Air Force had wanted to meet at the Goodrich plant, but that we—Goodrich—couldn't risk having them that close to the raw data.

"We don't want those guys in the plant," Mr. Sink said.

What happened at the meeting with the Air Force, I do not know. I did not attend.

On October 18, I submitted my resignation to Goodrich effective November 1.

I would like to read that resignation. This is addressed to Russell Line, manager of technical services:

In May of this year I was directed to participate in the preparation of qualification report for the A7D, 26031. As you are aware this report contained numerous deliberate and wilful misrepresentations which according to legal counsel constitutes fraud and therefore exposes both myself and others to criminal charges of conspiracy to defraud. In view of this fact, I must terminate my employment with the B. F. Goodrich Company effective November 1, 1968. I regret that this decision must be made, but I am sure that you will agree that events of the past seven months have created an atmosphere of deceit and distrust in which it is impossible to work effectively and productively.

On October 25 I was told that my resignation was to be accepted immediately, and within 20 minutes I had left the Goodrich Co.

Gentlemen, I am well aware that the B. F. Goodrich Co. is a well-known and well-respected firm with an almost impeccable reputation.

I am equally aware that the charges I have made are serious.

However, everything I have said to you is completely true and I can prove my statements with documentary evidence.

The unfortunate part of a situation such as this is that, invariably, many innocent persons are made to suffer along with the guilty.

Therefore, I should like to emphasize that three people whom I have mentioned here are, I feel, completely blameless and were implicated in this situation through no fault of their own.

Mr. Ralph Gretzinger from the very start fought this situation and tried very hard to use his influence to stop the issuance of the false report.

Mr. Richard Gloor, in his own handwriting, listed the irregularities occurring during the test and was outspoken in his opposition to the report.

This list was shown to B. F. Goodrich management.

Mr. Lawson, of course, was in a position similar to mine and the fact that he voluntarily disclosed the details of the A–7D test program to the FBI and GAO should stand upon its own merits. Thank you.

Chairman PROXMIRE. Thank you, Mr. Vandivier.

Mr. Lawson, you have heard the statement as read and I take it you have had a chance to see the full statement?

Mr. LAWSON. No, I have not.

Chairman PROXMIRE. The statement you have just heard read by Mr. Vandivier, do you agree with it fully or in part or do you disagree and can you tell us your reaction to it?

Mr. LAWSON. The factual data that Mr. Vandivier has presennted is correct, to the best of my knowledge.

Chairman PROXMIRE. There is no statement that you heard him read with which you would disagree in any part?

Mr. LAWSON. I really don't know. I haven't read the complete text.

Chairman PROXMIRE. Would you disagree with any part of what you heard him read right now in your presence?

Mr. LAWSON. No. I don't believe there is.

Chairman PROXMIRE. Now I would like to ask you, Mr. Vandivier, you gave us a picture which we may want to ask other witnesses about, so I want to qualify that picture. As far as we know, it is a picture which you say was taken of the brake that was tested?

Mr. VANDIVIER. That is correct.

Chairman PROXMIRE. But we would like to make sure that we qualify that, because it is going to be used later.

Now would you describe again, tell us how you came to have that, when the picture was taken and so forth?

Mr. VANDIVIER. Yes. This was taken just approximately an hour and a half or 2 hours before the worn brake RTO was conducted. This was for the qualification test, and I asked the plant photographer if he would take a Polaroid picture of this for me. He did so, and I took the Polaroid shot and I had it enlarged. I have a certification on this. I had the original Polaroid negative. I have the negatives that the photographer used.

Chairman PROXMIRE. Will you give us the date, the time that was taken, if you have that?

Mr. VANDIVIER. If you will give me just a moment, I can.

Chairman PROXMIRE. Meanwhile, may I ask Mr. Lawson, while Mr. Vandivier is looking up that, if you can confirm that this is in fact the picture of the A–7D brake that was undergoing qualification?

Mr. LAWSON. Yes, it appears to be.

Chairman PROXMIRE. It appears to be?

Mr. LAWSON. I would say it is.

Chairman PROXMIRE. It is. All right. Well, you can supply that a little later for the record, Mr. Vandivier.

Mr. VANDIVIER. All right.

Chairman PROXMIRE. Let me ask you this. You say you worked for Goodrich for 6 years?

Mr. VANDIVIER. That is correct.

Chairman PROXMIRE. What was your previous employment before you were hired by Goodrich?

Mr. VANDIVIER. I worked for the Food Machinery and Chemical Corp. at their Newport, Ind. plant.

Chairman PROXMIRE. Technical writer is a professional position that requires considerable competence and ability. What experience did you have that would qualify you to be a technical writer?

Mr. VANDIVIER. I had none.

Chairman PROXMIRE. Did you immediately go into this or did they give you a training course?

Mr. VANDIVIER. No. I had no training course. I kind of worked into the job I guess. It was—

Chairman PROXMIRE. You were not hired to be a technical—

Mr. VANDIVIER. No, I was actually hired as an instrumentation technician, and Goodrich engaged in a mass changeover of instrumentation techniques, and they wanted degreed people for this kind of work so I was switched over to the technical writing section.

Chairman PROXMIRE. How long did you work as a technical writer?

Mr. VANDIVIER. Approximately 3 years.

Chairman PROXMIRE. Three years. How many reports did you prepare for B. F. Goodrich?

Mr. VANDIVIER. At least 100, possibly 150.

Chairman PROXMIRE. Were any of these reports questioned in any way?

Mr. VANDIVIER. No, they were not.

Chairman PROXMIRE. Were they accepted? Did you get any reaction at all favorable or unfavorable in these reports that you wrote?

Mr. VANDIVIER. Occasionally we would get a question from the manufacturer about a wording or a clarification, and these would be supplied.

Chairman PROXMIRE. Was there any question as to the accuracy or competence of the report?

Mr. VANDIVIER. No, none whatsoever.

Chairman PROXMIRE. Were you criticized at any time that the reports were not adequate?

Mr. VANDIVIER. No; I was not.

Chairman PROXMIRE. In your statement, you say "Accordingly I wrote the report but in the conclusion I stated that the brake had 'not' met either the intent or the requirement of the specification and therefore was 'not' qualified." Then you add "When the final report was typewritten and ready for publication the two 'nots' in the conclusion had been eliminated, thereby changing the entire meaning of the conclusion."

Now it seems to me that you have testified before this that you and Mr. Lawson constructed this report based on your instructions from your superiors, and that this report was false in many ways that you knew, and that the report seemed to qualify the brakes, at least that was the impression I got, and yet you concluded, and I quote, "I stated the brake had not met either the intent or the requirement of the specifications and therefore was not qualified."

Doesn't it seem on the basis of your testimony that this is somewhat inconsistent? In other words, you had written a report that would qualify the brake and then you come in with a one-sentence conclusion in which you say it was not qualified? Do you see what I am getting at?

Mr. VANDIVIER. Yes. Mr. Chairman, this was probably one final gesture of defiance. I was so aggravated and sick at having to write this thing. I knew the words "not" would be taken out, but I put them in to show that, I do not know, that they had bent me to their will but they had not broken me yet. It was a foolish thing perhaps to do, but it was showing that I still had a little spirit left. At least this is how I felt.

Chairman PROXMIRE. What did you think your superiors at B. F. Goodrich would do when they found the "not qualified" in your report, when you had been told to show the brake qualified?

Mr. VANDIVIER. I knew it would be changed probably without question. I was not worried if you are trying—I was not worried at being called on the carpet for this. I knew they would just merely change it.

Chairman PROXMIRE. Was this the only time in the 3 years you worked as a technical writer with Goodrich the only time that you made false entries into a report of manufacture?

Mr. VANDIVIER. Yes it was.

Chairman PROXMIRE. So far as you know B. F. Goodrich's record is clean in every other respect with your experience?

Mr. VANDIVIER. With me—

Chairman PROXMIRE. With this single incidence being an exception?

Mr. VANDIVIER. That is right; that is correct.

Chairman PROXMIRE. They had never before asked you to do this?

Mr. VANDIVIER. No.

Chairman PROXMIRE. Do you know of any other technical writer you worked with, in which Goodrich had instructed them to take this kind of action?

Mr. VANDIVIER. If they had done this, I would know nothing of it. I could not say.

Chairman PROXMIRE. This was the only incident?

Mr. VANDIVIER. Yes, as far as I know, the only incident which I was asked to do this.

Chairman PROXMIRE. What was the normal procedure at Goodrich when a brake failed to meet all of the requirements or when normal procedures were not followed?

Mr. VANDIVIER. If for some reason or other the normal procedure was not followed or the brake simply could not meet a particular requirement, the report was written and a deviation was requested from the manufacturer, which in other words is a request to allow him to accept the brake with these noted deviations from the procedure.

I might add that there are many times that a brake just could not meet a certain requirement specified by the manufacturer, and it was always the customary procedure to ask for a deviation, and many times it was granted or some sort of a compromise was reached between the manufacturer and Goodrich.

Chairman PROXMIRE. I cannot understand what was going through the minds of Goodrich's management the way you have told the story. I cannot see what they have to gain by passing on a brake that would not meet qualifications. Somewhere along the line this is going to be shown as an unqualified brake. As you pointed out, it might be under disastrous circumstances, but in any event Goodrich would suffer and suffer badly by passing on a brake to LTV or the Air Force that was not going to work. What is their motivation?

Mr. VANDIVIER. I cannot tell you what their motivation is. I can tell you what I feel was behind this.

Chairman PROXMIRE. All right.

Mr. VANDIVIER. I feel in the beginning stages of this program someone made a mistake, and refused to admit that mistake, and in order to hide his stupidity or his ignorance, or his pride, or whatever it was, he simply covered up, you know, with more false statements, false information, and at the time it came time to deliver this brake, Goodrich was so far down the road there was nothing else to do.

They had no time to start over, I think it was a matter not of company policy but of company politics. I think that probably three or four persons within the Goodrich organization at Troy were responsible for this. I do not believe for a moment that the corporate officials in Akron knew that this was going on.

CATCH 20.5: CORPORATE MORALITY AS AN ORGANIZATIONAL PHENOMENON

JAMES A. WATERS

On a snowy February day in 1960 in Philadelphia, seven electrical equipment manufacturing company executives received jail sentences for their part in a widespread price-fixing and bid-rigging conspiracy in the industry. In reference to one of the defendants, a *Fortune* magazine writer noted: "gray-haired Westinghouse Vice-President, J.H. Chiles, Jr., vestryman of St. John's Episcopal Church in Sharon, Pennsylvania, got thirty days in prison, a $2000 fine."

The description is instructive. It is one thing to be caught with your hand in the till, but in our culture you're likely to receive a great deal more tongue clucking and scorn if you conspicuously represent a contrary set of values through some other activities; if, for example, you are a church elder, a political leader, a den mother, or a teacher. One suspects that the message of the clucking tongues was something like this: There goes Mr. Chiles. He was pretending to be an ethical, moral man, but he was really a crook. He was a hypocrite.

However, there might have been another response, reversed but equally valid, given the importance of situational determinants of behavior. People might have said: There goes Mr. Chiles. Really an ethical, moral man, he was pretending to be a crook. He was a pawn in the system.

INDIVIDUAL VERSUS ORGANIZATIONAL FOCUS

Over the past decade or so, corporate morality has been a subject of continual interest to managers, academics, social critics, and others. Much of this interest has focused on the ethical orientation or morality of corporate managers. However, there are hidden consequences to entering the topic from this perspective.

First, the approach leads to an individual level of analysis as distinguished from an organizational level of analysis. Both kinds of analysis are valid, but they lead to different ideas about action. Once started on an individual-level analysis, one is likely to end up with a kind of "moral exhortation" response to the issue—"What business needs are good people." The exhortation is appropriate, but it may divert attention from other substantive issues.

Second, a person-centered approach flies in the face of what is a subtle but altogether reasonable assumption that the people employed in the business world *are* good people. That is, taken as a whole, they are probably not any different from people in general. There are some crooks and some saints, but most people fall somewhere in between. Moreover, excluding a few businesses in which questionable practices are common, it is not unreasonable to say that the employees of most companies are typically good people within the limits and distribution of people in business, which is the same as people anywhere else.

But if the employees of any given organization are "typically good," why do various unsavory practices (graft, use of call girls, price fixing, and so on) keep reoccuring?

One answer is that sometimes the chief executive of an organization is directly involved. Most lower-level employees may not know what is going on or, if they do, they don't have anywhere within the organization to go with their concerns. A case in point would be the overseas bribery payments made by the Northrup Corporation. T. V. Jones, Northrup president, was central to the transactions in question. An assistant controller of the company was interviewed after the story broke. He noted that when he found out about the payments, he saw his choices as either to go along with them or to quit in protest.

However, another class of problem is probably more common and leaves us with more questions. That is when illegal or unethical activities take place in the organization *without* the knowledge and *against* the wishes of top management. What happens to the "typically good" employees then?

In a survey reported by Archie B. Carroll, 50 percent of the top-level managers who responded agreed to some degree with the statement that "Managers today feel under pressure to compromise personal standards to achieve company goals." In contrast, 84 percent of lower-level managers felt that way. Commenting on the survey results and his own experience, Carroll suggests that top management can "be inadvertently insulated from organizational reality." How can this happen?

ORGANIZATIONAL BLOCKS

As noted by K.D. Walters, the political right of employees to blow the whistle on employer practices that offend their consciences has been fairly well established, especially when they have exhausted internal grievance procedures. However, the question of *why they don't always do so,* that is, why they don't take steps internally to respond to their own disapproval of and discomfort with certain practices, even when they have no reason to believe that top management supports those practices, may be a more important consideration in understanding why those practices continue.

In the discussion that follows, the term "organizational blocks" will be used to describe those aspects of organizations that may get in the way of the natural tendency of people to react against illegal and unethical practices. The approach puts a positive value on internal whistle blowing. Note also that this way of getting into the topic leads to a different question about the disclosure of such practices. Rather than ask "What was going on with those *people* to make them act that way?" we ask "What was going on in that *organization* that made people act that way?"

The discussion is based on exploratory research. Disclosures of illegal and unethical practices were examined in an attempt to construct a picture of the organizational dimensions that seemed to make it difficult for people to get themselves disentangled from practices that made them uncomfortable. The analysis was based primarily on a study of the transcripts of testimony before various U.S. congressional investigating committees. As will be seen, a particularly suggestive source of information was the inquiry led by Senator Estes Kefauver in 1961 into price-fixing practices in the electrical equipment industry. The richness of these data for gaining insight into organizational practices springs in large measure from the fact that the inquiry took place *after* criminal charges had been settled in the courts.

In addition, three confidential interviews were held with informants who had been personally involved in activities they considered unethical. These three were all middle managers in large industrial organizations. One of the cases is used here, but the other two respondents decided to draw back from their initial willingness to contribute to the research.

As a methodological note, we must mention the difficulty of doing research in this topic area. The same organizational blocks that prevent people from internal whistle blowing act to block inquiry. As is discussed later, the fact that nobody asks questions reinforces the strength of some of the blocks.

What follows is a list of seven organizational blocks that seemed to be operating, though in differing degrees and not all in the same case. The blocks are discussed in terms of organizational needs, that is, as practices that are quite legitimate and inevitable in any complex organization. The fact that they also function as blocks can be looked on as an unintended consequence of organizational operating and control systems.

The first two blocks deal with aspects of supervisor-subordinate relations that can be found in many organizations. The next four relate to more broadly based organizational phenomena: cohesiveness of work groups, ambiguity regarding organizational priorities, separation of strategic and operating deci-

sions, and division of labor. The last block has to do with the relation of the organization to its environment. After a brief review of the nature and functioning of these seven blocks, we will turn to how the concerned manager might respond to the issues raised.

Block 1: Strong Role Models

One of the recurring tasks in organizations is teaching job incumbents the behavior that is required in their jobs. Written job descriptions and performance standards do part of the job, but a lot of teaching and training is accomplished less formally through the efforts of the jobholder's superior and more experienced peers.

Moving into a new job is a time of unusually high dependence on one's superior. To the extent that pressure, both internal and external, is exerted to "get on board and up to speed" quickly, the new jobholder must look to his or her superior for guidance and will attempt to imitate the superior's behavior.

When such socialization includes indoctrination into illegal and unethical practices, this same organizational dynamic makes it difficult for the executive to redefine the reality of his or her job so as to exclude such practices. He or she is led to conclude that nothing different can be done, that there is no way to disengage from such practices and still fulfill the requirements of the job.

Examples abound in the electrical equipment case. In describing how, as a proposition engineer-in-training for General Electric, he first became involved in meetings with competitors for purposes of price fixing, one man recalled that "I got into it in the beginning when I was young. I probably was impressed by the manager of marketing asking me to go on a meeting with him (where price-fixing discussions took place). I probably was naive" (16652). (In what follows, three- to five-digit references are to page numbers in testimony transcripts).

Another felt that when he became a sales manager for Wagner Electric, he was simply "filling a spot in carrying out a pattern that had been in existence for some time" (17823).

A socialization takes place. To varying degrees, one begins to see and value reality the way one's mentor does. The transition period may be the most crucial, but the socialization process is a continuing one. As one Westinghouse executive noted, after "living with Mr. Fuller almost continuously day by day and working directly with him for the six years where I was his assistant manager, I think we got pretty near thinking alike" (17293).

Block 2: Strict Line of Command

One of the popular principles of formal organization is establishment of a chain of command. Each person has one boss, and authority is vested in the office of that superior. It is a widespread belief that efficiency is best achieved through strict adherence to this approach, labeled the "one-over-one" in the General Electric vernacular of the 1950s.

Time and again, throughout the testimony, deeply ingrained respect for the line-of-command concept is evident. When asked directly why he did not report illegal activities to higher management, one witness simply replied: "I had no power to go higher. I do not report to anyone else except my superior" (16584).

Another consequence of the strict line of command is that assumptions are generated about where orders really come from:

I had to assume that whatever he told me came from his superior, just as my subordinate would have to assume that what I told him came from my superior. *That is the way business is run* (26864).

The power of the line of command is not simply a social norm: Unethical executives often have the raw power at their disposal to enforce compliance without tipping off higher-ups. Threats of transfer to lesser positions, subtle character assassination on appraisal forms, manipulation of rewards, and the like are used to keep the more conscience-troubled employee in line.

Whether or not such coercive power and control are necessary tools in the modern management tool bag can be argued. However, their existence may be a natural outgrowth of other dimensions of organizational life, such as task specialization, delegation of authority, and supervisor responsibility for performance appraisal and implementation of reward systems. A major effort would probably be necessary to eliminate them.

In any event, in terms of speed and efficiency, the existence of a strict line of command in the hierarchy has obvious payoffs. Similarly, the prevalence of a strong loyalty ethic allows an executive to deal more efficiently with the relations between his unit and the larger organization. Loyalty from the troops is a source of sustenance and power.

This same organizational dynamic becomes a block to the executive who wants to eliminate his involvement in illegal or unethical activities. Even if he gets past the ongoing socialization by his boss (Block 1) he is sitll in a bind. If he defies orders, he is subject to manipulation by his boss. If he exposes the practice, he is defying the organizational chain-of-command ethos and is likely to be stigmatized as disloyal. Also, since there is a logical presumption that his boss is simply passing along orders, to whom does he report the illegal goings-on?

Block 3: Task Group Cohesiveness

A ubiquitous phenomenon of organizational life is the presence of groups. People work in groups, draw their social support from groups, and look to groups as referents to define reality in vague and ambiguous situations.

When people work interdependently on

common tasks it is in the organization's best interest for them to be a cohesive group in order to facilitate communication and work. Investments are frequently made both formally (team-building programs) and informally (luncheons, travel together) to build group cohesion.

However, a posssible consequence of increased intragroup cohesion is reduced intergroup cohesion. Communication and cooperation among groups in the same organization can become restricted and reduce the impact or influence of some organizational directives. At the time, conspirators at General Electric referred to themselves as "members of the club" (17040). There is repeated testimony about how the group functioned to exclude outsiders. For example:

> We were continually reminded that whenever we got instructions that we were going to start this contracting up again, be sure not to let the lawyers know anything about it, and do not keep any records so that they can find out anything about it (16737).
>
> You were never to let the manufacturing people, the engineers, and especially the lawyers, know anything about it (17040).

While there are organizational gains to be made from tightly cohesive work groups, these groups can also function as organizational blocks. The group provides social support for continued involvement in the illegal activity. More importantly, efforts to disengage from such practices will conflict with the executive's loyalty to the group, especially if there is no way to get out without exposing the other members. Last, external pressure to expose illegal goings-on are a threat to the group, which in turn may cause it to draw even tighter and inhibit the executive still more from withdrawing from those activities.

Block 4: Ambiguity about Priorities

Richard Cyert and J. G. March have noted that organizations can often maintain mutually inconsistent or even conflicting objectives (for example, to increase market share *and* increase margin on sales) by devoting attention to them sequentially rather than simultaneously. When the directive to obey the law creates a tug-of-war with the general pressure for profits, *how* the organization presents these messages may be as important as *what* the messages contain. Subtle cues may determine the manner in which employees resolve perceived conflict among objectives and they may also determine the degree of uncertainty employees experience about how much social support they will receive if they expose some illegal practice. If I expose shady selling practices, will I be a hero or an outcast?

For example, General Electric had a very clearly written antitrust directive called "policy 20.5." But the directive received a curious treatment in the organization; it was often dominated by line-of-command directions to the contrary.

One executive was adamant about the ambiguity of the message in 20.5:

> I feel that if the company really meant that all the employees should follow this 20.5, that the company and all the officers of the company should take the same interest in that, and talk just as much about the 20.5 at every meeting as they talk about engineering, marketing, finance, profits, labor relations, and everything else. They never did that (16829).

Another executive suggested there was some question in his mind as to whether the top line-of-command people were behind the policy:

> At no time during this period did they use what we call the one-over-one system in the General Electric Company (concerning policy 20.5). That is the man over the other man, to sit down with that policy and say "You are to observe this policy and here, sign this." All they did was to issue that policy, and send [it] to us through the mail from the legal side of it, which was an advisory side, not a line-of-command side, and ask us to sign it (16788).

Two factors interact to create and maintain this ambiguity. First, hard, measurable performance criteria (for example, profitability, sales volume, costs) tend to drive out softer, less measurable criteria (for example, social responsiveness, ethical practices). Because the former are easier to discuss, agree on, and control for, they attract more executive time and energy than the latter. As Robert Ackerman points out, this is especially true for divisionalized structures, where the autonomy of operating divisions rests on their willingness to perform against hard, measurable financial targets, and communication with corporate management tends to be limited to those targets. It becomes easy to create the impression that the softer criteria are less important.

The general pressure within organizations to enhance profitability reinforces that impression. In GE at the time, there was considerable evidence that if a manager wanted to continue to have a profit-center responsibility, he would be well advised to keep achieving his profit budget.

Simply announcing that compliance with the law was a paramount value in the array of corporate objectives would have eliminated any ambiguity in the minds of employees about how they would be received if they blew the whistle. However, such a stance would have depressurized the forces exerted on employees for profits. The profit manager would have had an "out" about realized price levels. Thus the policy may have been perceived as being presented with an implicit message of "Do this, but make sure that doing it doesn't keep you from meeting your profit objectives." It would be a "Catch 20.5."

Block 5: Separation of Decisions

Ideally, the experiences of operating-level people in attempting to implement organization strategy are used as data input for the constant revision of basic strategy. Sometimes strategic decisions are made by middle managers.

However, in large, hierarchically structured organizations, lower-level people are usually expected to accept strategy as a given and to work to achieve the stated objectives. An executive might feel free to ask about objectives one or two levels up, but no avenues are available for routine questioning of more basic starting points in what amounts to a hierarchy of ends and means.

This organizational reality can function as a block when strategy constrains an executive to operate in a business or in a locale in which practices he perceives to be of questionable legality or ethicality are accepted as commonplace. The dilemmas faced by employees of multinational corporations with respect to payments that would be considered bribes (and illegal) in this country but are a way of life in others have been well publicized.

Analogies closer to home are available. One knowledgeable observer points out:

> . . . that in New York City it is well known that graft and bribes are an integrated part of "doing business" in the construction industry. At the opposite end of the scale, no graft is paid in Atlanta, Georgia, where it is considered inappropriate (417).

The point to be emphasized is that the lower-level executive who finds himself in a "New York City type of business" is in a peculiar bind. Suppose, for example, that as part of a diversification program, your company has acquired a subsidiary with completely new marketing channels. As part of your plan to integrate that acquisition into the corporate fold, you transfer some mid-level managers from the main business area to the new acquisition.

One executive who made just such a move discovered that selling practices in the new business routinely involved kick-backs, graft, elaborate promotional considerations (for example, giving buyers automobiles), and other, similar practices. The old-timers in the company had become desensitized to the ethical issues implicit in these practices. Moreover, they believed (quite correctly) that avoiding these practices would cause a drastic reduction in market-share.

What could this man do? It would be extremely costly for a single company to avoid such practices in this industry. The only realistic choices would be to stay in the business, to abandon it, or to sell the company to an unsuspecting buyer. This man's organization simply had no channels through which he could raise questions about the ethics of staying in this business.

Also, as James March and Herbert Simon point out, closely related to the idea of available channels is the issue of communication efficiency. Shared organizational vocabularies tend to develop such that large amounts of information can be communicated with relatively few words. For example, such short phrases as "ROI," "payback period," "he's a producer," "she's on a fast track," often convey a constellation of facts and judgments far beyond the literal meaning of the words. In contrast, anything that doesn't fit the system is communicated only with great difficulty.

In the organizations being discussed, as in most organizations, a widely shared organizational vocabulary concerning issues of morality and ethics does not exist. Just as the presence of a shared vocabulary facilitates identification and discussion of topics like market share, inventory levels, capital budgets, competitors' actions, and the like, the absence of a richly elaborated common language for issues of morality acts to block discussion.

Conversations about moral and ethical issues are almost doomed to be awkward, halting, and time-consuming to the point of painfulness. If an organizational environment normally demands snappy and efficient presentations and discussions, such conversations are unlikely to take place.

Block 6: Division of Work

The total work to be done in any organization must be subdivided. The most familiar division of work is horizontal in nature; this is the basis of task specialization. A consequence of rigid division is that things often get "left to channels." Employees in one part of an organization can be aware of illegal activities in another part, yet believe that they are in no position to do anything about it or that it just isn't done. As one witness put it: "I happen to have a great distaste for tale-bearing and I simply did not do that kind of thing" (17228).

Channels can also be changed to isolate and neutralize an executive who might be critical of a corporate practice. For example, Dale Console, former medical director for E. R. Squibb and Company, reported the following incident:

> The real eruption occurred in about 1955 when, as I understood it, Parke-Davis had offered Squibb a license to market chloramphenicol in some of Squibb's South American markets. ... I was presented with the prospect of marketing chloramphenicol under the Squibb label making all the excessive claims for the drug and excluding a warning statement since it was not required in the countries in which sale is proposed. I refused to approve the tentative copy and made it clear that I would tender my resignation before I would approve the copy. Apparently my colleagues thought I was sufficiently valuable and instead of making a confrontation out of the issue they decided to use an end play. The Overseas Division appointed its own Medical Director who was in no way responsible to me (4496).

Somewhat like the effect of a strict chain of command, exaggerated respect for channels could convince employees that they must *not* do what they're *not* told. A person who knows of or is associated with illegal or unethical practices may be blocked from reacting by the difficulty of working across channels and by the disfavor with which any such activity is viewed in a tight organization.

Vertical fractionation of work also occurs. Different levels in the hierarchy may make qualitatively different contributions to the organization. For example, the same information may mean different things to people at succeeding levels in the hierarchy. People at each level may filter or use selectively the data provided by the previous level because, by virtue of their position, they have a more accurate sense of the purpose for which the information was collected and/or have different factual input that supports revisions.

A possible consequence is that lower-level employees may have uncomfortable suspicions that what they are doing is illegal or unethical, yet not have enough command of the facts to report their suspicions without fear of finding that they have completely misread the situation. In short, the absence of sufficient knowledge of the "big picture" acts to immobilize the employee at the same time that the knowledge he does have about certain practices is spurring him to take action. In large organizations very few people have the "big picture." Each level tends to reserve a portion of the facts, perhaps in order to maintain differentiation of levels. Hence, the employee is afraid to act on what he knows.

In 1969, two former employees of the B.F. Goodrich wheel and brake plant in Troy, Ohio, told a congressional investigating committee a virtual horror story of changed test procedures, deliberate miscalculation of instruments, and changed data in test logs in connection with qualifying an experimental brake for test flights on the Air Force A-7D aircraft. Given the information they had, it clearly seemed appropriate for them to go to the FBI with their charges.

However, subsequent testimony by more senior officials of B.F. Goodrich suggested that the investigation was much ado about nothing. Changes in test procedures were routine in the business, and the ones in question were made with the approval of the prime contractor. Senior engineers had been working closely with this prime contractor and the test results had already been accepted. In addition, while the ex-employees were still at the plant, the company had begun testing an improved brake; the two simply were not privy to all the facts in the situation.

Given the conflicting testimony, the case remains ambiguous. Hierarchical control of information did not stop the two men from reporting their concerns. However, after considering the rebuttal testimony, it is suggested that such a control could certainly have deterred less intrepid souls.

Block 7: Protection from Outside Intervention

Any investigation into illegal and unethical practices by an organization only increases its risk of exposure to prosecution, damage claims, and soiled public image. Every pressure exists, even for the organization that wants to eliminate such practices, to avoid looking at what has happened in the past.

Thus the affidavit accompanying 20.5 in GE read in part as follows:

> I have received a copy of directive policy general no. 20.5 dated October 23, 1953. I have read and understood this policy. I am observing it and will observe it in the future (16737).

The focus of the affidavit is on the present and the future. It is certainly understandable that a sincere desire to obey the law would take its first form in a desire to clean things up from then on. It would take a qualitatively different type of motivation to engage in public confessions of past misdeeds, and that is probably what an organization would have to do if a full-scale investigation of past practices were launched.

One such case was that of the Northrup Corporation, which had been identified by the Watergate special prosecutor as having made illegal campaign contributions. The audit committee of the Northrup board of directors commissioned a study (by Ernst & Ernst) of how such transactions had taken place and been accounted for. By tracing the sources of funds and the "fundling" of cash back to the United States by foreign consultants, the investigation also spread to the bribing of foreign government officials.

At this point, the Multinational Subcommittee of the Senate Foreign Relations Committee subpoenaed Ernst & Ernst's carefully detailed notes and used them to expose Northrup's practices to the world. The chairman of the executive committee of Northrup's board of directors subsequently appeared before the subcommittee to "extend our public apologies to the government of Saudi Arabia for any embarrassment caused by this matter" (*The New York Times,* June 10, 1975). Thus Northrup Corporation officials were hardly rewarded for voluntarily undertaking an investigation of what had gone on. An unintended consequence of the Multinational Subcommittee's fine work might be to convince other executives that the last thing they should consider is a formal internal investigation of possible improprieties.

The way the organization is encouraged to exercise a tight control over its interface with the social system becomes an organizational block for the executive who wishes to stop illegal and unethical activities. To cease and desist, one must first clean house. Cleaning house could mean public exposure, which conflicts with reasonable organizational loyalty.

The tight control organizations are forced to maintain also limits research into instances of unethical behavior in organizational settings. The resulting lack of published cases and analyses limits public discussion and appreciation of the conflicting pressures on an employee with respect to illegal or unethical practices.

In something of a vicious cycle, this lack of open discussion in schools and among managers makes employees more susceptible to the organizational blocks. Conversely, to the extent that business school graduates and young managers have been able to read about and discuss cases in which people like themselves got mired in some unsavory practice, they are more capable of resisting pressures from inappropriate role models and simplistic norms about the chain of command.

The lack of open discussion also deprives the organizational policy-formulation process of important input. If there can be no data-based

analyses of the roots and flowering of past illegal and unethical practices, managerial attempts to eliminate such practices are forced to rely on vague and anecdotal feedback. The development of policies and change strategies that could reduce or eliminate organizational blocks is thus impeded.

RESPONSE: TIGHTENING DOWN OR LOOSENING UP?

As noted earlier, all these factors are natural concomitants of a complex organization. The extent to which they also act to block people from blowing the whistle on practices they find ethically objectionable might be described as an unintended consequence. In a few cases it might also be said that the same methods of control instituted by the leaders of an organization to achieve organizational objectives can be used by the occasional "bad apple" to block effective reaction by those who are offended by specific practices. How should the concerned manager react? Should he or she make the controls even more stringent?

Such an approach, however instinctive, can be seen to focus on the "bad guys" (assumed to be few in number) and to ignore the "good guys" (assumed to be most of the employees in the company). Based on a consideration of the notion of organizational blocks, I suggest that "battening down the hatches" can have exactly the opposite effect from the one intended. Increasing the clarity of control procedures may enable the few bad guys to navigate their way around the system more easily.

For example, establishing a "watch-dog" position, perhaps in the legal department, with great fanfare may enable those who are so inclined to rope that person off from crucial information more easily. Focusing guardianship in this way may also diminish the felt responsibilities in others to detect and report unethical practices. A mechanistic approach—such as having everybody sign a standard affidavit like

GE's "20.5"—can impersonalize and desensitize the issue. Such an approach can create the illusion that all is taken care of while the main effect may be to allow a few conspirators to lay low for a while or develop persuasive stories as to why this "routine staff request" should be treated lightly.

More importantly, such an approach doesn't tap into the tremendous reservoir of energy that exists among employees to root out such practices. By reversing the focus and thinking more about the "good guys," it may be possible to unblock some of the natural forces that exist in the organization to raise questions about practices of uncertain ethicality.

In other words, instead of asking how to block people from engaging in unsavory practices, it might be better to ask how to unblock the natural ethical instincts of most of your employees.

Action Planning

How can the concerned manager proactively approach the job of ensuring ethical business operations? A spirit of inquiry must be brought to a *preventive maintenance program*: just as you can do maintenance on a machine while it is running rather than wait for a possibly calamitous breakdown, you can work to reduce or eliminate the effects of organizational blocks before unethical practices take root or there is a costly scandal.

Any action programs of this kind must be tailored to the idiosyncracies of the particular organization. Such programs will flow from a diagnosis that starts with a question: Is it possible for nonethical practices to go on in my organization (or division, or department) without my knowing about it? Ask yourself the following questions:

- Does a vocabulary exist in our organization for discussing issues of morality and ethicality? Is it a topic that can come up for discussion, like market share or inventory levels?

- Just how rigid are our patterns of communication and norms against "nosiness"? Is it okay for me to ask questions or make comments about business areas other than my own?

- How much access is there to top management? When was the last time someone two or more levels down had the opportunity for a serious and open-ended dialog with me?

- How much information gets filtered in reporting up? Do I really have an appreciation of the practices of our field salesmen? Is it possible that we are operating in a business that condones unethical or illegal practices?

- How much do people depend on their boss for appraisals, promotions, salary increases? Do the people two levels down feel as if I know them well? Do I?

- How clear are our priorities? Do people really know where I stand, or might there be some "Catch 20.5" clauses connected with my general drive for performance?

Above all, to what extent are questioning, confrontation, and controversy valued in the organization? Although employees generally agree on what constitutes "pretty much OK" behavior, they are likely to be divided and to have different ideas of what the organizational stance should be on any specific issue. This is not a contradiction. Rather, it is a matter of fine tuning within a consensually determined range of acceptability. The manager who invites open discussion and challenge on what the acceptable range is almost certainly leaves himself open to a heated debate on very specific questions of morality. Before whistle blowers will feel welcome, that heat must be accepted as being constructive.

The challenge in all this for a concerned

management is to integrate a healthy pressure for performance and profitability with a healthy respect for individual consciences and differences of opinion. If top management has been relatively more articulate about the former than about the latter, there may be no more potent way of signaling a more balanced interest than to invest time and energy in a collaborative program aimed at minimizing the impact of organizational blocks.

What might such a program look like? As suggested earlier, it would have to be shaped to fit the organization, and it would be best if both its design and execution were carried out by the key people in that organization. Nevertheless, most programs contain some common basic elements.

1. *Removing ambiguity concerning organizational priorities.* If top management really wants to obey the law and operate according to the general ethical standards of society, it must say so unambiguously. It should state clearly that such constraints come *before,* and in that sense have a *higher priority than,* such traditional objectives as sales volume, market share, and profits.

Going back to A. B. Carroll's survey, 78 percent of all the managers responding agreed to some extent with the following statement: "I can conceive of a situation where you have sound ethics running from top to bottom but, because of pressures from top to achieve results, the person down the line compromises." To facilitate internal whistle blowing, everyone must be made acutely aware that organizational priorities will be maintained even when the pressure is on for profits and performance. This has to be a starting point.

2. *Moving from abstract generality to concrete example.* A presidential letter that stays at the "do good and avoid evil" level of abstraction can be a pretty ambiguous signal to people who are afraid to respond to their own distate for certain practices. "I wonder if he means this" will be the most common reaction. Avoiding specific examples that would be obvious to

anyone in the industry will create doubt about the seriousness of the message.

For instance, if your firm is involved in real estate transactions such as buying retail sites and working with zoning commissions, it is dysfunctional to pretend that bribery is not a frequent occurrence in this area and to avoid saying that you do not want your people to pay bribes of any sort, even if it hurts your business. If your firm is selling a relatively undifferentiated product to retail channels dominated by a few chains and their powerful buyers and buying/selling practices are notoriously corrupt, your field salespeople will feel uncertain about a message that does not acknowledge the existence of such practices and does not clearly state your views on how you want them to deal with the pressures they face.

Some brainstorming sessions with employees who have long and diverse experience in your industry can probably generate a lengthy list of examples. It can be done in a nonthreatening way by asking people what *could* be going on that shouldn't rather than what *is* going on. A corollary to Murphy's Law would be that illegal or unethical practices that could exist probably do.

3. *Providing concrete steps for internal whistle blowers.* If people are convinced of your position and want to take action on a questionable practice, what steps should they take? If you don't provide direction for them, they may still feel blocked. Leaving communications to the regular chain of command is obviously inadequate.

Should they ask for a meeting with you? Write you a memo? Call you at home? Perhaps you will want to establish an ombudsman in the organization. Although ombudsmen traditionally respond to employee complaints about such matters as compensation inequities, job performance appraisals, and benefit programs, it is not difficult to imagine the position also serving as a receiving point for internal whistle blowing.

Perhaps those who want to report wrongdoing could be encouraged by assurances that *initial* explorations would take place under the security of guaranteed anonymity. Subsequent serious action and change, if any, would necessarily and appropriately involve open discussion between the whistle blower and those engaged in the practice in question.

A system of secret informers is unthinkable, since it would destroy the spirit of openness and questioning that is being sought. However, an initial ice-breaking confidential discussion with a manager tuned in to these kinds of questions may help the would-be whistle blower to think through whether the issue in question warrants open investigation and, if so, may help him to gather his courage to proceed.

The exact channel used may be less important than the clarity with which the proper procedure is spelled out. The person who wants to take this action probably feels anxious and uncertain. Providing a reasonable procedure for reporting problems and a picture of what will happen to those reports will help to make the anxiety manageable and will facilitate action.

4. *Developing an appropriate organizational vocabulary.* As suggested earlier, one of the blocks to internal whistle blowing is the difficulty of discussing issues of morality and ethics in the absence of an appropriate organizational vocabulary. Training programs can be devised that focus directly on this problem. Peopled by employees from diagonal slices of the organization, so that different departments and hierarchical levels are involved, workshops can allow those attending to wrestle with cases that are directly pertinent to their own company and to see the issues from different perspectives.

Note that such programs would be organization-level interventions rather than attempts to change individuals. First, they would serve to legitimize the topic—ethical concerns or pangs of conscience would become proper subjects to bring up with one's boss or at a staff meeting.

Second, by being exposed to a common framework of cases and anecdotes, organiza-

tion members would begin to develop a shared appreciation of ethical questions and dilemmas. Analogies could be drawn. "The situation we're in here seems just like that of the sales manager in that XYZ Pump Company case we discussed." A crisper vocabulary could be used. "There appears to be a vast discrepancy between our intended values and our operational values in the case of this ad copy." In short, the purpose of these programs would be to create a rich and differentiated vocabulary within the organization so that when the time came to discuss ethical questions, everyone would be speaking the same language. They would *not* be set up to make people more ethical.

There are specific reasons for the diagonal-slice approach to selecting people for such workshops. If someone feels blocked because of strong pressure from a group of conspirators, working intensively with people from other parts of the organization can give that person a chance to build the social support necessary to break away from the old group.

Furthermore, the workshops, instead of being based on a one-way communication model, could be designed as deep-sensing sessions. Additional insights could be gathered about what might be going on in the way of illegal and unethical practices. Since people from different departments would be joining together on this work, norms that exist against commenting on business areas other than one's own would be challenged and revised. The cross-level nature of the participation would signal the seriousness of the commitment at all levels of the organization.

By having all *new* management employees participate in such training programs, you could bring about an evolutionary change. If appropriate norms about dealing with questionable practices could be instilled early in people's organizational careers, they would be less blocked from acting on their own ethical concerns.

In a longer-range effort to build appropriate

vocabularies and prepare new employees for the pressures they will face on the job, top management can also influence the training they receive *before* they reach the organization. They can demand that business schools explicitly devote research and teaching time to questions of ethics and morality. They can offer to work with serious researchers and to give guest lectures on the topic. It is hard to picture a contemporary management school faculty that would not be responsive to such influence.

5. *Launching sensitive investigative efforts.* Several firms (Seagram, Northrup, Gulf, and so on) have employed audit committees to search out and report illegal campaign contributions or overseas bribery payments. These have generally had a financial accounting orientation, but it seems reasonable to think that the mission of such audit committees could be expanded so that moral and ethical questions outside the existing financial control procedures are also explored.

In some ways, this would convert the ombudsman role mentioned earlier to a more proactive posture. Rather than being simply a receiving post for whistle blowers, such a person could go out into the organization and actively seek to uncover unintended organizational blocks. However, it would be important for this searching activity to be perceived as facilitating the general opening up of communication in the organization. If it is not part of an overall change program, it might be seen as detective work, and skillful operators will devise ways to circumvent it and rope it off from pertinent information.

Three Dilemmas

Let's say that a manager decides to start a program that builds on the elements described here. What pitfalls might he or she anticipate?

He or she may find some illegal practices already in existence in the organization. Price fixing, illegal rebates, unsafe products, grossly deceptive, advertising, bribery, or a variety of other illegalities could be uncovered. A first response can be to take the steps necessary to stop whatever it is. But the manager is probably still faced with the need to report the violation and the violators to the appropriate law enforcement agency.

Undoubtedly, he or she will want to get legal counsel (which is well beyond the scope of this article). At the same time, the manager will probably find himself or herself smack up against Block 7, "protection from outside intervention." There seems to be no alternative but to break through this block, report the problems, and suffer the consequences.

It does not seem unreasonable to expect legal authorities to take a more tolerant or lenient stance with respect to self-reported transgressions. In fact, it may be possible to discuss this topic beforehand with the appropriate agencies and negotiate specific arrangements in advance.

Given the understaffed and beleaguered state of most regulatory agencies, a case could be made that they would be better off encouraging penalty-free collaborative policing than maintaining the current hunter-huntee relationship with business organizations. In any event, until changes in the larger social system are brought about, the dilemma represented by Block 7 remains.

The second problem was hinted at earlier and concerns the questioning confrontation, and controversy that results when ethical issues are debated openly. Unblocking the natural ethical instincts of employees may unearth some black-and-white cases (conspiring to fix prices or bribing government officials, which are clearly illegal) but it will also bring a lot of gray cases up for consideration (what is excessive entertainment of a client or just how much emphasis should be given to explaining possible risks in promoting a new drug product?).

Who will be the final arbiter among competing definitions of what is ethical in a particular business setting? It is hard to avoid the conclusion that if debate on such questions is opened up, the chief executive officer is the one who will have to make the final decisions. Much has been written about how the CEO sets the moral tone of an organization, but if an organization truly sets out to unblock internal whistle blowing, he may have to do it at a much more visible and operational level.

More importantly, the dynamics of such open debate will engender a lot of feelings among the protagonists. Wishful thinking aside, there will be winners and losers. If the whistle blower is the loser, how can the act of blowing the whistle be rewarded at the same time that the substance of his allegation is denied?

It will be helpful if the fact that such debates will take place and such decisions will be made is clear at the beginning of a change program. An analogy would be the notion of consensus in group decision making. Consensus doesn't mean that everybody agrees with a decision, only that everybody is satisfied that his or her arguments have been heard and understood by all members of the group, and that, on this basis, they are willing to support the group decision.

If the whistle blower wins the debate, and an organizationally more powerful person (such as his boss), loses, how will it be possible to protect the winner from retribution, however subtle (see Block 2)? Again, the ground rules must be made clear to all concerned before internal whistle blowing is opened up. In any event, it is obvious that sincere reporters of wrong-doing who are acting on their consciences must be rewarded and protected if a change program is to survive. This second dilemma may require a CEO with the wisdom of King Solomon, but it must be resolved if an open organization is to be achieved.

Last, despite the most open discussion and debate and the most Solomon-like decision making, some whistle blowers will not be satisfied. If they are still conscience stricken, they may opt to report the practice in question to the press or to external authorities. Thus, reducing the effect of organizational blocks may also produce some external whistle blowing.

The result may be something analogous to so-called "sunshine laws" in government, opening all actions and deliberations to public scrutiny. If top management is convinced that organizational practices are ethically sound, it may also have to defend them in public forums. However, by encouraging internal action first, it will be considerably better prepared to deal with more public discussion.

BOUNDED COURAGE

Of course, some whistle blowing, does go on now. A radical critic may say that after all, if an employer's conscience were really bothered enough by a specific illegal or unethical practice, he or she would do something about it; others have.

However, such a criticism ignores the significant psychological and material costs that have to be paid by those people. In the general context of decision making, March and Simon have developed the notion of "bounded rationality," which directs attention to the fact that human beings are not omniscient creatures. They can't start from scratch on every problem, consider every alternative and possible contingency influence, and develop optimal solutions every time. As a result, organization design must respond to our limitations by developing set performance programs (for example, standard operating procedures for receiving customer orders or returned goods) and by limiting primary responsibilities (for example, you sell it, we'll make it).

In a similar way, human beings are not *always* universally capable of great acts of courage. The man or woman who has elderly parents and four children to support simply can't afford to be unemployed or underemployed, however heroic an act of disclosure may seem.

Is it reasonable to ask such a person to put aside his or her survival needs in the service of a more just and moral society?

To greater or lesser degrees, we all have boundaries on our courage. From an institutional leadership perspective, the individual as citizen is a natural integrating link between the organization and the laws and ethical customs of the larger society. Practices that are badly out of synchronization with the prevailing moral sense of society won't take place if they are exposed to the light of reasonable debate among "good people." The concerned manager might ask whether his or her organization makes it easy for employees to act on their consciences or whether it tests the boundaries of their courage.

1. Take Watergate, the escalation of the Vietnam War, or the B. F. Good-rich airbrake scandal, and discuss it in class. How would you handle each stage differently knowing what you know now? Do you think you would handle it differently at that stage now knowing the outcome of those three situations?

CHAPTER XII
REDESIGNING THE ORGANIZATION TO REDUCE THE SHOCK

ORGANIZATIONAL SHOCKS

- The structure of the organization as we know it today is not compatible with the dynamic nature of the marketplace.

- Organizations need to be restructured every two years or so in order to keep up with the demands of the marketplace.

- Power as a process can be so seductive for a manager that it destroys the organization.

- The position one holds in the organizational structure determines the power and influence one has rather than does the leadership characteristics of the individual.

- Theories of organizational structure and design as taught in most schools of administration are out of date when one considers the needs of the organization to survive.

In each of the chapters we have presented one or more shocks that we think the new manager will eventually face in his life with the organization. The various articles have presented solutions for reducing the shock and for managing the problems mentioned. For example, remember the last article on corporate morality by Waters. One of the solutions has often been to make sure the organization was designed in such a way that the potential of the problem was reduced. In the four readings in this chapter, specific suggestions are given for redesigning organizations so that they adapt to the needs of our current, social, and economic environment.

In the first reading Warren Bennis reiterates the problem with bureaucracy noted by Robert Frost in his poem "Departmental." He predicts that bureaucracy, as we know it today, will come to an end in the near future. He thinks that all organizations should regard their structures as temporary and should undergo change when needed.

The next article by Thomas Burns talks about a phenomenon called the "Darkness At Noon" atmosphere at ITT. In this period of control at ITT the senior staff management acted like the cross between secret police and a kindly family doctor. The ITT Staff was made up of graduates of the management consulting profession and, according to this article, were people who appreciated the manipulation of power almost as an academic exercise. Eventually, ITT had to change its emphasis on staff versus line management in order to meet the rule of the organization.

The article by Kanter describes how the position in the organizational structure determines the influence of the manager.

In the last article in this chapter Charles Perrow examines the question "Is business really changing?". In many cases not only have organizations failed to change their structure enough to keep up with the environmental needs, but also our theories of organizational structure have not kept up with the needs of organizations today. Perrow made the point that even though there may be a perceived need to change, organizations have not really changed in more than 100 years. This is partially because there is a difference between changing the organizational chart and changing the political, economic and social structure of institutions.

THE COMING DEATH OF BUREAUCRACY

WARREN G. BENNIS

Not far from the new Government Center in downtown Boston, a foreign visitor walked up to a sailor and asked why American ships were built to last only a short time. According to the tourist, "The sailor answered without hesitation that the art of navigation is making such rapid progress that the finest ship would become obsolete if it lasted beyond a few years. In these words which fell accidentally from an uneducated man, I began to recognize the general and systematic idea upon which your great people direct all their concerns."

The foreign visitor was that shrewd observer of American morals and manners, Alexis de Tocqueville, and the year was 1835. He would not recognize Scollay Square today. But he had caught the central theme of our country: its preoccupation, its *obsession* with change. One thing is, however, new since de Tocqueville's time: the *acceleration* of newness, the changing scale and scope of change itself. As Dr. Robert Oppenheimer said, ". . . the world alters as we walk in it, so that the years of man's life measure not some small growth or rearrangement or moderation of what was learned in childhood, but a great upheaval."

How will these accelerating changes in our society influence human organizations?

A short while ago, I predicted that we would, in the next 25 to 50 years, participate in the end of bureaucracy as we know it and in the rise of new social systems better suited to the twentieth-century demands of industrialization. This forecast was based on the evolutionary principle that every age develops an organizational form appropriate to its genius, and that the prevailing form, known by sociologists as bureaucracy and by most businessmen as "damn bureaucracy," was out of joint with contemporary realities. I realize now that my distant prophecy is already a distinct reality so that prediction is already foreshadowed by practice.

I should like to make clear that by bureaucracy I mean a chain of command structured on

Source: Reprinted by permission from *Think Magazine,* published by IBM. Copyright 1966 by International Business Machines Corporation.

the lines of a pyramid—the typical structure which coordinates the business of almost every human organization we know of: industrial, governmental, of universities and research and development laboratories, military, religious, voluntary. I do not have in mind those fantasies so often dreamed up to describe complex organizations. These fantasies can be summarized in two grotesque stereotypes. The first I call "Organization as Inkblot"—an actor steals around an uncharted wasteland, growing more restive and paranoid by the hour, while he awaits orders that never come. The other specter is "Organization as Big Daddy"—the actors are square people plugged into square holes by some omniscient and omnipotent genius who can cradle in his arms the entire destiny of man by way of computer and TV. Whatever the first image owes to Kafka, the second owes to George Orwell's 1984.

Bureaucracy, as I refer to it here, is a useful social invention that was perfected during the industrial revolution to organize and direct the activities of a business firm. Most students of organizations would say that its anatomy consists of the following components:

1. A well-defined chain of command.
2. A system of procedures and rules for dealing with all contingencies relating to work activities.
3. A division of labor based on specialization.
4. Promotion and selection based on technical competence.
5. Impersonality in human relations.

It is the pyramid arrangement we see on most organizational charts.

The bureaucratic "machine model" was developed as a reaction against the personal subjugation, nepotism and cruelty, and the capricious and subjective judgments which passed for managerial practices during the early days of the industrial revolution. Bureaucracy emerged out of the organizations' need for order and precision and the workers' demands for impartial treatment. It was an organization ideally suited to the values and demands of the Victorian era. And just as bureaucracy emerged as a creative response to a radically new age, so today new organizational shapes are surfacing before our eyes.

First I shall try to show why the conditions of our modern industrial world will bring about the death of bureaucracy. In the second part of this article I will suggest a rough model of the organization of the future.

FOUR THREATS

There are at least four relevant threats to bureaucracy:

1. Rapid and unexpected change.
2. Growth in size where the volume of an organization's traditional activities is not enough to sustain growth. (A number of factors are included here, among them: bureaucratic overhead; tighter controls and impersonality due to bureaucratic sprawls; outmoded rules and organizational structures.)
3. Complexity of modern technology where integration between activities and persons of very diverse, highly specialized competence is required.
4. A basically psychological threat springing from a change in managerial behavior.

It might be useful to examine the extent to which these conditions exist *right now*:

Rapid and Unexpected Change

Bureaucracy's strength is its capacity to efficiently manage the routine and predictable in human affairs. It is almost enough to cite the knowledge and population explosion to raise doubts about its contemporary viability. More revealing, however, are the statistics which demonstrate these overworked phrases:

a. Our productivity output per man hour may now be doubling almost every 20 years rather than every 40 years, as it did before World War II.

b. The Federal Government alone spent $16 billion in research and development activities in 1965; it will spend $35 billion by 1980.

c. The time lag between a technical discovery and recognition of its commercial uses was: 30 years before World War I, 16 years between the Wars, and only 9 years since World War II.

d. In 1946, only 42 cities in the world had populations of more than one million. Today there are 90. In 1930, there were 40 people for each square mile of the earth's land surface. Today there are 63. By 2000, it is expected, the figure will have soared to 142.

Bureaucracy, with its nicely defined chain of command, its rules and its rigidities, is ill-adapted to the rapid change the environment now demands.

Growth in Size

While, in theory, there may be no natural limit to the height of a bureaucratic pyramid, in practice the element of complexity is almost invariably introduced with great size. International operation, to cite one significant new element, is the rule rather than exception for most of our biggest corporations. Firms like Standard Oil Company (New Jersey) with over 100 foreign affiliates, Mobil Oil Corporation, The National Cash Register Company, Singer Company, Burroughs Corporation and Colgate-Palmolive Company derive more than half their income or earnings from foreign sales. Many others—such as Eastman Kodak Company, Chas. Pfizer & Company, Inc., Caterpillar Tractor Company,

International Harvester Company, Corn Products Company and Minnesota Mining & Manufacturing Company—make from 30 to 50 percent of their sales abroad. General Motors Corporation sales are not only nine times those of Volkswagen, they are also bigger than the Gross National Product of the Netherlands and well over the GNP of a hundred other countries. If we have seen the sun set on the British Empire, we may never see it set on the empires of General Motors, ITT, Shell and Unilever.

LABOR BOOM

Increasing Diversity

Today's activities require persons of very diverse, highly specialized competence.

Numerous dramatic examples can be drawn from studies of labor markets and job mobility. At some point during the past decade, the U.S. became the first nation in the world ever to employ more people in service occupations than in the production of tangible goods. Examples of this trend:

a. In the field of education, the *increase* in employment between 1950 and 1960 was greater than the total number employed in the steel, copper and aluminum industries.

b. In the field of health, the *increase* in employment between 1950 and 1960 was greater than the total number employed in automobile manufacturing in either year.

c. In financial firms, the *increase* in employment between 1950 and 1960 was greater than total employment in mining in 1960.

These changes, plus many more that are harder to demonstrate statistically, break down the old, industrial trend toward more and more people doing either simple or undifferentiated chores.

Hurried growth, rapid change and increase in specialization—pit these three factors against the five components of the pyramid structure described on page 391, and we should expect the pyramid of bureaucracy to begin crumbling.

Change in Managerial Behavior

There is, I believe, a subtle but perceptible change in the philosophy underlying management behavior. Its magnitude, nature and antecedents, however, are shadowy because of the difficulty of assigning numbers. (Whatever else statistics do for us, they most certainly provide a welcome illusion of certainty.) Nevertheless, real change seems underway because of:

a. A new concept of *man,* based on increased knowledge of his complex and shifting needs, which replaces an over simplified, innocent, pushbutton idea of man.

b. A new concept of *power,* based on collaboration and reason, which replaces a model of power based on coercion and threat.

c. A new concept of *organizational values,* based on humanistic–democratic ideals, which replaces the depersonalized mechanistic value system of bureaucracy.

The primary cause of this shift in management philosophy stems not from the bookshelf but from the manager himself. Many of the behavioral scientists, like Douglas McGregor or Rensis Likert, have clarified and articulated—even legitimized—what managers have only half registered to themselves. I am convinced, for example, that the popularity of McGregor's book, *The Human Side of Enterprise,* was based on his rare empathy for a vast audience of managers who are wistful for an alternative to the mechanistic concept of authority, i.e., that he outlined a vivid utopia of more authentic human relationships than most organizational practices today allow. Furthermore, I suspect that the desire for relationships in business has little to do with a profit motive per se, though it is

often rationalized as doing so. The real push for these changes stems from the need, not only to humanize the organization, but to use it as a crucible of personal growth and the development of self-realization.[1]

The core problems confronting any organization fall, I believe, into five major categories. First, let us consider the problems, then let us see how our twentieth-century conditions of constant change have made the bureaucratic approach to these problems obsolete.

Integration

The problem is how to integrate individual needs and management goals. In other words, it is the inescapable conflict between individual needs (like "spending time with the family") and organizational demands (like meeting deadlines).

Under twentieth-century conditions of constant change there has been an emergence of human sciences and a deeper understanding of man's complexity. Today, integration encompasses the entire range of issues concerned with incentives, rewards and motivations of the individual, and how the organization succeeds or fails in adjusting to these issues. In our society, where personal attachments play an important role, the individual is appreciated, and there is genuine concern for his well-being, not just in a veterinary-hygiene sense, but as a moral, integrated personality.

PARADOXICAL TWINS

The problem of integration, like most human problems, has a venerable past. The modern version goes back at least 160 years and was precipitated by an historical paradox: the twin births of modern individualism and modern industrialism. The former brought about a deep concern for and a passionate interest in the individual and his personal rights. The latter brought about increased mechanization of organized activity. Competition between the two has intensified as each decade promises more freedom and hope for man and more stunning achievements for technology. I believe that our society *has* opted for more humanistic and democratic values, however unfulfilled they may be in practice. It will "buy" these values even at loss in efficiency because it feels it can now afford the loss.

Social Influence

This problem is essentially one of power and how power is distributed. It is a complex issue and alive with controversy, partly because studies of leadership and power distribution can be interpreted in many ways, and almost always in ways which coincide with one's biases (including a cultural leaning toward democracy).

The problem of power has to be seriously reconsidered because of dramatic situational changes which make the possibility of one-man rule not necessarily "bad" but impractical. I refer to changes in top management's role.

Peter Drucker, over 12 years ago, listed 41 major responsibilities of the chief executive and declared that "90 percent of the trouble we are having with the chief executive's job is rooted in our superstition of the one-man chief." Many factors make one-man control obsolete, among them: the broadening product base of industry; impact of new technology; the scope of international operation; the separation of management from ownership; the rise of trade unions and general education. The real power of the "chief" has been eroding in most organizations even though both he and the organization cling to the older concept.

Collaboration

This is the problem of managing and resolving conflicts. Bureaucratically, it grows out of the very same process of conflict and stereotyping that has divided nations and communities. As organizations become more complex, they fragment and divide, building tribal patterns and symbolic codes which often work to exclude others (secrets and jargon, for example) and on occasion to exploit differences for inward (and always fragile) harmony.

Recent research is shedding new light on the problem of conflict. Psychologist Robert R. Blake in his stunning experiments has shown how simple it is to induce conflict, how difficult to arrest it. Take two groups of people who have never before been together, and give them a task which will be judged by an impartial jury. In less than an hour, each group devolves into a tightly-knit band with all the symptoms of an "in group." They regard their product as a "master-work" and the other group's as "commonplace" at best. "Other" becomes "enemy." "We are good, they are bad; we are right, they are wrong."

RABBIE'S REDS AND GREENS

Jaap Rabbie, conducting experiments on intergroup conflict at the University of Utrecht, has been amazed by the ease with which conflict and stereotype develop. He brings into an experimental room two groups and distributes green name tags and pens to one group, red pens and tags to the other. The two groups do not compete; they do not even interact. They are only in sight of each other while they silently complete a questionnaire. Only ten minutes are needed to activate defensiveness and fear, reflected in the hostile and irrational perceptions of both "reds" and "greens."

Adaptation

This problem is caused by our turbulent environment. The pyramid structure of bureaucracy, where power is concentrated at the top, seems the perfect way to "run a railroad." And for the routine tasks of the nineteenth and early twentieth centuries, bureaucracy was (in some respects it still is) a suitable social arrangement. However, rather than a placid and predictable environment, what predominates today is a dynamic and uncertain one where there is deepening interdependence among economic, scientific, educational, social and political factors in the society.

Revitalization

This is the problem of growth and decay. As Alfred North Whitehead has said: "The art of free society consists first in the maintenance of the symbolic code, and secondly, in the fearlessness of revision . . . Those societies which cannot combine reverence to their symbols with freedom of revision must ultimately decay . . ."

Growth and decay emerge as the penultimate conditions of contemporary society. Organizations, as well as societies, must be concerned with those social structures that engender buoyancy, resilience and a "fearlessness of revision."

I introduce the term "revitalization" to embrace all the social mechanisms that stagnate and regenerate, as well as the process of this cycle. The elements of revitalization are:

1. An ability to learn from experience and to codify, store and retrieve the relevant knowledge.
2. An ability to "learn how to learn," that is, to develop methods for improving the learning process.
3. An ability to acquire and use feed-back mechanisms on performance, in short, to be self-analytical.
4. An ability to direct one's own destiny.

These qualities have a good deal in common with what John Gardner calls "self-renewal." For the organization, it means conscious attention to its own evolution. Without a planned methodology and explicit direction, the enterprise will not realize its potential.

Integration, distribution of power, collaboration, adaptation and *revitalization*—these are the major human problems of the next 25 years. How organizations cope with and manage these tasks will undoubtedly determine the viability of the enterprise.

Against this background I should like to set forth some of the conditions that will dictate organization life in the next two or three decades.

The Environment

Rapid technological change and diversification will lead to more and more partnerships between government and business. It will be a truly mixed economy. Because of the immensity and expense of the projects, there will be fewer identical units competing in the same markets and organizations will become more interdependent.

The four main features of this environment are:

a. Interdependence rather than competition.
b. Turbulence and uncertainty rather than readiness and certainty.
c. Large-scale rather than small-scale enterprises.
d. Complex and multinational rather than simple national enterprises.

"NICE"—AND NECESSARY

Population Characteristics

The most distinctive characteristic of our society is education. It will become even more so. Within 15 years, two-thirds of our population living in metropolitan areas will have attended college. Adult education is growing even faster, probably because of the rate of professional obsolescence. The Killian report showed that the average engineer required further education only ten years after getting his degree. It will be almost routine for the experienced physician, engineer and executive to go back to school for advanced training every two or three years. All of this education is not just "nice." It is necessary.

One other characteristic of the population which will aid our understanding of organizations of the future is increasing job mobility. The ease of transportation, coupled with the needs of a dynamic environment, change drastically the idea of "owning" a job—or "having roots." Already 20 percent of our population change their mailing address at least once a year.

Work Values

The increased level of education and mobility will change the values we place on work. People will be more intellectually committed to their jobs and will probably require more involvement, participation and autonomy.

Also, people will be more "other-oriented," taking cues for their norms and values from their immediate environment rather than tradition.

Tasks and Goals

The tasks of the organization will be more technical, complicated and unprogrammed. They will rely on intellect instead of muscle. And they will be too complicated for one person to comprehend, to say nothing of control. Essentially, they will call for the collaboration of specialists in a project or a team-form of organization.

There will be a complication of goals. Business will increasingly concern itself with its adaptive or innovative-creative capacity. In addition, supragoals will have to be articulated, goals which shape and provide the foundation for the goal structure. For example, one might be a system for detecting new and changing goals; another could be a system for deciding priorities among goals.

Finally, there will be more conflict and contradiction among diverse standards for organizational effectiveness. This is because professionals tend to identify more with the goals of their profession than with those of their immediate employer. University professors can be used as a case in point. Their inside work may be a conflict between teaching and research, while more of their income is derived from outside sources, such as foundations and consultant work. They tend not to be good "company men" because they divide their loyalty between their professional values and organizational goals.

KEY WORD: "TEMPORARY"

Organization

The social structure of organizations of the future will have some unique characteristics. The key word will be "temporary." There will be adaptive, rapidly changing *temporary* systems. These will be task forces organized around problems to be solved by groups of relative strangers with diverse professional skills. The groups will be arranged on an organic rather than mechanical model; they will evolve in response to a problem rather than to programmed role expectations. The executive thus becomes a coordinator or "linking pin" between various task forces. He must be a man who can speak the polyglot jargon of research, with skills to relay information and to mediate between groups. People will be evaluated not vertically according to rank and status, but flexibly and functionally according to skill and professional training. Organizational charts will consist of project groups rather than stratified functional groups. (This trend is already visible in the aerospace and construction industries, as well as many professional and consulting firms.)

Adaptive, problem-solving, temporary systems of diverse specialists, linked together by coordinating and task-evaluating executive specialists in an organic flux—this is the organization form that will gradually replace bureaucracy as we know it. As no catchy phrase comes to mind, I call this an organic-adaptive structure. Organizational arrangements of this sort may not only reduce the intergroup conflicts mentioned earlier; it may also induce honest-to-goodness creative collaboration.

Motivation

The organic-adaptive structure should increase motivation and thereby effectiveness, because it enhances satisfactions intrinsic to the task. There is a harmony between the educated individual's need for tasks that are meaningful, satisfactory and creative and a flexible organizational structure.

I think that the future I describe is not necessarily a "happy" one. Coping with rapid change, living in temporary work systems, developing meaningful relations and then breaking them—all augur social strains and psychological tensions. Teaching how to live with ambiguity, to identify with the adaptive process, to make a virtue out of contingency, and to be self-directing—these will be the tasks of education, the goals of maturity, and the achievement of the successful individual.

NO DELIGHTFUL MARRIAGES

In these new organizations of the future, participants will be called upon to use their minds more than at any other time in history. Fantasy, imagination and creativity will be legitimate in ways that today seem strange. Social structures will no longer be instruments of psychic repression but will increasingly promote play and freedom on behalf of curiosity and thought.

One final word: While I forecast the structure and value coordinates for organizations of the future and contend that they are inevitable, this should not bar any of us from giving the inevitable a little push. The French moralist may be right in saying that there are no delightful marriages, just good ones. It is possible that if managers and scientists continue to get their heads together in organizational revitalization, they *might* develop delightful organizations—just possibly.

I started with a quote from de Tocqueville and I think it would be fitting to end with one: "I am tempted to believe that what we call necessary institutions are often no more than institutions to which we have grown accustomed. In matters of social constitution, the field of possibilities is much more extensive than men living in their various societies are ready to imagine."

NOTE

1. Let me propose an hypothesis to explain this tendency. It rests on the assumption that man has a basic need for transcendental experiences, somewhat like the psychological rewards which William James claimed religion provided—"an assurance of safety and a temper of peace, and in relation to others, a preponderance of living affections." Can it be that as religion has become secularized, less transcendental, men search for substitutes such as close interpersonal relationships, psychoanalysis—even the release provided by drugs such as LSD?

LINE AND STAFF AT ITT

THOMAS S. BURNS

With the emergence of the business conglomerate in America in the early sixties came the reemergence of centralized authority and the supervisory staff system of management.

President Ralph Cordiner's decentralized management system, as researched and perfected by the General Electric Company, was in vogue in the fifties—cheered on by management consultants and business school deans. The staff system robbed management of its entrepreneurial prerogatives, they said. It might be satisfactory for slow, cumbersome, military-type organizations, but it was unwieldy and unresponsive in the dynamic arenas of business. All of the negative adjectives were applied to centralized management. Professor Peter Drucker was hailed as the apostle of the new decentralized, line-oriented philosophy, and the rush was on to reduce staffs to lean operating crews of specialists. Staff people of any stripe or skill were suspect.

Then along came the conglomerate—a management organization that operated like a central bank for both funds and talent. As the conglomerates gobbled up company after company and grew ever more profitable, opinions changed with respect to their management policies. Conglomerates assembled large, knowledgeable staffs to audit and control the acquisitions in many diverse business activities. Companies that thought they had reached a happy medium began to doubt their staff-line relationships. As the conglomerates surged ahead, the desire to look like Litton or LTV or ITT was great enough to start the pendulum swinging. Gradually the circles of power became heavy with staff specialists, and the centralization of business management was back.

In understanding the *Darkness at Noon* atmosphere of ITT, it is necessary to understand how the staffs influenced policy. They operated like a cross between the secret police and a kindly family doctor. to a degree the staff was supreme so long as it reported all of the facts.

But it was also required to confess when it was technically incompetent for a particular assignment. So staff people apologized a lot and mitigated their advice. But top ITT management knew that there was no way to run the company on the formula devised by Harold Geneen, ITT chairman and chief executive officer, without heavy emphasis on the staff role.

ITT gradually developed a unique, efficient centralized operating system of line-staff management, both in organization and methods. In procedure it grew closer to the military general staff concept than any other major company, even to sporting an espionage organization and worldwide intelligence-gathering networks.

Unfortunately for Geneen's dreams and magnificent obsessions, ITT could never enjoy the leverage of General Motors or Dupont. It did not have the ability to dominate one or more major industries. The company seems destined to continue its piecemeal acquisition policies in diversified industries, ganging sales and profits to purchase the growth Geneen so dearly prizes. And with unrelated businesses in the assembly process at all times, management control problems become ever more complex, resulting in a tendency toward increased centralization and larger and more specialized staffs.

The ITT staffs were peppered with graduates of the management consulting profession, people who could appreciate the manipulation of power as almost an academic exercise. They seemed to have no psychic need for profit and loss responsibility and were the stuff great audit groups are made from. ITT claimed to run the largest and most efficient management consulting company in the world and continually proselytized some of the best talent away from the old-line management consulting houses.

"The only difference between a management consultant and an ITT staff man," a senior vice president said, "is that if you don't accept the consultant's advice, you leave." Another staff man said, "We get these MBAs from the Ivy League business schools all the time. But unless they learn our system, they don't last. We are taking the place of the Harvard Business School, so far as Geneen is concerned. He is proud of his Harvard tie, he lists the school's Advanced Management Program in his biography, but he balks at sending anyone back to the program. He believes that we are the trailblazers and the rest of the business world is 'sucking hind tit.' "

The staffs had taken over some functions to the point of completely emasculating company divisions management. Financial management and long-range planning were securely in staff hands. They also controlled the operations research, project management, and the market research and analysis which resulted in most of the company's acquisitions. Obviously, the staff chieftains reported directly to Geneen.

"To get to the top in this company you've got to go through one of the staffs," Frank Deighan said. He was a graduate of Booz, Allen & Hamilton, management consultants, and had been seasoned by two tours with ITT staff groups. "You may be operating well in the field, but it will only be a matter of time before they want you back in New York. If you're going to work on the top levels, the brass must be sure of your reactions, gut and otherwise. You've got to be able to hang though—they have to be sure. In short, you must become a known quantity. I thought the guys at Booz were ruthless until I joined H.S.G. and company. But Booz guys were little old ladies with bleeding hearts compared to these ITT guys."

As was intended, the staff struck fear into the hearts of the line management. There was a staff man always looking over your shoulder, and he was outside your jurisdiction and the control of your operating management. In fact, sometimes the staff man was outside of any authority or jurisdiction except the office of the president. The staff men were routinely rotated in assignments to avoid any rapport being achieved between division management and the staff. They were the Ogres of Operations, and headquarters intended to keep them that way.

The staff titles changed with the vogues of management policy. A fashionable one in the early seventies was "product line manager." to read the product line manager's job description you would assume he was a general manager, marketing manager, and financial specialist all rolled into one. And functionally his assignment was impressive, including a number of companies, usually scattered worldwide, assembled by industry or product line. But in fact the PLMs were spies, pure and simple. Their responsibility was to carry back to top management, and particularly Geneen, information concerning division operations.

The failing of these staff courtesans was often a superiority complex which allowed the line operators of the business to build up subtle defenses. Since the staff man could not know all of the key factors in the operation of the business, he was always vulnerable to a technological sandbag or conflicting expert opinion. Only if he reached some kind of peace with his line counterpart would he be fed "straight dope" insofar as the real problems were concerned. So often there developed an Alphonse and Gaston relationship not unlike the deals made between top management and labor leaders. when some controversy was inevitable, the scene was rehearsed by staff and line secretly before it got to the forum of a business plan or top management review. It was amusing to sit through such meetings, in which even the friction and dissent had been contrived.

On occasion the line and staff did battle without quarter. With so many people on both sides possessing a strong instinct for the jugular, such confrontations were usually mean, ugly, and counterproductive. But stimulated by top management interrogation, the staff had to make an occasional example of some errant or cocky division president.

"You watch your boss on the staff side and you get the signal," a North American staff manufacturing specialist said. "If Geneen and Executive Vice President Bennett start zeroing in on some guy, you had better be able to pull out the sheet of embarrassing questions from your little black notebook and join in. *Au contraire,* if H.S.G. is smiling, philosophizing, and telling stories about his old days in this or that industry, then we just clam up. No matter what we have on the division boss, we make some obvious comment concerning how brilliantly the division is being operated and suggest, *sotto voce,* some minor changes. This is a totalitarian government, buddy, and we don't ever forget it."

Criteria for selecting ITT staff men indicated, by nuance, the type of man that best fitted the role.

"Does he make recommendations based on a visibility of the situation not yet recognized by division management?"

"Does he keep cool, even during periods of violent disagreement with line managers?"

Other requirements ranged from technical grasp to social presence but came across as being much the same as those the CIA uses to select an agent.

The system of a staff man overseeing each major line function did not encourage an entrepreneurial business climate. But the staffs did provide direction and could marshal a number of diverse technical skills very quickly to solve a problem.

Geneen's concept of forcing the divisions to constantly run their businesses "on paper" was policed by the staffs. Reports submitted by each division monthly were examined in detail by the assigned staff man. A system of marginal notations was developed by the staffs which allowed top management to analyze the problems, opportunities, danger signals, and errors contained in the reports after only a cursory glance through the thick notebooks. More than a few "red flags" meant heavy going for the division managers involved.

The disadvantage, of course, was that such star-chamber procedures often eliminated the opportunity for line people to explain their business. It was a temptation for a line manager to accept the recommendations of the staff with mild reservations, even though he might feel strongly that they were in error. By carrying out the recommendations to illogical conclusions and requesting further staff direction as the losses mounted, the situation might become embarrassing enough to drive off the staff men and allow the manager to reap the rewards of setting things right.

"I gained a hell of a lot more respect for the staff after they fried us at the business plan review," a general manager said. "Mind you, not respect for their ability. Some of them don't know their ass from a hole in the ground. But let me tell you, they know how to play the game. They sat on the other side of the table with all the questions, while my managers sat over here and tried to come up with answers, poor bastards. I'm not fool enough to put us in that situation again, let me tell you!"

With the same clarity as they recall their first sexual experience, most managers remember their maiden voyage to New York for the annual business plan review. Mr. Geneen's "show and tell" parties take place for each and every division and company in the ITT fold once every year. The Europeans are reviewed in Europe, the North Americans are reviewed in New York, and other reviews are arranged at times and places convenient to Geneen. But everyone goes under the knife.

The ITT planning process, now famous among management consultants and business historians, began as a semiformal set of directives and guidelines accumulated over the years since the early days at ITT. Geneen took the system and honed it to a fine operating edge. His reverence for facts and figures was very much in evidence. The planning process was a no-nonsense philosophy of numbers. Every division or company president was re-

sponsible for preparing such an annual business plan—a book-length document of plans, graphs, financial exhibits, and analyses. The format was standardized for all, even to the preprinting of book covers and forms. The plan was conceived, written, and presented by division management—but it was approved successively by all levels of management between the division and Geneen before it was presented to him (personally, mind you) for final approval. The work of preparation was exhaustive; the requirements for planning specialists simply to keep the plan current was a financial burden for many of the smaller divisions. Most U.S. companies cannot or do not support such a planning function or take the time to assemble all the detailed information required in the Geneen system. And not surprisingly, this is exactly where Geneen sees ITT's competitive advantage. His managers know the down, the play, the score, and even the details of the referee's sex life in that grand game called business. By comparison, competitors seem to be standing in ticket lines or still suiting up while Geneen puts points on the board.

The performance put on by division management in front of Geneen during their once-a-year confrontation is the most important mark in their overall rating. He sees and hears them, and he knows whether or not they are good disciples of the Word. During the sessions—like a Pentagon briefing, advertising agency presentation, or political rally—the results of past actions and future projections are heavily colored by the personality and charisma of the actors on stage. So the production must be carefully planned and staged to achieve the maximum favorable exposure in the short time the division will have before the gathered New York staffs, ITT top management, and Geneen himself. The mighty have risen and fallen by the flickering lights of the slide projector and the whine of the microphone.

It was cold in New York in late December when our division's first business plan was finally scheduled for review. We had been twice delayed, confirming our suspicions that the staffs were saving their best chance at a massive humiliation to the last. There was black slush on the ground, and the sky was the color of old lead. We huddled in a mid-Manhattan Hamburger Heaven, catching a quick, pre-lunch meal, which we felt might be our last of the day. The division was scheduled to be "on" at four in the afternoon, so what with preparation, waiting in the wings, the presentation, and an interrogation, the day would be filled, with no time for the niceties of dining. Binks, the division controller recently elevated from the ranks, was shaken. "Have you ever done this before?" he asked Hayden Moore, the acting general manager.

"No," Moore said weakly. "Not alone. I've carried papers to a lot of the sessions."

"So have I," said Binks. "And given testimony and wrestled graphs and all that stuff. But this is different. Boy, just the three of us. And this goddam plan—it's full of holes. Maybe you guys don't know what can happen up there. I've watched guys get torn to pieces. I've seen Geneen scream at a general manager until I thought the guy was going to crawl under the table."

"Let's ask for a bye until next year," I said. "Plead nolo. Or why don't you have a seizure? No controller, no numbers."

The cab ride to headquarters had all the hardy camaraderie of a trip to the gallows. With our slides, graphs, and hats in hand we presented ourselves to the security guards on the meeting room floor and were duly identified and badged. We waited what seemed an interminable time in the lounge, then took our seats in the great chamber to watch the plans of other Defense Space Group companies unfold as we waited our turn.

Rumors drifted out from the business plan sessions in progress to the lounges and waiting rooms, alternately encouraging and discouraging.

"Geneen just said operations cash management is the most important consideration this year," a staff man announced. "Hope your operations cash management plan is sound." He nudged our controller with his elbow and cackled. Binks was now blanched and shaking. I began to wonder what we would do if he couldn't see it through. A year of planning only to pass out on the stage before Geneen. A tragic prospect: Binks lying there atop his forms and ledgers.

"No negative thinking. Forget about the goddam recession, that's the word," a friendly department manager said. "Rich Bennett doesn't want any 'can't do' shit. If you're looking for things to get worse, better tone it down."

Ushered successively closer to the podium, we watched the production with a partisan interest and awe. Geneen sat like an Oriental potentate, flanked by vice presidents in descending order of importance. The hierarchy was marvelously disciplined, speaking only when called on by Geneen or the interlocutor, Executive Vice President Rich Bennett. Bennett kept the harangue and monotonous division dialogues moving with questions, invitations for staff inquiries, and an occasional attempt at levity.

Finally, our turn came. As in the Mad Hatter's tea party, we had been moving our seats closer to the speaker's rostrum, and now we were there. Moving to stage center, the middle of the table, we now faced Geneen across the ten-yard expanse of green carpet. The *Caine* mutiny court-martial scene with Queeg on the wrong side of the green cloth.

We had been warned that everything would depend on Geneen's reactions. If he began serious questioning, the staff would be on us like a pack of hounds. We had tried to second-guess his curiosities—which areas to concentrate on and present with slide and story, where his chief interest might lie between the political and the practical. But it was impossible to cover all the holes and patches in the Cable Division program. If Geneen wanted our hides, he had only to delve a little.

Rich Bennett introduced us with a quip about leaving the good golf weather in San Diego to tell them all about our Silver Strand Plot. We were launched. Slowly, deliberately, we presented the plan. Geneen said nothing, nodding on occasion in agreement with some statement. Bennett asked a few questions of the product line managers on the staff responsible for cable and communications areas. They gave quick answers, referring to the piles of papers scattered over the table in front of them. As the last slide passed, our brevet general manager sat down, looking exhausted. His voice had cracked several times in the presentation, and the controller's replies to financial questions had been halting. But it was over, and we waited for the decision. Thumbs up or down.

Geneen rose and said, "These gentlemen are taking on some big people. This is probably the largest investment we've made in facilities in a long time." He turned to us. "Just get the goddam plant built and start turning out cable." He motioned to the staff. "These people will take care of the rest. Any questions?"

There were no questions.

"Watch those bastards from Western Electric in Washington," Geneen said to me, "and don't even have a cup of coffee with them. Or the other competition. No matter how well you know them. There can't be any smell of collusion. We may have some problems. . . ." His voice trailed off. He waddled slowly across the expanse of carpet that separated the tables, followed by a gaggle of corporate vice presidents. He shook hands with the three of us in what we later learned was an unprecedented gesture of support. Soft-spoken and pleasant, he chatted for a few minutes while the assembled gathering sat in silence. He asked me about the markets, the prospects for government business, AT&T plans, and the program schedules.

"Good work," he said. "I'll be out to see that beachfront property sometime, too." Then he paraded out of the room, receiving nods and smiles as he trouped the line. The meeting was temporarily adjourned. Then tension lifted like a curtain. A few brave souls lit cigarettes on their way to the refreshment tables in the lounges.

"I feel as though I've just had a battlefield decoration pinned on," I said.

The controller looked at his hand. "I've been with this company 20 years, and this is the first time I've ever met with the president. And I just shook hands with him."

"Fred will never wash that hand again," a staff assistant said. "Congratulations. You just had holy water sprinkled over you, and you will shortly be inundated with more cooperation than you can use."

After basking in the reflected glory of Geneen's approval in the lounge, we packed our exhibits and headed back to the Barclay Hotel. In the Gold Room we began a half-hearted victory celebration, but the emotional drain had been too much, and the evening went flat after two drinks.

"What won Geneen over, do you suppose?" the general manager asked, now out of shock.

"We showed a lot of confidence. That's important. You can't come on tentative with Geneen. He wants a team that is all for hard charging," Binks said, now high on Scotch and blessed relief.

"What a relief to have the bloody thing over," said Moore. "Here's how."

And he drained the last drink of our one and only victory celebration ever.

POWER FAILURE IN MANAGEMENT CIRCUITS

ROSABETH MOSS KANTER

Power is America's last dirty word. It is easier to talk about money—much easier to talk about sex—than it is to talk about power. People who have it deny it; people who want it do not want to appear to hunger for it; and people who engage in its machinations do so secretly.

Yet, because it turns out to be a critical element in efective managerial behavior, power should comeout from undercover. Having searched for years for those styles or skills that would identify capable organization leaders, many analzsts, like myself, are rejecting individual traits or situational appropriateness as key and finding the sources of a leader's real power.

Access to resources and information and the ability to act quickly make it possible to accomplish more and to pass on more resources and information to subordinates. For this reason, people tend to prefer bosses with "clout." When employees perceive their manager as influential upward and outward, their status is enhanced by association and they generally have high morale and feel less critical or resistant to their boss.[1] More powerful leaders are also more likely to delegate (they are too busy to do it all themselves), to reward talent, and to build a team that places subordinates in significant positions.

Powerlessness, in contrast, tends to breed bossiness rather than true leadership. In large organizations, at least, it is powerlessness that often creates ineffective, desultory management and petty, dictatorial, rules-minded managerial styles. Accountability without power—responsibility for results without the resources to get them—creates frustration and failure. People who see themselves as weak and powerless and find their subordinates resisting or discounting them tend to use more punishing forms of influence. If organizational power can

[1]Donald C. Pelz, "Influence: A Key to Effective Leadership in the First-Line Supervisor," *Personnel,* November 1952, p. 209.

"ennoble," then, recent research shows, organizational powerlessness can (with apologies to Lord Action) "corrupt."[2]

So perhaps power, in the organization at least, does not deserve such a bad reputation. Rather than connoting only dominance, control, and oppression, *power* can mean efficacy and capacity—something managers and executives need to move the organization toward its goals. Power in organizations is analogous in simple terms to physical power: it is the ability to mobilize resources (human and material) to get things done. The true sign of power, then, is accomplishment—not fear, terror, or tyranny. Where the power is "on," the system can be productive; where the power is "off," the system bogs down.

But saying that people need power to be effective in organizations does not tell us where it comes from or why some people, in some jobs, systematically seem to have more of it than others. In this article I want to show that to discover the sources of productive power, we have to look not at the *person*—as conventional classifications of effective managers and employees do—but at the *position* the person occupies in the organization.

WHERE DOES POWER COME FROM?

The effectiveness that power brings evolves from two kinds of capacities: first, access to the resources, information, and support necessary to carry out a task; and, second, ability to get cooperation in doing what is necessary. (*Exhibit I* identifies some symbols of an individual manager's power.)

Both capacities derive not so much from a leader's style and skill as from his or her location in the formal and informal systems of the organization—in both job definition and con-

[2]See my book, *Men and Women of the Corporation* (New York: Basic Books, 1977), pp. 164–205; and David Kipnis, *The Powerholders* (Chicago: University of Chicago Press, 1976).

Exhibit I Some common symbols of a manager's organizational power (influence upward and outward)

To what extent a manager can—
Intercede favorably on behalf of someone in trouble with the organization
Get a desirable placement for a talented subordinate
Get approval for expenditures beyond the budget
Get above-average salary increases for subordinates
Get items on the agenda at policy meetings
Get fast access to top decision makers
Get regular, frequent access to top decision makers
Get early information about decisions and policy shifts

nection to other important people in the company. Even the ability to get cooperation from subordinates is strongly defined by the manager's clout outward. People are more responsive to bosses who look as if they can get more for them from the organization.

We can regard the uniquely organizational sources of power as consisting of three "lines":

1. *Lines of supply.* Influence outward, over the environment, means that managers have the capacity to bring in the things that their own organizational domain needs—materials, money, resources to distribute as rewards, and perhaps even prestige.

2. *Lines of information.* To be effective, managers need to be "in the know" in both the formal and the informal sense.

3. *Lines of support.* In a formal framework, a manager's job parameters need to allow for nonordinary action, for a show of discretion or exercise of judgment. Thus managers need to know that they can assume innovative, risk-taking activities without having to go through the stifling multilayered approval process. And, informally, managers need the backing of other important figures in the organization whose tacit approval becomes another resource they bring to their own work unit as well as a sign of the manager's being "in."

Note that productive power has to do with *connections* with other parts of a system. Such systemic aspects of power derive from two sources—job activities and political alliances:

1. Power is most easily accumulated when one has a job that is designed and located to allow *discretion* (nonroutinized action permitting flexible, adaptive, and creative contributions), *recognition* (visibility and notice), and *relevance* (being central to pressing organizational problems).

2. Power also comes when one has relatively close contact with *sponsors* (higher-level people who confer approval, prestige, or backing), *peer networks* (circles of acquaintanceship that provide reputation and information, the grapevine often being faster than formal communication channels), and *subordinates* (who can be developed to relieve managers of some of their burdens and to represent the manager's point of view).

When managers are in powerful situations, it is easier for them to accomplish more. Because the tools are there, they are likely to be highly motivated and, in turn, to be able to motivate subordinates. Their activities are more likely to be on target and to net them successes. They can flexibly interpret or shape policy to meet the needs of particular areas, emergent situations, or sudden environmental shifts. They gain the respect and cooperation that attributed power brings. Subordinates' talents are resources rather than threats. And, because powerful managers have so many lines of connection and thus are oriented outward, they tend to let go of control downward, developing more independently functioning lieutenants.

The powerless live in a different world. Lacking the supplies, information, or support to make things happen easily, they may turn instead to the ultimate weapon of those who lack productive power—oppressive power: holding others back and punishing with whatever threats they can muster.

Exhibit II summarizes some of the major ways in which variables in the organization and in job design contribute to either power or powerlessness.

POSITIONS OF POWERLESSNESS

Understanding what it takes to have power and recognizing the classic behavior of the powerless can immediately help managers make sense out of a number of familiar organizational problems that are usually attributed to inadequate people:

Exhibit II Ways organizational factors contribute to power or powerlessness

Factors	Generates **power** when factor is	Generates **powerlessness** when factor is
Rules inherent in the job	few	many
Predecessors in the job	few	many
Established routines	few	many
Task variety	high	low
Rewards for reliability/ predictability	few	many
Rewards for unusual performance/innovation	many	few
Flexibility around use of people	high	low
Approvals needed for nonroutine decisions	few	many
Physical location	central	distant
Publicity about job activities	high	low
Relation of tasks to current problem areas	central	peripheral
Focus of tasks	outside work unit	inside work unit
Interpersonal contact in the job	high	low
Contact with senior officials	high	low
Participation in programs, conferences, meetings	high	low
Participation in problem-solving task forces	high	low
Advancement prospects of subordinates	high	low

- The ineffectiveness of first-line supervisors.
- The petty interest protection and conservatism of staff professionals.
- The crises of leadership at the top.

Instead of blaming the individuals involved in organizational problems, let us look at the positions people occupy. Of course, power or powerlessness in a position may not be all of the problem. Sometimes incapable people *are* at fault and need to be retrained or replaced. (See the rules insert on page 408 for a discussion of another special case, women.) But where patterns emerge, where the troubles associated with some units persist, organizational power failures could be the reason. Then, as Volvo President Pehr Gyllenhammar concludes, we should treat the powerless not as "villains" causing headaches for everyone else but as "victims."[3]

First-Line Supervisors

Because an employee's most important work relationship is with his or her supervisor, when many of them talk about "the company," they mean their immediate boss. Thus a supervisor's behavior is an important determinant of the average employee's relationship to work and is in itself a critical link in the production chain.

Yet I know of no U.S. corporate management entirely satisfied with the performance of its supervisors. Most see them as supervising too closely and not training their people. In one manufacturing company where direct laborers were asked on a survey how they learned their job, on a list of seven possibilities "from my supervisor" ranked next to last. (Only company training programs ranked worse.) Also, it is said that supervisors do not translate company policies into practice—for instance, that they do not carry out the right of every employee to fre-

quent performance reviews or to career counseling.

In court cases charging race or sex discrimination, first-line supervisors are frequently cited as the "discriminating official."[4] And, in studies of innovative work redesign and quality of work life projects, they often appear as the implied villains; they are the ones who are said to undermine the program or interfere with its effectiveness. In short, they are often seen as "not sufficiently managerial."

The problem affects white-collar as well as blue-collar supervisors. In one large government agency supervisors in field offices were seen as the source of problems concerning morale and the flow of information to and from headquarters. "Their attitudes are negative," said a senior official. "They turn people against the agency; they put down senior management. They build themselves up by always complaining about headquarters, but prevent their staff from getting any information directly. We can't afford to have such attitudes communicated to field staff."

Is the problem that supervisors need more management training programs or that incompetent people are invariably attracted to the job? Neither explanation suffices. A large part of the problem lies in the position itself—one that almost universally creates powerlessness.

First-line supervisors are "people in the middle," and that has been seen as the source of many of their problems.[5] But by recognizing that first-line supervisors are caught between higher management and workers, we only begin to skim the surface of the problem. There is practically no other organizational category as subject to powerlessness.

[3]Pehr G Gyllenhammar, *People at Work* (Reading, Mass.: Addison-Wesley, 1977), p. 133.

[4]William E. Fulmer, "Supervisory Selection: The Acid Test of Affirmative Action," *Personnel,* November–December 1976, p. 40.
[5]See my chapter (coauthor, Barry A. Stein), "Life in the Middle: Getting In, Getting Up, and Getting Along," in *Life in Organizations,* eds. Rosabeth M. Kanter and Barry A. Stein (New York: Basic Books, 1979).

WOMEN MANAGERS EXPERIENCE SPECIAL POWER FAILURES

The traditional problems of women in management are illustrative of how formal and informal practices can combine to engender powerlessness. Historically, women in management have found their opportunities in more routine, low-profile jobs. In staff positions, where they serve in support capacities to line managers but have no line responsibilities of their own, or in supervisory jobs managing "stuck" subordinates, they are not in a position either to take the kinds of risks that build credibility or to develop their own team by pushing bright subordinates.

Such jobs, which have few favors to trade, tend to keep women out of the mainstream of the organization. This lack of clout, coupled with the greater difficulty anyone who is "different" has in getting into the information and support networks, has meant that merely by organizational situation women in management have been more likely than men to be rendered structurally powerless. This is one reason those women who have achieved power have often had family connections that put them in the mainstream of the organization's social circles.

A disproportionate number of women managers are found among first-line supervisors or staff professionals; and they, like men in those circumstances, are likely to be organizationally powerless. But the behavior of other managers can contribute to the powerlessness of women in management in a number of less obvious ways.

One way other managers can make a woman powerless is by patronizingly overprotecting her: putting her in "a safe job," not giving her enough to do to prove herself, and not suggesting her for high-risk, visible assignments. This protectiveness is sometimes born of "good" intentions to give her every chance to succeed (why stack the deck against her?). Out of managerial concerns, out of awareness that a woman may be up against situations that men simply do not have to face, some very well-meaning managers protect their female managers ("It's a jungle, so why send her into it?").

Overprotectiveness can also mask a manager's fear of association with a woman should she fail. One senior bank official at a level below vice president told me about his concerns with respect to a high-performing, financially experienced woman reporting to him. Despite *his* overwhelmingly positive work experiences with her, he was still afraid to recommend her for other assignments because he felt it was a personal risk. "What if other managers are not as accepting of women as I am?" he asked. "I know I'd be sticking my neck out; they would take her more because of my endorsement than her qualifications. And what if she doesn't make it? My judgment will be on the line."

Overprotection is relatively benign compared with rendering a person powerless by providing obvious signs of lack of managerial support. For example, allowing someone supposedly in authority to be bypassed easily means that no one else has to take him or her seriously. If a woman's immediate supervisor or other managers listen willingly to criticism of her and show they are concerned every time a negative comment comes up and that they assume she must be at fault, then they are helping to undercut her. If managers let other people know that they have concerns about this person or that they are testing her to see how she does, then they are inviting other people to look for signs of inadequacy or failure.

Furthermore, people assume they can afford to bypass women because they "must be uninformed" or "don't know the ropes." Even though women may be respected for their competence or expertise, they are not necessarily seen as being informed beyond the technical requirements of the job. There may be a grain of historical truth in this. Many women come to senior management positions as "outsiders" rather than up through the usual channels.

Also, because until very recently men have not felt comfortable seeing women as businesspeople (business clubs have traditionally excluded women), they have tended to seek each other out for informal socializing. Anyone, male or female, seen as organizationally naive and lacking sources of "inside dope" will find his or her own lines of information limited.

Finally, even when women are able to achieve some power on their own, they have not necessarily been able to translate such personal credibility into an organizational power base. To create a network of supporters out of individual clout requires that a person pass on and share power, that subordinates and peers be empowered by virtue of their connection with that person. Traditionally, neither men nor women have seen women as capable of sponsoring others, even though they may be capable of achieving and succeeding on their own. Women have been viewed as the *recipients* of sponsorship rather than as the sponsors themselves.

(As more women prove themselves in organizations and think more self-consciously about bringing along young people, this situation may change. However, I still hear many more questions from women managers about how they can benefit from mentors, sponsors, or peer networks than about how they themselves can start to pass on favors and make use of their own resources to benefit others.)

Viewing managers in terms of power and powerlessness helps explain two familiar stereotypes about women and leadership in organizations: that no one wants a woman boss (although studies show that anyone who has ever had a woman boss is likely to have had a positive experience), and that the reason no one wants a woman boss is that women are "too controlling, rules-mided, and petty."

The first stereotype simply makes clear that power is important to leadership. Underneath the preference for men is the assumption that, given the current distribution of people in organizational leadership positions, men are more likely than women to be in positions to achieve power and, therefore, to share their power with others. Similarly, the "bossy woman boss" stereotype is a perfect picture of powerlessness. All of those traits are just as characteristic of men who are powerless, but women are slightly more likely, because of circumstances I have mentioned, to find themselves powerless than are men. Women with power in the organization are just as effective—and preferred—as men.

Recent interviews conducted with about 600 bank managers show that, when a woman exhibits the petty traits of powerlessness, people assume that she does so "because she is a woman." A striking difference is that, when a man engages in the same behavior, people assume the behavior is a matter of his own individual style and characteristics and do not conclude that it reflects on the suitability of men for management.

First, these supervisors may be at a virtual dead end in their careers. Even in companies where the job used to be a stepping stone to higher-level management jobs, it is now common practice to bring in MBAs from the outside for those positions. Thus moving from the ranks of direct labor into supervision may mean, essentially, getting "stuck" rather than moving upward. Because employees do not perceive supervisors as eventually joining the leadership circles of the organization, they may see them as lacking the high-level contacts needed to have clout. Indeed, sometimes turnover among supervisors is so high that workers feel they can outwait—and outwit—any boss.

Second, although they lack clout, with little in the way of support from above, supervisors are forced to administer programs or explain policies that they have no hand in shaping. In one company, as part of a new personnel program supervisors were required to conduct counseling interviews with employees. But supervisors were not trained to do this and were given no incentives to get involved. Counseling was just another obligation. Then managers suddenly encouraged the workers to bypass their supervisors or to put pressure on them. The personnel staff brought them together and told them to demand such interviews as a basic right. If supervisors had not felt powerless before, they did after that squeeze from below, engineered from above.

The people they supervise can also make life hard for them in numerous ways. This often happens when a supervisor has himself or herself risen up from the ranks. Peers that have not made it are resentful or derisive of their former colleague, whom they now see as trying to lord it over them. Often it is easy for workers to break rules and let a lot of things slip.

Yet first-line supervisors are frequently judged according to rules and regulations while being limited by other regulations in what disciplinary actions they can take. They often lack the resources to influence or reward people; after all, workers are guaranteed their pay and benefits by someone other than their supervisors. Supervisors cannot easily control events; rather, they must react to them.

In one factory, for instance, supervisors complained that performance of their job was out of their control: they could fill production quotas only if they had the supplies, but they had no way to influence the people controlling supplies.

The lack of support for many first-line managers, particularly in large organizations, was made dramatically clear in another company. When asked if contact with executives higher in the organization who had the potential for offering support, information, and alliances diminished their own feelings of career vulnerability and the number of headaches they experienced on the job, supervisors in five out of seven work units responded positively. For them *contact* was indeed related to a greater feeling of acceptance at work and membership in the organization.

But in the two other work units there was greater contact, people perceived more, not less, career vulnerability. Further investigation showed that supervisors in these business units got attention only when they were in trouble. Otherwise, no one bothered to talk to them. To these particular supervisors, hearing from a higher-level manager was a sign not of recognition or potential support but of danger.

It is not surprising, then, that supervisors frequently manifest symptoms of powerlessness: overly close supervision, rules-mindedness, and a tendency to do the job themselves rather than to train their people (since job skills may be one of the few remaining things they feel good about). Perhaps this is why they sometimes stand as roadblocks between their subordinates and the higher reaches of the company.

STAFF PROFESSIONALS

Also working under conditions that can lead to organizational powerlessness are the staff specialists. As advisers behind the scenes, staff people must sell their programs and bargain for resources, but unless they get themselves entrenched in organizational power networks, they have little in the way of favors to exchange. They are seen as useful adjuncts to the primary tasks of the organization but inessential in a day-to-day operating sense. This disenfranchisement occurs particularly when staff jobs consist of easily routinized administrative functions which are out of the mainstream of the currently relevant areas and involve little innovative decision making.

Furthermore, in some organizations, unless they have had previous line experience, staff people tend to be limited in the number of jobs into which they can move. Specialists' ladders are often very short, and professionals are just as likely to get "stuck" in such jobs as people are in less prestigious clerical or factory positions.

Staff people, unlike those who are being groomed for important line positions, may be hired because of a special expertise or particular background. But management rarely pays any attention to developing them into more general organizational resources. Lacking growth prospects themselves and working alone or in very small teams, they are not in a position to develop others or pass on power to them. They miss out on an important way that power can be accumulated.

Sometimes staff specialists such as house counsel or organization development people, find their work being farmed out to consultants. Management considers them fine for the routine work, but the minute the activities involve risk or something problematic, they bring in outside experts. This treatment says something not only about their expertise but also about the status of their function. Since the company can always hire talent on a temporary basis it is unclear that the management really needs to have or considers important its own staff for these functions.

And, because staff professionals are often seen as adjuncts to primary tasks, their effectiveness and therefore their contribution to the organization are often hard to measure. Thus visibility and recognition, as well as risk taking and relevance, may be denied to people in staff jobs.

Staff people tend to act out their powerlessness by becoming turf-minded. They create islands within the organization. They set themselves up as the only ones who can control professional standards and judge their own work. They create sometimes false distinctions betweeen themselves as experts (no one else could possibly do what they do) and lay people, and this continues to keep them out of the mainstream.

One form such distinctions take is a combination of disdain when line managers attempt to act in areas the professionals think are their preserve and of subtle refusal to support the managers' efforts. Or staff groups battle with each other for control of new "problem areas," with the result that no one really handles the issue at all. To cope with their essential powerlessness, staff groups may try to elevate their own status and draw boundaries between themselves and others.

When staff jobs are treated as final resting places for people who have reached their level of competence in the organization—a good shelf on which to dump managers who are too old to go anywhere but too young to retire—then staff groups can also become pockets of conservatism, resistant to change. Their own exclusion from the risk-taking action may make them resist *anyone's* innovative proposals. In the past, personnel departments, for example, have sometimes been the last in their organization to know about innovations in human resource development or to be interested in applying them.

Top Executives

Despite the great resources and responsibilities concentrated at the top of an organization, leaders can be powerless for reasons that are not very different from those that affect staff and supervisors: lack of supplies, information, and support.

We have faith in leaders because of their ability to make things happen in the larger world, to create possibilities for everyone else, and to attract resources to the organization. These are their supplies. But influence outward—the source of much credibility downward—can diminish as environments change, setting terms and conditions out of the control of the leaders. Regardless of top management's grand plans for the organization, the environment presses. At the very least, things going on outside the organization can deflect a leader's attention and drain energy. And, more detrimental, decisions made elsewhere can have severe consequences for the organization and affect top management's sense of power and thus its operating style inside.

In the go-go years of the mid-1960s, for example, nearly every corporation officer or university president could look—and therefore feel—successful. Visible success gave leaders a great deal of credibility inside the organization, which in turn gave them the power to put new things in motion.

In the past few years, the environment has been strikingly different and the capacity of many organization leaders to do anything about it has been severely limited. New "players" have flexed their power muscles: the Arab oil bloc, government regulators, and congressional investigating committees. And managing economic decline is quite different from managing growth. It is no accident that when top leaders personally feel out of control, the control function in corporations grows.

As powerlessness in lower levels of organizations can manifest itself in overly routinized jobs where performance measures are oriented to rules and absence of change, so it can at upper levels as well. Routine work often drives out nonroutine work. Accomplishment becomes a question of nailing down details. Short-term results provide immediate gratifications and satisfy stockholders or other constituencies with limited interests.

It takes a powerful leader to be willing to risk short-term deprivations in order to bring about desired long-term outcomes. Much as first-line supervisors are tempted to focus on daily adherenece to rules, leaders are tempted to focus on short-term fluctuations and lose sight of long-term objectives. The dynamics of such a situation are self-reinforcing. The more the long-term goals go unattended, the more a leader feels powerless and the greater the scramble to prove that he or she is in control of daily events at least. The more he is involved in the organization as a short-term Mr. Fix-it, the more out of control of long-term objectives he is, and the more ultimately powerless he is likely to be.

Credibility for top executives often comes from doing the extraordinary: exercising discretion, creating, inventing, planning, and acting in nonroutine ways. But since routine problems look easier and more manageable, require less change and consent on the part of anyone else, and lend themselves to instant solutions that can make any leader look good temporarily, leaders may avoid the risky by taking over what their subordinates should be doing. Ultimately, a leader may succeed in getting all the trivial problems dumped on his or her desk. This can establish expectations even for leaders attempting more challenging tasks. When Warren Bennis was president of the University of Cincinnati, a professor called him when the heat was down in a classroom. In writing about this incident, Bennis commented, "I suppose he expected me to grab a wrench and fix it."[6]

People at the top need to insulate themselves from the routine operations of the organization in order to develop and exercise power. But this very insulation can lead to antoher source of powerlessness—lack of information. In one multinational corporation, top executives who are sealed off in a large, distant office, flattered and virtually babied by aides, are frustrated by their distance from the real action.[7]

At the top, the concern for secrécy and privacy is mixed with real loneliness. In one bank, organization members were so accustomed to never seeing the top leaders that when a new senior vice president went to the branch offices to look around, they had suspicion, even fear, about his intentions.

Thus leaders who are cut out of an organization's information networks understand neither what is really going on at lower levels nor that their own isolation may be having negative effects. All too often top executives design "beneficial" new employee programs or declare a new humanitarian policy (e.g., "Participatory management is now our style") only to find the policy ignored or mistrusted because it is perceived as coming from uncaring bosses.

The information gap has more serious consequences when executives are so insulated from the rest of the organization or from other decision makers that, as Nixon so dramatically did, they fail to see their own impending downfall. Such insulation is partly a matter of organizational position and, in some cases, of executive style.

For example, leaders may create closed inner circles consisting of "doppelgängers," people just like themselves, who are their principal sources of organizational information and tell them only what they want to know. The reasons for the distortions are varied: key aides want to relieve the leader of burdens, they think just like the leader, they want to protect their own positions of power, or the familiar "kill the messenger" syndrome makes people close to top executives reluctant to be the bearers of bad news.

Finally, just as supervisors and lower-level managers need their supporters in order to be and feel powerful, so do top executives. But for them sponsorship may not be so much a matter of individual endorsement as an issue of support by larger sources of legitimacy in the society. For top executives the problem is not to fit in among peers; rather, the question is whether the public at large and other organization members perceive a common interest which they see the executives as promoting.

If, however, public sources of support are

---

[6]Warren Bennis, *The Unconscious Conspiracy: Why Leaders Can't Lead* (New York: AMACOM, 1976).
[7]See my chapter, "How the Top is Different," in *Life in Organizations.*

withdrawn and leaders are open to public attack or if inside constituencies fragment and employees see their interests better aligned with pressure groups than with organizational leadership, then powerlessness begins to set in.

When common purpose is lost, the system's own politics may reduce the capacity of those at the top to act. Just as managing decline seems to create a much more passive and reactive stance than managing growth, so does mediating among conflicting interests. When what is happening outside and inside their organizations is out of their control, many people at the top turn into decline managers and dispute mediators. Neither is a particularly empowering role.

Thus, when top executives lose their own lines of supply, lines of information, and lines of support, they too suffer from a kind of powerlessness. The temptation for them is to pull in every shred of power they can and to decrease the power available to other people to act. In-novation loses out in favor of control. Limits rather than targets are set. Financial goals are met by reducing "overhead" (people) rather than by giving people the tools and discretion to increase their own productive capacity. Dictatorial statements come down from the top, spreading the mentality of powerlessness farther until the whole organization becomes sluggish and people concentrate on protecting what they have rather than on producing what they can.

When everyone is playing "king of the mountain," guarding his or her turf jealously, then king of the mountain becomes the only game in town.

TO EXPAND POWER, SHARE IT

In no case am I saying that people in the three hierarchical levels described are always powerless, but they are susceptible to common conditions that can contribute to powerlessness. *Exhibit III* summarizes the most common

Exhibit III Common symptoms and sources of powerlessness for three key organizational positions

Position	Symptoms	Sources
First-line supervisors	Close, rules-minded supervision Tendency to do things oneself, blocking of subordinates' development and information Resistant, underproducing subordinates	Routine, rules-minded jobs with little control over lines of supply Limited lines of information Limited advancement or involvement prospects for oneself/subordinates
Staff professionals	Turf protection, information control Retreat into professionalism Conservative resistance to change	Routine tasks seen as peripheral to "real tasks" of line organization Blocked careers Easy replacement by outside experts
Top executives	Focus on internal cutting, short-term results, "punishing" Dictatorial top-down communications Retreat to comfort of like-minded lieutenants	Uncontrollable lines of supply because of environment changes Limited or blocked lines of information about lower levels of organization Diminished lines of support because of challenges to legitimacy (e.g., from the public or special interest groups)

symptoms of powerlessness for each level and some typical sources of that behavior.

I am also distinguishing the tremendous concentration of economic and political power in large corporations themselves from the powerlessness that can beset individuals even in the highest positions in such organizations. What grows with organizational position in hierarchical levels is not necessarily the power to accomplish—productive power—but the power to punish, to prevent, to sell off, to reduce, to fire, all without appropriate concern for consequences. It is that kind of power—oppressive power—that we often say corrupts.

The absence of ways to prevent individual and social harm causes the polity to feel it must surround people in power with constraints, regulations, and laws that limit the arbitrary use of their authority. But if oppressive power corrupts, then so does the absence of productive power. In large organizations, powerlessness can be a bigger problem than power.

David C. McClelland makes a similar distinction between oppressive and productive power:

"The negative . . . face of power is characterized by the dominance-submission mode: if I win, you lose. . . . It leads to simple and direct means of feeling powerful [such as being aggressive.] It does not often lead to effective social leadership for the reason that such a person tends to treat other people as pawns. People who feel they are pawns tend to be passive and useless to the leader who gets his satisfaction from dominating them. Slaves are the most inefficient form of labor ever devised by man. If a leader wants to have far-reaching influence, he must make his followers feel powerful and able to accomplish things on their own. . . . Even the most dictatorial leader does not succeed if he has not instilled in at least some of his followers a sense of power and the strength to pursue the goals he has set."[8]

[8]David C. McClelland, *Power: The Inner Experience* (New York: Irvington Publishers, 1975), p. 263. Quoted by permission.

Organizational power can grow, in part, by being shared. We do not yet know enough about new organizational forms to say whether productive power is infinitely expandable or where we reach the point of diminishing returns. But we do know that sharing power is different from giving or throwing it away. Delegation does not mean abdication.

Some basic lessons could be translated from the field of economics to the realm of organizations and management. Capital investment in plants and equipment is not the only key to productivity. The productive capacity of nations, like organizations, grows if the skill base is upgraded. People with the tools, information, and support to make more informed decisions and act more quickly can often accomplish more. By empowering others, a leader does not decrease his power; instead he may increase it—especially if the whole organization performs better.

This analysis leads to some counterintuitive conclusions. In a certain tautological sense, the principal problem of the powerless is that they lack power. Powerless people are usually the last ones to whom anyone wants to entrust more power, for fear of its dissipation or abuse. But those people are precisely the ones who might benefit most from an injection of power and whose behavior is likely to change as new options open up to them.

Also, if the powerless bosses could be encouraged to share some of the power they do have, their power would grow. Yet, of course, only those leaders who feel secure about their own power outward—their lines of supply, information, and support—can see empowering subordinates as a gain rather than a loss. The two sides of power (getting it and giving it) are closely connected.

There are important lessons here for both subordinates and those who want to change organizations, whether executives or change agents. Instead of resisting or criticizing a powerless boss, which only increases the boss's feeling of powerlessness and need to control, subordinates instead might concentrate on helping the boss become more powerful. Managers might make pockets of ineffectiveness in the organization more productive not by training or replacing individuals but by structural solutions such as opening supply and support lines.

Similarly, organizational change agents who want a new program or policy to succeed should make sure that the change itself does not render any other level of the organization powerless. In making changes, it is wise to make sure that the key people in the level or two directly above and in neighboring functions are sufficiently involved, informed, and taken into account, so that the program can be used to build their own sense of power also. If such involvement is impossible, then it is better to move these people out of the territory altogether than to leave behind a group from whom some power has been removed and who might resist and undercut the program.

In part, of course, spreading power means educating people to this new definition of it. But words alone will not make the difference; managers will need the real experience of a new way of managing.

Here is how the associate director of a large corporate professional department phrased the lessons that he learned in the transition to a team-oriented, participatory, power-sharing management process:

"Get in the habit of involving your own managers in decision making and approvals. But don't abdicate! Tell them what you want and where you're coming from. Don't go for a one-boss grass roots 'democracy.' Make the management hierarchy work for you in participation. . . .

"Hang in there, baby, and don't give up. Try not to 'revert' just because everything seems to go sour on a particular day. Open up—talk to people and tell them how you feel. They'll want to get you back on track and will do things to make that happen—because they don't really want to go back to the way it was. . . . Subordinates will push you to 'act more like a boss,' but their interest is usually more in seeing someone else brought to heel than getting bossed themselves."

Naturally, people need to have power before they can learn to share it. Exhorting managers to change their leadership styles is rarely useful by itself. In one large plant of a major electronics company, first-line production supervisors were the source of numerous complaints from managers who saw them as major roadblocks to overall plant productivity and as insufficiently skilled supervisors. So the plant personnel staff undertook two pilot programs to increase the supervisors' effectiveness. The first program was based on a traditional competency and training model aimed at teaching the specific skills of successful supervisors. The second program, in contrast, was designed to empower the supervisors by directly affecting their flexibility, access to resources, connections with higher-level officials, and control over working conditions.

After an initial gathering of data from supervisors and their subordinates, the personnel staff held meetings where all the supervisors were given tools for developing action plans for sharing the data with their people and collaborating on solutions to perceived problems. But then, in a departure from common practice in this organization, task forces of supervisors were formed to develop new systems for handling job and career issues common to them and their people. These task forces were given budgets, consultants, representations on a plantwide project steering committee alongside managers at much higher levels, and wide latitude in defining the nature and scope of the changes they wished to make. In short, lines of supply, information, and support were opened to them.

As the task forces progressed in their activities, it became clear to the plant manage-

THE REDISTRIBUTION OF POWER

The polarities that I have discussed are those of power and creativity. Workers who want to move in the direction of participative structures will need to confront the issues of power and control. The process of change needs to be mutually shared by all involved, or the outcome will not be a really participative model. The demand for a structural redistribution of power is not sufficient to address the problem of change toward a humanistic, as against a technological, workplace. If we are to change our institutional arrangements from hierarchy to participation, particularly in our workplaces, we will need to look to transformations in ourselves as well. As long as we are imbued with the legitimacy of hierarchical authority, with the sovereignty of the status quo, we will never be able to generate the new and original participative forms that we seek. This means if we are to be equal to the task of reorganizing our workplaces, we need to think about how we can reeducate ourselves and become aware of our own assumptions about the nature of our social life together. Unless the issue is approached in terms of these complexities, I fear that all the worker participation and quality-of-work-life efforts will fail.*

* From Robert Schrank, *Ten Thousand Working Days* (Cambridge, MA: The MIT Press, copyright © 1978 by The Massachusetts Institute of Technology). Reprinted with permission of the author.

ment that the hoped-for changes in supervisory effectiveness were taking place much more rapidly through these structural changes in power than through conventional management training; so the conventional training was dropped. Not only did the pilot groups design useful new procedures for the plant, astonishing senior managements in several cases with their knowledge and capabilities, but also, significantly, they learned to manage their own people better.

Several groups decided to involve shop-floor workers in their task forces; they could now see from their own experience the benefits of involving subordinates in solving job-related problems. Other supervisors began to experiment with ways to implement "participatory management" by giving subordinates more control and influence without relinquishing their own authority.

Soon the "problem supervisors" in the "most troubled plant in the company" were getting the highest possible performance ratings and were considered models for direct production management. The sharing of organizational power from the top made possible the productive use of power below.

One might wonder why more organizations do not adopt such empowering strategies. There are standard answers: that giving up control is threatening to people who have fought for every shred of it; that people do not want to share power with those they look down on; that managers fear losing their own place and special privileges in the system; that "predictability" often rates higher than "flexibility" as an organizational value; and so forth.

But I would also put skepticism about employee abilities high on the list. Many modern bureaucratic systems are designed to minimize dependence on individual intelligence by making routine as many decisions as possible. So it often comes as a genuine surprise to top executives that people doing the more routine jobs could, indeed, make sophisticated decisions or use resources entrusted to them in intelligent ways.

In the same electronics company just mentioned, at the end of a quarter the pilot supervisory task forces were asked to report results and plans to senior management in order to have their new budget requests approved. The task forces made sure they were well prepared, and the high-level executives were duly impressed. In fact, they were *so* impressed that they kept interrupting the presentations with compliments, remarking that the supervisors could easily be doing sophisticated personnel work.

At first the supervisors were flattered. Such praise from upper management could only be taken well. But when the first glow wore off, several of them became very angry. They saw the excessive praise as patronizing and insulting. "Didn't they think we could think? Didn't they imagine we were capable of doing this kind of work?" one asked. "They must have seen us as just a bunch of animals. No wonder they gave us such limited jobs."

As far as these supervisors were concerned, their abilities had always been there, in latent form perhaps, but still there. They as individuals had not changed—just their organizational power.

IS BUSINESS REALLY CHANGING?

CHARLES PERROW

Organizational theory has gradually developed a rather comprehensive paradigm for handling the impact of technological and environmental change upon organizations, which I have represented in Figure 1. Inventions and innovations in techniques and in goods and services have stimulated the growth of the "knowledge industry," and been stimulated by it. As a consequence, the environment of organizations has shown rapid and turbulent change and has led to new forms of competition. This, in turn, has stimulated both education and research, and resulted in still more innovations and inventions. The consequence for organizations, limited here to economic organizations, has been a change in the character of the workforce: more professionalization and higher skill levels; more rapid change in technologies and products; and more decentralization of authority, as those on the firing line have to make more decisions on their own and can do so because they possess the requisite skills. This creates greater instability in the environment, more innovations, and more growth in the knowledge industry. It is characteristic of our systems model that all the arrows are double-headed.

This model has been with us for several years now; it is celebrated in the works of almost all management theorists and popular authors, and is at least implicit in the work of most organizational theorists. Such widespread acceptance suggests there is a great deal in it, but I am no longer so sure, and what I want to do here is try to convince the reader that he should not be so sure, either. I am not certain that the dominant perspective is wrong, but I think it is greatly exaggerated. It takes as given many things that should be considered quite problematical. To create the necessary skepticism about it, I shall go to the other extreme and argue against it at every point.

In contrast to this view, and frankly in a spirit of controversy, I shall emphasize the stability of the system in Figure 1 and the glacial rate of change. Let me start with the symbol of futurol-

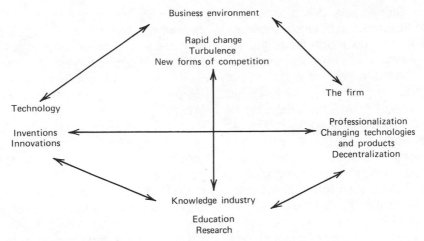

Figure 1. Organizational Theory Paradigm.

ogy that appears in the charts of Buckminster Fuller or Alvin Toffler and that pervades the writings of people like Daniel Bell and Zbigniew Brzezinski. Take the curve represented in Figure 2. Almost any behavior the futurologists are interested in can be plotted in this form. Nothing much happened for a long time, but then the increase in the behavior became exponential. The dates that one would enter at points A, B, C, et cetera would vary with the phenomenon, but the number of scientists that have been produced has increased at the rate suggested by the curve, as has the speed at which new innovations in industry can be made operational or new products marketed, the tons of metal or whatever that can be produced per hour, the velocity at which man gets about, and so on. We walked for thousands upon thousands of years on the plateau from point A to B, took horses and carriages around point B, steam engines and automobiles at C, aeroplanes and jet planes at D, and space capsules at point E, roughly 1969.

The fallacy is the evaporation of the de-

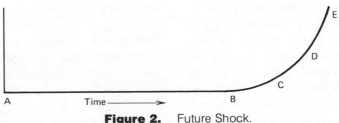

Figure 2. Future Shock.

nominator. The futurologists talk of mankind, but they ignore the world population of billions when they talk about how much faster the 10-or-so percent of Americans who use commercial flights get around today. Were they to put that small number in the numerator over the huge denominator of "mankind," the rate of change would be glacial indeed. In fact, most people in the world today don't even ride horses, let alone fly. And of course, the number who have orbited the earth is truly insignificant.

Only a tiny fraction of men are scientists. Regardless of whether this figure doubles or trebles in a few decades, the vast majority of men know nothing about what these scientists are doing, nor are their lives changed significantly by the scientists' actions, except in the case of radioactive fallout, pesticide poisonings, and so on.

The output statistics of steel for a few industrialized countries should be compared with the figures of the many nonindustrialized countries. The same is true of our organizations. When you take them all into account, rather than the few exotic ones we read about in the business journals or the exotic parts of large corporations, the overwhelming conclusion is one of stability or very slow rates of change.

PROFESSIONALIZATION

Turning now to the paradigm for organization and environment, let us start with one crucial item in Figure 1, the professionalization of the workforce, which has resulted from the knowledge explosion and education and training associated with it. It is a well-known fact that in industrialized countries the number of white-collar employees comes to exceed the number of blue-collar employees (if you count service workers as white-collar, although many are not). It happened several years ago in the United States. What is less well known is that this would not be true if females were excluded. They swell the ranks of the low-status white-collar positions

and hardly are there by virtue of technological breakthroughs. In 1970, 41 percent of the females in the labor force were in clerical or sales positions. Of those classified as "professional, technical, and kindred" by the Census Bureau in 1960, 43 percent were teachers. Women are in the workforce for a shorter time than men. All this suggests that they are marginal to industry in several respects—found mostly in low-status, low-skilled, high-turnover positions.

So let's leave them out of account and look only at males. If technological change and professionalization have had a significant effect, we should expect a considerable decline in the proportion of males in the blue-collar category. Professionals, technical specialists, engineers, and the like should be manning organizations, while blue-collar workers evaporated rapidly, dried up by automation and the rapid spread of higher education.

However, over the 70-year period from 1900 to 1969, from C to E in Figure 2—a period of massive technological and organizational change—we find that the percentage of the male workforce engaged in blue-collar and service activities declined by only 13 percent. It went from 70 percent in 1900 to 57 percent in 1969, and even in the 20-year period from 1950 to 1969, the period of postwar boom and knowledge explosion, it declined by only 5 percent. Indeed, if we exclude the service workers and deal only with male manual employees, the proportion of manual workers has actually been increasing slightly in the last decade.

The proportion of professional, technical, and kindred workers, the heart of the technological revolution, is indeed up; for males, it doubled from 7 percent in 1950 to 14 percent in 1969. But 14 percent is still a small percentage of the workforce; moreover, this category appears to be heavily concentrated in two areas: aerospace and "defense" industries (for example, 19 percent of the category are engineers), and the service sector, where technological change is scarcely rampant (for example, 14 percent are teachers). To make a rough estimate, about 30 percent of this group of males are in the high-technology sector of industry, while 35 percent are in the service sector. This suggests that most of industry is not greatly affected by the doubling of the professional and technical category. Most of industry is at level C in Figure 2. To point out that TRW or a nuclear engineering firm has a large proportion of scientists or engineers is like saying the Air Force has a large proportion of people who travel at very high rates of speed. Most of industry still plods along, and plods profitably.

DECENTRALIZATION

Nevertheless, you might say there has been an obvious increase in highly trained personnel in most firms, and it should lead to more decentralization in firms. This is because the market changes are more rapid, the technology more complicated, and the skills outdated sooner, so power must be delegated to those on the firing line with the latest skills and the latest information on the environment. Furthermore, there has been a management revolution, and there are all the T-groupers, sensitivity trainers, 9,9 Grid® men, matrix managers, and the integraters. Decisions have been shoved down to lower levels. Firms are becoming more decentralized.

A rigorous definition of decentralization is impossible at present; the closer one looks, the more it looks like a meaningless term. Sometimes we seem to associate it with what some have called "organization hygiene." I suppose that most organizations today are concerned that there be less smell, safer devices, more choices as to size or color or method, less roughness, irritation, and rudeness, and less secretiveness. The social sciences have marketed a lot of products to ease human interaction and make effort more benign. I think most will agree, however, that better working conditions and more humane supervision have little

to do with the decentralization of power or decision making.

The term participative management goes a bit further. It includes the hygiene sprays that are supposed to reduce alienation, but it also deals with feelings of powerlessness. The lower odors are consulted on decisions and encouraged to make their own in some areas, subject to the veto of superiors. The veto is important; it is like saying we have a democratic system of government in which people elect their leaders, but subject to the veto of the incumbent leaders. Workers and managers can have their say, make suggestions, and present arguments, and there is no doubt this is extremely desirable. It presumably results in the superior's making better decisions—but they are still his decisions.

We seem to have lost sight of something important in our packaging of pacifiers, namely, that good managements have *always* found it in their interests to utilize the skills, information, experience, and knowledge of people under them. These people know more about some things than management does, and failure to consult them not only is an affront to them, but also means that management must do much more work on its own to get the information. If it doesn't have the time or resources to do so, it makes inferior decisions. Max Weber, the much-maligned theorist of bureaucracy, was explicit about this some 60 years ago. He saw that a man has a set of skills, expertise, or experience and a sense of career with the firm. The skills, expertise, and experience can be developed, and he expects to utilize them—indeed, he wants to. It is wise, then, as we now see, to allow him the freedom to exercise these skills and to use his discretion, for that is why we employ experts and experienced people. However, he should exercise his skills in the service of organizational goals that are set for him. He is not expected, or encouraged, to inquire into the legitimacy of these goals.

Even if we move toward a more psychological model, such as the self-actualization one of Chris Argyris and others, it seems clear that self-actualization by the employee has to be on organizational terms. I don't think they would include the following as proper examples of self-actualization: organizing employees for better working conditions; exposing the cover-up of unjustified expenses in government contracts; opposing the development of chemical warfare techniques in a university research laboratory; advocating mass-transit subsidies as opposed to subsidies for highways while working for an automobile manufacturer; opposing price-fixing techniques or illegal campaign contributions at any number of large corporations; or calling for better testing of drugs and more accurate advertising in a pharmaceutical firm.

It is extremely difficult to get data demonstrating such restrictions, but one minor, though revealing, example was reported in *Look* magazine: At a stormy meeting concerning the activities of the Stanford Research Institute, a young physicist heard the president of SRI argue that no researcher was forced to undertake any project he found morally objectionable. The physicist contradicted him, saying that he had been pressured into doing chemical warfare research. The physicist was fired. As the executive vice-president of SRI put it, according to the article, "People like that have a decision to make—do they want to support the organization or not?"

Were actions such as these possible without penalty, I would agree that we would have decentralized firms. But as long as the superior can define the problem employees work on, he need not fear discussions of possible solutions. The fact that subordinates are using their expertise and skills more fully, and even with more enthusiasm, does not necessarily mean that authority or even decisions have been decentralized; it may merely mean a more effective organization (though I should add that careful critiques of research in the human relations

area have as yet been unable to firmly support even that conclusion).

We hear today that large organizations have become more democratic, in that subordinates are encouraged to set their own production goals, control methods, make up their own work teams, and so on. Dog food, pacemakers, television sets, even cars are being produced by "autonomous groups." Just as no one in his right mind would instruct the maintenance staff how many sweeps of the broom were to be taken for any 6' × 6' area of floor, no superior should dictate how an experienced work group should go about meeting the production (and quality and scrap) standards, unless the superior really has much more expertise or experience in the matter. The good supervisor-coordinator gets the resources and monitors outputs; he doesn't give orders about task sequences if his men are competent. But the standards are still there, and nonperformance brings sanctions. And the supervisors who set the standards are still there; the men cannot vote them out of office. The ideological confusion attending the gummy word democratic is well represented by Chester Barnard, who quoted with approval an army officer in World War I who remarked that the army is the greatest of all democracies, because when the order to move forward is given, each man decides on his own whether to obey or not.

No serious organizational theorists in the United States, to my knowledge, have advocated the form of decentralization of authority that democracy seeks to provide. That is, there are no calls for workers to elect management and to have the contenders for managerial positions run on platforms such as no speed-up, better washrooms, no defense contracts, no gifts to universities, or no price fixing, let alone less pay for managers and more for workers. In Europe, especially eastern Europe, where there seems to be more progressive management in this respect, the experiment with that most anemic form of democracy, workers' councils, has had only a slight impact on organizations.

TEMPORARY ORGANIZATIONS

A more serious usage of the term decentralization occurs in connection with the appearance of temporary work groups or matrix structures, associated mostly with the name of Warren Bennis. (Dr. Bennis has lost his vision on the way to an organizational presidency, but he had many followers in this Buck Rogers school of theory who still embrace the model with which I opened this article.) Proponents of his view argue that because of rapid environmental and technological changes, those with the most relevant skills and information are in the lower reaches of the hierarchy, and they also suggest that rapid changes call for task groups that have no fixed membership. The groups form and reform, depending on the problem at hand. One is a leader at one time and a subordinate at another. The organization, then, is made up of little cells or work groups that appear and disappear according to the cycle of innovation and implementation. Upper management merely provides the resources and offers what guidance it can.

Once again, I think that the ability of top management to formulate the problem other managers are assigned so limits the range of available solutions that we find very little decentralization of authority. But even if this were not true, I think that all we have here is a slight expansion of the size of the goal-setting unit. A few elite teams are added to the goal-setting unit, while the bulk of management personnel still remains outside of it. Granted, this would constitute a form of decentralization, but I suspect that the examples given in the literature are very special and deal with very special aspects of our large firms. They will cover only a tiny minority of corporations and only a tiny minority of the employees in them. Again, I should like to refer to Figure 2; because a few men have orbited the earth, does that mean that mankind is moving any faster?

There is another important consideration. Those who argue for the reality of organic structure and its expansion write as if innovations were the only things that corporations produce. (Roy Ash some time ago took this position, pointing to pop-top disposable cans and the SST.) But after the innovations and the design, production, and marketing decisions have been made by these elite teams, an army of personnel must carry them out on a volume basis. High-volume production, with masses of workers, clerks, technicians, and personnel men doing largely routine jobs, characterizes industry, not the floating, dissolving teams of innovators and troubleshooters. To suggest otherwise is to succumb to a myth about economic organizations.

DIVISIONALIZATION

Finally, let me come to the most interesting argument of all for decentralization, found in the literature on divisionalization of large corporations. There are a number of books about divisionalization that equate it with decentralization, and some of them are very scholarly and admirable books indeed. All of them deal, at least in part, with General Motors. The first was by Peter Drucker; then came Ernest Dale; then the very influential book *Strategy and Structure,* by Alfred Du Pont Chandler, Jr., and then one by Alfred Sloan himself on his years at General Motors. The evidence given in these books supports a quite different conclusion than the one that their authors put forth (though Chandler is more circumspect about actual decentralization than the rest). The evidence strongly suggests that General Motors was quite decentralized when it was run by William C. Durant—in fact, it was the very model of a present-day conglomerate or holding company, with the main office doing little more than allocate capital among the divisions.

When Sloan came in, he radically and continuously centralized the organization. He introduced inventory-control and production-control devices and internal pricing, allotted markets to the various units, controlled capital outlays, centralized advertising and personnel, standardized parts, and routinized innovation. At every step the divisions lost autonomy. At present there is hardly an area of policy- or goal-setting that is not controlled by the very large central headquarters, and in addition, it controls an enormous number of detailed decisions, including minute aspects of styling. The functionalized exception to divisionalization at General Motors has always been the Fisher Body plant, serving all divisions. That principle is now being extended to include multidivision assembly plants, further reducing the power of the division manager.

Sloan himself takes a characteristically ambiguous position about decentralization. His book opens with praise for decentralization in General Motors; a bit later, though, he criticizes Durant, his predecessor, for allowing General Motors to be too decentralized; and still later he calls for a happy medium between centralization and decentralization. Harold Wolff, in a perceptive discussion of the General Motors structure some years ago, concluded that reading the General Motors experience as an example of decentralization was an error: "If any *one* word is needed to describe the management *structure* of General Motors as it was recast by Sloan and the brilliant group around him, then that word is not decentralization, but *centralization*." He goes on to say that it is difficult to label the process, as distinct from the structure, but it is clear, he says, that it is not one of decentralization.

The usual way out of this labeling dilemma is to say the policy is centralized and the execution decentralized. But I contend that if policy is centralized, so is execution; the choice is execution through wasteful (and unpleasant) close supervision and direction, or execution through controlling the premises of decisions—through sharply delimiting the options available. Wolff captures it well: "The decentralized operating executives were left with smaller responsibilities than they had before. But the responsibility they did retain was total and sharply defined. They had the right to do only those things which would make the precise plans and policies of the top management work." This hardly fits the pattern of decentralized organizations that has lower-level people responding fully and freely to the turbulent environment.

There is another matter that clouds our perception of the realities of control in industry and organizations in general—the matter of scale, or volume of output, or number of things done. The head of an automotive division at General Motors is no puppet; he makes many decisions that have a great deal of impact on his division and on the corporation as a whole. But the facts that the divisions of General Motors are large and involved in very complex operations and that the division manager and his staff have a great deal to do and a great deal of responsibility do not mean that the controls exercised over them with regard to either means or ends are not great. There are simply more things to do in a large and complex organization such as a General Motors division.

The division manager is not, I understand, free to change legroom lengths, control auto frame production, formulate his own labor policies, raise capital, change the price range of his cars, engage in any significant research and development, or set up his own accounting system—let alone decide that General Motors should change its goals and policies with regard to pollution, highway sprawl, mass transit, product safety, or product warranties. Both his means and his ends are closely monitored and controlled by headquarters. There is nothing inconsistent with being both more closely controlled and having more decisions to make. As James March and Herbert Simon pointed out some time ago in their book *Organizations,* to shape the premises of decision is the key to control; it is unnecessary for members of the superior unit to make the decision themselves.

UNTANGLING THE ISSUES

I think we are only beginning to unravel some of the threads in the cloth we have woven for ourselves concerning the issues of control, delegation of authority, and decision making. I find it instructive that we can so readily assume, to use the words of Zbigniew Brzezinski, that "the increased flow of information and more efficient techniques of coordination need not necessarily prompt greater concentration of power," but can make possible a "greater devolution of authority and responsibility to the lower levels of government and society." Brzezinski's example of this summary of the model is as instructive as it is terrifying: "It is noteworthy that the U.S. Army has so developed its control systems that it is not uncommon for sergeants to call in and coordinate massive air strikes and artillery fire—a responsibility of colonels during World War II."

What Brzezinski does not note is that the ability of the U.S. Army to destroy more living things today than in World War II has increased. There are more decisions to make. The sergeant of today make more decisions than the colonel of World War II because the lethal output of the system is so much higher. I doubt that the colonel feels robbed of authority and I doubt that he has lost any in the process. Perhaps we should begin to pull apart these two strands in our cloth—control over the premises of decision, which makes the sergeant so ready to call in massive air strikes and artillery fire, and delegation of the authority that might have given

him the ability to say it is just not worth all that destruction.

The way we're conducting our research suggests, however, that we are not likely to disentangle these threads. The work of Peter Blau and his associates and of the Aston Group in England has concluded, to use Aston's terms, that the more structured the activities of an organization (that is, the greater the degree of bureaucracy), the greater the degree of decentralization of decision making or authority. But what has been measured when they speak of decentralization of authority?

I suspect that they have found that in large firms, with all their economies of scale and specialization and expert personnel, there has been an absolute increase in the output of the system. In consequence, lower managements have to make more important decisions than they do in weaker systems, but this also means that top managements have increased the importance and scope of their decisions, including those that shape the premises of lower management. It need not be a zero-sum game. Blau and Aston (and I, among many others) have not measured these kinds of decisions by top management because we are not privy to them, and, perhaps more important, not conceptually alert to them.

To say that lower management is more expert or experienced is to say that management will view the situation in the proper light and make the sensible decision in conformance with the interests of the organizational elites who control the organizations. The less the expertise, the more direct the surveillance and the more obtrusive or formal the controls; the more the expertise, the more unobtrusive the controls. The best situation of all is to hire professionals (though they do not come cheap), for someone else has socialized them and even unobtrusive controls are hardly needed. The professional, the prima donna of organizational theory, is really the ultimate eunuch, capable of doing everything well in that harem except what he should not do—and in this case that is to mess around with the goals of the organization or the assumptions that determine to what ends he will use his professional skills.

FLAWS IN THE ARGUMENT

I am quite aware that this argument has many weaknesses, and I will mention two of them. First, it is always possible to deny empirical generalizations, such as those by Blau and the Aston Group, on the grounds that the variables were not measured adequately. This is rightly called cheap criticism, but in an area as important as the centralization of authority I think it is worth raising the point quite strenuously. We should not measure decentralization by the level at which people may hire, fire, or spend a few thousand dollars without proper authorization. We must also measure the unobtrusive controls.

A more serious problem with my position is that it is difficult to know what would be a decentralized organization. Centralization seems to be inevitable, and variations in the degree are quite minor. Let me elaborate. I have argued that what we take to mean decentralization of authority generally means: (1) a larger, or more complex, or more busy organization, as there is more for people in the lower levels to do; (2) more effective bureaucratization, so that the virtues of experience, training, and expertise are more fully realized throughout the organization; (3) more effective control from the top, so that unobtrusive control has a wider scope—and this can include more effective control of the environment; and (4) better organizational hygiene, so that people are not treated so badly. This, I realize, tends to equate effective organizations with the centralization of organizations, and makes it difficult for me to be proved wrong.

This point bothers me. So let me remind you that my purpose is not to prove that the rosy

new view of firms emerging from the model of our social scientists is wrong, but merely to ask for a critical pause before we continue to rush headlong into that model. My extended remarks on centralization are meant to open up the debate a bit, in the face of an ever-enlarging consensus.

I have concerned myself mainly with decentralization, but the environment and technology themselves require some brief remarks to put that part of the pattern into a critical perspective, since they are important aspects of the general consensus.

ENVIRONMENT

Is the environment really turbulent? The most important fact, but one we seem to ignore systematically, is that the environment of organizations is primarily made up of other organizations that have similar interests. The shared interests are much greater than the competitive ones. Mobil Oil and Exxon may compete furiously at the intersection of two streets in any American town, but neither of them is really threatened by this marginal competition. They work very closely together in the important matter of oil depletion allowances, our foreign policy about the Mideast, federal tax policies, the pollution issues, and private transit-versus-mass transit. In fact, they cooperate quite well with large organizations in other industries that share their interests, such as the automobile industry. And the automobile industry cooperates with, and has a stake in, the steel industry, and so on. Where, then, is the furious rate of competition? At the lower levels in the organization—the levels of the regional manager who moves prices up and down a fraction and the station manager who washes the windshields and cleans the rest rooms. Who sets the parameters of their behavior and judges them in terms of their performance? Top management. Coping with the environment, then, not only is consistent with centralized control but requires centralized control if the turbulence is going to be minor and limited to the lower echelons.

A little reflection on some obvious behavior will illustrate the stability of large firms and their ability to do three things: select the environment they wish to deal with, create new environments if necessary, and change those that threaten to produce instability. Few firms move from the top 200 in the *Fortune* listing to the next 300; few drop out of the top 500 altogether except by merger, which is, of course, a device for increasing stability and gaining control over environments. Corporations resist technological change when it suits them, and quite successfully. After inventing the transistor, AT&T declined to use it, for it would have required scrapping too much existing equipment, even though the company asked the public to put up with increasingly poor service.

The techniques for managing the environment are so well known I would hesitate to mention them, were it not for the fact that the literature on organization-environment relations and on organizational change largely ignores them. Some obvious ones are administered pricing, government subsidies, price fixing, padded cost figures, planned obsolescence, tariffs, cartels, political payoffs, special governmental aid, takeovers and mergers, and, of course, monopsony, oligopoly, monopoly, and advertising.

In the United States there is overwhelming evidence that industries are able to regulate the regulatory agencies; that the vast majority of top officials in government have come from, and will return to, private business or the law firms that service business; that despite a briefly mobilized citizenry, the heat is off the pollution area, as the main polluters control the programs and advertise their dedication—and so on and so on. There are exceptions, I readily admit—industries where the competition extends to the very top of each firm and affects large areas of policy. But, surprisingly enough, these are generally not the professionalized,

technologically advanced firms, but those in the backward industries of food production, food distribution, auto parts and service, furniture, clothing, and the like. Their environments are relatively unstable because they lack size, standardization, centralized control, and mass production and mass marketing. They are 19th century industries, not 21st century industries.

TECHNOLOGICAL CHANGE

One might finally say in exasperation: "The evidence of technological change is overwhelming. Whether environments are controlled or not, surely there has been a great deal of technological change, and as a consequence, more influence on the part of technicians, engineers, scientists, and recently trained managers."

But just as the decline of the proportion of blue-collar workers in the workforce has been very slow and relatively even over the last 60 to 70 years, so has the rise in output per manhour. There have been fluctuations in this figure due to the depression of the 1930s, the war boom of the early 1940s, and more wars and recessions along the way right up to the present. Overall, though, the increase in productivity has not fluctuated greatly even from one environmental disturbance to the next. The impression is one of slow and stable change.

The reason seems to be that while most firms have routine technologies, they are only *somewhat* routine. Most are unable to automate extensively. In the large majority, new technologies have simply not created the condition for the decentralized, responsive, adaptive organization that organizational theorists seem to dream of.

I can only argue from examples here, and I shall give three of them. First, the automatic factory that was heralded as a possibility in the late 1940s and accepted as a reality by the mid-1960s is, as far as I know, still not with us. In 1965, a reporter for *Fortune,* Charles Silberman, tracked down the various references to startling examples of automation that had been served up by journalists and by social scientists. The results were very disappointing. Case after case turned out to be grossly overstated or simply not true. He could find, for example, no automated chemical complexes that had discharged their employees in droves. Most had experienced either no reduction in personnel or even some increase, and none were fully automated. After careful research, Silberman concluded that "no fully automated process exists for any major product in any industry in the U.S." Since we cannot seem to get social scientists to do this kind of work, I hope that *Fortune* magazine will send another crew out in 1975 to see if things have changed much since 1965. I don't think they will have.

The second example concerns the prima donna of technological change, computers. Again, it was *Fortune* that did the investigative work, rather than the social scientists. Tom Alexander, writing in the October 1969 issue of that magazine, concluded: "It turns out that computers have rarely reduced the cost of operations, even in routine clerical work. What they have accomplished is mainly to enable companies to speed up operations and thereby provide better service or handle larger volumes." He reported a survey by the Research Institute of America of some 2,500 companies that found that only half of those with in-house computers were certain that they were paying off—that heady enthusiasm about computers' providing total management information control systems had dissipated greatly.

Perhaps there is always waste with the adaptation of new technologies, but if so, we have been misled about its degree in this age of scientific and technological sophistication. When we look at developments like powdered metallurgy or numerically controlled machines, the story is the same. Fantastic progress is predicted but not realized, because we refuse to recognize the limits of routinization and the ability to control environments so that technological change is not required.

One last example is the Vega automobile produced by General Motors. It planned and built a completely new car and built a new plant to produce it. If automation could ever strike, it should strike here, in this key and wealthy company. (It turns out, incidentally, that the planning was completely centralized in the headquarters of General Motors and not handled by the division.) The computers in this supposedly computerized installation are limited to balancing production (though they were used in designing and making templates), and there are a few automatic welders on the production line. But as far as I can gather, there is nothing more radical in terms of technological change than this.

What allowed the company to use about 20 percent less direct labor in producing the cars was not the technology of the 1960s but that of the 1920s. First, there was the speed-up of the line, which could account for much of the labor-saving. Since it was achieved by having men work harder, we can hardly call it automation. (The line has since been slowed down as a result of high absenteeism, turnover, and wildcat strikes). Second, because there are many more interchangeable parts for all models, the number of parts was reduced and thus the complexity, allowing for longer production runs for parts. Third, the increased number of subassemblies simplified the assembly line. Fourth, there are streamlined assemblies, including the very important simplification of a one-piece roof. Finally, there is a basic model life of five years, rather than three. All of these innovations were made by the first Henry Ford, back in the 1920s. Yet the business press heralded the new plant as "the model of automation."

These examples suggest that technological change is not so widespread, continuous, and rapid as we tend to believe (as well as more wasteful of resources than we have been led to believe). I do not dispute the change that has occurred in, say, electronics, process firms, and even manufacturing, with its roller bearings and engine blocks. I am saying only that the striking examples are few, and that productivity has not taken the great leaps to be expected if these were the norm.

It is also quite possible that technological change is not impelled by market forces and scientific advancement so much as it is by government and corporate political strategy. Surely, the huge concentration of technical and scientific manpower in the defense, space, and atomic power industries is the result of political decisions. There is no free market for these products.

CONCLUSION

In conclusion, then, I have argued that there has been no rapid and drastic change in the workforce, except for the increasing employment of women in low-level, white-collar jobs in the service industry; that firms are more complex and larger, but not necessarily more decentralized, since we have been measuring only part of the control system; that the environment is not unstable and turbulent for the progressive and technologically advanced firms, but very stable, because it is controlled by the companies and managed in their common interests; and that technological change has been quite selective—far less extensive than is usually believed, resisted when it pleases firms, and well-controlled when it exists. At each point I have contradicted what I see as the dominant viewpoint on these matters in organizational theory.

Let me finally add a note to extend my contention to social and political theory. The evidence from our social and political systems also signifies overwhelming stability. The social structure of the United States has not changed much in a hundred years. There has been very little income redistribution; the class system is still quite intact; our political structures and mechanisms remain much as they were at the beginning of the century. It depends upon one's necromancy, but one interpretation of the similarity of the dominant economic, social, and political institutions is that if economic institutions do not change, we can't expect a change in the political and social ones.

QUESTIONS FOR DISCUSSION

1. Compare the poem by Robert Frost from an earlier chapter with the reading by Bennis in this chapter.
2. Treat the reading by Thomas Burns entitled "Line and Staff at ITT" as a case. Prepare it for a class discussion.